Behavior Dynamics in Teaching, Learning, and Growth

Don E. Hamachek

Behavior Dynamics in Teaching, Learning, and Growth

Behavior Dynamics in Teaching, Learning, and Growth

DON E. HAMACHEK
Michigan State University

Allyn and Bacon, Inc.
Boston

© Copyright 1975 by Allyn and Bacon, Inc.
470 Atlantic Avenue, Boston, Mass. 02210

Library of Congress Cataloging in Publication Data

Hamachek, Don E.
  Behavior dynamics in teaching, learning, and growth.

  Includes bibliographical references and index.
  1. Educational psychology.   I.   Title.
LB1051.H2278   370.15   74-20508

ISBN 0-205-04632-0

To Debbie and Dan:
    You are you.
  And that is nice.

Contents

Preface   ix

PART I   **A Psychological Framework for Understanding Behavior and Educational Processes   1**

   1   Major Views About the Psychology of Human Behavior   2

   2   Psychological Growth Models for Understanding and Interpreting Behavior   41

PART II   **Physical, Psychological, and Intellectual Growth Processes — Developmental Outcomes and Behavioral Consequences   91**

   3   Preschool Years: The Self Emerges   93

   4   Elementary and Middle School Years: The Self Expands   123

   5   Junior High and High School Years: The Self Matures   173

6   The Nature and Growth of Intelligence and Creative Functioning   231

PART III   Dynamics of Good Teaching and Healthy Teacher Behavior   287

7   Psychology and Behavior of Effective Teachers   288

8   Self-understanding: A Prerequisite for Good Teaching   331

9   Toward Making Teaching Meaningful, Relevant, and Lasting   372

PART IV   Learning Dynamics, Motivation Inputs, Self-concept Variables, and Evaluation Processes   427

10   Dynamics of Learning, Learning Processes, and Biochemical Developments   428

11   Motivational Processes and Human Learning   484

12   Self-concept Variables and Achievement Outcomes   532

13   Measurement and Evaluation of Learning: Concepts and Issues   580

PART V   The Psychology of Group Behavior, Classroom Dynamics, and Management Strategies   633

14   Psychology and Development of Healthy Classroom Group Dynamics   634

15   Understandings and Strategies for Achieving Positive Classroom Management   685

A Postscript   728

Author Index   731

Subject Index   743

Preface

    This is a book that addresses itself to some of the psychological aspects of human behavior that are reflected in teaching, learning, and growth. It focuses on ideas, research findings, issues, theories, and different points of view about such things as growth processes and developmental changes that occur over time, about what constitutes "good" or effective teaching, about what learning is, how it occurs, and how to enhance achievement outcomes, and about the social psychology of group behavior and classroom dynamics.

    Within these broad topical categories are more specific discussions related to the development of a psychological framework for understanding and interpreting behavior; an examination of physical, psychological, and intellectual growth processes as related to developmental outcomes and behavioral consequences; and a look at the dynamics of "good" teaching as this is associated with self-understanding and the ability to make instruction relevant and meaningful. It also includes a study of learning processes and relationships to motivational inputs, self-concept variables and measurement procedures, and an overview of ways for understanding and managing classroom groups.

    Inasmuch as my own personal leanings tend in the direction of being clinical and humanistic as opposed to experimental and behavioristic, the flavor of this volume is primarily humanistic. What this means is that I've deliberately focused on the *human* meanings, *human* understandings, and *human* experiences involved in growth, teaching, and learning. For me, classroom instruction — at any level — and teacher-student relationships are highly personal and individualized activities that demand that you not

ix

only know your subject area, but also that you have a good grasp of the basic principles related to effective teaching and learning practices and that you are willing to work on understanding your own interpersonal dynamics.

I've tried to write this text in a manner that combines ideas and information that are purely intellectual and cognitive with examples and experiences that are more informal and personal. With this overall stylistic objective in mind as a general guide, I set five specific goals for myself that I hoped would be reflected in the finished product. Let me share these with you so that the format might be better understood before you start reading. I wanted the book (1) to reflect a strong theoretical-philosophical overlay that was both adaptive and flexible within an essentially humanistic framework; (2) to have a solid informational base buttressed by clinical evidence and empirical research; (3) to have a fluid explanatory tone that sought to clarify ideas and concepts by both illustration (verbal and visual) and example; (4) to have a prescriptive core that offered possible solutions to a variety of classroom problems and teacher dilemmas; and (5) to include opportunities for reflective self-examination and self-discovery exercises. I'm not sure that each of these five goals has been achieved equally well, but I did strive for a reasonable balance.

I struggled with how to accomplish goal number five because I really wanted the exercises to be an evident and explicit expression of this volume's humanistic tone and emphasis on *human* behavior and *human* experiences that can be best understood, I feel, in personal terms. Thus, throughout the text there are what you might call "personal involvement" exercises that invite you to "Think About" an idea or experience in relation to yourself or "To Do" a specific exercise or task that is related to the material being discussed or "To Experiment With" a particular problem in a way to make it more personal to you. In addition, there is space at the end of each chapter for you to summarize in your own words the ideas and concepts that had particular meaning for you. Writing summary ideas immediately after reading a chapter, in this or any other book, is a good way to enhance long-term memory.

Research has shown that learning is enhanced when students are given what are called "advance organizers," which are usually in the form of short expository paragraphs, sentences, or labels that provide a general overview or introduction to new material. I've tried to put this "advance organizer" idea into practice in four ways: (1) I've divided the book into five separate but interrelated "parts," each of which deals with different ideas, issues, and concerns associated with the field of educational psychology. Each of the five major parts of this volume is preceded by an overview statement designed to help you anticipate what is coming and to help you relate each "part" to the other divisions of the book. (2) Each chapter is preceded by a chapter outline, which consists of the major headings and subheadings contained within the chapter. At a glance, you can have the "big picture" of the content flow and idea coverage included in any given chapter. (3) Each chapter is also preceded by a summation of what I considered to be the "important ideas" contained within any given chapter. I realize that there may be differences about what is and what is not important, so if you will consider my listing of "important chapter ideas" as reading guidelines and study organizers rather than as final conclusions, it may make it more possible to accept them in the spirit in which they are offered. (4) I've deliberately used many descriptive headings and subheadings in each chapter, the idea being to give you a reasonably good "headline overview" of the material immediately following.

I have no illusions about this volume covering all there is to know that is functional, useful information in the field of educational psychology. There is much to know and learn about—too much for one book to possibly include. I have, however, attempted to include a fair sampling of the research growing out of the various theoretical stances in educational psychology. Thus, this volume has an extensive research base because it is only through continuing research that our best or worst hunches can be validly used or tossed out, as the case may be.

I see teaching as an enormously complex professional activity. Neither research (if we look at it carefully) nor common sense (if we listen) allows us to believe that there is one particular way to be a good teacher—or, for that matter, a good learner. Rather, there are many different ways to be "good" at those things, and each has merit depending on the person, the moment, and, surely, the subject matter. If this volume is even a little bit successful in not only stimulating questions and discussion among and between students and instructors, but in helping you to really appreciate the idea that teaching and learning are challenging, complex, and intensely "human" activities, then I would be pleased indeed.

I would like to extend a very big thank you to Professor Jere Brophy (University of Texas), Gary Davis (University of Wisconsin), John Gaa (University of North Carolina at Chapel Hill), Paul Torrance (University of Georgia), Don Treffinger (University of Kansas), and Joanna Williams (Visiting Professor, Teachers College, Columbia University) for their careful, critical reviews of the manuscript and very helpful suggestions for its improvement.

I had the good fortune to have a secretary who could not only type, but draw as well. Hence, those sprightly cartoons appearing throughout the book with Hukill penned under them belong to Marilyn Hukill, whose intuitive sense of the ridiculous has added to the lighter side of this volume.

D.E.H.

No man can reveal to you aught but that which already lies half asleep in the dawning of your knowledge.

The teacher who walks in the shadow of the temple, among his followers, gives not his wisdom but rather his faith and his lovingness.

If he is indeed wise he does not bid you enter the house of his wisdom, but rather leads you to the threshold of your own mind.

The Prophet
Kahlil Gibran

I

A Psychological Framework for Understanding Behavior and Educational Processes

The title of Part I pretty well spells out the major objectives of the first two chapters of this book. In order to go about the business of teaching, helping students learn, and establishing relationships that facilitate the teaching-learning process, we need to be clear about what our assumptions are about why people—young and old, you and me—behave the way they do in the first place. Although we all have assumptions about the "nature" of human nature, these assumptions are not always at the fingertips of our awareness. Hence, the purpose of Chapter 1 is to encourage you to begin thinking about your assumptions about why people behave the way they do—indeed, why you behave the way you do—and to relate those assumptions to their possible implications for your role as a teacher and even for your behavior as a student. Chapter 1 is offered as a kind of backdrop for the stage on which subsequent chapters will follow.

Chapter 2 outlines five psychological growth models that may help you to more fully understand the processes and dynamics of healthy social-emotional growth and development. Also included is a discussion about what you can do to encourage healthy psychological development in your own classroom.

Together, chapters 1 and 2 are designed to serve as a theoretical backdrop for understanding the educational processes and behavioral outcomes that are discussed in greater detail in the chapters to follow.

What is the psychoanalytic position in psychology all about? How is the humanistic-perceptual view different? How are behavioristic principles translated into classroom practices? What does it mean to be "fully functioning" or "self-actualized"? What is the teacher's role in promoting a healthy, knowledgeable personality? Read on.

ONE

Major Views About the Psychology of Human Behavior

CHAPTER OUTLINE

PROLOGUE

THE PSYCHOANALYTIC POSITION

  Id, Ego, and Superego: Definition and Meaning

  The First Five Years Are Most Critical

  Much of Behavior Is Unconsciously Motivated

  Some Criticisms of the Psychoanalytic Position

  The Psychoanalytic Position in Summary

  Implications from Psychoanalytic Psychology for Teaching and Learning

THE BEHAVIORISTIC POSITION

  Behavior Can Be Predicted, Routed, and Controlled — Freedom a Myth

  Behavioristic Strategies for Controlling Behavior

Classical conditioning practices

Operant or instrumental conditioning practices

Some Criticisms of the Behavioristic Position

The Behavioristic Position in Summary

Implications from Behavioristic Psychology for Teaching and Learning

THE HUMANISTIC-PERCEPTUAL POSITION

Contributions of Phenomenology and Existential Psychology

Humanistic-Perceptual Concepts About the Nature of Man

Role of the Self in the Humanistic-Perceptual Framework

Some Criticisms of the Humanistic-Perceptual Framework

The Humanistic-Perceptual Position in Summary

Implications from Humanistic-Perceptual Psychology for Teaching and Learning

EPILOGUE

REFERENCES

REFERENCES OF RELATED INTEREST

IMPORTANT CHAPTER IDEAS

1. How you function as a teacher and how you relate to students will be influenced to a large extent by your beliefs about yourself and about the nature of man.

2. The psychoanalytic position emphasizes the importance of early life experiences.

3. From a psychoanalytic point of view, most of a person's individual dynamics are unconsciously motivated.

4. A major criticism leveled at the psychoanalytic view of man is that it overemphasizes pathological behavior and unconscious motivation.

5. Psychoanalytic psychology has contributed significantly to our understanding of how adult behavior can influence—for better or for worse—the behavior and self-attitudes of youth going through the formative years.

6. The behavioristic approach to understanding human behavior stresses outer experience, overt behavior, and action and reaction.

7. From a behavioristic point of view, behavior can be predicted, routed, and controlled—freedom is a myth.

8. Reinforcement procedures and conditioning practices are basic concepts related to the behavioristic position.

9. A major criticism of behaviorism is that it overstresses external control.

10. An important lesson growing from behavioristic psychology is that behaviors that are reinforced or rewarded are more likely to occur.

11. The humanistic-perceptual position emphasizes the subjective qualities of human experience and the personal meaning of an experience to a person.

12. Within a humanistic-perceptual framework, the emphasis is on conscious motivation and the fact that people behave the way they do as a consequence of how things *seem* to them.

13. A criticism leveled at humanistic-perceptual psychology is that it is too much common sense and too little science.

14. An important implication growing from humanistic-perceptual psychology is that one of the ways to facilitate good teaching is to help students understand and explore the personal meaning inherent in their learning experiences.

15. Each of the three psychological positions cited above is reflected in this volume, although the philosophical-psychological overlay is a humanistic-perceptual one.

PROLOGUE

We can begin with a given. Whatever you do as a teacher depends very much on what you think people are like, which is usually a generalized idea growing out of the kind of person you think you are. The goals you seek, the judgments you make, the hopes you have, and the risks you take are influenced in large measure by your beliefs about yourself and about the nature of man. Persons who feel unworthy, unable, or unwanted are not likely to have high goals or high hopes. It can be no other way. We behave in terms of what we believe to be true—about ourselves and about others. It has always been so. Teachers who believe students *can*, will try to teach, guide, or in some way extend students to the limits of their potential. Teachers who believe students are unable, unwilling, or "just too dumb" don't try very hard because they feel that what they do won't matter much anyway. Probably no beliefs will be more important to you as a person and in your role as a teacher than those you hold about the nature of man and the limits of his potentials.

You may be thinking, "What are my beliefs about the nature of man? For that matter, what are my beliefs about myself?" These are basic questions and they deserve attention. Once we examine them carefully, we find that many of our beliefs about ourselves specifically, and human nature generally, are embedded in one or more of three major psychological views about human behavior.

Before reading any further, take the nine-item inventory, "What Do You Believe?" There are no "right" or "wrong" answers as such. Just check the "yes" or "no" blank to each statement that seems most true for you.

What Do You Believe?	Yes	No
1. People are essentially evil by nature.	_____	_____
2. The first five or so years of life are probably the most important in shaping one's adult personality.	_____	_____
3. Unconscious forces are more dominant than the conscious ones in determining behavior.	_____	_____
4. Most people work better and harder when the reward for their efforts is given by another person.	_____	_____

5. Most people can be controlled by giving them ap-priate rewards or reinforcements when they behave the way you want them to.   _____   _____

6. It is easier to understand a person by watching his behavior than by listening to his feelings.   _____   _____

7. People are essentially good by nature.   _____   _____

8. Later life experiences are just as important as the early ones in determining the course of behavior.   _____   _____

9. A person's conscious life is more dominant than the unconscious in determining behavior.   _____   _____

These statements are related to one of the three psychological "camps" we will be discussing in the pages to come. A "yes" response to at least two of the first three may suggest a leaning toward psychoanalytic thinking about human behavior. A "yes" response to two or more of the statements from four through six may suggest an inclination to think along the lines of behavioristic psychology. A "yes" response to two or more of the items from seven through nine may reflect a humanistic position related to behavior. If you found yourself answering "yes" to six or more of the statements, this doesn't necessarily mean that your views about behavior are inconsistent. It may only mean that, for you, behavior can be viewed comfortably from different perspectives—even though at this point you may have no idea what those perspectives are.

You now have a general feel for what your own psychological leaning tends to be. My own thinking about the nature of man—how he learns, teaches, thinks and feels—is influenced significantly by what I call a "humanistic-perceptual" framework for looking at behavior, both inside and outside the classroom.

I am the first to admit, however, that my thinking is by no means rigidly humanistic. The humanistic-perceptual framework serves as the theoretical umbrella, which for me, at least, provides the sort of unifying framework and "tying together" I find necessary to function at some level of effectiveness as a teacher and therapist. It is the theoretical and philo-sophical "emphasis" that undergirds this entire volume. And that's exactly what it is—an "emphasis." Inasmuch as each of the other two major forces in psychology—the psychoanalytic and behavioristic—have made impor-tant contributions to our knowledge about human behavior, we would be both remiss and foolish to exclude the insights and understandings that have grown from these two great disciplines.

So what we will do now is take a critical look at the pros and cons of these theoretical positions, while at the same time making a particular ef-fort to examine their implications for teaching and learning.

Let's begin with the psychological position that practically everyone has heard about at one time or other.

THE PSYCHOANALYTIC POSITION

The origins of the psychoanalytic position go back to the pioneering efforts of Sigmund Freud (1856–1939) and extend over the fifty-year period of his clinical practice and writing. The picture of human nature that has grown out of classical Freudian psychology is not particularly kind or humanitarian but one, rather, that stresses man's evil and predatory manner. For example, Freud himself expressed the idea that:

> . . . men are not gentle, friendly creatures wishing for love, who simply defend themselves if they are attacked, but. . . . a powerful measure of desire for aggressiveness has to be reckoned as part of their instinctual endowment. The result is that their neighbor is to them not only a possible helper or sexual object, but also a temptation to gratify their aggressiveness . . . to seize his possessions, to humiliate him, to cause him pain. . . .
>   . . . Anyone who calls to mind the atrocities of the early migrations of the invasion of the Huns or by the so-called Mongols under Genghis Khan . . . of the sack of Jerusalem by the pious crusaders, even indeed the horrors of the last world war, will have to bow his head humbly before the truth of this view of man.[1]

Id, Ego, and Superego: Definition and Meaning

Freud was convinced that in every personality there is an area of untamed, untrammeled, animal-like motivation. In fact, orthodox psychoanalytic thinkers suggest that there is a universal set of violent urges that is an instinctual part of each man's heritage. This pattern of primitive aggressiveness coupled with what appeared to be an insatiable need for immediate gratification was termed the *id*. Freud thought he saw two different expressions of the id. On the one hand, there were urges to live, to create, to love. Expressions of this sort he called the *life wish* and the term *libido* was coined to symbolize that part of the life wish concerned with sexual or other affiliative relations with people. On the other hand, Freud also saw evidence of hostile and destructive impulses reflected in behavior. These, in Freud's continuing drama of personality dynamics, were called expressions of the *death wish*.

Now although the id can generate images and wishes related to immediate need gratification, it cannot begin the direct action necessary toward meeting its needs. Thus, a second key construct—the *ego*—develops to mediate between the demands of the id and the realities of the outside world. In the broadest sense of the word, the ego works something on the order of an intelligent administrator concerned with finding ways in which a person can maintain his survival in the face of the "I want it now!" demands of the id and the "Be careful what you do" cautions of the conscience.

This brings us to the third major psychoanalytic construct, namely the *superego*. This is what people usually refer to as their conscience, and it is concerned with the "good" and the "bad," the "right" and the "wrong." The superego grows and develops as a child gradually incorporates the values and social standards taught by parents and other significant persons in his life. In the psychoanalytic scheme of things, there are two divisions of the superego. One is the popularly referred to *conscience*, which discourages the expression of undesirable behavior, and the other is the *ego-ideal*, which encourages more desirable behavior. The conscience develops primarily through the influence of scorn and threats of punishment. For example, a parent may say, "You're a bad boy for doing that," or "You should be ashamed of yourself." The child, in turn, may conclude to himself, "I am bad for acting like that," or "I *am* ashamed of myself." Thus, over time a child learns to control his behavior much as his parents would control it. Similarly, the ego-ideal develops through continued positive statements and expressions of approval, such as "Good boy," or "I like it when you behave like that," or increased material rewards and privileges.

TO THINK ABOUT

Consider your own conscience for a moment. What relationships do you see between behavior you engage in that makes you feel guilty (conscience-pangs) and the sorts of expectations for being good that came from your parents? Usually, we are inclined to feel guilty when we do something that reminds us of behaviors we were punished for as we grew up. Is this true for you?

The First Five Years Are Most Critical

The psychoanalytic view of man has conceived the process of personality development as a continuous one and has consistently emphasized the first five years of life as the most critical stages of development. It is during these years, Freud maintained, that the foundations for adult personality are largely established. He believed that there is a predictable sequence of psychosexual stages through which the child passes. Individual differences in adult personality, he assumed, could be ultimately traced to the specific manner in which a child experiences and handles the conflicts aroused in these stages.

What Freud did was to take observable, biological facts and give them a dynamic psychological orientation. Perhaps we can understand this better by taking a brief look at the three stages a child passes through during his first five and a half years of life.

Development during the first years of life is called the *oral stage* and is so labeled because the infant's focus of attention and activity is centered mainly around his mouth, esophagus, and stomach. Freud further concluded that the baby has a great awareness of his pleasure in taking food and that the child soon comes to associate the feeding process (nursing) with the attitudes reflected by the mother as she feeds him. It was assumed that whatever attitudes shown by the mother during the feeding process were also attitudes the child was likely to associate with food, feeding, and the nursing process. On a broader scale, the psychoanalytic position maintains that a child psychologically "incorporates" much about life in general during this stage as he makes connections between his oral needs and his experiences with food. It is speculated, for example, that infants allowed to remain too often in a state of uncertainty (tension, hunger) tend to develop into the kind of person who in later life is perpetually uncertain about whether people or circumstances can be trusted. Indeed, the speculation goes further to suggest that excessive tension and/or frustration of oral needs may leave a child fixated at this level of development to the extent that later adult oral activities—excessive drinking, smoking, eating, or talking—become dominant expressions of his life-style. What happens to a child during his first year of life is seen as closely related to his sense of security.

During the *anal stage,* encompassing the second and third years of life, the infant's attention shifts mainly to anal activity, which is particularly emphasized through parental urges for toilet training. According to Freud, the tactics employed by the mother along with her attitudes about such matters as defecation, cleanliness, and control determine in large measure what kind of influence that toilet training will have upon personality and its development. Here again, there may be enduring anal fixations, which may result from punishment for failure to control elimination or from excessive rewards for successful control. Freud theorized that people who become fixated at this stage are inclined to show "anal" characteristics throughout their lives—for example, stinginess, stubborness, excessive neatness, compulsive perfectionism, and the like. The reasoning is that if a child is made to feel unduly guilty or anxious about neatness or cleanliness early in his life, these characteristics will persist into his adult years as well.

Along these lines I am reminded of a client who was obsessed with the idea of keeping herself and her possessions immaculately clean. In addition, everything had to be in a certain place and in a certain order or she would experience extreme anxiety. Among the early memories she recollected were those of a domineering and perfectionistic mother screaming, yelling, and becoming very upset whenever she (the client) soiled her diapers or training pants. Gradually, over years of living with a perfectionistic, compulsive mother this girl began to equate practically everything of her own that was out of place or untidy or in some way "not perfect" with being bad. So preoccupied was she with the possibility of being "dirty" that during the early months of therapy the first thing she would do after leaving a session was to use a spray disinfectant on the back of her coat in the event that there were germs picked up from the chair she had been sitting on! (She was able to relate this, by the way, only when she discovered that being perfect was not a necessary prerequisite to being a good or acceptable person.)

TO THINK ABOUT

The behavioral dynamics that psychoanalysts trace back to the preschool years may or may not be true from person to person. How about for you? The next time you see your parents it might be interesting to ask them how you were toilet trained, how old you were, and what their feelings were about it. And then look for relationships between how you were trained and your current attitudes toward being or not being compulsive. Do you find any?

The *phallic stage* is theorized to occur between three and five and one-half years of age. It is during this stage that the child grows increasingly aware of his own body and particularly of the pleasurable genital sensations he begins to experience. Indeed, Freud left a Victorian society flabbergasted in the wake of his assertion that childhood sexuality, with its sexual fantasy and masturbation, was a universal and normal phenomenon, a view that most people now take more or less for granted. At this stage typically occurs what Freud termed the *Oedipus complex* (so-called after the classical Greek myth of King Oedipus who unwittingly killed his father and married his mother). This is the "childhood romance" we've all heard about in which the boy experiences erotic feelings toward the mother and antagonistic feelings toward the father. This same phenomenon for girls, but in reverse, is known as the *Electra complex*. Thus, according to psychoanalytic theory, the boy and the girl place themselves in the fantasied role of father and mother, respectively, out of which grow their primary identifications with the parent of the same sex. If a young boy or girl were denied the opportunity to identify with an adult of the same sex because of, say, a parent's death or separation or noninvolved attitude then this makes it difficult for a child to assume the characteristics and behaviors appropriate to his or her sex role. One of the very important lessons that the psychoanalytic position has taught us about normal growth and development is that a boy learns how to be a man and how to give expression to normal male sexuality through a positive relationship to an adult male who is meaningful to him. This same phenomenon is true for a girl through her positive relationship to a meaningful adult female.

10

Much of Behavior Is Unconsciously Motivated

The concept of the *unconscious* occupies a central place in the traditional psychoanalytic view of man. Indeed, according to Freudian thinking, the origin of most of man's personal dynamics, like an iceberg, lies mostly beneath the conscious surface. Much of life, from the Freudian view, is living out unconscious wishes and conflicts, not only through the occupations we choose and the persons to whom we are attracted, but also in our hobbies, interests, preferences, and even such insignificant "accidents" as slips of the tongue, missed appointments, and lost articles. A very Freudian colleague of mine, for example, has observed that an indication of a successful class is the number of notebooks, texts, or other personal items left behind, which, he maintains, are really unconscious expressions on the part of students to return. (Or could it be that they are indications of a strong desire to leave in a hurry?) In any case, it is safe to say that the unconscious occupies an important position on the mantle of Freudian psychology.

Some Criticisms of the Psychoanalytic Position

Although psychoanalytic theory is now widely accepted, particularly among those who study and treat the emotionally disturbed, it nonetheless remains a controversial theory in the minds of persons who are inclined to assign more of man's behavior to conscious origins and who wish to understand the psychological systems of normal persons. Among the more common criticisms frequently leveled against the psychoanalytic view of man are the following:

1. The theory was generated out of a preoccupation with the pathology of abnormal people. It is doubtful whether such a theory can effectively deal with the normal personality.

2. The theory may overemphasize the breadth and depth of unconscious processes in behavior. It could well be that normal people are more aware of the origins of their motives for behaving than Freud gives them credit for.

3. The theory was established on the basis of emotional disturbances among middle-class people in Vienna over a half-century ago. There is no compelling evidence to suggest that the theory is equally applicable to other kinds of people in other cultural settings.

4. Although, as suggested by the theory, man can be characterized by his aggressive and sometimes vicious nature, studies of different cultures have shown that there are many peoples in the world who as a group are friendly and kind. For example, Margaret Mead found that the Arapesh, a primitive tribe living in the mountains of New Guinea, were peaceful people

11

who thought that ". . . all human beings. . . . are naturally unaggressive, self-denying . . . concerned with growing food to feed growing children."[2] Even though they lived in rocky terrain, Dr. Mead found the Arapesh to be gentle and cooperative, seldom showing hostile and aggressive behavior.

Along similar lines, Maslow[3] has described a notable lack of hostile aggressive behavior among the Northern Blackfoot Indians. In fact, he found a record of only five fist fights in fifteen years and no other signs of overt hostility!

Other evidence suggesting that man is not born with instinctual destructive urges is reflected in the behavior of African pygmies inhabiting the Ituri rain forests who neither hurt nor kill each other even though they are highly skilled with deadly blow guns and other weapons.[4] Also, data gathered in 1966 found that only three murders were committed in Iceland during a fifty-year period as compared to over 14,000 homicides each year in the United States alone.[5]

The Psychoanalytic Position in Summary

This is essentially a bio-psychological theory of human behavior that stresses the innate depravity of man, the over-riding influence of unconscious motivations, and the critical importance of the first five and a half years of life. As we have seen, each stage a child passes through (oral, anal, phallic) is linked to its biological counterpart (mouth, anus, genitals). In classical psychoanalytic terms, the term *sex* was used in the broadest way possible to include practically anything of a pleasurable nature—from eating, to holding a baby, to looking at a beautiful picture, to holding hands. Perhaps most importantly, the Freudian concept of man emphasizes the critical nature of past experiences as the primary and dominant forces influencing how one behaves in the present.

Not all psychoanalysts agree with Freud and many have struck out to develop their own views about the nature of man and the motivations behind his behavior. Among the contributors to the Neo-Freudian psychoanalytic movement who have given more emphasis to social and environmental factors—as opposed to purely innate or biological ones—in the development and function of personality are individuals such as K. Horney, E. Fromm, E. Erikson, C. G. Jung, A. Adler, and H. S. Sullivan, to name a few. (You will find basic references to each of these contributors in the "References of Related Interest" section at the end of this chapter.)

12   Now, then, let's turn our attention to a very important issue.

Implications from Psychoanalytic Psychology
for Teaching and Learning

This point of view reminds us of the critical importance of the early years and their contribution to later adult behavior. It also tells us that not all learning or motivation is conscious. Along this line, L. S. Kubie, a psychiatrist with a long and active interest in educational processes, has noted that:

> Traditional conceptions of how human beings think and learn have started from a natural but incorrect and misleading assumption *that we think and learn consciously*. This is not true. Conscious processes are important not for thinking but for sampling, checking, reality testing, correcting, ruminating, and communicating. Even the intake of bits of information, whether from the source or from the outer world, is predominately preconscious. It consists largely of an incessant subliminal bombardment which goes on unceasingly whether we are awake or asleep. . . . But whether the input is largely from distance and surface receptors (as in the normal waking state) or predominately from within the body (as in sleep), the major input is always subliminal. The conscious component is never more than a fragment of the total input. This neglected but basic psychophysiological fact is of major significance and is relevant to all educational processes.[6]

The psychoanalytic position does not deal directly with the sort of teaching and learning that goes on in a classroom. It is a theory of behavior, not of teaching and learning. Nonetheless, it can be useful to us not only in deepening our knowledge about unconscious motivations, but also for increasing our understanding of how adults serve as models for growing youth to imitate and identify with. Probably no theory of personality is more vigorous in underscoring the vast impact that adults, particularly "significant" (important, highly valued, highly esteemed) adults, can have on children and adolescents. Certainly parents are significant adults in the lives of their children. And so are teachers.

TO THINK ABOUT

Reflect back a moment. What one or two adults have had the most to do with how you felt about yourself as you grew up? Have they given you essentially positive or negative feedback about your worth as a person? How is that feedback reflected in your behavior and in your feelings of personal adequacy?

Growing children and adolescents are malleable. They want to grow up; they want to become like the adults around them and have more power, strength, status, privileges, and freedom.   What adults say to them matters. How adults behave around them makes a difference.   The sensitive first-grade teacher who says something like, "John, how well you read the words on that page!" may be the only positive, significant adult who has encouraged John in all his six years of living.   John's warm and trusting feelings toward that teacher may be the beginning of a healthy identification with an adult who can help him grow in positive ways.   On the other hand, a grouchy tenth-grade teacher who yells something like, "Sally, you never pronounce words right when you read" may nourish a fifteen-year-old girl's already existing seeds of self-doubt and self-disappointment.

One does not have to agree entirely with everything the psychoanalytic position declares about the nature of man and his growth and development in order to profit from it.   For many, it helps to make them more aware of the existence of unconscious motivations in themselves and others and to the possible connective links between adult behavior and childhood experiences.   How many students, for example, sit through entire terms and never say a word in their classes?   The reasons most frequently cited for the silence are along the lines of "I learn better by listening" or "I can learn so much more from other people's experiences" or "I really never had anything important to say."   These are usually the *conscious* reasons.   The less conscious ones are more likely along the lines of "I'm afraid of being laughed at or saying the wrong thing or being ridiculed."   More often than not being ridiculed or laughed at *was* a reality for the silent student.   Not infrequently experiences of this sort go back, way back, to those critical formative years.

There are at least two implications here for teachers:

1. Teachers are usually numbered among those significant persons in a child or adolescent's life who make a difference and who, in the context of an interpersonal relationship, can influence a youth's attitudes about himself for better or for worse.

2. Inasmuch as the basic framework for self-attitudes, which may last a lifetime, are established during the formative years, it is absolutely essential that teachers be positive and concentrate on what students *can do* — their strengths, possibilities, and potentials — rather than to be negative and focus on what students can not do — their weaknesses, shortcomings, and deficiencies.

Now then, let us turn our attention to another major theoretical camp in psychology.

THE BEHAVIORISTIC POSITION

The behavioristic position is an approach to human behavior stressing outer experience, overt behavior, action and reaction.   It is also referred to as stimulus-response psychology because it is an approach that seeks to understand behavior generally, and teaching and learning specifically, by studying the conditions (stimuli) *outside* a person that cause him to behave (respond) in certain ways.   Historically, it is a position that grew out of a reaction to what was called introspectionist psychology, which, as its name suggests, was an approach to understanding behavior through close and systematic examination of a person's conscious, introspective reports.

Whereas the introspectionists started out by asking, "What is being given in the *inner* experience?" the behavioristic approach is to ask, "What is being given in the *outer* experience?"   Thus, introspective study of conscious states or processes were rejected as being essentially mentalistic or prescientific because of the possibility of there being too much subjective error.

So, starting out with the basic assumption that man's behavior was shaped, molded, and maintained by forces outside himself, a psychologist by the name of John B. Watson[7] dramatically shifted the focus of psychology from inner psychic processes to outer behavior that is completely observable.   Watson asserted that the proper starting point for understanding man is through the study of his *behavior*—that is, what man *does*, not what he thinks or feels.

It may be interesting to briefly note that the early roots of stimulus-response theory were nurtured by the work of the Russian physiologist Ivan Pavlov,[8] who, in a classic experiment, conditioned a dog to salivate at the sound of a bell by associating that sound with the sight and smell of meat. Using a similar approach, Watson conditioned a child to fear a rat by substituting a loud, sudden noise for the rat.   He reasoned that if he could condition a child to fear a particular kind of animal, he could presumably condition him to fear anything else.   Indeed, he went on to assert that if he could condition a person to fear anything, he could also condition him to hate or love or do just about anything he (Watson) wanted him to do.   In Watson's own eyes his psychological system was such that "given a stimulus, psychology can predict what the response will be.   Or, on the other hand, given the response, it can specify the nature of the effective stimulus."[9]

Behavior Can Be Predicted, Routed, and Controlled—Freedom a Myth

As you can see, behavioristic psychology is very specific and very bold in its assertion that it can predict and route the course and expression of human behavior.   This view of the malleability of human behavior is probably best reflected in a very famous statement by John Watson back in 1919 when he said, "Give me a dozen healthy infants, well formed, to bring them up in any way I choose and I'll guarantee you to take any one at random and train him to become any type of specialist I might se-lect—doctor, lawyer, artist, merchant-chief and, yes, even beggar-man and thief, regardless of his talents, penchants, tendencies, abilities, vocations, and race of his ancestors."[10]

Although not all modern-day behaviorists would agree that Watson could do all that he promised in the above statement, there would none-theless be substantial agreement among those subscribing to behaviorism that behavior can be dramatically altered, shaped, controlled, and manipu-lated through the use of appropriate reinforcements.

Indeed B. F. Skinner, a Harvard psychologist who is one of the leading spokesmen for the behavioristic position, caused a national stir with his book, *Beyond Freedom and Dignity*,[11] in which he asserted that the idea of human freedom is really a myth. Skinner's thinking runs counter to the traditional humanistic image of man as an autonomous individual pos-sessed of a measure of freedom and personal dignity. According to Skinner, we attribute freedom and dignity to the human agent only because we retain the myth of the inner man who is somehow independent of the controlling influences of his environment. Skinner insists that no such creature exists. For example, Skinner has repeatedly asserted that *all behavior is lawful,* which, from a behavioristic perspective, means that an individual's behavior is entirely a product of, and can be understood purely in terms of, the objective world. We witness one individual commit a serious crime and still another perform a great service for humanity. *It is important to understand that to a behaviorist both expressions of behavior result from an interplay of identifiable variables that completely determine behavior.* In Skinner's words:

> We cannot apply the methods of science to a subject matter which is assumed to move about capriciously. Science not only describes, it predicts. It deals not only with the past but with the future. Nor is prediction the last word. To the extent that relevant conditions can be altered. If we are to use the methods of science in the field of human affairs, we must assume that behavior is lawful and determined. We must expect to discover that what a man does is the result of specifiable conditions and that once these conditions have been discovered, we can anticipate and to some extent determine his actions.
>
> This possibility is offensive to many people. It is opposed to a tradition of long standing which regards man as a free agent, whose behavior is the product, not of a specifiable antecedent condition, but of spontaneous inner changes of course. Prevailing philosophies of human nature recognize an in-ternal "will" which has the power to interfere with causal relationships and which makes the prediction and control of behavior impossible. To suggest that we abandon this view is to threaten many cherished beliefs—to under-mine what appears to be a stimulating and productive conception of human behavior.[12]

Is such a world of behavioral manipulation really possible? Skinner believes that it is. The way to do it, he thinks, is through "behavioral technology," a developing science of control that aims to change the environment rather than people, that seeks to alter actions rather than feelings, and that shifts the customary psychological emphasis on the world inside people to the world outside them. Central to the behavioristic approach is a method of conditioning, based on reinforcement, that has been used with uniform success on laboratory animals: giving rewards to mold the subject to the experimenter's will. According to Skinner and his followers, the same technique can be made to work equally well with human beings.

How would it work? Let's take a look at some of the basic principles involved in this.

Behavioristic Strategies for Controlling Behavior

Reinforcement is the critical concept in behavioristic psychology. Reinforcement can be defined as any event that strengthens the tendency for a response to be repeated. The idea of reinforcement is so important to behaviorism that it was recognized long ago as the law of effect.[13] Very simply, the law states that an act that has a satisfying effect—for instance, satisfaction of a motive state, escape from punishment, or relief from fear—will be learned, but an act that has an unpleasant effect or consequence—such as lack of reward, frustration of a motive, or fear—will not be learned.

In less weighty language, this means basically that one is more apt to repeat those behaviors for which he has been rewarded. If you study hard for an exam and receive what you consider to be a high grade, you will be likely to study hard for your next exam also. In other words, when a pleasant reward follows a specific behavior, then this behavior is likely to be repeated at some future time under similar conditions.

The consequences of reinforcement can be nicely seen in an informal experiment conducted by a group of psychology students who planned that on alternate days they would (1) laugh at anything even remotely funny in the instructor's lecture and (2) not even crack a smile no matter what the professor said or did. These experimenters (conspirators may be the more accurate term) reported that until the instructor caught on to the game there was vast day-to-day variation in the amount of humor or attempted humor in lectures. For instance, on days his humor was reinforced the instructor seemed to double his efforts to be funny. However, on days when his best jokes met with stony silence, lectures became grimly serious. Of course, similar effects of reinforcement on verbal behavior have been produced less dramatically but more quantifiably in laboratory investigations.[14]

Conditioning is another important concept associated with the behavioristic position. Basically there are two different conditioning processes—classical (or Pavlovian) and instrumental (operant). We should emphasize here that the two different types of conditioning processes do

17

not necessarily require two different sets of explanatory principles. A distinction is made between the two primarily because they make use of different techniques to elicit desired behaviors. Let's take some examples of how each of these conditioning processes work in actual practice.

Classical conditioning practices. Classical conditioning is probably the simplest of all forms of learning. It is what we see when a burned child fears the fire. Even more specifically it is what we see in the burned child's response to the *sight* of fire. What this means is that a *conditioned stimulus* (the sight of fire) comes to have the potential to evoke the *response* (fear) formerly reserved for the *unconditioned stimulus* (actual heat of the fire). Most people will automatically respond to anything that actually burns. But to react before being burned, to respond to the sight of fire, is learned behavior based on experience. It is a *conditioned response* much the same as Pavlov's dog salivating at the sound of a bell was a conditioned response.

An example closer to home would be that of a youngster who has been conditioned to fear school. Indeed, I know a high school student who is so fearful of school, that even the thought of going there causes him to tremble. What this means is that a *conditioned stimulus* (the thought of school and what happens there) comes to have the potential to evoke the *response* (fear, trembling) formerly reserved for the *unconditioned stimulus* (actual experiences with failure and humiliation). Most students will automatically respond to school failure experiences. But to respond *before* a failure (in other words, to the anticipation of a failure) is a learned behavior based on experience. Again, this is what you call a conditioned response. The boy had literally been "conditioned" to fear school because of his frequent experiences with failure. On the other hand, a teen-age neighbor of mine is "conditioned" the other way. He loves school because he associates it with success and positive feelings about himself.

Along a somewhat lighter vein, Guthrie[15] has reported the use of the principles of classical conditioning by two farm boys who systematically reeducated the minister's horse. Unhappy with their weekly assignment of grooming and feeding the horse while the preacher visited their parents, the boys conducted a small-scale learning experiment. For an hour, one boy held the horse between the shafts while his collaborator sat in the buggy and repeatedly yelled "whoa" and simultaneously poked the horse with the point of a hay fork. As you might suspect, the horse's retraining produced some serious surprises for the minister.

In each of these examples, the form of learning is the same. The unconditioned stimulus (the fire, the school, the pitchfork) evokes an unconditioned response (fear, trembling, jumping), which—when associated properly with the original unconditioned stimulus—leads to the conditioned response (fear, trembling, jumping).

18

Operant or instrumental conditioning practices. Where classical conditioning involves a change in the stimulus that evokes a response, operant conditioning involves a selection, from many responses, of the one that habitually will be given in a stimulus situation. The following statement by Skinner is indicative of the theoretical simplicity in operant conditioning:

> By arranging a reinforcing consequence, we increase the rate at which a response occurs; by eliminating the consequence, we decrease the rate. These are the processes of operant conditioning and extinction.[16]

In the classical conditioning process we just discussed, you saw that the person or animal in question receives his reinforcement no matter what he does in the learning situation. For example, the horse the boys were "retraining" got poked no matter what he did when the driver called "whoa." That is, the horse's behavior had nothing to do with whether he got poked. This programmed sequence of events occurred without alternation. By contrast, the behavior of the person in an operant conditioning situation has everything to do with his being reinforced. That is, his behavior is *instrumental* for the reward to occur. He must in some way *operate* within his environment for the reward to happen. Therefore, it is the person or animal's actions rather than another person's scheduling that determines the frequency and rate of reward.

A teacher friend of mine has nicely implemented the basic principles of operant conditioning in a technique to involve his more quiet students in class discussions. What he does is to direct his comments or questions to shy, bashful students whenever it appears that their hands are even close to being raised. For example, one of his quieter students had merely raised his hand to scratch his ear and the teacher wondered what his *opinion* was (not what he *knew*—that's a different order of question) about some of the ideas being expressed regarding the topic at hand. The student was a bit flustered at first, but he did express some opinions. Without making a big deal of it the teacher praised the boy for contributing and the class went on. By responding to a partially raised hand and publicly praising a quiet, shy boy, a wise teacher had planted the seeds of a healthy connection in this boy's mind between raising his hand and contributing and feeling good about the whole thing. True, this did not change the boy's quiet behavior overnight, but the boy did gradually increase the number of times he volunteered to participate in class.

TO THINK ABOUT

Not infrequently, students in my class take issue with the fact that a teacher deliberately does something—as in the example above—to

> change or alter a student's behavior. As one student put it, "I think it's damn unethical to deliberately manipulate a student through the use of rewards or what is called 'operant conditioning.' I don't care what the end result is. A student is no longer free when you do that."
>
> How do you feel about this issue? Would you do something like my teacher friend did? Why or why not?

Some Criticisms of the Behavioristic Position

Every theory has its critics. Behaviorism is no exception. As you may suspect, behaviorism has been variously criticized for allegedly depersonalizing or dehumanizing man's basic nature because of its emphasis on "quantifying" behavior and "objectifying" man.

Indeed it is precisely because of the emphasis on "quantifying" behavior and "objectifying" man that behaviorism meets its stiffest resistance. The whole idea of supporting an "objective" psychology that develops a technology for controlling and manipulating human behavior is frightening to some and appalling to many. Skinner is explicit about his feelings regarding the control issue:

> Science is readily increasing our power to influence, change, mold—in a word, control—human behavior. It has extended our "understanding" (whatever that may be) so that we deal more successfully with people in nonscientific ways, but it has also identified conditions or variables which can be used to predict and control behavior in a new, and increasingly rigorous, technology.[17]

Some of the major questions and criticisms regarding the control issue are raised by Carl Rogers, a psychologist with a far more humanistic bent:

> They can be stated very briefly: Who will be controlled? Who will exercise control? What type of control will be exercised? Most important of all, toward what end or what purpose, or in pursuit of what value, will control be exercised? . . . if we choose some particular goal or series of goals for human beings and then set out on a large scale to control human behavior to the end of achieving these goals, we are locked in the rigidity of our initial choice, because scientific endeavor can never transcend itself to select new goals. Only subjective human persons can do that. . . . If, however, a part of our scheme is to set free some "planners" who do not have to be happy, who are not controlled, and who are therefore free to choose other values, this has several meanings. . . It means that if it is necessary to set up an elite group which is free, then this shows all too clearly that the great majority are only slaves—no matter by what high-sounding name we call them—of those who select the goals.[18]

The criticism aimed at the behavioristic position always seems to revolve around two major issues: (1) Is there really no such thing as a subjective, inner man capable of making free choices? (2) Can people—and if it is possible—*should* people be controlled through an advanced behavioral technology that controls the environment? The critics say, yes there is an inner man, and no we should not control behavior. How do you feel about this?

TO THINK ABOUT

Consider it for a moment. If you had your choice between being able to make it possible for all youths to experience academic success by systematically controlling the school environment with the techniques discussed in this section or allowing all youths the freedom to learn or not as determined by their own free will, which would you choose? Why? Which system would you prefer to be a student in? Why?

The Behavioristic Position in Summary

Behaviorism is a psychological position that seeks to understand behavior in terms of those conditions and experiences that act on a person from the outside and cause him to behave in certain ways. The behavioristic model can interpret man so as to include those expressions of behavior that are good or evil, rational or irrational, depending on his conditioning. However, rather than say that behavior is caused or influenced by inferred constructs, such as an ego or a superego or a "self," which cannot be directly observed, seen, watched, or controlled, behavioristic psychology looks for the causes in the reinforcement history of a person. Thus it is that, from a behavioristic point of view, we are more or less at the mercy of our previous conditioning and present environment. Our freedom of choice in this frame of reference is really an illusion of something we only *think* we have.

Although we could certainly enlarge our picture of the behavioristic position with such related concepts as extinction, partial reinforcement, secondary conditioning, stimulus generalization, and so on, it is sufficient for our purposes to know that what we have discussed represents some of the basic tenets of the S-R view of man.

Actually there is no single behavioristic position, but rather a cluster of overlapping positions resembling each other more or less but at the same time each possessing certain distinctive characteristics. For example, there is one position that emphasizes the contiguity of stimulus and response—that is, the simultaneous occurrence of the two is regarded as a sufficient condition for a connection to be established. Psychologists associated with this position are W. K. Estes and E. R. Guthrie. There is still another position, very much related to the contiguity view, that stresses the importance of reinforcement in order to "stamp in" the desired response. Psychologists frequently associated with this position include E. C. Thorndike, J. Dollard, N. Miller, C. Hull, and K. Spence.

Still another behavioristic position asserts that there are at least two fundamental kinds of learning, and, therefore, theory must encompass both of them. Briefly, the position suggests that learning can be divided into two processes, conditioning or *sign learning*, with fear as a basic component, and *solution learning*, with habit formation as the key feature. This position is probably best known as Mowrer's revised two-factor theory. (Basic references to each of the men can be found in the "References of Related Interest" section at the end of this chapter. Also included in those references is an excellent volume by Glen Snelbecker titled, *Learning Theory, Instructional Theory, and Psychoeducational Design* [1974], which very skillfully discusses these and other positions related to the behavioristic model.)

To this point we have had brief glimpses of how the psychoanalytic view of man emphasizes early life experiences and unconscious motivations and how behaviorism emphasizes a person's reinforcement history and responses to external stimuli. The next question is what are the implications of the behavioristic position for better understanding the dynamics of teaching and learning?

Implications from Behavioristic Psychology for Teaching and Learning

Even if you happen to be uncomfortable with the emphasis on control and manipulation of behavior that emerge from this position, it can still offer a great deal in the way of helping you to improve teaching practices and learning outcomes.

One of the immediate implications of this view has to do with the use of reinforcement, especially positive reinforcement. This is something we use all the time except that most of us refer to positive reinforcement as praise, a compliment, a flattering remark, or a gift. The point is that whether we are the recipients or givers of positive reinforcement, it usually makes us feel good and helps us to be generally more available to experiences of a similar sort.

Percival Symonds, an educator of considerable note, has pointed out some of the specific implications growing from behaviorism for teaching and learning:

The most potent reward (reinforcement) for classroom learning is the teacher's acceptance of what the pupil does and the way he does it, because this acceptance becomes a guide in his future activities. This acceptance on the part of the teacher can take the form of tangible tokens, such as gold stars, honor rolls, and the like. But there is a tendency to short-circuit rewards so that a "correct" or "right" will do equally well. The effective teacher can communicate gestures of approbation to the slighted nod of the head, gleam in the eye, and general relaxed posture. . . .[19]

As we consider the implications of behaviorism for teaching and learning, we should keep in mind that reinforcement for learning in school does not necessarily have to be in the form of tangible tokens of approval such as stars, prizes, medals, money, or a place on the honor roll, although, to be sure, tangible rewards of this sort can be and are effective. Actually, the most effective rewards are embedded in satisfying relationships. Indeed, for most students (not to mention people generally), the most effective reinforcements for learning are a teacher's acceptance and approval. To reward a student's efforts does not require costly outlays for expensive gifts. Quite sufficient in most cases will be the teacher's attention, interest, pleasure, and satisfaction in what the student does.

TO THINK ABOUT

This is not something that has to be thought about in the abstract. Think about the last time an instructor gave you some attention or showed some interest in your work. How did that make you feel? How would you describe your attitude toward the instructor and the class generally. If you haven't received any attention, how does that make you feel? More importantly, how have you translated your feeling—good or bad—into observable behavior in class?

It is simple enough to use the concept of reinforcement in training animals because animals usually make a simple association between the reward and the act and then repeat the whole process again under similar conditions. In the case of human beings, however, one rewards not only the act but the person, so that the whole psychology of the self is involved. What this means is that reinforcement not only reinforces the specific act that is rewarded, but it also enhances the self. This leaves most students with an increased sense of self-satisfaction, self-confidence, and self-esteem, feelings we hope all students can experience.

Perhaps one of the most important implications of the behavioristic position for teaching and learning is the inherent stimulus potential of the teacher. The teacher is a stimulus and he does affect how students respond. How a teacher presents himself, his tone of voice, his manner of dress, his personality style, and so on all have stimulus potential in the sense that each characteristic will cause different students to respond in different ways and for different reasons. What this suggests is that we have

23

to be as aware as possible of how we are coming across to students. In other words, we have to understand what it is about ourselves that may be causing students to respond favorably or unfavorably. Once we begin to get in touch with ourselves as individuals then we're in a position to change those personal qualities ("quirks," even) that seem to be constricting and blocking student growth. At the same time, we can be looking for ways to refine those qualities that seem to have an expanding and facilitating effect.

> ### TO THINK ABOUT
>
> How about the instructors you have this term or semester? What is it about him, her, or them which is facilitating or blocking your learning? What is it about your instructor's(s') stimulus potential that encourages you to respond the way you do? What does this suggest for your own behavior as a teacher?

At least one big lesson growing from the behavioristic approach to teaching and learning is that behaviors that are reinforced or rewarded are more likely to recur. Watson, after a substantial review of research, concluded that "The type of reward [reinforcement] which has the greatest transfer value to other life-situations is the kind one gives oneself—the sense of satisfaction in achieving purposes."[20]

Let us turn now to still another and different view of man—one that considers the "inner man" rejected by the behavioristic position.

THE HUMANISTIC-PERCEPTUAL POSITION

The view of human behavior that grows out of a humanistic-perceptual framework is one that focuses on man, in a social context, who is influenced and guided by the personal meanings he attaches to his experiences. It is a point of view that focuses not so much on man's biological drives, but on his goals; not so much on stimuli impinging upon him, but on his desires to be or to do something; not so much on his past experiences, but on his current circumstances; not so much on "environmental forces" as such, but on his perceptions of those forces. Hence, the emphasis is on the *subjective* qualities of human experience, the personal meaning of an experience to a person, rather than on his objective, observable, measurable responses.

This humanistic-perceptual view of man represents what is sometimes called the "third force" in psychology insofar as it endeavors to go beyond the psychoanalytic and behavioristic views of man by focusing on the positive aspects of man, his inner-directed and conscious motivations, and his self-selected goals.

The late A. H. Maslow, a humanistic psychologist of considerable note, has observed that:

> From Freud we learned that the past exists *now* in the person. Now we must learn . . . that the future also exists *now* in the person in the form of ideals, hopes, goals, unrealized potentials, mission, fate, destiny, etc. One for whom no future exists is reduced to the concrete, to hopelessness, to emptiness. For him, time must be endlessly "filled." Striving, the usual organizer of most activity, when lost, leaves the person unorganized and unintegrated.[21]

This view considers man to be more than a hapless victim shackled to past experiences over which he has little control, and more than an automaton responding to conditions outside of himself. What has been done and what can be done within a humanistic-perceptual orientation has perhaps been most eloquently expressed by Gordon Allport, another very highly esteemed psychologist during his time:

> Some [views of man] are based largely upon the behavior of sick and anxious people or upon the antics of captive and desperate rats. Fewer theories have derived from the study of healthy human beings, those who strive not so much to preserve life as to make it worth living. Thus we find today many studies of criminals, few of law-abiders; many of fear, few of courage; more on hostility than on affiliation; much on blindness in man, little on vision; much on his past, little on outreaching into his future.[22]

Reasonable questions you may be asking at this point could be something on the order of: "Well why *haven't* we studied more healthy human beings? Why *have* we studied only select populations under special conditions in our effort to understand human behavior?" Perhaps the following observation by a clinical psychologist may help us understand the "whys" involved here.

> Because of our need to compete with the physical sciences, behavioral sciences have skipped over, by and large, the naturalistic stage from which other disciplines developed. We have not been people-watchers as biologists were bird- and bug-watchers. We have moved too quickly into the laboratory and looked only at special populations of people under special circumstances: we have thought we could derive generalizations about human behavior without first gaining the kind of understanding that could come only from years of performing normal tasks. Very few of us make any attempt to use our scientific training to investigate what people are really like when they are being

themselves. When one examines the literature in the behavioral sciences, one seldom has the feeling, "that's what it's like to be me." The *person* is usually missing and the findings have no reality or meaning for us because we cannot find ourselves.[23]

Contributions of Phenomenology and Existential Psychology

Since humanistic psychology, phenomenology, and existential psychology are frequently used in the same breath by psychologists discussing a humanistic-perceptual frame of reference, it might be well for us to briefly examine the meaning of each of these terms and their relationships to each other.

Let's begin with existentialism. This is basically a twentieth-century philosophy that stresses each person's responsibility for making himself what he is. It is a position that states that philosophizing must begin in an individual's intense awareness of the human predicament — *his own predicament* — which is the finitude and contingency of man's existence. More than this, it is an introspective philosophy that expresses each person's awareness of personal contingency and freedom to choose among alternatives for behaving. Indeed, the existential outlook states that a person's essence (being, behavior, personality, "self") is *created by his choices.* As Jean-Paul Sartre succinctly put it: "I am my choices." Within this framework, each individual is seen as having absolute freedom. In fact, even refusing to choose represents a personal choice. Thus the criteria for behavior is within the individual, which, in effect, makes each person the architect of his own life. The major pillars of the existential position have been stated in the form of three propositions:

1. I am a *choosing* agent, unable to avoid choosing my way through life.
2. I am a *free* agent, absolutely free to set the goals of my own life.
3. I am a *responsible* agent, personally accountable for my free choices as they are revealed in how I live my life.[24]

TO THINK ABOUT

Once again we have the freedom versus non-freedom issue. Skinner says: "The hypothesis that man is not free is essential to the application of scientific method to the study of human behavior. The free inner man who is held responsible for his behavior is only a pre-scientific substitute for the kinds of causes which are discovered in the course of scientific analysis; all these alternative causes lie *outside* the individual."[25]

Rogers, on the other hand, maintains that ". . . the freedom I am talking about is essentially an inner thing, something which exists in the living person. . . . It is the realization that I can live myself, here and now, by my own choice. It is the quality of courage which enables a person to step into the uncertainty of the unknown as he chooses himself."[26]

Two giants in psychology with opposing views—one says we are controlled by our environment, the other says we're free to choose. Where do you stand on this issue? Consider a simple here-and-now question. Why are you reading this book now? Do you *have* to, or is it your choice? How free do you feel *not* to read it? A larger question is: Who or what is it that determines what you do and when? What are the implications of your thinking about this for your work as a professional person?

A chief tenet of existentialism is the idea that man struggles to transcend himself—to reach beyond himself—always oriented to his possibilities. In this sense, the idea of transcendence boils down to what has been called man's capacity for "dynamic self-consciousness."[27] Another way of saying it is that not only can a person think but he can also think about (criticize and correct) his thinking. Not only can a person feel, but he can have feelings about his feelings. Man is not only *conscious,* he is self-conscious.

Phenomenology is a related position within the humanistic-perceptual framework and is derived from a school of philosophy known as, of all things, phenomenology. This view asserts that reality lies not in the event but in the phenomenon, that is, an individual's *perception* of the event. It is interesting to note that in its original usage, a phenomenon was "that which was known through the senses and immediate experience rather than through deductions."

Combs and Snygg, two psychologists who have been very influential in developing the phenomenological position have written that:

This approach seeks to understand the behavior of the individual from his *own* point of view. It attempts to observe people, not as they seem to outsiders, but as they seem to themselves. People do not behave solely because of the external forces to which they are exposed. People behave as they do in consequence of how things seem to them.[28]

This is a bit different from the behavioristic concept of behavior. Instead of perceiving behavior as associations between stimuli and responses, phenomenological psychology views it as a set of *cognitive structures* intervening between stimuli and responses. This could be expressed as S-O-R, the "O" (for organism) referring to those intervening or mediating factors.

Combs and Snygg[29] have developed the idea that each person behaves in a manner consistent with his "perceptual field," which is a more or less fluid organization of personal meanings existing for every individual at any given instant in time. Perceptual field has also been called one's private or personal world, one's psychological field or life space, or one's phenomenal field. The phenomenological outlook has been nicely captured by Carl Rogers' observation that "The organism reacts to the field as it is experienced and perceived. This perceptual field is, for the individual, 'reality.'"[30] In other words, a person responds not to the objective environment, but to the environment as he perceives and understands it. For the person in question, it is reality no matter how much he may distort and personalize it. The idea of how one's perception of "reality" can influence behavior is nicely illustrated in the following example cited by Combs and Snygg:

> Several years ago a friend of mine was driving in a car at dusk along a Western road. A globular mass, about two feet in diameter, suddenly appeared directly in the path of the car. A passenger screamed and grasped the wheel attempting to steer the car around the object. The driver, however, tightened his grip on the wheel and drove directly into the object. The behavior of both the driver and the passenger was determined by his own (perceptions). The passenger, an Easterner, saw the object in the highway as a boulder and fought desperately to steer the car around it. The driver, a native Westerner, saw it as a tumbleweed and devoted his efforts to keeping his passenger from overturning the car.[31]

Phenomenology is difficult to precisely define. It is an old term, now stewing in its own liberal metaphysical juices, that has to allow for such wide scope for change and individuality that there could be almost as many phenomenologies as there are phenomenologists. Why? Because the essential concern is with *meaning*, and meanings can vary extensively.

In sum, we could say that the emphasis of existential psychology is on personal choice, freedom, and responsibility, while the phenomenological emphasis is on perceptions, personal meanings, and subjective experiences. Since the humanistic-perceptual view of man is an orientation that centers on human interests and values, man's ability to make conscious choices, and man's perceptions of himself, the incorporation of existential and phenomenological ideas into this system is really a natural blending of overlapping concerns and views regarding the nature of man.

Humanistic-Perceptual Concepts About the Nature of Man

James Bugental[32] has suggested five basic postulates for the humanistic-perceptual view, which may help us give additional perspective to this frame of reference for understanding human behavior:

1. *Man, as man, supersedes the sum of his parts.* In other words, man is more than the accumulation of his various part-functions. I suppose you

could say that this is something like saying that Bernstein's score for *West Side Story* is more than the summation of the number of individual musical notes that went into composing it.

2. *Man has his being in a human context.* The unique nature of man is expressed through his relationship to his fellows and in this sense humanistic psychology is always concerned with man's "interpersonal potential."

3. *Man is aware.* This suggests that whatever the degree of consciousness man is aware of himself and his existence. He does not move from one experience to the next as if they were discrete and independent episodes unrelated to each other. How a man behaves in the present is related to what happened in his past and connected to his hopes for the future.

4. *Man has choice.* Phenomenologically, choice is a given of experience. That is, when man is aware, he can choose and thereby become not a bystander, but a participant in experience.

5. *Man is intentional.* Through his choices of this or that, of going here or there, man demonstrates his intent. He "intends" through having purpose, through valuing, and through seeking meaning in his life. Man's intentionality, his "conscious deliberateness" you might call it, is the basis on which he builds his identity and distinguishes himself from other species.

Bugental[33] has also articulated five basic characteristics of the human orientation in psychology, which are as follows:

1. Humanistic psychology cares about man.
2. Humanistic psychology values meaning more than procedure.
3. Humanistic psychology looks for human rather than nonhuman validation. (In other words, a psychologist working strictly from this frame of reference would not advocate studying rats, pigeons, or monkeys as a way for understanding human behavior.)
4. Humanistic psychology accepts the relativism of all knowledge.
5. Humanistic psychology relies heavily upon the phenomenological orientation. (That is, the major focus of concern is on *experience* of each individual.)

Role of the Self in the Humanistic-Perceptual Framework

With the emphasis on man as he perceives himself, on personal meanings, values, choices, and perceptions, it is not surprising to find that the idea of self occupies an important place in the humanistic-perceptual view of man. Although the use of the self-concept was first introduced by William James in his 1890 book, *Principles of Psychology*,[34] the concept of self idea all but dropped out of sight during the first thirty years or so of this century because behaviorists and other psychologists thought it too "internal" and hence to unobservable to be of much value.

It is true — the self is internal. It is that very private picture each of us has regarding who we think we are, what we think we can do, and who we think we can be. It is that part of each of us of which we are *conscious*.

The self is the individual known to the individual. It is that to which we refer when we say I. It is the custodian of awareness; it is the thing about a person which has awareness and alertness, which notices what goes on, and notices what goes on in its own field.[35]

> **TO THINK ABOUT**
>
> Is the way you see your "self" the way others see you? You can do a little experiment. Write down three adjectives that, from your point of view, best describe your physical, social, emotional, and intellectual self. Have one or two people who know you fairly well do the same thing for you. Compare the responses. Are they similar? Different? If they're different from your own, check this out with your friends. Why do they see you the way they do? What sorts of cues are you giving that they have responded to? Sometimes, the self we're conscious of is not the same one others are.

Over time the idea of self-concept has emerged as a kind of unifying principle of personality for psychologists and educators with a humanistic-perceptual bent. It offers a way for taking into account the subjective experience of each individual and for understanding the meaning of that experience from his point of view.

All in all, the self occupies a central seat of importance in the humanistic-perceptual view of man. It emphasizes the individual as he sees himself and, even more, it underscores the role of consciousness in human behavior. The self-concept idea has grown in popularity in recent years and promises to become even more so. But, as with most points of view, there are usually two sides to consider. Let's look at the other side of this one.

Some Criticisms of the Humanistic-Perceptual Position

A major criticism of this position is that it seems like too much of a common-sense psychology and too little of a scientific one. Another criticism is that it is allegedly based upon a naïve type of phenomenology. Essentially this criticism means that there is more to understanding human behavior than a study of conscious processes will allow us to observe. One psychologist, for example, notes that ". . . such a psychology of consciousness has an element of common-sense appeal. . . . It does make sense to the layman; it accords with what he is ready and able to recognize in himself. . . . Because it overstates its claims, however, it may tend to promote the state of affairs away from which we have been striving—every man his own psychologist."[36] Child[37] has discussed four, of what he calls, "defects" in the humanistic-perceptual position. They are, I think, fairly representative of the criticisms frequently leveled at this position by proponents of other psychological systems. Let's briefly examine them.

One of the criticisms is that the humanistic position is too vague, in the sense that the concepts used are far enough from relation to specific fact that they have a real ambiguity. *Authenticity,* a favorite concept among humanistic-perceptual psychologists and teachers, is a good example. Critics wonder how it is possible to recognize an "authentic" person or an "authentic" act. Child suggests that the concept may be capable of clarification but that it invites differences of interpretation. A person described as a "fully functioning" individual or a student engaged in a "real and meaningful learning experience" would be examples of other "vague" concepts.

A second criticism has to do with the difficulty in verifying conceptual conclusions. "How," say the critics "can we verify or confirm the existence of an authentic person or a fully functioning individual or a real and meaningful learning experience? How can we get beyond the subjectivity involved in deciding what, for example, is 'authentic.'"

A third criticism is related to the idea that it is difficult to accumulate objectively verified knowledge. Say the critics, "How can we objectify 'real' learning when what is 'real' is so subjectively determined? That is, what is real for one student may be unreal to another. How do we know who to believe?"

Still a fourth criticism leveled at humanistic-perceptual psychology is what Child calls a "trend toward sentimentality." What this means is that there is more to understanding human behavior than that which is embodied in simple religious optimism, emphasizing the power of positive thinking, and the infinite capacity of the human will to achieve good.

All in all, critics of the humanistic-perceptual position see it as being too "soft," not rigorous enough to encourage the sort of tough, objective scientific investigation necessary to render it more than a "common-sense" psychology.

The Humanistic-Perceptual Position in Summary

As a method for explaining the "why" of human behavior, teachers and psychologists who work within a humanistic-perceptual framework are inclined to take an organismic view of human behavior, which accentuates man's wholeness and uniqueness. It is a point of view that attempts to describe the conditions necessary for a full, productive life. In a more profound sense, it is an outlook that concentrates more on man's potential for caring than it does on his capacity for hating. The focus of attention is on man's striving for identity and perfection, his capacity for love and creativity, and his need to discover and develop and express his real self. In short, it is a point of view that emphasizes theories of motivation centering on the purposefulness of human behavior and man's need to "actualize" himself, to reach his highest potential.

As I see it, one of the genuine merits of the humanistic-perceptual approach is that it does, in fact, bring psychology closer to the world of common sense. There is always the danger that psychology, in its concern for rigor and neatness, may divorce itself too completely from the world of real people with real problems. Focusing scientific attention on the phenomenal world, the world we can see, sense, and experience, the world from which common sense is born, the humanistic-perceptual approach affords the psychologist access to information and problems too often left to common sense by default. Like common sense, and unlike some other varieties of psychological theory, it does deal with experience and thus presents itself as an attractive alternative to those who find psychoanalytic and behavioristic views of man uncongenial.

Psychologists whose work has been within a humanistic-perceptual framework and who have paid special attention to such distinctly human features of man's existence as his ability and need to know and judge, to love and choose include such men as A. H. Maslow, E. Fromm, G. W. All-port, H. A. Murray, and C. R. Rogers. (Each of these contributors is noted in the "References of Related Interest" section at the end of this chapter.)

Implications from Humanistic-Perceptual Psychology for Teaching and Learning

From the humanistic-perceptual point of view, the major purpose of education is to help develop the individuality of each person, to assist him in realizing himself as a unique individual, and to help him actualize his potentialities. These are broad goals and probably no more or no less than what any teacher would want regardless of his view of human behavior. The difference lies not in the goals, but in the means for achieving them. I think Maslow stated the difference most clearly when he wrote:

> . . . we are now being confronted with a choice between two extremely different, almost mutually exclusive conceptions of learning. [One] is what I want to call for the sake of contrast and confrontation, *extrinsic learning*, i.e., learning of the outside, learning of the impersonal, of arbitrary associations, of

arbitrary conditioning, that is, of arbitrary meanings and responses. In this kind of learning, most often it is not the person himself who decides, but rather a teacher or an experimenter who says, "I will use a buzzer," "I will use a bell," "I will use a red light," and most important,"I will reinforce this or that." In this sense, learning is extrinsic to the learner, extrinsic to the personality, and is extrinsic also in the sense of collecting associations, conditionings, habits, or modes of action. It is as if these were *possessions* which the learner accumulates in the same way that he accumulates keys or coins and puts them in his pocket. They have little or nothing to do with the actualization or growth of the peculiar, idiosyncratic kind of person he is.[38]

A major implication for educational processes growing from this point of view is the emphasis on helping each student decide for himself who he is and what he wants to be. The implication is that students can decide for themselves, that they have conscious minds that enable them to make choices, and that through their capacity to make choices they will develop the sense of self necessary for productive, actualizing lives. In other words, the job of the teacher is to assist a student toward finding out *what's already in him* that can be refined and developed further.

As you can probably sense, this implies a far more optimistic hope for man than is apparent in the psychoanalytic view. It also suggests that a person is as capable of responding to that which is in him in terms of inherent capacities, personal goals, hopes, and ambitions as he is capable of responding to that which is outside of himself, such as other's expectations, extrinsic rewards, and the like.

Another major implication growing from this point of view is the idea that in order to effectively teach a student we must ry to understand him from his point of view. This is consistent with a little truism growing out of perceptual psychology that asserts that a person will behave in terms of what he *believes* to be true. Not what *is* true, but what he believes to be true about reality as *he perceives it*. If we hope to be effective teachers, then the suggestion is that we attempt to see the world as the student sees it, accept it as truth for him, and not attempt to force him into changing. This doesn't mean that a teacher should not challenge what a student believes or avoid presenting him with alternatives, it only suggests that to be effective *a teacher should start where the student's perceptions are and not where his own happen to be at the moment*.

This point of view values individuality, personal choice, indeed, it values values. It starts with the idea that students are different, and it strives to help students become more like themselves and less like each other. The teacher's role is less that of a director, coercer, or manipulator and more that of one who assists, helps, and ministers to growing, living, dynamic human beings already in the process of becoming. A significant implication emerging from this point of view is that good teaching is best

I'm not sure we can say this is *all* we need, but it sure does help.

done through a process of helping students explore and understand the personal meanings that are inherent in all their experiences.

The humanistic-perceptual position is one that stresses the idea that adequate persons are, among other factors, the products of strong values. Recent efforts to include "value clarification" exercises in teacher education and public education reflect the growing response to the importance of recognizing how personal values influence human behavior.[39,40]

Sometimes students get the idea that how they feel and what they think is not very important compared to scientific and objective facts. From a humanistic-perceptual point of view, emphasizing narrowly scientific and impersonally objective learning tends to inhibit the development of personal meanings. As discussed in the important book, *Perceiving, Behaving, Becoming*, which outlined a basic "philosophy" for a humanistic approach to education:

34

Many students perceive school as a place where one is forced to do things which have little pertinence to life as he experiences it. Education must be concerned with the values, beliefs, convictions and doubts of students. These realities as perceived by an individual are just as important, if not more so, as the so-called objective facts. This does not mean that factual materials are not useful in making sound value judgments or in formulating constructive social policies, but rather that an overemphasis on the scientific and the objective impedes self-fulfillment. Facts have no value in themselves alone. It is only as facts find there way into human organization of convictions, beliefs, frames of reference and attitudes that they come to fruition in intelligent behavior.[41]

EPILOGUE

Each of the preceding three points of view has something important to say about the nature of man and his behavior. The psychoanalytic view helps us better understand the nature of unconscious motivations and the contribution of past experiences to current behavior. The behavioristic view gives us some insight into the basic processes of conditioning and how outside stimuli can influence behavior. The humanistic-perceptual view allows us some understanding of the nature of man's subjective experiences and the personal meanings he assigns to those experiences.

It would not be accurate to say that one point of view is better or more effective than another, but it is possible that you may find yourself *valuing* one particular view more than others. However, leaning one way or the other does not mean that we cannot listen to the lessons, the evidence, or the experience of points of view different from that to which we are inclined.

If, for instance, a teacher believes that his students are simply products of past experiences or victims of social conditioning then he is in a poor position to consider the motivation potential in the future goals students may set for themselves or in the personal aspirations they are striving to meet. Of course if a teacher believes that there is no such thing as intrinsic motivation then he may find himself expending much of his energy devising ways to extrinsically keep students awake, interested, and alert. On the other hand, a teacher could be so caught up in the idea of each student having maximum freedom to do his own thing, making his own choices, arriving at his own decisions, and so on that he may overlook those students who may need some direction, guidance, and structure in order to perform at their best.

The point is that different students learn in different ways and are motivated by different reasons. If this is true, and there is plenty of research evidence to suggest that it is, then it may suggest that as teachers we have to be as flexible in our view of man as possible.

We began with a given and we can end with that same given. Whatever you do in teaching and as a teacher depends very much on what you think people are like, which, in all likelihood, is a generalized idea growing out of the kind of person you think you are. If, for example, you see yourself as molded and shaped primarily by early life experiences, then you may find yourself trying to understand another person's behavior in terms of what happened in his past. You may even find yourself feeling somewhat pessimistic about the idea of another person, or yourself for that matter, ever being able to change in any significant way.

If you're the sort of person who works harder, studies longer, and learns best when the pressure of a deadline or an exam looms ahead or when a grade is at stake or when you want praise and approval, then you may be inclined to believe that most people work best when motivation is extrinsic.

On the other hand, if you're the sort of individual who is continually self-motivated and future oriented, relatively independent of others' praise and approval, and caught up in the idea of pursuing your own interests free of manipulation of other people, then you may find yourself among those who feel the motivation for learning is something that comes from within and, in that sense, is intrinsic.

Actually, it is natural to project those qualities we value in ourselves onto other people and to have the inclination to believe that most other persons learn, live, and behave as we do. However natural it is, our projections are not always accurate. The fact is that not all people are like each other. Each person is unique, although to be sure, each person shares many characteristics found in other people, too. The point is: In order to be an effective teacher one first of all has to be flexible and open enough to use the best of what various points of view regarding human behavior and human learning have to offer. No one approach is totally sufficient for a task as demanding as teaching or for an assignment as complex as understanding behavioral dynamics.

Each of the views about human behavior we've considered in this chapter has something to teach us—about ourselves and about others. The psychoanalytic position can help us better understand man in terms of what happens to him from the inside. The behavioristic view can assist us to better understand man in terms of what happens to him from the outside. The humanistic-perceptual approach can aid us to better understand man in terms of the meaning he attaches to his own behavior.

To some extent, each of these three positions will be reflected, both explicitly and implicitly, in this book. The philosophical-psychological overlay, however, will be a humanistic-perceptual one. The development of a healthy personality and a sense of personal adequacy are important educational goals within this framework, ideas to which we turn our attention in Chapter 2.

Write your own chapter summary (major points, ideas, and concepts that had meaning for you).

_____

_____

_____

_____

_____

_____

_____

_____

_____

_____

REFERENCES

1. Freud, S. *Civilization and Its Discontents.* London: Horgarth, 1930, pp. 85–86.
2. Mead, M. *From the South Seas: Studies of Adolescence and Sex in Primitive Societies.* New York: Morrow, 1939, p. xix.
3. Maslow, A. H. *Motivation and Personality.* New York: Harper and Row, 1954, p. 175.
4. Poppy, K. C. "The Generation Gap." *Look* 31(1967):26–32.
5. Winchester, J. H. "Iceland: A Nation Hurrying Toward Tomorrow." *Reader's Digest* 88(June 1966):197–200.
6. Kubie, L. S. "The Utilization of Preconscious Functions in Education." In *Behavioral Science Frontiers in Education*, edited by E. M. Bower and W. C. Hollister. New York: Wiley, 1967, p. 94.
7. Watson, J. B. *Behaviorism.* New York: Norton, 1925.
8. Pavlov, I. P. "The Scientific Investigation of the Psychical Faculties or Processes in the Higher Animals." *Science* 24(1906):613–619.
9. Watson, J. B. Op. cit., 1925, p. 82.

10. Watson, J. B. *Psychology from the Standpoint of a Behaviorist.* Philadelphia: Lippincott, 1919, p. 10.

11. Skinner, B. F. *Beyond Freedom and Dignity.* New York: Knopf, 1971.

12. Skinner, B. F. *Science and Human Behavior.* New York: Macmillan, 1953, p. 26.

13. Thorndike, E. L. *Animal Intelligence.* New York: Macmillan, 1911.

14. Verplanck, W. S. "The Operant Conditioning of Human Motor Behavior." *Psychological Bulletin* 53(1956):70–83.

15. Guthrie, E. R. *The Psychology of Human Conflict.* New York: Harper and Row, 1938.

16. Skinner, B. F. "Operant Behavior." *American Psychologist* 18(1963):503–515.

17. Skinner, B. F. "Some Issues Concerning the Control of Human Behavior." *Science* 30(1956):1058.

18. Rogers, C. "Some Issues Concerning the Control of Human Behavior." *Science* 30(1956):1063.

19. Symonds, P. M. *What Education Has to Learn from Psychology.* New York: Teacher's College, Columbia University, 1960, p. 19.

20. Watson, Goodwin. "What Psychology Can We Be Sure About?" *Teacher's College Record* (1960):253–257.

21. Maslow, A. H. "Some Basic Propositions of a Growth and Self-Actualization Psychology." In *Perceiving, Behaving, Becoming,* edited by A. W. Combs. Association for Supervision and Curriculum Development Yearbook, 1962, p. 48.

22. Allport, G. W. *Becoming: Basic Considerations for a Psychology of Personality.* New Haven: Yale University Press, 1955, p. 18.

23. Farson, R. E. (ed.). *Science and Human Affairs.* Palo Alto, California: Science and Behavior Books, 1965, p. 13.

24. Morris, V. C. *Existentialism in Education.* New York: Harper and Row, 1966, p. 135.

25. Skinner, B. F. *Science and Human Behavior.* New York: McGraw-Hill, 1953, p. 17.

26. Rogers, C. R. *On Becoming a Person.* Boston: Houghton Mifflin, 1961, p. 109.

27. Morris, Van Cleve. "Existentialism and Education." *Educational Theory,* 4(1954):252–253.

28. Combs, A. W., and D. Snygg. *Individual Behavior.* Rev. ed. New York: Harper, 1959, p. 11.

29. Combs, A. W., and D. Snygg. Op. cit., pp. 16–36.

30. Rogers, C. R. *Client-Centered Therapy.* Boston: Houghton Mifflin, 1951, p. 483.

31. Combs, A. W., and D. Snygg. Op. cit., p. 20.

32. Bugental, J. *The Search for Authenticity.* Holt, Rinehart and Winston, 1965, pp. 11–12.

33. Bugental, J. Op. cit., pp. 13–14.

34. James, W. *Principles of Psychology,* 2 vols. New York: Holt, 1890.

35. Jersild, A. T. *In Search of Self.* New York: Bureau of Publications, Columbia University, 1952, pp. 9–10.

36. Smith, M. B. "The Phenomenological Approach to Personality Theory: Some Critical Remarks." *The Journal of Abnormal and Social Psychology* 45(1950):516–522.

37. Child, I. L. *Humanistic Psychology to the Research Tradition: Their Several Virtues.* New York: Wiley, 1973, pp. 19–22.

38. Maslow, A. H. "Some Educational Implications of Humanistic Psychologies." *Harvard Educational Review* 38(Fall 1968):691.

39. Stewart, J. S. *Values Development Education.* Continuing Education Service, Michigan State University, 1973.

40. Simon, S. B., L. W. Howe, and H. Kirschenbaum. *Values Clarification.* New York: Hart, 1972.

41. Combs, A. W. (ed.). *Perceiving, Behaving, and Becoming.* Yearbook of the Association for Supervision and Curriculum Development. Washington, D.C.: National Education Association, 1962, pp. 68–69.

REFERENCES OF RELATED INTEREST

Adler, A. *The Practice and Theory of Individual Psychology.* New York: Harcourt, Brace and World, 1927.

Allport, G. W. *Pattern and Growth in Personality.* Holt, Rinehart, and Winston, 1961.

———. *Personality: A Psychological Interpretation.* New York: Holt, 1937.

Combs, A. W. "Educational Accountability from a Humanistic Perspective." *Educational Researcher* 2(September 1973):19–21.

Dollard, J., and N. E. Miller. *Personality and Psychotherapy.* New York: McGraw-Hill, 1950.

Erikson, E. *Childhood and Society.* New York: Norton, 1950.

Estes, W. K. "Stimulus-Response Theory of Drive." In *Nebraska Symposium on Motivation,* vol. 6, edited by M. R. Jones. Lincoln: University of Nebraska Press, 1958.

Freud, S. *A General Introduction to Psychoanalysis.* Garden City, N.Y.: Garden City Publishing Co., 1943.

Fromm, E. *Man for Himself.* New York: Holt, Rinehart, and Winston, 1947.

———. *The Sane Society.* New York: Holt, Rinehart, and Winston, 1955.

Guthrie, E. R. *The Psychology of Learning.* Rev. ed. New York: Harper and Row, 1952.

Hamachek, D. E. *Encounters with the Self.* New York: Holt, Rinehart, and Winston, 1970, Chapter 2.

Horney, K. *Neurosis and Human Growth.* New York: Norton, 1950.

———. *Our Inner Conflicts.* New York: Norton, 1945.

Hull, C. L. *Essentials of Behavior.* New Haven: Yale University Press, 1951.

Jones, E. *The Life and Work of Sigmund Freud,* vols. I, II. New York: Basic Books, 1953, 1955.

Jung, C. G. *Contributions to Analytical Psychology.* New York: Harcourt, Brace and World, 1928.

_____. *Psychological Types.* New York: Harcourt, Brace and World, 1933.

Lyon, H. C., Jr. *Learning to Feel—Feeling to Learn.* Columbus, Ohio: Merrill, 1971.

Maddi, S. R., and P. T. Costa. *Humanism in Personology.* Chicago: Aldine-Atherton, 1972.

Maslow, A. H. *Motivation and Personality.* 2nd ed. New York: Harper and Row, 1970.

_____. *Toward a Psychology of Being.* 2nd ed. Princeton, N.J.: D. Van Nostrand, 1968.

Mowrer, O. H. *Learning Theory and Behavior.* New York: Wiley, 1960.

Murray, H. A. "Prospect for Psychology." *Science* 136(1962):483–488.

Murray, H. H., and C. Kluckhohn. "Outline of a Conception of Personality." In *Personality in Nature, Society, and Culture,* 2nd ed., edited by C. Kluckhohn, H. A. Murray, and D. M. Schneider. New York: Knopf, 1956.

Olson, R. G. *An Introduction to Existentialism.* New York: Dover Publications, 1962.

Rogers, C. R. *On Becoming a Person.* Boston, Houghton Mifflin, 1961.

Royce, J. E. *Man and Meaning.* New York: McGraw-Hill, 1969.

Severin, F. T. *Discovering Man in Psychology: A Humanistic Approach.* New York: McGraw-Hill, 1973.

Skinner, B. F. *Science and Human Behavior.* New York: Macmillan, 1953.

Snelbecker, G. E. *Learning Theory, Instructional Theory, and Psychoeducational Design.* New York: McGraw-Hill, 1974.

Spence, K. W. *Behavior Theory and Learning: Selected Papers.* Englewood Cliffs, N.J.: Prentice-Hall, 1960.

Sullivan, H. S. *The Interpersonal Theory of Psychiatry.* New York: Norton, 1953.

Sutich, A. J., and M. A. Vich (eds.). *Readings in Humanistic Psychology.* New York: Free Press, 1969.

Thorndike, E. L. *The Fundamentals of Learning.* New York: Teachers College, 1932.

Weinberg, C. (ed.). *Humanistic Foundations of Education.* Englewood Cliffs, N.J.: Prentice-Hall, 1972.

TWO

Psychological Growth Models for Understanding and Interpreting Behavior

CHAPTER OUTLINE

PROLOGUE

ERIK ERIKSON'S PSYCHOSOCIAL STAGES MODEL

Phase I—Infancy: A Sense of Trust versus a Sense of Mistrust (Birth to Eighteen Months)

Phase II—A Sense of Autonomy versus a Sense of Shame and Doubt (Eighteen Months to Three Years)

Phase III—A Sense of Initiative versus a Sense of Guilt (Three to Six Years)

Phase IV—A Sense of Industry versus a Sense of Inferiority (Six to Twelve Years)

Phase V—A Sense of Identity versus a Sense of Identity Confusion (Twelve to Eighteen Years)

Phase VI—A Sense of Intimacy versus a Sense of Isolation (Eighteen to Thirty-five Years)

Phase VII—A Sense of Generativity versus a Sense of Self-absorption (Thirty-five Years to Retirement)

Phase VIII—A Sense of Integrity versus a Sense of Despair (Retirement Years)

HAVIGHURST'S DEVELOPMENTAL TASK MODEL

WHITE'S CONCEPT OF COMPETENCE MODEL

Self-esteem as Related to Competence

Growth of Competence during the Early School Years

Competence and Psychological Health

MASLOW'S SELF-ACTUALIZATION MODEL

The Basic Need Hierarchy

Influence of Needs on Behavior

The Degree of Fixity of the Hierarchy of Basic Needs

Examples of Self-actualized Persons

Characteristics of Self-actualized People

Self-actualization and Psychological Health

ROGERS' FULLY FUNCTIONING PERSON MODEL

Basic Propositions Related to the Model

The Fully Functioning Person and Psychological Health

WHAT CAN TEACHERS DO TO ENCOURAGE HEALTHY DEVELOPMENT?

Provide Opportunities for Classroom Interaction

Provide Opportunities to Express Emotions

Provide an Atmosphere of Acceptance

Provide Clearly Established Rules

Provide Ample Opportunity for Success

EPILOGUE

REFERENCES

REFERENCES OF RELATED INTEREST

IMPORTANT CHAPTER IDEAS

1. A prerequisite for healthy development is the successful passage through a series of psychosocial stages of development.

2. Erikson: An individual never *has* a personality, he is always redeveloping it as he moves from one development stage to the next.

3. Erikson's developmental stages focus on the successful and healthy solution of crises that occur at each stage of development.

4. Havighurst's developmental tasks consist of skills, attitudes, and understandings that a person is confronted with at various growth stages.

5. Each growth period is associated with specific "tasks" that must be met and accomplished before moving on to subsequent growth stages.

6. One's sense of competency is roughly proportional to the number of successes he has had in doing things that matter to him.

7. White: The drive or motivation to be competent is an inherent desire to have an effect on one's environment.

8. Positive self-esteem is related to feeling competent.

9. Feelings of being competent (or incompetent) begin in the early school years.

10. Maslow: Self-actualized living is achieved after a person is able to activate his potential to be that which he can become.

11. A person's basic needs must be satisfied before he is able to approach a self-actualized level of existence.

12. Rogers: A fully functioning individual has an internal rather than external locus of evaluation.

13. Each person has an inclination to strive, actualize, maintain, and enhance the experiencing organism.

14. A healthy, knowledgeable personality is the crowning effort of good teaching—the product of an educational system's best efforts.

PROLOGUE

Chapter 1 has given us a broad overview of three major theoretical camps within the field of psychology. We examined some of the major concepts related to each of those positions along with their implications for teaching and learning. Chapter 1 was our "psychological framework" chapter. This chapter will go a step further. What we will do here is to fill in the framework with greater detail as we look at five rather distinct, although in some ways, overlapping, psychological growth models.

Teaching is a complex professional endeavor, demanding as it does knowledge about how learning occurs and how physical and psychological growth processes are related to it. This will not be a chapter in which we concentrate very much on the physical aspects of development (more of that in chapters 3, 4, and 5), but it will be one in which we'll examine important psychological considerations.

At least one of the purposes of education is to teach students to know something. Most of us would probably agree that we want our students, whether in first grade or graduate school, to be more informed and better problem-solvers at the end of an educational experience than they were at the beginning of it. However, simply "being informed" or "having information" is only one kind of an educational objective. For example, we all know persons — young and old — who are bright, informed, and knowledgeable, but who seem not to be doing a good job of coping with the problems of life. One might say of such persons that their intellectual and problem-solving processes have run too far ahead of their adjustment and coping processes. Apparently it is one thing to *know* something but quite another to *be* something. Yet it would be erroneous to think that *behaving* and *knowing* are unrelated to each other. They *are* related — very much so. In fact, the whole idea of growing in emotionally healthy ways and of developing a sense of competency are highly related to learning and knowing. The question is: *How* are they related? Further, what do we mean by a "healthy personality" and a sense of competency? How are a healthy personality and a sense of competency achieved? What part can education play in all this? At the end of this chapter you should have a better idea about how to answer these questions.

Healthy development is a complex process that involves, among other things, integrating our own inner needs and genetic potential with the demands of the outside world. It also involves a reasonably successful passage through a series of psychosocial stages of development, each of which must be resolved in a satisfactory manner and to a sufficient enough degree to insure continued growth through subsequent stages in order to achieve one's maturity potential. This idea grows out of the psychosocial theory of Erik Erikson, a point of view about the course of normal growth and development to which we turn our attention first.

ERIK ERIKSON'S PSYCHOSOCIAL STAGES MODEL

Erik H. Erikson is a psychoanalyst who has developed a new and different way for looking at the developmental phases involved in psychological growth. Although Erikson was influenced by Freudian analytic theory, his own psychosocial growth model is more expansive and humanizing. Freud, for example, restricted himself to a person's inner dynamics in relation to the classical matrix of the child-mother-father triangle. Erikson, on the other hand, considers the individual in his relationship to his parents within the context of a family and in relation to a broader social setting within the framework of the family's cultural heritage. In Erikson's words, his psychosocial model is an effort to deal with "the relations of the ego to society"[1] and "to speculate the psychosocial implications of the human evolution."[2]

You may recall from Chapter 1 that the Freudian view of man is a somewhat dismal one that warns of man's social doom if left to innate strivings. Erikson doesn't see it that way. In fact, the main thrust of his psychosocial model is to point out the developmental opportunities that each of us has to triumph over the psychological hazards of living. While Freud gave his energies over to the study of pathological development, Erikson has focused upon the successful and healthy solution of developmental crises. I think it is important to note here that Erikson does not see human behavior as "good" or "bad," but rather he sees each human being as having the *potential to produce* "good" or "bad." Basically, however, Erikson is optimistic about man's potential to grow in a healthy direction. As Erikson says, "There is little that cannot be remedied later, there is much that can be prevented from happening at all."[3]

In general, Erikson's psychosocial phases coincide with standard ranges of chronological and sociocultural age groupings. During each phase of development, the individual must face and cope with a central

45

crisis that becomes dominant and that must be worked through before he can move on to the next level of development. An Eriksonian growth phase is notable for its own developmental theme, for its relationship to the previous and subsequent phases, and for the part it plays in the total scheme of developmental stages. For Erikson growth phases are in constant motion; an individual never *has* a personality, he is always redeveloping his personality.[4]

Altogether, Erikson has described eight successive developmental stages, each of which zero into focus at definite points in one's life. Let's look at these psychosocial phases one at a time and examine more closely the meanings and implications of each.

Phase I—Infancy: A Sense of Trust versus a Sense of Mistrust (Birth to Eighteen Months)

The first "task" of an infant is to develop what Erikson has called "the cornerstone of a healthy personality,"[5] a basic sense of trust—in himself and his environment. The first year of a child's life is a time when he is completely and utterly dependent on the outside world to tend to his most basic needs. If his assorted needs, say, for a bottle when hungry or dry diapers when wet or warm covers when cold or a protecting adult when frightened are not met with reasonably predictable consistency, he may gradually lose his sense of faith or "trust" in the world around him. Erikson goes on to note that:

> . . . the amount of trust derived from earliest infantile experience does not seem to depend on absolute quantities of food or demonstrations of love, but rather on the quality of the maternal relationship. [Parents] create a sense of trust in their children by that kind of administration which in its quality combines sensitive care of the baby's individual needs and a firm sense of personal trustworthiness. . . . This forms the basis in the child for a sense of being "all right," of being one's self, and of becoming what other people trust one will become.[6]

As conceived by Erikson, then, the whole idea of being able to depend on other people has its roots in the first year or so of life. This does not mean that if an infant is raised in a whimsical, willy-nilly, unpredictable environment during the earliest years of his life that he is irreversibly fated to grow into a non-trusting adult. It means only that if a basic sense of trust is not laid during the first year that it becomes increasingly difficult to establish it in later years.

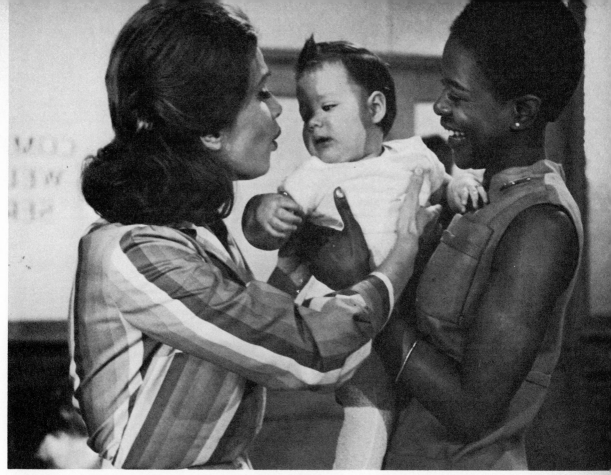

A sense of trust begins at a very early age and grows out of knowing that people care about you and can be depended on.

Phase II—A Sense of Autonomy versus a Sense of Shame and Doubt (Eighteen Months to Three Years)

This second phase of growth is a time when a child discovers that his behavior is his own. He begins to assert his newly discovered sense of autonomy in ways we're all familiar with—"No, let me do it." "Don't help

47

me." "Let me do it by myself." Erikson reasons that a child experiences conflicting pulls—one is to assert himself and the other is to deny himself the right and capacity to make this assertion. To live in a healthy way during this stage means to aggressively expand one's limits, to act on one's own terms, and to insist on one's own boundaries.

Adults can encourage a healthy sense of autonomy during this phase through a wise balance of firmness and permissiveness. Letting a young child do whatever he pleases is not a healthy way to help him find his strengths because he has nothing against which to measure himself. The responsibility for establishing reasonable limits rests with parents and teachers. A child is pliable; if he knows and fully understands the range of his limits, what he can do and what he can't do, his growth will be healthy. As one psychologist has noted:

> [The] imposition of limits serves to define the expectations of others, the norms of the group, and the point at which deviation from them is likely to evoke positive action; enforcement of limits gives the child a sense that norms are real and significant, contributes to self-definition, and increases the likelihood that the child will believe that a sense of reality is attainable.[7]

On the other hand, limits that are too restrictive, that are too punitive, and/or adults who are too protecting can interfere with a growing child's natural inclination to want to test his wings, to try himself out in different ways. A person—any age—who hasn't tested himself is invariably plagued with self-doubts because he is uncertain about what he can or cannot do. Shame is the other part of this feeling, which, as Erikson puts it, is an emotion that "supposes that one is completely exposed and conscious of being looked at: in a word, self-conscious."[8] I suppose we all know children (and adults) who feel terribly self-conscious and fearful when in a public setting (classroom, playground, party, etc.) where they are fearful of their weaknesses, real or imagined, being exposed. This sensation of fearful self-consciousness is probably no different than the one any of us has had as we've struggled with the decision of whether to say something publicly in class.

Suffice it to say that this is the time when a child develops the beginnings of a sense of independence or autonomy. It doesn't stop here, but it does start here. Developing autonomy is necessary for the emergence of initiative, which brings us to our next stage.

Phase III—A Sense of Initiative versus a Sense of Guilt (Three to Six Years)

At no time in a child's development is he ready to learn more quickly and avidly or to be more expansive in the sense of sharing obligation and performance than during this stage of his growth. This is also a time when a child begins to slowly but surely expand the geography of his social boundaries. Having acquired some measure of conscious control over himself and his environment, the child can now move rapidly forward to new challenges in ever-widening social and spacial spheres. Erikson reasons that the very act of moving out more aggressively into his social world is the beginning of a process that convinces a child that he *is* counted as a person, that he *does* have a certain amount of power (in terms of being able to make things happen), and that life has a purpose for him. Perhaps one way of expressing it is that this is a time when he can express his autonomy in behavior, a behavior we call *initiative*.

This is also the time in a child's life when he begins to develop a conscience, a sense of right and wrong, of "Should I or Shouldn't I?" If this tendency to feel guilty is overtaxed by moralistic and/or punitive parents and teachers, a child could easily develop a feeling of "badness" that could seriously inhibit healthy urges to test himself in an expanding social world. Some parents and teachers, however, fail to recognize the normal needs and inclinations of children this age and end up being over restrictive, sometimes in punitive ways. For example, I recall two parents during a parent-teachers' meeting proudly telling the others that they had successfully coped with their four year old's tendency to wander out of his back yard by putting up a fence. This surely will keep the youngster in, but it also will surely reduce his possibilities for seeing what the world beyond his backyard has to offer.

We might also keep in mind that this phase of expanding initiative goes hand in hand with rapidly growing physical and intellectual skills. Large muscle development is accelerating by leaps and bounds and 50 percent of a child's mature intelligence is completed before five years of age.[9] All in all, it is a period when a child engages in the complicated process of finding out who he is and what he can do, and he can only do this if he has a certain amount of freedom to do so without feeling guilty about it.

Phase IV — A Sense of Industry versus a Sense of Inferiority (Six to Twelve Years)

Before a child can grow up to become a parent himself, he must first learn to be a worker and potential provider. Not infrequently during this growth phase children are described as "too big for their boots" or "too cocky for their own good" and the like. Why? Well, this is the normal time for a growing child to devote his abundant energies to self-improvement and to the conquest of people and things. It is the time when, according to Erikson, a child "becomes ready to apply himself to given skills and tasks, which go far beyond the mere playful expression of his organ modes or the pleasure in the function of his limbs. He develops industry — i.e., he adjusts himself to the inorganic laws of the tool world."[10]

The major theme of this phase is reflected in a child's determination to master whatever he is doing. On the one hand, there is abundant energy to invest in every possible effort to produce, to be "industrious." On the other hand, there is the ever-present pull toward earlier levels of lesser production. The fear of the latter is reinforced by the very fact that he is still a child, an incomplete person, which feeds into feelings of inferiority. One way to combat the feelings of inferiority is to take advantage of all opportunities to learn by doing and to experiment with the rudimentary skills required by his culture. Play activities are an important part of a child's growth during this phase because it is through play that he begins to master some of the basic social and physical skills necessary for mature adult living. Maier observes that as a "child learns to wield his culture's tools and symbols, [he] seems to understand that this sort of learning will help him become more himself."[11]

In sum, this is a phase of growth during which time a child can learn to have a healthy view of himself through his increased competence in doing things. In learning to accept instruction and to win recognition and approval by producing "things," he opens the way for the capacity of work enjoyment in later years. The danger in this period is the development of a sense of inadequacy and inferiority in a child who does not receive recognition for his efforts.

> ### TO THINK ABOUT
>
> Do you see yourself as an "industrious" person or are you plagued with a sense of inferiority? What sorts of elementary school experiences encouraged your current feelings? What do you remember teachers doing to you that helped you feel good about yourself? Badly? If you intend to teach at the elementary level, what kinds of things do you think a teacher can do to help students feel "industrious"?

Phase V — A Sense of Identity versus a Sense of Identity Confusion (Twelve to Eighteen Years)

With the onset of sexual maturity, childhood comes to an end. This is a difficult and sensitive phase, as any parent or high school teacher will attest. Among other things, this phase of growth demands that the adolescent boy and girl shed the remaining remnants of a baby and child self as the first step toward establishing an identity uniquely his own. Wise parents and teachers help in this process, without making a young person feel guilty or wrong or bad as he takes his final steps toward ultimate independence.

As you may remember from personal experience, adolescence is an exciting time, but also a confusing one. Physical changes occur at a remarkable pace, boys and girls cause strange stirrings in each other, school work is more intense and competitive, expectations are more stringent, and questions about who am I? and what can I do? seem pressing and urgent. Erikson quotes an aphorism found in a western cowboy bar that seems to capture the spirit of this growth phase rather nicely:

I ain't what I ought to be, I ain't what I'm going to be, but I ain't what I was.[12]

The danger of this stage is role confusion, a possibility that is enhanced if a youngster takes deep unresolved questions about his sexual identity with him into adolescence. This does not mean that sex-role questions cannot be resolved during this stage, it means only that the identity crisis may be more severe and complicated. A young teen-age boy, for example, unsure about his maleness may spend a disproportionate amount of energy searching for his masculinity while other boys, more certain about their sex-role identification, are struggling with higher order questions involving future identification.

Generally speaking, this is a time for personality shopping, for trying on, as it were, different "identities" to see which one fits best. Personality shopping explains many of the dramatic shifts in dress, attitudes, moods, and language that can be reflected in a teen-ager's behavior as he courses his way through school. Trying one's self out, challenging adult authority, and puzzling through what to do with one's life are normal, healthy, indeed, necessary experiences an adolescent must have before he can figure out who he is, what he can do, and how best he can do it. When this is accomplished, then he is ready for the next stage.

TO THINK ABOUT

What are two or three considerations about adolescent psychological development you think are most important for teachers to know about? Or, to ask the question a little differently, what two or three things do you wish your high school teachers had been more sensitive to regarding your own psychological growth during those years? Why?

Phase VI—A Sense of Intimacy versus a Sense of Isolation (Eighteen to Thirty-five Years)

Childhood and youth are at an end. This is a time, if all has gone well, when each of us began our participation as "adult" members of Western society. According to Erikson, all one's growth experiences to this point in

51

time have prepared him for the readiness to participate in a close and trusting relationship with an opposite sex partner. Whereas graduation from adolescence requires a sense of identity; graduation from the first stage of adulthood requires a sense of shared identity. The experience of marriage can be, although it is not always, a healthy means for experiencing the sense of intimacy vital to this phase of development. As Erikson puts it, marriage can be "an experience of finding oneself, as one loses oneself, in another."[13]

Phase VII — A Sense of Generativity versus a Sense of Self-absorption (Thirty-five Years to Retirement)

This is that period in one's life when he literally "generates" or produces whatever it is that gives him a sense of personal creation. *Generativity* does not refer to the procreating individual, but rather to the route that a person may take to pass on to the next generation the wisdom and virtues he has accumulated. This sense of generativity is not necessarily specific to one thing, but rather involves an individual's total efforts to be useful as a father, a worker, a husband, a participant in the community, and so on. The danger in this period is that some individuals are unable to release themselves from the web of their own self-doubt.

Phase VIII — A Sense of Integrity versus a Sense of Despair (Retirement Years)

Finally, as an individual procreates and assures his contribution to this new generation, he accomplishes the fullest sense of trust that Erikson views as the "assured reliance on another's integrity."[14] As you can see, the first developmental theme (a sense of trust) evolves into the final one. In other words, this final phase is an outgrowth of the seven phases preceding it. It involves a sense of wisdom, a philosophy of life, an inner peace, all of which have roots in early trust, youthful independence, vigorous initiative, established identity, successful intimacy, and a sense of generativity. Erikson has nicely captured the spirit of this final phase with his observation that "healthy children will not fear life, if their parents have integrity enough not to fear death."[15]

TO THINK ABOUT

Death is not typically a subject that is openly discussed at school or at home. How would you feel about leading a group of students (any age) in a discussion involving their feelings and attitudes (yours, too) about death? Do you think that such a discussion would have any "educational" relevance? If yes, why, how, and in what ways? If your response is no, why do you feel as you do?

HAVIGHURST'S DEVELOPMENTAL TASK MODEL

Whereas Erikson talks about psychological growth in terms of progressing through a series of successful and healthy solutions of developmental crises, Havighurst focuses more on the specific "tasks" that a person is confronted with at different points in time. A major difference between the two is that Erikson talks more about the psychological meanings associated with various growth periods and Havighurst concentrates more on the intellectual and physical and social "tasks" that must be completed during various growth stages.

According to Havighurst, then, with each new stage of development there are certain "tasks"—skills, attitudes, understandings—that must be met before a person can move on to a higher level of development. Havighurst calls these *developmental tasks*, which he says occur:

. . . . at or about a certain period in the life of the individual, successful achievement of which leads to his happiness and to success with later tasks, while failure leads to unhappiness in the individual, disapproval by society, and difficulty with later tasks.[16]

Havighurst has divided the life-span into six periods. Each period is associated with specific "tasks" that must be met and accomplished before moving on to subsequent growth stages. Table 2–1 itemizes the specific tasks that are associated with each major growth stage.

As you can see, each series of developmental tasks is a complex organization of problems that all individuals encounter in some form or other at certain stages in their lives. Unless one meets the demands of these problems and resolves them adequately as they occur, it is likely that he will encounter difficulties with subsequent developmental problems that emerge in subsequent stages. For example, unless you achieve the developmental task of achieving new and more mature relations with the opposite sex during your preadolescent and adolescent years (twelve to eighteen), then it may be difficult to move to the next developmental task of selecting a mate, existing happily in a marriage, and starting a family. Indeed, many youthful marriages don't last precisely because one developmental task (getting married) was taken on before a prior developmental task (learning how to relate to members of the opposite sex) was completed.

TABLE 2–1. *Developmental Tasks from Infancy Through Later Life*

Infancy and early childhood (birth to 6 years)	Middle childhood (6–12 years)	Preadolescence and adolescence (12–18 years)
Learning to walk. Learning to take solid foods. Learning to talk. Learning to control the elimination of body wastes. Learning sex differences and sexual modesty. Achieving physiological stability. Forming simple concepts of social and physical reality. Learning to relate oneself emotionally to parents, siblings, and other people. Learning to distinguish right and wrong and developing a conscience.	Learning physical skills necessary for ordinary games. Building wholesome attitudes toward oneself as a growing organism. Learning to get along with age-mates. Learning an appropriate masculine or feminine social role. Developing fundamental skills in reading, writing, and calculating. Developing concepts necessary for everyday living. Developing conscience, morality, and a scale of values. Achieving personal independence. Developing attitudes toward social groups and institutions.	Achieving new and more mature relations with age-mates of both sexes. Achieving a masculine or feminine social role. Accepting one's physique and using the body effectively. Achieving emotional independence of parents and other adults. Achieving assurance of economic independence. Selecting and preparing for an occupation. Preparing for marriage and family life. Developing intellectual skills and concepts necessary for civic competence. Desiring and achieving socially responsible behavior. Acquiring a set of values and an ethical system as a guide to behavior.

Early adulthood (18–35 years)	Middle age (35–60 years)	Later life (60–)
Selecting a mate. Learning to live with a marriage partner. Starting a family. Rearing children. Managing a home. Getting started in an occupation. Taking on civic responsibility. Finding a congenial social group.	Achieving adult, civic, and social responsibility. Establishing and maintaining an economic standard of living. Assisting teen-age children to become responsible and happy adults. Developing adult leisure-time activities. Relating oneself to one's spouse as a person. Learning to accept and adjust to the physiological changes of middle age. Adjusting to aging parents.	Adjusting to decreasing physical strength. Adjusting to retirement and reduced income. Adjusting to death of spouse. Establishing an explicit affiliation with one's age group. Meeting social and civic obligations. Establishing satisfactory living arrangements.

(Adapted from R. J. Havighurst. *Human Development and Education.* New York: Longmans, 1953.)

TO THINK ABOUT

Consider your own progress through the developmental tasks outlined in Table 2-1. Where do you see yourself in your own growth and development? Do you feel pretty good about accomplishment of "tasks" to this point in your life? Where do you see yourself lagging behind some? What do you plan to do about it? What relationships do you see between successful passage through Erikson's psychosocial stages and successful accomplishment of Havighurst's developmental tasks?

Both Erikson and Havighurst's developmental models suggest that healthy growth and development tend to follow a certain order. Although this is not a fixed and rigid order, which all youths and adults follow in the same way at the same time, it does, nonetheless, give us a general picture of the hierarchy of the skills, attitudes, and understandings that are created by each person's maturing physical and mental capacities, the cultural forces around him, and his own personal motives, values, and level of aspiration. Learning to talk and walk, for example, are influenced by physical and mental readiness, parental expectations, and the child's own motivation to expand his social boundaries and communicate with others.

Among other reasons, the developmental task concept is important because it helps remind us that each individual functions as a "whole" person rather than as a hodgepodge of independent needs, skills, and impulses. It should also help remind us that one of the major goals of healthy, balanced homes and schools is the creation of experiences and opportunities to assist growing youngsters accomplish the tasks before them.

One thing is certain: Positive life experiences as one goes through his psychosocial stages and successful accomplishment of developmental tasks as they occur are necessary prerequisites for a sense of personal competency, a topic to which we now turn our attention.

WHITE'S CONCEPT OF COMPETENCE MODEL

A major expression of psychological health is the feeling of being a competent individual. The feeling of personal competency begins at home, is encouraged at school, and is reinforced by one's daily experiences. Indeed, in school a student learns not only about things and ideas, but he also learns about himself. One of the striking things we are currently discovering is that the most important ideas that affect a student's behavior are those ideas or conceptions he has about himself, which, in part, are a consequence of his school experiences. Unfortunately, thousands upon thousands of students graduate from high school with deep feelings of personal inadequacy. They do not feel very competent. During the 1960's for example, 7.5 million youngsters did not even finish high school—many because of the "I can't, others are smarter, so why try anyway?" attitude.

The negative effects of a low sense of competency begin their toll early in the elementary years. In fact, even though a youngster's self-perceptions start out on a positive note, there is no guarantee that they will end up that way. For example, Morse[17] found that to a statement like "I feel pretty sure of myself," 12 percent of the third graders say "unlike me," while 34 percent of the eleventh graders make that response. Morse further reported that 84 percent of the third graders felt good about their school work, while this was true for only 53 percent of the eleventh graders.

As we may know from personal experience, one's sense of competency is roughly proportional to the number of successes he has experienced in doing things that matter to him. Along this line, William Glasser, in his very sensitive book, *Schools without Failure*, makes the point that "regardless of his background, his culture, his color, his economic level, *he will not succeed in general until he can in some way first experience success in one important part of his life.*"[18]

In two provocative and still timely papers, Professor R. White,[19,20] a Harvard University psychologist, proposed a new way for looking at human motivation—a way that takes into account the whole question of competency. Quite simply, White has proposed the existence of a new drive or motivation, inherent in the child at birth, which is called *effectance*. This is what White calls the inherent desire to have an effect on the environment. It is what you might call a built-in motivation to be competent. Indeed, White regards man's usual primary drives such as hunger, thirst, and sex as relatively unimportant compared with the drive for effectance. It is reasoned that the effectance drive is as innate as other primary drives, which is to say that our most important motivated behaviors are *not* derivatives of sexual or erotic interests, as a more Freudian view would suggest, but have independent status. White notes, for example, that:

> The theory that we learn what helps us to reduce our viscerogenic drives will not stand up if we stop to consider the whole range of what a child must learn in order to deal effectively with his surroundings. He has much to learn about grasping and letting go, about the coordination of hand and eye.
> . . . He must learn many facts about his world, building up a cognitive map that will afford guidance and structure for his behavior. It is not hard to see the biological advantage of an arrangement whereby these many learnings can get underway before they are needed for instruments for drive reduction or for safety. An animal that has thoroughly explored its environment stands a better chance of escaping from a sudden enemy or satisfying a gnawing hunger than one that merely dozes in the sun when its homeostatic crises are past. Seen in this light, the many hours that infants and children spend in play are by no means wasted or merely recuperative in nature. Play may be fun, but it is also a serious business in childhood. During these hours the child steadily builds up his competence in dealing with the environment.[21]

As you can see, an individual's search for competence begins early. In fact, even during the first year of life when a child is most preoccupied with oral activities—sucking, feeding, mouthing, and the like—there are signs of behavior that suggest that he is doing more than simply seeking oral gratification. For example, have you ever noted the intensity with which a young child will investigate his eating utensils or explore spilled food or play with whatever toys or small objects are available throughout feeding? The older a child gets the more enthusiastic he grows for the "do it yourself" doctrine. In fact, around one year of age is when the "battle of the spoon" begins—when the baby grabs the spoon from the mother's hand and tries to feed himself. What purpose does behavior of this sort serve? Why do we see so much of it? Surely a child does not get more food in this manner. Indeed, White has noted that a child actually gets more food by letting mother do the feeding, but, and this seems to be the key, "he gets another kind of satisfaction—a feeling of efficacy, and perhaps already a growth of the sense of competence."[22]

The possibility that something more profound than direct oral gratification is going on is even more evident, according to White, if we look at a baby when he is not eating. Consider the following Gesell and Ilg description, for example, of a twenty-eight-week-old baby playing with a clothespin:

> The child wants to finger the clothespin, to get the feel of it. He puts it in his mouth, pulls it out, looks at it, rotates it with a twist of the wrist, puts it back in his mouth, pulls it out, gives it another twist, brings up his free hand, transfers the clothespin from hand to hand, bangs it on the high chair tray, drops it, recovers it, leans over to retrieve it, fails, fusses for a moment, then bangs the tray with his empty hand. . . . He is never idle because he is under such a compelling urge to use his hands for manipulation and exploitation.[23]

Hard to believe a clothespin could be so intriguing, isn't it?

Self-esteem as Related to Competence

To some extent the feeling of self-esteem (self-prizing, self-valuing) grows out of doing new things and doing them successfully. A child's initial acts of reaching, grasping, pulling, crawling, standing up, and eventually walking without help are done intentionally and, to the degree that they're successful, they can leave a child with a happy sense of efficacy, of being "good at something." You can check this out yourself. For example, the next time you have opportunity to observe a young child take his first tottering steps alone, don't watch his feet, watch his face because that's where you can see his feelings of efficacy and success related. As he tries to walk a few feet from one support to another, he knows whether he succeeds or fails. An appreciative adult audience may give him a huge social reward, but he does not require approval to know that he's succeeded. The fact is that mind and muscle have been pitted against an invisible force that tries to draw him to the floor, and they have proved equal to the task (competent) to triumph over this force.

Although it is true that one can enhance his own feelings of self-esteem by seeing for himself that he is good or successful in this or that, it would be erroneous to conclude that the dividends of self-esteem were minted entirely from within. There has to be a balance. Along this line, one psychologist has noted that:

> Throughout life self-esteem has these two sources: an inner source, the degree of effectiveness of one's own activity; and an external source, the opinions of others about oneself. Both are important, but the former is the steadier and more dependable one. Unhappy and insecure is the man who, lacking an adequate inner source of self-esteem, must depend for this almost wholly upon external sources.[24]

Fortunately, a healthy sense of self-esteem does not depend on being competent in all things one does. In school a young boy may find that he is particularly competent, let's say, in working math problems and reading, not so good in drawing, writing, and other fine motor coordination skills. We might reasonably expect that the ratio of success and failure is different in each activity and if the experiences of success and failure continue in a fairly consistent fashion there will eventually be differences in the confidence the boy feels in his ability to cope with each of these areas. He may run confidently around the playground, but enter the crafts room with great hesitation. He may approach penmanship drills with the uneasy feeling that he'll never be any good at this kind of stuff, either.

Although youths show decided differences in overall levels of confidence and self-esteem, they also typically differentiate their competence in different areas, and this tendency increases with age. In the normal course of growth, self-esteem is nourished more and more by one's stronger areas of competence and injured less and less by one's poorer spheres. In fact, each one of us probably has a goodly number of "poorer" spheres. Fortunately, however, most of us can live with this because our self-esteem is dependent on only a small range of excellencies. Failure in many areas may mean little if it is compensated by success in just one area. This point is eloquently made in a memorable observation by William James:

> I, who for a time have stacked my all on being a psychologist, am mortified if others know much more about psychology than I. But I am content to wallow in the grossest ignorance of Greek. My deficiencies there gave me no sense of personal humiliation at all. Had I "pretensions" to be a linguist, it would have been just the reverse. So we have the paradox of a man shamed to death because he is only the second pugilist or the second oarsman in the world.

Doing new things and being successful at them is one of the best ways to develop a feeling of competence.

That he is able to beat the whole population of the globe minus one is nothing; he has "pitted" himself to beat that one; and as long as he doesn't do that nothing else counts. He is to his own regard as if he were not, indeed he is not.

Yonder puny fellow, however, whom everyone can beat, suffers no chagrin about it, for he has long ago abandoned the attempt to "carry that tune" as the merchants say, of self at all. With no attempt there can be no failure; with no failure, no humiliation. So our self-feeling in this world depends entirely on what we *back* ourselves to be and do.[25]

In an integrated personality, which enjoys reasonable self-esteem growing from this effort and that success, feelings of incompetency will be relatively transient and of minor importance. When a person feels deeply incompetent, to the point of suffering an inferiority complex, we usually find him forever making unfavorable comparisons between himself and others, covering more lines of excellence than a single individual could ever hope to carry. There are many illustrations of this we all recognize. For example, there's the student who hears one of his peers make an intelligent response in class, and this causes him to lament what he considers to be his inferior intellectual status. At lunch someone talks happily about a high grade on a term paper, and he feels miserable because he cannot do likewise. A group wants him to join in a pinochle game, and he has a chance to deplore his medocrity at cards. A friend happens by with a pretty date and this causes him to squirm because, secretly, he would like to ask some pretty girls out but doesn't for fear of being turned down. In other words, a single day may provide him with opportunities to feel inferior in a dozen different ways. But it is not these dozen inferiorities that bother him. Rather, it is the more pervasive fact that he does not have a sufficient sense of competence about anything to help him form a nucleus of self-esteem necessary to make him feel worthy. Not feeling particularly competent in anything he feels somewhat incompetent in everything. In the absence of one or two things he could "back" himself to be good in, he behaves as if he had to back himself to be good in all things.

TO THINK ABOUT

How about your own feelings of competency? Do you feel you're better at one or two things than most other people? Or, do you find yourself feeling somewhat like the student in the paragraph above? Write down two or three things you think teachers should be responsible for in helping students feel more competent. Then, jot down two or three things you feel students should be responsible for to enhance their own competency.

_____

_____

_____

_____

_____

_____

Feelings of incompetency are apt to occur when obstacles, either internal or external, prevent the development of some personal pattern of excellence capable of supporting strong self-esteem. An attitude of competency that starts early and is reinforced over time is one of the best ways possible to develop a healthy personality and to avoid debilitating inferiority feelings. This brings us to our next point.

Growth of Competence during the Early School Years

There is little question that a child's sense of competence and self-esteem is strongly affected by his experience in the family circle. Stanley Coopersmith, in his very excellent book, *Antecedents of Self-Esteem,* notes from his research that children with high self-esteem are more likely to have parents who provide "direct experiences of success . . . [and who] provide the means of achieving success and of handling adversity in a realistic yet nondestructive manner."[26] Let's take an example of this. Not long ago I heard a father say to his four and a half year old son, "John, you're just not *good* enough to ride a two-wheel bike yet." A more appropriate and less ego-damaging response to his son's pleas for a new bike might have been something along the lines of, "John, you're not quite *big* enough yet. In another six months or so we'll see how much you've grown and then we'll test you out." To say that John is not good enough, which is, in fact, an assessment of his competency, does nothing to encourage him to think positively about his potential to *become* good. However, to say that John is not *big* enough is to more realistically appraise the problem for what it is—namely, a problem of size, not skill. This way John can see the problem for what it is and also retain good feelings about himself. There is little question that the experiences a child has during his preschool years play an incredibly important role in the development of feelings of competency. In 1,001 little entries an important chapter in establishing self-esteem can be already written before the child leaves the bosom of the family.

Eventually his social boundaries grow even larger, and it is whole new ballgame when a child goes off to school. In both the schoolroom and on the playground there are new things to do, new challenges to competence. Most children come to recognize that what they do has ultimate significance in the grown-up world, which gives them what Erikson has called "a token sense of participation in the world of adults."[27] At its best a school experience can serve to develop and enhance in the child "a sense of industry and a positive identification with those who *know* how to *do* things."[28] This opens the door for discovering new kinds of competency. Being pretty good at school work and finding oneself reasonably effective in accomplishing daily lessons can be a perpetual source of self-esteem for one student, while for another his school performance is a continual reminder of how dumb or how slow or how generally inadequate he is. Or, more accurately, perhaps, as he *thinks* or *feels* he is.

The impact of success and failure on one's feelings of competence is particularly critical during the early elementary years. For example, William Glasser, writing out of his many years of psychiatric experience with children, makes an observation which has deep, indeed, profound implications:

> The critical years are between five and ten. Failure, which should be prevented throughout school, is most easily prevented at this time. When failure does occur, it can usually be corrected during these five years within the elementary school classrooms by teaching and educational procedures that lead to fulfillment of the child's basic needs. The age beyond which failure is difficult to reverse may be higher or lower than ten for any one child, depending upon the community he comes from, the strength of his family, and his own genetic resources; regardless of these variations, however, it is amazing to me how constant this age seems to be. Before age ten, a good school experience can help him succeed. After age ten, it takes more than a good school experience, and unfortunately, shortly after age ten he is thrust into junior and senior high situations where he has much less chance for a corrective educational experience. Therefore, although children can be helped at any school level, the major effort should be made in the elementary school.[29]

Clearly, early school failure experiences and a sense of competency are incompatible. While it is true that not all children (or anyone else for that matter) can be equally competent in all things, it is also true that all children can be as competent (as good at, as skilled at) as most if not a bit better, in one or two areas.

A child's sense of competence during the early school years doesn't begin and end in the classroom. There is also the playground, where the feeling of being as good as the next guy depends on behavior of a different order. Strength, agility, and good coordination are important prerequisites for successful playground survival, and sometimes the child who is laughed at in the classroom for being among the slowest is lauded on the playground for being among the fastest. Most children pick and choose their playground activities with sufficient wisdom and foresight to avoid those activities in which they are destined to certain failure. Other children, particularly those who come from extremely permissive, child-centered homes, have a great deal of difficulty as they move into the competitive realities of even a friendly play group. Whatever the case, it is on the playground that children must show what they have in the way of physical prowess, manipulative skill, courage, assertiveness, friendliness, all in direct comparison with others their own age.   The penalties for failure are humiliation, ridicule, and even rejection from the group.

The fact is: Most children's playground groups and neighborhood play groups are to a large extent self-governing. As long as a child is relatively free to choose what activities to play in and who to play with he will very likely experience his fair share of success. Sometimes overzealous adults, fathers in particular, push their children too hard too soon and the consequences can lead to heartache. What is sadder than to watch a team of adult-supervised, adult-organized, adult-sponsored, and adult-umpired little league peewee baseball players leave the field in tears because they were defeated? It's one thing to lose a game, but it is quite another to lose face in front of Dad and his legion of friends who have been yelling "win, win, win" in its various disguises during the entire game. As one nine-year-old little league player expressed it, "My dad gets a little mad when we lose. That's alright I guess, except I can't tell whether he's mad at me or just mad at losing." Slowly, the boy is beginning to connect losing with his dad's angry feelings, which in the long run will serve only to increase the boy's anxiety and interfere with his playing well. Heavy emphasis during the early school years on winning (or getting high grades) does little to help a child concentrate on basic skill development.

In order for a child to acquire the basic skills demanded to enhance his feelings of competency, he must initially be free to make mistakes, indeed, to fail if necessary. Look at it this way: If a youngster feels that he will be punished (receive a low grade, be rejected) for making mistakes, he is not as likely to either (1) try as many new things or (2) try as hard in those activities he does assume. The psychology is simple (although self-defeating): "If I don't try, I can't fail. If I can't fail, I can't be rejected. If I am not rejected, I am okay." Or, if I try but don't try my hardest (give my best) I can always say, "I could have done better if I had tried harder" (or if I really wanted to).

Competence and Psychological Health

White's competence model is a point of view that suggests that there is more to man's motivational system than the urge to satisfy primary tissue needs. It is a view that allows us to tender the possibility that the really ubiquitous and important motives in human life are the drives to be active, to explore, to manipulate, to control one's destiny, to produce, and to accomplish. Implicit in this notion is the idea that many forms of cognitive and social behavior, which were originally thought to be derived from other, more instinctual qualities, may themselves have an innate or inborn basis in the structure of the nervous system. Thus, we may struggle to perform a task, read a difficult book, or complete a project not merely because

63

these are instrumental to the gratification of a primary drive, but, in part, each for its own sake because certain activities are intrinsically pleasureable. Man is not only a tension *reducer*, but also a tension *producer*. This particular model is a way of adding dignity to man's most unique and cherished accomplishment, namely, that of his competence in dealing with his intellectual and social environment.

Competence leads to positive self-esteem and positive self-esteem leads to psychologically healthier people. This being the case, we must spend more of our time and effort helping students, particularly at the elementary level, to discover their strengths and possibilities and spend less time penalizing them for their weaknesses and limitations. As a child or adolescent grows to know his strengths, it becomes increasingly more possible for him to "actualize" his potential to become what he can become, an idea to which we now turn our attention.

TO THINK ABOUT

Sometimes a teacher can emphasize a student's weaknesses and limitations without even being aware of it. Jot down two or three incidents growing out of your own experience when a teacher may have done this to you. How did they make you feel?

_____

_____

_____

Now, write down two or three incidences when a teacher made you feel really good about your strengths and possibilities. Compare your two lists. What are the essential differences between them?

_____

_____

_____

_____

_____

_____

MASLOW'S SELF-ACTUALIZATION MODEL

This is a point of view about healthy personality development that has a distinctly humanistic flavor. It is humanistic in the sense that it focuses primarily on human interests and values and human meanings and experiences. It is also a holistic-dynamic orientation in the sense of recognizing after all, that the cosmos is one and interrelated; that any society is one and interrelated; that all persons are individuals, but interrelated. Another way of saying this, I suppose, is that the deeper we explore into ourselves as particular and unique, seeking for our own individual identity, the more likely we are to find the whole human species.

Although self-actualization has been defined in various ways, there is nonetheless a reasonably stable core of agreement. For example, all definitions accept or imply (1) the acceptance or expression of an inner core or self and (2) a minimal presence of ill health, neurosis, psychosis, or loss of the basic human and personal capacities. It is, in the best sense of the word, each person's drive to reach the potential that is within him.

Man's "inner core" plays a substantial part in Maslow's view of human behavior. He concluded, from his years of study and research, that each individual has an essential inner nature that is intrinsic, given, "natural," and, usually, resistant to change. Maslow further observed that:

> . . . this inner nature rarely disappears or dies, in the usual person, in the United States (such disappearance or dying is possible, however). It persists underground, unconsciously, even though denied and repressed. Like the voice of the intellect, it speaks softly, but it *will* be heard, even if in a distorted form. That is, it has a dynamic force of its own, pressing always for open, uninhibited expression. Effort must be used in its suppression or repression, from which fatigue can result. This force is one main aspect of the "will to health," the urge to grow, the pressure to self-actualization, the quest for one's identity. It is this that makes psychotherapy, education and self-improvement possible in principle.[30]

Above all, self-actualization theory is an optimistic, hopeful view of human nature. That is, it is a theory that views man as essentially and innately good. Maslow admonished psychology for its pessimistic, negative, and limited conception of man. It was his view that psychology has examined man's frailties but has overlooked his strengths; that it has thoroughly investigated his sins while neglecting his virtues. Where is the psychology, Maslow asks, that takes account of such human conditions as joy, love, understanding, and well-being to the same extent that it deals with depression, hate, ill-will, and sickness? Why is it that we have a very rich vocabulary for psychopathology but a very meager one for health or transcendence?[31]   If man is bad it is because the environment is bad and not because of any inherent rottenness in man.   Destructiveness and violence, for example, are not indigenous to man.   He becomes destructive when his inner nature is twisted or denied or frustrated.   Although Maslow admits that the thin thread of man's potential for self-actualization may be overcome by a poor culture, bad parenting, or faulty habits, it never completely disappears.   Going even further, Maslow has written:

> All the evidence that we have (mostly clinical evidence, but already some other kinds of research evidence) indicates that it is reasonable to assume in practically every human being, and certainly in almost every newborn baby, that there is an active will toward health, and impulse towards growth or towards the actualization of human potentialities.[32]

Maslow's self-actualization theory and White's concept of competence model share interesting similarities.   White, you remember, established a substantial case for an inherent motivation he has called *effectance,* which, literally, is the desire to have an effect on, to make a difference in, one's environment.   That is, we humans have a need to do more than simply satisfy our basic needs.   Maslow, in a similar vein, has noted that

> . . . the gratification of basic needs does not in itself automatically bring about a system of values in which to believe and to which one may commit himself.   Rather, we have learned that one of the possible consequences of basic need gratifications may be boredom, aimlessness, anomie and the like. Apparently we function best when we are striving for something that we lack, when we wish for something that we do not have, and when we organize our powers in the service of striving toward the gratification of that wish.   The state of gratification turns out to be not necessarily a state of guaranteed happiness or contentment.   It is a moot state, one that raises problems as well as solving problems.[33]

As you can see, whether it is the desire to "have an effect" or the "striving for something we lack," both suggest what most of us know from experience—namely, the need to go beyond where we are at the moment. Indeed, Maslow has observed that "for many people the *only* definition of the meaningful life that they can think of is 'to be lacking something essential and to be striving for it.'"[34]   I suppose another way of saying this is that most people are never completely satisfied with what they have; they always want more.   It is like the fellow who dates a pretty girl, but as that relationship wears thin, he wants one who is even prettier.   It is like the seven year old who, upon being allowed to stay up ten minutes later on Monday night, wants to stay up fifteen minutes later on Tuesday night.   It is like a union, which having received an 8 percent increase in the last contract, wants a 10 percent increase in this contract.   Perhaps the best example of all is the student who approached his instructor after class one day after having received well-deserved A+'s on an exam and on a paper and asked, "If I do real well on the second paper and our second exam, would you give me an A and two pluses?"

Maybe it was with tongue-in-cheek that Maslow[35] labeled the need to get more than one already has as the "Grumble Theory." That is, some persons are just not satisfied unless they're grumbling about getting something they don't already have.

TO THINK ABOUT

How true does this ring for you, that is, the sense of lacking something essential and then striving for it? If you become competent in one area (bridge, piano, English composition, or whatever), do you grow somewhat bored with it and want to move on to something else? Or, is your sense of competence—being "good" at something—self-reinforcing," as Bruner[36] calls it? What are the implications for teachers who may have students just like you in their classrooms?

Striving, reaching beyond one's self, looking ahead, transcending the usual and mundane are important dimensions of the self-actualization model. Maslow states this idea nicely:

> The achievement of self-actualization [in the sense of autonomy] paradoxically make *more* possible the transcendence of self, and of self-consciousness and of selfishness. It makes it *easier* for the person to be homonomous, i.e., to merge himself as a part in a larger whole than himself. The condition of the fullest homonomy is full autonomy, and, to some extent, vice versa—one can attain to autonomy only via successful homonomous experiences. . . .[37]

Self-actualizing behavior, then, is aimed not at restoring the equilibrium or status quo but at some sort of improvement. Attainment of one goal usually unlocks new confidence and creates new incentives for further growth. However, it is important to realize that before any person can mobilize himself to aim for a goal as lofty or as noble as anything we might fit under the heading of "self-improvement," he first of all must have his more basic needs satisfied. At this point it might be well for us to take a look at those needs and the order in which they fall.

The Basic Need Hierarchy

Maslow's theory of self-actualization differentiates between basic needs and metaneeds. The basic needs are what he has called "deficiency needs" in the sense that a deficiency in any one or more of them prevents one from going on to higher level needs. These include such needs as basic tissue demands, hunger, security, and the like. Metaneeds, that is needs that are beyond and more transcending than the basic needs, are termed "growth needs." In other words, these are needs that are more directly connected to the sort of personal reaching or growing necessary to realize one's potential. Needs in this category might include justice, beauty, goodness, order, unity, and so forth. The point is: Within every personality structure there is a hierarchy of need priorities. These are degrees of personal functioning in which one must successfully achieve the first degree in order to go on to the second degree and then to the third degree and so on. There are six degrees of need priority arranged along a hierarchy of prepotency as Maslow defined them. Keep in mind that even though the first and second are lower order needs they are nonetheless most important. If these two are not met, the subsequent four cannot be met either.

Basic needs (lower order):

1. *Physiological needs.* These are the needs for air, food, water, and physical comfort, which must be met before the next needs can be approached.
2. *Safety needs.* This refers to the needs for protection from danger (physical and psychological), for routine, for familiarity of environment, and for a certain sense of freedom from excessive fear and insecurity.

Metaneeds (higher order);

3. *Belongingness and love needs.* These have reference to the needs for being wanted and appreciated, for being loved, and for being able to love.
4. *Esteem needs.* These are needs one has for being wanted because he is good, worthy, able—that he has a competence and an independence and a freedom and a feeling of being recognized for some type of endeavor.
5. *Self-actualization needs.* This is man's need to grow, to become, to develop, and to achieve his highest potential. In other words, what a man *can* be, he *must* be.
6. *Aesthetic needs.* These are needs for beauty, symmetry, closure, and a stable structure. This is a need perceived mainly in a very healthy person. Perhaps Einstein's search for some kind of universal order or Schweitzer's "reverence for life" would be examples of persons whose aesthetic needs were highly developed. Or, on a less lofty plane, reflections of an aesthetic need may be the simple but profound feelings of awe and wonderment any one of us may feel as we witness a sunset, a pretty flower, a quiet starlit night, or a new born baby.

Influence of Needs on Behavior

Maslow's hierarchical listing helps us understand many different expressions of human behavior. If, for example, six-year-old Tommy comes to school hungry, it's not likely that he will care much about learning how to read or learning how to play with his age-mates. If fifteen-year-old Sally is consistently yelled at by her mother and seldom sees her dad, it is not likely that she can feel free enough of the basic needs for love and belonging to be able to concentrate for extended periods on her school work. You probably don't have to go any further than your own life experiences to understand how the felt urgency of a lower-level need can make an upper-level need seem unimportant. For instance, have you ever noted how difficult it is to appreciate a really fine movie or play or lecture on an empty stomach? During a class discussion on this issue, a twenty-year-old female student expressed the idea in the following manner:

> You know, I find myself functioning best during those times when I know for sure that Bob loves me. I eat better, sleep better, and I even study better. I mean I seem freer to do the things that have to be done beyond just maintaining myself. I guess I take more of the everyday things for granted and I'm able to concentrate harder on just becoming more me. Really—I'm not fooling, when Bob and I are going right, I really have the feeling of being more like the person I can really be. Another thing I've noticed is that I'm more aware of more things around me. This may sound silly, but do you know that my roommate and I have a potted flower plant on our windowsill and it seems the times I notice it most— I mean really notice it—are when my relationship to Bob is going well. Sometimes when Bob and I fight or for some reason are not close, I just don't seem to notice that plant at all.

You may sense for yourself the freedom that this girl felt when she felt most confident and certain about Bob's love for her. Her comment, "when Bob and I are going right, I really have the feeling of being more like the person I can really be" has deep implications. What it means is that when she no longer has to worry about being loved, she is freer to energize her higher order needs to move in the direction of reaching toward whatever potentials reside within her. Interestingly, even her asesthetic appreciation of a simple flower was heightened when her lower-level needs were answered.

TO THINK ABOUT

An interesting experiment you can conduct in the next three or four days is to keep some sort of personal record of the relationship between your own need satisfactions and the amount of work or study you're able to do. As your lower-level needs are satisfied, do you find that you are freer to pursue higher-level ones? Keep track for a period and find out.

The Degree of Fixity of the Hierarchy of Basic Needs

So far we have spoken as if this need hierarchy were in a fixed order, but it is not nearly so rigid as it may seem at first glance. Although it is true that most people reflect these basic needs in about the order indicated, there can be exceptions.[38]

As one illustration, there are apparently innately creative people in whom the desire to creativeness seems to be more important than any other need. In fact, their creativeness might appear not so much as self-actualization released by basic satisfaction, but released in spite of a lack of basic satisfaction. For example, it is said that Irving Berlin frequently "forgot" his hunger pangs when in the midst of a new composition. As another illustration, sad but true, there appear to be some individuals in whom the level of aspiration may be permanently devitalized. That is to say, higher order goals seem lost forever, so that the individual who has experienced life at a very low level, such as chronic unemployment, drug addiction, or alcoholism, may continue to be satisfied for the remainder of his life if only he can get enough food, another fix, or something to drink.

There are some individuals—psychopathic personalities—who are examples of permanent loss of love needs. These are persons who, according to clinical studies, have been starved for love during their developmental years and have simply lost forever the desire and ability to give and receive affection. The idea here is well expressed by a delinquent boy who had lived with eight different relatives in his fourteen years of living and who had recently stabbed and killed two boys in a street fight. I asked him, "John, does anyone love you?" He replied, "What's that?"

A shift in the need hierarchy can also occur when a need has been so satisfied for so long a period of time that it ends up being underevaluated. Those of us, for example, who have never experienced long-term hunger are apt to underestimate its effects and to look upon food as a rather unimportant commodity. If, say, a person is dominated by a higher need, this higher need may seem to be the most important of all. In fact, there are instances when a taken-for-granted basic need becomes critical only when a person has been deprived of it for a long period of time. Thus, a recent college graduate who refuses to start at the bottom of a firm's salary schedule for fear of losing his self-respect and then practically starves for three or four months looking for a "suitable" job may be willing to take on the original low paying job even at the risk of losing his self-respect.

Among the notable exceptions to the need hierarchy are those that involve ideals, high social standards, high values, and the like. Under conditions such as this it is possible for a person to become a martyr, to give up everything for the sake of a prized ideal or a cherished personal value. Maslow reasons that persons who do this are likely to "have been satisfied in their basic needs throughout their lives, particularly in their earlier years, [and] seem to develop exceptional power to withstand present or future thwarting of these needs simply because they have a strong, healthy character structure as a result of basic satisfaction."[39] Martin Luther King's willingness to go to jail, if necessary, rather than back down in his civil rights struggle or Dr. Benjamen Spock's spirited inclination to get arrested to protest the Viet Nam War are both examples of exceptional men with exceptional ideals who were willing to suffer exceptional hardships to stand up for their beliefs.

It should be noted that Maslow's hierarchy of basic needs is not fixed in some kind of permanent staircase relationship. That is, it would not be correct to say that if one need is satisfied, then another automatically emerges.

The fact is: Most normal people are partially satisfied in all their basic needs and partially unsatisfied in all of their basic needs at the same time. A more realistic appraisal of the hierarchy would be in terms of decreasing percentages of satisfaction as we move up the need scale. According to Maslow, "it is as if the average citizen is satisfied perhaps 85 percent in his physiological needs, 70 percent in his safety needs, 50 percent in his love needs, 40 percent in his esteem needs, and 10 percent in his self-actualization needs."[40] As for the idea of the emergence of a new need after satisfaction of a lower need, this emergence is not a sudden, abrupt happening, but rather a gradual emergence by slow degrees from nothingness. A child who gradually comes to feel reasonably safe in a classroom doesn't, for example, suddenly feel that now he belongs and is loved and esteemed by all. This takes time. We might also keep in mind that the fact that the need that does not show itself clearly does not mean that it does not exist—it merely reflects the priority of lower-level needs.

Examples of Self-actualized Persons

In order to study the hierarchy of need structure, Maslow conducted a unique type of research. In the first place, he began with the notion that to study abnormal personalities would serve only to produce an abnormal psychology. And this would be one-sided. So, what he set out to do was to find a group of healthy, balanced, integrated, successful, "actualized" people. *Successful* here meant the full use and exploitation of talents, capacities, and potentialities. Within this framework, he came up with

forty-nine persons from public and private life, some contemporary personalities while others were historical figures. Examples of those included for
study were such persons as Lincoln, Jefferson, Walt Whitman, Thoreau,
Eleanor Roosevelt, Albert Einstein, Albert Schweitzer, Aldous Huxley,
and Adlai Stevenson, to name a few. Historical figures were studied via
biographical and autobiographical sources, while living contemporary
persons were investigated via personal interviews and contact with their
friends and relatives.

Upon studying these healthy, self-actualizing individuals, Maslow was
able to sort out fifteen basic personality characteristics that distinguished
them from, how shall we say, "ordinary" people. This is not to suggest
that each person he studied exhibited all fifteen self-actualizing characteristics, but each did, however, exhibit a greater number of these characteristics and in more different ways than might be expected in a less "self-
actualized" individual.

Characteristics of Self-actualized People

The personality characteristics which most frequently distinguished
"self-actualizing" people are as follows:[41]

1. They are realistically oriented.
2. They accept themselves, other people, and the natural world for what
   they are.
3. They are spontaneous in thinking, emotions, and behavior.
4. They are problem-centered rather than self-centered in the sense of
   being able to devote their attention to a task, duty, or mission that
   seems peculiarly cut out for them.
5. They have a need for privacy and even seek it out on occasion, needing
   it for periods of intense concentration on subjects of interest to them.
6. They are autonomous, independent, and able to remain true to themselves in the face of rejection and unpopularity.
7. They have a continuous freshness of appreciation and capacity to stand
   in awe again and again of the basic goods of life.
8. They have frequent "mystic" or "oceanic" experiences, although not
   necessarily religious in character.
9. They feel a sense of identification with mankind as a whole in the
   sense of being concerned not only with the lot of their own immediate
   families, but with the welfare of the world as a whole.
10. Their intimate relationships with a few specifically loved people tend
    to be profound and deeply emotional rather than superficial.
11. They have democratic character structures in the sense of judging peo-
    ple and being friendly not on the basis of race, status, or religion, but
    rather on the basis of who other people are as individuals.

12. They have a highly developed sense of ethics and are inclined to choose their behavior with reference to ethical implications.
13. They have unhostile senses of humor, which are expressed in their capacity to make common human foibles, pretensions, and foolishness the subject of laughter, rather than smut, sadism, or hatred of authority.
14. They have a great capacity for creativeness.
15. They resist total conformity to culture.

As you can see, this is an impressive list, and one of the most detailed conceptions of self-actualization yet developed.

TO THINK ABOUT

Which of these characteristics of self-actualizing persons seem to best fit you? Which ones would you like to have fit you, but at this point in your life do not? How do you suppose "self-actualized" persons get that way? What specific things can you do to lead a more self-actualized life? Or, to word it a bit differently, what sorts of things are you *willing* to do?

Self-actualization and Psychological Health

At first glance it may seem that the idea of self-actualization is too far removed from the grasp of the average youth or adult to be a realistic goal. Not true. In the first place, we must understand that psychological health does not necessarily mean possessing all the self-actualizing characteristics listed above to the same degree or, for that matter, even at the same time. Self-actualization is not a destination one stops at, but rather a goal toward which one is constantly moving. It is, in its broadest sense, a life-style, a manner for relating to oneself and others.

A sense of personal autonomy and capacity for independent judgment seem to be highly characteristic of self-actualizing persons. There is some evidence for this in the work of Rudin[42] who indicated that autonomous persons were guided by bodily cues to a greater extent than by visual cues, when these are pitted against each other in laboratory tests. It was shown that the more independent individuals change less under environmental pressures and that they yield less to group influence. Particularly, it was noted that they were able to pursue lines of actions that were somewhat nonconforming, a characteristic that is frequently related to self-actualizing behavior.

Before we go any further, we should be cautious to distinguish between pseudo- and authentic self-actualization. Healthy self-actualization does not mean that one goes about doing willy-nilly what he wants to do without regard for social customs or others' feelings. Pseudo self-actualization is very likely to be the undisciplined release of impulses of one who behaves something like a spoiled brat—who, in effect, "self-actualizes" at other people's expense. Pseudo-actualizing behavior says, in so many words, "I'm doing this for my sake, because it 'feels' right, no matter what the consequences." Authentic self-actualizing behavior says, "I've considered my feelings and yours, and as long as I do not hurt other people, I will go through with my plan." I am reminded of an interview with a tenth-grade sixteen-year-old boy who loved to paint and draw, and, in fact, was very good at it. I asked him if he painted much in school, and he said he did "as much as I can." I asked him if he drew pictures or doodled or in other ways pursued his artistry in academic classes and he said he didn't. I asked why and he replied, "Well, it's hard not to sometimes, but I wouldn't want to hurt the teacher's feelings by making him think I wasn't interested. And besides I know I can draw at other times." A small example perhaps, but a real one nonetheless. Here was a student sensitive enough to see that doing something just because he felt like doing it had to be weighed against its impact on another person. He was guided by sensitivity and good sense, not selfish impulses.

Being aware of the dynamics of self-actualizing behavior can serve as a guide in assisting us to develop in our students those attitudes and values and behaviors most conducive to healthy living. As an insightful student succinctly put it during a class discussion about this one day, "you know, it makes such good common sense—be sure a child's belly is full, help him feel safe, and make him feel like he belongs and then, maybe then, he might feel like learning something." I think this student had a point. Perhaps it would not be going too far to suggest that healthy self-actualizing behavior begins with a full stomach and reasonable freedom from fear-feeling states which, unfortunately, not all children and adolescents can take for granted.

When a student is encouraged to actualize his potentials, whatever they may be—science for this student, English for that student, metalworking for still a third student—he at the same time moves in the direction of what Carl Rogers has called a "fully functioning" individual. Let's examine what this means in greater detail.

ROGERS' FULLY FUNCTIONING
PERSON MODEL

"Fully functioning" is a concept that has evolved out of the many years of psychotherapeutic practice and research of Carl Rogers. In many ways it is similar to the idea of self-actualization in the sense that it refers to a behavior that is essentially "all together" to the point where one is able to maintain and enhance himself. Whereas Maslow studied healthy people in his effort to construct a model for healthy personality development and expression, Rogers' ideas about the healthy personality have come primarily from his work with clients in psychotherapy. Rogers' views of what constitutes a "fully functioning" person do not have their origins in his observation of clients at their lowest ebbs of despair, but rather in the processes they go through and the characteristics they reflect as they move in the direction of developing a "self" which is uniquely their own.

According to Rogers, a person en route to becoming "fully functioning" usually exhibits characteristics such as the following:[43]

1. He tends to move away from façades. That is, he moves away from a self that he is *not* and moves towards a self that he really *is*.
2 He tends to move away from "oughts," which is to say that he gradually relaxes his compulsion to do what he "ought" to be or "ought" to become.
3. He tends to move away from meeting others' expectations and moves toward meeting his own expectations.
4. He tends to move away from pleasing others and begins to be more self-directed.
5. He tends to be more accepting of himself and is better able to view himself as a person in the process of "becoming." That is, he does not as easily get upset by the fact that he does not always hold the same feelings toward a given experience or person or that he is not always consistent. The strivings for conclusions or end states seem to decrease.
6. He tends to move toward being more open to his experiences in the sense of not having to always blot out his thoughts, feelings, perceptions, and memories that might be unpleasant.
7. He tends to move in the direction of greater acceptance of others. That is, he seems more able to accept the experience of others even though they may differ from his own.

As you can see, the thrust of Rogers' fully functioning model is always in the direction of living in closer harmony with one's inner self. Another way of saying this is that as an individual grows healthier or more self-actualized or more fully functioning he is inclined to guide his behavior by the meanings that he discovers in the immediate feeling process that is going on inside him. He comes to want to tune into his inner courses of information rather than shutting them off. This means that persons moving in the direction of greater psychological health trust themselves and their own feelings more and more. Rogers says it nicely:

They accept the realization that the meanings implicit in their experiencing of a situation constitute the wisest and most satisfying indication of appropriate behavior. I think of one client who, toward the close of therapy, when puzzled about an issue, would put his head in his hands and say, "Now what is it I'm feeling? I want to get next to it. I want to learn what it is." Then he would wait, quietly and patiently, until he could discern the exact flavor of the feelings occurring in him. Often I sense that the client is trying to listen to himself, is trying to hear the messages and meanings which are being communicated by his own physiological reactions. No longer is he fearful of what he may find. He comes to realize that his own inner reactions and experiences, the messages of his senses and his viscera, are friendly.[44]

Basic Propositions Related to the Model

The self, which is a basic concept in Rogers' theory, has numerous features, the most important of which are these: (1) the self strives for consistency, (2) a person behaves in ways that are consistent with the self, (3) experiences that are not consistent with the self are perceived as threats and are either distorted or denied, and (4) the self may change as a result of maturation and learning.

The behavioral dynamics behind how a person's "self" is expressed in behavior are discussed in a series of nineteen propositions formulated by Rogers in his book, *Client-Centered Therapy*. To give you a feeling for how these propositions are related to Rogers' ideas about how a healthy person strives to function, seven of the most basic propositions are as follows:[45]

1. Every individual exists in a continually changing world of experience of which he is the center. In this sense, each person is the best source of information about himself.
2. Each individual reacts to his perceptual field as it is experienced and perceived. Consequently, knowledge of the stimulus and what it means to him.
3. Each individual has a basic tendency to strive, actualize, maintain, and enhance the experiencing organism.
4. As a result of interaction with the environment, and particularly as a result of evaluational interactions with others, one's picture of himself is formed—an organized, fluid, but consistent conceptual pattern of perceptions of characteristics and relationships of the "I" or the "me."
5. Perception is selective, and the primary criteria for selection is whether the experience is consistent with how one views himself at the moment.
6. Most ways of perceiving that are adopted by the individual are those consistent with his concept of self.
7. When a person perceives and accepts into one integrated system all his sensory and visceral experiences, then he is in a position to be more accepting and understanding of others as separate and *different* in-

dividuals. For example, a student who feels insecure about what he feels to be a lack in intellectual skills may tend to criticize or move away from those he considers to be "brighter" than he is. On the other hand, if he can accept his own intellectual skills as they are, then he may be less inclined to berate the intellectual skills of others.

The Fully Functioning Person and Psychological Health

A nuclear concept that is stressed time and again in Rogers' writings is that of trust, particularly trust in one's self. A way of putting it is that fully functioning persons are able to trust themselves enough to take more risks, which is simply a way of saying that they are able to put their best hunches on the line and follow their noses toward what feels "right" or "appropriate" to them. Perhaps we can understand this "trust in self" idea if we look at some of the existential choices with which many of us are faced from time to time: "Should I go out with him if he calls again?" "Should I have just one more drink?" "Shall I say yes if he asks me?" "Should I raise my hand and contribute to the class discussion?" What seems to be true of a fully functioning person who makes decisions in these situations is that he is open to his experiences and has access to all the available data on which to base his behavior. As observed by Rogers:

> He has knowledge of his own feelings and impulses, which are often complex and contradictory. He is freely able to sense social demands, from the relatively rigid social "laws" to the desires of friends and family. He has access to his memories of similar situations. . . . He is able to permit his total organism, his conscious thought participating, to consider, weigh and balance each stimulus, need, and demand, and its relative weight and intensity. Out of this complex weighing and balancing he is able to discover that course of action which seems to come closest to satisfying all his needs in the situation, long-range as well as immediate needs.[46]

As most of us can probably know from experience, sometimes a person makes his most ill-considered judgments and his greatest blunders when he remains closed to his inner feelings, his best hunches, or to that quiet but persistent voice of experience advising him to either go ahead or slow down. Thus an individual may persist in the idea that "I can handle liquor," when openness to his past experience with "just one more" would indicate that this was scarcely correct. Or a love-struck young man may see only the glorious qualities of his bride-to-be, whereas a more open attitude to his experience would indicate that she is not so perfect after all.

Speaking of being perfect, the whole idea of attaining this alleged state of bliss seems less important to a person who is functioning fully. Giving up the need for perfection is a difficult task for some persons because their lives seem to be so dominated by the fear of making mistakes (being imperfect) that they are unable to accept new challenges. And of course if an individual is haunted by the fear of making mistakes, it becomes increasingly more difficult to trust his inner feelings, much less his vague hunches. Perfectionistic students exist in every classroom at every level and their dynamics are never more apparent than at exam time. They are usually among the last to finish and the last to leave and usually, but not always, the most anxious. (Sometimes the most anxious students are the first to finish their exams as a means of terminating the source of their anxiety—the exam). After handing his exam in, one very anxious and perfectionistic student expressed it in somewhat the following way:

> I would have finished sooner, but I kept changing my answers. Boy, I hate exams. I never do as well as I could. If I put down an answer that I know has a 99 percent chance of being right, I'll still think it's wrong. Even when I know for sure, I'm not sure I know for sure. Isn't that stupid?

A word of caution may be in order here. We are not suggesting that a perfectionist individual is doomed to a life of neurotic straw grasping. The most we can say is that because of an exaggerated fear of failure he is less apt to reflect the sort of openness necessary for a more flexible life-style. In addition, he's less apt to discover his strengths because of his limited risk-taking behavior. He reduces his possibilities of discovering what many persons learn from experience, namely, that the way to grow in confidence and self-trust is to do those things now and then that you didn't think you could do in the first place and succeed. As one formerly petrified sophomore girl expressed it:

> You know, taking that public speaking course was the scariest experience of my life. Me, of all people, in front of thirty-five other people. Can you imagine! But I made it. The roof didn't cave in and my salivary glands didn't dry up after all. You know something else? I only got a C+, but I still feel great about myself.

Another trend Rogers has noted in the behavior of fully functioning persons is their increased trust in their own choices. Increasingly, this sort of person's locus of evaluation has an inner frame of reference. Rogers notes that:

> Less and less does he look to others for approval or disapproval; for standards to live by; for decisions and choices. He recognized that it rests within him-

self to choose; that the only question that matters is "Am I living in a way which is deeply satisfying to me, and which truly expresses me?"[47]

TO THINK ABOUT

Consider yourself for a moment. Where is your locus of evaluation? Out there? Inside yourself? How important is it to you what others think—about how you look, about your choice to be a teacher, about what you say in class, about what you wear? Whose evaluation is *really* most important to you? Yours? The other guy's? How do you feel about that?

Rogers' idea about the workings of an inner locus of evaluation in persons who move in the direction of being more truly themselves was nicely expressed by a fellow in a college encounter group talking about feelings and attitudes about exams. This is a fellow, by the way, who was working on his group dependency needs in an effort to be more, as he put it, "his own man." The question had just come up about cheating on exams, who did it, why, and how people felt about it. Someone said to him, "Bill, did you ever cheat on exams?"

Cheat? I used to work harder at cheating than studying. Honestly, I'd look on anyone's paper. (Pause) I'm not really sure why I was so frantic about it, but one of the feelings I had was that my answers couldn't possibly be right. I really felt that almost anybody's answers would be more likely to be correct than mine. Hell, that's the way I was with everything, though. I always had the feeling that what other people said or did or wore would be better than any choice I could ever make. I still feel that way to some extent, except now I feel like there are more things I can do. For example, I've found that in exams I feel more confident in terms of my answers having as good a chance of being correct as someone else's. I know they always won't be, but the nice thing is I know it won't be the end of the world if they're not.

All in all, growing in the direction of becoming a fully functioning person involves experiencing, trusting, and risking. As Rogers says so very well, "The process of healthy living is not, I am convinced, a life for the fainthearted. It involves the stretching and growing of becoming more and more one's potentialities. It involves the courage to be."[48] In order for any person, particularly a growing child or adolescent, to develop the courage to be (to be himself, to be what he *can* be), he must first of all have opportunities for learning about the world in which he lives, about himself, and about others. Which brings us to a logical question.

WHAT CAN TEACHERS DO TO
ENCOURAGE HEALTHY DEVELOPMENT?

A sense of competency, a self-actualizing spirit, and a fully functioning approach to life are acquired and learned through experience. What people acquire and learn, they can be taught. What can be taught is fair game for schools. An adequate, healthy personality is not a gift reserved for a chosen few, but a possibility available to every student who goes through school. At least this should be our goal.

One way of achieving this goal is to view it as a self-sustaining circular process. Consider Figure 2–1 as an example of what we mean here.

A healthy, positive school experience is both the product and producer of adequate, competent teachers and students. Again, we probably need go no further than our own school experiences to appreciate at a more personal level how school experiences can contribute to one's feelings of self-worth. A student ridiculed at the blackboard for misspelling a word or laughed at for not knowing the answer to a problem is unlikely to be among those who voluntarily participate in class on subsequent occasions.

Unfortunately, positive school experiences are not easy to come by. For example, John Holt, in his sensitive book, *How Children Fail*, recounts a time when he was talking to a group of elementary age children about their experiences in school. In Holt's words:

> We had been chatting about something or other, and everyone seemed in a relaxed frame of mind, so I said, "You know, there's something I'm curious about, and I wonder if you'd tell me." They said, "What?" I said "What do you think, what goes through your mind, when the teacher asks you a question and you don't know the answer?"
>
> It was a bombshell. Instantly a paralyzed silence fell on the room. Everyone stared at me with what I learned to recognize as a tense expression. For a long time there wasn't a sound. Finally Ben, who is bolder than most, broke the tension, and answered my question by saying in a loud voice, "Gulp!"
>
> He spoke for everyone. They all began to clamor, and all said the same thing. . . . I asked them why they felt gulpish. They said they were afraid of failing, afraid of being kept back, afraid of being called stupid. Stupid. . . . Where do they learn this?[49]

TO THINK ABOUT

Holt raises a good question, where *do* they learn this? Did you ever feel "stupid" in a classroom? What happened? What was your part in it? The teacher's? Or, think about the other side of it—what classroom situations allow you to feel really good about yourself? How did the teacher help with that?

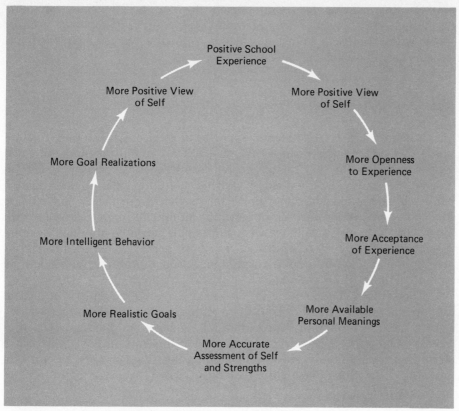

FIGURE 2–1. The Cycle of Positive Personal Growth

The fact is that every classroom at every level exists as a microcosm within a larger societal framework, and it dispenses praises and rewards, punishments and reproofs on a colossal scale. School is not only the theater in which much of the drama of a person's formative years is played, but it seats the most critical audience in the world — peers and teachers. Whether it is on an exam or speaking out in front of the class or working a problem at the board, each student has a certain amount of "stage time" as it were, in which in the face of his severest critics he is reminded again and again of either his failings and shortcomings or of his strengths and possibilities. Our task is to help students see that failing is not such a "gulp" experience as Ben says but that there is virtue and reward in the very act of trying. In order to try, to take a risk now and then, a student (or anyone else for that matter) must first be certain that he will not be called stupid or any other derivative of that label. A student has to feel reasonably positive about himself before he is able to risk doing those things or taking those courses he didn't think he could do or take in the first place.

Helping a growing young person develop into a "total" (self-actualizing, fully functioning, boundary expanding, competent feeling) person who can both know and feel is a process we can help facilitate. How? Let's look at some specific possibilities.

Provide Opportunities for Classroom Interaction

Sometimes we take students' opportunities for classroom participation more or less for granted, forgetting that not all young people have equal opportunity or, for that matter, equal assertiveness necessary to get involved. A study by Symonds[50] showed that the greatest need among adolescents was that of opportunity for participation, inside and outside the classroom. Boys need an opportunity to mingle in give-and-take with boys, girls with girls, and boys with girls. This could be provided by more democratic classroom organization, by more encouraged possibilities for free interchange of opinion in discussion, by small-group activities, and by activities that call for sharing and joint participation.

Coeducational sex education classes are a good example of a natural opportunity for boys and girls to share an experience in which they can interact, ask questions, and express mutual concerns and feelings. Unfortunately, some schools have separate classes of this sort for boys and girls, a condition hardly conducive to encouraging healthy sexuality as part of a growing child's total personality structure.

Provide Opportunities to Express Emotions

School should be a place where a growing child can test and expand the range of his emotional and intellectual potentials. It should be a place where he can express his deepest thoughts and his deepest feelings. Erich Fromm,[51] speaking from his many years as a practicing psychoanalyst, has observed that frequently those persons who are most alienated from themselves are those who have been taught to *think* feelings wihout having feelings. Consider, for example, the number of times you can recall students being asked, "What do you know about this?" or "What does the book say about that?" And then try to recall students being asked questions like "How do you *feel* about that?" or "What is your *attitude* toward this?" It certainly is true that helping students to *know* is a major task of schools. But so, too, should helping students to feel or at least allowing them to *feel* their anger, their joys, their hurts, or whatever when these emotions occur.

Ten-year-old Laurie no sooner walked in the door after school one day than she began to cry. Her mother asked her what was wrong and in sobbing tones

Laurie explained that the teacher chose another girl over her to play on the kickball team, and she [Laurie] felt terrible because she didn't know if the teacher just didn't like her or if she was too poor a kickball player.

A small example to be sure, but the point is that Laurie had held in her sad, confused feelings all day long for fear of someone seeing them. That's too bad, to have to hold back sad feelings for six hours before being in a setting safe enough to express them. School *can* be the best place in the world for a growing youngster to understand himself and the world in which he lives. In order to make this more possible we must provide the necessary conditions for helping him be open to all his feelings and not just part of them. One of the things a teacher can do is to provide the right atmosphere.

Provide an Atmosphere of Acceptance

This demands no elaborate machinery or organization. If you intend to be a teacher, an important requirement is that you like the age group you plan to teach. It means accepting a growing person not only for what he is, but for where he is. Does this mean we have to accept the youngster who kicks us in the shins or disrupts the class? Sure it does. Rejecting the person and rejecting the act are two different things. We may not like a specific behavior but that doesn't mean we have to reject the whole person. It is better to say, "John, your behavior is disrupting the class, and I will not tolerate any more of it" than to say, "John, you're a rotten kid, and I won't tolerate you any longer!"

Creating an accepting classroom climate and encouraging lots of group interaction is a way to promote healthy development. (Allyn and Bacon)

The point is: Children of all ages (adults, too) need to know that they are liked and accepted even though their behavior may be objectionable at times. A simple "Hi there, Mitch," or a friendly smile, or an encouraging note on a returned test, or just being able to call a student by his first name can work wonders in establishing a positive emotional classroom atmosphere.

An atmosphere of acceptance is important, but there is something else equally vital that is needed.

Provide Clearly Established Rules

Sometimes young people misbehave not because they are given too much freedom (although that could be a reason), but because they do not know the rules for what is appropriate behavior and what is not. Firmness and clearly defined limits are a very good way of making it clear to a young person that we *expect* him to live up to certain standards. Indeed, setting firm rules that are consistently enforced can leave a child with two kinds of messages. One is that we care enough about him and others to set them in the first place, and the other is that we can be counted on to be fair when enforcing them.

Having explicit rules and regulations does not inhibit freedom; in fact, students may feel even freer once they know what counts and what doesn't, where the boundaries are and how far they can go.

Provide Ample Opportunity for Success

Every student in every classroom needs a chance to be *successful* in something. We are not talking about success that is each student's own personal level of aspiration and assessed in terms of *his* feelings about it and not someone else's.

There has been a good deal of research related to the effects of failure on school achievement and almost without exception it points to the general conclusion that success tends to induce an individual to raise his level of aspiration, whereas failure generally causes him to lower it.[52] What better reason indeed for providing ample opportunity for success for every student in every classroom?

TO THINK ABOUT

Five specific approaches have been suggested to help encourage healthy development. What do you think is missing? What would you like to see included as approaches or ideas for teachers to think about as ways to encourage healthy development?

EPILOGUE

Although different people have different ideas about what constitutes a "healthy" personality, the effort in this chapter has been to stress the positive aspects of living and to underscore the *processes* that serve as available routes to positive mental health.

Frank Barron, who numbers among a growing cadre of psychologists interested in the study of emotionally healthy people, has suggested that psychological health is a *way of reacting to problems, not an absence of them*. He presents a picture of the healthy person, not as a paragon of moral virtues and uncommon personal strength, not in terms of coolness and efficiency, or freedom from emotional disturbances and symptoms of adjustive difficulty, but rather as a human being struggling to find his identity, forging beliefs out of disillusionment, dealing with everyday conflict, and allowing and even encouraging his more primitive urges to express themselves in creative realizations about the world and human life. He has observed about his high soundness (healthy) subjects:

> [They] are beset, like all other persons, by fears, unrealizable desires, self-condemned hates, and tensions difficult to resolve. They are sound largely because they bear with their anxieties, hew to a stable course, and maintain some sense of ultimate worthwhileness of their lives.[53]

From Erikson we learn that a person's "self" goes through different phases as he progresses through the eight stages of his psychosocial development. It is a developmental framework to help us understand that, even though growth is a continuous process, there are certain critical times or "crises" that occur at different points in the life cycle, each of which must be successfully resolved before one can effectively meet the subsequent psychosocial stage. Erikson's growth framework may help us to deeply appreciate the incredibly powerful influence that school can have on a growing youngster's sense of autonomy, initiative, industry, and certainly his sense of identity during adolescence.

The developmental task idea, described by Havighurst, is a framework for looking at the specific problems, undertakings, or "tasks" that occur at different stages of growth and that are necessary to master before moving to higher levels of development. As a simple example, the learning of the fundamental skills of reading, writing, and calculating are developmental tasks confronting all elementary age children during the middle childhood years. If they are unable to adequately cope with these tasks, they face difficulties in secondary school and in adult life. Each life stage has its own demands and expectations and if we are to be wise teachers and sensitive parents it would be well for us to be as aware of these as possible. Nothing is more conducive to healthy development than the sense of competency that naturally follows from successfully passing from one developmental task to the next.

The need to be effective or "good at something" is a need we all share and it is around this need that Robert White has built a strong case for competence being a primary stimulus for human motivation. Normal people *want* to be skilled, able, and effective with themselves, others, and their immediate surroundings. The need for competence or effectiveness, operating relatively independently of the physical drives, according to White, enables the human organism to find ways of adapting itself to an immensely complex environment. Children and adolescents need to have as many realistic success experiences as humanly possible. Success, as the saying goes, breeds success, but we must keep in mind that a student's striving for success or mastery can be quickly stifled or at least seriously inhibited if he learns at a young age that his best efforts to learn are either rejected or given low grades. Suffice it to say, a sense of competency is a primary prerequisite to a healthy development.

Maslow's self-actualization model is a direct outgrowth of investigations of healthy people. This is a point of view that focuses on human possibilities rather than human deficiencies. It is a theory of human motivation that underscores the hierarchical nature of needs behind human behavior.

Roger's fully functioning person model is similar to Maslow's in the sense that it, too, is a way for underscoring and highlighting the possible and positive in human behavior. Both indicate not only the signs but the possible routes to healthy development.

All in all, research and clinical evidence strongly suggests that psychological health and a sense of competency are goals within reach of every child and adult. Perfection is not our goal. Improvement is. And this is a goal toward which each of us can aim ourselves and the students we teach.

This concludes Part I of this volume. You have been introduced to three theoretical positions and five psychological models to help you better understand and interpret human behavior and to see some of the major implications for classroom practices.

Now that we have looked at some psychological models for growth, let's turn to a more detailed look at the actual developmental processes involved from birth through adolescence that will be our objective for Part II, coming up.

Write your own chapter summary (major points, ideas, and concepts that had meaning for you).

_____

_____

_____

_____

_____

_____

_____

_____

_____

_____

REFERENCES

1. Erikson, E. H. *Childhood and Society.* New York: W. W. Norton, 1950, p. 12.
2. Erikson, E. H. "The Roots of Virtue." In *The Humanist Frame*, edited by J. Huxley. New York: Harper and Row, 1961, p. 149.
3. Erikson, E. H. In *Symposium on the Healthy Personality,* edited by M. J. E. Senn. New York: Josiah Macy, Jr., Foundation, 1950, p. 104.
4. Maier, H. W. *Three Theories of Child Development.* New York: Harper and Row, 1965, pp. 27–29.
5. Erikson, E. H. "Youth and the Life Cycle. *Children 7* (March-April 1960):45.
6. Erikson, E. H. *Childhood and Society.* Op.cit., p. 221
7. Coopersmith, S. *The Antecedents of Self-Esteem.* San Francisco: W. H. Freeman, 1967, p. 238.
8. Erikson, E. H. *Childhood and Society.* Op. cit., p. 223.
9. Bloom, B. S. *Stability and Change in Human Characteristics.* New York: Wiley, 1964, p. 88.
10. Erikson, E. H. *Childhood and Society.* Op. cit., p. 227.
11. Maier, H. W. *Three Theories of Child Development.* Op. cit., p. 139.
12. Erikson, E. H. Symposium on the Healthy Personality. Op. cit., p. 139.
13. Erikson, E. H. "The Roots of Virtue." Op. cit., p. 158.
14. Erikson, E. H. *Childhood and Society.* Op. cit., p. 67.
15. Erikson, E. H. *Childhood and Society.* Op. cit., p. 67.
16. Havighurst, R. J. *Developmental Tasks and Education.* New York: McKay, 1952, p. 2.
17. Morse, W. C. "Self-Concept Data in the University School Project." *The University of Michigan School of Education Bulletin* 34(1963):49–52.

18. Glasser, W. *Schools without Failure.* New York: Harper and Row, 1969, p. 5.

19. White, R. W. "Motivation Reconsidered: The Concept of Competence." *Psychological Review* 66(1959):297–333.

20. White, R. W. "Competence and the Psychosexual Stages of Development." In *Nebraska Symposium on Motivation,* edited by M. R. Jones. Lincoln, Nebraska: University of Nebraska Press, 1960.

21. White, R. W. Op. cit., 1960, p. 102.

22. White, R. W. Op. cit., 1960, p. 110.

23. Gesell, A., and F. L. Ilg. *Infant and Child Care in the Culture Today.* New York: Harper and Row, 1943, pp. 108–109.

24. Silverberg, W. V. *Childhood Experience and Personal Destiny.* New York: Springer Publishing Co., 1952, p. 29.

25. James, W. *The Principles of Psychology,* vol. 1. New York: Holt, Rinehart and Winston, 1890, p. 310.

26. Coopersmith, S. Op. cit., 1967, p. 117.

27. Erikson, E. H. "Growth and Crises in the 'Healthy Personality,'" In *Personality in Nature, Society and Culture,* 2nd ed., edited by C. Kluckholm, H. A. Murray, and D. M. Schmeider. New York: Knopf, 1953, p. 212.

28. Erikson, E. H. Op. cit., 1953, p. 214.

29. Glasser, W. *Schools without Failure.* Op. cit., 1969, pp. 27–28.

30. Maslow, A. H. "Some Basic Propositions of a Growth and Self-Acualization Psychology." In *Perceiving, Behaving, Becoming,* edited by A. W. Combs. Yearbook of the Association for Supervision and Curriculum Development. Washington, D.C.: National Education Association, 1962, pp. 35–36.

31. Maslow, A. H. *Motivation and Personality,* 2nd ed. New York: Harper and Row, 1970, pp. 281–293.

32. Maslow, A. H. "A Theory of Metamotivation: The Biological Rooting of Value Life." *Journal of Humanistic Psychology* 7(1967):93–117.

33. Maslow, A. H. *Motivation and Personality.* Op. cit., 1970, p. xv.

34. Maslow, A. H. *Motivation and Personality.* Op. cit., 1970, p. xv.

35. Maslow, A. H. *Eupsychian Management: A Journal.* Homewood, Ill.: Irwin-Dorsey, 1965.

36. Bruner, J. S. *The Relevance of Education.* New York: Norton, 1973, p. 77.

37. Maslow, A. H. "Some Basic Propositions of Growth and Self-Actualization Psychology." Op. cit., 1962, p. 48.

38. Maslow, A. H. *Motivation and Personality.* Op. cit., 1970, pp. 51–53.

39. Maslow, A. H. Op. cit., 1970, p. 53.

40. Maslow, A. H. Op. cit., 1970, p. 54.

41. Maslow, A. H. Op. cit., 1970, pp. 153–180.

42. Rudin, S. A., and R. Stagner, "Figure-Ground Phenomena in the Perception of Physical and Social Stimuli." *Journal of Psychology* 45(1958):561–564.

43. Rogers, C. R. *On Becoming a Person.* Boston: Houghton Mifflin, 1961, pp. 163–198.

44. Rogers, C. R.   "Toward Becoming a Fully Functioning Person."   In *Perceiving, Behaving, Becoming*, edited by A. W. Combs.   Yearbook of the Association for Supervision and Curriculum Development.   Washington, D.C.: National Education Association, 1962, p. 28.

45. Rogers, C. R.   *Client-Centered Therapy*.   Boston: Houghton Mifflin, 1951, pp. 483–520.

46. Rogers, C. R.   "Toward Becoming a Fully Functioning Person.   Op. cit., 1962, p. 118.

47. Rogers, C. R.   *On Becoming a Person*.   Op. cit., 1961, p. 119.

48. Rogers, C. R.   "Toward Becoming a Fully Functioning Person."   Op. cit., 1962, p. 32.

49. Holt, J.   *How Children Fail*.   New York: Dell Publishing Co., 1964, pp. 38–39.

50. Symonds, P. M.   "Education for the Development of Personality."   *Teachers College Record* 50(December 1968):163–169.

51. Fromm, E.   "On Bringing Up Children Who Love Life."   In *Human Dynamics in Psychology and Education*, edited by D. E. Hamachek.   Boston: Allyn and Bacon, 1968, pp. 397–416.

52. Hamachek, D. E.   Effect of Early School Failure Experiences on Self-Image Development and Implications for School Counselors,"   American Educational Research Association paper.   Chicago (April 1972).

53. Barron, F.   *Creativity and Psychological Health*.   Princeton, N.J.: Van Nostrand, 1963, pp. 64–65.

REFERENCES OF RELATED INTEREST

Bischof, L. L.   *Interpreting Personality Theories,* 2nd ed.   New York: Harper and Row, 1970.

Chiang, H., and A. H. Maslow (eds.).   *The Healthy Personality*.   New York: Van Nostrand, 1969.

Clarizio, H. F., R. C. Craig, and W. A. Mehrens, (eds.).   *Contemporary Issues in Educational Psychology*.   Boston: Allyn and Bacon, 1970, Unit Six.

Foote, N. N., and L. S. Cottrell, Jr.   *Identity and Interpersonal Competence*.   Chicago: University of Chicago Press, 1955.

Gergen, K. J.   *The Concept of Self*.   New York: Holt, Rinehart and Winston, 1971.

Grebstein, L. C. (ed.).   *Toward Self-Understanding*.   Glenview, Ill.: Scott, Foresman, 1969.

Hamachek, D. E.   *Encounters with the Self*.   New York: Holt, Rinehart and Winston, 1971, Chapter 7.

Harris, R. A.   *I'm OK—You're OK*.   New York: Harper and Row, 1967.

Hass, K.   *Understanding Ourselves and Others*.   Englewood Cliffs, N.J.: Prentice-Hall, 1965.

Jersild, A. T.   *In Search of Self*.   New York: Bureau of Publications, Teachers College, Columbia University, 1952.

Johnson, D. W. *Reaching Out.* Englewood Cliffs, N.J., Prentice-Hall, 1972.

Lyon, H. C. *Learning to Feel—Feeling to Learn.* Columbus, Ohio: Charles E. Merrill, 1971.

May, R. *Man's Search for Himself.* New York: W. W. Norton, 1953.

Merbaum, M., and G. Stricker (eds.). *Search for Human Understanding.* New York: Holt, Rinehart and Winston, 1971.

Moustakas, C., and C. Perry. *Learning to Be Free.* Englewood Cliffs, N.J.: Prentice-Hall, 1973.

Putney, S., and G. J. Putney. *The Adjusted American.* New York: Harper and Row, 1964.

Rogers, C. R. *Freedom to Learn.* Columbus, Ohio: Charles E. Merrill, 1969.

Sahakian, W. S. (ed.). *Psychology of Personality,* New York: Rand McNally, 1965.

Schmuck, R. A., and P. A. Schmuck. *A Humanistic Psychology of Education.* Palo Alto, Calif.: National Press Books, 1974.

Strom, R. D. (ed.). *Teachers and the Learning Process.* Englewood Cliffs, N.J.: Prentice-Hall, 1971, Chapter 7.

II

Physical, Psychological, and Intellectual Growth Processes — Developmental Outcomes and Behavioral Consequences

Having established an overall theoretical framework in Part I, it seemed to me a logical next step to turn our attention to the developmental outcomes and behavioral consequences associated with physical, psychological, and intellectual growth. Before we can hope to be successful teachers, we must first know as much as possible about the growth dynamics of the age group with whom we'll be working.

The four chapters included in this part of the book are designed to acquaint you with some of the basic developmental principles related to the preschool years, the elementary school years, and the high school years. Each of these growth "stages" has its own unique characteristics and each leaves an indelible mark on growing youths as they progress through them.

Among other things, we'll take a look at the physical changes that are related to each growth stage, the personality and behavioral changes that occur over time — particularly as these changes are related to parent practices and peer influences; we'll examine the developmental tasks that should be completed during each stage; plus we'll study the intellectual functioning and personality expressions most commonly associated with each major growth stage.

Intellectual growth is a big part of a youngster's growth, a part in which parents and teachers, naturally enough, have a large interest. Some of the specific changes in intellectual functioning associated with each growth stage are dealt with in chapters 3, 4, and 5. The larger questions related to how intelligence, in its variety of expression grows, develops, and how it is measured is taken up in Chapter 6. The controversial issue of the relative impact of genes and environment on intellectual growth is also considered.

When does "self"-awareness begin? What part does identification play in personality development? When does a growing youngster shift from concrete thinking to abstract reasoning? Do different child-rearing practices produce different kinds of behavior? Are there differences between alienated and activistic youths? Can a person be "creative" without being "intelligent"? Can IQ be raised or lowered by environmental conditions? Can teachers do anything that will significantly enhance psychological and intellectual growth processes?

It is to these and related questions that chapters 3 through 6 are directed.

THREE

Preschool Years: The Self Emerges

CHAPTER OUTLINE

PROLOGUE

PHYSICAL DEVELOPMENT AND MATURATIONAL CHANGES

Physical Growth and the Beginnings of Self-Awareness

DEVELOPMENTAL STAGES IN THINKING AND LANGUAGE DEVELOPMENT

Effect of the Environment on Language Development

Changes in Language Usage

PERSONALITY AND THE EMERGING SELF

Behavioral Consistency Over Time

The Role of Identification and Sex-Typing

Adult Models Are Important

Dynamics of Dependent and Independent Behavior

FOUR BASIC NEEDS OF GROWING CHILDREN (AND ALL OTHER LIVING THINGS)

The Need for Achievement (Competence)

The Need to Be Loved and Esteemed

The Need to Be Understood

The Need to Belong

EPILOGUE

REFERENCES

REFERENCES OF RELATED INTEREST

IMPORTANT CHAPTER IDEAS

1. There are more dramatic physical growth changes during the first five years than in any subsequent five-year period thereafter.

2. School readiness varies from child to child; all children are *not* ready when they're five years of age.

3. Self-awareness is related to body-awareness.

4. Comprehension of language precedes expression of language.

5. Environmental factors (social class, parenting, schooling) play an important part in language and intellectual development.

6. Healthy growth during the preschool years involves moving away from an "egocentric" stage of development toward "decentration" (Piaget).

7. The preschool years play an important role in determining the initial direction of a child's total growth and development as a physical and psychological person.

8. Appropriate adult models are necessary for healthy identification and sex-typing to occur.

9. Indulging, overprotecting adults inhibit a child's growth toward independence.

10. A preschool child's personality normally grows in the direction it starts if his basic life conditions remain essentially the same.

Somewhere between the ages of two and three, the child moves out of his toddlerhood years and becomes a preschool child. In many ways the years between two and five are the magic years of childhood. Probably at no other time in his life will a child experience so much that is new, exciting, and pleasurable. And at no other period in his life will he be confronted with so many new challenges, conflicts, anxieties, and fears. Indeed, at no other time in his life will he experience so many changes within himself in such a short span of time. For example, by the time he is five years of age, the typical child is usually about twice as tall as he was at two and weighs about five times more than he did at birth. Developmental changes are so rapid during these early years that fully half of a child's future height is reached by age two-and-one-half. By the age of four, his IQ becomes so stable that it is a fairly accurate indicator of his IQ at seventeen. In many ways, then, the preschool years are foundational to the subsequent developmental phases that are soon to follow.

Actually, the "preschool" label is somewhat of a misnomer because the fact is that not all preschool children attend preschool; nor is there any reason to believe that the child who does attend school is "pre" anything, any more than he is "post" something else. Although it is true that each growth phase is a building block for the next growth phase, it is also accurate to say that each growth period needs to be recognized in terms of its own identifying characteristics. In the case of the developmental years between two-and-one-half and five, which we're considering in this chapter, getting ready to go to school is not so much a specific task to be accomplished as it is a natural consequence of increasing curiosity and broader explorations into an ever-expanding physical and social environment. Perhaps because of the premium we place on education in our society, the "preschool" label serves best to both foretell and highlight the importance of formal schooling in the total development of a child's emerging self.

Probably the most observable signs of a child's emerging self are reflected in the dramatic and hurried changes we can see in his evolving physical growth status, a topic to which we turn our attention first.

95

PHYSICAL DEVELOPMENT AND MATURATIONAL CHANGES

Growth in early childhood, from ages two through five, is not as accelerated as that experienced in infancy although it does continue at a relatively rapid pace. Slowly but surely the developing preschooler loses his pot-belly and begins to assume the body proportions he will ultimately have as an adult. A glance at Figure 3–1 will give you a good idea of the dramatic changes that occur in body proportions between birth and twenty-five years of age.

As you can see, the new born baby has a disproportionately large head and very short legs, while his head makes up practically a fourth of his total height and his legs only about a third. Since the legs are disproportionately short in relation to the rest of the body at birth, they grow the most and eventually represent about half of one's total height. The head, on the other hand, which started out so disproportionately large, grows the least and eventually represents only about one-tenth of one's total height. During the preschool years, head growth is slow, limb growth is rapid, and trunk growth is intermediate.[1]

The average three-year-old boy weighs about thirty-three pounds and is about thiry-eight inches tall. Girls at this age are just a bit lighter and

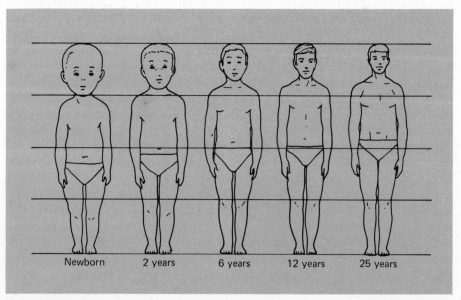

| Newborn | 2 years | 6 years | 12 years | 25 years |

(Adapted from B. J. Anson [ed.], Morris' Human Anatomy, 12th ed. Copyright © 1966 by McGraw-Hill, Inc.)

FIGURE 3–1. Development and Change of Body Proportions

Preschoolers typically have robust appetites. (Eric L. Brown)

shorter. By age five, the average height for boys is between forty-three and forty-four inches and the average weight is around forty-three pounds. At age five, the average girl's measurements are roughly comparable, though again the boy is slightly taller and heavier.[2]

Generally speaking, the tall, thin, short, or heavy child of two will hold his position relative to his peers at three, four, and five, and his height during the preschool years is a fairly good indicator of his adult stature. Developmental research has shown, for example, that a boy will ordinarily grow about twice again as tall as his height at two-and-one-half years, and a girl to about twice again her height at one-and-two-thirds years. This is less apt to be the case, however, if a growing child has experienced severe nutritional deficiencies or an unusual and prolonged illness along the way. In general, tall preschoolers tend to be tall grownups; tall parents tend to have tall children, and vice versa. But not always, and this is because of the complicating influences of those other ancestors to one's genetic endowment. That is, we cannot simply calculate a mother and father's average height and conclude that this reflects the probable adult stature of their children. The reason for this can be explained, in part at least, by

Galton's principle of hereditary regression.   Basically, the theory postulates that a child receives only one-half of his heredity from his immediate parents, one-fourth from his grandparents, one-eight from his great-grand-parents, and so on.   Sooner or later the ancestry of, in this case, tall children and those who are less tall becomes common stock.   Thus, the principle of hereditary regression suggests that children of tall parents will not be exactly as tall nor will the children of short parents be equally as short.   Rather, children will tend to regress toward the *average*.   Children whose parents are rather tall will tend to be somewhat shorter, although probably still above average.   Children whose parents are rather short will *tend* to be somewhat taller.   A similar argument could be made for any other human characteristic influenced by hereditary considerations as, indeed, Galton did in the case of intelligence.[3]

A FORMULA FOR PREDICTING A CHILD'S HEIGHT

Although it is not possible to predict exactly what a child's stature will be in adulthood, there is a formula for making a reasonably accurate prediction about this based on the 12/13 ratio of heights of women as compared with the heights of men.[4]   Thus, to estimate the average heights of daughters, we first of all reduce the father's height by multiplying by 0.923.   Then this is averaged with the mother's height.   To predict the height of sons, multiply the mother's height by 1.08 and average this with the father's height.   As an illustration of this, let's say we know that five-year-old Sally's father is six feet tall, or 72 inches, and that her mother is five feet four, or 64 inches.   First we multiply 72×0.923, which equals 66.4.   Then we average the father's adjusted height with the mother's actual height $64.4 + 64$ which equals 65.2, or about five feet five inches for Sally's predicted height.   This prediction would also be true for any of Sally's sisters.   To get the prediction for any of Sally's brothers, multiply $64 \times 1.08 = 69$.   Then $\dfrac{69 + 72}{2} = 70.5$ inches, or just a few tenths short of five foot nine inches.   Give or take an inch, this is usually a fairly good predictor of height.   Use this formula to figure out your own height in relation to your parents.   How close are you?

In addition to increase in size, the child undergoes other physical changes as he moves through his preschool years.   Among the more significant changes are those that occur in muscular development during this period.   Up until about four years of age, growth in the muscular system is roughly proportional to all other aspects of physical growth.   From that point on, however, the muscles develop at a faster rate, so that about 75 percent of the child's weight increase during the fifth year can be attributed to muscle development.   An important consideration to remember is that the larger muscles are far better developed than the small, fine muscles, which accounts for the fact that although the preschooler may run and tumble with abandon, he will have trouble with complex coordination tasks, such as, say, balancing on a narrow board or even staying within the lines in his coloring book. In fact, development of all the smaller, finer muscles, whch gives a person his ultimate strength and manipulative capabilities, is not complete until adolescence.

Other physiological changes also increase the child's stamina and endurance, which enable him to engage in increasingly more strenuous activities. For example, during this period respiration becomes deeper and slower, the heart rate slows down and becomes less variable, and blood pressure goes up steadily.[5] Indeed, per pound of body weight the preschooler burns more calories per day—between 1,300 and 1,400—than at any other time in his growing years.[6]

By age five, the child has about 75 percent of his ultimate brain weight, and by age six the brain has developed to about 90 percent of its adult weight.[7] At the same time, nerve fibers in the brain and subcranial areas are nearing maturity by the end of the preschool period, which represents an important and necessary physiological change preparatory to a child's formal learning experiences in the school years immediately ahead. Let's remember that we're talking about *average* growth rate here and that there are many exceptions to this. From a purely physiological or biochemical point of view, some children may be "ready" for formal school experiences when they're only four years old. Others may not be "ready" for formal school experiences until they're six or even older.

All in all, the growth changes that occur during the preschool years are remarkable for both their pace and expression. In a short span of three years or so, a child moves from being a high stepping, wobbley, uncertain toddler to a more confident, free-swinging, jungle gym-climbing preschooler. He also begins to develop some ideas about who he is.

Physical Growth and the
Beginnings of Self-Awareness

All these growth processes and experiences we've discussed so far feed into a child's growing sense of "self"-awareness. That is, as his physical capabilities (or lack of them) unfold so, too, does his feeling of competency and ableness (or incompetency and unableness) become a more conscious part of his everyday life.

The roots of a person's self-awareness very likely extend all the way back to his earliest distinctions between the self and not-self, between his physical body and the remainder of his visible environment. A child's surrepetitious discoveries of the various parts of his body and their functions,

Learning to use one's body is an important part of a preschooler's growth.
(Darry Dusbiber)

and the recognition of his own voice are the genesis of his mounting awareness of personal properties and resources. For the preschooler in particular, body-awareness furnishes a common core around which self-reference and identity becomes organized, although later he does learn to distinguish self from the physical body. When children are young, however, they are inclined to think about themselves and describe themselves in terms of what they can do or make or accomplish, all of which imply an active physical involvement with the world. The point is that a child's emerging sense of self or personal identity begins with a sense of body awareness that grows out of natural experimentations with his developing physical capabilities.

Of course, not only do the preschooler's physical skills increase, but so, too, do his thinking and language skills.

DEVELOPMENTAL STAGES IN THINKING AND LANGUAGE DEVELOPMENT

A door to a lifelong learning process is gradually opened during the preschool years as the growing youngster begins to understand what he hears, communicate what he feels, and question what he sees. A child's capacity to deal with his developing verbal skills is composed of two separate processes: *comprehension,* or the understanding of words, and *expression* or speaking them. Not only are they different processes, but research has shown that they seem to be controlled by different parts of the brain.[8] A child's comprehension precedes his use of words, although his expression very rapidly catches up after about two-and-one-half years of age. The average child, for example, can understand 3 or so words by 1 year, around twenty-two words by 18 months, over 270 words at age 2, and 2,000 or more words by age 5.[9] This may not seem like a great number of words, but when you consider that a child's comprehension vocabulary increases about 74 percent between 2 and 5 years of age, then this is a dramatic increase indeed.

More recent research related to the growth of language skills suggests that, with the advent of television, better books, improved teaching methods, and advanced educational technology, childrens' vocabularies are developing more rapidly than ever before. Although there are no dramatic or consistent sex differences in language development, girls do, however, tend to excel slightly in articulation skills, while boys usually reflect slightly higher scores in vocabulary level and word knowledge.[10]

Most attempts to understand developmental stages in thinking and language development draw on studies by Piaget. Although most developmental psychologists do not distinguish the different stages of language development as clearly as does Piaget, they readily acknowledge the importance of his contributions to our understanding of the language and thoughts of children.

According to Piaget,[11] a child's language and thought are interrelated aspects of a total cognitive process. The intellectual development of the child can be best understood through a study of his thought and language processes. Through this method, three levels of intellectual activity may be observed: (1) exploratory, (2) egocentric, and (3) rational thought.

During the first stage of development of thinking, the child is perpetually exploring the world through a variety of sensorimotor experiences and manipulations. At this time he learns to differentiate important dimensions of his environment. Among other things, he learns that his world includes those who play special differentiated roles. He learns that different symbols are used to label different events, objects, and experiences.

During his early years, he develops a vocabulary. However, the world of people, things, and events is interpreted largely in terms of self. Language and thought during this second stage, the preschool years, are largely egocentric. The third stage (more will be said about this in Chapter 4) involves rational thought and usually occurs somewhere between age seven to age eleven, although rational thought may be observed among some intellectually advanced preschool children. Often as a child begins school and develops increased mental maturity, his language and thought become more social and logical in nature. Increased social experiences with adults and older children lead to an increase of logical thinking and a decrease of egocentric thinking.

Effect of the Environment on Language Development

There are, as you might suspect, some marked social-class differences in language development and usage. For instance, children from lower-class families, in comparison to those from upper-class homes, typically have lower vocabulary scores, less advanced sentence structure, poorer sound discrimination, and less clear articulation. In light of the finding that young children from the lower-class families are encouraged to vocalize less than is the case for those from the middle- and upper-middle class, it should not be surprising that middle-class children come out somewhat ahead in terms of overall language development. According to Deutsch,[12] an early deficit in language development and continued environmental stimulation frequently result in an increase with age in language differences between lower- and middle-class children.

There is little question that a child's language skills grow more proficient if he is raised in an environment that both encourages and rewards his use of the language. For example, it has been noted that institutionalized children, who were rewarded only infrequently or inconsistently for their early attempts to use words, displayed marked deficiencies in all speech areas measured—including word sounds, intelligibility, and level of language organization—when compared to preschool children who lived in foster homes.[13,14]

Still other evidence pointing to the impact of environment on language development suggests that there is a positive relationship between the amount of time and effort a mother spends in encouraging her preschooler's verbal abilities (talking to him, answering questions, etc.) and his language proficiency.[15] One very good way that parents can use to facilitate their children's skills is to encourage them to use the proper words when asking for something. If, for instance, two-year-old Randy wants a cookie it would be better to help him say "cookie" rather than responding to his pointing to the cookie jar and saying "ga-ga."

TO OBSERVE

Next time you have the chance, make a special effort to listen to the interaction between a preschool child and an adult, preferably his own parent. How does the parent talk to him? What does the parent say? Does the parent answer the child's questions? Does he or she encourage the proper use of words? If you could arrange it, an observation would be to compare the interactions of a middle-class parent and child with those of a lower-class parent. What differences would you expect to hear?

The only adequate explanation for what we call "knowing a language" is that the child learns a limited set of rules. On the basis of these rules most preschoolers can produce and comprehend an infinite number of sentences. Of course, when we say that a child knows a set of rules, this does not imply that he knows them in any conscious way. The rules are known unconsciously, out of awareness, as a kind of tacit knowledge. This is because the proper use of tenses, parts of speech, and the appropriate use of adjectives, nouns, verbs, adverbs, and so on are usually acquired without any direct teaching. This way of knowing is also true for adults. For example, there aren't too many adults who could state the rules for adding /s/ or /z/ or /iz/ sounds to form plural nouns. Yet if asked to give the plural forms of such nonsense words such as *wik* or zug or *gutch,* most whose native tongue is English could do so with relative ease.[16] Most five year olds can too.

The common sense view of how children learn to speak is that they imitate the language they hear in their immediate environment. To some extent, this is true. A child raised in a English-speaking home grows up to speak English, not German or Hindu or some other language not his own. We cannot simply say, however, that the language stages that children pass through are merely partial versions of adult knowledge. Indeed, one of the most significant findings of studies of child language acquisition is that these stages not only reflect strong similarities across different children, but equally strong deviations from adult grammar.[17]

For example, while in the process of learning to form noun and verb endings, at a certain stage in their development preschoolers will say *foots* instead of *feet, goed* instead of *went, shooted* instead of *shot,* and so on. Perfectly good English to the inventive, happy-go-lucky preschooler could well be on the order of "I runned all the way to the school and I swimmed in the swimming pool there." Actually, these words are overgeneralizations of rules that each child is somehow extracting from the language he hears around him.

We sometimes forget that young children are newcomers to the language and that learning the proper rules for correct language usage takes time. When a preschooler hears words like *his, hers, ours, yours,* and *theirs,* he naturally enough concludes that the first person singular should be *mines.* Humans are pattern- or rule-seeking animals, and these overgeneralizations of tacitly discovered rules are actively tucked away in each child's mind as economical representations of how he should construct future sentences. Once the rule system is established, it is not easy to change—at least during the preschool years—as the following delightful dialogue between a psychologist and a four year old indicates:

> She said, "My teacher holded the baby rabbits and patted them."
> I asked, "Did you say your teacher held the baby rabbits?"
> She answered, "Yes."
> I then asked, "What did you say she did?"
> She answered again, "She holded the baby rabbits and we patted them."
> "Did you say she held them tightly?" I asked.
> "No," she answered, "she holded them loosely."[18]

Changes in Language Usage

A child's language usage undergoes two basic kinds of changes during his preschool years. In the first place, his words increasingly come to stand for specific objects and events. Whereas the three year old might call all animals with four feet "dogs," the five year old is beginning to distinguish between different kinds of animals and dogs. Whereas the three year old calls all four-wheeled vehicles "cars," the five-year-old knows the difference between a car and a truck, or a Ford and a Volkswagen. During the early phases of a child's language development, his language usage is what one psychologist called *undifferentiated* and *syncretic,*[19] which means using a word or phrase to represent several concepts or ideas. Only later does he come to realize that different words have different meanings.

A second characteristic change during the preschool years is an increase in the abstract quality of the language. For instance, every language has words that stand for specific and concrete objects (e.g., bear, deer, orange, apple, car, truck) and other words that stand for classes of objects that share qualities in common (e.g., animals, fruit, vehicles). It is the appropriate use of these latter words that is another characteristic of the language changes occurring during this period. On the one hand, the child is learning to use specific words for specific objects (e.g., he calls a horse a "horse" and does not apply it to all other farm animals), while on the other hand he is learning abstract words that reflect common characteristics shared by dissimilar objects (e.g., he understands that, while not all farm animals are horses, they are, nonetheless, "animals").

A young child's perception of reality is different from ours. (Donna Harris, The Merrill-Palmer Institute)

A child's conceptual development is roughly assessed by the number of abstract concepts he uses as labels for the sub-categories making up each abstract concept. Between age two-and-one-half to about four, a child's concepts are typically defined in terms of their actions or functions (e.g., water is to drink or makes you wet, a ball is for throwing, fire is a thing that burns you). Somewhere between four and five years of age, the child gradually begins to define or conceptualize objects in terms of abstract labels (a ball is ued for many games and sports) or descriptive properties (kittens are cute and furry).

All in all, the growth of language during the preschool years involves learning (1) specific events or objects to which a word applies, (2) the abstract category in which a word belongs, (3) the proper grammatical usage of a word, and (4) the descriptive properties of objects and events. As a child's language skills grow, so, too, does his personality and sense of self.   **105**

PERSONALITY AND
THE EMERGING SELF

The preschool years are important in many ways in terms of in-fluencing the future shape and direction of a child's life. It is a time when the preschool child learns to use words and develop concepts; when he begins to expand the boundaries of his social world and develop new friendships; when he develops his first twangs of guilt and experiences that rather strange sensation called *conscience;* when he learns that people are divided into males and females and that the expectations for each are somewhat different; when he begins to sense that he is an individual person with an increasing awareness of self as a *choosing* person, *doing* person, and *causing* person. That is, he gradually comes to see that he can make choices, he can do more things, and he can more consciously *cause* more events to happen as a consequence of his doing and choosing. In a sense, the preschool child moves away from being a passive vessel, totally dependent on others, to being more of an activator with a power of his own.

TO THINK ABOUT

The next time you see your parents (or whoever raised you), you might want to ask them what their memories are of you as a "doing" and "causing" person. That is, what sorts of things did you do as a preschooler that signaled your exit from being dependent and passive to being more independent and assertive? How did your parents respond to this?

This emerging sense of power is greatly enhanced when the maturation of a child's expanding intellectual capacities unites with his improving motor skills and muscular coordination. The more a preschooler tries that is new and different, the more aware he becomes of his strengths and weak-nesses, his potentialities and limitations, all of which contribute to a more clear and differentiated sense of self. A young child's "inner world" as we might call it, embraces more and more of the outer world. Psychological inputs and interpersonal relationships are important at this time because only on the basis of broad experience can the child learn that both people and events have an external reality. This process enables him to shift from Piaget's "egocentric" stage toward "decentration," which enables him to move from being so utterly self-centered to being more conscious of the fact that he may not be the center of the universe after all.[20]

It would not be stretching it to say that the basic footings of an overall personality structure are laid during the preschool years. Although healthy development during the preschool years means that a child grows more independent, we have to remember that independence is a relative term. Don't forget, the child has to move from the total dependency of infancy and that he still has a good way to go beyond the preschool years. This means that he is still quite dependent on the nature and quality of his relationship to the significant people in his life, which means he is in a highly impressionable, suggestible, malleable stage of personality development. Perhaps another way of saying this is that once a basic personality characteristic is established in early childhood, that same characteristic is likely to persist over time. What does research say about this? Let's take a look.

Behavioral Consistency Over Time

In a long-term study of twenty-five babies during the first two years of life, Shirley[21] observed that even very young children showed a high degree of behavioral consistency on a month to month basis. It was noted, for example, that even though their behavior changed as they matured, there were always "identifying earmarks." That is, a given expression of behavior "would lapse only to be supplemented by another which was its consistent outgrowth." One baby, for instance, was unique at an early age for his continuous, "timorous crying." As time passed, the crying stopped, but he then showed a lot of "apprehensive watching" and, at a later age, reflected similar fearful behavior by hiding behind his mother and by refusing to play and talk in the presence of a stranger. Even though the specific responses are different (timorous crying, apprehensive watching, hiding behind his mother), each grows out of basic feelings of insecurity and fear. Once we understand that the child in question is a fearful child, then we can see that much of his behavior is similar even though the overt responses *seem* different.

Another study revealed a high degree of constancy in social behavior patterns among nursery school children. During each of four semesters of nursery school, fifty-three middle-class children were rated in terms of their dependency, nurturance, aggression, control-dominance, autonomous achievement, avoidance behavior, and friendship patterns. Only nine of the fifty-three children were markedly inconsistent over a two-year period. The investigator concluded that:

. . . during a period in the life span when instrumental behavior is demonstrably changing, in response to modifications in individual capabilities and

107

social expectations, and—more specifically in the nursery school setting—a pattern of individual social behavior that is strikingly unchanging emerged. It is as if each child has his own *behavioral economy* which persists through time.[22]

Probably one of the most extensive studies of consistency of behavior over time was done by Kagan and Moss, who compared the infant ratings for eighty-nine subjects with self-ratings and scores on various personality tests, and interview data of these same individuals during adulthood. The major variable they looked at was the stability from infancy to adulthood of such aspects of behavior as passivity, aggression, need for achievement, and sexuality. One characteristic that proved to be relatively stable was passivity, a characteristic usually apparent during the early nursery school years and expressed in various ways during the school years; e.g., general timidity, shyness, avoidance of rough and tumble activities, conformity to parents. It was also noted that boys were more stable when it came to aggressive behavior and girls more stable in terms of dependency. That is, the aggressive behavior observed in preschool boys and the dependent behavior seen in preschool girls were likely to persist into adulthood. Regarding the overall study, Kagan and Moss concluded that:

> Many of the behaviors exhibited by the child aged six to ten, and a few during the age period three to six, were moderately good predictors of theoretically related behaviors during early adulthood. Passive withdrawal from stressful situations, dependency on family, ease-of-anger arousal, involvement in intellectual mastery, social interaction anxiety, sex-role identification, and pattern of sexual behavior in adulthood were each related to reasonably analogous behavioral dispositions during the early school years. . . . These results offer strong support for the generalization that aspects of adult personality begin to take form during early childhood.[23]

All in all, there is abundant research evidence to suggest that certain basic personality characteristics are fairly well established by the age of six.[24] However, it is important to keep in mind that, as impressive as the evidence for the early determination of personality may seem, there are also grounds for believing that personality ordinarily remains open to change over extended periods. In the first place, the findings do not indicate that traits are *completely* formed during the preschool years and early childhood. The best we can say is that the preschool years play an important role in determining the *initial direction* of a child's total growth and development as a physical and psychological person. If the basic life conditions and experiences of a fearful or a venturesome preschooler remain essentially the same, chances are good that these behavioral characteristics will not only continue to grow in the direction they started, but will become more permanently impressed as a part of each child's overall personality style.

TO THINK ABOUT

The idea of behavioral consistency is something you can research on your own. For example, think of four or five basic personality characteristics that best describe you as you know yourself. Compare those characteristics with descriptions you obtain from relatives and parents who knew you when you were still a preschooler. Are there similarities? If there are gross differences, how do you account for them? You can do this same kind of research with others in your family. You will find it fascinating to trace the evolvement of a personality over time.

A question we might ask at this point is: What influences the direction of a child's personality in the first place? There is no simple answer to this, but we know that identification and sex-typing play strong roles.

The Role of Identification and Sex-Typing

Identification is a concept derived from psychoanalytic ideas about how personality evolves and develops over time. Essentially, identification refers to a process that is largely unconscious in nature and that influences a growing child to think, feel, and behave in ways similar to the primary people in his life. More specifically, it is a process whereby a growing child takes on the behavior of another significant individual in his life and behaves as if he were that person. Indeed, a child's emerging sense of self is built on the foundation of his earliest and most primary identification with people (or a person) most meaningful to him.

Identification is preceded by what is commonly referred to as *sex-typing*, which is more on the order of *modeling* or *imitative* behavior. Whereas identification is largely an unconscious process of incorporation of an entire personality, sex-typing is a more conscious process of copying specific behaviors. Examples would include such behavior as the four-year-old boy's "mowing" the lawn with his toy mower just as his dad does with the real thing, or the little three year old girl "preparing" dinner in her make-believe kitchen just as her mom might do it in the real kitchen. Sex-typing is evident when the preschool youngster begins to express the psychological and social behavior appropriate to his/her own biological sex.

At what age does sex-typing and identification occur? Since both of these processes occur without any direct teaching, it is difficult to say exactly. However, by the time a child moves into his preschool years, he has already begun to develop interests and attitudes similar to his parents. By the time a child is two-and-a-half or so, he or she typically experiences certain subtle and obvious pressures to behave in ways appropriate for his or

109

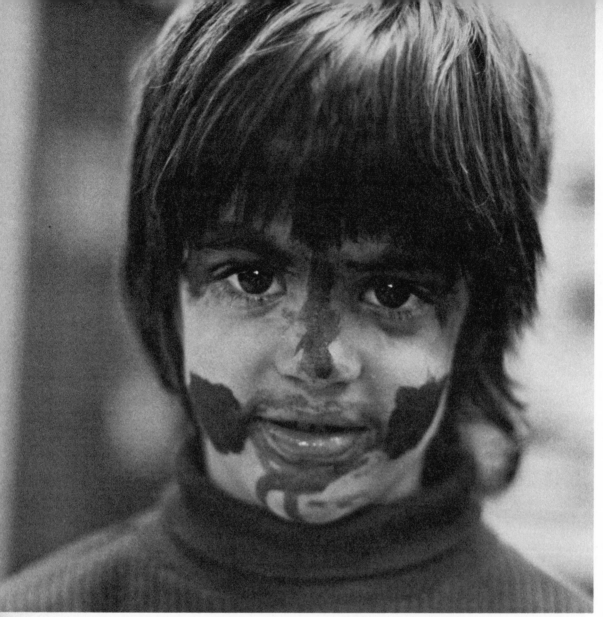

Young children have their own ideas about which cosmetic effect looks best. (Darry Dusbiber)

her sex; e.g., little girls are given dolls and cut-outs to play with and little boys, trucks and cars. By the time most girls and boys conclude their preschool years, they're usually fairly certain what sex they are and what is expected of them in that sex role. Research shows, for example, that we're not likely to find a five-year-old boy assuming the "mother" role as they play house.[25,26] Indeed, a great deal of the playacting we see during the preschool years is something akin to miniature dress rehearsals preparatory to boys and girls assuming their eventual status as adult men and women.

110

Adult Models Are Important

As you might suspect, parents are enormously important in determining a child's sex-role preference. Probably the most fortunate preschooler is the one who has so adequate a father (male model) and mother (female model) that he comes early to prefer the sex-role dictated by his physiology, moves along naturally and easily with its development, and eventually identifies thoroughly with it. There seems little question that the basic components of sex-typing are undoubtedly acquired at home, largely through imitation of, and identification with, the parent of the same sex. One psychologist put it this way:

> In the ideal family constellation, a little boy finds it very natural and highly rewarding to model himself in his father's image. The father is gratified to see this re-creation of his own qualities, attitudes, and masculinity; and the mother, loving the father, finds such a course of development acceptable in her son. Tentative explorations, conscious and unconscious, in the direction of being "like mother" quickly convince the boy that this is not his proper or approved destiny; and he speedily reverts to his identification with father. In the well-ordered, psychologically healthy household, much the same picture in reverse, holds for the little girl.[27]

Theoretically, the extent to which a child identifies with a parent's behavior is dependent on that parent's nurturance and affection, competence and perceived power. Research supports this theoretical stance. For example, Sears[28] found that five-year-old boys of fathers who were relatively warm, permissive, easy-going, in other words, *rewarding*, tended to behave in a manner appropriate for their sex. On the other hand, boys who were more effeminate were likely to come from homes in which the mother, but not the father, was high in warmth and nurturance.

In another study, it was found that a group of preschool children would imitate even the irrelevant behaviors and responses of an adult teacher if she was viewed as warm, nurturant, and rewarding. Preschoolers in a non-nurtured group, led by an aloof, detached, and disinterested teacher imitated significantly *fewer* of her behaviors.[29] They were not, in other words, motivated to be like her. These same results have been found in research that had mothers teaching their daughters simple maze problems. That is, the more nurturant mothers were imitated more, even to the extent of their irrelevant behaviors being copied; e.g., the nurturant mother might make some unnecessary loops or curves in her maze lines and find her daughter doing the same thing.[30]

When both parents are perceived as nurturant, warm, and powerful (in the sense of being able to make decisions, stick to them, and have convictions), and competent (in the sense of being able to do, accomplish,   **111** achieve, and to be dependable), the child will identify with both of them. Typically, however, even a preschool child will perceive greater similarity to the parent of the same sex and will identify more strongly with him or her, as the case may be. We should emphasize that identification is not an all-or-none phenomenon. Not only does each preschooler identify with both parents, but as his social contacts become wider, he identifies with other adults and peers outside the family as well.

TO OBSERVE

Examples of modeling behavior are all around us. In the weeks to come, try to pay particular attention to children who are with adults, wherever that may be—playground, supermarket, school. Watch how young children tend to mimic the adults they're with —how the boy walks like dad, how the girl talks and acts like mother, the roles that boys and girls take when they play house, and so forth. Usually, the closer a child feels to an adult, the more he will tend to model (copy, mimic, imitate) that adult's behavior. This is something you can begin checking out for yourself.

All in all, the evidence is clear and consistent in pointing to the preschool years as a time in a child's life when, as a consequence of identifications he has with the primary adults in his/her life, he may form some of his strongest and most enduring attitudes about sex-role concepts and sex-type values.[31]

Dynamics of Dependent and Independent Behavior

It is truly remarkable when you stop to consider that in a span of three short years or so a child moves from being a totally helpless, flailing infant to being a reasonably coordinated (relatively speaking), assertive preschooler. Indeed, a not uncommon phrase in the typical three year old's language bag is "No, I do it" or "No, I get it" or just plain "No." This change from dependency to more independent behavior is sometimes startling to parents because they sometimes jump to the mistaken conclusion that their child's increased assertiveness and negative behavior is something only "naughty" children do. Nothing could be further from the truth. It is a perfectly natural expression of normal behavior for the preschool child to do increasingly more things for himself with a minimum of adult interference. Of course, it doesn't always work out that way.

That is, some children are very independent in their behavior, while others are clinging, fearful children who seem too timid and passive to do anything assertive.

Dependent and independent children can be distinguished from each other in very clear-cut ways. Symptoms of dependence in children are expressed in behaviors such as the following: seeking help, seeking physical contact, seeking attention and recognition, and hanging around one or both parents. More independent children are more notable for taking the initiative, working through problems by oneself, finishing things once they're started, and trying to do routine tasks by oneself. The independent child is relatively more detached from outside sources of appraisal and relies more heavily on his own resources for getting things done. The dependent child, on the other hand, is more at the mercy of others and there are some sources, possibly as few as one, from whom he cannot dismiss himself and who have the capacity to raise, lower, threaten, or stabilize his self-esteem.

As we discuss the dependency-independency continuum of behavior, we should keep in mind that even though some children display generally more dependent behavior than others, some of both kinds of behavior can be seen in all children. The fact remains that some preschoolers (and older children, too) are much more dependent acting than their peers. Why?

Although no single explanation accounts for why some children are overly dependent, child development research points strongly to the conclusion that dependent behavior is likely to grow from too much parental overconcern and overprotectiveness. Research has found, for instance, the homes of dependent youngsters usually rate high on child-centered practices and "babying" behavior.[32] Coopersmith[33] concluded from his study of over 1,700 children that "One of the more striking expressions of dependency-inducing behavior is the mother's protectiveness of the child." Excessive contact between parent and child and withholding the child from normal outside contacts are behaviors typically found in homes of dependent youngsters. The fact is: Indulgent home conditions do not provide an opportunity for the growing, expanding preschooler to test his abilities. Neither, for that matter, do overly indulgent nursery schools or day-care centers. In the absence of being able to test his abilities, the child more often than not grows increasingly uncertain of his adequacy and effectiveness in the world at large. Indulgence and overprotectiveness, in effect, produce illusions of grandeur and omnipotence but do not permit these illusions to be tested in the broader and more objective arenas of performance. The parent or preschool teacher who overplays his or her inclinations to be the protecting and encompassing adult runs the heavy risk of encasing the child in a cacoon-like shell that severely limits his opportunities for discovering new strengths and developing new skills.

We shouldn't leave this discussion with the mistaken notion that a child should be allowed, willy-nilly, to do as he pleases under the guise of encouraging independent behavior. A preschool child needs reasonable limits established for his behavior, and he needs to know that the significant adults in his life care enough for him to enforce the rules when he breaks them and have expectations that he must live up to.

FOUR BASIC NEEDS OF GROWING CHILDREN (AND ALL OTHER LIVING THINGS)

The years from birth to five are when a growing child begins to form his most fundamental and perhaps his most lasting attitudes about himself or herself as a person. As discussed in Chapter 1, it is a time in a child's life when it is natural for the qualities of trust, autonomy, and initiative to be incorporated as dynamic features of an emerging life-style. That's the happy side of the coin. The other is that a youngster may grow through his preschool years learning to mistrust his environment and the significant people in it; he may learn to doubt his abilities and even to feel ashamed of himself because of what he senses as his lesser worth; and he may feel so inferior that he is unable to take the usual risks necessary for doing things on his own intitiative.

In order for this not to happen, every young child has certain basic needs that must be met if he is to have any chance at all for psychological survival. I suppose another way of expressing this idea is to say that there are certain "life conditions" that must be present if he is to move in the direction of accomplishing his developmental tasks enroute to a healthy, balanced personality.

Whether we look at a growing child from a psychoanalytic, behavioristic, or humanistic frame of reference, the four needs below are universal—they cut across theoretical positions. They are critical at any age, but they are especially critical during the preschool years because a child's personality is just in the process of being formed. Every teacher at every level can help meet these needs. Can you?

The Need for Achievement (Competence)

A child needs a sense of achievement, accomplishment, or mastery over at least some aspect of his external world. The conditions that make the satisfaction of this need possible are opportunities for learning, materials to work with, a word of encouragement now and then, and lots of praise for fledgling efforts and even the smallest accomplishment. A child isn't born with pride in himself and his achievements; that comes later as he identifies with the significant people in his life and gradually internalizes their pride as his own. Eventually, he moves from the feeling,"They are proud of me" to "I am proud of myself."

The Need to Be Loved and Esteemed

A child needs to know that he is loved and esteemed. That is, he needs to know that he matters to someone enough so that what he does and how he behaves makes a difference to that person or persons. The condition that makes the satisfaction of this need possible is the presence of concerned, caring adults who make it a point to let the child know that he is prized, valued, and loved. We're not talking here about an unconditional love that says, "Do what you want" but rather one which says, "I may not always allow you to do all the things you want to do, but that does not mean I do not love you. It means not just saying 'yes' to your requests, but sometimes saying 'no' and meaning it."

The Need to Be Understood

A child needs to know that he is understood. He needs to know that someone older and wiser will at least try to understand his most erratic behavior. A necessary condition for the satisfaction of this need is the presence of not just a tolerant and patient adult, but an adult who appreciates the idea that when a child is young he makes mistakes, he does the "wrong" thing not necessarily because he's bad, but because he just doesn't know any better yet. He has to learn. And in order for this to happen he has to be understood and accepted for where he is on the maturity scale. I am reminded of an incident related to me by a friend who apparently was

115

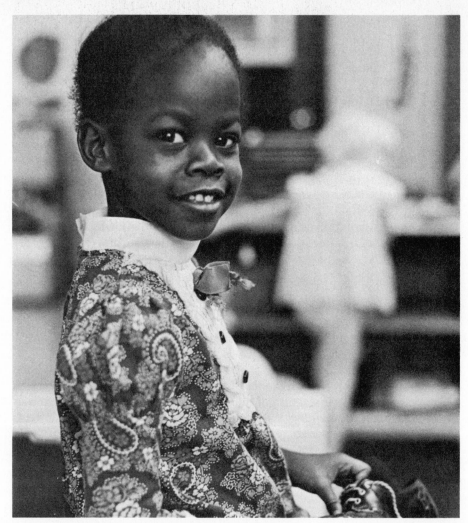

A child's face can tell us a lot about how he feels about himself, school, and life generally. (Darry Dusbiber)

working late one night in his study when suddenly his three-and-one-half year old boy walked into the room, stood before his father, and without saying a word, preceded to wet his pants—actually, his pajamas. This, from a boy toilet trained for over one year. The youngster started to cry and his father simply hugged the boy and reassured him that "accidents do happen now and then." This sensitive adult was wise enough to know that his boy was not deliberately being naughty, but rather he was responding to the new baby his mother brought home just the week before. With behavior, not words, the boy was saying, "Hey, don't forget me. I'm

116

Playing with others and working cooperatively in groups are important learning experiences for young children. (Steve Kopke)

here too." Of course the boy was not conscious about what his behavior meant, but the point is, that his father was aware and rather than punish him for wetting, he tried to understand the deeper meaning of the behavior. The happy ending to this story is that both my friend and his wife made an effort to help the boy to see that he was important too, and pretty soon the boy began to see that his baby brother wasn't such an intruder after all.

The Need to Belong

A child needs to know that he belongs, that he is an important part of a primary group. The necessary condition for the satisfaction of that need is the existence of a sustained and continuous family grouping. In this day and age of increasing numbers of divorces and instances of both parents working, this need is not so easy to satisfy as it may seem. However, it is by no means impossible. A child's mother doesn't have to be present twenty-four hours a day in order for him to feel a sense of belonging. Indeed, some at-home mothers (and fathers) very successfully communicate to the child that he *doesn't* belong which is translated by the rejected child to mean that he's not *important* enough to belong. Actually, it is not simply the quantitative total of the total number of hours that an adult spends with a child that helps him to feel as though he belongs to a primary group (which may be the traditional family group or it might be an orphanage), but rather the *quality* of that relationship. Probably one of the best ways to help a child to know that he really belongs is to make it clear to him that sometimes things are done in a certain way just because he is part of a primary group. For example, one mother I know periodically offers each of her children the opportunity to pick out their favorite dinner

117

dish, which she then prepares.   A neighbor friend of mine put the choice of color for a new car in the hands of his three children (one of whom was four years old) and had them pick it out.   Small things, these, but over time they add up to help the child feel that his membership in the primary group really does make a difference.

Reasons for the importance of need satisfaction in the preschool years are essentially the same as for other life stages.   In order for a child to grow psychologically healthy, his basic physiological needs must be met, his needs for safety and shelter must be assured, he should be loved and accepted, and he must be able to satisfy his need for self-esteem.   If a child is rejected or neglected, he very likely will come to think of himself as inadequate and unworthy.   If he is loved, accepted, and given expectations to live up to, he stands a good chance of moving into his elementary school years with a positive sense of self.

EPILOGUE

At no time in a child's life are there more changes in his person and personality than during the preschool years.   In the short span of five years or so he achieves half of his intelligence, half of his height, and by the time he moves into kindergarten he has developed certain personality characteristics that make him unique and like no other person except himself.

The preschool years are basic learning years.   Everything a young child learns is new and fresh to him.   He is incredibly impressionable, and this is so primarily because his lack of experience with living renders him more susceptible to its events.

Although every preschool child has a unique personality, we should keep in mind that it is by no means totally formed during the preschool years.   The most accurate thing we can say is that a child's personality usually grows in the direction it starts if his basic life conditions remain essentially the same.   By and large, behavior is relatively consistent over time, and the personality characteristics we see in the preschool youngster are likely to persist if they are reinforced and encouraged by the significant people in his life.

One of the most important dimensions of healthy growth during the preschool years is the emergence of independent behavior.   Indeed, it should be cause for some concern if a child does not become increasingly independent as he approaches his elementary school years.   Movement in the direction of independent behavior is a sign that a child is able to trust others (i.e., he is able to count on someone being there in case his independence wears thin.   I'm reminded of the little four year old who said angrily to his mother, "I'm going to run away and never come back—right after dinner") and that he values his own resources highly enough to do more and more things on his own.

There is surely much more we could say about the preschool child, but our purpose here has been to draw a general picture of the preschool child and the more salient features of his overall development. During the preschool years a child's basic personality framework is sketched out. During the elementary years, as we shall see in the next chapter, it is filled out.

Write your own chapter summary (major points, ideas, and concepts that had meaning for you).

_____

_____

_____

_____

_____

_____

_____

_____

_____

REFERENCES

1. Tanner, J. M. "Physical Growth." In *Carmichael's Manual of Child Psychology,* vol. 1, 3rd ed., edited by P. H. Mussen. New York: Wiley, 1970, pp. 77–84.

2. Tanner, J. M. *Education and Physical Growth.* New York: International Universities Press, Inc., 1970, pp. 17–18.

3. Galton, F. *Hereditary Genius.* London: Macmillan, 1869.

4. Bayley, N. *How They Grow, Grow, Grow.* U.S. Department of Health, Education and Welfare. Washington, D.C.: U.S. Government Printing Office, 1959.

5. Tanner, J. M. "Physical Growth." Op.cit., 1970, pp. 84–86.

6. Strang, R. *An Introduction to Child Study*, 4th ed. New York: Macmillan, 1959, p. 137.

7. Tanner, J. M. *Education and Physical Growth*. Op.cit., 1970, p. 72.

8. Lenneberg, E. H. *Biological Foundations of Language*. New York: Wiley, 1967.

9. Smart, M. S., and R. C. Smart. *Child Development and Relationships*, 2nd ed. New York: Macmillan, 1972, p. 256.

10. Templin, M. "Certain Language Skills in Children, Their Development and Interrelationship." *Institute of Child Welfare Monograph Series*. Minneapolis: University of Minnesota Press, 1957, no. 26.

11. Piaget, J. *Factors Determining Human Behavior*. Cambridge, Mass.: Harvard University, 1937.

12. Deutsch, M. P. "The Disadvantaged Child and the Learning Process." In *Education in Depressed Areas*, edited by A. H. Passow. New York: Bureau of Publications, Teachers College, Columbia University, 1963.

13. Goldfarb, W. "The Effects of Early Institutional Care on Adolescent Personality." *Journal of Experimental Education* 12(1943):106–129.

14. Goldfarb, W. "Personality Privation in Infancy and Subsequent Adjustment." *American Journal of Orthopsychiatry* 15:(1945)247–255.

15. Moss, H. A., and J. Kagan. "Maternal Influences on Early IQ Scores." *Psychological Reports* 4(1958):655–661.

16. Berko, J. "The Child's Learning of English Morphology." In *Psycholinquistics*, edited by S. Saporta. New York: Holt, Rinehart and Winston, 1961, pp. 359–375.

17. Cazden, C. B. "Suggestions for Studies of Early Language Acquisition." In *As the Twig Is Bent*, edited by R. H. Anderson and H. G. Shane. Boston: Houghton Mifflin, 1971, pp. 196–201.

18. Gleason, J. B. "Do Children Imitate?" *Proceedings of International Conference on Oral Education of the Deaf*, vol. II, June 1967, pp. 1441–1448.

19. Werner, H., and E. Kaplan. "The Acquisition of Word Meanings: A Developmental Study." *Monograph of the Society for Research in Child Development*, (serial no. 51) 15(1952).

20. Beard, R. M. *An Outline of Piaget's Developmental Psychology for Students and Teachers*. New York: Basic Books, 1969, pp. 59–70.

21. Shirley, M. M. "The First Two Years: A Study of Twenty-five Babies." *Personality Manifestations*. Institute of Child Welfare Series. Minneapolis: University of Minneapolis, vol. III, no. 8, 1933.

22. Martin, W. E. "Singularity and Stability of Profiles of Social Behavior." In *Readings in Child Behavior and Development*, edited by C. B. Stendler. New York: Harcourt, Brace and World, 1964, p. 465.

23. Kagan, N., and H. A. Moss. *From Birth to Maturity: A Study in Psychological Development*. New York: John Wiley and Sons, Inc., 1962, pp. 266–268.

24. Hamachek, D. E. *Encounters with the Self*. New York: Holt, Rinehart and Winston, 1971, pp. 62–100.

25. Fauls, L., and W. D. Smith. "Sex-Role Learning of Five-Year-Olds." *Journal of Genetic Psychology* 89(1956):105–117.

26. Brown, D. G. "Sex-Role Preference in Young Children." *Psychological Monographs* 70(1956):1–19.

27. Mowrer, O. H. *Learning Theory and Personality Dynamics.* New York: Ronald Press, 1950, p. 596.

28. Sears, P. S. "Child-Rearing Factors Related to Playing of Sex-Typed Roles." *American Psychologist* 8(1953):431 (abstract).

29. Bandura, A., and A. C. Houston. "Identification as a Process of Incidental Learning." *Journal of Abnormal and Social Psychology* 63(1961):311–318.

30. Mussen, P., and A. Parker. "Mother Nurturance and Girls' Incidental Imitative Learning." *Journal of Personality and Social Psychology* 2(1965)94–97.

31. Kohlberg, L. "A Cognitive-Developmental Analysis of Children's Sex-Role Concepts and Attitudes." In *The Development of Sex Differences,* edited by E. E. Maccoby. Stanford, Calif.: Stanford University Press, 1966, p. 82.

32. Heathers, G. "Emotional Dependence and Independence in a Physical Threat Situation." *Child Development* 24(1953):169–179.

33. Coopersmith, S. *The Antecedents of Self-Esteem.* San Francisco: W. H. Freeman, 1967, p. 223.

REFERENCES OF RELATED INTEREST

Anderson, R. H., H. G. Shane (eds.). *As the Twig Is Bent.* Boston: Houghton Mifflin, 1971.

Edge, D. (ed.). *The Formative Years.* New York: Schoeken Books, 1970.

Frost, J. L. (ed.). *Early Childhood Education Rediscovered.* New York: Holt, Rinehart and Winston, 1968.

Ginott, H. *Between Parent and Child.* New York: Macmillan, 1965.

Herron, R. E., and B. Sutton-Smith (ed.). *Child's Play.* New York: Wiley, 1971.

Jersild, A. T. *Child Psychology,* 6th ed. Englewood Cliffs, N.J.: Prentice-Hall, 1968.

Kagan, J. *Understanding Children.* New York: Harcourt Brace Jovanovich, 1971.

Lavatelli, C. S., and F. Stendler (eds.). *Readings in Child Behavior and Development,* 3rd ed. New York: Harcourt Brace Jovanovich, 1972.

Mussen, P. H., J. J. Conger, and J. Kagan. *Child Development and Personality,* 3rd ed. New York: Harper and Row, 1969.

Mussen, P. H., J. J. Conger, and J. Kagan (eds.). *Readings in Child Development and Personality,* 2nd ed. New York: Harper and Row, 1970.

Nixon, R. H., and C. L. Nixon. *Introduction to Early Childhood Education.* New York: Random House, 1971.

Parker, R. K. *The Preschool in Action.* Boston: Allyn and Bacon, 1972.

Read, K. H. *The Nursery School Years,* 5th ed. Philadelphia: Saunders, 1971.

Salk, L. *What Every Child Would Like His Parents to Know.* New York: McKay, 1972.

Seidman, J. M. (ed.). *The Child*, 2nd ed. New York: Holt, Rinehart and Winston, 1969.

Smart, R. C., and M. S. Smart (eds.). *Readings in Child Development and Relationships*. New York: Macmillan, 1973.

_____. *Children: Development and Relationships*, Part II, 2nd ed. New York: Macmillan, 1973.

_____ (eds). *Preschool Children*. New York: Macmillan, 1973.

Todd, V. E. and H. Hefferman (eds.). *The Years Before School*. New York: Macmillan, 1970.

Yamamoto, K. *The Child and His Image*. Boston: Houghton Mifflin, 1972.

Young, L. *Life Among Giants*. New York: McGraw-Hill, 1966.

FOUR

Elementary and Middle School Years: The Self Expands

CHAPTER OUTLINE

PROLOGUE

PHYSICAL DEVELOPMENT AND MATURATIONAL CHANGES

Body Build as Related to Personality

Implications for teachers

Accidents and Health Considerations

INTELLECTUAL GROWTH AND COGNITIVE FUNCTIONING

Vocabulary Grows Larger

Ability to Conceptualize Develops

Concepts become more valid

Concepts have more status

Concepts become more accessible

Development of Rules in Relation to Concepts

Formal and informal rules

Development of Concrete Thinking (Piaget's Stage III)

The principle of conservation

The principle of transformation

The process of equilibration

Erikson's Stage Four: Industry versus Inferiority

Parents' Influence on Cognitive Functioning and Intellectual Performance

Child Rearing Across Social Classes: Relationships to Cognitive Development

Intellectual and Cognitive Growth: Implications for Teachers

INFLUENCES ON A CHILD'S EMOTIONAL-SOCIAL DEVELOPMENT

Child-rearing Practices: Varieties and Consequences

Authoritarian parenting

Authoritative parenting

Permissive Parenting

Influence of Different Parenting Styles

Warm-restrictive versus warm-controlling parents

Influence on children's behavior

Functional versus interpersonal adult power

Peer Group Involvement: Influence and Outcomes

Three major peer group functions

Children's Play: Function and Meaning

Psychological significance of games

UNDERSTANDING MIDDLE CHILDHOOD FOR WHAT IT IS

EPILOGUE

REFERENCES

REFERENCES OF RELATED INTEREST

IMPORTANT CHAPTER IDEAS

1. The self further expands from its undifferentiated and diffuse infant state into a more identifiable cluster of behavior patterns that we associate with a child's personality.

2. Physical growth slows considerably.

3. Body build can influence personality development because it can influence, to some extent, how peers and adults respond.

4. Middle childhood is generally a healthy period, disease-wise, although accidents are numerous.

5. Children during this age are gluttonous learners.

6. Approximately 80 percent of a child's intelligence is developed by age eight or so.

7. Vocabulary, particularly language recognition, grows dramatically.

8. Ability to conceptualize improves significantly.

9. Flexibility of thought is crucial for normal cognitive development to occur.

10. It is important to both allow and encourage children to be "industrious" during this growth stage.

11. Parents significantly influence—for better or for worse—a child's intellectual development.

12. The gap between middle- and lower-class child-rearing practices is getting increasingly smaller.

13. Each home is like a miniature school with its own individual curriculum and each parent shares part of the "teaching" role in a kind of team-teaching arrangement.

14. Authoritarian control and permissive noncontrol tend to inhibit healthy growth.

15. High self-esteem among children is associated with parental (and teacher) love, firmness, and reasonable expectations to meet.

16. A middle-years child looks more and more to his peers for identity.

17. Parents value behaving appropriately; peers value performing adequately.

18. A child's play is an important aspect of his overall socialization insofar as he must both relate and perform with peers.

19. A major outcome of middle childhood is not improvement, but disorganization.

PROLOGUE

The age period from six to twelve is a rather remarkable one in a child's life. It is a time in a child's development when he becomes increasingly more aware of and responsive to an ever-widening variety of influences ranging all the way from his mother, to his teacher, to his buddies up the street, to comic books, to television. It is a time when little boys don't particularly care for little girls, when little girls are equally indifferent to little boys (but not as much so), and when both sexes find their greatest satisfaction and pleasure in being with other kids, preferably of the same age and gender. It is a time for large-muscle development and small-muscle refinement, and for an energy supply with such giant reserves that it leaves some parents wondering why they ever wanted children in the first place. Depending on his culture and where he lives, the typical American middle-years youngster learns to ride a two-wheeler (with no hands, standing up, sideways, and some even backwards), to swim and dive, to dribble a basketball, to play kick-the-can, to hang by his knees, to play baseball, football, or soccer, and to master simple small-muscle acrobatics such as crossing his eyes, snapping hs fingers, winking one eye, whistling, and, if he is truly talented, even wiggling his ears. It is also a time when, within a broader social context, he continues to develop the personality characteristics that began to emerge during the preschool years. In a very real sense of the word, the self we had brief glimpses of during his early years begins to expand and unfold from its undifferentiated and diffuse infant state into a more differentiated and identifiable cluster of behavior patterns that we gradually associate with a child's personality. It is a slow, inevitable, even fateful process, and one that involves a continual interaction between what a child inherits and the environment in which he lives.

The elementary and middle school years are consolidation years— they're years when a growing child is still "putting himself together," which is why it's important for teachers to understand the basic dynamics associated with physical, intellectual, and social-emotional development at this time. In Chapter 3, we saw how the self emerges. Now let's turn to how it expands.

"AND JUST HOW LONG HAVE YOU BEEN DRIVING THIS SCHOOL BUS?"

Elementary school age youths have endless supplies of energy and enthusiasm. It takes patient and well-integrated teachers (and bus drivers) to cope with them on a daily basis. (NAT, reprinted by permission of Masters Agency)

As is the case during the preschool years, a very observable and measureable aspect of an elementary age child's expanding self is reflected in his evolving growth status, a topic to which we turn our attention first.

PHYSICAL DEVELOPMENT AND MATURATIONAL CHANGES

The physical changes occurring during the middle years of childhood are primarily ones of proportion rather than sheer increase in size. The rapid growth experiences during the preschool days slows considerably. For example, by eight years of age the arms and legs are nearly 50 percent longer than they were at age two, yet the overall height has increased by only 25 percent. Arm and leg muscles develop slowly during this period, which is why so many children this age look spindly and undernourished.

Increases in height during the middle years of childhood is usually at the rate of two to three inches annually. By the onset of puberty, the

127

The elementary school years are a time for more growing, more learning, and for silly postures and faces, too.

average girl of eleven years is around 58 inches tall and the average boy of the same age about 57.5 inches.[1] By the time the average boy reaches twelve years of age he will have attained approximately 84 percent of his mature adult height. Girls, on the other hand, reach approximately 92.6 percent of their mature adult height at that same age.[2] Actually, boys are slightly shorter than girls throughout the middle childhood period, a distressing fact for many boys until they eventually catch up and finally surpass girls during the adolescence growth spurt.

There are also some striking changes in the general cast of a child's facial features during the middle childhood years. The fat pads that fill out the preschooler's cheeks gradually dwindle away leaving a formerly rounded face with a far leaner appearance. The oversized forehead housing a rapidly growing brain gets progressively smaller as the rest of the child's face catches up with cranial development. And then, of course, there are those years between six and eight, depending on the child, when the baby teeth are lost (or does the tooth fairy take them?), and what was once a cute smile becomes a silly toothless grin. When permanent teeth arrive to fill the gaps, they frequently appear disproportionately large in relation to the jaw available to them. The baby teeth go approximately in the order in which they came, beginning with the lower front teeth and moving systematically back. Later losses of baby teeth are not so noticeable, since they occur farther back in the mouth, but the shedding of old teeth and the eruption of permanent ones goes on until age ten or twelve. Actually, it is not until adolescence, when the nose cartilage expands and the jaw develops further that the face at last catches up to the teeth in size, and the child begins to look like the person he will be in adulthood.

TO OBSERVE

You could, of course, make it a point to observe for yourself some of the striking physical changes that go on between ages six and twelve by visiting a school and making a specific effort to compare children in different grades. Another way to do this is to get pictures that were taken of you during your "growing up" period. Put them in chronological order. Compare the changes and you will soon see how dramatic those changes can be.

As with height, weight increases are also slow and fairly uniform at this age. At the end of these middle years, the average twelve-year-old girl weighs approximately 100.5 pounds and the average boy of the same age, 96 pounds.[3] Again, as with height, girls tend to be slightly heavier at every age during these middle years than boys, and this difference is exaggerated even more when girls begin their puberty spurt earlier than boys during the

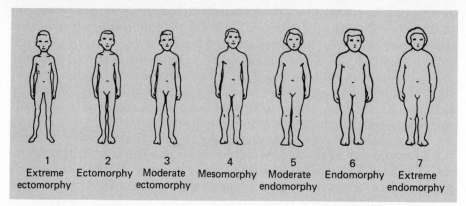

1 Extreme ectomorphy
2 Ectomorphy
3 Moderate ectomorphy
4 Mesomorphy
5 Moderate endomorphy
6 Endomorphy
7 Extreme endomorphy

(From M. Massler and T. Suher. "Calculation of "Normal" Weight in Children." Child Development 22[1951]:75–94. Used by permission.)

FIGURE 4–1. Differences in Body Build during Childhood

closing years of childhood.[4]   How much a child weighs depends to some extent on his particular body build, which can range all the way from extreme ectomorphy (thin) to extreme endomorphy (fat).   Figure 4–1 will give you a pretty good idea of the seven basic body builds or types that characterize the physical structure of different children (and adults, for that matter).

Body Build as Related to Personality

Knowing something about body build and its relationship to height, weight, and total appearance is not merely of academic interest, but of considerable practical importance as well.   For example, research has shown that even among children as young as six to ten years of age they are already in close agreement when it comes to assigning certain personality characteristics to particular body types.   This suggests that how elementary age children respond to each other is at least partially determined by physical characteristics.   One psychologist, for instance, found that among six- to ten-year-old boys there is a strong tendency to stereotype certain body types in predictable ways.   For example, these boys described those with endomorphic build (obese, heavy) as socially offensive and delinquent; those with mesomorphic build (athletic, muscular) as aggressive, outgoing, active, and having leadership skills; and those with ectomorphic builds (tall, thin) as retiring, nervous, shy, and introverted.   In addition, it was also found that ectomorphs and mesomorphs were more apt to be chosen as the most popular.   On a less happy note, the endomorphic children were not only inclined to be less popular, but they more often were among those who have negative, rejecting feelings about their body image.[5]   Other research has shown that relationships between body type and personality is evident even among preschool children.[6,7]

The positive relationships between body build and personality are more evident for boys than for girls. That is, neither girls nor boys are inclined to stereotype a girl's personality according to perceived body build. This is particularly true among preschool and elementary age children. When it comes to being judged on the basis of physical appearance, the latitude allowed girls is apparently greater than is the case for boys. It may also be that these relationships are more definite for boys because we are clearer about what the physical standards are for what a boy should look like than we are for girls—at least young girls. This does not mean that there are no relationships whatsoever between body build and personality for girls; it only means that these relationships are not as strong as is the case for boys.

We cannot say that a child's personality is *caused* by this or that body type, but we can say that a child's physical skill plays an important part as far as the kind of feedback he gets is concerned. Indeed, considering the feedback that any person—young or old—both gives and receives on the basis of purely physical appearances, it is not difficult to see how an individual's physical proportions can influence his feelings about himself simply by affecting how other people react toward him. Consider the chubby or obese child who grows up in the face of monikers like "Tubby," "Chubby," "Fatso," or "Lard-belly," or the thin, lanky child who is variously tagged with "Beanpole," "Skinny legs," or "Big ears." Descriptive labels, these, and, as you may recall from your own childhood days, children are masters at picking out those one or two physical characteristics that stand out on one another and then exaggerating them to the level of defamatory caricatures. If used for a long enough period of time—particularly if they come from significant people in a child's life like parents and teachers—the names that were originally meant to describe a person's physique can also have the effect of describing and defining, to some extent, his personality. Thus, the overweight little boy who frequently hears adjectives such as "fatso," "awkward," "clumsy," or "heavyfooted" ascribed to him may in fact grow up to be that kind of person—clumsy and self-consciously awkward not only in social situations, but in his interpersonal relationships as well. Let's keep in mind that a child going through his middle years is extremely receptive to both adult and peer input regarding both his person and performance. Another way of saying this is that he more readily believes and incorporates what is said about him during these middle years than he ever will again. It behooves all of us who work with or teach growing children to remind ourselves that what we consider to be harmless *perceptions* ("John, you're so dumb about the way you do things" or "Sally, your feet seem to be a major obstacle course for you") may, if a child hears them often enough, be converted in the child's mind as self-*conceptions*. Over time, John may conclude, "I'm pretty dumb" and then set out to behave in dumb ways. And

131

Sally may conclude, "I'm pretty clumsy" and then fulfill that conception by tripping over her own feet.

Implications for teachers. Whether we are aware of it or not, part of our response to other people is determined by how they look to us. Physical appearance and body dimensions can make a difference. As teachers we must work at being aware of our biases regarding physical appearance so we don't end up rejecting some students and favoring others because they happen to offend or please our eyes. Every child and adolescent deserves to be treated with equal respect and caring—regardless of what his physical appearance happens to be. A teacher's acceptance is sometimes all a growing youngster needs to be more self-accepting.

Accidents and Health Considerations

Middle childhood is generally a healthy period. Although most children are prone to minor diseases such as measles, mumps, chicken pox, and whooping cough (many of which can be avoided completely by inoculation), the happy fact remains that the death rate during this period is the lowest of any comparable span of years. Research shows that the dreaded diseases that used to fill pediatric wards in hospitals, such as rheumatic fever and rheumatic heart disease, osteomyelitis, mastoiditis, pneumonia, streptococcal infections, meningitis, and polio, to name a few, have sharply declined over the past twenty years.[8]

Unfortunately, there is no vaccine to render a child immune to accidents. This is too bad because it is middle childhood's stumbles, tumbles, and falls and not germs and viruses that most frequently plague children in this age bracket. Accidents are the largest single cause of deaths during middle childhood, responsible for about 50 percent of boys' deaths and 25 percent of girls' deaths.[9] As a rule, the older child has fewer accidents than the younger child, but they tend to be more serious than the younger child's. This is not surprising since the older child can use his superior coordination and advanced muscle development to play harder, run harder, and, alas, fall harder. It has been reported that approximately two-thirds of all childhood accidents occur before children are nine years old, with more before six than after six.[10]

It is not surprising to note that boys have more accidents at all ages than do girls.[11] This is consistent with the differences commonly seen between boys and girls when it comes to the sort of play activities they engage in. Naturally enough, boys, who participate in more all-out rough and tumble games than is usually the case for girls, are more apt to bang a head, twist an ankle, or even break an arm than their female counterparts. Figure 4-2 will give you a quick overview of the frequency of childhood injuries to various parts of the body. As you can see, head injuries are far

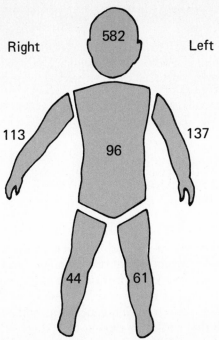

Right

Left

582

113

137

96

44   61

(*From H. Jacobziner.* "*Accidents—A major child health problem.*" *Journal of Pediatrics 46*[1955]:419–436. *Used by permission.*)

FIGURE 4–2. Parts of the Child's Body Most Often Injured in Non-fatal Accidents. Numbers Indicate Frequency of Injuries in One Survey

ahead of other types of injuries. There is no clear explanation for why this should be, but one pretty good possibility is that a child's reflexes simply have not yet developed enough to enable him to respond with sufficient speed to protect himself.

Research has shown that some children seem to be more "accident prone" than others and that this proneness is related to certain personality characteristics. Accident-prone children, it appears, are more inclined to be overactive, restless, anxious, impulsive, adventuresome, and resistant to authority. Children with fewer accidents, on the other hand, are found to be more timid, submissive, and well controlled.[12,13] It makes sense: The more active and assertive a child is, the more bumps and bruises he's going to have.

All told then, the middle years of childhood are a time of good health, slower growth, large muscle development and small muscle refinement, and increased skill development. It is a time when a child sheds his baby physical self and gradually assumes the body proportions and facial dimensions of his future adult physical self. Physical growth is one aspect of middle childhood; intellectual growth is still another, a topic to which we now turn.

133

TO FIND OUT ABOUT

In your continuing effort to learn more about growth and development and yourself in the process, this is another area you can check out about your own development. That is, what was your health and accident record like between the years of six and twelve? Make an effort to get the information about this from parents and others who knew you back then. If you were accident-prone, are you still?

INTELLECTUAL GROWTH AND COGNITIVE FUNCTIONING

A child between the ages of six and twelve characteristically begins to divert his attention away from home involvements and aim it outward toward the world at large. We know from Piaget's[14] developmental studies that this is a perfectly natural course for a growing child to make as he moves slowly but surely away from his egocentric, self-centered preschool years. We also know that children during this stage of growth are gluttonous learners—or at least they can be if encouraged, helped, directed when needed, and challenged when necessary. They learn everywhere and from everyone—from the gang, from conversations at home either as participants or listeners, from their reading, television, and, most certainly, in schools.

Sometime during the beginning of the school years, which for some children is around age four, while for others it is as late as age seven or eight, a major change in cognitive functioning takes place and is reflected in various general and specific learning readinesses—general school readiness, reading readiness, number readiness, and so forth. This means that different children at different times enter what we might call a state of general intellectual readiness and cognitive preparedness to do school-related work. This is partly a function of physical maturation and partly a function of the life experiences a child has had (an enriched, above-average environment, an average environment, or an impoverished, below-average environment). Both of these factors, physical maturation and life experiences, play important parts in determining when a child is "ready" for readin', 'ritin', and 'rithmetic.

Although middle-years children are hungry learners, research also tells us that intellectual development slows down some during this period. You may recall from Bloom's studies, for example, that it has been estimated that about half of one's mature intelligence is developed by age four, another 30 percent by age eight, and the remaining 20 percent during the

A youngster's ability to conceptualize and think things through grows rapidly during the elementary school years. (Allyn and Bacon)

remainder of the middle childhood years.[15]   Let's be sure we understand
this. To say, for instance, that about 80 percent of a child's intelligence is
developed by age eight does not mean that he knows 80 percent of all that
he can learn about. It *does* mean, however, that by age eight most children
have developed about 80 percent of their *innate ability* for learning. How
that innate ability is used, of course, depends very much upon the environment (home, schools, parents, opportunities, etc.) to which a child is exposed. Suffice it to say, middle-years children have a great deal of learning
readiness that good schooling and stimulating teachers can do much to
develop.

Vocabulary Grows Larger

Intellectual development is revealed in vocabulary growth, which,
after reaching a high point at three, maintains a remarkably steady increase
in number of words gained per year up through the elementary years.
Indeed, the number of words that the average elementary age child can
recognize, which means he may be able to give some meaning to although
not necessarily be able to use, has increased dramatically over the past
40 years or so. For example, research in the 1930's indicated that the
recognition vocabularies of sixth graders was around 14,000 words.[16] By
the late 1940's this was approaching 15,000 words.[17] Research in the
1960's indicates that a sixth grader's recognition vocabulary may now be as
high as 50,000 words.[18,19] Improved teaching methods, the gradual but
sure demise of the constricting, limiting, dull *Dick and Jane* type books in
the early grades, plus enlightened ideas about what young children are

really able to learn have all undoubtedly contributed to the steady increase in childrens' vocabularies over time. As you might suspect, children from better-educated families increase their vocabularies more than do those from families where parents have less education, and girls, on the whole, continue to build up larger vocabularies than boys.[20,21]

How a child chooses to use his vocabulary depends largely on who he is talking to.[22] If with his own peers, a child's conversations are usually related to home, family, games, sports, television programs, sex, sex organs and their functions, and to boastful commentaries about his own latest accomplishments. Boys, between nine and twelve years particularly, are notorious braggarts as they go through this span in their growth when newly expressed physical and intellectual skill discoveries leave them heady with success. As one 10-year-old boy recently said to me in relation to the touch football team he was playing on, "I'm on a pretty good team, but the reason we're pretty good is that I score lots of touchdowns." And then, something as an afterthought, he added, "And lots of times I do it even when there's no blocking." When a child is with adults, what he talks about is largely determined by the adult.

In general, the middle-years child wants both knowledge and know-how. He wants information (although, at this age, he does not discriminate very well between *correct* information and *mis*information), and he grows increasingly more skilled at classifying, conceptualizing, and discovering the general rules that help him to understand relations among concepts.

Ability to Conceptualize Develops

A concept allows a child—or anyone else for that matter—to react more or less the same to different stimuli. For instance, once a child possesses the concept "fruit," he can categorize apples, oranges, bananas, grapes, and so on, under "fruit" and react to them in an equivalent way—i.e., he may eat them. A concept, then, is a symbolic outgrowth of grouping similarities among events and objects that are, on the surface, different. Three attributes of a concept that change markedly during the middle childhood years include the *validity* of a concept, the *status* of a concept, and the *accessibility* of a concept.[23]

Concepts become more valid. You may have noted how a two year old's concept of the word *toy* or *father* is often personalized and reference-specific to *his* toys and *his* father. He doesn't understand yet that "toy" and "father" are concepts that have reference to many different types of play objects and adult males which, once they meet certain criteria, can be generally classified under the label of "toy" or "father." An eight year old, on the other hand, has no problem with this whatsoever. He knows right

136

away that toy or father can either refer to something of his or someone else's. In that sense, these concepts become more *valid* for him insofar as their meaning is more similar for all people.

Concepts have more status. Secondly, concepts assume greater *status* during the middle years as a child is able to more clearly articulate their meaning. For instance, a three year old's concept of "weather" is fuzzy at best, whereas a nine year old's understanding of this concept is more exact, clearer, and more stable over time so that he can talk about different kinds of weather, given different conditions and seasons of the year. A three year old says, "Weather is all over outside." A nine year old says, "It can be cold weather or hot weather, but it depends on if the sun is out." In this sense, concept development during middle childhood grows to have more status, or perhaps we could say more "power," in helping a child become more astute in seeing the difference between objects or events that seem similar, while at the same time perceiving similarities between objects or events that seem different.

Concepts become more accessible. Finally, it is during these middle childhood years that a youngster becomes increasingly able to talk about his concepts. That is, they become a more *accessible* part of his intellectual skills and cognitive repertoire. If you ask a five year old about the concept of "badness" or the concept of "size," he very likely will say that he doesn't know—although his behavior might very well suggest that he does have some comprehension of these concepts. For instance, two five-year-old boys were building different size forts out of wet sand at a beach. One said to the other, "Your fort is bigger than mine." The other answered, "Yes, mine's the biggest in the whole world." A few moments later I asked the first boy how he would compare the size of those two forts. His answer, "I don't know—they're just forts, that's all." His friend was equally as puzzled by the idea of comparing size, although each had made obvious references to "size" in their earlier spontaneous comments. A ten year old, even an eight year old, would have little difficulty talking about the concept of size and using it in his reasoning to conclude something like, "Well, Greg's fort is larger than Dan's."

In sum, during the middle childhood years, a concept increases its *validity, status,* and *accessibility,* a fact of great importance when it comes to understanding a child's learning process. Sometimes adults forget that the ability for conceptual learning is not something that happens all at one time the moment a child begins school, but that it is a gradual process that evolves slowly during a child's middle years—slowly for some children and faster for others.

Development of Rules in Relation to Concepts

Whereas all concepts are symbols that represent a set of common attributes of persons, places, objects, events, or experiences, rules are ways of categorizing relations among concepts. This, too, is a major intellectual skill and cognitive activity that commences with vigor during middle-hood.[24]

A rule can function in one of two ways. In one instance, it can state a relation between aspects of two or more concepts. Consider a simple rule like "lemons have a bitter taste," which states a relation between the two concepts lemon and bitter. A lemon has many qualities, one of which is bitterness. Bitterness is a quality of many qualities, one of which is a lemon. Therefore, a lemon implies bitterness and vice versa. I remember one eight-year-old third-grader stretch the concept lemon about as far as it would go when he raised his hand and asked the teacher, "Could lemon also be the name of a car?" (It would've been interesting to know more about the car the boy's father was driving.)

In a second instance, a rule can also state a routine function that is imposed on concepts to form a new concept. Division, for example, is a rule imposed on two numbers to yield a new concept.

Formal and informal rules. There are also *formal* and *informal* rules, both of which play important parts in the child's cognitive functioning. Actually, most of a child's beliefs are informal rules, and their major purpose is to help him bring some order and predictability to what he experiences in an increasingly more complex life. Once a child leaves the refuge of his mother's apron strings, life *does* get more complicated, and in the absence of adults who understand life for him he must work harder to understand it better himself. Hence, the evolvement of many informal rules. "Crosswalks are dangerous," "Ovens can burn," and "Ice is cold" are all informal rules that describe the dimension shared by the concepts crosswalks and dangerous, oven and burn, and ice and cold.

Formal rules, on the other hand, state a relation between different aspects that is always true and specifiable. The rules we find in mathematics and physics are good examples of this. For instance, the formal rule $3 \times 10 = 30$ implies a fixed relation between the concepts 3 and 10 when subjected to the process of multiplication. Similarly, the formal rule that the weight of a piece of clay remains the same no matter how its external shape is changed states a fixed relation between the quantity of an object before and after an alteration in its appearance.

The development of increasingly more sophisticated concepts and rules are major cognitive outcomes growing out of the intellectual activities of middle childhood. Piaget's research indicates that these are the years when a child comes into his own when it comes to constructing mental images and thinking symbolically, both of which are necessary prerequisites for mature conceptual processes. Let's turn our attention briefly to a discussion of what this means and how we can see it in actual practice.

Development of Concrete Thinking (Piaget's Stage III)

Piaget has studied intellectual growth and cognitive processes of children for over forty years. Out of his many years of study he has evolved a theory of cognitive development that he sees as being broken into four major stages of intellectual growth: (1) sensorimotor stage (birth to eighteen months of life), (2) preoperational stage (eighteen months to age seven), (3) concrete operational stage, and (4) the stage of formal operations (twelve years onward).[25] As the child passes through these definable stages on his way to achieving mature adult thinking processes, Piaget maintains that there is an ongoing resolution of the tension between assimilating old knowledge and accommodation of new knowledge, which, in practice, refers to the ability to alter old strategies or make new ones to solve unfamiliar problems. A key to understanding Piaget's view of intellectual growth is the idea that *flexibility of thought is crucial for normal cognitive development to occur.*

The principle of conservation. A basic principle related to the idea of flexibility is what Piaget has called the operation of *conservation,* or the rule that liquids and solids can be transformed in shape without changing their volume or mass. For example, in the preoperational stage (eighteen months to age seven) a child is able to talk about and to form simple concepts of such things as the quantity of a liquid, but he is easily confused once the apparent quantity is changed. For instance, a twelve year old who watches water being poured from a tall narrow glass into a short broad glass knows that this operation could be reversed to return the water to the tall narrow glass. Furthermore, he knows that the amount of water is the same regardless of the glass in which it is held. A preoperational child, on the other hand, will judge that there is more water in one glass than there is when it is poured in the other glass. In other words, he wouldn't understand the *operations* involved in the sense of being able to see that the volume remains the same even though the distribution of volume is changed. In a similar sense, the four year old who watches his mother receive a five dollar bill and four one dollar bills at a store in change for a ten may be convinced that this mother now has "a lot more money." Again, it is a matter of not understanding the *operations* involved, not to mention not understanding the concept of money.

139

TO OBSERVE

If you can arrange to have access to some children who are seven and younger and others who are eight and older, you can actually see the principle of conservation in action. All you need is a tall narrow glass and a short broad glass. How does a four year old respond to water being poured from one to the other? Will he suddenly "see more" if the water is poured from the short glass to the tall one? What are his responses? What does he give as reasons? Compare with an older child. What are the differences?

The principle of transformation. For Piaget, then, this stage of concrete operations is a time in a child's life when he is both *ready* and *able* to perform the necessary physical and sometimes trial-and-error operations so necessary for the development of concepts. For instance, the middle-years child can begin to learn about the concept of money by actually giving and getting change for a specified amount. He can actually learn about, say, rectangles or circles or triangles by rotating them, cutting them into two pieces, refitting them, and so on. He learns to make what Piaget calls *transformations*, which involve practice and ability in changing the structure of objects in order to better understand them. For example, an eight year old of my acquaintance painted a higher number over the last speed indicator of his bike speedometer to see if that would make it go faster. Then, in a race with a friend who also had a speedometer he discovered that his own speed, alas, was the same as his friend's even though he'd changed his speed indicator. His conclusion: "That speedometer doesn't make me go fast—I do." This is precisely what is meant by a concrete operation.

Another example I am reminded of occurred while my son and a friend of his (seven and eight at the time) and I were fishing. Both wanted to cast out from the boat as I was doing, but both were frustrated at their lack of success at doing this, particularly since I was able to cast my own lure for what seemed to them to be quite a distance. Actually, the problem was that they had no sinker attached to their lines, refusing to do so because in their words, "It would splash and scare the fish away." However, as they observed that (1) splashing did not scare fish from my hook and that (2) I could cast much farther and closer to the weedbed than they could, I heard one say to the other (shortly after I caught a second fish), "Let's try a small sinker." A small sinker didn't work out too well either and a few casts later they had mounted larger sinkers and soon were casting with accuracy to the edge of the weedbed. After they caught several fish apiece I heard one say (almost too casually it seemed) to the other, "I think these big sinkers work better."

In the best sense of the word, these are both examples of the sorts of the actual doing, trying, testing, experimenting, and trial-and-error operations associated with middle childhood years. It is during this time when a child's thinking begins to stabilize in the sense that over time his external behavior and perceptual schemes begin to get organized into logical, conceptual internal systems. That is, operations quickly become internal to the extent that one does not always have to perform a physical, external operation to understand it.

The process of equilibration. Although in Piaget's theory of intellectual growth, cognitive processes are organized into four definable stages associated with certain age ranges, it is important to note that these ranges are by no means precise and binding. At best they are approximations that overlap each other and vary from child to child. They are also continuous, which means that we should not assume that one developmental stage ends and then another begins, but that at each stage other capabilities are beginning to be actively acquired. Thus, from infancy to adulthood, through a process Piaget calls *equilibration* — an active internal process of self-regulation in which there is an organizing and coordinating of one's own intellectual development — the organized system, or cognitive structure — is constantly changing, enlarging, and reorganizing as the growing child goes through a continuous process of accommodation and assimilation.[26-28]

Although it may sound something like a platitude, there is more truth than fiction to the old saying that a child learns best by doing. He learns not only about himself, in terms of skills, competencies, strengths, and weaknesses, but he also learns to form the necessary rules and concepts so vital to successful day-to-day living and eventual higher-level thinking. He learns to appraise his own and other's behavior objectively as well as subjectively. He becomes able to think about things distant in time and space so that during this growth period there are increasingly more questions related to such abstract time-space issues as: "Where do people go when they die?" "How high is the sky?" "How far is the sun?" Why does it take so long to get to the moon when it is so close?" By actually doing things, by going through the concrete operations of seeing how things are made and how they work, a middle childhood youngster slowly abandons the magic and make-believe of his preschool years for the reality of rational thinking. Erik Erikson has made the astute observation that during the preschool years a child's personality crystallizes around the conviction "I am what I can imagine I will be." During middle childhood this conviction changes to "I am what I learn."[29] Let's examine what this means more closely.

Erikson's Stage Four: Industry versus Inferiority

It is during middle childhood that a youngster learns that the best way to achieve recognition and self-esteem is by actually producing things or, in

Erikson's terms, by being industrious and achieving some concrete, tangible results.   Along these lines, Erikson observes:

> Nothing could better express the fact that children at this age do like to be mildly coerced into the adventure of finding out that one can learn to accomplish things which one would never have thought of by oneself, things which owe their attractiveness to the very fact that they are *not* the product of play and fantasy but the product of reality, practicality, and logic; things which provide a token sense of participation in the world of adults.[30]

Middle childhood is a natural time in a child's life for trying himself out, for taking on new challenges, for testing his wings, as it were.   It is through the process of being "industrious" that a child finds out what he is good at and what he can do best.   Erikson's observation above is well taken.   That is, children not only do not mind, but, in fact, rise to the challenge of being mildly coerced, whether it is at home or in school.   The danger of an overly permissive school or home atmosphere is that a child is too seldom stretched to his limit.   Success or accomplishment too easily attained can be quickly discarded as not important because too little effort went into getting it in the first place.

It is very important that a child going through this age period be provided with as many opportunities and experiences as possible to discover his competencies for that is the only way he can avoid the inevitable feelings of inferiority that evolve out of feeling less able than others in most, if not all, endeavors.   If children between six and twelve seem restless, perpetually curious, and anxious to try out new activities and learn new things, be assured that these are perfectly normal behaviors reflecting a child's innate needs to discover himself and master what he sees as an increasingly more complex environment.   I recall a second-grade boy, who, in response to the teacher's question, "What would you like to do during free period today?" replied, "I don't care what I want."   In other words, he was game for anything—a major characteristic of middle childhood.

As you might suspect, parents play a significant part in a child's overall intellectual development and cognitive performance in school, an idea to which we now turn.

Parents' Influence on Cognitive Functioning and Intellectual Performance

There have been many interesting studies investigating the influence that parents have on their children's achievement and intellectual performance.   We very likely do not have to go any further than our own childhood memories to appreciate the enormous impact that parents can have on the course and direction of a child's intellectual development. It is no coincidence that parents who read and enjoy reading are more likely than not to have children who also grow to like books. If parents both raise and answer interesting questions in the course of their day-to-day living, it is not unusual to find that children coming from verbally curious families also raise many questions and aggressively seek answers in books, experience, and trial-and-error learning. The fact is: How parents relate to children and adolescents can and does influence their general intellectual functioning and orientation toward achievement. The nature of this relationship is particularly crucial during middle childhood because it is during this time that a child is stabilizing the cognitive style and attitudes toward achievement that conceivably could follow him for the rest of his life.

TO THINK ABOUT

What relationships can you see between your own intellectual functioning and that of your parents? Do they like to read? Do you? Are they intellectually curious about the why and how of things? Are you? Did they encourage you to ask questions, to solve problems, to figure things out? How are you intellectually like your parents? How are you different?

One question we can ask is: What is it that parents of high achievement-oriented children do to make them that way? Rosen and D'Andrade[31] were interested in just this sort of question and, through observation of family interactions, investigated the relationship between achievement behaviors of children and the child-rearing practices of their parents. Forty boys, age nine to eleven, white, native-born, and matched for IQ and social class, were studied along with their parents. Half the boys had high achievement-oriented scores and half low achievement-oriented scores. In each achievement category, high and low, half of the boys were middle-class and half lower-class. Tasks were devised for the boys that also involved the parents, which made it possible to gather data by observing the parent-child interactions while the problems were being solved. For the most part these observations concerned the way in which the parents enforced their demands and the amount of autonomy or independence they gave to the child. Some of the more interesting results follow:

1. Parents of a high achievement-oriented boy tend to have high aspirations for him and have a high regard for his problem-solving abilities. Indeed, what these parents tended to do was to establish certain standards of excellence that they *expected* the boy to reach. This, by the way, is consistent with a later study by Coopersmith[32] who found that medium and

low self-esteem children are much more likely to come from homes where parents have *low* expectations for their children's school achievement. Again, evidence to suggest that when children are so permissively raised as to feel neither pressure nor obligation to attain and maintain a certain standard of behavior, they may be seriously deprived of growth-promoting opportunities to test out the upper reaches of their abilities.   Children in middle childhood need help when it comes to establishing standards for their behavior, and research points strongly to the conclusion that when they have few, if any, expectations to live up to they are apt to end up with a low need for achievement *and* low self-esteem.   In spite of what the old maxim, "The child knows best," would have us believe, there is a notable absence of any evidence to support that statement.   A child may know when he's full, or when he's had enough sleep, or when he's cold (even these statements are on shaky ground when you think about the times a child may, for example, eat more sweets than is good for him, deny he is tired even though half asleep, or play outside with no jacket even though it's only thirty degrees), but he needs active adult assistance when it comes to establishing higher order standards of behavior.   The fact is that children both need and want adult guidance, and research and common sense tell us that those who get it fare better in all ways than those who do not.

2. Fathers of high achievement-oriented boys allow more autonomy and independent thinking than fathers of low achievement-oriented boys. The fathers of achievement-oriented boys were neither passive nor overbearing in their relationship to their sons; they offered suggestions and guidance, not mandates and orders.

3. Mothers of boys with high achievement motivation engage more actively in achievement training.   That is, they have higher aspirations for their sons than mothers of boys having low achievement needs and are more concerned over their sons' success.   They are more likely to reward and punish than the more indifferent mothers.

4. Mothers of high achievement-oriented boys, like the fathers, allow their children more autonomy and independence and give their children more options about how to go about completing a task.   However, they also expected that it would be done well.

The general picture that emerges here is this: The children who have a high achievement orientation and who function best intellectually are likely to be those whose parents give active guidance; who *expect* good work; and who, at the same time, allow considerable independence and freedom for doing the work.   Perhaps the key to understanding this is that parents of high achievement-oriented children can be actively involved with them without being either so permissive that they communicate an "I don't care" attitude or so authoritarian that they frustrate a child's efforts to be his own kind of person.

Along these same lines, Winterbottom[33] studied the relationship between the achievement motivation among a group of eight-year-old boys and their mothers' standards of training in independence and mastery. Three results stood out:

1. Mothers of high achievement-motivated boys did not necessarily make more demands on their boys than mothers with low achievement-motivated sons, but they did make them *earlier*.

2. Related to this was the finding that mothers of high achievement-motivated boys were not particularly more restrictive than mothers of low achievement-motivated boys, but the high achievement mothers did impose more early restrictions and make more demands on their children up to age seven.   It should be noted that although restrictive training (teaching boundaries, limits, what is acceptable behavior and what isn't) comes earlier for achievement-oriented boys, this was found to be accompanied by a good deal of opportunity for autonomous and independent thinking. However, this was not the free-floating, do-as-you-please approach practiced by permissive parents, but, rather, a you-can-do-many-things-within-certain-prescribed-reality-boundaries approach that made it clear to the child that he had to stay within reasonable limits.

3. Mothers of boys with high achievement motivation used all types of rewards—verbal, gifts, and particularly physical affection—more frequently.   Whether you use the language of behavioristic psychology and call this the rewarding or reinforcing of correct responses, or the language of humanistic psychology and call it the encouragement or validation of self-actualizing behavior, the net effect is the same.   When a child (or anyone else for that matter) is acknowledged or rewarded for something he has done that is judged or valued as appropriate or right, he is more likely to repeat that same behavior in the future.

In sum, it seems clear that mothers whose sons directed their intellectual functioning in achievement-oriented ways were more demanding during their sons' early years, more overtly responsive to their sons' successes, and more willing to allow their sons to become increasingly independent as they grew older.

In addition to examining parental variables related to a child's intellectual functioning and school performance, several research efforts have sought to specify more exactly the particular kinds of parental influence that affect specific aspects of a youngster's achievement.   Bing,[34] for example, investigated a group of elementary-school children who showed marked discrepancy between verbal and mathematic ability.   She found that high verbal children experienced much more verbal stimulation in the preschool years, as evidenced by such variables as amount of play time the mother had with the infant, verbal stimulation of the infant, mother's responsiveness to the child's early questions, and interest shown in the child's good speech habits.   Although the *mothers of high verbal children were rather controlling and pressuring, the mothers of those children high in mathematical ability were less interfering and permitted greater indepen-*

dence. Bing concluded that high verbal ability is encouraged by intensive interaction between parent and child, while number and spatial abilities, on the other hand, develop from interaction with the physical rather than the interpersonal environment. The development of these latter abilities apparently requires greater independence to investigate and explore one's surroundings.

TO THINK ABOUT

Think about your own mathematical and verbal abilities for a moment. Are you good with numbers but less skilled with words? Or is it the other way around for you? Or maybe you see yourself about the same in each area. How did your mother interact with you? Do you see any relationships between Bing's research findings and your own life experiences?

In another study, Baer and Rogosta[35] found that those males showing high verbal ability were more likely to perceive their fathers as less caring and less attentive than those showing less verbal ability. They also perceived their mothers as less caring. A similar finding was noted in a study with elementary school girls, in which those who scored high on reading achievement had less affectionate and less nurturant mothers than those less proficient in their academic skill.[36] Taken together, the findings of these two studies do not contradict those obtained by Bing, but suggest, rather, that mothers who are intrusive and pressuring also engage in a high level of verbal interaction with their children.

Although, in general, parents who value intellectual achievement for themselves stress intellectual achievement for their children, some areas of achievement are emphasized more than others. In a study of parental values for achievement in the intellectual, physical, artistic, and mechanical areas, parents who valued achievement in the artistic and mechanical areas tended also to value such achievement for their children.[37]

So far, the studies we've looked at reflect primarily middle-class values and behavior. There are some interesting social class differences related to child rearing and cognitive development that may help us better understand differences in intellectual functioning among school age children.

Child Rearing Across Social Classes: Relationships to Cognitive Development

One distinct characteristic about middle-class child-rearing practices is that it is future oriented. Although middle-class parents may in some ways be more permissive in catering to the needs of the growing child, they are also generally insistent on his performing as well as possible in school. Middle-class children, regardless of their ethnic origins or skin color, are taught to believe in success and taught to be willing to take the steps that make that achievement possible.[38,39] One research effort, for instance, found that middle-class fathers expected their sons to have middle-class, or higher, positions in the occupational structure and, consistent with that aspiration, are inclined to emphasize and encourage scholastic achievement, emotional stability, and athletic prowess. Middle-class fathers are inclined to provide clear guidelines for expected behavior, reward it when it occurs, and be critical when it does not.[40]

Probably the best known and most recent studies related to cognitive development as related to child-rearing practices across different social classes was done by Hess and Shipman,[41-44] who followed a group of 163 black mother-child pairs over a four-year period, beginning when the children were four years old. Families studied came from four different social-class levels, from professionals to welfare families. What the investigators found were very substantial differences between social-class groups in the way mothers interacted with their children and the subsequent cognitive functioning of those children. For example, in comparison with lower-class mothers, middle-class mothers more often gave rationales with their instructions, used more praise, took more time orienting the child to the tasks he was to do, and gave more specific feedback to the child. The general impression I get from reviewing this research is that there is more interaction of all kinds going on in middle-class homes with the focus being on relating (talking, helping, being friendly) with the child rather than simple coping (yelling, ordering, being angry) with him. There were also significant relations between the mothers' interaction styles and the child's cognitive functioning, and these relations were apparent within social-class groups as well. That is, the very poor mothers who used more "middle-class" interaction styles in relating to their child had the most successful children. Similarly, middle-class mothers who were more "lower class" in style had the least successful children. So, we cannot conclude that it is the social class itself that is responsible for high or low cognitive functioning and intellectual growth, but rather the particular kind of parent-child relationship *within* a class level. Make no mistake about it: How a mother behaves with a child has a powerful impact on that child's cognitive functioning, an impact that grows increasingly more apparent during the middle childhood years. For instance, the research we're examining here has found that a child's school performance during the early elementary years can be predicted from how the mother interacted with him at age four. Indeed, Hess and Shipman have noted that a mother's teaching style is just as good, if not a better, predictor of the child's school performance and cognitive functioning than his social class or his mother's

147

IQ. It may be important to note here that similar conclusions have been reached using samples of black and white families across different social classes.[45,46]

Looking at the total picture, it is clear that two distinct child-rearing patterns emerge from the two social groups. Middle-class fathers and mothers ask and answer more questions, have higher expectations for academic achievement, use more praise and less criticism, orient their children toward the future, and less frequently interfere in their children's work and play. Further, these behaviors, or their opposites, cluster together for individual parents. That is, parents—be they middle class or lower class—who use praise liberally, also tend to ask and answer many questions and to point the child toward the future. Elementary age youngsters coming from middle-class homes probably have a better chance to identify with Erikson's *Industry* end of the behavioral continuum because industriousness (achieving, performing, accomplishing) is both demanded and rewarded to a greater degree than is the case in lower-class homes. However, we should note that there is increasing evidence to suggest that the gap between lower- and middle-class child-rearing practices is getting increasingly smaller, particularly as educational opportunities are expanded for children at all social-class levels, which means that over time middle-class values and practices will belong not just to those in the middle class, but to all classes.[47,48] (Not infrequently it is implied by some that middle-class values are less than honorable standards for any person to strive to attain. If you would like to read an interesting and forceful defense of middle-class values, it can be found in an article appropriately titled, "In Defense of Middle Class Values" by James E. Heald and published in *Phi Delta Kappan* 46[October 1964]:81–83.)

Intellectual and Cognitive Growth: Implications for Teachers

Intellectual and cognitive development is a blend of maturation and learning and varies in rate from child to child. A major implication for teachers is that different children mature at different rates. Although the majority of elementary age children increase their vocabularies and conceptual skills, the pace is not uniform for all children. This means that we must constantly keep in mind the idea that different children learn at different rates. Sometimes one group of children learn slower than another group not because they are "dumb," but because (1) they have not had the necessary experiential background to prepare them for new learning or (2) they are not developmentally "ready" to learn as rapidly as some others.

INFLUENCES ON A CHILD'S
EMOTIONAL-SOCIAL DEVELOPMENT

There are two key principles of growth basic to understanding underlying developmental processes and dynamics. The first of these is that the human personality is constantly in the process of formation and reformation and that this process occurs most rapidly and most dramatically during the growing years. The second is that growth is a product of interaction between the individual and his environment. It would surely simplify our understanding of emotional-social development if we could point to a time in a child's life and say, "Now he is formed," but human development is far too complicated for that. Nor is it possible to point to any one interaction and conclude, "That interaction is most important." The fact is that there are many times and many interactions in a child's life that can influence, shape, redirect, or change him for better or for worse. Although, in this chapter, we cannot hope to identify all the possible moments and interactions in a child's life that most effect the course of his emotional-social development, we will identify and discuss at least three very important ones: (1) parent's child-rearing practices, (2) influence of peer relations, and (3) influence of play activities.

Child-rearing Practices:
Varieties and Consequences

There is little question that how a child is raised has an enormous impact on his overall personality development. Indeed, we need go no further than our own lives to see that how we feel about ourselves and how we relate to others has been significantly effected by how our parents treated us as we were growing up. It is no accident that the woman with problems relating to men was the little girl who had trouble relating to her father or that the little boy rejected by his mother grows into the man fearful of close relationships with women. In our adult lives we tend to mirror the interaction patterns of our parents (a startling revelation for some who don't particularly care for their parent's interaction patterns), and, further, we tend to raise our children as we were raised.[49] It doesn't *have* to be this way, but it very likely will continue to be as long as parents are unaware of the relationship between their old experiences as growing children and their new experiences as parents.

When you think about it, each home is like a miniature school with its own individual curriculum. And each parent shares part of the "teaching" role in a kind of team-teaching arrangement. When stretched over a period of seventeen years or so, a child cannot help but be profoundly affected and markedly influenced by the day-to-day exposure to the "curriculum" demands of his home. Although it is not likely that any single family event

149

or child-rearing experience will be totally responsible for how a child turns out, it *is* possible that a single experience or person for that matter may stand above all others as far as its personal impact and importance is concerned.   Perhaps we should remind ourselves that although it is difficult to find a case history of a grossly disturbed or neurotic adult without some childhood traumatic experience, it is equally difficult to find a case history of a normal person without such an experience.   What makes a difference to the growing child is *accumulative* effect of *similar* life experiences over time, for these are what have the greatest influence on his feelings about himself and others.

It is probably safe to say that the vast majority of parents who consciously choose to have children do not deliberately set out to make their children more unhappy than happy, more fearful than adventuresome, more closed-minded than open-minded, or more neurotic than adjusted. Most parents, naturally enough, want to give their children the best they can give them.

In spite of good intentions, children don't always turn out for the best. Some turn out to be hostile, hateful, and suspicious; others are chronic complainers; still others are fearful and anxious; and some turn out to be unhappy, shy adults wondering who they are and what they stand for.   On the other hand, many children turn out to be productive, integrated, self-actualizing adults.   The question is: What kind of child-rearing style produces what kind of children?

Although there is by no means a simple answer to this question, parent-child research over the past ten years or so has given us a pretty good idea about what we might reasonably expect given certain child-rearing styles.   One of the most active and productive investigators of parent-child relations in recent years has been Diana Baumrind, who, among other things, has identified three distinct patterns of how parents relate to their children and use the authority implicit in the parental role. She has called these parental patterns *authoritarian, authoritative,* and *permissive.*   Let us turn to Baumrind's own descriptions of how each of these relationship-authority patterns are actually reflected in the behavior of parents identified with each.   (By the way, Baumrind noted that to avoid confusion, the pronoun "she" was used to refer to the parent and the pronoun "he" to refer to the child, although the statement applies to both sexes equally.)

Authoritarian parenting.   The *authoritarian* parent is one who attempts:

> to shape, control and evaluate the behavior and attitudes of the child in accordance with a set standard of conduct, usually an absolute standard, theologically motivated and formulated by a higher authority.   She values obedience as a virtue and favors punitive, forceful measures to curb self-will at points

150

where the child's actions or beliefs conflict with what she thinks is right conduct. She believes in inculcating such instrumental values as respect for authority, respect for work, and respect for the preservation of order and traditional structure. She does not encourage verbal give and take, believing that the child should accept her word for what is right.[50]

Authoritative parenting. The *authoritative* parent, by contrast with the above, attempts:

to direct the child's activities but in a rational, issue-oriented manner. She encourages verbal give and take, and shares with the child the reasoning behind her policy. She values both expressive and instrumental attributes, both autonomous self-will and disciplined conformity. Therefore, she exerts firm control at points of parent-child divergence, but does not hem the child in with restrictions. She recognizes her own special rights as an adult, but also the child's individual interests and special ways. The authoritative parent affirms the child's present qualities, but also sets standards for future conduct. She uses reason as well as power to achieve her objectives. She does not base her decisions on group consensus or the individual child's desires; but also, does not regard herself as infallible, or divinely inspired.[51]

Permissive parenting. The *permissive* parent, on the other hand, attempts:

to behave in a nonpunitive, acceptant and affirmative manner towards the child's impulses, desires, and actions. She consults with him about policy decisions and gives explanations for family rules. She makes a few demands for household responsibility and orderly behavior. She presents herself to the child as a resource for him to use as he wishes, not as an active agent responsible for shaping or altering his ongoing or future behavior. She allows the child to regulate his own activities as much as possible, avoids the exercise of control, and does not encourage him to obey externally-defined standards. She attempts to use reason but not overt power to accomplish her ends.[52]

TO THINK ABOUT

Which of these three parent types best fits your own parents? It would be interesting to have your own parents read each of Baumrind's descriptions and choose the one they see best fitting themselves and each other. How would their choices square with yours? Next time you see your parents, why not try this and find out. It might lead to some interesting and worthwhile discussion.

Influence of Different Parenting Styles

In what ways did each of these parent-child patterns influence children growing up under their influence? Consider some of the findings. Both authoritative and authoritarian parents demanded socially responsible behavior (following certain rules, controlling impulses, listening when talked to, behaving, etc.) from their children but encouraged it in different ways. Authoritarian parents, for instance, permitted their own needs to take precedence over those of the child, assumed a stance of personal infallibility, and in other ways showed themselves to be more concerned about their own ideas being right than with the child's welfare. Thus, although they preached socially responsible behavior, they were not likely to practice it themselves. Authoritative parents, on the other hand, both preached and practiced responsible behavior and, as a consequence, their children were significantly more responsible than those of authoritarian parents.

Permissive parents were different still. They neither demanded socially responsible behavior nor were they particularly aggressive in rewarding it when it did occur. They issued few directives and those that were issued were seldom enforced by either physical means or verbal influence. Indeed, permissive parents seemed to make it a point to avoid confrontations when the child disobeyed. The children of permissive parents, particularly the boys, were found to be clearly lacking when it came to socially responsible and achievement-oriented behavior.[53] One reason for this is that, in the absence of negative sanctions ("This is something you must not do") or positive expectations ("I expect you to listen when the teacher talks"), the child is left with the impression that either there are no rules to follow or, if there are, it is okay to go ahead and disobey them anyway. Indeed, Siegel and Kohn[54] found that when adults do not react at all to a child who disobeys or breaks an existing rule, the child is even more likely on subsequent occasions to repeat that same behavior. If, for example, a seven-year-old boy punches his four-year-old sister every time he's mad at her, his behavior is not likely to change unless someone older and, presumedly, wiser steps in and points out that hitting one's sister simply is not allowed under any circumstances. The fact is that some children misbehave not because they're necessarily "bad," but because no one has ever taught them correct or more appropriate behavior.

All in all, research strongly indicates that both authoritarian control and permissive noncontrol *tend to inhibit* a growing child's opportunities to engage in vigorous interaction with people. Demands that cannot be met, refusals to help, and unrealistically high standards all tend to roadblock normal, healthy commerce with the environment. On the other hand, expecting little if anything from a child or establishing unchallenging low standards for behavior may understimulate him. Is there a reasonable balance between total control and no control? Apparently there is. However, it is not so easy as saying that the best kind of parents are those who combine just the right mixture of being tough and being permissive. The qualities of explicit warmth and caring are important ingredients in that mixture. For example, Baumrind[55] has noted from her research that it is a combination of parental warmth *and* firm discipline that is likely to produce a self-reliant, self-controlled, adequate-feeling child. Coopersmith's[56] research also supports this observation. One of his important findings was that the most notable antecedents of high self-esteem among elementary age children were directly related to parental behavior and the consequences of the rules and regulations that parents establish. As an illustration, he observed that definite and consistently enforced limits on behavior were associated with high self-esteem; that families who maintained clear limits utilized less drastic forms of punishment; and that parents who produce high self-esteem children deeply cared about their children and were not afraid to show it.

It should also be noted that parents of high self-esteem children had attitudes of total or near total *acceptance* of their children (which does not mean that they accepted or even tolerated all their behaviors), but they also allowed considerable flexibility *within* established limits.

The point here that is extremely important is that explicit love, warmth, and acceptance from parent to child are absolutely necessary qualities for establishing and maintaining a relationship built on mutual love and respect. When a child is not loved and accepted—or even if he believes this is the case when it actually isn't—he can easily conclude that any sign of parental restrictiveness or demands are simply further indications of not being loved. The child, for example, disciplined by a cold and even punitive parent may think to himself, "Dad's punishing me because he doesn't love me." Another child, disciplined by a warm, caring parent, may think to himself, "The reason I am being grounded is because I've done something wrong. I will try to be more careful in the future." If a child cannot trust his parent's (or his teacher's) caring, then it is equally difficult for him to trust their motivations for disciplining and/or restricting him.

Unfortunately, the parent who is both hostile and restrictive tends to encourage a vicious cycle of hostility and counter-hostility in the parent-child relationship. Too frequently, in this parent-child pattern, the child is not allowed to directly express his own feelings of anger and hostility and, as a consequence, is forced to lock them away in a safe place in his unconscious. It is perhaps not surprising that hostile-restrictive parents are found to have more than their share of neurotic children.[57,58] Indeed, there is evidence to suggest that a cold, detached, hostile-restrictive parenting style is linked to problems among children ranging from self-punishment to suicide, and accident proneness,[59] as well as shyness, social withdrawal, difficulties relating to peers, and little confidence in, or motivation toward, assuming more mature behavior with age.[60,61]

Warm-restrictive versus warm-controlling parents. It is not enough, however, to say that sufficient amounts of parental warmth is the answer to raising healthy, balanced children. It depends on what the warmth is combined with. On the one hand there are the warm-*restrictive* parents, while on the other hand there are the warm-*controlling* parents—each having a different effect on children. In the first place, there's a difference between restrictive control and firm control. *Restrictive control* is associated with the use of extensive proscriptions and prescriptions covering practically all areas of a child's life and severely limiting his autonomy to test himself out in new ways and to learn new skills. There are many "No's," "Keep off" signs, and "Don't touch" signals in this child's life. *Firm control* is different in the sense that the emphasis is less apt to be one which says, "You will be a bad boy if you don't mind" and more apt to be one which says, "I *expect* you to be a good boy." There is firm and consistent enforcement of the rules, effective resistance against the child's demands, and generally more guiding and showing as opposed to the ordering and telling behavior of restrictive-controlling parents.

Influence on children's behavior. What kind of child behaviors are likely to be associated with each parenting style? Becker[62] reported that warm-*restrictive* parents tended to have passive, fearful, dependent children who were generally well-behaved. (It is difficult for a passive, fearful, dependent child *not* to behave.) Baumrind[63] found, however, that warm-*controlling* (by contrast with warm-*restrictive*) parents were likely to have responsible, assertive, self-reliant, and independent children. Parents of these children consistently enforced their directives and resisted the child's demands. Lots of times parents "give in" to their children because it's the easiest thing to do but feel guilty for having done so, and, then, to make up for this lapse get "tough" with the child the next time he asks for something. This not only confuses the child, but makes the parent look inconsistent and more restricting than ever. As teachers, we must be cautious not to be guilty of this same inconsistency.

Functional versus interpersonal adult power. An important principle for both parents and teachers that grows out of research related to child-rearing practices is that it is better for adults to use their power in a *functional* rather than in an *interpersonal* context. That is, the emphasis should be on the task at hand or the rule to be followed rather than upon the special status of the powerful adult. For example, it would be better to say, "You must complete your math assignment before going to recess" than to say, "You had better complete your math assignment or I'm going to give you a low mark." By concentrating on what the *child* should do rather than on what *you* will do, the focus is where it should be, namely, on his responsibility rather than on your power. Focus on adult power does one of two things to children. One, it encourages them to be very submissive (out of fear) or, two, very rebellious (out of anger) neither of which bode well for the actualization of one's full potentials as a mature adult.

Finally, we should recognize that there are both desirable and undesirable aspects to any particular child-rearing style. There is no one kind of home atmosphere that guarantees the "perfect" child. For example, although fearless, curious, and self-directed children are likely to come from homes in which a psychological climate of democracy and autonomy prevails, these same children are also inclined to be aggressive, rebellious, and nonconforming. On the other hand, the obedient well-behaved child of a home characterized by strict, unbending control may show signs of a constricted personality and high dependency needs.

A reasonable question at this point is whether there is a *pattern* of conditions necessary to produce healthy social-emotional growth or whether there is any single condition, or set of conditions, that plays a greater role than others. In answer to this question, Coopersmith observes:

> First and foremost, we should note that there are virtually no parental patterns of behavior or parental attitudes that are common to all parents of children with high self-esteem. Examination of the major indices and scales of *acceptance, limit definition, respect,* and *parental self-esteem* provides explicit support for the view that not all of these conditions are essential for the formation of high self-esteem. . . . [The data] suggest that combinations of [these] conditions are required — more than one but less than the four established for this study. . . . In addition it is likely that a minimum of devaluating conditions — that is, rejection, ambiguity, and disrespect — is required if high self-esteem is to be attained.[64]

Parents, as you can see, play an incredibly important part in determining the course of a child's total personality development. So do his peers, a phenomenon to which we now turn our attention.

Peer Group Involvement: Influence and Outcomes

Although a child's transition from "family centeredness" to "peer centeredness" is a slow, gradual process, it is, nonetheless, an inevitable process. Indeed, research indicates that a growing child spends increasingly larger blocks of his waking hours with kids his own age and that these time blocks get bigger as he moves from kindergarten through high school.[65] Whereas the preschool child takes his identity from his parents,

Doing things with the gang becomes increasingly important.

the middle-years child looks more and more to his peers for identity. Not only is this a natural process, but a healthy one—healthy in the sense that it affords a growing child increased opportunities to test his wings outside the protective confines of the family nest.

Peer group involvement and relatedness is valuable to a child in many ways. He gets practice in learning how to behave in interpersonal relationships, how to deal with kids who are either stronger or weaker than he is, and how to cope with the conflicts and tensions that invariably occur when any group, any age, work and play together. There is little question that a vast amount of learning occurs among children immersed in a common peer culture. Although the peer group has neither the traditional authority of the family nor the legal authority of the schools for formal teaching, it nonetheless manages to convey a substantial body of information to its members. A delightful passage from Robert P. Smith's sensitive book, "*Where Did You Go?*" "*Out.*" "*What Did You Do?*" "*Nothing.*," in which he talks about his childhood years and what he learned in a "house" he and his friends built, captures nicely the sort of interpersonal "learning" experiences that go on in a child's peer culture:

It was a pitiful wreck of a tarpaper hut, and in it I learned the difference between boys and girls, I learned that all fathers did that, I learned to swear, to play with myself, to sleep in the afternoon, I learned that some people were Catholics and some people were Protestants and some people were Jews, that people came from different places. I learned that other kids wondered, too, who they would have been if their fathers had not married their mothers, wondered if you could dig a hole right to the center of the earth, wondered if you could kill yourself by holding your breath. (None of us could.) I learned that with three people assembled, it was only for the briefest interludes that all three liked each other. Mitch and I were leagued against Simon. And then Simon and I against Mitch. And then—but you remember. I didn't know then just how to handle that situation. I still don't. It is my coldly comforting feeling that nobody still does, including nations and that's what the trouble with the world is. That's what the trouble with the world was then—when Mitch and Simon were the two and I was the one. What else did I learn in the hut? That if two nails will not hold a board in place, three will probably not either, but the third nail will split the board. I think kids still do that. I think objects made of wood by children, left to their own devices, if such there be, will assay ten percent wood, ninety percent nails.

In the hut we looked and we learned. And drooled. I remember a picture of Clara Bow with one shoulder strap—and then there was Toby Wing—and look at Lily Damita—she's bending way over. . . .[66]

Most particularly, peer group involvement helps a child develop an accurate concept of himself. In the process of interacting with others who approximate his own age and size, a child cannot help but arrive at a clearer, and perhaps more realistic, picture of his assets and liabilities. The following excerpt may help us understand this better:

It is fair to say that the crucial arena for self-esteem is the arena of one's agemates. At home there is an age hierarchy. Even the siblings are bigger or smaller, so that differences of competence are expected. The home, moreover, continues to be the source of love and provision of basic wants, even when the child ventures forth to play-ground and school. At home he must be *love-worthy*. This may include being competent but it is heavily weighted on the side of being good, obedient and affectionate. On the playground the values are different; he must be *respect-worthy*, able to command respect because he shows competence and handles himself with ease. It is a sharp strain for many children when they pass from the atmosphere of a child-centered home into the competitive realities of even a friendly play group. They must now show what they have in the way of physical prowess, courage, manipulative skill, outgoing friendliness, all in direct comparison with other children of their age. The penalties for failure are humiliation, ridicule, rejection from the group.[67]

As you can see, the expectations of a child's peers are different from those of his parents. At home the emphasis is usually on the child being *lovable* (obedient, good, somewhat restrained), while with peers the emphasis is more on being *able* (competent, skilled, somewhat rebellious). Parents place a higher premium on a child *behaving appropriately,* while peers place a greater premium on his *performing adequately.* The difference between peer and parent expectations are by no means as black and

157

white as they may sound. The fact is that these are overlapping expectations with the primary distinction being a matter of emphasis. That is, parents typically expect both appropriate behavior and adequate performance, but the stress is on behavior. For example, it is not uncommon for a parent to say to a child, "Now if you behave yourself and listen to the teacher and follow the rules, there is no reason why you shouldn't do well in school." Notice that being good and obedient (behavior) precedes the doing well (performance). A child's age-mates, on the other hand, are far less demanding when it comes to behavior. In fact, it is not uncommon for the worst behaved (by adult standards) fifth-grade boy to be among those most readily accepted by peers because he is the best football player or the longest hitter in softball or simply the most courageous, gutsy kid in free play activities. I remember my nine-year-old boy saying to me about one of his classmates, whom he admired, "None of the teachers like Tom real well cause he's always sassing back." I asked how that made him feel about Tom, to which he replied, "Heck, that doesn't make me feel anything. If he gets in trouble with the teachers that's too bad I guess. All I know is that he got lots of points in helping our school to win the track championship last year." The point couldn't be clearer — who cares how he behaves; he's fast and that's what counts.

Peer group involvement is important for many reasons, but there are three that stand out.

Three major peer group functions. 1. *Evaluation and feedback opportunities:* The peer group is perhaps the only group with whom a growing child can compare his developing talents, skills, and know-how. At home he's either the only child, the youngest or oldest, or somewhere in between, which means that he cannot fairly compare himself with siblings because of age differences. But evaluation of self is possible in the society of peers. Not only can a child evaluate himself more accurately, but he can get honest feedback from his age-mates.

Elementary age youngsters are harsh but relatively unbiased judges of each other. An undesirable characteristic is quickly diagnosed by them, and they are usually frank to both point it out and deride it, thus heightening the possibility for change. I remember a playground incident involving a fourth-grade boy who was thrown out at home during a kickball game. He was a reasonably skilled lad in most athletic ventures, but he was also an overindulged, somewhat spoiled boy who was accustomed to having things his own way. At home, when he wanted his own way, he either sulked or threw a minor tantrum. He tried the same tactics at the kickball game. First he threw what amounted to a tantrum (kicked the ball into centerfield, cried) and when that didn't work, he went off to the side to sit and sulk threatening to "never play with you kids ever again." Not only were the other kids content to let him play his manipulation game, but they soon were taunting him for being a "sissy," a "momma's boy" and a "crybaby poor sport." Within ten minutes a former sulking eight-year-old boy was back playing again, a bit wiser for the lesson that only kids his own age could have taught him, namely, behaving like a four-year-old when you're eight doesn't work, so I better act my age. If this lad had chosen to go home to "momma," it may not have turned out so well. Although peer feedback is usually direct and to the point, it is by no means always harsh or critical. For example, shortly after the boy mentioned above (John) entered the game again he kicked a long one for a triple and received the plaudits of his teammates for "really wacking one." In fact, a boy on the opposing team let it be known that "Next time John is on our team." Standing on third base stood John, with a big grin. Acting one's age did indeed have its rewards.

Evaluation and assessment by one's peers is by no means arbitrary or haphazard. As an illustration of the accuracy of peer evaluation, the results of one study showed that among adults who were considered behavior problems in their own childhood, one of the best predictors of adult adjustment was acceptance by peers.[68] It was found that if a child is judged to be a problem child by adults but is accepted by peers, his chances of achieving a normal adjustment are good. However, if the peer group also considers him a problem, his chances for later adult adjustment fall drastically. Although peer judgment is harsh and its penalties severe, both are relatively fair and accurate.

TO THINK ABOUT

Reminisce for a moment about your own elementary and middle school years. How did you relate to your peers? What sorts of feedback stand out in your memory? How were you treated by your agemates? Were you liked? Accepted? Do you recall any labels they gave you back then that still fit today? What resemblances do you see between the way you got along with kids in your younger years and the way you get along with people today?

2. *Opportunities for practicing different roles:* In order for a child's self to grow and expand during this stage of his growth, he must have as many opportunities as possible for not only *doing* things (becoming able), but for *being* different roles (becoming a person). It appears characteristic of all levels of human society that every group has a leader and assorted rankings for influence, strength, and intellectual ability. Every group has its most influential member, its strongest, and its brightest or wisest. These roles, into which individuals naturally gravitate or are pushed by others, are found in groups of children as well as of adults. Once a child has either been assigned or has assumed a role in his group, he usually takes it

159

seriously, receives a certain degree of satisfaction from it, and begins to take on more of the behaviors characteristic of that role. The popular third-grade girl, admired for her initiative, zest, and spark is likely to develop many of the techniques of skilled leadership roles, while the class clown develops an increasingly buffoonlike personality.

3. *Opportunities for being assertive and rebellious:* Middle childhood is the normal time in a child's life when he begins preparing what amounts to his declaration of independence. This is an unconscious process and one that grows naturally out of a child's growing sense of personal competency. A child's declaration of independence is more than merely a withdrawal from adults, it is also in some part a turning against them. This can, however, be a lonely and even threatening process, which is another reason why affiliation with the peer culture is important during middle childhood. Within the confines of the group a youngster can find both support and encouragement for his fledgling efforts to be freer of adult restrictions — particularly those restrictions on the display of hostility and the demands for cleanliness, order, quiet, and being in bed at a certain time. (As one seven year old said in response to what he wanted to be when he grew up: "I want to be able to stay up as late as I want.") In the society of his peers, the growing child finds a place where he can express his hostilities, make messes, get dirty, and do all the other things that the big adult world forbids — and receive the commendations of his classmates rather than their disapproval.

Interestingly, peer group rebelliousness against adult standards as we find in the United States is not characteristic of all cultures. This fact has been demonstrated in an experiment that had American and Russian children respond to a questionnaire about how they would behave if some of their friends urged them to do such things as go to a movie disapproved of by parents, run away after accidently breaking a window, steal fruit from an orchard, or cheat on a school examination. Some of the children were told that no one would see their answers except the experimenters, others that their parents would see the answers, and still others that their classmates would see the answers.

In every case, the American children proved far more inclined than the Russian children to do the forbidden. An even more striking finding was that when the Russian children believed that their peers would see the answers, they were less willing to admit an inclination to want to do forbidden acts then when they thought *no one* would see their answers. There was little doubt that the peer group acted as a restraint. For American children, on the other hand, the finding was the opposite; when they believed that only their peers would see the answers, they were even *more* inclined toward forbidden or rebellious behavior.[69] Not surprisingly, perhaps, in the Soviet Union the peer group serves to help enforce compliance with adult standards, while in the United States it serves to foster rebelliousness.

The rebelliousness we're talking about here is not the consequence of something pathological, but it is, rather, the outgrowth of normal developmental processes. Actually, a certain amount of rebellious behavior is both expected and encouraged in the American culture as a child outgrows his baby self and expands the boundaries of his personal competencies and interpersonal skills. This is, as we have mentioned earlier, the natural time in a child's life for him to be active and industrious, a process that is both encouraged and supported through involvement and experience in the peer group culture. One of the ways this is facilitated is through play.

Children's Play: Function and Meaning

Games and play activities are an important factor in a child's overall socialization. Actually, records of the sorts of games children play go back thousands of years, and many of the games popular today trace their histories back to the dawn of recorded time. While Socrates was lecturing on the street corner, it is likely that young Greek children were playing tag and hide-and-seek among the trees in the groves of Academe.

In a delightful book titled, *Children's Games in Street and Playground*, Iona and Peter Opie[70] have traced the history of children's games and analyzed their social significance as well. Altogether, the Opies talked to and observed over 10,000 children in a variety of play settings and activities and found that there were two major objectives associated with all unorganized play. These are not necessarily conscious objectives in a child's mind, but they exist nonetheless. The first objective is a social one, which means that the game produces a structure within which it is possible for a child to have interpersonal contacts with children his own age. Part of children's interpersonal transaction time is spent making the rules for the games they play, and it is usually very important to them that the rules are stuck to once formed. What seems to be an inordinate amount of time making and enforcing rules probably serves the child well in many ways. Among other things, he learns that social commerce must be regulated if interactions are to be sustained for any length of time (younger children merely drift on to other things if they don't like the rules); he also learns that once a more-or-less formal structure has been enacted, he can relax and enjoy himself within its boundaries without having to worry about breaking a rule and being rejected.

An immediate implication here for teachers is that it is important to allow children both time and opportunity to make their rules and set their own boundaries. They get to know each other better this way, and it also allows them valuable practice time in being, as Erikson would say, "industrious," as they work out their own limits and solve their own problems.

Another important function of games is that they allow the child to experience adult life in easy bits and nonthreatening pieces. Although the rules for a particular game are usually rather rigid, there nonetheless is enough variety in both games and rules so that even the most timid and ineffective child has a chance somewhere to fit into games.

Through games a child has a chance to try his powers, to take risks to compete without losing too much face (unless he loses constantly), to accept defeat like a good sport, and to win without being pompous. It is important for us to understand that a growing child gets an enormous sense of satisfaction from merely participating in games. Adults usually get most of their enjoyment of games from winning, not from experiencing. Children are different. Their games do not require umpires, and they seldom bother to keep score. Unless overzealous adults prompt them to do otherwise, children attach only minor significance to who wins or loses; they don't worry about prizes or trophies and in fact are not particularly concerned about whether or not a game is finished when they stop. One of the points made by the Opies is that children prefer some games in which there is an element of luck, so that individual abilities cannot be directly compared. All in all, games not only serve to instruct a child in how to relate better to his peers, but also allow him to test his physical abilities both in relation to others and to his own personal standards. (A gift, for example, which most elementary age boys derive a great deal of enjoyment from is a stopwatch. An amazing variety of performances suddenly get measured and compared, and they range all the way from beating last night's time in getting out of clothes and into pajamas to beating yesterday's time in running to the corner and back.)

A series of interesting studies by Sutton-Smith[71-73] has given us some provocative insights into the characteristics of children who choose certain games and not others. There is one group of children, the "fortunists," who prefer games of chance (e.g., bingo, musical chairs, dice, spin-the-bottle) in which their chances for success depend more on luck than skill. There are the "potents" who endeavor to succeed through their physical prowess and/or strength (e.g., in games such as hopscotch, jacks, horse-shoes, running, darts, jump rope). There are the "strategists" who try to win by out-guessing and out-thinking their opponents (e.g., in games such as marbles, wrestling, pick up sticks, soccer) and the "potent strategist." The children in these studies were all between eight and twelve years of age, and they reflected a good deal of consensus in their views regarding the characteristic type of play preferred by their age-mates, as well as in their naming of some children as failures.

As it turned out, the "strategists" and "potent strategists" were higher than the chance-takers or failures in socioeconomic status and intelligence. Their peers also described them as being quieter, more serious, "not getting mad easily," and better sports. This supports other research that suggests that brighter children are inclined to more frequently enjoy quiet and even solitary games. They are, in a sense, better able to devise their own entertainment and their own self-competitive activities.[74] "Potent" boys, on the other hand, were characterized as being more restless, bossy, more easily angered, and more inclined to take chances. That is, they would not be afraid to, say, mix it up in a football game or wager their allowance on the outcome of a hopscotch contest.

According to Sutton-Smith, a child's play style is connected to the sort of parenting he has received. A child, for example, who has had "high obedience" training is likely to become the "strategist" in his play; a potent physical skill type of preference was found to be related to early "achievement training"; the "fortunists," on the other hand, were comprised mostly of children of low socioeconomic status who had not been reared to prize achievement (or to think they were capable of it), but who believed, rather, that success depends more on lucky breaks than on savvy and know-how.

Psychological significance of games. In a lucid discussion about the psychological significance of games, Sutton-Smith pointed out a variety of ways that a child might be encouraged to get involved in games related to his needs and that might help him cope with his difficulties.[75] For example, a child who has problems following rule games because of his social immaturity might succeed in "cheating games" in which it is possible to fool your opponent and get away with behavior he ordinarily is supposed to guard against. The card game "I Doubt It" would be an example of such a game. As you may recall from your own childhood experiences with this game, here a player "declares" the alleged cards in his hand without showing them. If unchallenged, he receives the score he declared. If, however, he's challenged after a false declaration, he loses the points he declared. Thus suspicion and legitimate "cheating" are central features of this game. Children who are good at picking up nonverbal cues particularly enjoy the "behavior watching" associated with this activity.

There are other examples of how a game with a certain structure may be more gratifying to some than others. For instance, a hesitant or insecure child may enjoy a game like simple tag more so than, say, cross tag. The person who is it in simple tag can chase any player he wishes to tag, which gives him more opportunities to succeed. In cross tag, on the other hand, the "It" person does not have this choice—he must tag the player who passes between him and someone he is chasing. Hence, the reluctant, uncertain child has fewer chances to succeed and may drop out to avoid further frustration.

Modes of personal expression, along with ways of relating to and controlling one's environment are partly learned through play and game activities as a child grows up. Children become good at what they've had most practice doing. For example, given two youths with comparable physical development, motor coordination, and intellectual ability, the youngster who is more physical in relating to his world may grow up to be superior in activities demanding physical dexterity than the youngster who puts a heavier emphasis on verbal skills. Sometimes a lower-class young-ster grows up with outstanding athletic skills because he has learned from an early age that his use of physical strength, skill, and agility is the primary way he can feel able, competent, and good about himself.

A middle-class youngster, on the other hand, may spend more of his time playing problem-solving or intellectual skill type games, both of which enhance verbal skills. It's a matter of degree. Most children don't just do one thing and not another, but most children do tend to emphasize certain play activities over others that may be available. You can learn a great deal about children by watching what they do in their leisure time. Some children are forever active and doing things. Others are involved in quieter pastimes, while still others do little more than read. The point is that a growing child needs a balance of activities in his life, and, as teach-ers, we can be sensitive to those children who may be overbalanced in one area. It is as important for quiet, bookish type children to test their physical capacities now and then as it is for the active, physical children to test their intellectual abilities. This does not mean that our aim should be to change the bookworm into a jock or the athletic hero into an intellect but, rather, to have each growing child test his expanding self in as many ways as pos-sible in order to both develop and encourage talents he may not have thought were there in the first place.

TO THINK ABOUT

Again, go back in time. What sorts of games did you enjoy as a growing youngster? Active games? Quiet ones? Thinking games? Chance games? Do you see relationships between the sorts of games you were attracted to as a child and the sorts of games or pastime ac-tivities you enjoy now? What sorts of games did you (or do you) avoid? Why?

UNDERSTANDING MIDDLE CHILDHOOD
FOR WHAT IT IS

Probably one of the most important points to understand about the psychology of middle childhood is that it is a time when the previously es-tablished pattern of a child's personality is broken up or loosened, so that emerging adolescent changes can be incorporated into it. The outcome of this developmental phase is not *improvement* but *disorganization*. Not

permanent disorganization, of course, but disorganization for future growth. Indeed, disorganization must occur, or else a higher level of organization and integration cannot be achieved. In short, a child cannot become an adult by simply growing bigger and better. When you think about it, if all a child did was to "improve" his personality, then he very likely would end up as an over-sized child, an infantile adult. Among other things, "growing" into a adult means leaving behind, or drastically modifying some of what the child has been, and becoming something else in more mature and complex ways.

The middle years are primarily "disassembly" years and are designed to prepare a child for the physical and psychological changes that occur during adolescence. Existing personality patterns are loosened up so that change can take place.

EPILOGUE

Middle childhood is a remarkable age. The changes that occur are so slow in coming and so subtle in happening that a youngster can go from childhood into adolescence almost before we are aware of it. Indeed, more than one parent has asked him- or herself, "What ever happened to my little boy/girl?" Middle childhood goes so quickly, but, yet, as it is happening it seems hardly to be moving at all. Actually, there is a good reason for this and has to do with the fact that physical growth does not spurt so dramatically as it did during the infancy and preschool years. During middle childhood physical growth is less "spurty" and more steady, which makes month to month changes less apparent to the eye of the beholder. But grow a child does, until by age twelve the average boy has attained about 84 percent of his full height and a girl about 92 percent of hers.

A child's self expands and develops in many ways during these years. He not only grows bigger and stronger, but he grows smarter and more knowing. It has been estimated that a child reaches about 80 percent of his innate ability for learning when he is about eight years of age. That may be true, but he also reaches about 150 percent of his curiosity when he's about six years of age and continues his insatiable hunger for knowing through his middle childhood years. Not all children, of course, have the same kind of hunger. One child, for example, may enjoy doing things that are more physical in nature and that allow him to use his body. At the same time, another child may appreciate activities that are more intellectual in nature and that encourage him to use his mind. Most growing children, if given half a chance, will try out both their minds and their bodies during middle childhood and, somewhere along the way, discover those talents

165

and interests and personal strengths that eventually will help them uncover their own individual identities.

Middle childhood has been called the latent period in a child's total growth because it is a time of relatively little in the way of sexual development. Actually, it would probably be more accurate to say that this is a time of relatively little in the way of sexual interests. Boys and girls continue in their development as sexual persons, but, for the time at least, they have neither interest nor hormones to be much more than wary of each other's differences or platonic in their close relationships.

On the other hand, a child's sex-role development continues at a rapid pace. The identification process that began during the preschool years usually continues in the direction it started. That is, boys with available significant male models and girls with available significant female models will continue to identify and "become like" that model of the same sex. It is especially important during these middle childhood years that boys and girls have the opportunity for meaningful relationships with a same-sex adult in order for them to continue the rehearsal and identification with the sex-role dictated by their respective physiologies.

Piaget has taught us a great deal about how children function intellectually. For example, Piaget has observed that most elementary age children operate on the naive assumption that the world *is* as it *seems* to be from their own angle of judgment. Hence, most children during these years are not very skilled at verbal logic. Until he finds that there *are* contrary opinions and that things may appear differently to other people, the child has no spur to reflecting upon the *way* in which he thinks. And without such reflections upon the way he thinks, logical thinking is difficult.

In addition, his verbal thinking lags behind his verbal logic. For instance, he can deal with the problems of right and left, of degree and order, and of social relations *in practice,* long before he can handle the same issues in words and in thought separate from action. It isn't until the end of the elementary years, so says Piaget, that a child begins to show any *verbal* facility in reasoning. Although he may begin to be curious about mechanical causes and effects somewhere between seven and ten years of age, he probably will have little success with causal *thinking* until eleven or twelve years. The implication for teachers is clear: The more opportunities there are for elementary age youngsters, in particular, to actually *do* things—manipulate, experiment, touch, feel, examine, and so forth (as opposed to simply thinking about things abstractly)—the more likely it is that learning will occur.

A child's allegiance to children his own age, whether they happen to be a couple of kids down the street or the neighborhood "gang," is a perfectly normal outgrowth of a self that is expanding its social boundaries and interpersonal contacts. It is behavior that says, "I am growing up, I can take care of myself, I need to talk to other kids with parent problems, I want to see how strong I am and what my chances for survival are with those who will judge me impartially." It's all part of the process of maturing and becoming independent—processes that can't happen unless a child has as many opportunities as possible for relating to his own kind and holding his own under a variety of conditions and circumstances.

Middle childhood is another stage in a continuous cycle of growth. It is a time when most children begin to consolidate a self-image and integrated a personality style which, for better or worse, will serve as the foundation upon which a framework for a more complex personality structure will be built.

Right around the corner is adolescence—perhaps the most complex growth stage of all. We'll turn our attention to this in Chapter 5.

Write your own chapter summary (major points, ideas, and concepts that had meaning for you).

_____

_____

_____

_____

_____

_____

_____

_____

_____

_____

_____

REFERENCES

1. Tanner, J. M. *Education and Physical Growth.* New York: International Universities Press, 1970, pp. 67–70.

2. Bayley, N., and S. R. Pinneau. "Tables for Predicting Adult Heights from Skeletal Age: Revised for Use With the Greulich-Pyle Hand Standards." *Journal of Pediatrics* 40(1952):423–441.

3. Bayley, N. "Individual Patterns of Development." *Child Development* 27(1956):45–74.

4. Tanner, J. M. "Physical Growth." In *Carmichael's Manual of Child Psychology*, vol. I, 3rd ed., edited by P. H. Mussen. New York: Wiley, 1970, pp. 87–90.

5. Staffieri, J. "A Study of Social Stereotypes of Body Image in Children." *Journal of Personality and Social Psychology* 7(1957):101–104.

6. Walker, R. N. "Body Build and Behavior in Young Children: I Body Build and Nursery School Teachers' Ratings." *Monographs of the Society for Research in Child Development,* no. 3, 27(1962).

7. Walker, R. N. "Body Build and Behavior in Young Children: II Body Build and Parents' Ratings." *Child Development* 34(1963):1–23.

8. *Health of Children of School Age.* Washington, D.C.: U.S. Department of Health, Education and Welfare, 1964.

9. Scheifeld, A. "The Mortality of Men and Women." *Scientific American* 198(1958):22–27.

10. Goddard, J. L. "Childhood Accidents." *Children* 6(1959):83–85.

11. Jacobziner, H. "Accidents—A Major Child Health Problem." *Journal of Pediatrics* 46(1955):419–436.

12. Marcus, I. M., et al. "An Interdisciplinary Approach to Accident Patterns in Children." *Monographs of the Society for Research in Child Development,* no. 2, 25(1960).

13. Slovic, P. "Risk-taking in Children: Age and Sex Differences." *Child Development* 37(1966):137–176.

14. Piaget, J. *The Construction of Reality in the Child.* New York: Basic Books, 1954.

15. Bloom, B. S. *Stability and Change in Human Characteristics.* New York: Wiley, 1964, p. 88.

16. Seashore, R. H., and L. D. Eckerson. "The Measurement of Individual Differences in General English Vocabularies." *Journal of Educational Psychology* 31(1940):14–38.

17. Mandel, F. L. "Vocabulary Growth in Children." *School and Society* 66(1947):163–164.

18. Ervin, S. M., and W. R. Miller. "Language Development." *62nd Yearbook of the National Society for the Study of Education* (1963):108–143.

19. Wolman, R. N., and E. N. Barker. "A Developmental Study of Word Definitions." *Journal of Genetic Psychology* 107(1965):159–166.

20. McCarthy, D. "Language Development." *Monograph of the Society for Research in Child Development,* no. 3, 25(1960):5–14.

21. Schwebel, A. I. "Effects of Impulsivity on Performance of Verbal Tasks in Middle- and Lower-Class Children." *American Journal of Orthopsychiatry* 36(1966):13–21.

22. Dreger, R. M. "Spontaneous Conversation and Story-Telling in a Naturalistic Setting." *Journal of Psychology* 40(1955):163–180.

23. Flavell, J. H. "Concept Development." In *Carmichael's Manual of Child Psychology*, vol. I, 3rd ed., edited by P. H. Mussen. New York: Wiley, 1970, pp. 983–1060.

24. Mussen, P. H., J. J. Conger, and J. Kagan. *Child Development and Personality*, 3rd ed. New York: Harper and Row, 1969, pp. 430–445.

25. Beard, R. M. *An Outline of Piaget's Developmental Psychology for Students and Teachers*. New York: Basic Books, 1969.

26. Ginsburg, H., and S. Opper. *Piaget's Theory of Intellectual Development*. Englewood Cliffs, N.J.: Prentice-Hall, 1969.

27. Flavell, J. H. *The Developmental Psychology of Jean Piaget*. Princeton, N.J.: Van Nostrand, 1963.

28. Baldwin, A. L. *Theories of Child Development*. New York: Wiley, 1967.

29. Erikson, E. H. "Industry versus Inferiority." In *Growth and Crisis of the Healthy Personality*, Supplement II, Transactions of the 4th Conference on Infancy and Childhood, Josiah Macy, Jr., Foundation, 1950, p. 130.

30. Erikson, E. H. "Industry versus Inferiority." Op. cit., 1950, p. 131.

31. Rosen, C. R., and R. D'Andrade. "The Psychological Origins of Achievement Motivation." *Sociometry* 22(1959):185–218.

32. Coopersmith, S. *The Antecedents of Self-Esteem*. San Francisco: W. H. Freeman, 1967, pp. 226–227.

33. Winterbottom, M. R. "The Relation of Need for Achievement to Learning Experiences in Independence Mastery." In *Motives in Fantasy, Action and Society*, edited by J. W. Atkinson. New York: Van Nostrand, 1958.

34. Bing, E. "The Effect of Child Rearing Practices on Development of Differential Cognitive Abilities." *Child Development* 34(1963):631–648.

35. Baer, D., and T. Ragosta. "Relationship Between Perceived Child-Rearing Practices and Verbal and Mathematical Ability." *Journal of Genetic Psychology* 108(1966):105–108.

36. Crandall, V., et al. "Parent's Attitudes and Behaviors and Grade-School Children's Academic Achievements." *Journal of Genetic Psychology* 104(1964):53–66.

37. Katkovsky, W., A. Preston, and V. Crandall, "Parent's Attitudes Toward Their Personal Achievements and Toward the Achievement Behaviors of Their Children." *Journal of Genetic Psychology* 104(1964):67–82.

38. Rosen, B. C. "The Achievement Syndrome: A Psycho-Cultural Dimension in Social Stratification." *American Sociological Review* 21(1956):203–211.

39. McClelland, D. C. *The Achieving Society*. New York: D. Van Nostrand, 1958.

40. Aberle, D. F., and K. D. Naegele, "Middle-Class Fathers' Occupational Roles and Attitudes Toward Children." *American Journal of Orthopsychiatry* 22(1952):366–378.

41. Hess, R. D., and V. C. Shipman. "Early Experiences and the Socialization of Cognitive Modes in Children." *Child Development* 36(1965):869–886.

169

42. Hess, R. D. "Cognitive Elements in Maternal Behavior." In *Minneapolis Symposia on Child Psychology,* vol. I, edited by J. P. Hill. Minneapolis: University of Minnesota Press, 1967, pp. 58–81.

43. Hess, R. D. *Maternal Influences on Early Learning: The Cognitive Environments of Urban Preschool Children,* In *Early Education,* edited by R. D. Hess and R. M. Baer. Chicago: Aldine, 1968, pp. 91–103.

44. Hess, R. D., et al. *The Cognitive Environments of Urban Preschool Children.* Chicago: University of Chicago Press, 1969.

45. Bee, H. L., et al. "Social Class Differences in Maternal Teaching Strategies and Speech Patterns." *Developmental Psychology* 1(1969):726–734.

46. Bee, H. L., et al. "A Study of Cognitive and Motivational Variables in Lower and Middle Class Preschool Children: An Approach to the Evaluation of Head Start, vol. I. *University of Washington Social Change Evaluation Project,* Contract 1375, Office of Economic Opportunity, 1968.

47. Behrens, H. D., and G. Mayhard (eds.). *The Changing Child,* Part IV. Glenview, Ill.: Scott, Foresman, 1972.

48. Bronfenbrenner, U. "The Changing American Child: A Speculative Analysis." *The Journal of Social Issues* 17(1961):6–18.

49. Symonds, P. M. *The Psychology of Parent-Child Relationships.* New York: Appleton-Century-Crofts, 1939.

50. Baumrind, D. "Authoritarian vs. Authoritative Parental Control." *Adolescence* 3(1968):261.

51. Baumrind, D. Op. cit., 1968, p. 261.

52. Baumrind, D. Op. cit., 1968, p. 256.

53. Baumrind, D. "Socialization and Instrumental Competence in Young Children." In *The Young Child,* vol. II, edited by W. W. Hartup. Washington, D.C.: National Association for the Education of Young Children, 1972, pp. 202–225.

54. Siegel, A. E., and L. G. Kohn. "Permissiveness, Permission, and Aggression: The Effects of Adult Presence or Absence on Aggression in Children's Play." *Child Development* 36(1959):131–141.

55. Baumrind, D. "Parental Control and Parental Love." *Children* 12(1965): 230–234.

56. Coopersmith, S. Op. cit., 1967, pp. 236–242.

57. Kessler, J. W. *Psychopathology of Childhood.* Englewood Cliffs, N.J.: Prentice-Hall, 1966.

58. Rosenthal, M. J., M. E. Finkelstein, and G. K. Berkwits. "Father-Child Relationships and Children's Problems." *AMA Archives of General Psychiatry* 7(1962):360–373.

59. Sears, R. R. "The Relation of Early Socialization Experiences to Aggression in Middle Childhood." *Journal of Abnormal and Social Psychology* 63(1961): 466–492.

60. Kagan, J., and H. A. Moss. *Birth to Maturity: The Fels Study of Psychological Development.* New York: Wiley, 1962.

61. Medinnus, G. R. (ed.). *Readings in the Psychology of Parent-Child Relations,* Section III. New York: Wiley, 1967.

62. Becker, W. C. "Consequences of Different Kinds of Parental Discipline." In *Review of Child Development Research*, vol. I, edited by M. L. Hoffman and L. W. Hoffman. New York: Russell Sage Foundation, 1964, pp. 239–271.

63. Baumrind, D. "Child Care Practices Anteceding Three Patterns of Preschool Behavior." *Genetic Psychology Monographs* 75(1967):43–88.

64. Coopersmith, S. Op. cit., 1967, pp. 239–240.

65. Campbell, J. D. "Peer Relations in Childhood." In *Review of Child Development Research*, vol. I, edited by M. L. Hoffman and L. W. Hoffman. New York: Russell Sage Foundation, 1964, pp. 289–322.

66. Smith, R. P. *"Where Did You Go?" "Out." "What Did You Do?" "Nothing."* New York: Pocket Books, 1958, pp. 78–80.

67. White, R. W. *The Abnormal Personality: A Textbook.* New York: Ronald Press, 1948, pp. 144–145.

68. Roff, M. "Childhood Social Interactions and Young Adult Bad Conduct." *Journal of Abnormal and Social Psychology* 63(1961):333–337.

69. Bronfenbrenner, U. "Reaction to Social Pressure from Adults versus Peers Among Soviet Day School and Boarding School Pupils in the Perspective of an American Sample." *Journal of Personality and Social Psychology* 15(1970): 179–189.

70. Opie, I., and P. Opie. *Children's Games in Street and Playground.* New York: Oxford University Press, 1969.

71. Sutton-Smith, B. "The Psychology of Children's Games," Part I. *National Education* (New Zealand) 37(1955):228–229, 261–263.

72. Sutton-Smith, B. "Child Training and Game Involvement." *Ethnology* 1(1962):167–185.

73. Sutton-Smith, B., and J. M. Roberts. "Rubrics of Competitive Behavior." *Journal of Genetic Psychology* 105(1964):13–37.

74. Wang, J. D. "The Relationship Between Children's Play Interests and Their Mental Ability." *Journal of Genetic Psychology* 93(1958):119–131.

75. Herron, R. E., and B. Sutton-Smith. *Child's Play.* New York: Wiley, 1971, pp. 73–82.

REFERENCES OF RELATED INTEREST

Bernard, H. W. *Child Development and Learning.* Boston, Mass.: Allyn and Bacon, 1973.

Binter, A. R., and S. H. Frey (eds). *The Psychology of the Elementary School Child.* Chicago, Ill.: Rand McNally, 1972.

Charles, D. C., and W. R. Looft (eds.). *Readings in Psychological Development Through Life.* New York: Holt, Rinehart and Winston, 1973.

Clarizio, H. F., and G. F. McCoy. *Behavior Disorders in School-Aged Children.* Scranton, Pa.: Chandler, 1970.

Edge, D. (ed.). *The Formative Years.* New York: Schocken Books, 1970.

Elkind, D.   *A Sympathetic Understanding of the Child Six to Sixteen.*   Boston: Allyn and Bacon, 1971.

Frost, J. L. (ed.).   *Early Childhood Education Rediscovered.*   New York: Holt, Rinehart and Winston, 1968.

———.   *Revisiting Early Childhood Education.*   New York: Holt, Rinehart and Winston, 1973.

Hawkes, G. R., and D. Pease.   *Behavior and Development from 5 Through 12.*   New York: Harper and Row, 1962.

Herron, R. E., and B. Sutton-Smith.   *Child's Play.*   New York: Wiley, 1971.

Hertling, J. E., and H. G. Getz (eds.).   *Education for the Middle School Years: Readings.*   Glenview, Ill.: Scott, Foresman, 1971.

Hurlock, E. B.   *Child Development,* 5th ed.   New York: McGraw-Hill, 1972.

Lavatelli, C. S., and F. Stendler (eds.).   *Readings in Child Behavior and Development,* 3rd ed.   New York: Harcourt Brace Jovanovich, 1972.

McCandless, B. R., and E. D. Evans.   *Children and Youth: Psychosocial Development.*   Hinsdale, Ill.: Dryden Press, 1973.

Maier, H. W.   *Three Theories of Child Development.*   New York: Harper and Row, 1965.

Munsinger, H. (ed.).   *Readings in Child Development.*   New York: Holt, Rinehart and Winston, 1971.

Mussen, P. H., J. J. Conger, and J. Kagan (eds.).   *Readings in Child Development and Personality.*   New York: Harper and Row, 1970.

Nash, J.   *Developmental Psychology.*   Englewood Cliffs, N.J., Prentice-Hall, 1970.

Redl, F.   *When We Deal with Children.*   New York: The Free Press, 1966.

Rogers, D.   *Child Psychology.*   Belmont, Calif.: Wadsworth, 1969.

——— (ed.).   *Issues in Child Psychology.*   Belmont, Calif.: Brooks/Cole, 1969.

Salk, L.   *What Every Child Would Like His Parents to Know.*   New York: David McKay Co., 1972.

Seidman, J. M. (ed.).   *The Child,* 2nd ed.   New York: Holt, Rinehart and Winston, 1969.

Smart, R. C., and M. C. Smart (eds.).   *Readings in Child Development and Relationships.*   New York: Macmillan, 1973.

Smart, M. S., and R. C. Smart.   *Children: Development and Relationships,* Part III, 2nd ed.   New York: Macmillan, 1973.

Sutton-Smith, B.   *Child Psychology.*   New York: Appleton-Century-Crofts, 1973.

Watson, R. I., and H. C. Lindgren.   *Psychology of the Child,* 3rd ed.   New York: Wiley, 1973.

Yamamoto, K. (ed.).   *The Child and His Image.*   Boston: Mass.: Houghton Mifflin, 1972.

FIVE

Junior High and High School Years: The Self Matures

CHAPTER OUTLINE

PROLOGUE

ADOLESCENCE HAS MANY MEANINGS

What Is "Adulthood"?

Physical Adolescence

Psychological Adolescence

PHYSICAL DEVELOPMENT: VARIATIONS AND CONSEQUENCES

Growth Spurts in Adolescence

Hormone Secretions Accelerate

Youths Are Growing Bigger

Adolescence Is a Healthy Period

RELATION BETWEEN PHYSICAL GROWTH AND SELF-CONCEPT DEVELOPMENT

Appearance Can Influence Self-Perception

Effect of Early versus Late Physical Maturity on Boys

Effect of Early versus Late Physical Maturity on Girls

DEVELOPMENTAL TASKS OF ADOLESCENCE

IMPACT OF PARENTS ON THE ADOLESCENT'S GROWING SELF

Parent Relationships and the Development of Independence

Religion and Social Class as Variables in Independence Training

Sex of Parent and Child as Factors

Males and Females Are Treated Differently

Sex-Role Identification Is Important

Autonomy a Major Goal

Parental Influence Is Strong

IMPACT OF PEER RELATIONSHIPS ON THE ADOLESCENT'S GROWING SEL

Major Functions of the Peer Group

Peer Acceptance and Social Adjustment

Peer Acceptance Related to Academic Success

Personal Adjustment not Necessarily Related to Social Success

Importance of Peer-Group Culture

YOUTH ALIENATION: ANTECEDENTS, EXPRESSIONS, AND OUTCOMES

Antecedents to Adolescent Protest and Alienation

The Student Activist

Why activists protest

The Culturally Alienated

Implications for Teachers

INTELLECTUAL PROCESSES AND COGNITIVE FUNCTIONING

Shift to Abstract Thinking: Piaget's Stage IV

Piaget's assumptions tested

Virtues to Adolescent Idealistic Thinking

EPILOGUE

REFERENCES

REFERENCES OF RELATED INTEREST

IMPORTANT CHAPTER IDEAS

1. Adolescence is not a universal happening and is a relatively recent phenomenon in Western societies.

2. "Psychological" adolescence varies from person to person.

3. Not all adolescents grow at the same rate and pace.

4. Physical growth can influence self-concept development for better or for worse.

5. Effects of early versus late maturing has different effects on males and females.

6. There are at least ten important developmental tasks to accomplish during adolescence.

7. Either *too* much or *too* little parental involvement can interfere with an adolescent's growth toward independence.

8. The religious orientation of parents influences their attitudes about when they think adolescents' independence training should begin.

9. The effects of different social-class backgrounds on parenting practices is not so great as it used to be.

10. Opportunities for same-sex identification is an important prerequisite for healthy psychological development.

11. Peer-group influence reaches a peak around middle adolescence and then begins a slow decline.

12. Feeling accepted and being recognized is important at any age, but it is particularly crucial during adolescence.

13. Affiliation with a peer-group culture helps a growing adolescent to separate himself from his parents—a necessary first step to being autonomous and independent.

14. A majority of activist youth are attempting to live out the political aspirations of their parents.

15. Culturally alienated youth have usually rejected parental values.

16. During adolescence there is a shift from a specific, black and white thinking to more abstract reasoning.

17. As an adolescent grows in his ability to think and reason symbolically, it becomes more possible to transcend the concrete here and now and enter the world of ideas.

18. An adolescent's idealism is a normal, healthy way for testing his dreams of what could be against the reality of what is.

PROLOGUE

However you look at it, adolescence is a remarkable and complex phenomenon. There is virtually no aspect of a growing youngster's physical being, social existence, or cognitive functioning that is not subject to change. Consider a few examples. Between eleven and fifteen and depending on whether one is a boy or girl, a youngster may grow up to six inches taller and up to 30 pounds heavier. That's just for openers. Hair begins growing all over the place, acne makes its appearance on the facial scene (for reasons not entirely clear most adolescents hate the word *pimples* — as one sixteen-year-old girl expressed it, it just sounds "yechy"), boys experience wet dreams and girls begin menstruation. On the social front, friendships grow deeper and more profound, cliques develop, groups form, and boy-girl relationships grow simultaneously more confusing, tempting, and exciting through the complex chemistry of awakening sexuality. Cognitively, the typical adolescent moves from being able to think only in concrete, "here and now" terms to the more sophisticated intellectual ability of making logical deductions from a hypothetical state of affairs. All in all, adolescence is a time for adjusting to an incredible welter of biochemical and psychological changes that make separate and sometimes collective withdrawals on the growing youngster's energy bank. It is a time for raising such questions as who am I, how am I coming across to others, how did I ever get to be this way in the first place, and what do I want to do with my life? It is a time when the adolescent self reaches for maturity.

Adolescence can be a confusing time and partly this is related to adult confusion about what adolescence means. Let's turn our attention to this first of all.

ADOLESCENCE HAS MANY MEANINGS

To begin with, adolescence is neither a universal happening nor does it have lengthy historical credentials. The *Oxford English Dictionary*, for example, traces the term only to the fifteenth century. Prior to that the idea of childhood hardly existed, let alone childhood beyond puberty, as the term *adolescence* suggests. The early Greeks and Romans, for instance, did not view what we call adolescence as a separate growth stage, except for the relatively brief one- to two-year period it took to change from sexual immaturity to sexual maturity. Although the Roman Emperor Claudius was regarded by his relatives in the Claudian and Julian families to be somewhat dull and slow in developing, he nonetheless married at twelve and was made high priest at thirteen. You may also recall that Shakespeare's tragic heroine Juliet was only fourteen at the time of all the fateful events in her abbreviated life.

The leap from childhood straight into adulthood with no adolescent apprenticeship was typical not only of classical culture, but characteristic of the Middle Ages and Renaissance as well. Aries,[1] who has studied the history of adolescence in great detail, notes that in the 1300 and 1400's young elementary age boys frequently went to school armed with sabers no less! Thus, age has not always been a yardstick for deciding what a growing youngster could do or what he should be taught. Indeed, it has been noted that, in 1677, students in some of the French primary grades ranged in age from nine to seventeen, and those in the highest grade were anywhere from twelve to twenty.[2] Early cultures were not age-graded. For both those who went to school and those who did not, seven years of age was considered to be the age of adulthood in most of early Western culture. Even today adolescence as a separate growth stage is often absent in entire cultures. For example, within certain hunting cultures childhood is considered over by age eight, and within certain agrarian cultures it ceases anywhere between ten and twelve.[3]

What Is "Adulthood"?

Actually, the prolonged postponement after puberty to full adult status is a relatively recent phenomenon in Western societies. Up to several hundred years ago in Western society, and persisting even today in many tribal cultures, the physical changes accompanying puberty, usually celebrated by some kind of ceremonial observance, automatically opened the doors to adulthood. However, as Western societies grew more complex, industrialized, and technological, the total period of childhood apprenticeship has been extended and lengthened to the point where this stage we call adolescence is now a bona fide and important developmental period. It has been lengthened because as the number of adult roles and responsibilities multiplied, an increasingly longer period of learning in preparation for adult status has become necessary. Unfortunately, there has been a notable lack of agreement among the elders of Western culture as to when

178

this adolescence apprenticeship should be terminated.   Although our culture contains numerous micro-*rites de passage* to signal a youngster's entrance to adulthood, there is no universal indicator of adulthood.   Indeed, those micro-rites that do exist may even conflict with each other.   For example, although it is now possible via the twenty-sixth amendment for all eighteen year olds to vote in all elections, the age at which a young person can buy alcoholic beverages may be set at eighteen, nineteen, twenty, or twenty-one depending on the state he lives in.   In some states the minimal age for a driver's license is sixteen while in others it is eighteen.   Indeed, up to 1972 it was possible for a young person living in Minnesota to obtain a driver's license when he was only fourteen!   And, of course, one needed to be only eighteen to be eligible for the draft, when the draft was still in effect.

All in all, there is a good bit of confusion about what adolescence means and when it ends.   What seems to happen is that adult ambiguity about the adolescent reinforces his own ambiguity about himself.   For instance, what is one to do when he must address a group of adolescents?   How should the salutation be expressed?   "Teen-agers?", "Ladies and Gentlemen?", "Boys and Girls?"   It's hard to know.

Physical Adolescence

In a purely *physical* sense, adolescence is a universal phenomenon. What varies are the meanings and expectations that different cultures and subcultures within a culture place upon a growing youngster as he moves through this growth stage.   In terms of physical development, adolescence commences with the prepubertal growth spurt and ends with the attainment of full physical maturity. Although physical maturity is difficult to define with precision, it usually refers to the idea that one has reached the upper limits of his genetic potential for endocrinal development, skeletal growth, and total height.

Psychological Adolescence

In a purely *psychological* sense, the meaning of adolescence refers more to a state of mind, an attitude, a style of existence that begins with puberty and ends when one is relatively independent of parental control. As you may know from your own observations, the cessation of *psychological* adolescence varies from individual to individual.   For one person, psychological adolescence is terminated when he is about eighteen, while for another person his psychological adolescence persists into his twenties or thirties or, sadly enough, even later.

179

Adolescence, then, begins with signs of sexual maturity in both physical and social development and ends when the individual becomes self-supporting, responsible, and is accepted in most ways by the reference group peers toward whom he looks for some measure of approval, recognition, and advice. I want to emphasize the importance of shifting one's needs for approval, recognition, and advice to the peer group because of the major symptoms of persisting *psychological* adolescence, particularly when physical adolescence has been completed, is continued dependence on parents as a major source of approval, recognition, and guidance. One study, for example, found that many of the undergraduate college students who used the counseling center facilities had *more* trouble talking to their peers than to their parents, which would suggest that later adolescent youths who have not weaned themselves away from parents are more apt to have social-emotional problems than those who are more independent and peer-related.[4] This is not to say that one must give up completely the idea of needing anything from his parents, whether it be their counsel or their love, in order to be a mature adult. It is more a matter of the *degree* to which an individual remains dependent on his parents and "needs" them for emotional and social support when physical adolescence is completed. A twenty-five-year-old woman who whines home to her mother every time she has a rift with her husband or a twenty-three-year-old male who gives up his vocational plans because his parents disapprove could very well be psychologically adolescent in their dependency ties and inability to think for themselves.

What does adolescence mean in terms of behavior? Well, the specifics may depend on who you talk to and what state you live in, but in a more general psychological sense it means that this is a time for a growing youngster to test his intellectual, social, emotional, and physical limits in order to consolidate a mature self-image.

TO THINK ABOUT

When you think about all the things that you had to "test" about yourself as an adolescent, what two or three things stand out? Or, as another way of looking at it, what two or three things were most difficult for you to test? Jot them down and then refer back to them after reading this chapter to see if you're clearer about why they were difficult.

_____

_____

_____

Adolescence is a time for wondering what life is all about and who one is as a person. (Allyn and Bacon)

Although there are many important inputs to an adolescent's maturing self-image, one to which he is extremely sensitive is his physical growth, a topic we turn to next.

PHYSICAL DEVELOPMENT: VARIATIONS AND CONSEQUENCES

As a stage of physical development, adolescence includes several distinct periods of change.   Pubescence—or preadolescence as it is sometimes called—refers to the two years preceding puberty and to the physical changes occurring during that time.   Puberty follows pubescence and is marked by specific indicators of sexual maturity.   For girls it is the onset of menstruation and for boys the most valid indicator is probably the presence of live spermatozoa, or male reproductive cells, in the urine.   This may or may not coincide with the emergence of pigmented pubic hair, which is the more easily observable sign of sexual maturity in boys.[5]

For the majority of young persons, the years from about eleven to sixteen are the most eventful ones of their lives insofar as their growth and development is concerned.   Although a child's growth is more rapid and dramatic during the first three years of life, he was not the fascinated, delighted, or horrified spectator who watches the developments, or lack of developments, of adolescence.   The typical adolescent spends a great deal of time in front of the mirror—the boy looking for muscles he is sure will never develop, the girl worrying about whether her figure is too much, too small, or not at all.

181

Growth is a very regular and highly regulated process, and from birth onward the growth rate of most body tissues decreases steadily. Body shape changes gradually, since the growth rate of some parts, such as the arms and legs, is greater than the rate of growth of others, such as the trunk. As you know from your own experience, arm and leg growth reach their peak during early adolescence, which accounts for the long gangly look that some youngsters have at this time. Overall, however, growth changes represent a steady process, a smoothly continuous development rather than a passage through a series of discrete stages. In addition, there is evidence to suggest a general "going-togetherness" of growth. For example, there is a close correspondence between the onset of menstruation for the girl and the age when bones of the fingers become fused. Similarly, appearance of pubic hair in boys is closely associated with skeletal development of the hand.[6] Similar relationships are apparent among other aspects of skeletal and muscle growth, on the one hand, and primary and secondary sexual development, on the other.[7]

Growth Spurts in Adolescence

At puberty, there is a very considerable alteration in growth rate. There is a swift increase in body size, a change in the shape of body composition, and a rapid development of the reproductive organs. These body changes vary widely in intensity, duration, and age of onset from one young person to the next.

Research has consistently shown that in every age group some youngsters will be ahead of their peers in terms of physical, mental, social, and emotional development and others will lag behind.[8] For example, in a typical sixth-grade class of forty students (twelve and thirteen year olds), you would very likely find two fully adolescent, eight preadolescent, and ten childish girls, four preadolescent boys, and sixteen childish boys. A ninth-grade class (fourteen and fifteen year olds) of the same size would likely consist of sixteen adolescent young ladies, four preadolescent girls, two childish boys, eight preadolescent boys, and ten fully adolescent young men.[9] Figure 5–1 may help give you a visual idea of the variations in growth rate among youngsters of the same age.

Developmental studies have shown that the growth spurt may begin as early as nine and one half years or as late as thirteen and one half years in boys. Most boys, however, begin their growth acceleration at about thirteen years, reach a growth peak between thirteen and one half and fourteen years, and decline sharply to pregrowth-spurt rates by about fifteen and one half. Growth goes on at a slower pace for several years thereafter.

For girls, the adolescent growth spurt may be as early as seven and one half years (seldom) or as late as eleven and one half. The average girl,

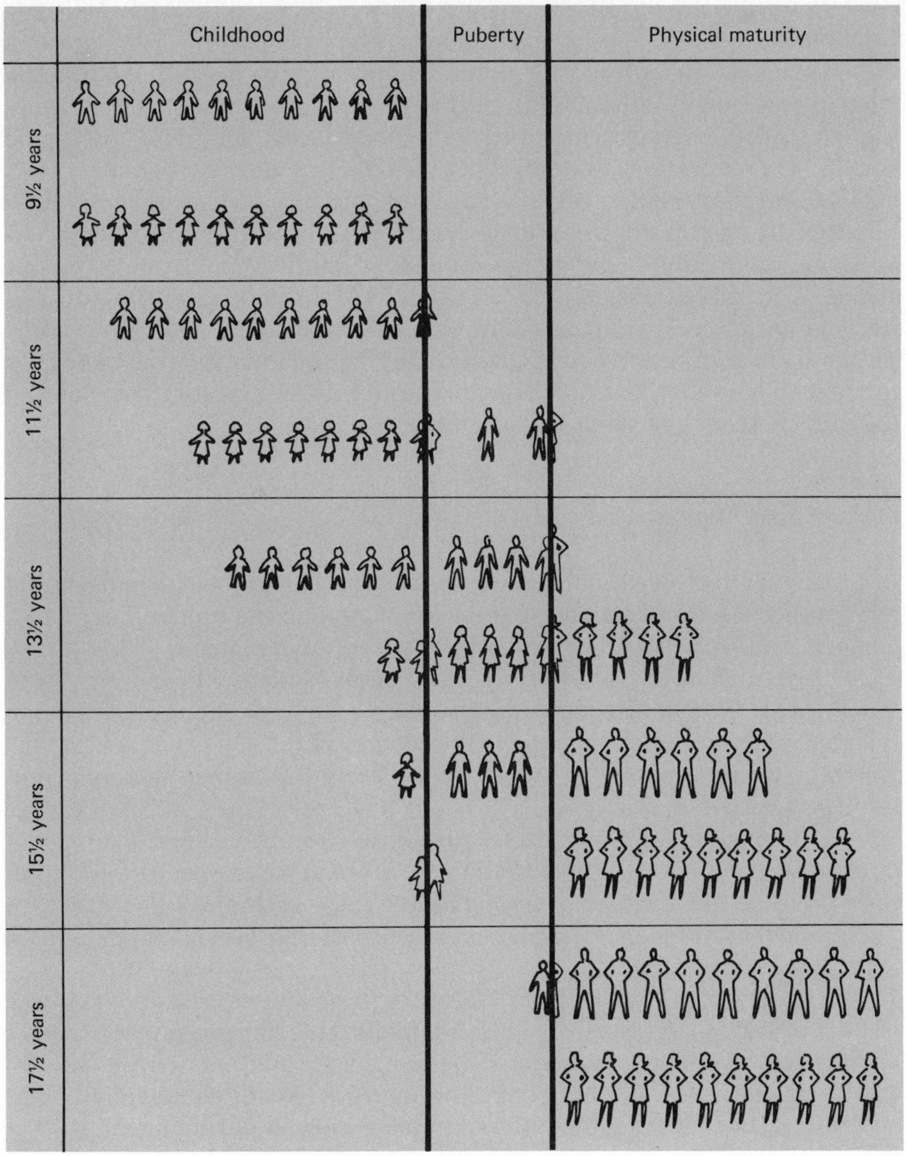

	Childhood	Puberty	Physical maturity
9½ years			
11½ years			
13½ years			
15½ years			
17½ years			

FIGURE 5–1. When Boys and Girls Mature

however, begins her period of rapid acceleration about age eleven, reaches a peak between eleven and one half and twelve years and then decreases to pregrowth-spurt rates by about age thirteen. As with boys, growth continues on, but at a slower pace, for the next several years.[10,11]

Along with the increases in height and weight during this period, some less dramatic changes are occurring too. For example, the low forehead becomes higher and wider, the mouth widens and the lips fill out, and the slightly receding childhood chin begins to assert itself more. In addition, the large head, characteristic of the childhood years, continues to become smaller in proportion to total body length. It doesn't actually grow smaller, but it appears to because the trunk and extremities are growing so rapidly. By age fifteen, the average head has reached its adult size.

Even more subtle changes go on during this period. In boys, for instance, there is a decrease in the width of fatty tissue beneath the skin and body fat decreases significantly during their growth spurt. Not so for girls. To the dismay of many a young lady, they not only develop thicker fatty tissue than boys, but "fat widths in girls continue to increase in size during the prepubescent and adolescent years."[12]

Hormone Secretions Accelerate

Many of the most noteworthy physical changes that occur during adolescence are those stemming from altered endocrine functioning due to an increased output of hormones from the pituitary gland. This gland, located in the brain, is primarily responsible for growth and serves to monitor the hormone balance of the body. The gonadotropic hormone secreted by the pituitary stimulates the activity of the gonads or sex glands, which, in turn, produce the sex hormones and the growth of mature sperm in males and ova in females.

In the female, hormones from the ovaries (estrogens) stimulate development of the breasts, uterus, Fallopian tubes, and vagina. In addition, they produce the secondary sex characteristics, including the growth of pubic and auxillary hair, increased activity of the sweat glands, and a broadening of the hips.

In the male, hormones from the testes (testosterone) stimulate growth of the prostrate gland, seminal vesicles, penis, and such secondary characteristics as broadened shoulders, deeper voice, and, as in the female, growth of pubic and auxillary hair, and increased sweat gland activity. In addition, male hormonal activity stimulates muscle development so that they grow both stronger and larger. In many cases, the plumpness of late childhood is replaced by a firmer more angular build.

Youths Are Growing Bigger

184   Although developmental psychologists are pretty much agreed that the sequence of growth has remained the same over time and that there was

probably as much variation in growth rate among children in the past as there is now, several changes stand out: (1) youths are not only maturing at an earlier age, but (2) they are bigger when they do mature. For example, forty years ago or so the average girl experienced her first menstruation (menarche) at about her fifteenth birthday; nowadays it is somewhere between her twelfth and thirteenth.[13] This is interesting, particularly when you consider that the average age of menarche in northern Europe at around 1800 was between seventeen and one half to eighteen years.[14]

In regard to physical size, evidence suggests that, over the past forty years in the United States, fifteen- to sixteen-year-old boys are averaging almost two inches taller and ten pounds heavier than their forbears. At the same time, girls, on the average, have gained better than one half inch and one and one fourth pounds. Interestingly enough seventeen to nineteen-year-old girls average about three pounds lighter than their counterparts forty years ago, a fact that very likely reflects changes both in dietary habits and changing ideas of physical attractiveness.[15]

For the most part, this change in the onset of puberty and alteration in physical size are related to improved vitamin-enriched diets and health.

If we were to assume that the present rate of change of one inch per generation continues and then project this trend to the year 4000, we would find that the average man would be between eleven and twelve feet tall. If the age of menarche were to continue to decrease by four months per decade, a girl would be around four years old when she experienced her first menstrual period. Fortunately, there is evidence to suggest that, just as other species seem to have growth boundaries, so, too, does man. Experts in physical anthropology and genetics predict that the growth trends we've been discussing will level off when man reaches an average height of six feet.[16,17]

Adolescence Is a Healthy Period

The adolescent years are among the healthiest of our entire life-span, when compared to later years and judged in terms of mortality rates and the causes of death. Most deaths of teen-age boys are due to violence—some suicide and homicide, but mostly they occur as a consequence of accidents with cars, drowning, firearms, and misfortunes at home rather than as a result of poor health. On the other hand, accidents account for only about one-fifth of the mortality rate for girls, while various diseases account for the other four-fifths. The toll of accidents rises throughout the teen years until in the eighteen- and nineteen-year-old group about two-thirds of the boys who meet death and about one-third of the girls die from accidents. Motor vehicle accidents are responsible for the deaths of five of eight adolescent boys, while for girls motor vehicle mishaps account for

five of seven accidental deaths.   In case you've ever wondered why car in-
surance premiums are so high for teen-agers, the above figures should
speak for themselves.   Table 5–1 gives you a general overview of the ages,
causes, and rates of death per 1,000 youngsters.   The adolescent years
may be the healthiest, but they are also the most accident-prone, a fact that
likely reflects the robustness of teen-age living.

RELATION BETWEEN PHYSICAL
GROWTH AND SELF-CONCEPT
DEVELOPMENT

Like all other aspects of one's self-image, the conception a person has
of his body is subjective.   An individual may have a generally positive
body-image—he likes the way he looks, or he may have a negative body
image (how he looks falls short of his expectations for himself).

When you think about it, no aspect of one's "self" is more available for
public assessment and careful scrutiny than his physical shell.   Indeed, the
most material and visible part of the self is our physical body.   Like any
other object in our physical environment, our bodies are perceived through
the various senses.   Occupying as it does a large segment of our visual and
auditory experiences, we see and hear a lot of ourselves.   In this important
way, one's body comes to assume a central role in his self-perceptions.

The particular *way* a person perceives his physical body—whether distorted or not—may have important psychological consequences for him.
For example, an adolescent boy may be so frightfully self-conscious about
his awkward coordination that he refuses to attend dances or participate in

TABLE 5–1.   *Ages, Causes, and Rates per 1,000 for Deaths*

Causes	5–14 years	15–24 years
All accidents	18.7	61.7
Cancer and malignant neoplasms	6.5	8.2
Congenital malformations	2.8	2.4
Influenza and pneumonia	2.1	2.2
Diseases of the heart	.9	3.2
Cerebral hemorrhage	.7	1.5
Homicide	.6	6.8
Suicide (fourth in rank, age 15–24)		6.2

(From *Facts of Life and Death*.   Public Health Service Publication no. 600.   Washington, D.C.:
U.S. Department of Health, Education and Welfare, 1967, p. 15.)

sports; a sixteen-year-old girl may be so overly sensitive to what she feels is inadequate breast development that she refuses to date; a young man who feels intellectually inferior spends so much time developing his muscles that he neglects to do anything about expanding his mind or growing socially. Perceptions of the body are related intimately to perceptions of larger aspects of the self.

Appearance Can Influence
Self-Perception

Indeed, there is research evidence to suggest that one's appearance is an important determiner of self-esteem, both among men and women. For example, in one study it was found that the feelings an individual had about his body were similar to those he had about himself as a person.[18] That is, the person who had positive feelings about his body was likely to feel positively about himself as a total person and vice versa. Another series of studies found that later adolescent male and female youths who were satisfied with their bodies were also apt to be fairly secure and self-confident.[19,20] In other words, individuals who like and accept their bodies are more apt to "like" themselves (have higher self-esteem) than those who dislike their bodies.

Other research has indicated that an individual's physical attractiveness is an important social cue used by others as a basis for social evaluation. It has been demonstrated, for example, that physically attractive young adults, both male and female, are assumed to possess more socially desirable personalities and to lead more successful and fulfilling lives than are those of lesser attractiveness.[21] There is evidence to suggest that the effects of a physical attractiveness stereotype may begin at an early developmental level. For instance, it has been found that, even among nursery school children, popularity is related to physical attractiveness.[22] Indeed, it has also been noted that when an attractive child misbehaves he is evaluated less negatively than is the case for an unattractive child.[23]

The point is that physical growth and how one appears to others play important parts in determining how an adolescent boy or girl (or anyone else for that matter) feels about him- or herself. Although the typical adolescent worries a good deal about how he stands on a number of measures — intelligence, wit, popularity, daringness, and so on — his primary concern is with his progress toward social maturity. The fact is: Whether physical growth is too much or too little, too fast or too slow, it can be the source of great anxiety. Hence, the rate of a boy's total growth in relation to other boys in his class or the extent of a girl's overall development in comparison to other girls her age are highly influential inputs to how each youngster feels about himself.

Individual differences in physical growth have been found to affect personal and social adjustment not only during adolescence, but beyond that time as well. Since the effects of early or late growth are different for boys than for girls, perhaps we can more clearly see these differences if we separate the two and examine them one at a time. Let's take the boys first.

Effect of Early versus Late Physical Maturity on Boys

Highly significant and classical growth studies have emerged from the Institute of Human Development at the University of California. One of these studies, conducted by Jones and Bayley,[24] focused on a group of boys who were the sixteen most accelerated growers and the sixteen who were the most consistently slow growers for a four-and-a-half year period between the ages of twelve and seventeen. Figure 5-2 will give you a pretty good idea of the physical differences between a typical fast growing boy and a slow growing boy.

Many significant differences between the two groups were found. For example, when rated by adults, the slower growing boys were judged as lower in physical attractiveness, less masculine, less well groomed, more animated, more affected, and more tense. They did not, however, differ from the more advanced boys in ratings of popularity, leadership, prestige, or social effect on the group. In addition, slow growing boys were considered to be less mature in heterosexual social relations.

When rated by their peers, the slower growers were judged to be more restless, talkative, and bossy. In addition, peer ratings showed them to be less popular, less likely to be leaders, more attention-seeking, and less confident in class situations. Significantly, perhaps, they were also judged by their peers as being shorter on a sense of humor about themselves.

In contrast, boys who were physically accelerated were usually more accepted and treated by adults and peers as more mature. They were more matter-of-fact about themselves and had less need to strive for status and recognition, although from their ranks came the outstanding student body leaders in high school. The investigators concluded:

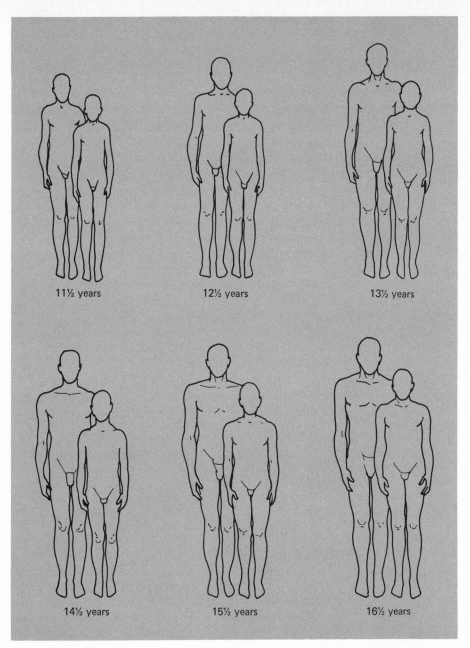

11½ years   12½ years   13½ years

14½ years   15½ years   16½ years

(From F. K. Shuttleworth. "The Adolescent Period: A Pictorial Atlas." Monographs of the Society for Research in Child Development [Ser. no. 59] 14[1949]. By permission of The Society for Research in Child Development, Inc.)

FIGURE 5-2. Differential Growth of an Early Maturing and a Late Maturing Boy

The findings give clear evidence of the effect of physical maturing on behavior. Perhaps of greater importance, however, is the repeated demonstration of the multiplicity of factors, psychological and cultural as well as physical, which contribute to the formation of basic personality patterns.[25]

In a study designed to see if there were any differences between the self-conceptions, motivations, and interpersonal attitudes of late and early maturing boys, it was found that boys who mature late in adolescence are more likely to be insecure and dependent than their faster growing peers. In addition, they more frequently behave in childish, affected, attention-getting ways.[26]

These findings are consistent with those in another study that investigated the motivations of late and early maturing boys.[27] In general, it was discovered that high drives for social acceptance and for aggression are more characteristic of the slower growing than the faster growing boys. This may suggest that a later-maturer's high needs for social visibility may stem from feelings of insecurity and dependence, which conceivably serve as the basic motivators for recognition in order to compensate for underlying feelings of inadequacy and rejection. It is as if these boys were saying in many different ways, "Hey lookit me!"

In line with the evidence thus far, Weatherly, in a study related to physical maturation and personality in late adolescence, concluded:

> . . . the late maturing boy of college age is less likely than his earlier-maturing peers to have satisfactorily resolved the conflicts normally attending the transition from childhood to adulthood. He is more inclined to seek attention and affection from others and less inclined to assume a position of dominance and leadership over others. Yet he is not ready to accept the dictates of authority gracefully; he is inclined, rather, to deny authority and assert unconventional behavior in a rebellious vein. In view of the evidence of these potentially competing forces within him [it is not] surprising that he tends to see himself different from his peers and parents.[28]

Taken together, these findings make it clear that the rate of physical maturing may affect self-concept development specifically and personality development generally in crucially important ways. We can reasonably infer that adult and peer attitudes toward the adolescent, as well as their treatment and acceptance of him, are related to some extent to his perceived physical status. This suggests that the sociopsychological environment in which a late-maturer grows may be significantly different and less positive from that of their early maturing peers. As a consequence, early maturing and late maturing boys acquire different patterns of overt social behavior.

On the basis of both observation and research, we can reasonably conclude that during adolescence late maturing is a handicap for many boys and rarely offers special advantages. Early maturing, on the other hand, is a two-sided coin. On the positive side it frequently lends itself to certain competitive advantages, but on the negative side it sometimes means that the adolescent has to respond to expectations that are determined more by size and appearance than other aspects of maturing. All in all, however, the early maturing boy is likely to have a better time of it both in terms of certain physical advantages and more positive self-concept outcomes as he moves through his adolescent years than is his later maturing counterpart.

Effect of Early versus Late Physical Maturity on Girls

Relationships between developmental maturity and personality variables in girls are much less dramatic than those for boys. For girls, early maturing provides no obvious prestige gaining advantage. Indeed, at the peak of their growth, early maturing girls are not only taller than their girl classmates but are actually taller than most of the boys in their class. In addition, there is evidence to suggest that many early maturing girls consider their accelerated growth status to be a physical stigma that interferes with their opportunity for wider social experiences.[29] Such girls have also been judged to have little influence on their peers and seldom attain a high degree of popularity, prestige, or leadership.[30] Figure 5-3 will give you an idea of the growth differences between a typical early maturing and late maturing girl.

In an effort to determine whether the psychological impact on girls of early or late growth persisted into later adolescence, Jones and Mussen[31] studied the self-conceptions, motivations, and interpersonal attitudes of thirty-four seventeen-year-old girls—sixteen who had been consistently fast growers and eighteen who had been consistently slow growers. They assumed that since the early maturing girl had a harder time of it during her peak growing years that she might be expected to reveal negative self-feelings and poor interpersonal attitudes in late teen years. However, when the results of psychological testing of early and late maturing girls were compared it was found that early maturing girls had significantly more positive self-concepts. From the picture we have to this point, we would have expected early maturing girls to have negative self-concepts. Although this was not true, the fact that early maturing girls did have a higher self-concept in later adolescence is consistent with the conclusion of Faust,[32] who found that, for girls, precocious physical development tends to become a decided asset as the girl moves from junior high and into the high school years. On the other hand, Weatherly's[33] efforts to find whether late physical maturation was a liability or asset to the personality development of girls did not result in a definite answer to the question. He did,

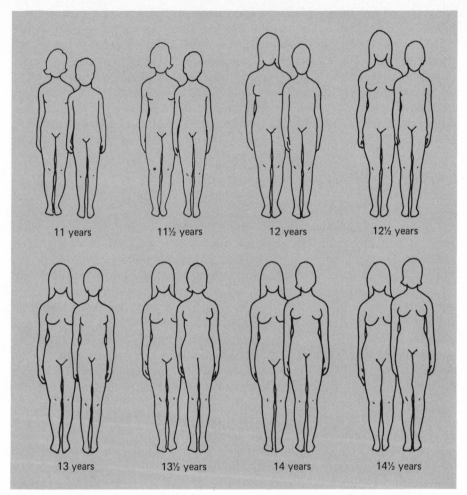

11 years   11½ years   12 years   12½ years

13 years   13½ years   14 years   14½ years

(From F. K. Shuttleworth. "The Adolescent Period: A Pictorial Atlas." Monographs of the Society for Research in Child Development [Ser. no. 50] 14[1949]. By permission of the Society for Research in Child Development, Inc.)

FIGURE 5-3. Differential Growth of an Early Maturing and a Late Maturing Girl

however, observe that late physical maturation had adverse effects on personal adjustment in *both* sexes in late adolescence. This is consistent with the conclusion reached by Jones and Mussen:

> When the differences between early- and late-maturing girls are compared with the differences between early- and late-maturing boys, they are found to be in the same direction more often than in the opposite. These findings are interpreted to indicate that late-maturing adolescents of both sexes are characterized by less adequate self-concepts, slightly poorer parent-child relationships, and some tendency for stronger dependency needs.[34]

The relationships between physical maturation and personality variables is much less definite for girls than boys. A logical conclusion is that rate of physical maturation is a less influential variable influencing personality development in girls than for boys. This is not surprising, particularly when you consider that the cultural sex-role prescription for males in our society is relatively clear and is one which places a high value upon attributes associated with physical strength, coordination, and athletic deftness, especially in the adolescent and young adulthood years. For girls, however, the feminine sex-role prescription is less definite and stereotyped and is, therefore, not as likely to be connected to any specific pattern of physical attributes. In addition, whereas people seem to respond more to a boy or a man's total physical makeup the response to a girl's physical makeup is apt to be more specific. That is, the physical qualities of a girl capable of eliciting a favorable response includes her face, bosom, hips, legs, and total proportions (although not necessarily in that order). For example, one girl might have a pretty face and very little else, but this could be sufficient to win her many signs of approval. Another girl may have an extremely attractive figure and only very plain facial features, but her nice legs or substantial bosom may be enough to win her some feeling of social approval. In other words, it may be possible for a girl than for a boy to elicit different responses to different parts of her body so that even though she may fall short in one area, she can make it up in another. Girls are expected to do little else with their bodies except adorn them and make them as attractive as possible.

This concept, however, of what the girl is *expected* to do may change as the basic principles of the Women's Liberation movement are incorporated into contemporary child-rearing practices. Boys, on the other hand, are expected to *do* something with their bodies and are judged more on that basis. Another way of stating it would be to suggest that when it comes to the physical side of the self, at least, girls tend to be judged more in terms of how they look and boys more in terms of how they perform. If this is true, then a tentative speculation about why it is that the rate of physical maturation has less dramatic effect on girls than boys is that girls have greater flexibility for altering or changing their looks than boys do for altering or changing their performances. Even a somewhat plain girl can look attractive with the aid of proper dress, padding, and cosmetics.

TO THINK ABOUT

Reflect back over your own adolescent years. Were you an early- or late-maturer? In what ways did your growth status affect your interpersonal relationships? What sorts of feedback about the physical "you" did you receive from your parents and teachers? How did that make you feel about yourself as a total person? In what two or three ways will your own experiences influence how you behave towards students you have in the future?

The pace and rate of an adolescent's physical development does make a difference in his personality evolvement and self-concept development. However, emergence of the adolescent self does not happen simply because a developing youngster grows older and taller but occurs, rather, because of the accomplishment of certain developmental tasks, an idea to which we turn next.

DEVELOPMENTAL TASKS OF ADOLESCENCE

As you may recall, Havighurst[35] has suggested that there are certain rather specific developmental "tasks" that a youngster must accomplish at his various stages of growth in order to reach the next level of development. A *developmental task,* then, is an event that occurs at a certain point in the life of an individual, successful achievement of which spurs him to further growth and probably success with later tasks, while failure inhibits growth and leads to disapproval by society and difficulty with later tasks.

The major developmental tasks confronting the adolescent boy and girl include the following:

1. Achieving new and more mature relations with age-mates of both sexes.
2. Achieving a masculine or feminine social role.
3. Accepting one's physique and using the body effectively.
4. Achieving emotional independence of parents and other adults.
5. Achieving assurance of economic independence.
6. Selecting and preparing for an occupation.
7. Preparing for marriage and family life.
8. Developing intellectual skills and concepts necessary for civic competence.
9. Desiring and achieving socially responsible behavior.
10. Acquiring a set of values and an ethic system as a guide to behavior.

In a sense, these ten developmental tasks are the prerequisite learnings and accomplishments necessary for successful adult living. Each task, in its own way, contributes to one's expanding sense of self, of who he is, of what he wants to be, and how he can best achieve his goals. Unless, for example, the adolescent boy and girl achieves greater maturity and confidence in his or her relations with the opposite sex during adolescence it becomes increasingly difficult to acquire these qualities as one moves into adulthood. The adolescent girl, let's say, who remains emotionally attached to her parents, who dates hardly at all, who fails to test her feminine self in different social roles, and who persists in attaching too much importance to what other people think is a poor risk to leave the psychological safety of perpetual adolescence.

Just as there are some individuals who remain psychological adolescents most of their lives, there are others who, unfortunately enough, scramble headlong into adulthood without completely working through the tasks of adolescence. An example of this could be the boy who drops out of school before he's either emotionally or educationally ready for economic independence. Another example could be the teen-age boy and girl who marry before they understand themselves well enough to know that the person they are marrying is really the one they can live with in an intimate relationship. One twenty-three-year-old girl, unhappily married after six years, expressed it this way during a counseling session:

> When Bill and I got married right after high school it was great. We dated each other all through high school and never really considered dating others. Marriage just seemed a natural outgrowth of our relationship. But now, I don't know, it's sorta like we've missed out on something—at least I feel that way and I think he does, too. Isn't it stupid? Here I've been married six years and I feel I'm into something I wasn't ready for in the first place.

This young lady is saying what many young adults feel as they look back over their adolescent years, namely the wish to have done things differently or at least to have had more heterosexual experiences while the opportunity was available.

The developmental tasks of adolescence are not simply hurdles that must be jumped in some mechanical way, but they are, in a deeper sense, highly personalized experiences, each of which helps the adolescent define himself to himself as a person and develop a recognizable and reasonably predictable "self."

Despite romantic or hostile assertions to the contrary, the single most important external influence in aiding or hindering the average adolescent in the accomplishment of these tasks are his parents. How important are parents? Let us now turn our attention to that question.

Parents continue to play a strong part in an adolescent's total growth and development.

IMPACT OF PARENTS ON THE ADOLESCENT'S GROWING SELF

Inasmuch as a major developmental task of adolescence is that of progress toward greater self-sufficiency and self-direction, it is not surprising that an air of tension exists between the adolescent and his parents as he struggles to find himself in his expanding social world. Parents, of course, are anxious to have their children grow up. Indeed, as you may have noticed yourself, when parents criticize an adolescent it is likely to include the observation that he is acting childishly. Although the young person is continually prodded toward adulthood, parents sometimes behave as if his reaching it is in some remote and far-off future. One frus-

196

trated sixteen-year-old boy expressed it this way during a group discussion: "Oh, I think my parents want me to be independent and think for myself alright, but apparently not while I'm still living at home." This youth's remark is probably true for many homes in which adolescents reside. Perhaps the observation that adulthood comes about two years later than the adolescent claims and about two years earlier than his parents will admit is more accurate than we realize.

The fact is that most parents do not easily let go of their children, a reality that has both good and bad points. The positive side is that the adolescent boy and girl must work harder and withstand stiffer challenges to prove to their parents and *themselves* that they really can make it on their own and that their self-concepts are sturdy enough to withstand both the responsibilities and setbacks accompanying independent adult living. The negative side is that parents who hang on too tightly can cause a young person struggling to be free to either feel guilty (My parents need me so—how can I leave them?), or inadequate (They don't trust me on my own—maybe I'm not able enough). As Douvan and Adelson[36] point out in the results of their study of a large number of adolescents, either too much or too little involvement can inhibit the adolescent's achievement of independence. If parents are too little involved, the security necessary for self-direction is underdeveloped. On the other hand, too much involvement may generate dependency needs that interfere with the growth of independence. Let's see what research has to say about the relationship between parent-child relations and the development of independence.

TO THINK ABOUT

How do you feel about the amount of independence you experienced as an adolescent at home? About right? Too little? If it was what you consider to be too little, did this cause you difficulties after you left home for college? How do you think high school teachers can respond most effectively to an adolescent's growing needs for independence and freedom? Jot down two or three ideas you'd like to recommend to high school teachers.

_____

_____

_____

Parent Relationships and the
Development of Independence

The achievement of independence, of finally "being on one's own," is a major developmental task of adolescence. A very important variable in the accomplishment of that task involves the parents' overall behavior along the dimension of authority and control versus freedom and autonomy.

In an effort to study how parental behavior influences the development of independence in adolescence, Elder[37] studied 7,400 adolescents and identified the following parent-child relationships:

Autocratic. No allowance is provided for the youth to express his views on a subject nor for him to assert leadership or initiative in self-government.

Authoritarian. Although the adolescent contributes to the solution of problems, his parents always decide issues according to their own judgment.

Democratic. The adolescent contributes freely to discussion of issues relevant to his behavior and may even make his own decisions; however, in all instances the final decision is either formulated by parents or meets their approval.

Equalitarian. This type of structure represents minimal role differentiation. Parents and the adolescent are involved to a similar degree in making decisions pertaining to the adolescent's behavior.

Permissive. The adolescent assumes a more active and influential position in formulating decisions that concern him than do his parents.

Laissez faire. The position of the adolescent in relation to that of his parents in decision making is clearly more differentiated in terms of power and activity. In this type of relationship the youth has the option of either subscribing to or disregarding parental wishes in making his decisions.

Ignoring. This type of structure, if it can be legitimately considered as such, represents actual parental divorcement from directing the adolescent's behavior.

You can see that as the parent-child relationships move from the autocratic to the ignoring type there is a gradual increase in the adolescent's making his own decisions and a concurrent decrease in parents making decisions for him. Just as these relationship styles represent variations in the allocation of power between parents and the adolescent, so, too, do they represent different patterns of communication. In the autocratic structure communication is primarily from parent to child, while in the permissive structure it is primarily from child to parent.

As might be expected, more fathers were rated as authoritarian or autocratic (35 percent) by the adolescents in this study than were mothers (22 percent). This is fairly consistent with other research that shows that normal adolescents see their fathers as the harsher disciplinarian and more aggressive and their mothers as more emotionally supportive, affectionate, and protective.[38-40] Another interesting finding was that both mothers and fathers were inclined to treat older adolescents more permissively than younger ones, although, again, it was the mother who was judged as shifting more toward permissiveness than the father.

How did 7,400 adolescents respond to these varying patterns of parent-child relationships? It was found that those exposed to *democratic* practices considered their parents most fair (approximately 85 percent for both mother and father), with equalitarian parents ranking second. Autocratic parents (those who "just tell" their children what to do) ranked lowest. These results are consistent with other findings which, together, support the hypothesis that democratic communication between parents and adolescents encourages identification and closeness, while autocratic communication fosters resentment and distance.[41,41]

TO THINK ABOUT

How do the findings mentioned above square with your feelings about your own parents? What implications can you see here for teachers? Indeed, what implications can you see here for yourself as a teacher?

In a related study, Elder[43] subdivided the three major categories of child-rearing patterns (autocratic, democratic, laissez faire) into those parents who frequently explained their rules for conduct and expectations, and those who did not. As you might expect, democratic and permissiveness parents were more apt to give explanations than autocratic parents. Indeed, it is precisely *because* democratic and permissive parents gave more explanations for their rules and expectations that they were perceived as exercising a "legitimate" use of their power. Consistent with other research results, this suggests that adolescents are more likely to have positive feelings toward their parents and be more likely to behave on the basis of internalized standards of behavior if parents make some effort to "legitimatize their power"—in other words, are willing to both explain and listen.[44,45]

All in all, the evidence points strongly to the conclusion that lack of confidence and low independence are apt to occur most frequently among adolescents of autocratic parents who seldom make either their parental rules of conduct or expectations clear. Conversely, democratic practices, which are associated with explanations by parents for their rules of conduct and expectations, enhance the possibility of learning to be independent in several different ways: (1) by providing opportunities to participate in the family's decision-making machinery; (2) by encouraging positive identification with the parent, based on love and respect for the child, rather than rejection or indifference; (3) by themselves being models of reasonable independence.

A growing child cannot very well learn to think for himself unless he has some opportunity to actually practice thinking for himself as he grows up. The very autocratic parent who says "Do it my way" or the very permissive parent who says, "Do whatever you want" offer little in the way of either constructive alternative or direct guidance, both of which are necessary and helpful prerequisites to the development of independent living.

Another phenomenon that interferes with the development of healthy adolescent independence is what seems to be the existence of a parental lag in many parent-child relationships. That is, many parents find it difficult to change their behavior toward the children as the children grow older. Many times parents tend to use external events, such as a sixteenth birthday or graduation from high school, as indicators of when their children are "grown up." Bowerman and Kinch[46] have noted that a "law of preservation" seems to be dominant in many human relationships. That is, people are inclined to behave in a certain way toward others until they are forced to change by the pressure of external circumstances. Whether one calls this lag, a law of preservation, or a principle of social inertia, the phenomenon seems plain enough, and it is part of the explanation for why parents sometimes continue to treat their adolescents as younger than they really are. A serious consequence of this, of course, is that independence training is stifled when parents act as if their adolescent children are too immature to assume new responsibilities. For example, some high school age youths are still told by their parents what to wear, when to study and for how long, who they can date and who they can't, who they should and shouldn't be friends with, and on and on. There is a vast difference between *telling* an adolescent what he should do or be or what to wear, etc., and expressing an active but noncoercive interest in his tastes and activities. Along this line, Rosenberg[47] found that confidence and self-esteem were highest among adolescents whose parents expressed strong interest in, and knowledge about, their opinions and activities and who encouraged independent behavior and active participation in family affairs.

Religion and Social Class as Variables in Independence Training

As a general rule, Protestant parents begin independence training earlier than do Catholic parents, which suggests that Catholic parents are more reluctant to give their adolescents freedom in self-direction than Protestants.[48]   Research indicates that Catholic and Protestant parents are similar in the sort of control they exercise over their *younger* sons and daughters and that only Catholic and Protestant fathers (but not mothers) differ in their relationships to *older* adolescents.[49]   When the children are older, proportionately more of the Protestant youths perceive their fathers as democratic, equalitarian, or permissive, and proportionately more of the Catholic youths perceive their fathers as either autocratic or authoritarian. This appears to indicate that there is a tendency among Catholic fathers, but not Catholic mothers, to increase limits and controls as the children get older—a practice that is reversed among Protestant fathers.   Keep in mind that this is a statistical generalization and there are many individual variations within it.

With respect to social-class effects, there is evidence suggesting that differences (though present) are not so great as they once used to be.[50,51] Urie Bronfenbrenner, a well-known developmental psychologist, has noted:

> As of 1957, there are suggestions that the cultural gap may be narrowing. Spock has joined the Bible on the working-class shelf. . . .   Apparently "love" and "limits" are both watchwords for the coming generation of parents.   As Mrs. Johnson, down in the flats, puts away the hairbrush and decides to have a talk with her unruly youngster "like the book says," Mrs. Thomas, on the hill, is dutifully striving to overcome her guilt at the thought of giving John the punishment she now admits he deserves.[52]

Overall, there is a tendency for middle-class parents to be perceived as more democratic, equalitarian, or permissive, while lower-class parents are seen as more autocratic and authoritarian.   When class differences in frequency of parental explanations are examined, it is generally found to be the case that the lower-class autocratic mothers and middle-class democratic and permissive mothers are more likely to explain rules and give reasons for existing family policies.[53]

In summary, autocratic and authoritarian parents are most likely to be fathers with older sons and daughters; to be of lower-class status; to have a high school education or less; to be Catholic; and to have three or more children.   Democratic and equalitarian parents are most apt to be mothers; to be parents of older youths; to be in the socioeconomic middle-class bracket; to have at least some college education; to be Protestant; and to have one or two children.   In short, middle-class Protestant parents in one- or two-child families seem most inclined to allow their high school age children greater responsibility and freedom for directing their own behavior in life.

201

> **TO THINK ABOUT**
>
> In what ways does the research related to social class and religious background square with your own experiences? How does it differ? If it does differ, think about *why* it does and who the important people were in your life who contributed to it being different?

Sex of Parent and Child as Factors

Research shows that the specific impact that parents have on an adolescent's emerging self depends not only on whether the youngster is a boy or girl, but also on the sex of the parent. For example, there is evidence to indicate that a boy's adjustment during adolescence depends to some extent on the level of affection existing in his relationship to his father. As an illustration of this, an interesting cross-cultural study of a group of adolescent boys found that boys who experience "insufficient parental affection" were less secure, less self-confident, and less well adjusted socially than boys whose fathers showed sufficient affection.[54]

An investigation by Bronfenbrenner[55] examined parental behaviors and the development of responsibility and leadership qualities in a large group of fifteen- and sixteen-year-old youths. It was found that three parental behavior variables were related to the development of responsibility in young people, these being rejection, neglect, and affiliative companionship. The adolescent who was judged to be the least responsible was most likely to describe his parents as inclined to complain about and ridicule him, compare him unfavorably with other children, and spend little time with him. An interesting sex difference was observed, however. For example, responsibility in boys was associated with nurturance, affection, and companionship, especially from the mother, and with relatively high amounts of discipline and authority from the father. At the same time, these same variables were found to deter the development of responsibility in girls, for whom heavy paternal discipline, in particular, was deleterious to a high rating on responsibility.

The antecedents of a self-attitude that encourages leadership qualities in the adolescent were not too different from those related to responsibility. It was noted, however, that parental overprotectiveness seemed to undermine an adolescent's leadership attempts. Again, a marked sex difference was apparent. Specifically, it was noted that ". . . affiliative companionship, nurturance, principled discipline, affection, and affective reward appear to foster the emergence of leadership in sons but discourage it in daughters."[56]

In terms of personality needs, this sex difference in antecedents of the self-attitudes leading to a high level of responsibility and leadership ap-

202

parently means something different for the adolescent girl than for the adolescent boy. At least one explanation is that in our culture both responsibility and leadership are important and rewarded aspects of the male sex role but less so for the female sex role. Thus, the explicit expression of these characteristics in a girl is not so likely to win her the praise and encouragement of a proud father or a pleased mother as might more likely be the case for a boy.

Males and Females Are Treated Differently

The fact is that boys and girls within and outside the family units are treated differently by adult men and women and this contributes significantly to how the adolescent views him- or herself. For example, there is increasing evidence to suggest that expressions of affection and punishment, as two major factors in parent-child interactions, are used in somewhat different ways, for somewhat different purposes, and with somewhat different effects when applied to boys and girls. An illustration of this is in the evidence showing that girls are more likely than boys to be subjected to "love-oriented" child-rearing techniques and that such techniques are effective in encouraging healthy social adjustment.[57,58] In contrast, a rather different child-rearing style is used for boys. That is, parents are more likely to use physical punishment, to be permissive of and even encourage aggressiveness, to minimize the emphasis on conformity, and to stress the value of independence and achievement. With boys, parent-child interactions seem to be focused more specifically on *directing him toward the environment*, while with girls the emphasis is more on *protecting her from the environment*. These contrasting means and ends help explain why it is that girls are usually found to be more obedient, cooperative, and, in general, better socially adjusted than boys of comparable ages.[59,60]

TO THINK ABOUT

To what extent do you think that the impact of the Women's Liberation Movement will change the nature of parent-child interactions so that growing boys and girls will be treated more or less equally and with less regard for sex differences? As it is, boys and girls are treated somewhat differently by their parents and teachers. How do you feel about this? Some say that's the way it should be and others say treat both the same. What's your stance on this?

At the same time, research also indicates that adolescent girls also tend to be more anxious, dependent, and sensitive to rejection. Apparently characteristics such as independence, self-confidence, initiative, and self-sufficiency, which are included among the top criteria of an adolescent boy's successful socialization in our culture, require for their development a different balance of authority and affection than is found in the more "love-oriented" strategies employed with girls.   Although parental affection is important for a boy's overall socialization and self-concept development, it must be accompanied by and be compatible with a strong blend of parental discipline.   Otherwise, the adolescent boy is likely to find himself in the same situation as the girl, who, having been the object of greater affection, is also more sensitive to its withdrawal.   In other words, since a girl is likely to *receive* more affection than the boy, she is also likely to be *more responsive* to its loss, which is, in fact, why her self-attitude is marked by predispositions to greater anxiety, dependency, and sensitivity to rejection.   Along this same vein, Hoffman and others[61] have noted that ". . . It seems likely that assertiveness in girls is less valued by others," and that girls are more likely to "respond to the emotional rejection that coercion (being aggressive, getting others to do what she wants, etc.) implies."   This is not the sort of behavior normally encouraged in an adolescent boy and as you might suspect, dependent behaving boys at any age have a more difficult time developing a healthy self-concept than those boys who are more independent, aggressive, and able to hold their own. Returning to Bronfenbrenner again, he makes the point that "for boys, who tolerate and require higher levels of discipline on an affectional base, problems derive most commonly from the failure on the part of parents to provide adequate emotional support and—especially firm authority."[62]

In general, research is showing that the emergence of a healthy adolescent self-image is a function of an optimal balance of affection and control, which is different for boys and girls and involves different risks in the process of child rearing.   A healthy self-concept, at least as it is expressed in getting along with others, being accepted as a leader and assuming responsibility, is most likely to be encouraged when sons and daughters experience the *parent of the same sex* taking an active part in the child-rearing process.

Sex-Role Identification Is Important

There are definite indications that appropriate sex-role identification results in better adjustment to the day-to-day demands of living.   For example, Heilbrum[63,64] found that male college students who identified with their fathers were better adjusted and had a stronger sexual identity (were more certain about their "maleness") than males who were not so identified with their fathers.   In a similar vein, another researcher found that the degree of "likeness" or "identification with" the father was related to the popularity of high school boys.[65]   That is, popular, likeable boys were more identified with their fathers. Just as the father plays an increasingly important role in the boy's life as he grows older, there is also evidence to show that mother assumes a more prominent role in the girl's life as she grows older.[66] In sum, boys thrive in a patriarchal context and girls in a matriarchal one.

Autonomy a Major Goal

Although adolescent boys and girls both share the goal of emotional independence as a major developmental task, the data reported by Douvan and Adelson[67] suggest sex differences in the expression and achievement of autonomy.

Surprisingly, adolescent girls seem to be more advanced in behavioral autonomy despite the fact that they are somewhat more restricted and protected by parents. For example, by the time they are eighteen more girls than boys report holding jobs, dating earlier, and taking a greater share of household responsibilities. Even though girls mature earlier than boys, socially as well as physically, they remain closer emotionally to the family. Contrary to what popular and fictional literature may lead us to believe, few adolescents of either sex go through a dramatic struggle for independence, and such an occurrence is even less prevalent among girls. Although an early or middle adolescent girl may have disagreements with her parents about such things as clothes, makeup, dating, how late she stays out, and so on, most of these issues are pretty well resolved by the time the girl is seventeen or eighteen. Conflicts that occur after that point are more likely to center around differences in attitudes and values related to the more general and ambiguous area of philosophy of living or life-style.

This route toward emotional independence is not so smooth for boys. They are more inclined to actively rebel against their parents and look to their peers as a primary reference group. In fact, you may recognize this behavior as being consistent with the earlier observation of boy's greater aggressiveness and the extent to which dependency is approved of in girls and disapproved of in boys. All in all, mild expressions of antisocial activity, especially if engaged in with a gang of friends, seems to be a pretty normal way for the adolescent boy to test his emotional biceps and burgeoning masculinity.

Parental Influence Is Strong

On the whole, the main trend during the adolescent years as far as influence of parents is concerned is toward a more thorough internalization of parental values, even though there may be considerable hassling about particular points. This generalization is especially true for girls, who are more apt to be identified with the parental point of view.

In fact, the influence of parents on an adolescent's developing self extends well into adult life. It is not uncommon that the very boy who battles his parents' beliefs and values so ferociously in his teens comes to adopt those same beliefs and values as his own as he enters his twenties.[68] Others retain undercurrents of bitterness toward their parents and still others acquire a deeper feeling of respect. Some, when they have children of their own, recognize and appreciate for the first time what their parents mean to them. As one young mother expressed it, "I never had parents until I had children." Suffice it to say, parents play a critical part in influencing the shape and direction of an adolescent's growing self. So do peers, an idea to which we turn next.

IMPACT OF PEER RELATIONSHIPS ON
THE ADOLESCENT'S GROWING SELF

It is no secret that an adolescent's peer relationships become increasingly more important as he moves into his junior high and high school

"NOW, MR. FILBRICK, JUST WHAT'S WRONG WITH THE WAY MY DAUGHTER DRESSES FOR SCHOOL?"

Parental behavior has a strong effect on how growing children and adolescents dress and behave. (A. L. Kaufman, reprinted by permission of Masters Agency)

Long telephone conversations (to the dismay of many parents), girl-talk, boy-talk, and boy-girl talk are all important inputs to an adolescent's growing and maturing self. (AT&T Co.)

years. Peer group influence hits a peak around middle adolescence and begins to decline after that, when young people go their separate ways, marry, and begin setting up standards for their own nuclear families. However, during the junior high and high school years, adolescents have a "youth culture" of their own, overlapping with, and yet separate from, the larger society in which they live.

There is little question that the peer group has an enormous impact on an adolescent's developing sense of self. Why is the adolescent peer culture successful in shaping the behavior and self-attitudes of young people? Medinnus and Johnson look at it this way:

> It succeeds because it is dangerous and exciting and it requires real skills . . .; because it is *not* based on such things as class distinctions, which are contrary to our expressed adult values system but not to our actual behavior; because it *is* based on the idea that the individual should be judged in terms of personal attributes and accomplishments because it is in many ways more humane and accepting of individual differences than adult cultural values; because it is concerned with expanding self-awareness at a time when people have few means of discovering themselves; because it is against sham; and because it fulfills the needs of young people better than does the adult culture.[69]

Major Functions of the Peer Group

Ausubel[70] has identified seven basic functions the peer group serves during adolescence. In somewhat modified form, in view of research that has appeared since Ausubel's discussion, these functions are as follows:

1. To some extent, *the peer group takes the place of the family,* which is to say that a youngster can feel a certain status, or lack of it, independent of what or who his family is. As you might suspect, this is invaluable preparation for adulthood because it gives one a chance for more objective feedback than parents can usually provide.

2. *Peer group membership is a useful stabilizer* during a period of rapid transition. In light of the incredible endocrinal, developmental, and social changes that occur during the brief period of adolescence, it is comforting to know that others are going through the same thing. As one sixteen-year-old boy put it, "I hate these dumb pimples, but I'd hate them more if I was the only one who had them."

3. *The peer group can be an important source of self-esteem* in the sense of being important to someone outside the primary family unit. Of course it can work the other way, too, particularly for the adolescent who is isolated or scapegoated.

4. Ausubel takes more or less for granted an issue over which there is some disagreement, namely, that *adolescents allow their peer group the authority to set standards.* The reasoning is that adolescents thereby affirm their own right to self-determination, since the peer group basically represents what they value in the first place.

This may be, but it is not certain that the impact of the peer group is any more intense than the influence of the family. Although the adolescent moves initially in the direction of the more liberal peer group, there is evidence to suggest that, for basic life decisions, the standards of the family carry more weight than the peer group when the two are in conflict.[71-74]

There are exceptions to this. For example, where parental warmth and a sense of "equal rights" within the home are at a minimum, as is sometimes the case, the peer group may provide both the security and the models that youngsters need. We can say with some certainty that the greater the wall between the adolescent and his family, the more elaborate the peer culture becomes and the more he will turn to it for support and identity. Not infrequently those teen-age youths who are most involved and identified with their peer culture are those who have strained and difficult relationships with their parents.

5. *The peer group insulates and protects* adolescents to some extent from the coercions that adults are likely to impose on young people. When the adolescent says something on the order of "Well everyone else is going (or doing it, or wearing it, or whatever), why can't I?", he is raising what has become an almost universal wail of defensive protest designed to

208

implore restricting adults to change their minds. As you can imagine (or remember from your own adolescent years), there is a certain safety in lodging this protest while holding membership within the security of one's peer group. Being able to say, for example, that "everyone" is doing it is a much more persuasive statement than "he" or "she" is doing it. There is both safety and strength in numbers and membership in the peer culture provides a little of each.

6. Another thing *the peer group provides is an opportunity to practice by doing.* Dating, participation in extracurricular activities, and bull sessions about life, sex, future goals, and the world generally are all important rehearsal experiences for eventual adulthood. As one practices by doing, the peer group is a source of instant feedback; it is an audience of self-proclaimed critics watching for flaws in the performance of their own kind and in themselves. Feedback from peers is important because it is objective (sometimes unmercifully so), and it provides cues and information that can be used to modify and refine the adolescent's emerging concept of who he is as a person.

7. Particularly for disadvantaged youngsters, *the peer group offers a psychosocial moratorium* that many parents simply cannot provide. For example, Hoffman and Saltzstein's[75] research relating parent discipline to a child's moral development found that although middle-class youngsters used their parents as models for moral and conscience development, there was very little of this parental modeling among lower socioeconomic status youths. It may very well be that lower socioeconomic youths are more psychologically dependent on their peers and thus use them as models "to be like" more extensively.

Peer Acceptance and Social Adjustment

Being liked and accepted is important at any age, but it seems particularly crucial during the adolescent years. Sometimes the dependency on group approval is so severe that it seems something on the order of a "popularity neurosis." Being noticed and feeling reasonably accepted are important prerequisites to getting feedback and to taking the necessary risks to try out different personalities or relationship "styles" from time to time. Boys show themselves off in what they consider to be their masculine best, and girls in their most feminine and alluring best. No matter how interested in their own group various clusters of boys and girls seem to be, at a deeper level they are really proclaiming and advertising how interesting they are. Individuals within any given peer group may be busy politicking and making time, but so is everyone else. In a sense, they are all campaigning for office, for the esteem and acclaim and recognition that will tell them where they finished in the voting. Actually, the adolescent's concern

209

about getting along with others or having a "good personality" is not so much a search for inner strength as it is a rummaging for the tricks that will gain him approval and acceptance, whether it be in making the varsity team, playing a musical instrument, getting high grades, developing into the class clown, being active in extracurricular activities, and so on.

> ## TO THINK ABOUT
>
> What do you remember about your own needs for approval and popularity in high school? Was being approved and accepted pretty important to you? What did you do to get it? As you think back on the way you recall yourself as being, what would you change about yourself if you had to relive your high school days again? Why?

Ironically, the occasional adolescent who is mature enough to be more independent of the whims, wishes, and fads of his contemporaries and goes his own way may find that his peers flock around him as if he were a tower of strength. It is almost as if they want to find what his secret is so as to be more that way themselves. When you think about it, there are very few people—young or old—who enjoy the ingratiating submissiveness demanded of them when they are dependent on another person or group of people as their source of self-esteem and self-worth. Perhaps this is one of the reasons that most of us admire and even feel a bit envious of the strong person able to hold his own in the face of strong adversity and/or group pressure.

The intense need to be liked and accepted during adolescence is neither a negative characteristic nor is it in any sense abnormal. In fact, the youngster who reflects the qualities that make him more or less acceptable to his peers has many advantages. In a study involving over 2,000 adolescents, it was found that young persons who were accepted by others had, on the whole, a more favorable view of themselves than the rejected ones. In addition, they had better relationships with their parents and teachers.[76]

Peer Acceptance Related to Academic Success

There is also evidence to show that peer acceptance is related to success in high school, at least as far as its completion is concerned. For example, Gronlund and Holmlund[77] examined the high school careers of children who had high or low sociometric status as determined by tests administered when they were in the sixth grade and compared these with the records of these same individuals seven years later. What they found was that 82 percent of the high-status pupils, as compared to low-status pupils, graduated from high school. In other words, about three times as many students in the low-status group as in the high status group dropped out of high school. We might also note that the difference in intelligence between the two groups (high-status average IQ was about 109; low-status average IQ, about 101) was not large enough to account for this difference in the number of dropouts. Although we cannot conclude from this that low social acceptance causes poor high school performance or that high social acceptance leads to superior high school performance, we can conclude that low peer-group acceptance may be one of the contributing factors to a particular adolescent's subpar academic achievement record. Significantly, it was also noted that a considerably large number of those who had been most accepted by their sixth-grade peers joined clubs and organizations, participated in varsity sports, and held various leadership positions in high school.

Personal Adjustment not Necessarily Related to Social Success

Although it is true that acceptance by one's peers very often leads to social success, we cannot take for granted that social success, as indicated by high popularity ratings, automatically leads to healthy personal adjustment. Nor, for that matter, can we assume that a low degree of acceptance by peers is indicative of current or future social maladjustment. Why?

In the first place, to judge the meaning of high or low peer acceptance it is necessary to consider the criteria of standards and values being applied. In some high schools, as you know, athletics are prized above all else and in fact the morale of an entire school may fluctuate with the won-loss column of the current varsity sport. In still other high schools, honor rolls and a college-orientation are so highly esteemed that even the team's best fullback has to show academic promise to be fully accepted.

In the second place, to understand the meaning of high peer acceptance it is also necessary to consider the price a person may pay to get it. For example, the adolescent who gives up his own natural bent and inclinations so he can "go along with the crowd" may be the very one who so lacks confidence in himself that he will do almost anything to be liked, no matter what the price. Sometimes the most popular members of a crowd include those whose sense of personal adequacy and mental health is so tenuous that they can feel worthwhile only by being a friend to all and enemy to none. Indeed, there is evidence to show that among those who attain a high level of social acceptance on a sociometric test, there are some who are "seriously disturbed."[78] In order to assess all the implications of peer acceptance or lack of it, we have put it in perspective by first of all determining its criteria and its price. We probably all know persons with whom we went to high school who never really "made" it with their peers during that stage of growth, but who went on to be successful—educationally, socially, and economically—as they moved into young adulthood when being popular, in terms of getting along with people, was less important than being competent, in terms of accomplishment and getting things done.

Importance of Peer-Group Culture

All in all, the peer group and the youth culture provide the medium within which one secures an identity, however tentative it may be. Because the adolescent must separate himself from his parents, he must initially at least, reject their dictates and, occasionally, their values. Why should this be? As you may recall from personal experience, "achieving" an identity is an active process, not one of passively purchasing the achievements of others. The typical adolescent is driven by a strong need to become who *he* is, not who his parents are. In order to do this, the adolescent becomes less like his parents and more like his peers. Unfortunately some parents overreact to this shift in affiliation by behaving as if their youngsters had sworn a blood allegiance to a group of youthful desperadoes bent on overthrowing the entire concept of parenthood. Nothing could be further from the truth. It is simply a necessary phase that all adolescents go through (just as each of us did) in finding themselves. If a growing adolescent boy or girl is psychologically healthy, each must fill the need of being his or her own man or woman before he can be anyone else's.

Another reason behind the peer group's being an important medium for the adolescent's total socialization and self-definition is that adults have been negligent in providing clear landmarks and in institutionalizing systematic steps to autonomy. Not surprisingly, the adolescent constitutes his own society. The result has been a youth culture that provides a series of eccentric, substitute vehicles toward the achievement of independence and maturity which, though characteristically non-adult, nonetheless encourages many of the same behaviors found in the adult world such as conformity and stereotyping. What is important is that the adolescent peer culture develops its own criteria of good and bad, right and wrong, successful and nonsuccessful and thereby offers its own series of demarcations to identity. Thus, through an elaborate system of rewards and punishments, the vast social system of the peer culture is defined and constituted.

YOUTH ALIENATION: ANTECEDENTS, EXPRESSIONS, AND OUTCOMES

The label *alienated youth* has come to have general reference to all those young people who, for one reason or other, feel somewhat estranged from and betrayed by, the larger society in which they live.

Actually, the problem of disenchanted youth is not a new one (although each new generation of parents acts as if it is), having as it does roots into the distant past. Aries,[79] for example, has noted that in 1649 in Die, England, headmasters barricaded themselves inside the college when students fired cannon shots, threw desks out windows, and tore up books. At Rugberg, in 1768, students burned the books and desks and took refuge on an island where they were finally subdued by an army assault. In 1818, two companies of troops with fixed bayonets were called in to suppress an uprising of students at Winchester. More recently, of course, came the pranks and shenanigans of the 1930 and 1940's followed by doldrums and apathy of the 1950's. While adults were lamenting about the mid-century youth's lack of spirit, his souped-up successor of the late sixties sneaked up on us, thumbed his nose, and proclaimed, "Hey, let's change things!"

Antecedents to Adolescent Protest and Alienation

The wave of youthful protest and alienation that has surfaced in the past ten years or so grew primarily as a response to the struggle of southern black students to achieve their basic civil rights. It expanded rapidly "to include such issues as nuclear testing and the arms race, attacks on civil liberties, the problems of the poor in urban slum ghettos, democracy and educational quality in universities, and the war in Vietnam."[80]

What are some of the underlying antecedent conditions and feelings of such protests? On the basis of his research into the problem, Flacks[81] has suggested seven possibilities: (1) *romanticism*—a quest for "free" self-expression, with an emphasis on "experiencing" and "knowing," unrestrained by highly rational pursuits and attitudes; (2) *anti-authoritarianism*—a decided hostility toward what is perceived as "establishmentmade rules" and centralized decision making; (3) *equalitarianism, populism*—a strong belief in the need for direct participation in the making of decisions by those affected by them; (4) *antidogmatism*—a fairly intense resentment toward doctrinaire ideological interpretations of contemporary events; (5) *moral purity*—a strong antipathy to self-serving behavior, which many view as pervading the adult culture, as well as a particularly strong

213

aversion to "hypocritical" or "phoney" behavior; (6) *sense of community* — a need to break through traditional barriers that discourage the establishment of warm, open, and honest human relationships; and (7) *anti-institutionalism* — an aggressive distrust of conventional institutional, "establishment" roles, whether in industry, the professions, science, or politics.

There is little doubt that high school and college youths are changing. It would, however, be a mistake to conclude that student protest and alienation are characteristic of the majority of young people. Facts do not support rampant protest and alienation. At most, only a small percentage, probably not more than 9 to 15 percent, of any student body is involved in protest movements.[82,83]

The fact that student "activists" are in the minority does not mean that their contributions to the youth culture are not important. Indeed, their cries of protest have started many social changes. There are, however, different expressions of student activitism and alienation. Let's look at these differences.

The Student Activist

The student activist does not always fit the popular stereotype of the bearded, long-haired, unkept, Marxist-influenced, unconventional, unhappy, parentally rejected young person. Actually, the student activist tends to be raised in an upper-class family with a relatively high income. His father is apt to be a professional (college faculty, lawyer, doctor), and his mother is likely to have a career of her own.[84,85]

It is interesting to note that the views of activist young people rather than being in opposition to those of their parents, tend to be rather similar to them. Research shows, for instance, that activist sons not only tend to have liberal fathers and to share their father's liberal values, but they tend to carry these values further and to act on them in a more assertive or "radical" fashion.[86] Thus, the popular notion that activist youths are either overtly or covertly involved in a "rebellion" against parental values is not supported. A more tenable view is that a great majority of activist students are attempting to live out the political aspirations of their parents.

It is worth noting that parents of activists have generally been found to be more "permissive" in child-rearing practices than nonactivists. The likelihood of parents' "intervening strongly" in the decisions of their adolescent sons and daughters has been found to be significantly less among activist parents.[87]

Compared to nonactivists, activist students have been found to be brighter, more successful academically, more flexible, and more au-

214

tonomous. In addition, they have also been found to be more anxious, more imaginative, more concerned with reflective and abstract thinking, and more liberal and less conventional in religious values.[88,89]

Why activists protest. We might ask, if activist youths are not rebelling against parental values, if they come from reasonably affluent backgrounds, and if they are generally brighter and more successful than their peers, why are they prone to protest? There are several possible reasons for this. One is that in the absence of parental values that are different from their own, and in the absence of parents who say "you must do it my way," they turn to the social world around them as the arena within which to test themselves. Another possibility is that activist youths get caught up in living out the expressed but unimplemented values of their liberal, socially conscious parents. Indeed, there are indications that the youthful activist is more likely to criticize his parents' failure to practice what they preach than he is to criticize the values themselves. It has also been suggested that parents may be "secretly proud of their children's eagerness to implement the ideals they as parents have only given lip-service to."[90]

Most young people see no reason to question the current sociopolitical system primarily because they have never visualized any other. But a small minority of activist youths have succeeded far beyond their limited strength or political wisdom because, as psychoanalyst Erik Erikson has observed, they "draw out and inflame the latent aggravations of that majority of young people who would otherwise choose only to help themselves."[91]

Unfortunately, some student activists get so caught up in their goals that almost any means to appear to be justified in reaching them. The point has been made that in pursuit of his own personal principles, an activist "may ride rough-shod over others who do not share these principles, will disregard human beings or even destroy human life."[92] What is advertised as a lofty personal principle may in fact be constituted as dogmatic and destructive moral self-righteousness. There are some activists who would not hesitate to injure either people or property in order to fulfill their own moral principles. Consider, for example, the zealous Pre-Nazi German youth movement in which their perception of right and proper morality went hand in hand with vicious anti-Semitism. Pascal expressed it best: "Evil is never done so thoroughly or so well as when it is done in good conscience."

The point is that the ultimate success of youthful activist movements depends on whether the degree of potential destructive zealotry, which seems inherent in most activist ventures, is matched by development of other human dimensions, most especially compassion, love, and empathic understanding of the total human condition.

215

The Culturally Alienated

Whereas the activist aggressively attempts to change the world around him, alienated young people are inclined to have the dismal and sometimes hopeless feeling that meaningful change of the social and political world is impossible. Although alienated and activist youth come largely from the same social-class and educational backgrounds, there are important psychological and ideological differences that separate them. Unlike the activist youth who shares his parents' values, an alienated young person is likely to reject his parents' values. Indeed, the father of an alienated youth is frequently viewed "as a man who has 'sold out' to the pressures for success and status in American society."[93]

Like the activist, alienated youths are frequently bright and talented, although they are typically less committed to academic values and intellectual pursuits. They are also more likely to be disturbed psychologically, particularly in their mother relationships. In the case of the activist, the mother is apt to be an important force in helping the son or daughter to become increasingly independent. The mother of the alienated adolescent, however, is inclined to be controlling and intrusive—oversolicitous and limiting, qualities that are not noted for helping a growing youngster develop a healthy self-image.[94,95]

Perhaps the most conspicuous characteristics of the culturally alienated student are his unwillingness to make any real commitment to either himself or to others; his abject scorn and contempt for society; his pervasively nihilistic, chaotic view of the world; and his emphasis on "inner experience" and "aesthetic awareness," as opposed to "achievement-oriented, practical, and disciplined doing."[96] The fate of the alienated adolescent is not a particularly bright one. In the face of uncertain and shifting values, Keniston correctly observes that this is the sort of youth who is likely to be "confused, disoriented, and unhappy. . . . The defiant face of public scorn and opposition soon gives way to clear unhappiness, depression, self-doubt, and apprehensiveness."[97]

Implications for Teachers

Every generation of youth has had, has, and will very likely continue to have its own expression of uniqueness. Whether we call them flappers, bobby-sockers, beatniks, hippies, yippies, or Jesus freaks, they will always be an active and innovative part of the contemporary scene. As teachers, we have to recognize that growing up means more than just growing bigger. It means growing away from authority and towards independence; it means growing different and being an individual with a self of one's very own; it means identifying to some extent with current youthful ideologies as a way

Growing away from authority and towards independence is not easy. Sometimes adolescents feel that the odds against them making it are overwhelming. (Dave Webb, *The State Journal*)

of establishing a philosophical framework within which a more personal concept of self can grow and develop.

Both parents and peers have important roles in the unfolding drama of an adolescent's life-style and self-image development. It is, however, worth noting that much of the evidence points to the parents as very likely the most crucial to a child's development. Their influence is incredibly powerful. If we hope to understand the child, we would do well to know as much as possible about the parents and their treatment of the child.

Adolescence is that time in a youngster's growth when he goes through a stage of psychosexual development that Erik Erikson[98] has identified as that of "identity versus identity diffusion." What he is suggesting is that every adolescent is faced with the basic developmental tasks of settling on the sex-role (masculine or feminine) and the tentative occupational identity with which he feels most comfortable, or, to put it a little differently, most himself. If he is unable to make these basic choices during his teen years, then he runs the risk of concluding his adolescence with an identity so dif-

217

fuse that he is unable to "take hold" of either a personal identity or occupational choice that makes sense to him.

The point is: The behavior of most normally developing adolescents will at different times reflect components of each of the two general youth styles we've just discussed. This is not only healthy, but necessary behavior. It is so because it means that a youngster is actively "trying himself out"; he's testing his emotional and mental muscle in a variety of roles and against entrenched social institutions such as parents, teachers, traditional lines of authority, traditional ways for doing things, and so on. As teachers, we need to keep in mind that it is only by testing himself in these ways that an adolescent can begin to realistically assess what is within his potential to be and become.

TO THINK ABOUT

Did you experience a certain amount of "alienated" behavior yourself during high school? How did you express it? How did you feel about it? How did teachers respond to it? As you think about the different ways students can be alienated to some extent from home, school, even society at large, what two or three suggestions can you offer teachers to help them handle alienated behavior constructively when it occurs?

INTELLECTUAL PROCESSES AND COGNITIVE FUNCTIONING

As you by now know, the Swiss biologist-psychologist Jean Piaget has made important contributions to our understanding of the intellectual development of children. His studies of mental development have identified four rather specific stages in a growing youngster's capacity for thinking and problem solving. Stage one begins with the sensorimotor phase of the toddler, whose mental growth centers around motor exploration, simple play activities, imitative behavior, and the translation of mental images into language. From this humble beginning, intellectual development proceeds through a preoperational stage, a state of concrete operations, and, finally, in adolescence, attains a level of intellectual maturation known as formal operations. Let's examine this more closely to understand what this means in practice.

Shift to Abstract Thinking: Piaget's Stage IV

According to Piaget,[99,100] a child at eleven or twelve years of age begins what he calls the "period of propositional or formal operations." This

In adolescence there is a shift away from concrete thinking to more abstract ways of conceptualizing. (Allyn and Bacon)

means that the child shifts away from the concrete, specific, black and white thinking of the preadolescent years into the more mature hypo-thetico-reasoning skills associated with adult problem solving. That is, a youngster between eleven and fifteen years of age slowly refines his ability to think in terms of "possible" rather than "here and now actual" states of affairs. It is during adolescence that one develops his capacity for imagining or hypothesizing that a certain situation exists, and this, then, is followed by reasoning that considers what might result from such a situation. Or, to phrase it another way, thinking behavior evolves from doing, to doing knowingly, to conceptualization. The rate of this development will vary from adolescent to adolescent because it is not only dependent on the maturation of the nervous system, but influenced heavily by each adolescent's specific social environment and experiential history.

Piaget's research on the development of thinking and intelligence has made it fairly clear that the evolution of formal thinking processes reaches its completion during adolescence.[101] Evidence indicates that it is between the years of about eleven to fifteen that a youngster develops and refines his capacity to think in terms of symbols. That is, real or concrete entities are able to be symbolically represented so that spatial and temporal limitations can be transcended. In this way, symbols enable him to think at a level detached from concrete reality. Whereas an elementary age child in the concrete thinking stage might ask, "What is it that makes me live?", a 15-year-old tenth-grader might ask, "What is the meaning of life?" The devel-

219

opment of the ability to think in terms of abstractions and symbols is one of the essential conditions for being able to operate at this formal, logical level. Thus, the symbols of language and mathematics can be used, beginning in early adolescence, to represent what *might* be the case, what *might* happen, and what outcomes *might* result.

Piaget's assumptions tested. In order to test Piaget's assumptions and findings about the development of formal thinking, Case and Collinson[102] presented a group of boys and girls from seven to eighteen with written materials in history, geography, and literature. Each child was asked questions about the material and then scored as giving an *intuitive* answer (lowest level of thinking), a *concrete* answer (next highest level), or a *formal* answer (highest level).

For instance, after reading a passage about an English church reformer by the name of Dunstan, the child was asked, "Was Dunstan a good man? Why?" If a child either failed to reply or said something like: "Because he was a good man and did as he was told, so that made him good," the child was said to be giving an intuitive answer. If on the other hand, the child answered: "Yes, he was a good man because he made the church better," he was scored as giving a concrete answer. It was scored this way because the child gave a very specific and concrete example of why Dunstan was good. A child was scored at the formal operation level if he gave a response such as: "He was good in some ways, but not in others, because he was trying to make the church powerful, although I don't think he was right in being cruel to those who disagreed with him." Here the child is able to appropriately use words such as "powerful," "cruel," and "disagreed," which are really conceptual labels that stand for complex behaviors. This sort of reasoning enables a child to see that Dunstan was neither all good nor all bad and that although it may be a legitimate aim to make the church powerful (a hypothesis), it does not necessarily follow that it is desirable to cruelly squash disagreement (a deduction).

The results were clear. Age eleven was the earliest age at which children gave more formal or concrete answers, rather than intuitive responses. Between eleven and thirteen years of age the children were giving more formal answers than either intuitive or concrete. However, it was also noted that the combined number of intuitive or concrete answers was greater than or equal to the number of formal answers given between eleven and thirteen. It was no contest between the ages of fourteen and eighteen. Here, formal answers outweighed intuitive and concrete responses by about eleven to one.

The results generally support Piaget's theory of intellectual development and the relationship between certain ages and stages of thinking. However, we should note that the findings of Case and Collinson also suggested that many children are at times able to engage in formal verbal reasoning before age eleven. What seems to happen is that, from ages seven through fifteen, there is a steady increase in the tendency to think formally rather than a sudden appearance of this higher level way of thinking.

Most children do, in fact, begin to reflect a formal, hypothetico-deductive thinking style around age eleven or so, but it is a thinking style that develops gradually, until it reaches full dominance by age fifteen or sixteen. However, the evidence suggests that eleven years may be roughly the age when it becomes a *favored* way of thinking, and not when it *first* begins to develop or be used.

Depending on the occasion and circumstances, the young adolescent may, therefore, think intuitively, concretely, or formally. The older he is, the more likely he or she is to think formally. How soon formal thinking makes its appearance and becomes dominant will vary from person to person because like all other behavioral expressions, it is a function of not only innate intelligence, but of experience, social class, ethnic background, and previous learning.

Not all psychologists agree with Piaget's assumption that the ability to think in different ways and at different levels is a developmental phenomenon. Bruner,[103] for example, has been a stout advocate of the notion that almost any way of thinking can be taught to children at any age, after they have learned to use the language.

Virtues to Adolescent Idealistic Thinking

In sum, when the adolescent acquires the capacity to think and reason symbolically, it becomes possible for him to escape the concrete here and now present of childhood and enter the world of ideas. This is an important prerequisite for future growth. A person does not become a true individual, in the sense of developing a reasonably accurate and positive self-image, until he reaches this stage of development and can integrate thoughts and feelings about himself into a total life philosophy that expands beyond the egocentric self-interest of childhood.

Adolescents are frequently accused of being idealistic thinkers. That may be the case, but they are not simply playing at idealism. Characteristically, most adolescents have a strong belief in the omnipotence of reflection, which is frequently coupled with a firm belief that the world can be remade through idealistic solutions. As pointed out several years ago by a group of child psychiatrists, we should not be too alarmed by either the intensity or extravagance of adolescents' idealistic thinking.[104] As adulthood settles in, ideas and behavior are tempered by experience and reality. For most, equilibrium is eventually restored and the individual is a better and probably wiser person for having lived through the idealism of youth.

221

EPILOGUE

However you look at it, adolescence represents a very special time in the chronology of a young person's developmental history. As a youngster moves from his junior high through his high school years, he not only grows as a physical person, but he develops as a psychological person as well. Middle childhood was a time when he began to consolidate and pull together a more definitive self-image. Adolescence is a time in his life when he works on refining that self-image and when he begins to develop, at a deeper level, that special feeling of being a unique individual.

A great many changes go on in an adolescent's life between eleven and eighteen years of age. He grows bigger, taller, and heavier; glandular eruptions convert him from an indifferent sexual person to one whose awakening sexuality adds a whole new dimension to how he sees himself as a total person; parental authority (and practically all else can be associated with parents) is questioned with increasing frequency and intensity; what one's friends are thinking, doing, and wearing becomes a reference base for both thought and action; intellectual processes grow from being able to think only about everyday, concrete, here-and-now happenings to complex social issues and the meaning of life itself.

Although the adolescent self seldom reaches full maturity during adolescence, it nonetheless makes significant strides in that direction. In order to mature completely, an adolescent has to outgrow his child self so he can assume the posture and responsibilities of an adult self.

The adolescent self is a tenuous, fragile thing which, not uncommonly, is marked by continual shifts in emphasis, direction, and expression. When we talk about the adolescent "self," what we have reference to is a kind of experimental personality "style" that may change, chameleon-like, on a moment's notice, depending on the strength of current social fads. Probably the most important considerations to keep in mind regarding the adolescent self is that it is incompletely formed and that many of its expressions are simply temporary mimicries of the youth culture in which it is nurtured. Persons who either work with or are the parents of adolescent youths would do well to keep in mind that a teen-ager must necessarily experience a great deal of changing and growing during his adolescent years. Sometimes we forget this and act as if the normal signals and stresses of growing up were symptoms of personality malfunction and disorder.

All in all, growing up is no simple task. One part of the adolescent boy or girl wants to feel safe and protected by parents who love him and tell him what to do, while another part of him wants to reach out for new experiences and take on new challenges. In a sense, it's like a kind of personal civil war. The conflict would not be half so troublesome if it were just a simple struggle between children and parents. Its complexity grows from the revolt of the maturing self against the baby self. Frequently, parents, teachers, and other authority figures get dragged into the strife because they are all mixed up in a young person's mind with the baby self. It may be helpful to keep this in mind so that we can understand that some of the rebel behavior of the adolescent is not so much a rebelling against his parents as against his love for his parents and his dependency on them and other authority figures. When you think about it, falling out of love with one's parents is the first step an adolescent boy or girl must take toward falling in love with a mate and beginning a new family.

A significant thing about many of today's young people is that they are not so much in revolt as they are in search of workable guidelines for their lives, their work, and their relationships—goals not unreasonable for any stage of development.

Write your own summary (major points, ideas, and concepts that had meaning for you).

_____

_____

_____

_____

_____

_____

_____

_____

_____

_____

REFERENCES

1. Aries, P. *Centuries of Childhood* (translated by R. Baldic). New York: Knopf, 1962.
2. Aries, P. *Centuries of Childhood.* Op. cit., 1962, p. 219.

3. Landis, P. H. *Adolescence and Youth.* New York: McGraw-Hill, 1945.

4. S. M. Jourard. "Healthy Personality and Self-Disclosure." In *Interpersonal Dynamics,* rev. ed., edited by W. G. Bennis et al. Homewood, Ill.: Dorsey Press, 1968, pp. 720–730.

5. Tanner, J. M. *Growth at Adolescence.* Springfield, Ill.: Thomas, 1955.

6. Greulich, W. W. "The Rationale of Assessing the Developmental Status of Children from Roentgenograms of the Hand and Wrist." *Child Development* 21(1950):33–44.

7. Olson, W. C. "Developmental Theory in Education." In *The Concept of Development,* edited by D. B. Harris. Minneapolis: University of Minnesota Press, 1958, pp. 259–274.

8. Eichorn, D. H. "Variations in Growth Rate." *Childhood Education* 44(January 1968):286–291.

9. Wattenberg, W. W. "The Junior High School — A Psychologist's View." *Bulletin of the National Association of Secondary School Principals* 49(April 1965):34–44.

10. Maresh, M. M. "Variations in Patterns of Linear Growth and Skeletal Maturation." *Journal of the American Physical Therapy Association* 44(1964):103–106.

11. Tanner, J. M. "Sequence, Tempo, and Individual Variation in Growth and Development of Boys and Girls Aged Twelve to Sixteen." *Daedalus* 100(Fall 1971):907–930.

12. Maresh, M. M. "Changes in Tissue Width During Growth." *American Journal of Disturbed Children* 3(1966):154.

13. Tanner, J. M. "Sequence, Tempo, and Individual Variation in Growth . . . Op. cit., 1971, p. 108.

14. Muuss, R. E. "Adolescent Development and the Secular Trend." *Adolescence* 5(1970):267–284.

15. Stone, L. J., and J. Church. *Childhood and Adolescence,* 3rd ed. New York: Random House, 1973, p. 422.

16. Muuss, R. E. "Adolescent Development and the Secular Trend." Op. cit., p. 269.

17. Jensen, A. R. "Reducing the Heredity-Environment Uncertainty." In *Environment, Heredity, and Intelligence,* Reprint Series no. 2 compiled from *Harvard Educational Review,* 1969, pp. 209–243.

18. Secord, P. F., and S. M. Jourard. "The Appraisal of Body-Cathexis: Body-Cathexis and the Self." *Journal of Consulting Psychology* 17(1953):343–347.

19. Jourard, S. M., and P. F. Secord. "Body-Cathexis and Personality." *British Journal of Psychology* 46(1955):130–138.

20. Jourard, S. M., and P. F. Secord. "Body-Cathexis and the Ideal Female Figure." *Journal of Abnormal and Social Psychology* 50(1955):243–246.

21. Dion, K., E. Berscheid, and E. Walster. "What Is Beautiful Is Good." *Journal of Personality and Social Psychology* 24(1972):285–290.

22. Dion, K., and E. Berscheid. *Physical Attractiveness and Sociometric Choice in Young Children.* Mimeographed. Minneapolis: University of Minnesota, 1971.

23. Dion, K. K. "Physical Attractiveness and Evaluation of Children's Transgressions." *Journal of Personality and Social Psychology* 24(1972):207–213.

24. Jones, M. C., and N. Bayley. "Physical Maturing Among Boys as Related to Behavior." *Journal of Educational Psychology* 41(1950):129–148.

25. Jones, M. C., and N. Bayley. Op. cit., 1950, p. 146.

26. Mussen, P. H., and M. C. Jones. "Self-Conceptions, Motivations and Interpersonal Attitudes of Late- and Early-Maturing Boys." *Child Development* 28(1957):243–256.

27. Mussen, P. H., and M. C. Jones. "The Behavior-Inferred Motivations of Late- and Early-Maturing Boys." *Child Development* 29(1958):61–67.

28. Weatherly, D. "Self-Perceived Rate of Physical Motivation and Personality in Late Adolescence." *Child Development* 35(1964):1209.

29. Stolz, H. R., and L. M. Stolz. "Adolescent Problems Related to Somatic Variations," Part I. *Yearbook of the National Society for the Study of Education* 43(1944):80–99.

30. Jones, M. C. "A Study of Socialization at the High School Level." *Journal of Genetic Psychology* 93(1958):87–111.

31. Jones, M. C., and P. H. Mussen. "Self-Conceptions, Motivations, and Interpersonal Attitudes of Early- and Late-Maturing Girls." *Child Development* 29(1958):491–501.

32. Faust, S. "Developmental Maturity as a Determiner in Prestige of Adolescent Girls." *Child Development* 31(1960):173–184.

33. Weatherly, D. Op. cit., 1964, pp. 1191–1210.

34. Jones, M. C., and P. H. Mussen. Op. cit., 1958, p. 498.

35. Havighurst, R. J. *Human Development and Education.* London: Longmans, Green, 1953.

36. Douvan, E., and J. Adelson. *The Adolescent Experience.* New York: Wiley, 1966.

37. Elder, G. H., Jr. "Structural Variations in the Child Rearing Relationship." *Sociometry* 25(1962):241–262.

38. Dubbé, M. C. "What Parents Are not Told May Hurt: A Study of Communication Between Teenagers and Parents." *Family Life Coordinator* 14(1965):51–118.

39. Fitzgerald, M. P. "Sex Differences in the Perception of the Parental Role for Middle and Working Class Parents." *Journal of Clinical Psychology* 22(1966):15–16.

40. Meissner, W. W. "Parental Interaction of the Adolescent Boy." *Journal of Genetic Psychology* 107(1965):225–233.

41. Chorost, S. B. "Parental Child Rearing Attitudes and Their Correlates in Adolescent Hostility." *Genetic Psychology of Monographs* 66(1962):49–90.

42. Cooper, J. B. "Parent Evaluation as Related to Social Ideology and Academic Achievement." *Journal of Genetic Psychology* 101(1962):135–143.

43. Elder, G. H., Jr. "Parental Power Legitimation and Its Effect on the Adolescent." *Sociometry* 26(1963):50–65.

44. Hoffman, M. L. "Power Assertion by the Parent and Its Impact on the Child." *Child Development* 31(1960):129–143.

45. Raven, B. H., and J. R. P. French. "Group Support, Legitimate Power, and Social Influence." *Sociometry* 21(1958):83–97.

46. Bowerman, C. E., and J. W. Kinch. "Changes in Family and Peer Orientation Between the Fourth and Tenth Grades." *Social Forces* 37(1959):206–211.

47. Rosenberg, M. *Society and the Adolescent Self-Image.* Princeton, N. J.: Princeton University Press, 1965.

48. McClelland, D. C., A. Rindlisbacher, and R. DeCharms. "Religious and Other Sources of Parental Attitudes Toward Independence Training." In *Studies in Motivation,* edited by D. C. McClelland. New York: Appleton-Century-Crofts, 1955, pp. 389–397.

49. Elder, G. H., Jr. *Family Structure and the Transmission of Values and Norms in the Process of Child Rearing.* Doctoral Dissertation. University of North Carolina, 1961.

50. Miller, D. R., and Swanson, G. D. *The Changing American Parent.* New York: Morrow, 1958.

51. Klatsin, E. H. "Shifts in Child Care Practices in Three Social Classes Under an Infant Care Program in Flexible Methodology." *American Journal of Orthopsychiatry* 22(1952):52–61.

52. Bronfenbrenner, U. "Socialization and Social Class Through Time and Space." In *Readings in Social Psychology,* 3rd ed., edited by E. E. Maccoby, T. M. Newcomb, and E. L. Hartley. New York: Holt, Rinehart and Winston, 1958, p. 423.

53. Hess, R. D. "Social Class and Ethnic Influences on Socialization." In *Carmichael's Manual of Child Psychology,* vol. II, 3rd ed., edited by P. H. Mussen. New York: Wiley, 1970, pp. 473–482.

54. Mussen, P., et al. "The Influence of Father-Son Relationships on Adolescent Personality and Attitudes." *Journal of Child Psychology and Psychiatry* 4(1963):3–16.

55. Bronfenbrenner, U. "Some Familiar Antecedents of Responsibility and Leadership in Adolescents." In *Leadership and Interpersonal Behavior,* edited by L. Petrullo and B. Bass. New York: Holt, Rinehart and Winston, 1961, pp. 239–271.

56. Bronfenbrenner U. Op. cit., 1961, p. 256.

57. Sears, R. R., E. E. Maccoby, and H. Levin. *Patterns of Child Rearing.* Evanston, Ill.: Row, Peterson, 1967.

58. Miller, D. R., and G. E. Swanson. *Inner Conflict and Defense.* New York: Schocken Books, 1966, pp. 73–76.

59. Terman, L. M., and L. E. Tyler. "Psychological Sex Differences." In *Manual of Child Psychology,* edited by L. Carmichael. New York: Wiley, 1954, 1064–1114.

60. Mischel, W. "Sex-Typing and Socialization." In *Carmichael's Manual of Child Psychology*, vol. II, 3rd ed., edited by P. H. Mussen. New York: Wiley, pp. 3–72.

61. Hoffman, L., R. Rosen, and R. Lippin. "Parental Coerciveness, Child Autonomy, and Peer Group Role at School." Paper presented at 66th Annual American Psychological Association Convention, Washington, D.C., September 1958, p. 5.

62. Bronfenbrenner, U. "Some Familiar Antecedents of Responsibility and Leadership in Adolescents." Op. cit., 1961, p. 260.

63. Heilbrum, A. B. "The Measurement of Identification." *Child Development* 36(1965):111–127.

64. Heilbrum, A. B. "The Measurement of Identification." *Child Development* 36(1965):789–799.

65. Helper, M. M. "Learning Theory and Self-Concept." *Journal of Abnormal and Social Psychology* 51(1955):184–194.

66. Schaefer, E. S., and N. Bayley. "Maternal Behavior, Child Behavior, and Their Intercorrelations from Infancy Through Adolescence." *Monographs of the Society for Research in Child Development* 28(1963) (3, Whole no. 87).

67. Douvan, E., and J. Adelson. *The Adolescent Experience*. Op. cit., 1966.

68. Bath, J. A., and E. C. Lewis. "Attitudes of Young Female Adults Toward Some Areas of Parent-Adolescent Conflict." *Journal of Genetic Psychology* 100(1962):241–253.

69. Medinnus, G. R., and R. C. Johnson. *Child and Adolescent Psychology*. New York: Wiley, 1969, p. 709.

70. Ausubel, D. P. *Theory and Problems of Adolescent Development*. New York: Grune and Stratton, 1954.

71. Hartup, W. W. "Peer Group Interaction and Social Organization." In *Carmichael's Manual of Child Psychology*, vol. II, 3rd ed., edited by P. H. Mussen. New York: Wiley, 1970, pp. 361–456.

72. Reiss, A. L. "America's Sex Standards—How and Why They're Changing." *Trans-action* 5(March 1968):26–36.

73. McDill, E. L., and J. Coleman. "Family and Peer Influences in College Plans of High School Students." *Sociology of Education* 38(1965):112–126.

74. Levitt, E. E., and J. A. Edwards. "A Multivariate Study of Correlative Factors in Youthful Cigarette Smoking. *Developmental Psychology* 2(1970):5–11.

75. Hoffman, M. L., and H. D. Saltzstein. "Parent Discipline and the Child's Moral Development." *Journal of Personality and Social Psychology* 5(1967):45–57.

76. Feinberg, M. R. "Relation of Background Experience to Social Acceptance." *Journal of Abnormal and Social Psychology* 48(1953):206–214.

77. Gronlund, N. E., and W. S. Holmlund. "The Value of Elementary School Sociometric Status Scores for Predicting Pupils' Adjustment in High School." *Educational Administration and Supervision* 44(1958):255–260.

78. Northway, M. L., and A. Wigdor. "Rorschach Patterns Related to the Socioeconomic Status of Children." *Sociometry* 10(1947):186–199.

79. Aries, P. *Centuries of Childhood*. Op. cit., 1962.

80. Sampson, E. E. (ed.). "Stirrings Out of Apathy! Student Activism and the Decade of Protest." *Journal of Social Issues* 23(1967):52.

81. Flacks, R. "The Liberated Generation: An Exploration of the Roots of Student Protest." *Journal of Social Issues* 22(1967):52–75.

82. Peterson, R. E. *The Scope of Organized Student Protest in 1964–1965.* Princeton, N. J.: Educational Testing Service, 1966.

83. Trent, J. W., and J. L. Craise. "Commitment and Conformity in the American College." *Journal of Social Issues* 22(1967):34–51.

84. Flacks, R. Op. cit., 1967.

85. Halleck, S. L. "Hypotheses of Student Unrest." In *Human Dynamics in Psychology and Education*, 2nd ed., edited by D. E. Hamachek, Boston: Allyn and Bacon, 1972, pp. 366–383.

86. Flacks, R. Op. cit., 1967.

87. Flacks, R. Op. cit., 1967.

88. Rogers, D. *The Psychology of Adolescence*, 2nd ed. New York: Appleton-Century-Crofts, 1972, pp. 336–338.

89. Keniston, K. *The Uncommitted: Alienated Youth in American Society.* New York: Dell, 1960.

90. Keniston, K. "The Sources of Student Dissent." *Journal of Social Issues* 22(1967):119–120.

91. Erikson, E. H. "Reflections on the Dissent of Contemporary Youth." *Daedalus* 99(1970):171–172.

92. Rossman, M. "The Two Faces of Youth." *Saturday Review* (17 August 1968):50.

93. Keniston, K. "The Sources of Student Dissent." Op. cit., 1967, p. 113.

94. Keniston, K. Op. cit., 1967, p. 113.

95. Vogel, W., and C. G. Lauterbach. "Relationships Between Normal and Disturbed Sons' Percepts of Their Parents' Behavior, and Personality Attributes of Parents and Sons." *Journal of Clinical Psychology* 19(1963):52–56.

96. Keniston, K. *The Uncommitted: Alienated Youth in American Society.* Op. cit., 1960.

97. Keniston, K. Op. cit., 1960, pp. 101–102.

98. Erikson, E. *Childhood and Society.* New York: Norton, 1950, pp. 227–229.

99. Piaget, J. *The Psychology of Intelligence.* London: Routledge and Kegan Paul, 1950.

100. Inhelder, B., and J. Piaget. *The Growth of Logical Thinking.* New York: Basic Books, 1958.

101. Beard, R. M. *An Outline of Piaget's Developmental Psychology for Students and Teachers.* New York: Basic Books, 1969, pp. 92–122.

102. Case, D., and J. W. Collinson. "The Development of Formal Thinking in Verbal Comprehension." *British Journal of Educational Psychology* 31–32(1961–62):103–111.

103. Bruner, J. *Toward a Theory of Instruction.* Cambridge, Mass.: Harvard University Press, 1966.

104. Committee on Child Psychiatry, Group for the Advancement of Psychiatry, *Psychopathological Disorders in Childhood: Theoretical Considerations and a Proposed Classification,* Report no. 62, vol. VI. New York: Mental Health Materials Center, June 1966.

REFERENCES OF RELATED INTEREST

Adams, J. F. (ed.). *Understanding Adolescence,* 2nd ed. Boston: Allyn and Bacon, 1973.

Bardwick, J. M., et al. *Feminine Personality and Conflict.* Belmont, Calif.: Brooks/Cole, 1970.

Cole, L. *Psychology of Adolescence,* 6th ed. New York: Holt, Rinehart and Winston, 1964.

Conger, J. J. *Adolescence and Youth.* New York: Harper and Row, 1973.

Cusick, P. A. *Inside High School.* New York: Holt, Rinehart and Winston 1973.

Frey, S. H. (ed.). *Adolescent Behavior in School.* Chicago: Rand McNally, 1970.

Ginott, H. G. *Between Parent and Teenager.* New York, Macmillan, 1969.

Goethals, G. W., and D. S. Klos. *Experiencing Youth: First-Person Accounts.* Boston: Little, Brown, 1970.

Golburgh, S. (ed.). *The Experience of Adolescence.* Cambridge, Mass.: Schenkman, 1965.

Grinder, R. E. *Adolescence.* New York: Wiley, 1973.

Gross, R., and P. Osterman (eds.). *High School.* New York: Simon and Schuster, 1972.

Hill, J. P., and J. Shelton (eds.). *Readings in Adolescent Development and Behavior.* Englewood Cliffs, N. J.: Prentice-Hall, 1971.

Hurlock, E. B. *Adolescent Development,* 3rd ed. New York: McGraw-Hill, 1967.

Jersild, A. T. *The Psychology of Adolescence,* 2nd ed. New York: Macmillan, 1963.

Josselyn, I. M. *Adolescence.* New York: Harper and Row, 1971.

Kagan, J., and R. Coles (ed.). *12 to 16: Early Adolescence.* New York: Norton, 1972.

Lambert, B. G., et al. *Adolescence: Transition from Childhood to Maturity.* Monterey, Calif.: Brooks/Cole, 1972.

Libarle, M., and T. Seligson (eds.). *The High School Revolutionaries.* New York: Vintage Books, 1970.

Lowe, G. R. *The Growth of Personality: From Infancy to Old Age.* Baltimore: Penguin Books, 1972.

McCandless, B. R. *Adolescents: Behavior and Development.* Hinsdale, Ill.: Dryden Press, 1970.

Mead, M. "Adolescence in Primitive and Modern Society." In *Readings in Social Psychology,* edited by E. Maccoby, T. Newcomb, and E. L. Hartley. New York: Holt, Rinehart and Winston, 1958.

Muuss, R. E. (ed.). *Adolescent Behavior and Society: A Book of Readings.* New York: Random House, 1971.

————. *Theories of Adolescence,* 2nd ed. New York: Random House, 1968.

Peel, E. A. *The Nature of Adolescent Judgment.* New York: Wiley, 1972.

Perez, J. F., and A. I. Cohen. *Mom and Dad Are Me.* Belmont, Calif.: Brooks/Cole, 1969.

Purnell, R. F. (ed.). *Adolescents and the American High School.* New York: Holt, Rinehart and Winston, 1970.

Ralston, N. C., and G. P. Thomas. *The Adolescent: Case Studies For Analysis.* New York: Chandler, 1974.

Rogers, D. (ed.). *Issues in Adolescent Psychology,* 2nd ed. New York: Appleton-Century-Crofts, 1972.

————. *The Psychology of Adolescence,* 2nd ed. New York: Appleton-Century-Crofts, 1972.

Rosenberg, M. *Society and the Adolescent Self-Image.* Princeton, N. J.: Princeton University Press, 1965.

Scott, E. M. *The Adolescent Gap.* Springfield, Ill.: Thomas, 1972.

Stone, L. J., and J. Church. *Childhood and Adolescence,* 3rd ed. New York: Random House, 1972.

Thornburg, H. D. (ed.). *Contemporary Adolescence: Readings.* Belmont, Calif.: 1971.

Wattenberg, W. W., *The Adolescent Years,* 2nd ed. Harcourt Brace Jovanovich, 1973.

Wesley, F. *Childrearing Psychology.* New York: Behavioral Publications, 1971.

Westley, W. A., and N. B. Epstein. *The Silent Majority.* San Francisco: Jossey-Bass, 1969.

Winter, G. D., and E. M. Nuss (eds.). *The Young Adults.* Glenview, Ill.: Scott, Foresman, 1969.

SIX

The Nature and Growth of Intelligence and Creative Functioning

CHAPTER OUTLINE

PROLOGUE

WHAT IS INTELLIGENCE?

Intellectual Growth Is Orderly and Cumulative

Intelligence Is Related to Learning

Four Different Views of Intellectual Functioning

The case for general and specific intelligence (E. Spearman)

Intelligence determined by neural network (E. L. Thorndike)

Intelligence consists of seven primary mental abilities (T. G. Thurstone)

Intelligence is a complex three-dimensional structure (J. P. Guilford)

Intelligence Is a Combination of Many Different Abilities

THREE TYPES OF INTELLIGENCE MEASURES: GROUP, INDIVIDUAL, AND APTITUDE TESTS

RANGE, CLASSIFICATION, AND INTERPRETATION OF MENTAL ABILITIES

Caution: Different Intelligence Tests May Measure Different Factors

Percentile Ranking Indicates Relative Position

The Mental Age Concept and Relationship to IQ

The Deviation IQ: A New Approach for Reporting Intelligence

Intelligence Test Reliability: A Word of Caution

How Stable Is IQ Over Time?

Socioeconomic Status Can Affect IQ Stability

Personality Characteristics Are Related to Changes in IQ

HEREDITY, ENVIRONMENT, AND IQ: CONTROVERSY, DEBATE, AND JENSEN

Some Reflections of My Own

Jensen's Basic Ideas

Arguments Against the Jensen Point of View

Influence of Heredity on Intelligence

The Impact of Environment on Intelligence

Improvement of environment leads to improvement in IQ

A Final Word on the Heredity-Environment Issue

THE GROWTH AND DECLINE OF INTELLIGENCE OVER TIME

Crystallized and Fluid Intelligence Differ in Rate of Decline

SOME RELATIONSHIPS BETWEEN INTELLIGENCE AND SCHOOL PERFORMANCE

There Are Limitations to What an IQ Test Can Predict

IQ, School Achievement, and Minority Groups: A Note of Caution

VARIETIES AND EXPRESSIONS OF CREATIVE BEHAVIOR

What Is Creativity?

Approaches to the Measurement of Creativity

Intelligence and Personality Factors Related to Creativity

Creative persons are open to personal feelings and subjective impressions

A creative person is more a perceiver than a judger

Creative persons are less tradition-bound

Ways to Encourage Creative Activity

Learn to value that which is different

Be cautious not to reject nonconformity

Teach students to ask extending questions

Be willing to accept that which is new, different, and even imperfect

Us praise liberally and modify assignments to fit the student

Make your guidance available, your expectations clear, and let your flexibility set the tone

Ten Commandments for Enhancing Creative Expression

EPILOGUE

REFERENCES

REFERENCES OF RELATED INTEREST

IMPORTANT CHAPTER IDEAS

1. There is some doubt about what it is exactly that "intelligence" is supposed to be; it means different things to different people.

2. Intelligence is best thought of as being a combination of many different abilities, talents, and competencies, which can vary from person to person.

3. Intelligence tests are more appropriately called "scholastic aptitude" tests, since they measure one's aptitude or "aptness" for learning school-related materials.

4. Different intelligence tests measure different intellectual and cognitive factors.

5. A person's mental age may be higher or lower than his chronological age.

6. Youngsters whose IQ's fluctuate the most during their developmental years are likely to have life histories that show unusual variations with respect to disturbing and stabilizing factors.

7. IQ gains are most likely to occur among youth who are independent, competitive, and self-initiating.

8. Overall, IQ development tends to move in the direction of the family norm.

9. Although IQ tends to remain fairly stable, it can change—particularly during the school years.

10. The longer a child remains in a deprived environment, the lower his IQ score is likely to be.

11. Research indicates that the cumulative effect of environmental influences during the first seventeen years of life is on the order of about 20 IQ points.

12. Research evidence suggests that, whereas heredity probably determines a top and a bottom limit on each person's IQ score, environment very likely has the final say as to where within this range the score will actually fall.

13. There is a positive relationship between intelligence test scores and school performance.

14. Variables such as drive, interest, motivation, opportunity, and self-concept greatly influence how intellectual ability is developed and used.

15. Personality characteristics such as boldness, courage, freedom, spontaneity, and self-acceptance are linked to creative behavior.

16. In general, research indicates that individuals with high IQs show a great range of creative talent, from high to low, whereas persons with low IQs are more apt to score lower on creativity tests.

17. The more perceptive a person is, the more creative he is apt to be.

18. Teachers can encourage creative thinking by valuing and accepting that which is different, new or novel, by making their expectations clear, and by being flexible.

PROLOGUE

Intelligence and creativity are elusive personal qualities that can vary a great deal from person to person. Some people, we know, are extremely intelligent when it comes to thinking things through, solving problems, or remembering factual details, but are somewhat inept when it comes to doing things in any kind of different, novel, or "creative" way. Still others are extremely imaginative when it comes to dreaming up ideas that no one's ever thought about before, but somewhat ineffectual in handling the problems of everyday living. For whatever else they may be, intelligence and creativity are relative qualities. That is, "intelligent" behavior may be in one individual's deftness with numbers or another person's agility with words; it may be in one individual's skill in repairing damaged interpersonal relationships or in another person's talent for repairing damaged car engines. Creative behavior can be as profound as Einstein's $E = mc_2$, as sensitive as Shelley's Tress, or as simple as grandma's apple pie. (Maybe as good, too.) The point is that both creativity and intelligence can be expressed and nurtured in different ways. It will be our objective in this chapter to better understand how these processes grow, develop, and function in human behavior. This brings us to an important first question.

WHAT IS INTELLIGENCE?

It would be nice if there were a simple, universally accepted working definition of intelligence, but, alas, there is not. Although most definitions refer in one way or other to one's ability, there is some disagreement as to what kind of ability and ability to do what. Some of the more commonly cited definitions, for example, include the following:

The ability to profit from experience.
The ability to solve problems.
The ability to adjust and relate to one's environment.
The ability to perceive relationships.

The ability to think abstractly.
The ability to behave competently and effectively.
The ability to learn.

TO THINK ABOUT

How would you define intelligence? Consider the definitions cited above, and then write your own comprehensive definition of intelligence—a definition which, for you, includes what you feel being intelligent *really* means. You will find it interesting to get others' ideas about this to compare your ideas with.

_____

_____

_____

As you can see, none of these definitions is mutually exclusive of the others, and, in fact, the better a person is able to do any one of the seven things mentioned, the better he is able to do others. That is, if one can perceive relationships, he very likely can learn. If he can learn, he can profit from experience. Although there may be certain semantic distinctions among the seven definitions, in terms of human behavior they are more alike than different. Nonetheless, there remains some doubt what it is exactly that intelligence is supposed to be—at least as measured by intelligence tests. An interesting illustration reflecting the confusion around the concept of intelligence was recently dramatized by the dilemma facing the Mensa Society, an international organization that limits membership to those who score at the 98th percentile or above in intelligence. The Society's officers found that roughly three of four prospective members selected on one kind of intelligence test failed to be selected by a second test, and three out of four chosen by the second type could not meet the standards of the first test. Eventually, the officers had to make a policy decision about *which* kind of intelligence the society would consider.

Intellectual Growth Is Orderly and Cumulative

Intelligence is made up of more than one ability, which is why it is difficult to define (or measure) with precision. Rather than being a single or simple capacity for learning, it appears more accurately to be a succession

Intelligence is reflected in a person's capacity for abstract thinking and ability to solve problems. (Allyn and Bacon)

of constantly developing functions. The successful development of each new function depends on the combination of a number of simpler ones that have matured earlier. Intelligence, like other developing functions and skills seen in a growing child, proceeds in a more or less orderly fashion. For instance, in order for a three year old to successfully do something as simple as copy a square, he must first of all be able to grip a pencil and hold it in an upright position; he must perceive the relationship between moving it along the paper and producing a mark; he must have sufficient sensory awareness of the relation between the visual image of four corners,

237

four straight lines, and then he must have the necessary eye-hand coordination to produce this same picture on paper. So, copying a square is not so simple as it may appear at first glance. A three year old can draw an "intelligent"(reasonably correct, accurate) square to the extent that he has learned certain lower-level functions.

Intelligence Is Related to Learning

Once again we come back to the idea of learning in relation to intelligence. Something like Mary's little lamb, wherever learning is, intelligence is too. We couldn't put it the other way and say that wherever intelligence is, learning is sure to follow because, unfortunately, it doesn't always work out that way. We probably all know persons—young and old—who by most standards are intelligent enough, but who, for one reason or other, simply refuse to learn either from their own experience or someone else's. An "intelligent" person does not always learn, or at least use his capacity for learning (they're frequently labeled "underachievers" in school), but whenever learning does occur there has to be some measurable degree of intelligence.

Four Different Views of Intellectual Functioning

There are a variety of ways for describing and understanding the various components of intelligence. A. Binet and T. Simon,[1] whose work in the early 1900's in developing a test for predicting academic achievement for the French public school system led to the first successful attempt to measure intelligence, were among the first to conceptualize intelligence as a composite of many abilities rather than as a specific trait.

The case for general and specific intelligence (E. Spearman). At about the same time, an American psychologist by the name of Charles E. Spearman[2,3] was publicizing the notion that intelligence was not made up of many abilities, but rather than it included one general (g) factor and several specific (s) factors. He made a case for the g factor being a kind of mental energy that a person draws upon for everything he does. Essentially, a person's g factor is considered to be his ability to perceive relationships. S factors, on the other hand, are specific to given tasks. For example, the s factors involved in arithmetic are the same as those involved in spelling or reading, although a certain amount of the g factor is necessary for dealing with and understanding all three subjects. Within this framework it is possible for a person to have a high level of general intelligence but still be less capable in a certain area than someone who has a high s

238

factor in that particular area.   Usually, however, the more g factor a person has, the more s factors are at his command.   This is consistent with other research that suggests that persons with above average (or below average, as the case may be) aggregate intelligence scores tend to be somewhat above average (or below average) in most things they attempt.[4,5]

Intelligence determined by neural network (E. L. Thorndike). Edward L. Thorndike[6] differed sharply with Spearman by asserting that there are no such things as general intelligence or general mental ability.   Thorndike's theorizing was somewhat more abstract, but essentially it involved the idea that intelligence was due to the number and kind of neural connections. According to the theory, a bright person simply has more neural connections of an adequate nature than a dull person, a view which, in light of recent brain research evidence[7,8] may have more merit than even Thorndike thought was possible.   Although Thorndike perceived every mental act to be different from every other one, some were seen as having enough elements in common to justify three general groupings or components of intelligence, which included: (1) concrete thinking—the ability to deal with things; (2) social thinking—the ability to deal with people; and (3) abstract thinking—the ability to deal with ideas.

Intelligence consists of seven primary mental abilities (T. G. Thurstone).   A somewhat better known view is Thurstone's[9-11] theory of primary mental abilities, which conceptualizes intelligence as being made up of seven components or families of closely related abilities.   Although not all psychologists would agree with Thurstone's seven primary mental abilities, they nonetheless have weathered the test of both time and scientific scrutiny long enough to qualify among the more generally accepted components of intelligence.   They are as follows:

1. *Space factor*—Refers to the ability to visualize objects in space, e.g., it's the ability a good quarterback uses to complete long passes or the ability a pilot uses to land an airplane or the ability anyone of us uses to judge whether or not we have time and room to pass a car when another one is approaching in the other lane.   Although most intelligent people seem to be reasonably well supplied with the space factor, some highly intelligent people are lacking in this primary ability.   (Some intelligent people, for example, have trouble just parking a car.)

2. *Number factor*—Those who rate high in this are usually good at manipulating numbers like, for example, balancing a checkbook, making change, or even keeping a mental tab of the grocery bill while shopping. We would expect that accountants and cashiers, for example, would be high in this ability.

3. *Verbal comprehension*—People high in this typically read faster, have large vocabularies, and, naturally enough, seem to understand more of

what they read. They would be more likely to be able to quickly interpret a proverb like, say, "All that glitters is not gold," than one whose verbal comprehension was not as high.

4. *Word fluency*—People high in this seem to have a knack for using words. A simple test for word fluency is to ask someone to write as many girls' or boys' names (beginning with something like Ch- or Fr-) as he can in a few minutes. Some, you'll find, can produce a string of names while others have a terrible time.

5. *Ability to memorize*—Oddly enough, the ability to memorize doesn't seem to be very much related to other mental abilities. That is, those with good memories may or may not be blessed with other primary abilities. More than that, there seems to be several distinct kinds of memory abilities. For example, there appears to be a difference between the ability to memorize intentionally—a list of presidents, let's say—and the ability to recall casual past experiences one has had.

6. *Inductive reasoning*—This is the ability to discover the underlying rule or principle in the material one is working with. It is the ability to arrive at useful generalizations from limited information. We would suspect, for example, that successful football coaches or field generals or school board members would be high in this ability.

7. *Perceptual speed*—This is the ability to identify objects quickly. For example, those high in this can more easily understand entire sentences without having to examine each word carefully and are more able to comprehend entire paragraphs without microscopically looking at each sentence. It is, if you will, the ability our good quarterback uses when he is able to scan his entire field of potential receivers to find an open man without spending undue time on each individual receiver.

TO DO

Rate yourself as high, medium, or low on each of these seven factors to get some feel for how you regard your own intelligence. Invite two or three persons who know you fairly well to do the same thing for you. Compare their ratings with yours. Do you see yourself as others do?

These abilities, which Thurstone considers as aspects of a person's general intelligence, are thought to be relatively independent, so that a person proficient in one is not necessarily in another. However, statistical relationships among them are almost always found to be positive, which indicates that a person who is average (or above or below) in one is usually average (or above or below) in the others. Again, this is evidence to suggest that different types of mental activity share something in common and that they may all be influenced, at least in part, by a general intellectual power or ability. Nonetheless, the differences in a person's performance in these seven areas suggest that each depends upon the operation of a separate ability or factor. Research has confirmed Thurstone's findings for some of these factors, but, as discussed below, other studies have pointed to the existence of an even finer division of the components of intelligence.

Intelligence is a complex three-dimensional structure (J. P. Guilford). Probably the most comprehensive conceptualization of the variety of components that may make up human intelligence is the "structure of intellect" model developed by J. P. Guilford.[12,13] As you can see from the $5 \times 4 \times 6$ three-dimensional model in Figure 6-1, Guilford's components of intelligence include 5 intellectual *operations*, 4 *contents*, and 6 *products*, which interact to produce 120 separate abilities. The *content* dimension has reference to the particular medium in which a person happens to be operating at the moment. It may be symbolic, figural (graphic), semantic, or behavioral (motor). The *operations* dimension refers to the particular cognitive processes being used, such as cognition (thinking), memory, and divergent or convergent idea production. The final dimension of intellect is *products*—the results of operations and content. Examples of these would include classes, relations, transformations, and evaluations.

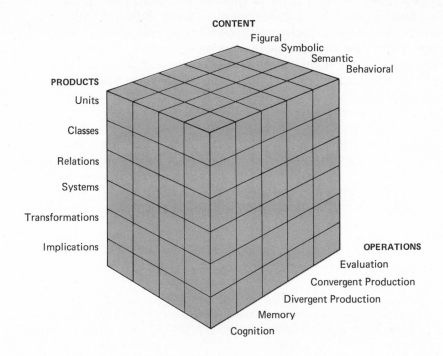

(From *J. P. Guilford. The Nature of Human Intelligence. New York: McGraw-Hill, 1967. Copyright 1967 by McGraw-Hill, Inc.*)

FIGURE 6–1. Guilford's Model for the Structure of Intellect

Guilford's model of intelligence has important implications for teaching and learning inasmuch as it offers a valuable framework for exploring and further defining the many components that make up intelligence. Among other things, it suggests that in relatively complex forms of learning, such as problem solving, several combinations of abilities may be required, depending upon the nature of the problem being solved. It is a model that supports the idea of the learner who acquires information, stores it, uses it as necessary in the form of divergent or convergent thinking for the generation of new information, and evaluates his results. It helps explain why John is good at solving math problems but not so hot in memorizing formulas or history dates, or why Bob is good at thinking of new ideas but less skilled in evaluating and integrating the ideas of others.

Intelligence Is a Combination of Many Different Abilities

The point is that intelligence is not something that comes all in one piece. From whatever point of view we look at it, intelligence is not just one thing but, rather, a combination of many different abilities or components tied up in a package that we label as intelligence. You and your close friend may have the same score on an intelligence test, for instance, but yet have very different skills, talents, and competencies. The idea of intelligence being more than one thing is a hopeful and positive way of looking at intelligence. Just as it is possible for people to have different kinds of personalities, interests, and values, so, too, it is possible for people to have different kinds of intelligence. Alice is good with words, Al is skilled with numbers, and Deb expresses herself best with pictures. Alice may end up as a writer, Al, an accountant, and Debbie, an artist. Does this mean that one is necessarily any brighter or smarter than the other? Not at all. It may mean simply that each has followed his or her own natural bent and curiosities in the actualization of the intellectual potential that was within each of them.

TO THINK ABOUT

I have the impression that our educational system does not place equal value on different "types" or "expressions" of intelligence. For example, the college-bound high school student is more valued (esteemed, has higher status) than the trade school-bound student. To the extent that you also share these impressions, what would you recommend we do to begin changing that system of values — if, indeed, you think it should be changed at all? In either case, why do you think we should change or not change?

THREE TYPES OF INTELLIGENCE MEASURES: GROUP, INDIVIDUAL, AND APTITUDE TESTS

There are many different types of intelligence tests and many different versions of each type. For example, *The Seventh Mental Measurement Yearbook*[14] reviewed 130 different intelligence tests or instruments similar to intelligence tests. There are two main types: individual and group. An individual test is administered to only one person at a time and requires the skill of a specially trained examiner. As you might suspect, an individually administered intelligence test takes longer to administer and score (about one and one-half to two hours altogether), but it has the advantage of offering useful diagnostic information since the examiner is right there to observe the examinee's responses and behavior as he takes the test. If, let's say, a youngster taking an individual test obtains a low score and has been observed to be extremely fidgety and restless throughout the testing session, this may be useful information to include in the test report as additional observations that may help to understand this youngster's total performance. This kind of information wouldn't be available from a group test because, as the name implies, it is a test administered to large groups, which eliminates the possibility of being able to observe any one person's behavior for extended periods. Usually, group tests are administered in large auditoriums to hundreds at a time.

Group tests do, however, have some distinct advantages. Literally hundreds can be tested at one sitting; any mature person who can read and tell time can administer the test, and the tests may be machine-scored in a matter of minutes. Disadvantages include the possibility of misunderstanding the directions, putting answers in the incorrect place, copying from someone else's paper, or for a variety of real or imagined reasons failing to put forth as much effort as possible.

Some of the more popular and widely used group tests you may encounter in your professional work include the *California Tests of Mental Maturity* (six levels of these, all the way from preprimary to advanced), *Terman-McNemar, Henmon-Nelson, SRA* (Science Research Associates), *Kuhlman-Anderson,* and various forms of the *Otis.* Although these tests differ somewhat with respect to the kind of items they include, they each include subtests in vocabulary, sentence understanding, general information, analogies (e.g., "Good is to bad as love is to . . ."), arithmetic reasoning, following directions, and the perception of similarities and differences (e.g., "In what way are an orange and banana alike? In what way are they different?").

The *Stanford-Binet*[15] is probably one of the most popular and widely used individually administered intelligence tests. It consists of twenty groups of tests for age two through the adult level. There are tests for ages two through four and one-half at half-year intervals; tests for five through fourteen at yearly intervals; and tests for those above fourteen designated Average Adult, Superior Adult I, II, and III. It is primarily a verbal test of intelligence inasmuch as most of the items deal with vocabulary, general information, comprehension, and similar tasks requiring verbal responses to verbally presented questions.

Other individually administered intelligence scales that are widely used include the *Wechsler Adult Intelligence Scale* (WAIS) for persons between sixteen and seventy-five, the *Wechsler Intelligence Scale for Children* (WISC) for those between five and fifteen, and the *Wechsler Preschool and Primary Scale of Intelligence* (WPPSI).[16] Each of these tests yield three scores, one being a verbal IQ, another the performance IQ (this requires nonverbal responses), and a third a total IQ, which is the average of the first two. Actually, the verbal and performance batteries are composed of individual tests that are scored separately and then combined to give an overall measure of one's ability to deal effectively with his environment. The verbal part of the scale consists of subtests of (1) general information, (2) comprehension, (3) arithmetic reasoning, (4) memory span, (5) similarities, and (6) vocabulary. The performance part includes tests of (1) picture completion items, (2) picture arrangement, (3) block design, (4) object assembly, and (5) digit-symbol manipulation.

The tests we've just referred to are all intended to measure and predict a student's ability to learn the sorts of things a school has to offer. In this sense, they could be more accurately called scholastic aptitude tests rather than "intelligence" tests, since they do, in fact, measure a student's aptitude or "aptness" for learning school-related materials. Whereas intelligence tests are a more general assessment of one's scholastic aptitude, a regular *aptitude test* attempts to measure a person's specific or potential for achievement in a specific field. Thus there are a large number of aptitude tests available to measure one's aptness in areas as art, music, math, mechanical dexterity, foreign languages, engineering, and so on. Reading readiness tests are a particular kind of aptitude measure inasmuch as they are designed to assess whether the young child has developed the necessary readiness to profit from reading instruction.

RANGE, CLASSIFICATION, AND INTERPRETATION OF MENTAL ABILITIES

If a large enough random sample of the population were administered an IQ test, it is theoretically possible that the resulting scores would fall

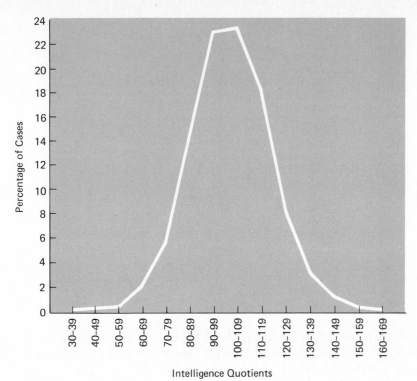

Intelligence Quotients

(From L. M. Terman and M. A. Merrill. Stanford-Binet Intelligence Scale, 3d rev.
ed. Boston: Houghton Mifflin Company, 1960. By permission of the publisher.)

FIGURE 6-2. Distribution of the IQs of 2,904 Children in the Stanford-Binet Standardization Group

more or less in line with the normal curve, which will be discussed in Chapter 12. What this means is that most of the scores would cluster around the middle with fewer and fewer toward the extremes above and below. In fact, it has been determined that about two-thirds of the population would obtain IQ's between 84 and 116, leaving about a sixth with higher scores and another sixth with lower scores. Figure 6–2, which shows the actual distribution of IQ scores of 2,904 children who constituted the standardization group for the *Revised Stanford Binet Scale*, will give you a visual idea of how a normal curve of scores actually looks.

Most other intelligence tests are so constructed as to yield somewhat comparable distributions. On the Wechsler tests, for instance, 50 percent of those who take it fall within the 91 to 110 IQ range as compared with the 47 percent who score between 90 and 109 on the Stanford Binet.

Most intelligence tests results can be divided into at least seven different categories, with each category having its own range of scores. A mental abilities classification system that reflects most intelligence tests results is shown in Table 6–1.

TABLE 6–1. *Intelligence Classifications*

Classification	IQ
mentally defective	69 and below
borderline defective	70–79
low average	80–89
average	90–110
high average	111–120
superior	121–130
very superior	131 and over

A score of, let's say, 115 falls within the high average range, which, as we can approximate from Figure 6–2, is achieved by about 18 percent of the population.

Caution: Different Intelligence Tests May Measure Different Factors

We must be careful, however, not to assume that identical scores from different tests mean the same thing. For example, if a person achieved a score of 109 on the *SRA Primary Mental Abilities* test and a similar score on the *Stanford-Binet,* the best we could conclude—to be accurate—would be that they were identical scores and both fell with the average range. They are not equivalent. Why? The reason for this is that they measure somewhat different factors and assign somewhat different weightings to those factors. The SRA test, for instance, is specifically a measure of five factors—verbal meaning, spatial perception, reasoning, number facility, and word fluency—whereas the *Stanford-Binet* samples measure many more abilities and, in addition, weight the verbal factors much more heavily.

Percentile Ranking Indicates Relative Position

It is important to keep in mind that no test is an absolute measure of *how much* ability or aptitude or skill a person has. It would not be accurate to say that a person has only so many points worth of intelligence, but it would be appropriate to look for how his ability compares with that of others who have taken the same test. A common way of expressing the relative status of an IQ score is to report it in terms of its percentile ranking. As you will see in the discussion in Chapter 10, percentiles indicate the relative standing of an individual in his group by specifying the percentage of those who scored lower than he did on the same test. If, for example, Mary, a high school senior, surpasses in performance 85 percent of the other high school seniors throughout the country who have taken the same test, she is at the 85th percentile. If John, a college freshman, scores at the 40th percentile, this means he has excelled 40 percent of the other college freshman who have taken the test, while 60 percent excelled him. The highest percentile rank is the 99th, the lowest is the first. The correspondence betwen IQ and percentile rank on most intelligence tests is about as shown in Table 6–2.

TABLE 6–2.

IQ	Percentile
140	99th
130	96th
120	87th
110	69th
90	23rd
80	8th
70	3rd

Thus, an individual with an IQ of 90, for example, excels approximately 23 percent of those of his age as measured on that particular test. The average and the medium (midpoint) IQ is always about 100. An advantage of reporting and talking about an IQ score in terms of its corresponding percentile ranking is that it reflects an individual's performance on a given test relative to others who took it.

TO THINK ABOUT

Jot down several advantages you can think of for students at all levels being told the results of IQ tests they take.

_____

_____

_____

_____

What disadvantages can you see?

_____

_____

_____

Would you like to know your IQ? Would you want your parents to know? Your loved one? Why or why not?

_____

_____

_____

The Mental Age Concept and Relationship to IQ

Before an intelligence test is ever used in the public schools, it is tried out on thousands of youngsters of all ages. By doing this the performance of the average child of a given age is determined, and norms or criteria for comparing performance are established. For example, in standardizing one test, measurement experts may find that the average 10 year old answers 90 questions correctly. Any individual, then, regardless of his chronological age, who does as well as the average 10 year old is said to have a *mental age* of 10. In other words, if a 16 year old and a 14 year old both answer 90 questions correctly, they would reflect a mental age of 10. On the same test, the average raw score or number of correct responses of 12 year olds may be 120. As in the above example, an individual, regardless of age, who obtains a score of 120 would be said to have a mental age of a 12 year old. The higher the score, the higher the mental age; the lower the score, the lower the mental age. By definition then, mental age refers to a given individual's level of ability, expressed in terms of the age at which the *average* person attains that ability. Hence, an average child of 13 has a mental age of 13.

The mental age idea is derived from the demonstrable fact that there are noticeable differences in the problem-solving skills and thinking abilities of children at various age levels, even at monthly intervals. Although a six-month age difference between you and your friend has practically no effect on what either one of you are able to accomplish as far as mental ability is concerned, a difference of only three or four months in age can significantly influence what two young children can do. The average three year old, for example, has matured sufficiently to do things that the average two and one-half year old is incapable of doing. Given the fact that all babies are born with zero knowledge, but with differences in genetic potential and environmental opportunity for acquiring knowledge, it is not difficult to see that a matter of a few months in age can make a big difference in how and what they learn and also the rapidity of their learning. Comparing an individual child with others of his age, then, can be a meaningful source of information about his rate of mental development and current state of maturity.

By itself, however, mental age gives no clue to a child's *rate* of mental growth. Suppose that three children—Valarie, Bob, and Allen—all take the same IQ test and end up with mental ages of ten. We now know something about their mental ability and have some idea of what can be expected of them. However, until we consider their chronological ages we cannot reliably estimate their smartness or dullness. Let's suppose that Valarie is eight, Bob is ten, and Allen is twelve. This tells us that Bob is about average in intelligence; Allen is a bit below; and Valarie somewhat above. We're also in a position to estimate their ability in terms of the conventional IQ by considering their chronological ages in relation to their mental ages. This is done by dividing the mental age (MA) by the chronological age (CA) and multiplying by 100 in order to eliminate decimals. Thus, the formula is expressed as $IQ = \dfrac{MA}{CA} \times 100$. Now we can calculate the IQ of the three youngsters above in the following manner:

$$\text{Valarie} \quad \frac{10}{8} \times 100 = 125$$

$$\text{Bob} \quad \frac{10}{10} \times 100 = 100$$

$$\text{Allen} \quad \frac{10}{12} \times 100 = 83$$

As you can see, the higher the MA in relation to the CA the further above average the obtained IQ will be.

The Deviation IQ: A New Approach for Reporting Intelligence

The approach we've just discussed is called the *ratio IQ formula* inasmuch as resulting intelligence quotient is the ratio between one's mental age and chronological age. Although the ratio IQ formula is still widely used, the *deviation IQ* is being used more and more as a way of reporting intelligence test results.

There are several reasons for this trend to using deviation IQ's. One is that the standard deviations of ratio IQ's were not constant for different ages, which means that an IQ score of, say, 110 would be equal to a different percentile at one age than another. A second issue involving the ratio IQ was around the problem of what the maximum value of the denominator should be. That is, when does a person stop growing intellectually—twelve years, eighteen years, fifty years? Because of these problems, increasing numbers of test constructors now report deviation IQ's, which means that deviation IQ's *are calculated separately for each group within each norm sample.* Typically, these deviation IQ's have a mean of 100 and a standard deviation of 15 or 16, although this may vary from test to test. As presently computed, an IQ of 115 or 116 means that the person is one standard deviation above the average for his age group. To determine the deviation IQ you would consult the table of norms printed in the manual of the test that had been used.

Intelligence Test Reliability: A Word of Caution

As will be discussed in Chapter 13 a reliable instrument is a dependable one; it gives reasonably consistent results. If your bathroom scale weighed you out at 140 pounds yesterday, 155 pounds the day before, and 147 pounds today, it is probably not very reliable. (Assuming, of course, you really *didn't* add and subtract all those pounds.) In order to believe your bathroom scale, or your boyfriend or girlfriend's expressed love and devotion for you, or the score on an IQ test, it is first necessary to know that what you are weighing, hearing, or reading is dependable. The dependability of an IQ test is expressed by what is called a *reliability coefficient,* which usually has to be in the neighborhood of .90 in order for us to "believe" it. (A perfect reliability coefficient is 1.00) A high reliability coefficient simply means that we can depend on scores to be fairly similar on repeated administrations of the same test. It is, however, important to keep in mind that coefficients of reliability are based on the performance of large groups, which means that *individual* scores might vary to some extent either on the same test or from one test to another. Since an effort is made to produce intelligence tests that are consistent with one another, it is important that they be as reliable as possible.

Actually, it is not likely that a person who scores well below average on one IQ test will score average or above on another test. But there would be nothing particularly surprising in the fact that a person whose IQ is 110 on one test obtains an IQ of, say, 103 or 117 on another test taken on the same day. Indeed, differences larger than these have been found when individuals take the same test twice. For example, one research effort found that of forty students who scored between 90 and 94 on Form L of the Stanford-Binet, only eleven received the same IQ when retested a short time later on Form M. Fourteen students gained IQ points the second time around while fifteen lost points.[17]

On the whole, however, IQs tend to be relatively stable and therefore relatively reliable. That is, the chances are fairly good that a youngster's IQ at age twelve will be within seven or so points of his IQ at age nine. If his intelligence performance at age nine was somewhat above average for nine year olds, he will in all probability be somewhat above average at age twelve as well. Although fairly reliable, we have to keep in mind that IQ scores for the same person can and do change over time. Which brings us to an important question.

How Stable Is IQ Over Time?

In a classic longitudinal study, Majorie Honzik and her co-workers[18] studied a group of 252 children, who comprised a representative sample of children living in an urban community, by giving them mental tests at specified ages between twenty-one months and eighteen years. Four important findings emerged from that investigation:

1. The IQs of almost 60 percent of the participants changed 15 or more points between the ages of six and eighteen; a third of the group changed 20 or more points; and the IQs of 9 percent changed over 30 points.

2. Some individuals showed consistent upward or downward trends in IQ over a long period resulting in changes of as much as 50 IQ points.

3. Changes in mental test scores tended to be in the direction of the family norm as indicated by the parents' education and socioeconomic status. To put it another way, children with middle- and lower-range IQs tended to have higher IQs as they matured if they had parents with college educations and upper-middle-class status. On the other hand, children who had middle-to-high-range IQs tended to have lower IQs if they grew up in lower-class surroundings with parents of limited education.

4. Children whose IQ scores reflected the most marked fluctuations had life histories that showed unusual variations with respect to disturbing and stabilizing factors—e.g., sickness, death, or separation, or divorce of parents, etc.

TO DO

If you were able to arrange it (and risk it), an interesting thing you could do is to obtain permission from the schools you attended to examine your own mental scores over the years. How stable are they? If there are shifts, do they correspond to life experiences that may have encouraged a decrease or increase in your test performance?

The importance of these findings is stressed in the authors' concluding remarks when they noted that:

The observed fluctuations in the scores of individual children indicate the need for the utmost caution in the predictive use of a single test score, or even two such scores.   This finding seems of especial importance since many plans for individual children are made by schools, juvenile courts, and mental hygiene clinics on the basis of a single mental test score.   Specifically, it should be noted that a prediction based on a 6-year test would be wrong to the extent of 20 IQ points for one out of three children by the age of 18 years, and to the extent of 15 IQ points for approximately six out of ten children.[19]

In a recent monograph by McCall et al.,[20] developmental changes in mental performance were reported for large samples of youth from different social classes from the time they were two and one-half to seventeen years of age.   Among the more interesting findings of this study were the following:

1. Among home-reared middle-class children, one of every three displayed a progressive change of more than 30 points, and one in seven shifted more than 40 points.

2. High-IQ children were more likely to show greater amounts of change than low-IQ children.

3. This was some indication that boys were more likely to show increases in IQ over time than girls and that girls who were relatively more favorably disposed to traditional masculine roles tend to increase in IQ more than girls who are less so. (It may well be that contemporary changes in the female role in society may modify this conclusion in the not to distant future.)

4. While most samples studies showed increases in IQ over age, not all subjects nor groups of subjects followed that trend.   For example, the predominant pattern was one of no change or decline in IQ over age for low-income and culturally isolated groups.   (Environment *does* make a difference!)

5. Persons whose IQ increased over time differed in personality from those who showed decreases, and these personality correlates were related in part to age and sex.   Preschool children whose IQ's increased were described as independent and competitive.   Elementary grade students who made the greatest IQ gains were described as independent, scholastically competitive, self-initiating, the problem solving.

6. Parents of children who reflected the greatest IQ gains were found to encourage intellectual activities and to take a moderate, rationally structured approach to discipline.

Socioeconomic Status Can Affect IQ Stability

There is evidence to suggest that IQ stability is more pronounced among lower- and middle-range scores.   For example, Stennett[21] compared the IQs of 800 boys and girls, who were divided into equal groups on the basis of sex and socioeconomic status (SES) and found a tendency for the IQs of children above average in SES to rise over time, while the IQs of below average SES children tended to decline.

These findings were supported by Lindholm,[22] who analyzed the IQs for five groups of children tested ten times between the ages of three and twelve and found that children in the lowest IQ groups (90 to 109) showed the least amount of change, whereas those in the highest group (140 to 169) showed the greatest change toward higher scores. Children in the low-middle, middle, and high-middle groups showed some change, but the overall effect was one of general stability. Perhaps one of the reasons that high IQ children tend to move in the direction of higher IQs as they get older is due to what could be their natural curiosity and quickness about learning new things. It could also be that they are the benefactors of a positive self-fulfilling prophecy that began when they were very young; e.g., "My, what a bright boy Mitch is. He surely will do well in school," or "Marilyn is such a smart little girl. School will probably be a snap for her."

Personality Characteristics Are Related to Changes in IQ

Having a high IQ is apparently not the only factor that contributes to positive changes over time. Research conducted at the Fels Institute for Human Development has demonstrated that personality characteristics such as independence, aggressiveness, self-initiative, and competitiveness are associated with increases in IQ over time. (You will recall that McCall's research found the same thing.) For instance, Sontag[23] and his co-workers investigated factors associated with IQ shifts from infancy to ten years of age and found that the child who is encouraged to meet some of his needs through aggressive, independent problem solving is apparently laying the groundwork for a high need for achievement that, in turn, is related to an accelerated mental growth rate. This is consistent with an observation made from Coopersmith's research[24] in Chapter 11, namely, students are more likely to do well in school if their parents *expect* them to do well and make this expectation clear. Consistent with what we've said already, Sontag also observed that children between the ages of three and six who were the most emotionally dependent on their parents were more apt to experience slower intellectual growth. Look at it this way—if a young child is waited on, pampered, and worse, babied, by the primary adults in his life, it is not likely that he will be terribly motivated to fend for himself by the way of spirited competitiveness, interest in solving his own problems (Mom does it—why worry?), and self-initiated behavior.

What these studies indicate is that certain kinds of conditions are favorable for influencing changes in IQ, thereby influencing its stability over time.   Perhaps the most important things to remember about this are that IQ development tends to move in the direction of the family norm, and the encouragement of independent behavior during early childhood may be a necessary condition for helping a youngster stretch his mental muscle by solving more and more of his own problems.   Although IQ tends to be relatively stable, it can change, which is why it is so incredibly important not to label a young child as "too stupid to learn" on the basis of limited IQ evidence.   If anything, it is better to err in the direction of hope than despair.   This brings to mind an interesting study by Strauss,[25] who found that among 500 successful scientists with Ph.D. degrees, 7 percent had been in the lowest quarter of their high school graduating classes and many had obtained IQ scores assumed to be too low for college graduation!

The question remains: How does one get his IQ or "intelligence" to begin with?   Does it come from heredity, environment, or both?

HEREDITY, ENVIRONMENT, AND IQ: CONTROVERSY, DEBATE, AND JENSEN

Although the heredity-environment issue has been an ongoing debate for over fifty years in psychological and educational circles, it has escalated to new peaks of polemics in recent years.   The catalyst for this new controversy about whether it is environment or genes that contribute the most to one's intellectual development has been Arthur R. Jensen, an educational psychologist from the University of California, whose 1969 article in *The Harvard Educational Review,* "How Much Can We Boost IQ and Scholastic Achievement?"[26] landed on the social-psychological-political scene like a ton of TNT.   Only rarely do scientific reports appearing in scholarly journals get the sort of play and press that Jensen did with his article.

Some Reflections of My Own

The Jensen controversy is a heated, emotional issue.   Professor Jensen has been publically berated in scores of newspapers and journals by both newswriters and his own colleagues.   He has been physically assaulted in public lectures by alleged "liberals" and, at various times, he has been under police guard because of threats to his life.   For persons looking for ways to support an essentially racist stance, Jensen's efforts have been applauded and vigorously encouraged.

Those persons interested in soothing racial tensions and in building a more equal America have viewed Jensen's research findings with attitudes ranging from severe skepticism to utter disbelief. I, for one, am not comfortable with Jensen's basic conclusion (heredity determines most of intelligence) because it is, for me, a fatalistic one; it offers little promise for improvement and sets the tone more for an attitude of resignation than for hope. I am, however, comfortable with Jensen the man; although I do not know him well, I know him well enough to know that he is an honest, sincere human being interested in the discovery of new knowledge through scientific inquiry.

Ignorance helps make no man wise, and with this in mind I'll do my best to give you some of the evidence on both sides of the heredity-environment debate. (An excellent synopsis, by the way, of Jensen's position is Lee Edson's "Jensenism, N. The Theory That IQ Is Determined Largely by the Genes," *New York Times Magazine,* 31 August 1969.)

Jensen's Basic Ideas

Jensen's article begins with an appraisal of the alleged failure of compensatory education programs in their goal to help preschool ghetto youngsters overcome years of cultural deprivation in order to compete more favorably with middle-class youngsters in school. Basically what he does is to question the central premise behind these programs, namely, that differences in IQ are due primarily to environmental influences, and brings evidence to bear to support the opposite point of view, which is that genetic factors are much more important than environmental ones in causing differences in intelligence. One of Jensen's major theses is that extreme environmental deprivation can keep a child from reaching his genetic potential, but an enriched educational program cannot necessarily push a child beyond his potential. So far so good; these are reasonable, plausible conclusions with which one may or may not agree.

But Jensen went further with his analysis, and, in what has turned out to be the most controversial aspect of his 123-page article, he asserted that certain kinds of learning abilities seem to be characteristic of particular ethnic groups and independent of social class and that these differences are genetically determined. Jensen's central position is basically this: Intelligence is a natural trait, which is part of the total genetic pool and unequally distributed among individuals. Theoretically, a genius or a dullard can be found anywhere, regardless of race or social milieu. In practice, however, Jensen insists that in terms of the average IQ, whites score about 15 points higher than blacks on IQ tests. He makes the further assertion that Indians, who are even more disadvantaged than blacks, are nevertheless more intelligent. Further, he asserts that blacks as a group—as opposed to any single individual black—test out lower than white or Orientals on that aspect of general intelligence that involves abstract thinking and problem-solving ability. He goes on to add that this ability (which he equates with ability measured by IQ tests) is largely inherited and therefore not very accessible to environmental manipulation such as compensatory preschool education programs.

According to Jensen, what is critically missing among blacks is what constitutes formal intelligence: conceptual learning and problem-solving ability. Based on this conclusion, he recommends that we distinguish between two genotypically distinct processes underlying a continuum ranging from "simple" associative learning, which he labels *Level I*, to complex conceptual learning, which he calls *Level II*. Memorizing the names of objects, learning by rote, and trial and error learning are examples of Level I. Learning concepts and solving complex problems are good examples of Level II. With the idea in mind that heredity plays the largest part in determining intelligence, the ideal educational world of Jensen would provide two types of education: one directed toward the acquisition of certain basic skills and information and the other directed toward concept learning and complex problem-solving skills.

In spite of what seems to be an unshakable stance, Jensen himself is among the first to admit to the uncertainty of our knowledge of the causes of race differences in mental abilities. In Jensen's words:

> I do not claim any direct or definite evidence, in terms of genetic research, for the existence of genotype intelligence differences between races or other human population groups. I have not urged acceptance of a hypothesis on the basis of insufficient evidence. . . . Let me stress that none of the research I have discussed . . . allows one to conclude anything about the intelligence of any individual black or white person.[27]

Jensen is by no means alone among researchers who feel that intelligence is largely hereditary. Psychologist Richard Herrnstein[28] avoids the racial issue but concludes from his studies on intelligence that not only is it for the most part genetically determined, but that IQ influences social status to the extent that the nation already has a high IQ ruling class and a lower class with IQs below average. He believes, moreover, that these differences will become sharper. That is, the better a nation succeeds in encouraging each man to reach his level of ability, the more will wealth and prestige be concentrated at the top. At the bottom he predicts there will be a human residue that will have difficulty mastering the common occupations and who, in all likelihood, will be born to parents who have similarly failed.

A dismal view, this, and one which offers little optimism for either remedial or compensatory education programs. Perhaps this is one of the reasons that the heredity point of view fans the flame of so much controversy and debate. It seems like such a deterministic view — even fatalistic in some ways — and it runs counter to what seems to be a basic human need for hope and at least a cautious optimism about things being a little better tomorrow than they are today.

TO THINK ABOUT

Before reading further, think about your own feelings and views about the heredity-IQ issue. Is intelligence mostly the result of heredity, environment, or an equal combination of the two? Why do you believe the way you do? How do you suppose these beliefs — assuming they don't change — will influence your behavior as a teacher?

Arguments Against the Jensen Point of View

As you might suspect, Jensen's views about intelligence being determined by factors which are 80 percent hereditary and 20 percent environmental have not gone unchallenged. Psychologist Gilbert Voyat, for example, observes that Jensen's strategy in demonstrating the roles of heredity and environment is to use exclusively statistical evidence and goes on to say, "It is a typical case of validation by quantification. It is impressive, precise, and wrong headed."[29] Harvard psychologist Jerome Kagan[30] analyzed the same data from which Jensen derived his conclusions and suggested — in an article aptly titled, "Inadequate Evidence and Illogical Conclusions" — that the Jensen data can also be interpreted to indicate that environmental differences are *more*, not less, significant than genetic ones. In fact, Kagan's article was one of seven papers appearing in a subsequent issue of the *Harvard Educational Review*, which was devoted entirely to counter-arguments to the Jensen position.

Among other things, Kagan observes that the low IQs reported for youngsters from disadvantaged backgrounds may be the result of poor rapport between test administrators and children, which may contribute to many children failing to understand directions and what is expected of them when tests are administered. This is not idle speculation. For example, recent research by British psychologist Peter Watson has shown that when a white person gives an IQ test to black children, the tendency is for scores to drop.

. . . we found that with a younger age group — the seven to eight year olds — a white tester made their performance worse, no matter what the instructions were. Further, this drop in performance was greater with older children. We infer that young black children in predominately white schools see white persons as threatening. Later on, the children learn that assessment by whites is sometimes valuable; however they function well only in those conditions in which they feel secure. As black children come to learn the significance of the IQ test, it becomes more threatening. . . .[31]

Watson does not suggest that heredity plays no part at all in determining intelligence test differences between black and white youth, but he does present some rather intriguing evidence to indicate that a black child may feel more stress when tested by a white examiner, which can adversely influence his performance. This is a consequence of poor testing conditions and not poor genes. Indeed, Cazden[32] has shown that when testing conditions are improved, that is, where test administrators were given instructions to make certain that disadvantaged children understood the nature of the test and felt comfortable with the tester before the test was begun, the subjects' scores were eight to ten points higher than those not so prepared.

As you can see, there are those who argue that heredity plays the bigger part in determining intelligence and those who say that environment does. It may help our total understanding of the heredity-environment issue if we take a look at some of the research related to it.

Influence of Heredity on Intelligence

Research efforts stretching back as far as 1869, when Francis Galton published his book, *Hereditary Genius,* have repeatedly demonstrated that a child's intelligence is usually related to that of his parents. While evidence of this sort offers strong support for the idea that intelligence follows family lines, they neither prove nor disprove that it is inherited, for good heredity is typically accompanied by good environment and poor heredity by poor environment. Thus, it is difficult to tell under these conditions exactly which comes first — good heredity or good environment.

One approach psychologists have used to investigate the "which comes first?" question is to study a variety of sibling and non-sibling relationship combinations ranging all the way from identical twins raised together to unrelated children raised together. The advantage to studying identical twins is that we know from the outset that they share exactly the same genes for all the attributes they will ever develop, including mental ability. The assumption is that when children of the same heredity are brought up in different environments, any tested differences in their abilities must be due to their environments. On the other hand, when children representing different genetic backgrounds are raised in the same environment, differences in their tested intelligence can be more reasonably attributed to heredity. The correlations between various sibling and non-sibling relationships are summarized in Table 6–3. (Note: A perfect positive correlation or relationship between hereditary factors and intelligence would be +1.00. With data of this sort, correlations between .80 and .92 express a very high rela-

TABLE 6–3. *Hereditary Relationship and Correlation Between IQ Scores*

1. Identical twins reared together	.929
2. Identical twins reared apart	.829
3. Fraternal twins reared together	.539
4. Siblings reared together	.514
5. Siblings reared apart	.473
6. Unrelated children reared together	.267

Average Correlations Between Various Hereditary Relationships and IQ scores. (From C. Burt. "The Inheritance of Intelligence and Mental Ability." *American Psychologist* 13(1958):1–15, reprinted by permission.)

tionship; correlations between .40 and .79 an above average relationship, and the .26 correlation you see would express a rather low relationship between heredity and intelligence.)

These correlations indicate that, at least to some extent, intelligence as reflected in IQ does tend to have a genetic base. The correlation between the IQ of one child and another chosen at random would be zero, but the correlations between siblings are always positive. Other research has shown that even such distant family relationships such as first cousins and grandparents and grandchildren show IQ correlations between .30 and .35.[33] For identical twins reared in the same home, it can reach .92. This is a very high correlation indeed, especially when we consider that even the same person's IQ scores, calculated at different times, do not show a perfect correlation. For example, when the same child takes the Stanford-Binet test at one-year or two-year intervals, the correlation is around .90.

There seems little question that heredity plays a part in determining intelligence. The question is: How much of a part and to what extent can a good environment enhance intelligence or a poor environment depress it? Let us turn now to the other side of the coin.

The Impact of Environment on Intelligence

All in all, there is abundant evidence to indicate that an environment that does not encourage or provide stimulation for the kinds of skills and abilities measured by intelligence tests is likely to result in a lower IQ score than a growing youngster would be capable of attaining under better circumstances. Moreover, the longer a child remains in a deprived environment, the lower his IQ score is likely to be. For example, after an extensive review of research evidence, Professor Bloom[34] of the University of Chicago estimates that exposure to extreme environments—i.e., either a very good environment or a very poor one—during the first four years of life may affect the development of intelligence by about 2.5 IQ points per year, which over that four-year period is about 10 points. He further estimates that the cumulative effect of environmental influences during the first seventeen years is on the order of 20 IQ points, when one contrasts deprived and enriched environments as they exist today.

Psychologists are not the only ones who have studied the IQ issue and its relationships to heredity and environment. For instance, regarding IQ test differences between races, geneticist Irving Gottesman writes:

> My evaluation of the literature on race differences has led me to conclude that the differences between mean IQs of Negro Americans and other Americans can be accounted for almost wholly by environmental disadvantages that start in the prenatal period and continue through a lifetime.[35]

Support for Gottesman's conclusions is found in several different research efforts. In one instance, no IQ differences were found among groups of black male children three years old who had been born to families of different social status.[36] If it is true, as hereditarians claim, that differences in IQ among children from different socioeconomic backgrounds are because of genetic rather than environmental differences, then we would not expect that children born to families of different social status to be the same. Still other research shows that tested IQ differences between black and white children rarely appear before the age of twenty months or so.[37] These results indicate that differences appearing later are the result of environmental rather than hereditary factors.

Improvement of environment leads to improvement in IQ. The incredible impact that environment can have on intellectual growth is dramatically illustrated in the findings of an important longitudinal study conducted by developmental psychologist Harold Skeels.[38] For over thirty years he followed the lives of twenty-five children, thirteen of whom were transferred from an orphanage to an institution for the mentally retarded before they were three years old where they received special care, attention, and stimulation. The average IQ for this group was 64. After about a year and a half in their new "home," their average IQ had risen by 28 points to 92 and they were judged suitable for adoption into foster homes. In Skeel's follow-up study thirty years later, he found that the children had completed an average of about twelve years of schooling and that all were living at about the average level of occupation and income for their area of the nation.

This investigation also tracked the life histories of twelve other children who, for lack of opportunity to be moved elsewhere, had to remain in what was described as a "relatively nonstimulating orphanage environment over a prolonged period of time." As it happened, these children actually began with higher average IQs than the others, 87. However, in the two years immediately following their placement in the orphanage this average dropped

26 points to 61.   A followup study thirty years later found that these youngsters had completed an average of only four years of school, that a third of them were still institutionalized, and that only one of them worked at a job above the level of dishwasher or napkin-folder in a cafeteria.

The evidence for the impact of environment on intelligence is striking when we consider that the trends toward intellectual stimulation or retardation were enhanced or facilitated depending on where the children in each of these groups were placed during their early developmental years.   Skeels speculated that if the children who remained in the orphanage had had an opportunity to be placed in suitable adoptive homes while they were growing up, most or all of them may have developed along more normal lines.

A Final Word on the Heredity-Environment Issue

The endless rhetoric about whether it is environment or heredity that contributes the most to IQ development is probably more academic than practical.   The fact is that man's pool of the various genes affecting his performance on an intelligence test is infinitely varied.   Although no two people except identical twins share the same inheritance, it is also true that no two people *including* identical twins are ever subject to exactly the same environmental influences every hour of the day and every day of their lives.

Another factor that fogs the heredity-environment issue is the use and construction of IQ tests.   As one psychologist put it, "When Chicano (or black) children score lower than Anglos on a test made of Anglo items there's no need for debate about heredity and environmental factors."[39]   The point is well taken: Frequently intelligence tests are unfair to many non-white, non-Anglo-Saxon, and even poor white persons because of language, background, and cultural differences.

IQ averages between this group or that group do not tell us much about individual potential.   More than that, even if the amount of intellectual heredity were known for an individual, an IQ score is by no means an indicator of an individual's willingness to work hard, of his capacity to persist at a task until it is completed, or — as my track coach used to say — his ability to "gut it out."

Most psychologists and educators accept the more moderate view, which is that in the constant interaction between heredity and environment, heredity probably determines a top and a bottom limit on each person's IQ score and that environment then determines where within this range the score will actually fall.[40]

We might also keep in mind that there is nothing about the assertion that 80 percent of IQ is determined by heredity that implies anything about the changeability of IQ.   We know, for example, that there is a very high correlation (approximately .90, which is not far from perfect +1.00 correlation) between height and hereditability. In spite of the high correlation between these two factors, the average height of people in the United States and Japan has increased several inches in the past seventy years. Better nutrition and sounder health practices have contributed to this increase in height. In other words, by improving certain environmental conditions genetic structure has been changed. Tuberculosis once had high hereditability, but now the bacillus is so rare that contracting TB depends less upon one's genetic susceptibility and more on one's likelihood of exposure. The hereditability is now low. Therefore, a hereditability of .80 for IQ in the broad sense of the word says nothing about our ability to influence such performance in the future.

The debate about heredity and environment will very likely continue, but as it does an observation by Bloom may be a good one for those of us concerned with teaching and learning to pay attention to:

> The psychologist and geneticist may wish to speculate about how to improve the genetic pool — the educator cannot and should not. The educator must be an environmentalist — bridled or unbridled. It is through the environment that he must fashion the educational process. Learning goes on by proving the appropriate environment. If heredity imposes limits — so be it. The educator must work with what is left, whether it be 20 percent of the variance or 50 percent.[41]

THE GROWTH AND DECLINE OF INTELLIGENCE OVER TIME

A great many investigations have been conducted to study the development of intellectual growth over time. Overall, the evidence strongly indicates that intellectual development is most rapid during the early years and slows with increasing age. This evidence leads to some interesting questions: At what age do the abilities measured by intelligence tests reach their peak? Once any given peak is attained, does the ability then decline during middle to old age?

As you can see in Figure 6–3, more than 40 percent of mature intellectual growth has been reached by ten and one-half years of age and that growth from then on is progressively slower.[42] As is evident in Figure 6–4, mental growth follows a rather shallow, steeply slanted S-shaped path, which means that growth occurs very rapidly during infancy and the preschool years and then gradually slows down after that point. We might add here that intellectual growth or "power" (ability to think, solve problems, understand complex issues) does not necessarily stop at some magical age. Indeed, we probably all know persons up in years whose sharp minds and quick wit seem not at all diminished by their advanced years. There is, in fact, research to indicate that intellectual growth continues

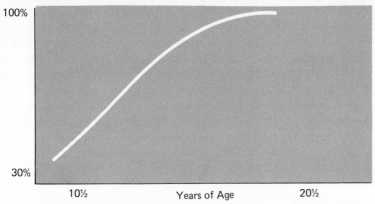

(From H. E. Jones and H. S. Conrad. "Mental Development in Adolescence." National Society for the Study of Education, 43rd Yearbook, Part I, 1944, pp. 146–163. Reprinted by permission.)

FIGURE 6-3. Intellectual Growth from Ten and One-half to Twenty and One-half Years of Age

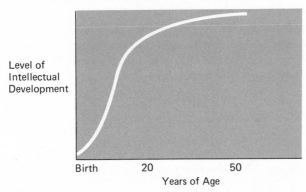

(From N. Bayley. "On the Growth of Intelligence." American Psychologist 10(1955):805–818. Copyright 1955 by the American Psychological Association. Reprinted by permission.)

FIGURE 6-4. A Hypothetical Composite Age Curve Showing the Growth of Intelligence from Birth to the Middle Years

longer for the bright and well-educated than is the case for those of lower intelligence.[43,44]   Other research shows that intellectual growth continues until well into one's later years for both superior and above average persons.[45–48]

Crystallized and Fluid Intelligence Differ in Rate of Decline

The intellectual capacity that seems to have the greatest resistance to deterioration over time is what Cattell[49] has called *crystallized* intelligence.

This refers to that part of our intellectual capacity that is a precipitate out of experience. It includes such abilities as verbal, numerical, and reasoning skills, all of which are taught by, honed, and enhanced through both formal and informal experiences. Crystallized intelligence increases with one's experience and with the education that provides new methods and perspectives for dealing with that experience.

Another component of intelligence discussed by Cattell is *fluid* intelligence, that aspect of intellectual ability most apt to slow down and decrease with age. This dimension of intelligence is relatively independent of formal education and is determined by one's endowment in cortical, neurological-connection count development. Not surprisingly, research shows that the older a person is the more likely he is to receive lower scores than younger persons on those parts of an intelligence test which emphasize perceptual or manual speed, close attention to detail, or long periods of concentration.

On a happier note, and by way of contrast, research also indicates that crystallized intelligence increases throughout most of adulthood. Here alternative mechanisms are used. Compensating for the loss of one ability for the surplus of another, the older person uses crystallized intelligence in place of fluid intelligence.[50-53] Although he may be short on speed and brilliance, he may be long on insight and wisdom, qualities frequently associated with the older person who continues to grow intellectually. An old dog can not only be taught new tricks, but he may even understand them better.

SOME RELATIONSHIPS BETWEEN INTELLIGENCE AND SCHOOL PERFORMANCE

A question of considerable practical importance has to do with whether or not one's measured IQ is related to one's measured achievement. At the elementary level, the correlations between IQ and reading and arithmetic are about +.50, which is a moderately high statistical relationship. In high school, the correlation between intelligence and reading may be as high as the +.80's, while the correlations between intelligence and achievement in English, social studies, and the sciences range in the +.50's and +.60's.[54]

Actually, it should not be surprising to find that a positive relationship exists between IQ and achievement, particularly when we consider that there is anywhere from a 90 to 95 percent overlap between material included in tests of intelligence and that incorporated in both standardized and teacher-made tests of achievement.[55]

Intelligence test scores tend to be related to other kinds of success, too, but not as highly as with school marks. For example, one investigator found that fourth and sixth graders who scored in the top 10 percent on intelligence tests were likely to be perceived as leaders by their classmates and to show above average artistic ability. They were also noted to have high emotional adjustment.[56] Another study found that high IQ students usually scored lower on test anxiety,[57] and still other research has shown that a quality shared in common by high school boys outstanding in athletics, science, fine arts, leadership, and academic achievement was their tendency to score high on intelligence tests.[58]

All in all, research indicates a positive relationship between intelligence test performance and success both inside and outside the classroom. This relationship is not always high, but it is almost always in a positive direction. A characteristic about the relationship between intelligence test scores and achievement is that it tends to be highest for subjects heavily dependent on verbal and reasoning ability, perhaps reflecting the fact that the tests probably sample these abilities more than others. Another characteristic about this relationship is that it is higher at the high school level than at earlier levels. Apparently, the higher one goes up the educational ladder, the more directly relevant intelligence testing becomes to the sort of cognitive skills necessary for at least average achievement in high school and post-high school study.

There Are Limitations to What an IQ Test Can Predict

It is important to note that in no case is there a perfect correlation between measured ability and achievement. There are just too many variables other than sheer intelligence that enter into how a student performs. Other factors, such as drive, interest, motivation, opportunity, not to mention one's self-concept, greatly influence how intellectual ability is developed and used. Strong determination and hard work can make up for many deficiencies. Also, not every student has the necessary qualities or psychological makeup for high achievement, nor does every student with a low IQ lack them. There is many a boy, for instance, who is highly skilled at fixing gadgets or repairing engines (mechanical intelligence) or in conducting class meetings or organizing parties (social intelligence) who scores only average on standardized intelligence tests. An endless number of teachers have puzzled over why a boy or girl with the highest IQ is doing only average work or even failing. The point is that a single IQ score can't begin to tell us all there is to know about a student. At best, an intelligence test result can indicate the possible range of a student's potential, but it is practically useless for telling us whether or not he will achieve his potential. We have to begin to know our students more personally to discern that. When considering the relationship between mental ability and school achievement, there is an important consideration we shouldn't overlook.

IQ, School Achievement, and Minority Groups:
A Note of Caution

Although the findings we discussed above are rather typical in studies involving middle-class white students, there is evidence that they do not necessarily apply to non-white or poor white disadvantaged students. For example, one study found no relationship between academic aptitude test scores and grades in a Detroit area high school for black male students, although the usual positive relationships did appear for white and black female students. On the other hand, tests of achievement motivation were positively correlated with grades for black and white students of both sexes, thus indicating that a student's need for achievement was better than intelligence tests as a predictor of academic success for black students.[59] Again, we're back to the idea that intelligence tests may unfairly assess certain children whose lack of opportunity for learning puts them at a disadvantage when it comes to taking standardized mental tests.

There is other evidence to suggest that even when the IQ of disadvantaged youth is positively correlated with standardized achievement tests, they still get lower marks from teachers than do advantaged children with IQ's similar to the disadvantaged. For example, one study found that the IQ of lower-class children correlated consistently low with teachers' marks than did the IQ of higher-class children. At the same time, correlations between IQ tests and achievement test scores for lower-class children were higher than correlations between IQ and teacher marks, which suggests that bright lower-class students who may have been doing a fairly good job of learning were less apt to be recognized and rewarded by their teachers as were higher-class students.[60] One explanation for this may be that some teachers, either consciously or unconsciously, have negative attitudes or low expectations for lower-class or disadvantaged students and thereby fail to recognize what could very well be average or above average achievement. Mercer[61] and Rosenthal,[62] among others, have demonstrated that once a child is *labeled* as disadvantaged or slow or retarded or whatever, this could be the beginning of a self-fulfilling prophecy in which not only the teacher, but the child behaves in such a way that it ends up being true. A distinct possibility, this, and one which all of us who teach would do well to keep in mind.

So far we've focused our attention on the various dimensions and expressions of intelligence. Let's turn our attention now to another aspect of cognitive behavior related to achievement and performance in school.

VARIETIES AND EXPRESSIONS
OF CREATIVE BEHAVIOR

Over the past fifteen years or so a great deal of writing and research has gone on regarding the nature and growth of creativity. The whole idea of why and how some persons are "different" than others in terms of how they think, plan, organize their perceptions, and carry out their work seems a fascinating question to study. From whence comes the man who marches to a different drummer, to whom the gathered wisdom of the ages is but chaff upon the wind? Is he really different or is it an illusion? Who, and what, is the "creative person?"

To begin with, we cannot be certain that there even is such a creature—at least in some pure form. Actually, we have a semantic difficulty here. For example, "ordinary" persons may be highly creative under certain circumstances—as witness the performance of prisoners in concentration camps or even a man preparing his income tax forms. On the other hand, quite potentially gifted persons may not do anything particularly creative—i.e., may not do anything one might call original in a whole lifetime but will cling to the safe and accepted. The world is full of them.

Before going further we should examine an important question.

What Is Creativity?

D. W. MacKinnon,[63] a psychologist at the University of California who has studied creativity extensively, suggests that a creative act is one which (1) involves the production of something new and rare, (2) helps to reach some recognizable goal, and (3) is carried through to completion. Thus, the glib dilettante who seldom sees his ideas through to completion is not creative, and neither, for that matter, is the madman out of touch with reality or the idiot savant. Thus, when we talk about a creative person, we are generally referring to someone who generates not only many good ideas, but also many unusual, unexpected, or unique ideas that are "good" with respect to some quality criterion. When we speak of creativity we could be speaking of Einstein, Beethoven, Confucius, or we could be speaking of a college sophomore's analysis and proposed solutions for the unemployment problem or a fifth grader's poem about Christmas or even a Fran Tarkington broken-play improviso that went for a touchdown.

Whereas MacKinnon focuses on the product of creative behavior, Maslow[64] preferred to focus on the process itself. For Maslow, creativity—particularly the self-actualizing kind—grows naturally out of certain personality qualities such as boldness, courage, freedom, spontaneity, integration, and self-acceptance.

267

Among other things, creative thinking can result in finding new uses for old things. (Ohio Development Department)

Creative expression can take many different forms. One does not necessarily have to be a great composer or painter or writer or scientist in order to be creative. Maslow, in his discussion of creativity in self-actualizing people talked about one of his subjects, an uneducated, poor woman, who was a full-time housewife and mother:

[She] was a marvelous cook, mother, wife and homemaker. With little money, her home was somehow always beautiful. She was a perfect hostess. Her meals were banquets. Her taste in linens, silver, glass, crockery, and furniture was impeccable. She was in all of these areas original, novel, ingenious, unexpected, inventive. I just *had* to call her creative. I learned from her and others like her that a first-rate soup is more creative than a second-rate painting.[65]

Approaches to the Measurement of Creativity

Creativity tests attempt to measure what has been called "divergent" thinking, which, as described earlier, is a cognitive process that diverges — bends, varies, moves away from the usual ways of perceiving and thinking. Actually, this is easier said than done because of the endless controversy about what is and what is not creative. Unfortunately, it is simpler to measure and study sheer originality of response than other qualities necessary for true creativity. Mere novelty, remember, is not enough. Aside from being different and unusual, a creative response must also be appropriate. Even Einstein's theory of relativity was in accord with and relevant to information known about energy, mass, and the speed of light.

An intelligence test measures convergent thinking — i.e., thinking which analyzes, draws together, synthesizes, and "converges" on the most correct answer. Intelligence, no matter how it is defined, is usually easier to measure because the answers on an intelligence test are either right or wrong. One either knows or he doesn't. Not so with tests of creativity, which are less concerned with what one knows and more concerned with *how one thinks.* Perhaps some examples from some creativity tests will help understand this better. Consider Figures 6–5 and 6–6.

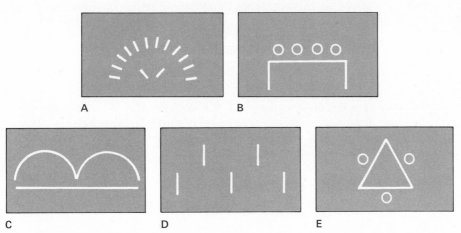

A   B

C   D   E

(From M. A. Wallach and N. Kagan. Modes of Thinking in Young Children. New York: Holt, Rinehart and Winston, 1965. Used by permission.)

FIGURE 6-5. A Test of Creativity

These drawings are shown to fifth-grade children, who are asked to try to imagine what they might look like when completed. Most children make routine responses, but a few come up with original and creative ideas. The usual responses are: (A) the sun, (B) table with glasses on it, (C) two igloos, (D) raindrops, and (E) three people sitting at a table. Unusual responses would be: (A) a lollipop bursting into pieces, (B) a foot and toes, (C) two haystacks on a flying carpet, (D) worms hanging, and (E) three mice eating a piece of cheese.

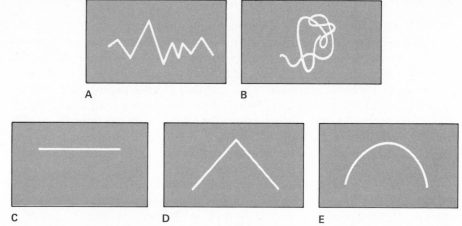

(*From M. A. Wallach and N. Kagan.* Modes of Thinking in Young Children. *New York: Holt, Rinehart and Winston, 1965. Used by permission.*)

FIGURE 6-6. A Variation of the Creativity Test

In this variation of the creativity test, children are asked what these lines suggest to them—the lines as a whole, not just in part. Ordinary responses would be: (A) mountains, (B) string, (C) stick, (D) arrow, and (E) rising sun. Unusual and original responses would be: (A) squashed piece of paper, (B) squeezing paint out of a tube, (C) stream of ants, (D) alligator's open mouth, and (E) fishing rod bending with a fish.

TO DO

Another type of test wherein creative individuals function differently from less creative persons is the word association test; the more creative person associates a larger number of categories with each word.[66] Sample test: What is the fourth word that is the associative link with the other three words?

1. Dog   out   cat   —The answer is HOUSE. House is the connective link in the word pairs—e.g. doghouse, out-house, and house-cat.

A few others for you to puzzle over are:*

2. rain   pay   mate   _____

3. maid   graph   candy   _____

4. house   ship   tennis   _____

5. hole   master   board   _____

6. knife   milk   fingers   _____

Still other kinds of items used to measure divergent production abilities are the following:

1. Give as many unusual uses as you can think of for a brick; a rubber band (or some other common object).
2. Make up an original title for the story about Goldilocks and the Three Bears.
3. Formulate as many sentences as you can, the words of which begin with the letters: T M R S P B L W.
4. List as many items as you can think of that are red (or some other color or specified quality).

ANSWERS: 2. check, 3. bar, 4. court, 5. key, 6. butter

Another interesting way to get a creative output is to ask a person to draw two parallel lines and to use these lines in making a design. (Stop. Before reading further, draw two parallel lines and draw a design utilizing them. Then, read on.) Some designs look something like those in Figure 6–7.

All these tests, as you can see, have in common a variety of requests for the unusual, different, and unique—at least they provide opportunities for a person to be different if he wants to be, or if, for that matter, he can be. As we can probably testify to from personal experience, not all people are creative. The question is: What kind of individuals are they and how can we identify them?

Intelligence and Personality Factors Related to Creativity

Highly creative individuals are usually above average in measured intelligence but not necessarily outstanding in this respect. While the relationship between IQ and creativity, as assessed by tests of divergent production, is generally found to be positive,[67,68] it is by no means strikingly high. Although a certain level of intelligence seems necessary for creative output, this level can vary from one field to another and in some may be low. In general, research indicates that individuals with high IQs show a great range of creative talent, from high to low, whereas persons with low IQs are more apt to score lower on creativity tests.[69,70] We might also mention that beyond an IQ of 120 the relationship between intelligence and creativity gets increasingly smaller, which is to say that being more intelligent does not necessarily lead to corresponding increase in creativeness.

Usually, the stereotype of the highly creative youth or adult is that he has an extraordinarily high IQ, is eccentric not only in his thinking, but in appearance, dress, and behavior as well. Sometimes these descriptions do fit a highly creative person, but most of the time they do not.

Creative persons are open to personal feelings and subjective impressions. Regardless of the level of his measured intelligence, what seems to

271

Starting with two parallel lines

A. Some persons draw designs that look like this:

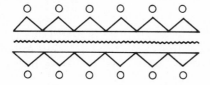 

(Less creative tend to stay inside the "boundaries.")

B. Others look like this:

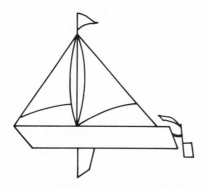 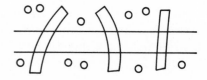

(More creative go outside boundaries, but stay close.)

C. Still others look like this:

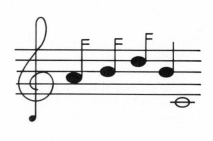

(Highly creative persons go even further outside boundaries—in fact, seem not at all constricted.)

FIGURE 6-7.

characterize the creative person is the relative absence of repression and suppression as mechanisms for the control of his impulses and mental images. Repression, which is a way of keeping rein on one's consciousness, operates against creativity because it keeps significant aspects of a person's subjective experiences from awareness. Before Picasso could paint or sculpt, for example, he had to first be able to deal with his subjective feelings and perceptions with total consciousness. Indeed, before grandma can create an apple pie from scratch, she must first be fully aware of its blend of

ingredients and ultimate taste.   This openness to personal feelings and subjective experiences is one of the most striking characteristics of the creative
person.   Indeed, a fundamental psychological condition for constructive
creativeness is openness to experience for creative effort is essentially a natural consequence of self-realization rather than something one strives for
directly.   Nonetheless, people can be taught to be *more* creative, an idea
we'll deal with shortly.

A creative person is more a perceiver than a judger.   MacKinnon's[71]
research with creative individuals found more of them to be introverted
than extroverted, although those who were extroverts were no less creative
than introverts.   Apparently, creative persons—particularly those who are
highly creative—have rich inner lives and are inclined to spend more time
ruminating among the sensory happenings of their own internal world of
subjective experiences.   MacKinnon also noted that although everyone perceives (can become aware of something) and judges (can come to conclusions about something), a creative person tends to prefer using his mind in
perceiving ways than in judging ways.   That is, where a judging person
emphasizes the control and regulation of experience, the perceptive creative
individual is apt to be more interested and curious, more open and receptive, seeking to experience life in the full.   In a way, the perceptive creative
person sounds a bit like Rogers'[72] fully functioning person, in the sense that
his openness to his world and trust in his perceptual processes enable him to
be the kind of person from whom creative products and creative living are
likely to emerge.   All in all, the more perceptive a person is, the more creative he tends to be.
     There are no one or two personality characteristics associated with crea-
tivity; rather there seem to be many different, but overlapping characteristics.   Consider, for instance, the following two categories of personality
variables and their relationship to creativity:

A. Personality characteristics positively related to creativity:
    1. flexibility
    2. spontaneity
    3. sense of humor
    4. perceptiveness
    5. playfulness
    6. radicalness
    7. intelligence
    8. independence

B. Personality characteristics negatively related to creativity:
    1. rigidity
    2. control

3. neatness
4. logic
5. thoroughness
6. respect for tradition and authority
7. reason
8. tendency to routinize tasks

Creative persons are less tradition-bound. Comparing these two lists of personality characteristics, you can see that a less creative person is typified by a more constrained, orderly, and even predictable life-style.   That is, it is difficult to be too much concerned about, say, logic, neatness, and tradition, while at the same time being open to unique and new ideas, different possibilities, or novel innovations.   As is apparent in Figures 6–5, 6–6, 6–7, more creative persons seem less responsive to conventional perceptions and traditional boundaries.   For example, the response of three mice eating a piece of cheese to box E of Figure 6–5 is surely less conventional and more unique (even humorous, playful sounding) than a more routine response of three people sitting at a table.   Or the parallel lines responses in part C of Figure 6–7 are certainly more imaginative, further out, daring even, than the more

"HE'S A GOOD STUDENT, BUT HIS MIND WANDERS."

The cartoon stretches the point, but the fact is that the minds of creative students do wander more divergently into other (and not always related) content areas.   (A. L. Kaufman, reprinted by permission of Masters Agency)

constrained and boundaried responses in part A. Some personal characteristics, then, of a creative person is his willingness to gamble, take risks, and go beyond established boundaries.

Two other personal characteristics that can be associated with creative persons (actually, they can probably be associated with *any* person who makes something of his life and himself) are a sense of dedication and willingness to work hard. These qualities may not express themselves in the number of hours put in on the job, or in obvious labor, but in the fact that even in sleep or reverie the creative person may be working for a solution.[73] The willingness to spend years simply accumulating data about which a creative question may be asked (Darwin, George Washington Carver, and Thomas Edison are good examples of this) is characteristic of the creative person.

As Maslow notes from his research, creative persons:

> . . . are inhibited, less constricted, less bound, in a word, less enculturated. In more positive terms, they are more spontaneous, more natural, more human. This too would have as one of its consequences what would seem to other people to be creativeness. If we assume, as we may from our study of children, that all people were once spontaneous, and perhaps in their deepest roots still are, but that these people have in addition to their deep spontaneity a superficial but powerful set of inhibitions, then this spontaneity must be checked so as not to appear very often. If there were no choking-off forces, we might expect that every human being would show this special type of creativeness.[74]

Which raises an important question for all of us who teach: How can we encourage and enhance creative output in the classroom? Let's look at some possibilities for this.

Ways to Encourage Creative Activity

If we accept Maslow's basic premise, which is that every person has the capacity for some level of creative expression — and there seems little reason why we cannot accept it — then the problem of education is not necessarily the *production* of creativity, but rather the *release and encouragement* of the creativity that is already present. Here are some suggestions for doing that.

Learn to value that which is different. Make explicitly clear that you *value* creative, different, novel, innovative, and unique ways for doing projects, writing papers, or conducting experiments. Sometimes students are hesitant to be different precisely because they are fearful of rejection, ridicule, or low grades, and they need to be told, to be given "permission" as it were, by the teacher that it is okay to be daring, adventuresome, novel, or in other ways "different." There will, of course, be times when doing things in a different way are *not* appropriate, and they need to be told that, too. In a word, a student needs to know that the teacher *values* creative effort. I have noted in my own teaching, for example, that I invariably receive more creative, "colorful," and off-beat papers or class reports when I have said directly something along the lines of "Be yourself—be different—don't be afraid." Not all students believe that, of course, but it seems to help those who have a readiness to believe it.

Be cautious not to reject nonconformity. Recognize within yourself any tendency to reject or dislike students who are by nature less conforming. It's pretty well known that traits that characterize the creative student—adventuresomeness, nonconformity, impulsiveness, and the like—tend to be traits teachers associate with students they feel negatively toward. Indeed, research has shown that many teachers, if given a choice, would prefer to work with high-intelligence rather than high-creative students.[75] Neither a creative effort nor a creative person is likely to be encouraged in the face of a rejecting teacher demanding total obedience. It may be worth noting that other research indicates that a teacher's effort to be creative himself is the very quality most likely to enhance the creativity of his students.[76] Perhaps if a teacher can work on developing his own creative potential, he can be more tolerant of it in others.

Teach students to ask extending questions. Encourage students to ask "extending" questions, that is, questions that take them from what they know to new and different ways to think about problems. Some examples:

a. Are there ways we can borrow or adopt from ideas or objects that already exist? (e.g., Rudolf Diesel got the idea for his engine from a cigar lighter).
b. Can we think of a new twist or new shape? (e.g., like the buggy-maker who tapered the roller-bearing Leonardo da Vinci had invented 400 years before).
c. Can we make something "less so" by elimination? (e.g., gliders, tubeless tires, and even bikinis).
d. Can we make something "more so" by increasing strength or adding on? (e.g., reinforced heels or toes in hosiery, elbows on jackets, or knees on boys' pants).
e. Can we think of ways to substitute or replace? (e.g., synthetic rubber during World War II, powdered milk for the liquid form, solar energy instead of fossil fuels).
f. Can we reverse the usual process and do the opposite? (e.g., Elias Howe perfected his sewing machine by designing a needle with a hole at the bottom rather than the top).
g. Can we think of ways to combine or put together? (e.g., Ben Franklin, to

avoid changing from one pair of spectacles to another, cut the lenses of each in half and stuck them together for the world's first bifocals).

Be willing to accept that which is new, different, and even imperfect. Recognize that mistakes and imperfections are typically natural consequences of learning activities that are new, different, and original. Youngsters imbued by overzealous teachers and parents with the idea that one should be thoroughly competent and adequate in all possible respects hesitate to talk about their imaginative ideas or display their creative products for fear of ridicule and censure. Above all, a student needs to feel that taking a risk from time to time or doing something different now and then will not lead to some ego damaging personal disaster. All too often, a student fails to make an additional effort because he has received the impression that because an earlier idea or product was not perfect he is a failure. This reminds me of an incident I saw involving a first-grade boy who had just finished a multicolored abstract looking finger painting. He beamed with delight upon finishing it, proudly showed it to his friends, and then took it to his teacher for her to see, too. Her response, "John, what in the world is that?" totally erased John's happy smile and sent him frustrated, put-down, and maybe even a bit angry back to his seat. And that was the end of John's "different" looking finger paintings for the rest of the school year.

An encouraging smile, a helping hand, a word of praise, an accepting attitude, alternative suggestions—each of these represents the sort of human touch necessary for helping a student experience the upper limits of his creative expression. Usually, motivation for learning is more effective, and creative effort more possible, if a teacher can help students concentrate on improvement rather than perfection.

TO DO

Answer yes or no to each of the following:

	yes	no	
1.	_____	_____	I enjoy trying new foods.
2.	_____	_____	I like meeting new people.
3.	_____	_____	I usually look forward to going to new places.
4.	_____	_____	I'm among the first to try new clothing styles.
5.	_____	_____	I like abstract painting that can be interpreted in different ways.

6. _____   _____   I usually appreciate and understand ideas and points of view different than my own.

If you've answered no to four or more of these, what might this suggest about your openness?

Use praise liberally and modify assignments to fit the student.   As the purveyor of rewards and punishments for social and intellectual skills, a teacher is in a very advantageous position for encouraging creativity, curiosity, independence, and self-reliance.   When a student shows some independent thinking a teacher can praise him, and when a student shows signs of boredom a teacher can modify the assignment enough to include his interests.   A fifth-grade boy I know is fascinated by the sea, which, for him, includes all those things that live in it and float on it.   Fortunately he has a wise, sensitive teacher who is able to encourage that interest in creative ways.   For example, when the class was studying Colonial history, the teacher suggested that he either write or report about the *Mayflower.*   For an assignment that had to do with the first Thanksgiving, the teacher suggested that he write about the Pilgrims' use of fish as a fertilizer to grow corn.

Make your guidance available, your expectations clear, and let your flexibility set the tone.   Establishing a climate of total permissiveness is not a good method for encouraging maximum creative expression from all students.   As we will discuss in Chapter 8, research indicates that some students do their best work, indeed, their most creative work when they are clear about the boundaries they are to work within and the teacher's expectations for them.   A fact of life is that few students know what to do when exposed to a totally permissive classroom and that most need the assistance of both a teacher's guidance and expectations to do their best.   I think it is safe to say that there is *no one best* way of teaching for creativity any more than there is one best way for creative expression.   Some students flourish in a totally open, permissive, student-centered classroom, while others function better in more structured circumstances.   There seem to be many different ways for encouraging creative effort and for being creative.   Most of all, perhaps, students need to know that expressing themselves in new and different ways is not only possible, but *valued,* so that those who want to can and those who are somewhat more hesitant may at least try.

Ten Commandments for Enhancing Creative Expression

The author of the following "ten commandments," Joan Brunswick, is a first-grade teacher.   After taking a course on creativity, she reevaluated her own teaching and decided that there were certain things she should and should *not* do that would increase the possibility of creative behavior on the part of her students. I think Ms. Brunswick's "commandments" are very likely relevant for *any* teacher at *any* level, and they seem just the right note on which to conclude our discussion of creative behavior and ways to encourage it in the classroom. What "shalt" a teacher do? In Ms. Brunswick's words:

1. Thou shalt not acknowledge ANY blindly accepted answers by students but shall become a wondering questioning echo saying, "Is it? . . . Are you sure? . . . How can you tell? . . . Did it?"
2. Thou shalt bite thy tongue every time thou wants to settle a disagreement between two children quickly by telling them the right answer.
3. Thou shalt turn thy ears up to HIGHEST to be sure thou doesn't miss any child's comment which might lead to a self-initiated learning opportunity.
4. Thou shalt not remove the string from thy finger to always remind thou to let the learning come from the children's interests, the children's motivations, the children's wonderings.
5. Thou shalt write on the chalkboard 100 times, "I must not let an alarm clock run my classroom activities."
6. Thou shalt honor thy own "crazy" ideas, curiosity and divergent thinking to cultivate a taste for those of others.
7. Thou shalt hold thy breath until the feeling passes if thou ever feel like saying, "We don't have time to waste or fool around with this idea."
8. Thou shalt remember to make every day the day to offer that encouraging word, that pat of security, that smile of comfort.
9. Thou shalt not commit thyself to rigidity in content, method or materials.
10. Thou shalt recite these every day so that thou will come to practice what thou preaches.[77]

EPILOGUE

Intelligence and creativity are elusive concepts, and there seems to be no end to the debate about what each of them means, how each is defined, and how each can best be measured. Psychologists and educators are generally in agreement, however, when it comes to the notion of there being more than one kind or one expression of intelligence and creativity. We can see these different expressions of intelligence and creative effort in our everyday lives. Some persons, for instance, are high in concrete intelligence, which may be expressed in their skills in dealing with things and objects; other individuals are above average in social intelligence, which may be reflected in how they handle group situations or one-to-one interpersonal relationships; still other persons are high in abstract intelligence, which may be shown in their ability to handle ideas expressed in verbal or mathematical concepts.

Intelligence is made up of different components—spatial perception, number facility, verbal comprehension, word fluency, memory ability, inductive reasoning, perceptual speed being the ones underscored in this chapter—and different people can have different amounts of each of these components of intelligence. However we look at it, intelligence is not just one thing, but rather a combination of many different abilities wrapped up in a package we call *intelligence*. Different people can be intelligent in different ways, which, when you think about it, is a hopeful view for any of us who teach or in other ways work with young people because it allows us more latitude when it comes to identifying each individual's strengths and skills.

At best, an intelligence test score gives us a gross estimate of an individual's overall aptitude for scholastic endeavor. All things being equal, it allows us to make a rather general prediction of how well an individual may do in school in relation to others with similar scores. But we have to take a person's intelligence test score with a grain of salt because there are so many things it *doesn't* tell us—e.g., how hard he will work, what his level of motivation is, what his interests are, how he feels about himself, what goals he has set for himself, and so on. These are all very important things to know about a student, which is why there is no substitute for actually *knowing* every one of our students in a more personal way so we can make the best plans possible for his total growth and development.

There is little question that *both* heredity and environment play important parts in determining intellectual growth and development. There is also little question that teachers represent an incredibly important part of each student's environment, particularly when you consider that teachers, for approximately nine months of every year for a twelve-year period, are exposed to growing children and youths during more of their waking hours than are parents: Heredity may determine each person's upper intellectual limits, but environment, it is safe to say, determines how close an individual comes to realizing his outer limits.

Creativity is an aspect of human behavior that cannot be measured by an intelligence test. By definition, a creative effort is one that is novel, unique, different, and unlike anything done before. The mark of a well-rounded educational system is that it teaches not only what we know, but it encourages creative probes into the unknown; it encourages students to not only answer questions, but to ask questions.

The growth, development, and expression of intelligence and creativity is a problem and challenge to each individual teacher. A teacher surely cannot give a young child or adolescent more than he was born with, but he or she can surely be one of the nicer happenings in his environment that allowed him to reach the potential that was there in the first place.

This, then, completes our examination of how children and adolescents grow physically, psychologically, and intellectually. Let's turn our attention now to how good teachers teach these youths and what it takes to become a good teacher.

Write your own chapter summary (major points, ideas, and concepts that had meaning for you).

_____

_____

_____

_____

_____

_____

_____

_____

_____

_____

REFERENCES

1. Binet, A., and T. Simon. "Upon the Necessity of Establishing a Scientific Diagnosis of Inferior States of Intelligence." *The Annuals of Psychology* 11(1905):163–190.
2. Spearman, C. E. "General Intelligence Objectively Determined and Measured." *American Journal of Psychology* 15(1904):201–293.
3. Spearman, C. E. *The Abilities of Man: Their Nature and Measurement.* New York: Crowell-Collier and Macmillan, 1904.
4. Hoepfner, R., and M. O'Sullivan. "Social Intelligence and IQ." *Educational and Psychological Measurement* 28(1968):339–344.
5. Kolstoe, O. P. "A Comparison of Mental Abilities of Bright and Dull Children of Comparable Mental Ages." *Journal of Educational Psychology* 54 (1954):161–168.
6. Thorndike, E. L. *The Measurement of Intelligence.* New York: Columbia University Press, Teachers College, 1927.

7. Rosenzweig, M. R., D. Krech, and E. L. Bennett. "A Search for Relations Between Brain Chemistry and Behavior." *Psychological Bulletin* 57(1960):476–492.

8. Krech, D. "Psychoneurobiochemeducation." *Phi Delta Kappan* 50(March 1969):370–375.

9. Thurstone, L. L. *Vectors of the Mind.* Chicago: University of Chicago Press, 1935.

10. Thurstone, L. L., and T. G. Thurstone. "Factorial Studies in Intelligence." *Psychometric Monograph,* no. 2. Chicago: University of Chicago Press, 1941.

11. Thurstone, T. G. *Your Child's Intelligence.* Washington, D.C.: National Education Association, 1962.

12. Guilford, J. P. "Three Faces of Intellect." *American Psychologist* 14(1959):469–479.

13. Guilford, J. P. *The Nature of Human Intelligence.* New York: McGraw-Hill, 1967.

14. Buros, O. K. (ed.). *The Seventh Mental Measurements Yearbook.* Highland Park, N.J.: The Gryphon Press, 1972.

15. Terman, L. M., and M. A. Merrill. *Stanford-Binet Intelligence Scale.* Boston: Houghton Mifflin, 1960.

16. Wechsler, D. *The Measurement and Appraisal of Adult Intelligence,* 4th ed. Baltimore: Williams and Wilkins, 1958.

17. Terman, L. M., and M. A. Merrill. *Measuring Intelligence.* Boston: Houghton Mifflin, 1937, p. 45.

18. Honzik, M. P., J. W. MacFarlane, and L. Allen. "The Stability of Mental Test Performance Between Two and Eighteen Years." *Journal of Experimental Education* 17(1948):309–324.

19. Honzik, M. P., et al. Op.cit., 1948, p. 322.

20. McCall, R. B., M. I. Appelbaum, and P. S. Hogarty. "Developmental Changes in Mental Performance." *Monographs of the Society for Research in Child Development,* no. 3, 38(1973).

21. Stennett, R. G. "The Relationship of Sex and Socioeconomic Status to IQ Changes." *Psychology in the Schools* 6(1969):385–390.

22. Lindholm, B. W. "Changes in Conventional and Deviation IQs." *Journal of Educational Psychology* 55(1964):110–113.

23. Sontag, L. W., C. T. Baker, and V. L. Nelson. "Mental Growth and Personality Development: A Longitudinal Study." *Monographs of the Society for Research in Child Development,* no. 68, 23(1958).

24. Coopersmith, S. *The Antecedents of Self-Esteem.* San Francisco: W. H. Freeman, 1967.

25. Strauss, E. "High School Backgrounds of Ph.D.'s." *Science Education* 44(1960):45–51.

26. Jensen, A. R. "How Much Can We Boost IQ and Scholastic Achievement?" *Harvard Educational Review* 39(Winter 1969):1–123.

27. Jensen, A. "The Differences Are Real." *Psychology Today* (December 1973):86.

28. Herrnstein, R. J. *Preface to IQ in the Meritocracy.* Atlantic-Little, Brown, 1973, pp. 3–59.

29. Voyat, G. "IQ: *God-Given or Man-Made?*" *Saturday Review* 52(17 May 1969):74.

30. Kagan, J. S. "Inadequate Evidence and Illogical Conclusions." *Harvard Educational Review* 39(1969):126–129.

31. Watson, P. "IQ: The Racial Gap." *Psychology Today* 6(September 1972):99.

32. Cazden, C. B. "The Situation: A Neglected Course of Social Class Differences in Language Use." *Journal of Social Issues* 26(1970):35–60.

33. Burt, C. "The Evidence for the Concept of Intelligence." *British Journal of Educational Psychology* 25(1955):158–177.

34. Bloom, B. S. *Stability and Change in Human Characteristics.* New York: Wiley, 1964.

35. Gottesman, I. "Beyond the Fringe—Personality and Psychopathology." In *Genetics,* edited by D. Glass. New York: Rockefeller University Press, 1968.

36. Palmer, F. H. "Socioeconomic Status and Intellectual Performance Among Negro Preschool Boys." *Developmental Psychology* 3(1970):1–9.

37. Schaefer, E. A. *The Need for Early and Continuing Education.* Unpublished paper presented at the American Association for the Advancement of Science, Chevy Chase, Md., December 1969.

38. Skeels, H. M. "Adult Status of Children with Contrasting Early Life Experiences." *Monographs of the Society for Research in Child Development,* no. 3, 31(1966).

39. Garcia, J. "IQ: The Conspiracy." *Psychology Today* 6(September 1972):43.

40. Gottsman, I. I. "Biogenetics and Social Class." In *Social Class, Race, and Psychological Development,* edited by M. Deutsch, M. Katz, and A. B. Jensen. New York: Holt, Rinehart and Winston, 1968, pp. 25–51.

41. Bloom, B. S. "Replies to Dr. Jensen's Article." *ERIC Clearinghouse on Early Childhood Education* 3(May 1969):50.

42. Jones, H. E., and H. S. Conrad. "Mental Development in Adolescence." *National Society for the Study of Education,* Part I, 43rd Yearbook, 1944, pp. 146–163.

43. Miles, C. C., and W. R. Miles. "The Correlation of Intelligence Test Scores and Chronological Age from Early to Late Maturity." *American Journal of Psychology* 44(1932):44–78.

44. Gurwitz, M. S. "On the Decline of Performance on Intelligence Tests with Age." *American Psychologist* 6(1951):295. (Abstract.)

45. Bayley, N. "Development of Mental Abilities from Birth through 36 Years." *Roche Report: Frontiers in Hospital Psychiatry* 5(November 1968):5–6, 11.

46. Green R. F. "The Age-Intelligence Relationship Between Ages 16 and 64: A Rising Trend." *Developmental Psychology* 1(1969):618–627.

47. Schaie, K. W., and C. R. Strother. "A Cross-Sequential Study of Age Changes in Cognitive Behavior." *Psychological Bulletin* 70(1968):671–680.

48. Nisbet, J. D. "Intelligence and Age: Retesting with Twenty-four Years Interval." *British Journal of Educational Psychology* 27(1957):190–198.

49. Cattell, R. B. "Theory of Fluid and Crystallized Intelligence: A Critical Experiment." *Journal of Educational Psychology* 54(1963):1–22.

50. Cattell, R. B. "Are IQ Tests Intelligent?" *Psychology Today* (March 1968):56–62.

51. Horn, J. L. "Organization of Abilities and the Development of Intelligence." *Psychological Review* 75(1968):242–259.

52. Horn, J. L. "Intelligence—Why It Grows, Why It Declines." *Trans-action* 5(November 1964):23–31.

53. Owens, W. A. "Age and Mental Abilities: A Second Adult Follow-Up." *Journal of Educational Psychology* 57(1966):311–325.

54. Ketcham, W. A. "Student Characteristics and Growth: Research Findings in National Conference on Higher Education." In *Current Issues in Higher Education.* Washington, D.C.: National Education Association, 1956.

55. Coleman, W., and E. E. Cureton. "Intelligence and Achievement: The 'Jangle Fallacy' Again." *Educational and Psychological Measurement* 14(1954): 347–351.

56. Liddle, G. "Overlap Among Desirable and Undersirable Characteristics in Gifted Children." *Journal of Educational Psychology* 49(1958):219–223.

57. Denny, T., and J. Feldhusen. "Anxiety and Achievement as a Function of Daily Testing." *Journal of Educational Measurement* 1(1964):143–147.

58. Clarke, H. H., and A. L. Olson. "Characteristics of 15-Year-Old Boys Who Demonstrate Various Accomplishments or Difficulties." *Child Development* 36(1965):559–557.

59. Green, R. L., and W. W. Farquhar. "Negro Achievement Motivation and Scholastic Achievement." *Journal of Educational Psychology* (1965):241–243.

60. Phillips, B. N. "Sex, Social Class, and Anxiety as Sources of Variation in School Achievement." *Journal of Educational Psychology* 53(1962):316–322.

61. Mercer, J. R. "IQ: The Lethal Label." *Psychology Today* 6(September 1972):44–47, 95–97.

62. Rosenthal, R., and L. Jacobson. *Pygmalion in the Classroom.* New York: Holt, Rinehart and Winston, 1968, pp. 47–60.

63. MacKinnon. D. W. "Personality and the Expression of Creative Potential." *American Psychologist* 20(1965):273–281.

64. Maslow, A. H. Toward a Psychology of Being, 2nd ed. Princeton, N.J.: D. Van Nostrand, 1968, pp. 135–145.

65. Maslow, A. H. *Toward a Psychology of Being.* Op. cit., 1968, p. 136.

66. Mednick, S. A. "The Associative Basis of the Creative Process." *Psychological Review* 69(1962):220–232.

67. Moss, J., Jr., and L. G. Duenk. "Estimating the Concurrent Validity of the Minnesota Tests of Creative Thinking." *American Educational Research Journal* 4(1967):386–396.

68. Seitz, T. L. "The Relationship Between Creativity and Intelligence, Personality, and Value Patterns in Adolescence." Unpublished doctoral dissertation. University of Denver, 1964.

69. MacKinnon, D. W. "Personality Correlates of Creativity." In *Productive Thinking in Education,* edited by M. J. Aschner and C. E. Bish. Washington, D.C.: The National Education Association, 1965.

70. Wallach, M. A. *The Intelligence/Creativity Distinction.* New York: General Learning Press, 1971.

71. MacKinnon, D. W. "What Makes a Person Creative?" *Saturday Review* (10 February 1962):15–17, 69.

72. Rogers, C. R. "Toward Becoming a Fully Functioning Person." In *Perceiving, Behaving, Becoming,* edited by A. W. Combs. Washington, D.C.: Association for Supervision and Curriculum Development, 1962, pp. 21–33.

73. Guilford, J. P. "Creativity: Its Measurement and Development." In *A Source Book for Creative Thinking,* edited by S. J. Parnes and H. F. Harding. New York: Charles Scribner's Sons, 1962, pp. 151–168.

74. Maslow, A. H. *Motivation and Personality,* 2nd ed. New York: Harper and Row, 1970, p. 171.

75. Getzels, J. W., and P. W. Jackson. *Creativity and Intelligence.* New York: Wiley, 1962.

76. Torrance, E. P. "Education and Creativity." In *Creativity: Process and Potential,* edited by C. W. Taylor. New York: McGraw-Hill, 1964.

77. Brunswick, J. M. "My Ten Commandments for Creative Teaching." *The Journal of Creative Behavior* 5(1971):199–200.

REFERENCES OF RELATED INTEREST

Barron, F. *Creative Person and Creative Process.* New York: Holt, Rinehart and Winston, 1969.

_____. *Creativity and Psychological Health.* Princeton, N.J.: Van Nostrand, 1963.

Clarizio H., R. C. Craig, and W. A. Mehrens (eds.). *Contemporary Issues in Educational Psychology,* 2nd ed., Unit 7. Boston: Allyn and Bacon, 1974.

Combs, A. W. "Intelligence form a Perceptual Point of View." *Journal of Abnormal and Social Psychology* 47(1952):662–673.

Crockenberg, S. B. "Creativity Tests: A Boon or Boondoggle for Education?" *Review of Educational Research* 42(1972):27–45.

Davis, G. A. "Teaching for Creativity: Some Guiding Lights." *Journal of Research and Development in Education* 4(1971):29–34.

Eysenck, H. J. *The IQ Argument.* New York: Library Press, 1971.

Gartner, A., C. Greer, and F. Riessman (eds). *The New Assault on Equality.* New York: Perennial Library, 1974.

Gottesman, I. I. "Heredity and Intelligence." In *The Young Child: Reviews of Research,* vol. 2, edited by W. W. Hartup. Washington, D.C.: National Association for the Education of Young Children, 1972, pp. 24–53.

Hamachek, D. E. (ed.). *Human Dynamics in Psychology and Education,* 2nd ed. Boston: Allyn and Bacon, 1972, Chapter 5.

Hoyt, D. P. "The Relationship Between College Grades and Adult Achievement: A Review of the Literature." *ACT Research Report,* no. 7. Iowa City, Iowa: American College Testing Program, 1965.

Kagan, J. (ed.). *Creativity and Learning.* Boston: Houghton Mifflin, 1967.

Krippner, S. "The Ten Commandments That Block Creativity." *The Gifted Child Quarterly* (Autumn 1967):144–151.

Lesser, G. S., G. Fifer, and D. H. Clark. "Mental Abilities of Children from Different Social-Class and Cultural Groups." *Monographs of the Society for Research in Child Development,* no. 30, 1965.

MacKinnon, D. W. "Selecting Students with Creative Potential." In *The Creative College Student: An Unmet Challenge,* edited by P. Heist. San Francisco: Jossey-Bass, 1968.

Maslow, A. H. "Creativity in Self-Actualizing People." In *Creativity and Its Cultivation,* edited by H. H. Anderson. New York: Harper & Row, 1959.

Parnes, S. J. *Creative Behavior Guidebook.* New York: Scribner's, 1967.

Pine, P. "What's the IQ of an IQ Test?" *American Education* 5(November 1969).

Richardson, K., and D. Spears (eds.). *Race, Culture and Intelligence.* Baltimore: Penquin Books, 1972.

Rower, W. D., Jr., P. D. Ammon, and P. Cramer. *Understanding Intellectual Development.* New York: Holt, Rinehart and Winston, 1974.

Spuhler, J. N. (ed.). *Genetic Diversity and Human Behavior.* Chicago: Aldine, 1966.

Torrance, E. P. *Creativity.* Washington, D.C.: National Education Association Pamphlet no. 28, "What Research Says to the Teacher" series, 1963.

————. *Guiding Creative Talent.* Englewood Cliffs, N.J.: Prentice-Hall, 1962.

Wallach, M. A., and J. Kagan. *Modes of Thinking in Young Children: A Study of the Creativity—Intelligence Distinction.* New York: Holt, Rinehart and Winston, 1965.

Watson, P. "How Race Affects IQ." *New Society* 16(16 July 1970):103–104.

Wing, C. W., Jr., and M. A. Wallach. *College Admissions and the Psychology of Talent.* New York: Holt, Rinehart and Winston, 1971.

III

Dynamics of Good Teaching
and Healthy Teacher Behavior

Although I would be among the first to admit that all five parts of this volume are important in terms of what we need to know, think about, and practice in order to enhance the possibilities of good teaching and learning, I must confess to a special affinity for the next three chapters. Why? Well, for me, knowledge about psychological theories or growth principles or learning processes or savvy about classroom group dynamics doesn't really make that much difference unless that knowledge is explicitly translated into "good" or effective teaching and healthy teacher behavior.

Hence, our major objectives in the next three chapters are to look more closely at how effective versus ineffective teachers behave and teach in the first place. In addition, we'll look at why self-understanding seems to be such an important prerequisite for good teaching, along with some ways you may want to think about to achieve the sort of self-knowledge that enables one to be not just a more complete and fully developed teacher, but a more complete and fully developed person as well.

Finally, we'll examine some rather specific strategies for helping to make teaching more meaningful, relevant, and lasting. As we do this we'll also take into account social-class factors so as to keep in mind the certain reality that what is meaningful and relevant to one student may not be to another.

In what basic ways do "good" teachers differ from "poor" teachers in their approach to students and subject matter? How do teachers in each of these categories feel about themselves and others? What are some ways to encourage transfer of in-school learning to the "real" world outside? Are there ways to exploit the "psychological" content of a curriculum? How important is "freedom" in a classroom? What are the symptoms of teacher maladjustment? How can I make learning seem more alive?

These are some of the questions raised to be discussed. You will find many more of a related sort in the three chapters ahead.

SEVEN

Psychology and Behavior
of Effective Teachers

CHAPTER OUTLINE

PROLOGUE

GOOD TEACHING IS MORE THAN ONE THING

PERSONAL CHARACTERISTICS OF GOOD TEACHERS

Cognitive and Intellectual Dimensions

Good teachers have broad interests

Good teachers are intellectually prepared

Good teachers know students

Good teachers use advance organizers

Good teachers are noted for conceptual simplicity

Personality Dimensions

Good teachers are stable, warm

Good teachers express more friendly feelings

Good teachers are nonpunitive

Good teachers are responsible, systematic, and imaginative

Good teachers are enthusiastic

Good teachers are not perfect

Good teachers are "human"

Perceptions of Self and Others

Good teachers value students

Good teachers see themselves as self-confident

Good teachers see themselves as good people

Good teachers have favorable perceptions of others

INSTRUCTIONAL PROCEDURES AND INTERACTION STYLES

Good Teachers Challenge and Encourage

Good Teaching Is Enhanced Through Personalized Feedback

Impact of Autocratic, Laissez-faire, and Democratic Approaches

Good teachers are learner-centered

Democratic teaching related to positive student behavior

Different psychological climates produce different behavior

Interaction of Different Student-Teacher Personality Types

Dominative versus Integrative Teacher Behavior

Examples of dominative teacher behavior

Examples of integrative teacher behavior

Impact of dominative and integrative behavior on students

A teacher's behavior does not change easily

Effects of Indirect and Direct Teacher Influences

Good Teachers Are Flexible

EPILOGUE

REFERENCES

REFERENCES OF RELATED INTEREST

IMPORTANT CHAPTER IDEAS

1. Good teachers and the consequences of good teaching can be identified.

2. Good teaching is both an art and a science.

3. Two teachers of equal intelligence, training, and subject-matter mastery may differ considerably in the results they achieve with students.

4. Being a knowledgeable teacher is important; ability to effectively communicate knowledge is equally as important.

5. A teacher's personal characteristics play a very large part in determining how students respond to him or her.

6. Teacher enthusiasm is related to high student achievement.

7. One does not have to have a perfect or unassailable personality to be an effective teacher.

8. Good teachers value themselves and students.

9. Good teachers are more concerned with people and their reactions than they are with things and events.

10. Students tend to perform better when they know that teachers view them favorably.

11. Good teaching is characterized by democratic classroom practices.

12. A teacher's instructional procedures and interaction style can affect both a student's intellectual performance and social development.

13. The type of student one is in relation to particular teacher types may, depending on the combination of types, positively or negatively influence a student's performance.

14. Once established, a teacher's teaching style does not change easily.

15. Research indicates that students in all subjects tend to learn more when taught by flexible teachers.

PROLOGUE

Teaching is an incredibly demanding and complex task. To the casual observer, the man on the street, or the parent at home it may seem easy enough, but it is not when one begins to look at the smaller units of behavioral dynamics within the larger and more complex picture of a functioning classroom. The fact is that classrooms are not neat and orderly places where students, like automatons, flow without resistance from one activity to the other. This does not mean that there is no order in educational affairs (indeed, some teachers work so hard to keep their charges orderly that they lose sight of all else), but it does suggest that not all events can be predicted before they happen or easily controlled when they do. However you look at it, the typical teacher, for 5 or 6 hours a day, 5 days a week, 40 weeks a year, is immersed in an environment of real people and events whose demands on him or her are continuous and insistent. For example, there is evidence to show that a teacher can have as many as 200 or 300 interpersonal transactions *every hour* of a working day. This totals to something in the neighborhood of 1,000 interpersonal interchanges every day.[1] Suffice it to say, in the small and sometimes crowded quarters of a classroom, events come and go with astonishing rapidity, and it takes savvy, skill, and patience to keep up with the shifting tides of class activities, students' needs, and one's own personal desires.

What sort of individual does it take to be an effective teacher under such demanding circumstances? The purpose of this chapter is to help us understand this question more fully.

GOOD TEACHING IS MORE THAN ONE THING

As early as 1950, two researchers underscored the vastness of teacher effectiveness research with their annotated bibliography of over 1,000 studies.[2] And it is likely that a similar number of similar studies have been conducted since that time. Nevertheless, in spite of the incredible welter of research evidence surrounding us about the nature of effective and ineffective teaching, we still have trouble spelling out exactly what it is that separates the good guys from the bad guys. For example, Biddle and Ellena[3] in their book, *Contemporary Research on Teacher Effectiveness*, begin by stating that "the problem of teacher effectiveness is so complex that no one today knows what *the competent teacher is*."

But is this really true? Are the qualities of good or positive or effective teaching really that elusive? I don't think that they are. Arthur Combs, speaking from his experience as an educator and psychologist, has observed:

> . . . you and I know who good teachers are. In a very short time in a new school or faculty we are able to state with a high degree of confidence who are the very best teachers in the group. We can do this even when we have never entered a teacher's classroom. Somehow we pick up the information we need to make such judgments by a kind of osmosis. Why, then, can't we *measure* good teaching? The answer is simple; because they are unique human beings. Like the children they teach, teachers, too are individuals. No good teacher is like any other.[4]

However you look at it, teaching is a highly individualized activity. Some argue that it is an art, others stress that it is a science, but to get caught in whether it is this or that ends up in a semantic game that gets us nowhere. The fact is that *good teaching is both an art and a science.* Or, another way of saying this is that good teaching is done by an artist, who is able to "actionize" the best that scientific research has to teach us about how to use our human resources and technological advances to the fullest in a classroom setting.

It is not the intent of this chapter to argue that there is one best kind of teacher or teaching methods, but rather to suggest that there are many "best" kinds of teachers and teaching methods. Although it is certainly true that good teachers are not alike, it is also true that they nonetheless share certain characteristics in common. That is, whether it is in the way they manage their instructional activities or the manner in which they view themselves or in their style for interacting with students, they tend to resemble each other. What makes each teacher entirely unique and *unlike* any other teacher is the precise expression and final execution of any act or interaction that goes on in the classroom.

One of the best ways for learning how to do something, whether it be plumbing, quarterbacking, or teaching is to observe and study carefully the behavior of those who are successful at their craft. Research and experience have taught us a great deal about why successful teachers are successful and even why certain teachers are more effective with certain types of students. There is a great deal to be learned from the vast array of evidence gathered to date. Even though no one can tell you precisely what you must do to be a good teacher, there are nonetheless many excellent guidelines for you to consider and follow as you develop and grow into your own unique "style" of teaching.

TO OBSERVE

Reading what research has to teach us about effective teaching and studying a variety of teaching "strategies" that seem to work are several ways to learn more about what good teaching is all about. Another excellent way is to study carefully those teachers you currently have and will have in the future whom you regard as tops in their craft. What do they do that sets them apart? How do they talk, gesture, illustrate ideas, and so forth? Observe them carefully. What makes them so special? Think about the things they do that you might like to someday incorporate into your own teaching behavior.

By and large, most research efforts aimed at investigating teacher effectiveness have attempted to probe one or more of the following dimensions of teacher personality and behavior: (1) personal characteristics, which includes cognitive dimensions, personality dimensions, perceptions of self and others and (2) instructional procedures and interaction styles.

So, let us take each of these areas one at a time and begin to explore in greater depth what research has to tell us about the psychology and behavior of effective teachers.

PERSONAL CHARACTERISTICS OF GOOD TEACHERS

We would probably agree that it is possible to have two teachers of equal intelligence, training, and grasp of subject matter who nonetheless differ considerably in the result they achieve with students. Part of the difference can be accounted for by the effect of a teacher's personality on students. Personality is not easy to define. One psychologist, for example, has listed fifty-seven known definitions of the word *personality* in his analysis of the subject![5] However, for our purposes, when we talk about personality we will consider it as having reference to the whole person as most others see him, particularly in terms of his characteristic interests, attitudes, and general behavior.

Inasmuch as "personality" is such a global construct, it may help if we break it down into some of its component parts. Let's start with one which, no matter how you look at it, is a very important dimension of any teacher's personal characteristics.

Cognitive and Intellectual Dimensions

How much a teacher knows, how well he thinks on his feet, how stimulating he is to his students—these are all considerations that must be taken into account while looking at the cognitive dimensions involved in good or poor teaching. The part that cognitive or intellectual dimensions play in effective teaching is difficult to assess because it not only depends on how much a teacher knows but how well he can communicate what he knows. We have probably all had our share of brilliant teachers, in terms of

Keeping students interested and motivated is not easy. It takes careful planning and preparation. (Allyn and Bacon)

their sheer store of knowledge, but who nonetheless were frightfully dull in getting what they knew across to students or anyone else, for that matter, in any meaningful way.

Good teachers have broad interests. I suppose it will come as no surprise to you to see repeated here what you no doubt have heard many times before, namely, "If you don't know anything go on out and teach, where it doesn't make any difference anyway." Thankfully, there is more myth than truth to that saying because, the fact is, good or successful or effective teaching—at any level—is not possible unless a teacher is thoroughly knowledgeable in his major area or areas of interest. Research is pretty clear about that. Good teachers are well informed.[6]

There is good evidence for this. For example, an investigation by Ryans[7] focused on, among other things, the cognitive characteristics of two groups of teachers chosen from a larger sample who had been designated as "good" or "poor" on the basis of ratings of trained observers on twenty-two dimensions of classroom behavior. (Not only is this study significant because it was well planned and carried out, but because of its comprehensiveness, involving as it did 2,043 teachers, 987 elementary and 1,065 secondary schools.) He found that effective or "high" teachers in comparison with "low" teachers, had strong interest in literary matters, enjoyed music, painting and the arts in general, and had superior verbal intelligence.

Good teachers are intellectually prepared. Preparation that teachers have had in their major subject-matter areas has always been considered to be highly related to effective teaching. Although the relationship between academic grade point average and varied measures of teaching effectiveness has never been very high, it nonetheless is usually a positive one.[8-10] This means that how well a teacher candidate performs in college does indeed

294

have some bearing as to how well he will do in teaching. Perhaps it would be more accurate to suggest that students who end up being the "better" teachers are better for the very reasons that they were good students; that is, they study more, work harder, prepare longer, and read more widely than those who are less able as teachers.

Good teachers know students. A particularly important variable among the congitive characteristics of effective teachers is the amount of information they possess about their students. That is, not only do good teachers know about their subject area(s), but they also know about their students! For example, in a study by Ojemann and Wilkinson,[11] it was found that students in classes with teachers who had a great deal of information about their students made significantly greater academic gains than students who had teachers who knew very little about their pupils.

TO THINK ABOUT

How does it make you feel when a professor knows you by name? Or when an instructor takes a moment to talk with you in an effort to find out something about you as a person? How does it make you feel about him or her? About being in that instructor's class? Good feeling, isn't it?

"HAWKINS, YOU'VE BEEN WITH US A LONG TIME..."

Keeping pace with current developments is a characteristic of good teachers. (A. L. Kaufman, reprinted by permission of Masters Agency)

Good teachers use advance organizers. There is also evidence to indicate that effective teachers do a better job than less able teachers when it comes to cognitively preparing their students for the presentation of new material.[12-14] That is, the effective teacher is more apt to give students what are called "advance organizers," which are usually in the form of general overviews or short bits of relevant reading material prior to a complex learning task. Primarily the organizers or pre-learning activities provide the transitional bridge by which familiar material facilitates the discrimination and understanding of new material. Suffice it to say, good teachers usually do a good job of priming their students for new material; that may be one of the reasons why they are good. Poor teachers don't; that may be one of the reasons why they are poor.

Good teachers are noted for conceptual simplicity. If you ever hear a group of teachers talking, particularly elementary teachers, you won't usually hear much discussion about sociograms, reinforcement schedules, role expectations, psychosocial stages, and the like, even when it may be appropriate for them to do so. Right away you might say, "Well, that sort of squares with my notion about the simplicity of elementary teachers anyway." You would be partly right if you did think that way, but very likely for the wrong reasons. It does seem to be true that teachers lean toward what Jackson's[15] research with elementary teachers, superior ones, by the way, has led him to call *conceptual simplicity*. The reasons for this, however, have more to do with the job than may be apparent at first glance.

Jackson found that there were four major aspects of conceptual simplicity revealed in teachers' language. These are: (1) an uncomplicated view of causality; (2) an intuitive, rather than rational, approach to classroom events; (3) an opinionated, as opposed to open-minded, stance when confronted with alternative teaching practices; and (4) a narrowness in the working definitions assigned to abstract terms.

Even though Jackson's generalizations were derived from teachers who were highly respected practitioners of the teaching craft, we nonetheless are left with the image of a teacher who not only approaches educational matters in a simple sort of way, but who is pretty tough to change once his mind is made up. To the extent that people are reasonably consistent in their behavior, it is entirely possible that the typical elementary teacher's cognitive style is pretty well established by the time he begins to teach and that the classroom does little more than exaggerate those cognitive characteristics he brought to it in the first place. This is very likely only part of the truth of the matter. The other part of it lies in the nature of the teacher's complex and often chaotic environment. Considering that the elementary school teacher engages in 200 or 300 interpersonal interchanges every hour of the working day and considering that these interchanges cannot be preplanned or predicted with any exactitude, it is easy to see that the dynamics underlying these kaleidoscopic events are neither readily discerned, nor are they, except superficially, under the control of the teacher. Small wonder that there is so little time for "intellectual" meanderings. Jackson, I think, has summed it up nicely:

> There is a certain appropriateness, even charm perhaps, in the image of the absent-minded professor. If he is to do his work well he must be able, at least figuratively, to free himself for long periods of time from his physical and social surroundings. But the image of the absent-minded elementary school teacher is not nearly so appealing.[16]
> . . . By being less than completely rational and methodical in his dealings with students the teacher may help to soften the impact of the impersonal institution. In a world of time schedules and objectives and tests and routines, the teacher's humanness, which includes his feelings of uncertainty and his Boy Scout idealism, stands out in bold relief.
> . . . in some classrooms the teacher not only knows students as persons, he also *cares* about them.
> . . . As we all know, a favorite device of young children when dealing with competitive claims or threats from their peers is to respond with the query: "Who cares?" The answer to that question, when it refers to matters dealing with school and school work, is usually, "The Teacher."
> (Another) way in which the teacher might help dull the sharp edges of classroom life is by presenting his students with a model of human fallibility. Unlike the computer in the records office and the electrical system that regulates the bells and buzzers, classroom teachers sometimes get angry or laugh or make mistakes or look confused.
> . . . Thus teachers are able to personify the virtue of possessing knowledge while at the same time demonstrating the limits of that virtue. In this way, the abstract goals of learning are given a human referent. Students cannot aspire to become a computer or a teaching machine or a textbook but they can aspire to become [like] a teacher.[17]

From the evidence before us it seems clear that cognitive dimensions do play an important part in the work of a successful teacher. Good intelligence, reading habits that are wide and varied, skill in using advance organizers, and a willingness for plenty of hard work and sound preparation are major cognitive variables related to effective teaching.

This is one part of the total teaching process. There is another and even more complicated aspect.

Personality Dimensions

Whether we're talking about doctors, lawyers, next-door neighbors, roommates, or teachers, it seems to be true that different people tend to create different climates of feeling in their interpersonal relationships. As any of us can remember from our early school days or college classes, this most certainly appears to be the case with teachers. Some teachers seem to have the sort of personality that radiates a pleasant psychological aroma in all directions. Indeed, it probably wouldn't be going too far to say that the whole psychological tincture of a classroom experience is sweet or sour, fragrant or foul, tangy or stifling, according to the moods we inhale from the teacher in charge.

Good teachers are stable, warm. The impact that a teacher's personality can have on a student's emerging self and intellectual output is staggering. For example, it has been found that children and adolescents who have experienced difficulty at home and in school have been able to improve greatly when they encountered teachers who were capable of giving them responsibility.[18] From a study of 70 teachers and over 1,000 fifth and sixth graders, Boynton and his associates[19] found that children begin to be affected by the characteristics of teachers in as little time as two months. The pupil who had stable teachers showed markedly good mental health and emotional security, while those with tense and unstable teachers revealed poor mental health and instability on every measure.

TO COMPARE

Before you read the next several paragraphs, jot down the five or six traits or characteristics you associate with "teachers who have helped you most."

_____

_____

_____

Compare them with Hart and Witty's finding. If yours are vastly different, why are they? What do the characteristics you wrote down suggest about what you value in yourself as a potential teacher?

An interesting investigation was conducted by Hart[20] that was based upon the opinions of 3,725 high school seniors concerning best-liked and least-liked teachers. A total of 43 different reasons were listed for "Liking Teacher A Best" and 30 different reasons were listed for "Liking Teacher Z Least." Consider the first four most frequently cited reasons in each category.

Four Most Frequently Mentioned Reasons for Liking
"Teacher A" Best Reported by 3,725 High School Seniors

1. Is helpful in school work, explains lessons and assignments clearly and thoroughly, and uses examples in teaching. 51%
2. Cheerful, happy, good-natured, jolly, has sense of humor, and can take a joke. 40%
3. Human, friendly, companionable, "one of us." 30%
4. Interested in and understands pupils. 26%

Four Most Frequently Mentioned Reasons for Liking "Teacher Z" Least Reported by 3,725 High School Seniors

1. Too cross, crabby, grouchy, never smiles, nagging, sarcastic, loses temper, and "flies off the handle." 50%
2. Not helpful with school work, does not explain lessons and assignments, not clear, and work not planned. 30%
3. Partial, has "pets" or favored students, and "picks on certain pupils." 20%
4. Superior, aloof, haughty, "snooty," overbearing, does not know you out of class 20%

You will note that personality traits monopolize the top rankings after the first items that deal with teaching technique as it immediately affects students. Interestingly enough, mastery of subject matter, which is vital but badly overemphasized by specialists, ranks sixteenth on both lists.

Hart's general findings have been corroborated time and again by later studies. For example, Witty[21] in connection with the "Quiz Kids" program, received 12,000 letters on the theme, "The Teacher Who Helped Me." An analysis of those letters revealed that the top ranking traits were the following:

(1) Cooperative, democratic attitudes; (2) kindliness and consideration for the individual; (3) patience; (4) wide interests; (5) personal appearance and pleasant manner; (6) fairness and impartiality; (7) sense of humor; (8) good disposition and consistent behavior; (9) interest in pupil's problems; (10) flexibility; (11) use of recognition and praise; (12) unusual proficiency in teaching a particular subject.

Even at the college level there is evidence to suggest that students still rank first the professor's interest in his students and their problems and his willingness to give attention to them.[22]

So far, we have been examining desirable personal characteristics of teachers as these characteristics are identified by students. For the most part, these characteristics group themselves under the general heading of capacity for warmth, patience, tolerance, and interest in students. What happens when these personal qualities are related to the more rigid test of whether having them or not makes any difference in the actual performance of students?

299

Sears,[23] for one, found that there are positive correlations between the extent to which a teacher reflects a personal interest in and willingness to listen to students' ideas and the creativity shown by students. As a further example, Cogan[24] found that warm and considerate teachers got an unusual amount of original poetry and art from their high school students. Reed[25] found that teachers higher in a capacity for warmth favorably affected their pupils' interest in science.

Good teachers express more friendly feelings. Ryans[26] directed a second monumental research effort, this one involving more than 6,000 teachers in 1,700 schools at 450 school systems over a period of 6 years, in an effort to study both the cognitive and personality dimensions of teacher behavior. A major intent of the investigation was to find out how the effective or "high" teachers and the less effective or "low" teachers differed from each other. Tables 7–1 and 7–2 summarize some of the major findings relevant to our consideration of personality dimensions related to differential teacher behavior.

Good teachers are nonpunitive As you can see, the "high" group was more generous in their appraisals of the behaviors and motives of others and expressed friendly feelings for others. All in all, "high" teachers are warm, friendly, and sociable, characteristics frequently associated with effective teaching. For example, Kounin and Gump[27] have shown that elementary school children exposed to punitive teachers, compared with those exposed to nonpunitive teachers, manifested more aggression, were less concerned

TABLE 7–1. *Personal Characteristics of Teachers with Low Ratings**

Elementary-secondary teachers combined

A. "Low" group members more frequently (than "high"):
   1. Are from older age groups.
   2. Are restricted and critical in appraisals of the behavior and motives of other persons.
   3. Value exactness, orderliness, and "practical" things.
   4. Indicate preferences for activities that do not involve close contacts with people.
B. "Low" group on the average (compared with "high" group):
   1. Is less favorable in expressed opinions of pupils.
   2. Is less high with regard to verbal intelligence.
   3. Is less satisfactory with regard to emotional adjustment.

* Adapted from D. G. Ryans. *Characteristics of Teachers: Their Description, Comparison, and Appraisal.* Washington, D.C.: American Council on Education, 1960, pp. 360–361.

with learning, and generally got into more trouble of various sorts. Apparently teachers with punitive, harsh, or aggressive personalities bring out similar behavior in their students. We surely cannot assume that all students will behave more aggressively if they have aggressive, punitive teachers, but this could well be the case among students who have a readiness to be more overtly aggressive in the first place. This certainly is not all-inclusive evidence, but it is, I think, another indication of how a teacher's personality can influence a student's affective behavior. Although there probably isn't a teacher alive who has not been punitive at one time or other, it would not seem unreasonable to suggest that good teachers are inclined to be less punitive than poor teachers.

The other qualities in which both the "high" elementary and secondary teachers excelled were judging themselves in ambition and initiative and having more satisfactory emotional adjustment. This is similar to the findings of Symonds and Dudek,[28] who found that effective teachers were inclined to have superior personality organization, a well-developed capacity for relating to others, and a low need to express aggression. This is consistent with the results of a study that found that elementary school age children perceived good teachers as being friendly, warm, supportive, and skilled at communication.[29]

Good teachers are responsible, systematic, and imaginative. Returning to Ryans' work again: He identified three major categories of personal characteristics of teachers, which were characterized as:

TABLE 7–2.   *Personal Characteristics of Teachers with High Ratings**

Elementary-secondary teachers combined

A. "High" group members more frequently (than "low"):
   1. Manifest extreme generosity in appraisals of the behavior and motives of other persons; express friendly feelings for others.
   2. Indicate strong interest in reading and in literary matters.
   3. Indicate interest in music, painting, and the arts in general.
   4. Report participation in high school and college social groups.
   5. Judge selves high in ambition and initiative.
B. "High" group on the average (compared with "low" group):
   1. Indicates greater enjoyment of pupil relationships (i.e., more favorable pupil opinions).
   2. Indicates greater preference for nondirective classroom procedures.
   3. Is superior in verbal intelligence.
   4. Is more satisfactory with regard to emotional adjustment.

* Ibid.

1. Warm, understanding, friendly or aloof, egocentric, restricted
2. Responsible, businesslike, systematic or evading, unplanned, slipshod
3. Stimulating, imaginative, enthusiastic or dull, routine [30]

Among elementary teachers in general, the three patterns of behavior were highly interrelated. In other words, warm, understanding, friendly behavior went along with being businesslike, responsible, and systematic, and also with stimulating, imaginative behavior.

The comparisons for high school teachers (English, social studies, science, mathematics) found that the interrelationships among the three behavior patterns were not as high as was the case for elementary teachers. However, when high school teachers were compared to each other it was found that men and women social studies teachers and women English teachers were highest on warmth, understanding, and friendliness. Women mathematics teachers were high in responsible, systematic, and businesslike behavior, while women social studies and science teachers surpassed other groups in being stimulating and imaginative. It is not surprising to find that, in general, teachers who are friendly and warm, organized, and provide

"MR. HIGGLEBY, ABOUT THIS COURSE YOU'RE CONDUCTING IN SEX EDUCATION..."

Effective teachers are not afraid to try out new ideas and different approaches. (Gallagher, reprinted by permission of Masters Agency)

stimulating and imaginative experiences are judged to be the more effective teachers.

Ryans' study of teachers' personal characteristics was done by having trained observers watch and record the behavior of teachers in action. In contrast to this procedure, Veldman and Peck[31] had junior and senior high school students rate their student teachers immediately after the student teachers had completed their assignments. Then the students' ratings of their student teachers were compared with the supervisors' ratings of the effectiveness of the same student teachers. The students and the supervisors were in high agreement that personal behavioral clusters such as friendly and cheerful and knowledgeable, poised and firm and strict were characteristic of effective teachers. (Notice how the idea of being friendly keeps popping up as a desirable teacher characteristic.)

Good teachers are enthusiastic. You and I both know from personal experience that a teacher's enthusiasm, or lack of it, can have a lot to do with either making or breaking a class. And there is evidence to support this. For example, Mastin[32] noted that in nineteen or twenty classes in ten schools teacher enthusiasm was related with high student achievement. In addition, the students indicated more favorable reactions to the enthusiastic teacher and to material that was presented enthusiastically by teachers. The differences in student achievement and in attitudes were large and consistent, all of which suggest that teacher enthusiasm may be the most powerful personality characteristic of all when it comes to effective teaching.

TO THINK ABOUT

"Enthusiasm" is an elusive quality, particularly as related to teacher behavior. Whatever it is, it's important. What does it mean for you? How do you judge a teacher's enthusiasm? What cues do you look for?

_____

_____

_____

_____

_____

You may find it interesting to compare your ideas about "enthusiasm" with other students you know. Where are you similar? Different?

Good teachers are not perfect. There are many different, but, none-theless, acceptable personality characteristics that can go into making a good teacher. Morse and his associates[33] interviewed students from grades three and ten and noted two major trends. The pupils tended to rate a teacher as good on such matters as one, "She helps us learn" even if she was considered tough, and two, "She cares about us" even if the lessons were somewhat confused. It was found that there were wide differences in the consideration the students used for judgment. But let a teacher be too near the extreme on one dimension, say, "mean" rather than merely "strict," or "chaotic" rather than merely "lax," or arbitrary rather than merely "quite demanding" and the students would more often than not overlook the teacher's more positive characteristics. In other words, a student's otherwise positive perceptions were frequently lost because of some overriding negative characteristic of the teacher that blocked out his good points. The important thing is that students were tolerant of a wide range of differences in a teacher's behavior unless the behavior became too extreme. I suppose another way of looking at this is that a teacher does not have to have some kind of perfect or unassailable personality to be regarded as an effective teacher — at least by students.

Good teachers are "human." In summary, the evidence seems clear when it comes to sorting out good or effective from bad or ineffective teachers on the basis of personality characteristics. Effective teachers appear to be those who are, shall we say, "human" in the fullest sense of the word. They have a sense of humor, are fair, empathetic, friendly, enthusiastic, more democratic than autocratic, and apparently more able to relate easily and naturally to students on either a one-to-one or group basis. Their classrooms are something akin to miniature enterprise operations in the sense that they are more open, spontaneous, and adaptable to change. Teachers who are less effective apparently lack a sense of humor, grow impatient easily, use cutting, reducing comments in class, are less well integrated, are inclined to be somewhat authoritarian, and are generally less sensitive to the needs of their students. As suggested by the studies on the authoritarian personality by Adorno and his associates,[34] one has to wonder whether the bureaucratic conduct and tone of the ineffective teacher's classroom is not merely a desperate measure to support the weak pillars of his own personal superstructure.

In the event the thought has crossed your mind, be assured that a teacher does not have to be all the good things ordinarily associated with a good teacher all at the same time. No one is perfect. When it comes to assessing a teacher's personal characteristics, students are pretty much like everyone else in the world — they look for a reasonable degree of consistency and a whole lot of fairness and then judge on that basis.

Perceptions of Self and Others

This is, perhaps, one of the most significant differences between good and poor teachers. Once again we very likely do not have to go any further than our own personal experiences to know that the way we see, regard, and feel about ourselves and others has an enormous impact on both our private and public lives. How about good versus poor teachers? First of all, how do they see themselves?

Good teachers value students. Bowman[35] uncovered some interesting evidence regarding teachers' self-perceptions after asking a group of high school students to indicate what teachers had made a significant contribution to their lives and also what teachers they would try to avoid in future courses. In this way, a small number of teachers rated as inspiring and a small number rated as poor were chosen. Then both groups of teachers were administered a value inventory. Although the good teachers had higher scores on every value (except one), their scores were only slightly higher than those of the poorer teachers and in many cases not even significantly different. On two items, however, there were great differences. On the word *yourself*, the good teachers averaged a 30 percent higher score; and on the word *student*, a 74 percent higher score. In other words, those selected as good and inspiring teachers seemed to be differentiated mostly by the positive perceptions they had of their students and themselves. Teachers chosen as inspiring valued (cherished, prized, esteemed) themselves and their students more highly than teachers chosen as poor. This surely does not mean that valuing one's self and others magically causes one to be a good teacher, but it does suggest that good teaching and self-other acceptance may go hand in hand. For example, a male high school teacher, who had been teaching for fifteen years, candidly expressed the idea somewhat along the following lines during a graduate seminar:

> I think the days I seem to fire on all six in my classes have a lot to do with how I feel toward myself. If I like me, I seem to like the kids better, too. On the other hand I think there are some specific days when I don't like myself very well—like one time when I spanked my six-year-old little girl for some small thing that didn't deserve a spanking—and on those days I have a great deal of trouble accepting or tolerating any goofing off or variation from the rules whatsoever. I'm not sure I can explain it very well, but it has something to do with my own deviation of my own rules, and it makes it more difficult for me to accept deviations in anyone else.

What this seasoned teacher was saying is very true and it happens to all of us from time to time. That is, the inability to like ourselves gets generalized and spills over onto other people. For some persons, negative self-other perceptions are situation-specific, which means that, like our teacher in the example above, the incident that triggers negative self-other perceptions is more or less specific to a particular experience. As an illustration from your own life, you may have noted how difficult it is to have positive, not to mention loving, feelings toward yourself or others following a big fight with, say, a loved one (or former loved one), or a nasty letter from home. On the other hand, some persons have negative self-other perceptions that are chronic, nonspecific, and rooted in life experiences that can be traced all the way back to early life experiences.

Good teachers see themselves as self-confident. There is still other research bearing on the question of how good versus poor teachers view themselves. Ryans,[36] for example, found that there were, indeed, differences between the self-related expressions of high emotional stability teachers versus low emotional stability teachers. For example, the more emotionally stable teachers were more apt to have the following kinds of self-reports: (1) frequently named self-confidence and cheerfulness as dominant traits in themselves; (2) said they liked active contact with other people; (3) expressed interests in hobbies and handicrafts; and (4) reported their childhoods to be happy experiences.

On the other hand, teachers with lower emotional maturity scores (1) had unhappy memories of childhood; (2) seemed not to prefer contact with others; (3) were more directive and authoritarian; and (4) expressed less self-confidence.

TO THINK ABOUT

How do Ryans' research findings about high and low emotional stability teachers' self-perceptions square with your own self-perceptions? If you happen to be a person who feels less confident than others, what have you done of an active sort to change that feeling? What would you like to do about it?

Why not do it?

We can be even more specific. For example, Arthur Combs[37] in his book, *The Professional Education of Teachers*, cites several studies that reached similar conclusions about the way good teachers typically see themselves.

1. Good teachers see themselves as identified with people rather than withdrawn, removed, apart from, or alienated from others.
2. Good teachers feel basically adequate rather than inadequate. They do not see themselves as generally unable to cope with problems.

3. Good teachers feel trustworthy rather than untrustworthy. They see themselves as reliable, dependable individuals with the potential for coping with events as they happen.
4. Good teachers see themselves as wanted rather than unwanted. They see themselves as likable and attractive (in personal, not physical sense) as opposed to feeling ignored and rejected.
5. Good teachers see themselves as worthy rather than unworthy. They see themselves as people of consequence, dignity, and integrity as opposed to feeling they matter little, can be overlooked and discounted.

Good teachers see themselves as good people. In the broadest sense of the word, good teachers see themselves as good people. Their self-perceptions are, for the most part, positive, tinged with an air of optimism, and colored with tones of healthy self-acceptance. I dare say that self-perceptions of good teachers are not unlike the self-perceptions of any basically healthy person whether he be a good bricklayer, a good manager, a good doctor, a good lawyer, a good experimental psychologist, or you name it. Clinical evidence has told us time and again that any person is apt to be happier, more productive, and more effective when he is able to see himself as fundamentally and basically "enough."

Good teachers have favorable perceptions of others. Research, as you have seen, is showing us that not only do good and poor teachers view themselves differently, but they are also somewhat unique in the way they perceive others. Ryans,[38] for example, reported several studies that have produced findings that are similar and in agreement when it comes to sorting out the differences between how good and poor teachers view others. He found, among other things, that outstandingly "good" teachers rated significantly higher than notably "poor" teachers in at least five different ways with respect to how they viewed others. The good teachers had (1) more favorable opinions of students, (2) more favorable opinions of democratic classroom behavior, (3) more favorable opinions of administrators and colleagues, (4) a greater expressed liking for personal contacts with other people, and (5) more favorable estimates of other people generally. That is, they expressed belief that very few students are difficult behavior problems, that very few people are influenced in their opinions and attitudes toward others by feelings of jealousy, and that most teachers are willing to assume their full share of extra duties outside of school.

Interestingly, the characteristics that distinguished the "lowly assessed" teacher group suggested that the relatively "ineffective" teacher is self-centered, anxious, and restricted. One is left with the distinct impression that poor or ineffective teachers have more than the usual number of paranoid-like defenses. For example, turning to Ryans[39] again, we find that he reports that his "ineffective teachers believe a substantial portion of parents' visits to school are made to criticize the teacher or the school and that a fairly large portion of people (40 to 60 percent) are influenced in their opinions and attitudes toward others by feelings of jealousy."

Combs [40] has also studied the perceptual differences between good and poor teachers, and he suggests that good teachers can be clearly distinguished from poor ones with respect to the following perceptions about people:

1. The good teacher is more likely to have an internal rather than external frame of reference. That is, he seeks to understand how things seem to others and then uses this as a guide for his own behavior.
2. The good teacher is more concerned with people and their reactions than with things and events.
3. The good teacher is more concerned with the subjective-perceptual experience of people than with objective events. He is, again, more concerned with how things seem to people than just the so-called or alleged "facts."
4. The good teacher seeks to understand the causes of people's behavior in terms of their current thinking, feeling, beliefs, and understandings rather than in terms of forces exerted on them now or in the past.
5. The good teacher generally trusts other people and perceives them as having the capacity to solve their own problems.
6. The good teacher tends to see other people as being of worth rather than hostile or threatening.
7. The good teacher tends to see other people as being of worth rather than unworthy. That is, he sees all people as possessing a certain dignity and integrity.
8. The good teacher sees people and their behavior as essentially developing from within rather than as a product of external events to be molded or directed. In other words, he sees people as creative and dynamic rather than passive or inert.

I am sure it comes as no surprise to any of us that how we perceive others is highly dependent on how we perceive ourselves. If a potential teacher (or anyone else for that matter) likes himself, trusts himself, and has confidence in himself, he will likely see others in this same light. Research is beginning to tell us what common sense has always told us, namely, people grow, flourish, and develop much more easily when in relationship with someone who projects an inherent trust and belief in their capacity to become what they have the potential to become.

It is one thing to say that good teachers have a generally more positive view of others, but does this have anything to do with how students achieve and behave? There is evidence to suggest that it does. For example, Davidson the Lang[41] found that among the boys and girls in grades four through six, those children with the more favorable self-images were those who more likely than not perceived their teacher's feelings toward them more favorably. They also found the more positive the perception of their teacher's feelings, the better was their academic achievement, and the more desirable their classroom behavior as rated by teachers.

It seems to me that we can sketch at least five interrelated generalizations from what research is telling us about how good teachers differ from poor teachers when it comes to perceptions of others. In relation to this, good teachers can be characterized in the following ways:

1. They seem to have generally more positive views of others—students, colleagues, and administrators.
2. They do not seem to be as prone to view others as critical, attacking people with ulterior motives, but rather see them as potentially friendly and worthy in their own right.
3. They have a more favorable view of democratic classroom procedures.
4. They seem to have the ability and capacity to see things as they seem to others—i.e., the ability to see things from the other person's point of view.
5. They do not seem to see students as persons "you do things to," but rather as individuals capable of doing for themselves once they feel trusted, respected, and valued.

Having the necessary intellectual skills, a friendly attitude, and relatively positive self-other perceptions are important considerations when it comes to figuring out what it is that contributes to the psychology and behavior of effective teachers. However, intelligence, friendliness, and positive self-other perceptions are practically useless possessions if they are not translated into learning that makes a difference and relationships that matter through a teacher's instructional procedures and interaction style. This brings us logically to our next point.

INSTRUCTIONAL PROCEDURES
AND INTERACTION STYLES

If there really are such polar extremes as "good" or "poor" teachers as both research and observation suggest, then we could reasonably assume that they might differ not only as far as personal characteristics are concerned, but also in the way they conduct themselves in a classroom.

A teacher's interpersonal relationships provide the medium of exchange for either good will or hostility, depending on how relationships are handled. And the nature of a teacher's relationships does make a difference. For the example, a teacher's relationships with a particular student can even influence whether or not that student is accepted by his classmates.[42] Research also indicates that the high school teacher with poor teacher-student relations, who creates an atmosphere of fear and tension, and who thinks primarily in terms of *content to be covered* rather than in terms of what his charges need, feel, know, and can do, is more likely to fail students than a teacher who is able to maintain reasonably good rapport with his students and is interested in them as individuals.[43]   The point is that a teacher's instructional procedures and interaction style can affect both a student's intellectual performance and social development.   To be sure, a teacher is not the sole input in a student's life, but he is a highly significant one.   Let's turn our attention more specifically now to how effective and ineffective teachers differ in their instructional procedures.

Good Teachers Challenge and Encourage

An earlier effort to investigate the differences in the use of instructional procedures and teaching styles between good and poor teachers was conducted by Barr.[44]   Detailed stenographic records, observation charts, and various time charts were kept on forty-seven teachers of social studies in high school deemed to be superior and forty-seven deemed well below average in teaching skills.   Practically every conceivable act and every expression of teacher and pupil interaction was considered, about thirty-seven factors in all.   What follows are some characteristic comments made by good and poor teachers.

Characteristic Comments Made by Poor
But not by Good Teachers

Are you working hard? . . . Aren't you ever going to learn that word? . . . Everyone sit up straight, please. . . . I'm afraid you're confused. . . . No, that's wrong. . . . Oh, dear, don't you know that? . . . Oh, sit down. . . . Say something . . . and so on, through nearly 100 different expressions. Note the overtones of frustration, futility, and impatience that leak through most.

Characteristic Comments Made by Good
But not by Poor Teachers

Aha, that's a new idea. . . . Are you going to accept that as an answer? . . . I should like more proof. . . . Do you suppose you could supply a better word? . . . Can you prove your statement? . . . Don't you really think you could? . . . I'm not quite clear on that—think a moment. . . . Let's stick to the question. . . . Probably my last question wasn't a good one . . . and so on, through a long list. Note here the emphasis on challenging the student, on pushing and encouraging him to go beyond where he may be at the moment.

TO EXPERIMENT WITH

Although *what* a teacher says is important, so, too, is *how* he says it. With a willing friend as your listener, it may be an interesting experiment for you to try to change the *meaning* of the comments cited above by changing the voice inflection accompanying any one of them. If you change the inflection, can your friend tell whether it came from a "good" or "poor" teacher? Words convey messages, but inflection conveys feeling. Try it and see.

This study also demonstrated that not only did poor teachers give more assignments than good teachers but, almost without exception, they gave some sort of textbook assignment as a part of their daily procedure. In contrast, the majority of good teachers used something other than textbook assignments, and when the text was assigned good teachers were more likely to supplement it with topics, questions, or other references. Poor teachers usually gave far more assignments, but they took less time in giving them. The better teachers, however, were more likely to give fewer assignments, each one covering a topic or unit of respectable size and taking some time to develop.

Good teachers are able to make learning challenging and interesting. (Allyn and Bacon)

Good Teaching Is Enhanced
Through Personalized Feedback

There is also evidence to suggest that when a teacher is able to personalize his teaching he is apt to be more successful, particularly when it comes to motivating students to do better work. For example, Page[45] conducted an experiment with high school and junior high school students and teachers in which the teachers graded objective tests of their pupils and then randomly assigned each paper to one of three groups. The group-one student was given back his paper with no comment except a mark. Each group-two student was given a streotyped, standard comment from "excellent" if his score was high to "let's raise this grade." Every C student, for example, received his mark with the notation, "perhaps try to do still better." For those in group three, the teacher wrote a personal comment on every paper saying whatever he thought might encourage that particular student. On the next objective test, groups two and three outperformed group one. This suggests that the personalized comments had a greater effect than standardized comments and that even a very short standard comment written on the paper produced measurable achievement gains. The greatest improvement was made by the failing students in group three who received encouraging personal notes on their papers. This study points up the motivational implications of evaluative practices that go far beyond the simple indication of right or wrong answers. It certainly does seem to be true that teachers who reflect an active personal interest in their students' progress and who show it are more likely to be successful than teachers who are more distant and impersonal.

Impact of Autocratic, Laissez-faire,
and Democratic Approaches

Whether one likes the idea or not, teaching demands that a teacher assumes a certain responsibility for leadership of the class, and it is by examining a teacher's function as leader that we can perhaps see most clearly how he or she relates to a group and affects its members. The autocratic-democratic continuum of teacher behavior is variously called directive-non-directive or teacher-centered–learner-centered, but they all refer to essentially the same thing, namely, a teachers' leadership style in a classroom.

Good teachers are learner-centered. What happens when a teacher uses either learner-centered or teacher-centered approaches? In an investigation by Flanders,[46] experimentally produced climates simulating the two approaches mentioned above were designed. In the learner-centered climate the teacher was acceptant and supportive of the student and problem-centered in approach; in the teacher-centered climate the teacher was direc-tive and demanding, often deprecating in his behavior toward students. The major conclusions reached were: (1) The teacher-centered behavior of directing, demanding, and using private criteria in deprecating a student leads to hostility to the self or teacher, aggressiveness, or sometimes with-drawal, apathy, and even emotional disintegration; (2) the learner-centered behavior of accepting the student, being usually supportive, elicited problem-orientation, decreased personal anxiety, and led to emotionally readjusting and integrative behavior. Again, evidence to suggest that teach-ers are likely to be more successful with learner-centered democratic ap-proaches.

Democratic teaching related to positive student behavior. Stern[47] reviewed thirty-four studies (largely college classes) comparing nondirective instruction in influencing two types of learning outcomes: (1) gain in cogni-tive knowledge and understanding and (2) attitude change toward self and others. In regard to cognitive gains, he concludes: "In general, it would ap-pear that the amount of cognitive gain is largely unaffected by the autocratic or democratic tendencies of the instructor." However, when he summarizes the findings related to attitude change toward the self and others, the conclusion is somewhat different: "Regardless of whether the investigator was concerned with attitudes toward the cultural outgroup, toward other participants in the class, or toward the self, the results generally have in-dicated that nondirective instruction facilitates a shift in a more favorable, acceptant direction." Once more we find evidence to support the notion that, at least as far as affective variables are concerned, a more nondirective, democratic teaching style is likely to be associated with positive changes in student behavior. As a further example of this, Tiedeman[48] found that the teacher who was disliked most by students was a domineering, authoritarian person. As a matter of fact, the older the student (hence the greater need for autonomy?), the more intense the dislike.

Probably one of the most famous and widely cited leadership studies was conducted by Lippitt and White,[49] who carried on a series of ex-periments to ascertain the effects of various forms of leadership in the individual and group behavior of eleven-year-old boys in a club situa-tion. Three "styles" of leadership—autocratic, democratic, and laissez faire—were experimentally arranged. In addition, there were two different expressions of authoritarian or autocratic leadership, one of which was an aggressive or hard-boiled autocracy and the other a more benevolent or apathetic autocracy. The situations were so arranged that the groups of boys experienced each type of leadership, making possible comparisons of the leadership effects on the same boys.

These three major leadership styles were expressed in many different ways. For example, in regard to setting policy and the goals of the club, the leader of the autocratic group personally indicated the purposes of the club and the activities to be undertaken. The democratic leader, in contrast, discussed the goals and purposes with the boys. The laissez-faire leader offered no direction at all, and his interactions contained few or no suggestions as to the goals toward which the club should work. While the autocratic leader remained somewhat aloof from active participation except when demonstrating a technique, the democratic leader made an effort to be a regular group member without actually doing the boys' work for them. The laissez-faire leader, on the other hand, offered practically no specific direction or made any attempt to appraise or regulate the course of events.

Different psychological climates produce different behavior. The important question is: How did the boys in each of these three groups behave? Generally speaking, members of the autocratic group had two kinds of reactions toward the leader; they were either rebellious or submissive. When the group submitted it showed high work output while the leader was present and in charge of activities. The rebellious group accomplished less but was still effective in reaching some of its goals. However, what frequently happened in the autocratic group was that the social controls dis-

The consequences of good teaching results in busy, involved students.
(Allyn and Bacon)

solved and productivity decreased when the leader was absent. Not only that, but autocratic group members, more so than members of the other two group conditions, did more bickering, scapegoating, and aggressive acting out. At the end of the experiment it was also observed that some members of the autocratically led groups destroyed the products of their enterprise.

Democratically led group members behaved differently. They were more work-minded, showed greater initiative and independence, and reflected a higher level of frustration tolerance. This was true even when the leader was not present. On the whole, there was more friendliness, cooperation, and good feeling among members of the democratic group. This was, for example, illustrated by more expressions of, "We should . . . ," rather than, "I think you should . . . ," more amiable praise between members, and more sharing of group property. Laissez-faire group members engaged in more "horseplay," showed more intragroup friction, and generally reflected less in the way of a consistent goal orientation in their work. Table 7–3 provides a brief thumbnail sketch of the characteristics associated with each of the leadership styles along with the typical reactions of students to each kind of leadership.

In regard to their research, Lippitt and White conclude with the following observations:

> The adult-leader role was found to be a very strong determiner of the pattern of social interaction and emotional development of the group. Four clearcut types of social atmosphere emerged, in spite of great member differences in social expectation and reaction tendency due to previous adult-leader (parent, teacher) relationships.
>
> It was clear that previous group history (i.e., preceding social climates) had an important effect in determining the social perception of leader behavior and reaction to it by club members. A club which had passively accepted an authoritarian leader in the beginning of its club history, for example, was much more frustrated and resistive to a second authoritarian leader after it had experienced a democratic leader than a club without such a history. There seem to be some suggestive implications here for educational practice.[50]

TO THINK ABOUT

What implications do you see here for your own work as a teacher and the way you want to conduct a classroom? Jot down three or four ways you will try to implement these research findings in your own behavior as a teacher. How do they compare with what others in your class have written?

_____

_____

_____

TABLE 7-3.   *Types of Leadership, Characteristics of Leaders, and Students' Reactions*

Type of leadership	Characteristics of this type of leadership	Typical reactions of students' to this leadership
Hard-boiled Autocrat	1. Constant check on students. 2. Expects immediate acceptance of all orders—rigid discipline. 3. Little praise is given as he believes this would spoil children. 4. Believes students cannot be trusted when on their own.	1. Submission, but there is incipient revolt and dislike of the leader. 2. "Buck-passing" is a common occurrence. 3. Pupils are irritable and unwilling to cooperate and may indulge in "backbiting." 4. The work slips markedly when the teacher leaves the room.
The Benevolent Autocrat	1. Is not aware that he is an autocrat. 2. Praises pupils and is interested in them. 3. The crux of his autocracy lies in the technique by which he secures dependence upon himself. He says, "that's the way *I* like it," or "how could you do this to me?" 4. Makes himself the source of all standards of class work.	1. Most students like him, but those who see through his methods may dislike him intensely. 2. There is great dependence upon the teacher for all directions—little initiative on part of pupils. 3. There is submissiveness and lack of individual development. 4. Amount of class work may be high and of good quality.
The Laissez-faire Teacher	1. Has little confidence in dealing with pupils or a belief that they should be left alone. 2. Has difficulty in making decisions. 3. Has no clear-cut goals. 4. Does not encourage or discourage students, nor does he join in their work or offer help or advice.	1. There is low morale and poor and sloppy work. 2. There is much "buck-passing," "scapegoating," and irritability among students. 3. There is no teamwork. 4. No one knows what to do.
The Democratic Teacher	1. Shares planning and decision making with the group. 2. Gives help, guidance, and assistance to individuals gladly but not at the expense of the class. 3. Encourages as much group participation as possible. 4. Praise and criticism given objectively.	1. Pupils like work, each other, and teacher better. 2. Quality and quantity of work are high. 3. Students praise each other and assume responsibilities on their own. 4. There are few problems of motivation whether teacher is in the room or not.

* Adapted in part from L. P. Bradford and R. Lippitt. "Building a Democratic Work Group." *Personnel*, vol. 22. American Management Association, Publisher, 1954, pp. 142–148.

Interaction of Different Student-Teacher Personality Types

It surely does seem clear that the particular leadership style that a teacher either consciously or unconsciously reflects while going about the business of "teaching" can have an enormous effect on the attitudes and behavior of students. There is even evidence to suggest that teachers' beliefs can influence classroom atmosphere and alter student behavior.[51,52]   A student can feel cooperative and friendly or hostile and aggressive or even bewildered and confused depending, to some extent at least, on the kind of teacher he has at the moment.   However, the type of student one is in relation to particular teacher types also makes a difference in a student's behavior.

An interesting study along this line was done by Neil and Washburne[53] who identified three teacher styles, which they referred to as: Type A, turbulent, impulsive, and variable; Type B, self-controlling, orderly, and work-oriented; and Type C, fearful, anxious, and unsure of self.   The greatest differences were noted between the Type B and Type C teachers.   Type B was warm and empathic, set standards for himself and others, and then saw to it that those standards were maintained and achieved.   Type C was colder, more distant, lower in originality and leadership, but higher in hostility and aggression.

What happened to students exposed to these three teacher types?   As far as academic achievement was concerned, they did best with Type B teachers, least well with Type C teachers, while those with Type A fell somewhere in between.   Type B teachers were especially successful with children who seemed unsure of themselves.   Type A teachers—turbulent, impulsive, and variable—got different results with different kinds of children.   For example, students who were somewhat hesitant and uncertain did poorly with Type A teachers.   At the same time, students as a total group performed well in the subjects in which these teachers were interested.   Type C teachers—fearful, anxious, uncertain—were not successful with any students.

What relationships can we predict between the type of teacher a student has and his feelings toward self and authority?   Type B—goal setting, orderly, and work-oriented—was particularly effective with negative and hostile students.   Toward the end of the school year, these children reflected more positive feelings toward authority and were less anxious.   This suggests that hostile children develop better in an orderly, work-oriented environment.   An anxious person—child or adult—functions better in a more structured setting because, among other things, it reduces uncertainty.

Finally, it was noted that different teacher types influence students' feelings toward one another.   Students with Type B teachers behaved in a more friendly way toward them than did children under either of the other two types of teachers.   One further point should be noted.   While the self-controlling (Type B) teacher was definitely superior to either of the other two types in obtaining academic achievement and social acceptance, students under this type of teacher appeared to be less self-reliant.   In other words, they were prone to disclaim responsibility and put it back in the hands of the authority figure.   The message here seems to be that a certain amount of teacher orderliness and control is fine, but not so much so that a student's reliance on the teacher serves as a substitute for his own self-reliance.

Dominative versus Integrative Teacher Behavior

A fact of life that we can probably all attest to from our personal school experience is that some teachers try to dominate a class by demanding, ordering, and coercing, while others attempt to integrate or pull a class together by suggesting, supporting, and encouraging. The effect of the interaction that teachers with these styles have upon a class over a period of time is nicely illustrated by Anderson and Brewer's[54] intensive study and comparison of the characteristics of second-grade children in classes of two quite different teachers. One was a domineering sort of individual who more frequently than the other met aggression with aggression and initiated contacts with pupils rather than helping them to be more assertive and seek out contacts with her.

Examples of dominative teacher behavior

1. Arbitrarily prescribes some activity: "Don't do it that way. I'll tell you what to do."
2. Answers "No" when a pupil asks if he can do something.
3. Orders a student to go to another part of the room.
4. Postpones something without giving any reason: "We can't do that now."
5. Uses disapproval, blame, shame, obstruction, or interruption as methods of controlling students.
6. Resorts to warnings, threats, conditional promises: "If you can't do what you're supposed to do, you'll have to go out in the hall."
7. Demands attention: "John, face this way, won't you?"
8. Deprives children of specific materials, rights, activities, or privileges, sometimes spanks or slaps, keeps students after school, and/or sends them to the principal's office.

The other teacher, described as "integrative" gave more friendly guidance and encouraged, rather than demanded, pupils to join in class activities.

Examples of integrative teacher behavior

1. Helps student to define, re-define, or make progress with problems.
2. Agrees with, approves of, and non-judgmentally accepts the student's contribution.

3. Extends invitation to go ahead in response to a student's wish, suggestion, or expression of need.
4. Asks questions regarding the student's expressed interest or activity.
5. Comments on such interest or activity.
6. Admits to his own ignorance or incapacity.

Impact of dominative and integrative behavior on students. In classes where the teacher's style was essentially dominative rather than integrative, there was more evidence of nonworking behavior among students such as looking up, whispering, and playing with "foreign objects." In addition, there was more specific incidents of *both* conforming and nonconforming behavior, submissiveness and rebelliousness. On the other hand, the integrative teachers produced more spontaneity in students such as volunteering suggestions and contributions, expressions of appreciation, sharing experiences, working on their own problems, and effective problem solving. Fewer instances of children dominating others and fewer nervous habits were also reported. Although slight differences occurred from one classroom to another, the results followed the same pattern. What happened with consistent regularity was the circular effect of teacher behavior. That is, dominative teacher behavior provokes dominative student behavior, and interactive teacher behavior encourages integrative student behavior. In short, *how a teacher behaves has a great deal to do with how his students behave.*

A teachers' behavior does not change easily. I think it is important to note here that when teachers were observed throughout the same year, the dominating behaviors did not "soften" and the "integrative" behaviors did not "harden." In fact, when teachers were observed from one year to the next, the same pattern of behavior existed, suggesting that teachers remained the same even though the groups of children changed. It seems to suggest that once a teacher's instructional procedures and interaction styles are established they are likely to remain more or less constant. What does this mean? Among other things it means that if we're going to be the best kind of teacher we can be then we would do well to listen to our early teaching mistakes and correct as many errors as possible in the beginning while there's still time.

Effects of Indirect and Direct Teacher Influences

Two different methodologies were investigated by Flanders'[55] studies of indirect versus direct teacher influence as it was related to student attitudes and resulting achievement in seventh-grade social studies and eighth-grade mathematics. A central focus of the study was to determine the amount of freedom or lack of it teachers granted students during the course of their everyday instructional activities. In order to do this, Flanders developed what has turned out to be a very useful tool for analyzing interaction patterns existing between teachers and students. As you can see in Table 7–4, the interaction analysis system provides a means for categorizing student talk and for identifying periods of silence or confusion. Notice, too, how different expressions of verbal behavior of teacher and students are subdivided in order to make the total pattern of interaction vivid. Flanders remarks that inaction analysis:

> . . . consists simply of observing, recording, and counting events as they occur. The usefulness of such a simple procedure will depend on congruence between the purpose of observing and the nature of the categories. The proper application of interaction analysis begins by identifying the purposes of observation clearly and then designing a set of categories that fits purposes. Only rarely will an existing set of categories be appropriate.[56]

One of the major outcomes of Flanders' research is what has been termed the "rule of two-thirds," which, appropriately enough, has three parts to it: (1) generally, about two-thirds of classroom time is spent in talking; (2) the chances are two out of three that the person is the teacher; and (3) the teacher spends roughly two-thirds of his "talking" time expressing facts or his own opinions, giving directions, or criticizing students. Furthermore, it was noted that the teacher talk was usually of the kind that merely calls for students to respond to the initiative of the teacher, rather than teacher talk that responds to students in such a way as to cause them to take the initiative. Gallagher,[57] for example, showed that many student responses indicated that they were simply parroting back something the teacher asked them to recall.

It was also found, however, that in classrooms where there is greater freedom for intellectual curiosity, more open expression of ideas, more positive feelings, and higher achievement, the rule of two-thirds is more likely to be the rule of one-half. Indeed, in such classrooms the teacher was observed doing more of those things named in the first four interaction categories cited in Table 7–4, which include spending more time asking questions, clarifying, praising, encouraging, and developing student ideas and opinions.

TO EXPERIMENT WITH

An interesting and revealing effort in "action research" would be for you to actually collect some classroom interaction data by using Flanders' ten categories cited in Table 7–4. For example, you could tally

TABLE 7-4.   *Direct versus Indirect Teacher-Student Interaction Patterns**

Teacher Talk—Indirect Influence
1. *Accepts feelings:* accepts and clarifies the feelings of the pupils in a nonthreatening manner. Feelings may be positive or negative. Predicting or recalling feelings are included.
2. *Praises or encourages:* praises or encourages pupil action or be-havior. Jokes that release tension, but not at the expense of another individual, as well as nodding head or saying "um-hum" or "go on" are included.
3. *Accepts or uses ideas of pupil:* clarifies or developes ideas sug-gested by a pupil. As the teacher brings more of his own ideas into play, shift to category 5.
4. *Asks questions:* asks a question about content or procedure with the intent that a pupil answer.

Teacher Talk—Direct Influence
5. *Lecturing:* gives facts or opinions about content or procedures; ex-presses his own ideas; asks rhetorical questions.
6. *Giving directions:* directs, commands, or orders with the intent that the pupils comply.
7. *Criticizing or justifying authority:* makes statements intended to change pupil behavior from nonacceptable to acceptable pattern; criticizes or rebukes; states why he is doing what he is doing; refers extensively to himself.

Student Talk
8. *Response:* pupil makes a predictable response to teacher. Teacher initiates the contact or solicits pupil's statement and sets limits to what the pupil says. Shift from 8 to 9 as pupil introduces own ideas.
9. *Initiation:* a pupil initiates communication with the teacher in-cluding unpredictable statements in response to teacher.

Undirected Activity
10. *Silence or confusion:* pauses, short periods of silence, and periods of confusion in which communication cannot be understood by the observer.

* Adapted from N. A. Flanders. *Interaction Analysis in the Classroom: A Manual for Ob-servers,* rev. ed. Ann Arbor: University of Michigan School of Education, 1964.

the interactions you see going on in the classes of two different in-structors to compare the results. You may even want to interview a sample of students from each class to assess their attitudes towards each class. How do their attitudes relate to your observational data? Do your findings square with Flanders'?

Another major finding was that direct influence by a teacher tends to restrict and inhibit students, while indirect teacher influence tends to encourage students to more freely express themselves. It was also noted that teachers who used direct influence methods were somewhat deficient in accepting, clarifying, and making use of the ideas and feelings of students. (Which may, in fact, be why they use direct methods in the first place.) In addition, it was observed that teachers who used direct influence methods needed to give directions and orders twice as often as the indirect teachers and criticism about eight times as often. In line with this, Flanders writes:

> Our data show that higher standards can be achieved not by telling students what to do in some sort of misguided "get tough" policy, but by asking questions and then using student ideas, perceptions, and reactions to build toward greater self-direction, student responsibility and understanding. If "getting tough" means helping students face the consequences of their own ideas and opinions, contrasted against living with the consequences of the teacher's ideas and opinions, then our indirect teachers are much tougher.[58]

Good Teachers Are Flexible

Another variable used by Flanders to differentiate superior from less superior patterns of teacher influence was the degree of teacher *flexibility*. Not only were superior teachers apt to be more flexible, in the sense of being able to be direct or indirect as the occasion demanded, but it was also found that *students in all subjects learned more working with more flexible teachers.*

Good teachers are flexible in their approach and relate easily to many different types of students. (Darry Dusbiber)

Interestingly, those teachers who were not successful were the very ones who were inclined to use the same instructional procedures and methodology in a more or less rigid fashion. That is, there seemed to be little variation from one classroom situation to the next. In particular, unsuccessful teachers seemed to lack the ability to expand or restrict the freedom of action of the students through the use of their own verbal influence.

All in all, one of the most significant results of Flanders'[59] study and others with a similar focus is that, with only a few exceptions, indirect teaching as opposed to direct teaching was more likely to be associated with higher student achievement, more favorable student attitudes toward the teacher, the subject matter, and other aspects of the school situation.

EPILOGUE

It might be well at this point to remind ourselves that with comprehensive studies such as those cited in this chapter, there is much overlap between the classroom behaviors of good and poor teachers. Nevertheless, there are characteristics that seem to appear more consistently with one group than the other. For example, when it comes to classroom behavior, interaction patterns, and teaching styles, good or effective teachers seem to be superior in the following ways:

1. Willingness to be flexible, to be direct or indirect as the situation demands.
2. Ability to perceive the world from the student's point of view.
3. Ability to "personalize" their teaching.
4. Skill in asking questions (as opposed to seeing self as a kind of answering service).
5. Willingness to experiment, to try out new things.
6. Knowledge of subject matter and related areas.
7. Provision of well-established examination procedures.
8. Provision of definite study helps.
9. Reflection of an appreciative attitude (evidenced by nods, comments, smiles, etc.).
10. Use of conversational manner in teaching—informal, easy, style.

Neither empirical research nor common sense support the belief that successful teaching is possible only through the use of some specific methodology. A reasonable inference from existing data is that methods that provide for adaption to individual differences, encourage student initiative,

323

and stimulate individual and group participation are superior to methods that do not.   In order for the former methods to come about, perhaps what we need first of all is to work toward becoming more flexible, "total" teachers as capable of planning around people as around ideas.

What, then, is a good teacher?   Number one, a good teacher is a good person.   Simple as it sounds, a good teacher does, indeed, seem to be, first and foremost, a good person.   He rather likes life, is reasonably at peace with himself, has a sense of humor, and enjoys other people.   If I interpret the research correctly, what it seems to be saying is that there is no one best better-than-all-others type teacher.   Nonetheless, there are clearly distinquishable "good" and "poor" teachers.   As a general statement, a good teacher is good because he does not seem to be dominated by a narcissistic self that demands a spotlight, or a neurotic need for power and authority, or a host of unconscious fears and tremblings that demote him from the master of his class to its mechanic.   Number two, the good teacher is flexible.   Either implicitly, or, most often, explicitly, this characteristic emerges time and again over all others when good teaching is discussed in the research.   In other words, the good teacher does not seem to be overwhelmed by a single point of view or approach to the extreme of being afflicted by a kind of intellectual myopia.   A good teacher knows that he cannot be just one sort of person and use just one kind of approach if he intends to meet the multiple needs of his students.   He seems able to move with the shifting tides of his or her own needs, the student's, and do what has to be done to handle the situation.   A "total" teacher can be firm when necessary (say "No!" and mean it) or permissive (say "Do it your way!" and mean that, too) when appropriate.   It depends on many things and good teachers use their knowledge about themselves, their students, the dynamics of learning, and group dynamics in order to move fluidly and effectively with the tides of shifting classroom circumstances.

In sum, the psychology and behavior of effective teachers are complex and varied.   There very likely is no one *best* kind of teaching because there is no *one kind* of student.   When it comes right down to it, good teachers are basically warm, responsive individuals who seem as sensitive to relationships variables as they are to cognitive variables.   Good teachers view teaching as more than an objective presentation of facts—they also see it as a subjective, existential process of guiding a student to the threshold of his own potential for understanding.

A good teacher not only knows his subject area and something about his students, but he also knows something about himself—a topic we head for in Chapter 8.

Write your own chapter summary (major points, ideas, and concepts that had meaning for you).

_____

_____

_____

_____

_____

_____

_____

_____

_____

_____

REFERENCES

1. Jackson, P. W. *Teacher-Pupil Communication in the Elementary Classroom: An Observational Study.* Paper read at the American Educational Research Association Meeting, Chicago, February 1965.

2. Domas, S. J., and D. Tiedeman. "Teacher Competence: An Annotated Bibliography." *Journal of Experimental Education* 19(1950):101–218.

3. Biddle, B. J., and W. J. Ellena. *Contemporary Research on Teacher Effectiveness.* New York: Holt, Rinehart and Winston, 1964, p. 2.

4. Combs, A. W. "Teachers Too Are Individuals." In *The Self in Growth, Teaching and Learning,* edited by D. E. Hamachek. Englewood Cliffs, N. J.: Prentice-Hall, 1965, p. 458.

5. Allport, G. W. *Personality: A Psychological Interpretation.* New York: Holt, Rinehart and Winston, 1937.

6. Hamachek, D. E. "Characteristics of Good Teachers and Implications for Teacher Education." *Phi Delta Kappan* 50(February 1969):341–345.

7. Ryans, D. G. "Some Correlates of Teacher Behavior." *Educational and Psychological Measurement* 19(1959):9–10.

8. Gould, G. "Predictive Value of Certain Selective Measures." *Educational Administration and Supervision* 33(1947):208–212.

9. Cowan, J. C., C. Conner, and P. Kennedy. "Follow-up Study of Teaching Candidates." *Journal of Educational Research* 54(1961):353–355.

10. Simun, P., and J. W. Asher. "The Relationship of Variables in Under-Graduate School and School Administrators' Rating of First-Year Teachers." *Journal of Teacher Education* 15(1964):293–302.

11. Ojemann, R. H., and F. R. Wilkinson. "The Effect on Pupil Growth of an Increase in Teachers' Understanding of Pupil Behavior." *Journal of Experimental Education* 8(1939):143–147.

12. Ausubel, D. P. "The Use of Advanced Organizers in the Learning and Retention of Meaningful Verbal Learning." *Journal of Educational Psychology* 51(1960):267–272.

13. Ausubel, D. P., and D. Fitzgerald. "Organizer, General Background, and Antecedent Learning Variables in Sequential Verbal Learning." *Journal of Educational Psychology* 53(1962):243–249.

14. Wittrock, M. C. "Set to Learn and Proactive Inhibition." *Journal of Educational Research* 57(1963):72–75.

15. Jackson, P. W. *Life in Classrooms.* New York: Holt, Rinehart and Winston, 1968, pp. 144–155.

16. Jackson, P. W. Op. cit., 1968, pp. 149–150.

17. Jackson, P. W. Op. cit., 1968, pp. 152–153.

18. Anderson, H. H. "Creativity in Perspective." In *Creativity and Its Cultivation,* edited by H. H. Anderson. New York: Harper and Row, 1959, p. 34.

19. Boynton, P. L., H. Dugger, and M. Turner. "The Emotional Stability of Teachers and Pupils." *Journal of Juvenile Research* 18(1934):223–232.

20. Hart, F. W. *Teachers and Teaching.* New York: Macmillan, 1934, pp. 131–132, 250–251.

21. Witty, P. "Analysis of the Personality Traits of the Effective Teacher." *Journal of Educational Research* (May 1967):662–671.

22. Bousfield, W. A. "A Student's Rating on Qualities Considered Desirable in College Professors." *School and Society* 24 (February 1940):253–256.

23. Sears, P. S. "The Effect of Classroom Conditions on Strength of Achievement Motive and Work Output of Elementary School Children." In press.

24. Cogan, M. L. "The Behavior of Teachers and the Productive Behavior of Their Pupils." *Journal of Experimental Education* 27(December 1958):89–124.

25. Reed, H. B. "Implications for Science Education of Teachers Competence Research." *Science Education* 46(December 1962):473–486.

26. Ryans, D. G. *Characteristics of Teachers: Their Description, Comparison and Appraisal.* Washington, D.C.: American Council on Education, 1960.

27. Kounin, J. S., and P. V. Gump. "The Comparative Influence of Punitive and Nonpunitive Teachers upon Children's Concepts of School Misconduct." *Journal of Educational Psychology* 52(1961):44–49.

28. Symonds, P. M., and S. Dudek. "Use of the Rorschach in the Diagnosis of Teacher Effectiveness." *Journal of Projective Techniques* 20(1956):227–234.

29. Beck, W. "Pupils' Perceptions of Teacher Merit: A Factor Analysis of Five Postulated Dimensions." *Journal of Educational Research* 61(1967):127–128.

30. Ryans, D. G. Op. cit., 1960, p. 77.

31. Veldman, D. J., and R. F. Peck. "Student Teacher Characteristics from the Students' Viewpoint." *Journal of Educational Psychology* 54(1963):346–355.

32. Mastin, V. E. "Teacher Enthusiasm." *Journal of Educational Research* 56(1963):385–386.

33. Morse, W. C., R. Bloom, and J. Dunn. *A Study of School Classroom Behavior from Diverse Evaluative Frameworks: Developmental, Mental Health, Substantive Learning, Group Process*, USOE #SAE-8144. Ann Arbor: University of Michigan, 1961.

34. Adorno, T. W., et al. *The Authoritarian Personality*. New York: Harper and Row, 1950.

35. Bowman, P. H. "Personality and Scholastic Underachievement." In *Freeing Capacity to Learn*, edited by A. Frazier. Washington, D.C.: Association for Supervision and Curriculum Development, NEA, 1960, p. 51.

36. Ryans, D. G. "Prediction of Teacher Effectiveness." *Encyclopedia of Educational Research*, 3rd ed. New York: Macmillan, 1960, pp. 1486–1490.

37. Combs, A. W., et al. *The Professional Education of Teachers*, 2nd ed. Boston: Allyn and Bacon, 1974, pp. 83–84.

38. Ryans, D. G. "Research on Teacher Behavior in the Context of the Teacher Characteristics Study." In *Contemporary Research on Teacher Effectiveness*, edited by B. J. Biddle and W. J. Ellena. New York: Holt, Rinehart and Winston, 1964, pp. 87–90.

39. Ryans, D. G. Op. cit., 1964, p. 89.

40. Combs, A. W. Op. cit., 1974, p. 63.

41. Davidson, H. H., and G. Lang. "Children's Perceptions of Their Teachers' Feelings Toward Them Related to Self-Perception, School Achievement, and Behavior." *Journal of Experimental Education* 29(1960):107–108.

42. Flanders, N. A., and S. Havumaki. "The Effects of Teacher-Pupil Contacts Involving Praise on Sociometric Choices of Students." *Journal of Educational Psychology* 51(1960):65–68.

43. Rocchio, P. D., and N. C. Kearney. "Teacher-Pupil Attitudes as Related to Non-promotion of Secondary School Pupils." *Educational and Psychological Measurement* 16(1960):244–252.

44. Barr, A. S. *Characteristic Differences in the Teaching Performance of Good and Poor Teachers of Social Studies*. Bloomington, Ill.: Public School Publishing Co., 1929.

45. Page, E. P. "Teacher Comments and Student Performance." *Journal of Educational Psychology* 49(1958):173–181.

46. Flanders, N. A. "Personal-Social Anxiety as a Factor in Experimental Learning Situations." *Journal of Educational Research* (October 1951):100–110.

47. Stern, G. C. "Measuring Non-Cognitive Variables in Research on Teaching." *Handbook of Research on Teaching*, edited by N. L. Gage. Chicago: Rand McNally, 1963, p. 427.

48. Tiedeman, S. C. "A Study of Pupil-Teacher Relationships." *Journal of Educational Research* (May 1942):657–664.

49. Lippitt, R., and R. K. White. "An Experimental Study of Leadership and Group Life." In *Readings in Social Psychology*, edited by E. E. Maccoby, T. M. Newcomb, and E. E. Hartley. New York: Holt, Rinehart and Winston, 1958, pp. 496–511.

50. Lippitt, R., and R. K. White. Op. cit., 1958, pp. 510–511.

51. Harvey, O. J., et al. "Teachers' Belief Systems and Preschool Atmospheres." *Journal of Educational Psychology* 57(December 1966):373–381.

52. Harvey, O. J., et al. "Teachers' Beliefs, Classroom Atmosphere and Student Behavior." *American Educational Research Journal* 5(March 1968):151–166.

53. Neil, L. M., and C. Washburne. "Brooklyn College Research in Teacher Effectiveness." *Journal of Educational Research* 55(1962):347–351.

54. Anderson, H. H., and J. E. Brewer. "Studies of Teachers' Classroom Personalities: II. Effects of Teachers' Dominative and Integrative Contacts on Children's Classroom Behavior." *Applied Psychological Monographs*, no. 8. American Psychological Association, Stanford University Press, June, 1946.

55. Flanders, N. A. *Teacher Influence, Pupil Attitudes, and Achievement.* U.S. Department of Health, Education and Welfare, Office of Education, Cooperative Research Project no. 397. Minneapolis: University of Minnesota, 1960.

56. Flanders, N. A. *Interaction Analysis in the Classroom: A Manual for Observers.* Rev. ed. Ann Arbor: University of Michigan School of Education, 1964, p. 30.

57. Gallagher, J. J. "Expressive Thought by Gifted Children in the Classroom." *Elementary English* 42(1965):559–568.

58. Flanders, N. A. Op. cit., 1960, p. 111.

59. Flanders, N. A. "Teacher Effectiveness," In *Encyclopedia of Educational Research*, edited by R. L. Ebel. New York: Macmillan, 1969, pp. 1423–1437.

REFERENCES OF RELATED INTEREST

Anderson, R. C., et al. (eds.). *Current Research on Instruction.* Englewood Cliffs, N. J.: Prentice-Hall, 1969.

Bower, E. M., and W. G. Hollister. *Behavioral Science Frontiers in Education.* New York: Wiley, 1967, Chapter 6.

Brophy, J. "Stability of Teacher Behavior Over Time." *American Educational Research Journal* 10(1973):2.

Brophy, J. E., and T. L. Good. *Teacher-Student Relationships: Causes and Consequences.* New York: Holt, Rinehart and Winston, 1974.

Broudy, H. S. "Can We Define Good Teaching." *The Record* 110 (1969):583–592.

Bruner, J. S. *The Process of Education.* Cambridge, Mass.: Harvard University Press, 1961, pp. 81–92.

———. *Toward a Theory of Instruction.* New York: Norton, 1966.

Clarizio, H. F., R. C. Craig, and W. A. Mehrens (eds.). *Contemporary Issues in Educational Psychology.* Boston: Allyn and Bacon, 1974, Unit One.

Coop, R. H., and K. White. *Psychological Concepts in the Classroom*. New York: Harper and Row, 1974.

Duffy, W. "The Problems of Defining the Good Teacher." *SPATE Journal* (Winter 1969):49–52.

Dunkin, M. J., and B. J. Biddle. *The Study of Teaching*. New York: Holt, Rinehart and Winston, 1974.

Gage, N. L. *Handbook of Research on Teachers*. Chicago: Rand McNally, 1963.

———. "A Method for Improving Teacher Behavior." *Journal of Teacher Education* 14(September 1963):261–266.

Glock, M.D. (ed.). *Guiding Learning*. New York: Wiley, 1971, chapters 2 and 4.

Greenberg, S. B. *Selected Studies of Classroom Teaching: A Comparative Analysis*. Scranton, Pa.: International Textbook Co., 1970.

Hallman, R. J. "Principles of Creative Teaching." *Educational Theory* 15(October 1965):306–316.

Hamachek, D. E. (ed.). *Human Dynamics in Psychology and Education*, 2nd ed. Boston: Allyn and Bacon, 1972, Part II.

———. "Personality Styles and Teacher Behavior." *The Educational Forum* 36(1972):313–322.

Henderson, G., and R. F. Bibens. *Teachers Should Care: Social Perspectives of Teaching*. New York: Harper and Row, 1970.

Hough, J. B., and J. K. Duncan. *Teaching: Description and Analysis*. Reading, Mass.: Addison-Wesley, 1970.

Lewis, G. M. *The Evaluation of Teaching*. Washington, D.C.: National Education Association, 1966.

McKeachie, W. *Teaching Tips*. Ann Arbor, Mich.: G. Watir Publisher, 1963.

McKeachie, W. J., Y. G. Lin, and W. Mann. "Student Ratings of Teacher Effectiveness: Validity Studies." *American Educational Research Journal* 8(May 1971):435–445.

Moustakes, C. *The Authentic Teacher*. Cambridge, Mass.: H. A. Doyle, 1966.

Murphy, P. D., and M. M. Brown. "Conceptual Systems and Teaching Styles." *American Educational Research Journal* 7(November 1970):529–540.

Nelson, L. N. (ed.). *The Nature of Teaching*. Waltham, Mass.: Ginn, 1969.

Raths, J., J. R. Pancella, and J. S. Van Ness. *Studying Teaching*. Englewood Cliffs, N.J.: Prentice-Hall, 1967.

Rogers, C. R. *Freedom to Learn*. Columbus, Ohio: Charles E. Merrill, 1969.

Shulman, L. S., M. J. Loupe, and R. M. Piper. *Studies of the Inquiry Process*, Final Report, Project no. 5-0597. U.S. Department of Health, Education and Welfare. East Lansing, Mich.: College of Education, Michigan State University, 1968.

Shumsky, A. *In Search of Teaching Style*. New York: Appleton-Century-Crofts, 1968.

Sprinthall, N. A., J. M. Whiteley, and R. L. Mosher. "A Study of Teacher Effectiveness." *The Journal of Teacher Education* 17(Spring 1966):93–106.

Strom, R. D. (ed.). *Teachers and the Learning Process*. Englewood Cliffs, N.J.: Prentice-Hall, 1971.

Weigand, J. E. (ed.). *Developing Teacher Competencies.* Englewood Cliffs, N.J.: Prentice-Hall, 1971.

White, W. F. *Psychosocial Principles Applied to Classroom Teaching.* New York: McGraw-Hill, 1969.

Yamamoto, K. "Evaluating Teacher Effectiveness: A Review of Research." *Journal of School Psychology* 2(1963):60–71.

EIGHT

Self-understanding: A Prerequisite for Good Teaching

CHAPTER OUTLINE

PROLOGUE

TEACHER MALADJUSTMENT: SOME FACTS AND CONSEQUENCES

Nervous Tension High Among Teachers

Many Students Are Affected

A Teacher's Work Is Long and Demanding

Symptoms of Possible Teacher Maladjustment

Tense, overactive

Punitive and aggressive

Anxious, quiet, shy

A Cautionary Note

Effects of Teacher Maladjustment on Students

Physical harm can result

Inferiority feelings can be reinforced

A Teacher's Adjustment Does Make a Difference

THE MEANING AND IMPLICATIONS OF SELF-UNDERSTANDING

How Can Self-understanding Be Acquired?

Observe and study the behavior of others

Practice empathy

Be honest with others

Self-disclosure helps

Cultivate friends who can be honest with you

Take some risks now and then

Be aware of your use of defense mechanisms

Defense mechanisms can be self-defeating
rationalization (excuses, excuses) / denial of reality (the old head-in-the-sand trick) / projection (not my fault—it's yours) / reaction formation (behavior different than feelings) / fantasy (personality's Walt Disney) / displacement (someone safer gets it) / compensation (emphasizing the position)

Defense mechanisms in summary

Take a personal inventory

Avail yourself to therapy

How Can Self-understanding Help?

It helps to understand transference phenomena

It helps to understand countertransference

It can reduce unhealthy transference transactions

It helps avoid unnecessary personalization

It helps one to be at peace with oneself

INSTITUTES THAT STRESS SELF-UNDERSTANDING

EPILOGUE

REFERENCES

REFERENCES OF RELATED INTEREST

IMPORTANT CHAPTER IDEAS

1. The kind of teacher you become depends on the kind of person you are.

2. Teachers are no better or no worse in regard to mental health than the population in general.

3. Teacher maladjustment is serious because of the number of students involved.

4. Difficulty speaking in public is a big problem for many teachers and teacher candidates.

5. Teacher maladjustment can have a profound effect on students.

6. The more self-knowledge a person possesses, the more options he has for choosing to act differently.

7. Self-understanding refers to specific knowledge about how one's unique individuality develops in an interpersonal context.

8. Overused defense mechanisms can interfere with greater self-understanding.

9. Counseling or therapy can facilitate healthy self-other understanding.

10. Becoming what one is involves a continual tension between accepting our basic nature and limitations while at the same time struggling to realize our full potentialities.

PROLOGUE

The kind of teacher you become depends on the kind of person you are. This may seem apparent enough on the surface of it, but sometimes, in our frantic quest for better teaching methods, more efficient instructional strategies, specifically defined behavioral objectives, and more effective methods of inquiry, we lose sight of the fact that the success of those things "better" we dream up depends very much on the psychological makeup and self-understanding of the teacher who uses them.

I think you would probably agree that the urgency for understanding oneself is probably not as important for some as it is for others. In the case of, say, the construction worker or the accountant or the engineer or the chemist or the plumber, where the relationship is between man and buildings or numbers or bridges or test tubes or pipes, then I suppose we could suggest that knowledge about one's personal dynamics is not so critical. But where the relationship is between man and man or, in our case, between teacher and student then the matter of understanding oneself is more crucial. Why? Well, because the processes involved are more personal in nature involving as they do feelings, emotional states, subjective views, and personal preferences.

In Chapter 2, we took the position that an essential function of good education is to help students, at all levels, to become not only knowledgeable, but also to develop healthy attitudes of positive self-acceptance. Teachers can help with this. However, as pointed out by Arthur Jersild in his study of what happens when teachers face themselves:

A teacher cannot make much headway in understanding others or in helping others to understand themselves unless he is endeavoring to understand himself. If he is not engaged in this endeavor, he will continue to see those whom he teaches through the bias and distortions of his own unrecognized needs, fears, desires, anxieties, hostile impulses, and so on.

The process of gaining knowledge of self and the struggle for self-fulfillment and self-acceptance is not something in which he himself must be involved.[1]

Unfortunately, not all persons who become teachers end up being enlightened paragons of mental health secure in the warm embrace of self-understanding. Some, in fact, are miserable, wretched individuals who use the classroom as a convenient podium for their neurotic wailings and negative outlooks about themselves specifically and life generally. Their numbers are not large, but then they don't have to be in order to adversely influence countless numbers of students at various grade levels. How serious is the problem of teacher maladjustment? Let's turn our attention now to that question.

TEACHER MALADJUSTMENT: SOME FACTS AND CONSEQUENCES

Lest we too hastily conclude that teachers as a group are a pretty sick lot, let us be clear at the outset in acknowledging that teacher mental health studies show that the great majority are well-adjusted men and women who exert a wholesome influence on the overall development of their students. Some. however, do not fit this description, and we probably do not have to reminisce long among our school memories to pick out a teacher or two whose emotional stability and interpersonal relations seemed shakey at best or irrational at worst. The fact is that almost anyone who has gone through public or parochial schools can relate instances of having been exposed to some unstable teachers. As one high school junior expressed to me recently, "Man, I've got one teacher this term who's strange — man, that dude's strange."

TO THINK ABOUT

Do you recall any teachers you've had who were "strange"? Jot down the three or four major characteristics about such teachers that stand out for you. What did they do, how did they behave?

_____

_____

_____

How did you feel about being with teachers such as you've just described?

Although reliable evidence is difficult to find, maladjustment is by no means unknown among teachers. The evidence that is available points to the existence of a relatively small group of teachers whose presence in the classroom is a chronic sore spot in education. Indeed, Ringness,[2] who has written extensively in the area of mental health in schools, has suggested that the studies we do have indicate teachers to be no better or no worse in regard to psychological health than the adult population in general.

Nervous Tension High Among Teachers

However, the evidence we do have strongly indicates that many teachers are working under what they consider to be considerable strain and nervous tension. Illustrative of the studies that suggest this as a possibility is one conducted at the Mayo Clinic where patients admitted for various physical ailments were examined for neurotic symptoms. Among the different groups examined it was found that 54 percent of the teachers admitted to the clinic reflected neurotic symptoms, 42 percent of the clergyman and nuns were so, 36 percent of the lawyers and housewives, 30 percent of the dentists, and 17 percent of the physicians.[3]

Another indication of the emotional well-being of teachers has been derived from an analysis of the reasons for teacher resignations and absences. These studies reveal that emotional disturbances underlie many of the physical complaints of teachers and are often the cause for absence from the classroom.[4,5]

Many Students Are Affected

The import of these findings does not lie in the numbers of teachers involved, but rather in the number of students who are exposed to them each day. For example, an investigation by the National Education's Research division of over 4,100 teachers found that about 20 percent of them were so unhappy, worried, or dissatisfied with teaching that they would not choose teaching again if they were to do it over.[6] What happens when we project that figure against the total teaching population? In 1971 to 1972 there were approximately 2,250,000 teachers employed in the public elementary and secondary schools. The average pupil-teacher ratio for that year was about 24 students for every teacher.[7] When we apply the National Education Association's 20 percent figure to the total teaching population of 1971 to 1972, we find that this involves approximately 450,000 teachers, who, over the course of a single academic year are exposed to roughly 10,700,000 elementary and secondary students!

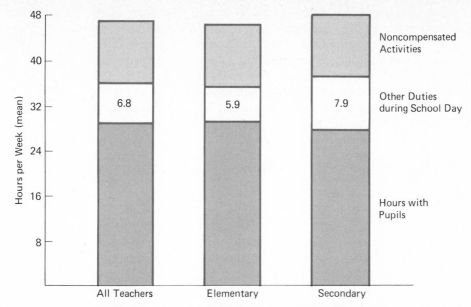

FIGURE 8–1. The Work Week of a Teacher, 1965–1966

(*Source:* NEA Research Bulletin [*October 1967*]:*77. Redrawn by permission.*)

Although we cannot say that a teacher who sees himself as unhappy, worried, or dissatisfied is emotionally unbalanced, we can reasonably speculate that he will very likely experience more difficulty staying emotionally steady than a teacher who is at peace with himself and his work.

A Teacher's Work Is Long and Demanding

The fact is that the task of teaching is long, complex, and demanding. It's not a forty-hour per week job. Indeed, research shows that teachers spend almost fifty hours a week on duties connected with their work, ranging all the way from correcting homework and tests, planning and preparing for daily classes, conferring with and about students, maintaining records and writing reports, attending meetings, sponsoring student activities, and so on.[8]

Not only is the usual work day for teachers longer than the school day, but better than half a teacher's time is spent in active interaction with a group of lively and often unpredictable young human beings. This requires a continuous output of emotional and physical energy. Figure 8–1 will give you a pretty good idea of what we mean here. Small wonder that a national survey found about one-third of the teachers describing their workload as very heavy and involving considerable strain and tension.[9]

In conclusion, we can say that in terms of numbers alone, personality disturbances among teachers is not an overwhelming problem. The seriousness of the situation is not that some teachers are victims of one sort of emotional problem or another, but rather that they are exposed to large numbers of school age students at all grade levels. Clearly, the task of working toward positive mental health and sound self-understanding is not only a responsibility a teacher has to himself as a professional person, but an obligation he owes to his students.

Teachers who are not mentally healthy reflect the symptoms of this lack in a variety of ways. Let's turn our attention now to what some of these symptoms are.

Symptoms of Possible Teacher Maladjustment

Sometimes the personal difficulties of teachers are revealed in their primitive and punitive treatment of students. As an illustration of this, one investigator found that some experienced teachers engaged in practices like:

1. Jerking a child from his seat by his hair.
2. Kicking a youngster in the shins.
3. Forcing a student to push chalk around the room with his nose.
4. Forcing a child to apologize on his knees.
5. Mimicking a child with a stuttering problem.
6. Calling students names like "spaghetti," "lard," "garbage," and "tattler."[10]

Tense, overactive. Another investigator studied fifty female teachers who were hospitalized because of psychotic behavior and found that, while they were in the classroom, these women were characteristically tense, overactive, and unable to relax. They drove themselves and they drove their students. Thirty of these teachers were hypochondriacs, consulting doctor after doctor and seeking out health cults. In addition, fourteen had reflected increasing signs of sensitiveness, suspiciousness, and social withdrawal over a long period of time.[11]

Punitive and aggressive. Symptoms of maladjustment that are reflected in punitive and aggressive behaviors come in a wide assortment of expressions. For example, in Altman's[12] observations of classroom teachers he found some who indulged in vicious temper tantrums, others who humiliated and antagonized children through the use of sarcasm, nagging, and shouting, and some who were almost sadistic in their disciplinary treatment of students.

Speaking of discipline reminds me of an incident that occurred when I was in the sixth grade and sent to the principal's office for scuffling with another boy in the back of the classroom. Shortly after I arrived, the principal, a tall, somewhat broad-shouldered—or so it seemed to me at the time—woman in her fifties (now deceased) marched in, placed a chair in the center of her vast office, and ordered me to lie over it. I had little choice, particularly since the school custodian—all 220 pounds of him—was standing in the corner to witness what I thought might conceivably be my last day on earth. To make a long story short, Ms. principal fetched a long rubber hose from her desk drawer and promptly administered four good whacks to my protruding posterior. She then asked the custodian if he would like to administer a similar dosage—since the hose was out and I was conveniently there—for any misdeed of mine he was aware of and for which justice had not been served. Although justice may have been shortchanged, I am happy to report that my custodian friend deferred and in fact offered, "I think he's probably had enough." If at that moment he would have asked me to sweep out every room of the school with a two–inch wide broom, I would have gladly done it.

Needless to say, I survived that rubberhosing, although for a time it was difficult for me to clearly discern whether it was my ego or my behind that had been most severely scathed. Probably a bit of both. The point is that what happened to me, happens in some form, to many youth in schools across the country. It may not be as dramatic as four smacks with a rubber hose, but it can be every bit as sadistic an expression of anger and aggression. It's safe for me to talk about what happened now. It's over and done with. However, when it occurred I was a terrified young man. I survived it because other significant adults in my world did not do that to me, and I knew that I was loved by people who mattered.

Sad to say, there were children in my elementary school who, before, during, and after my tenure there, received lashes with that ominous rubber hose and who should never have been touched—at least in that way. Some of the boys who received the hose were already victims of harsh and cruel adults, and this principal's primitive administrations of justice did little more than reinforce what these boys were beginning to believe in the first place—namely, adults can't be trusted and they will treat you unfairly every chance they get. I remember one boy in particular—probably one of the most frequently punished boys in school, not just by the principal but by most teachers who had him—who at age twenty-three killed a man during a holdup and is at this moment in state penitentiary where he will very likely spend the rest of his life. No, the teachers who spanked him, kept him after school, and hollered at him cannot be blamed for his life of crime. His other negative experiences included bad parenting. As teachers, we cannot do much about a parent's maladjustment, but we can surely do a great deal about our own. It is certainly true that children and adolescents can be exasperating to even the most well-integrated teacher. However, when a teacher (or anyone else for that matter) indulges his frustration and/or anger in vicious temper tantrums or sadistic sarcasm or extremes such as rubberhosing, then we have good reason to suspect that something, at a deeper level, may be seriously awry with the teacher who behaves in such a manner.

Anxious, quiet, shy. There seems to be a certain pattern of symptoms of maladjustment that we might examine. For example, a study of 733 men and women teachers confined to mental hospitals found that, while they were in classrooms, these teachers manifested the following expressions of behavior (listed in rank order of importance):[13]

Men Teachers	Women Teachers
Introversion	Overambition
Overambition	Hyperactivity
Hyperactivity	Efficiency
Efficiency	Quiet and retiring disposition
Unreal fears	Irritability
Quiet and retiring disposition	Introversion
Anxiety	Neuroticism
Irritability	Anxiety
Selfishness	Selfishness
Eccentricity	Eccentricity

Although the order of particular expressions for men and women varies slightly, the pattern is still somewhat the same. In both instances, the general picture that emerges is that of an anxious, somewhat quiet and fearful individual who may be ambitious enough, yet lacks the necessary inner strength to seek out goals that really matter.

The results of another study closely corroborate those cited above. In a survey by Peck[14] of the mental health of 110 women teachers, it was found that there were sixteen symptoms of maladjustment. Among the most frequently cited symptoms were the following:

Symptom	Percentage Mentioning It
Difficulty speaking in public	46
Discouraged easily	45
Feelings easily hurt	37
Moody	37
Nervous	33
Shy	33
Disturbed by criticism	31
Lack of self-confidence	30

Again, the behavioral pattern emerging here is that of a somewhat withdrawn, quiet, low self-confidence individual who gives up more easily than he would perhaps like to and who finds it difficult to be assertive. It is probably significant that "difficulty speaking in public" heads the list, since this is, after all, one of the more dramatically manifested feelings of shyness, low self-confidence, and anxiety. As any of us who has ever felt uncertain of himself in the face of a group can attest, one of the most traumatizing feelings in the world is the fear of talking to a group of people when one isn't sure of himself to begin with. The deeper level fear is that of not being accepted or approved of and this fear is even more intensified if a person cannot accept himself.

TO THINK ABOUT

Would you rank your participation in class discussions as high, medium, or low? If medium or low, why? What is it about you that makes active class involvement difficult? What two or three positive steps can you take (would you like to take, will you take) to overcome your fear (if that's what it is) of speaking in public?

_____

_____

_____

It is interesting to note here that just as retiring, shy, and low assertive behavior is linked to maladjusted teachers, a more dominant, out-going personality is likely to be found among teachers rated as effective. For example, in a study of qualities related to effectiveness in teaching, Ryans reported that dominance was a characteristic of effective teachers and he went on to observe:

> Dominant—People scoring high on this factor think of themselves as leaders, capable of taking initiative and responsibility. They are not domineering. They enjoy public speaking, organizing social activities, promoting projects, and persuading others.[15]

A Cautionary Note

Let's not rush to the hasty conclusion that all shy, quiet teachers are maladjusted. Nothing could be further from the truth. In the first place, no one or two behavioral expressions can tell us all there is to know about another person's total personality, whether that person is a teacher or anyone else. In the second place, to conclude that a person's quietness or shyness, for example, is symptomatic of maladjustment is premature unless we know more about the motivational well from which his alleged shyness is fed. One person may be shy and somewhat withdrawn in social settings because he is uncertain, fearful of rejection, and ambivalent about his strengths. Another person's shy, quiet behavior, on the other hand, may reflect the carriage of a confident individual who knows what he's doing, what he wants, where he's going, and how to get there.

The accuracy of our diagnoses of ourselves and other people is not in the labels we attach to our perceptions, but in the totality of the observable behavior that follows. If, for example, you look at your own behavior and conclude that you are basically a person with a strong sense of personal adequacy and reasonable assertiveness, the test of the accuracy of that self-perception is the extent to which your behavior is consistent with what you see yourself as being. The point is: We must learn not to hastily judge either ourselves or others on the basis of limited information.

Usually, if emotional maladjustment exists it is usually manifested in a more or less similar pattern of congruent behaviors. As an illustration, if a person is not only shy, but nervous in groups, easily upset at signs of rejection, unduly disturbed by criticism, and reluctant to speak in the company of more than three people then we might tentatively conclude that something may be emotionally awry. There is, as you can see, a certain sameness to his behavior and feelings even though each is expressed a bit differently.

The fact is that some teachers do have deep emotional problems and their effects on students can be long lasting. Let's look at this.

Effects of Teacher Maladjustment on Students

In spite of the fact that many emotionally maladjusted teachers are to be found in our classrooms, the extent to which such teachers affect the lives of the students under their tutelage is difficult to determine. The research that has been done, however, indicates that the effects can be far-reaching. For example, in an early study carried out in the classrooms of 73 fifth- and sixth-grade teachers it was found that the students of teachers in the best mental health were more stable than students whose teachers were rated as being in poor mental health.[16] In a later study, it was shown that kindergarten children in the charge of a teacher considered to be poorly adjusted changed for the worse, while a comparable group taught by "an adjusted teacher with good mental health" suffered no such loss.[17] An investigation by Baxter[18] clearly showed that the way teachers conducted their classes was usually reflected in the security and greater freedom from tensions of students and that much of the teacher's behavior appeared to be tied up with factors related to personal adjustment.

The varieties of physical violence and mental havoc inflicted on students of emotionally unbalanced teachers are endless.

A teacher in Oklahoma resented very bright children, and when Janie came into her third-grade class with a perfect report card from the year before, "the teacher isolated her completely from the other children, would never let her participate or recite, ignored her hand when she tried to volunteer," according to an administrator's report. The child suffered a nervous breakdown. It was further reported that the school administration recommended that exceptionally bright youngsters be kept out of her classes "for their own welfare."[19]

The problem is not new. As far back as 1942, the National Education Association's division of school administrators concluded that "the emotionally unstable teacher exerts such a detrimental influence on children that she or he should not be allowed to remain in the classroom."[20]

Physical harm can result. Consider the teacher in Cleveland, Ohio, who became enraged when a boy left a seat without permission to peer out over a windowsill at something going on in the street below. Without a word, this teacher left his desk, walked over to where the boy was, and slammed the window down on the boy's neck. The boy suffered a broken collarbone. His parents were dissuaded from filing a lawsuit only by a Board of Education promise to place the teacher on leave and arrange for him to go to a psychotherapist.

Inferiority feelings can be reinforced. The misfortune of another student who had the ill-luck to have a maladjusted teacher is presented by Wallin. The following case was described by the person involved some years after the unfortunate incident occured:

> My friends are always talking about my inferiority complex. I have always considered myself dumb and had little confidence in my ability to get high grades or to achieve much in school, in spite of the fact that I continue to find my university courses very interesting. I think my inferiority feelings sprang up in the third grade, when I had a teacher whom I hated. She is the one who mocked and made fun of my thumb sucking. . . . She said I was naughty, inattentive, and unable to get my work, and kept me in the third grade for three years, while my classmates with probably no more ability than I had were advanced. When the fourth-grade teacher got hold of me and became aware of the injustice done me, she shoved me on as fast as she could, so that I made up about a year that way. Although I advanced a grade every year thereafter, as long as I was in that particular school I always felt I was a dumb-bell. When I transferred to another school, where I had no bad record, I worked with real zest and during the last few years of grammar school I was among the first six or seven in the class. But this did not entirely eliminate my deeply implanted inferiority feeling. In my heart I felt I was dumb but the

343

teachers in this school didn't know it, and I felt I was putting something over on them. My inferiority feeling is still with me, although my later successes have helped some to overcome it.[21]

A Teacher's Adjustment Does Make a Difference

Suffice it to say, the effects of teacher adjustment or lack of it play an important part in determining the interpersonal dynamics occurring within any classroom. In a concluding remark summarizing numerous studies of the effects of teacher adjustment on child development, Synder observed that there is no question that the teacher's emotional health can profoundly influence the behavior of his students. He went on to say:

Adjusted teachers do much to bring about pupil adjustment, and the converse is also true. Probably the most satisfactory way of measuring whether or not a classroom is smooth-running and effective would be to measure the degree of personal adjustment of the teacher.[22]

Snyder's observations were supported by Laycock, who studied 157 different classrooms in an effort to examine the effect of the teacher's personality on the behavior of students. The major thrust of his conclusions were that "the effect of many teachers on the mental health of their pupils is definitely bad."[23]

It is important to keep in mind that it is not the teacher's adjustment per se, but rather the way it is reflected in his or her behavior towards students that makes a difference. Thus, the teacher who is aware of his own problems is in a position to be more sympathetic and sensitive to those of his students and more capable of controlling his own behavior. We might also remember that there are many other inputs into the lives of students, and it is not fair to blame any particular teacher's lack of adjustment for all the problems of students. Nonetheless, it is true that some teachers are so busy trying to hold their own emotional lives together that they have hardly any energy at all left over to work effectively in guiding their students' growth.

We might conclude from everything said so far that only normal, well-adjusted persons should be teachers. To a great extent this is true. The evidence does suggest that healthy, balanced teachers who are warm, flexible, and interested in students seem better able to positively affect the attitudes and leanings of students than do teachers in whom these personal characteristics are less evident. The point can be argued, however, that some teachers are successful precisely because of their neuroticism. For example, the compulsive-obsessional teacher who places a high premium on order, accuracy, and precision may teach students the value of order in their lives. Or, we may find another teacher with strong needs for power and

Healthy, adjusted teachers help students feel like this. (Allyn and Bacon)

domination who vigorously carries students along with his own high standards of achievement. Still another teacher may have strong self-punishing tendencies who whips himself by the long hours and hard work he puts into the job. This does not mean, however, that we should recruit more neurotic teachers or that we should feel more comfortable about our own unresolved personal hangups. Absence of self-understanding and flexibility are the two conspicuously lacking personal qualities that make it difficult for the neurotic or emotionally unbalanced teacher to be successful with any group except that narrow band of students who meet his strong personal needs.

TO THINK ABOUT

What personal characteristic(s) of yours do you see as having the potential to cause some difficulties for you as a teacher? Or, let's ask the same question a bit differently. If you could choose a teacher who had essentially the same personal characteristics (general personality) as you, would you choose him or her? Why or why not?

The key to better human relationships, whether it is in being a friend, a boss, a spouse, or a teacher is in understanding oneself. Let's consider that idea more carefully.

THE MEANING AND IMPLICATIONS OF
SELF-UNDERSTANDING

If you are like most other people, there are many facets about yourself and your relationships with others that are difficult to understand. For example, why do you sometimes dislike a person you've just met even when there is no apparent cause for feeling that way? Why do you sometimes lose your temper for no good reason? Why do you sometimes deliberately behave in such a way as to hurt the person you love even though you know you'll regret it later?

The fact is that we don't always know the answers to questions like these because the motives for our behavior may reside outside our conscious awareness. Sometimes, for example, we dislike a person we've just met because he may (1) unconsciously remind us of something in ourselves we don't like, or (2) he may trigger the buried memory of some individual in our past experience with whom we had a bad experience. We may lose our temper because we have unconsciously linked tantrum-like behavior to (1) getting attention, or (2) to getting our own way. We may hurt the person we love knowing we'll regret it later because of an unconscious need to be punished. There are all sorts of possible reasons for behavior which, on the surface, seems incomprehensible to us (and others).

Because of the vast complexity of human behavior, it is not likely that anyone can ever totally understand himself. But everyone, *if he tries,* can understand himself better. In the struggle to cope with the reality of day-to-day living and to deal firmly with threats, frustrations, and conflicts, we must have a firm grip on our own identity. Indeed, the admonition to "Know thyself" has been passed down through the ages as a major antecedent to wisdom and peace of mind until it has emerged in our present day from a religious-philosophical notion into a slogan for better mental health. Why is it important to know oneself? I think Nathaniel Branden has stated it nicely:

When a person acts without knowledge of what he thinks, feels, needs or wants, he does not yet have the option of choosing to act differently. That option comes into existence with self-awareness. That is why self-awareness is the basis of change.

When a person becomes self-aware, he is in a position to acknowledge responsibility for that which he does including that which he does to himself, to acknowledge that *he* is the cause of his actions — and thus to take ownership of his own life. Self-responsibility grows out of self-awareness.

When a person becomes aware of what he is and takes responsibility for what he does, he experiences the freedom to express his authentic self. Self-assertiveness becomes possible with the achievement of self-awareness and the acknowledgement of self-responsibility.[24]

Healthy, positive self-understanding is not a mystical psychic station at which one stops during a particular point in life, but rather it is (or at least it can be) a dynamic, ongoing process that never really ceases. Now, then, let us turn to a critical question.

How Can Self-understanding Be Acquired?

Sometimes it is assumed that one can learn about himself by learning about man in the abstract, i.e., man as a psychological, social, biological, economic, and religious being. Necessarily, then, the so-called "knowledgeable person" ends up learning about the hypothetical man constructed from theories, research, and other people's experiences, not the man, like themselves, who lives and breathes and to whom the personal pronouns "I" and "me" apply. I think you might agree that it is possible to take a great many psychology courses and wind up knowing a vast amount about psychology, but very little about oneself.

Clearly, such information is not wisdom, nor does it bring peace of mind, nor does positive self-understanding prevail because of it. Self-understanding appears to be specific knowledge about how one's unique individuality develops in an interpersonal context. The question is: How can we gain such knowledge? Let's look at some ways for doing this.

Observe and study the behavior of others. At first glance this may seem an odd suggestion, particularly since our emphasis is on "self"-understanding. But is it? Perhaps a maxim of Goethe's may help here. "If you want to know yourself, observe what your neighbors are doing," he said. "If you want to understand others, probe within yourself." When you think about it, most of us are inclined to do exactly the opposite. We observe the other person in order to understand him, and we probe within ourselves in order to understand ourselves better. Seems an obvious enough route to take, but it doesn't always work quite that simply. Why? Mostly it is because we look at other people objectively, but look at ourselves subjectively. We perceive others with the 20-20 vision of sanity and realism—no blind spot here—we behold their shortcomings, flaws, self-deceptions, and even recognize their prejudices masquerading as principles.

TO EXPERIMENT WITH

If you would like to see how your subjective views of yourself compare with someone else's more objective view, try a little experiment. Write down at least three things you hunch that most people are aware of or in some way respond to in the "physical you." Do the same for the "social" you. Have two or three friends share their perceptions of what they respond to in the physical and social you. How closely do your perceptions square with someone else's?

However, when we look within ourselves, we are not inclined to see the same personal distortions. Indeed, most of us "see" only our good intentions, our purest motives, and our most altruistic inclinations. To the extent that we allow our unremitting calls for love and recognition to distort our self-perceptions, then we can never really change anything about ourselves which may, in the interests of more accurate self-understanding, need correcting. There are however, ways for seeing ourselves more accurately as Goethe suggests, through "observing what our neighbors are doing." And there is something specific we can do to enhance this process.

Practice empathy. Empathy, quite simply, is the capacity to put ourselves in another person's shoes and to try to understand what his problems and difficulties are as he feels them. The idea of "social feeling" developed by the psychiatrist Alfred Adler[25] provides us with a useful conceptual tool in understanding the empathic process. Essentially, the idea of social feeling refers to a person's ability to empathize with another—to see, hear, and feel with him. The usefulness of this concept lies in the fact that it combines the idea of social, which is an objective reference to common experiences, with the idea of feeling, which is a subjective reference to private experiences. The synthesis of the objective "social" with the subjective "feeling" is one way, then, of narrowing the gap between "you" and "me."

Social feeling is an attempt to understand oneself through the empathic understanding of others. It means becoming less involved with one's own inner feelings and tuning in more sensitively to how the other person thinks and feels. Along this line, Erich Fromm,[26] one of the most sensitive observers of the human condition in our time, has remarked, "I discover that I am everybody, and that I discover myself in discovering my fellow man and vice versa."

There is a great deal we can learn about ourselves through being empathic observers of the human scene. If we can recognize the common threads that weave us together as a common humanity, then some measure of self-understanding is available to us by participating and sharing mutual concerns with another, or more succinctly, being an "I" for a "Thou" as Buber[27] would say.

Be honest with others. The idea here is a tricky one because it can too easily be misinterpreted to mean that being honest gives one license to do and say pretty much as he pleases without regard to how, when, or to whom the "honesty" is expressed. Practicing honesty in interpersonal relationships does not mean that one can do or say as he pleases regardless of the opinions or feelings of others. Being honest does not mean "self-actualizing" at the expense of other people's feelings, nor does it imply being brutally and indiscriminately frank. But it does mean showing some of yourself to another person and exhibiting some of your own feelings and attitudes. This isn't particularly easy because from early childhood most people learn to mask their inner feelings, as if being honest about them would only hurt others and destroy relationships.

Self-disclosure helps. As you may have noted in your own interpersonal relationships, it is easy enough being honest about the other guy, but it is more difficult to be as honest or revealing about yourself. Actually, the inevitable consequence of exposing and sharing feelings is usually greater interpersonal closeness. If I am honest with you about myself, this encourages you to be more honest with me about yourself. If you are honest with me about yourself, I am freer to be honest with you about myself. And so the cycle goes.

The principle here can be simply stated: The more information you give other people about yourself, the more accurately they can respond to you and the more certain you can be that they are responding to that which comes closer to being the "real" you and not some superficial role. Jourard, a psychologist who has studied the phenomenon of self-disclosure in some depth, has made the following observations that may help us at this point:

> We get to know the other person's self when he discloses it to us. . . . This, of course, takes courage,—the "courage to be." I have known some people who would rather die than become known. In fact, some did die when it appeared that the chances were great that they would become known. . . . When I say that self-disclosure is a means by which one achieves personality health, I mean something like the following: It is not until I *am* my real self and I act my real self that my real self is in a position to grow. . . . People's selves stop growing when they repress them. . . . Alienation from one's real self not only arrests one's growth as a person; it tends also to make a farce out of one's relationships with people.[28]

What this means is that when we repress something, we are not only withholding awareness of this something from someone else, but we are also withholding from ourselves. We might note here what students of psychosomatic medicine have known for a long time, namely, that those individuals who chronically *repress* certain needs and emotions, especially hostility and dependency, are likely candidates for ulcers, asthma attacks, colitis, migraine problems, and even heart trouble.[29,30] One way or the other, it appears, our feelings get expressed.

TO EXPERIMENT WITH

You can easily try out the self-disclosure idea. If you're not a self-disclosing type person to begin with, you may have to try it out for awhile to get the feel of it. Whatever kind of person you are, make a specific effort in the next week or so to be more self-disclosing. Note what happens to your interpersonal relationships. Do you find yourself feeling closer or more distant from people? How about their feelings toward you when you become more self-disclosing? Check it out—see what happens.

You might wonder how this idea can be related to teaching. Consider an example.

A high school teacher friend of mine had the unfortunate experience of losing his pet dog, to which he was very attached, in a hit and run car accident. He was both sad because he lost "Charlie" and angry that the driver made no pretense at stopping, even though he clearly knew that a dog had been hit. This happened right before he was to leave for class one morning and needless to say he was in no mood to teach. (Working productively is difficult enough when one is deeply depressed and/or angry about something, and it is even more difficult when one is in the kind of work where close interpersonal relationships are necessary while one is feeling that way.) He had two alternatives for handling his feelings. One, he could choose to say nothing either about the event or his feelings and mechanically go through the day as if there were nothing wrong. (The risk here is that he would have periodically snapped at his students as if they were the source of his depression and anger.) Or, two, he could frankly admit to his troubled feelings, why they existed, and thereby give his students a chance to respond to his honesty. He chose the latter because he felt that once his students knew that his generally down mood was for a reason, they would be less apt to be defensive and/or depressed themselves. And this is exactly what happened. They responded by expressing their sorrow and sympathy and, in addition, were exceptionally well-behaved. As my friend said, "There was a certain gentle quality about the whole class that day." That teacher's decision was a wise course of action because what usually happens is that *once the students learn that the teacher has feelings, not all of which are buoyant, pleasant, or good, then they are more apt to face up to and admit feelings within themselves*, which opens the door to vastly improved communications. Suffice it to say, if a teacher is honest with his students, shares with them some of his own personal self, he can be much more assured of his students giving him honest feedback about the conduct of the course, its content, and him or her as a teacher.

All in all, self-revealing honesty is one way of facilitating healthy self-understanding because it encourages greater freedom and openness of interpersonal exchange, the medium in which self-knowledge grows. Of course, all the honesty in the world would be fruitless unless we can be reasonably assured of honest feedback in return. This brings us to our next point.

Cultivate friends who can be honest with you. One of the most consistent findings in mass communications research is that *people tend to relate to other people with whom they agree.*[31] A basic principle of social interaction is the idea that most people, if given the choice, will tend to associate with those who think well of them and to avoid those who dislike them, thus guaranteeing more or less favorable feedback about themselves. The outstanding example of this is friendship, which is, perhaps, the purest form of selectively choosing one's propaganda. Usually, not only do we like our friend, but he likes us. In fact, it is possible that we may like him *because* he likes us. And then, of course, friends are typically disposed to say friendly things, which serve to increase the likelihood of hearing more of what we like to hear about ourselves. Friendship is at least to some extent a "mutual admiration unit," in which each party helps to reinforce the desired self-image of the other.

This is all well and nice, but unless we're careful our friendship experiences can end up being superficial, glib interactions. Inasmuch as self-understanding grows best in an interpersonal stream of reflected appraisals, the opportunity for this kind of nurturance is severely reduced when the selectivity of friends is too guarded. The point is: *If we count as friends only those who agree with us and seldom challenge us, then we are seldom forced into the position of having to reevaluate ourselves and our positions on different issues.* Perhaps the best kind of friend is one who can, when it seems appropriate, challenge our most cherished beliefs without being threatened by the possibility of being rejected if he does.

Take some risks now and then. Risk-taking behavior is a fairly relative matter, since what may appear risky to me could seem to you to be child's play. What is risky for one may be everyday behavior to others. However relative it may be, a risk is a risk to the extent that the person engaging in the risk-taking behavior feels uncertain about the outcome and fearful about the possibility of some form of ego damage, whether it be in a sense of shame, humiliation, embarrassment, or rejection. The risk-taking, frightened feeling probably would not be unlike the butterflies we all feel from time to time as we consider the possibility of doing something which, for us at least, is different than what we're accustomed to doing. It could be as simple as raising one's hand in class for the first time or as profound as choosing an occupation.

As an example of how risk-taking can affect behavior, I remember a student who, after having sat without uttering a word for eight weeks of a ten-week term, made his first voluntary contribution during a class discussion. Although visibly nervous about his new verbal venture, he nonetheless managed to express his ideas clearly and with force. Several students responded to him and for a short while there was a spirited discussion between this hitherto quiet young man and his peers. After class he approached me and said, "You know, it wasn't easy for me to talk out tonight as I did. God, I was terrified. I could even feel my heart pound. But you know what? I think I learned some things about myself. One, I can talk in a class like this [about thirty-five students] and survive and, two, I may not be so fearful as I thought I was." He chuckled a bit at that and then added, "Damn, wouldn't that be great if I really did discover I'm not so fearful as I thought."

On the threshold of a new insight about himself, this student left with a small feeling of exhilaration and renewed courage to try himself another time. *By risking failure he discovered strength.* It was not a giant insight destined to change him overnight, but it was nonetheless a small victory over fears that all too frequently shackled him to silence.

Of course, risk-taking behavior can lead not only to the discovery of strengths, but to the revelation of one's limitations as well. An example: A sophomore girl is unsure of her choice of teaching as a major and about her ability and desire to manage a classroom of twenty-five to thirty elementary age children. In order to test her choice, she arranged with her former school to spend three weeks prior to college classes starting in the fall as a teacher-aide. It was a bad experience—the children got on her nerves, she was miserable, but she discovered an essential fact about herself. Teaching was not for her. It was not a happy discovery, but a realistic one that enabled her to concentrate on discovering her strengths while there was still time to prepare for a more compatible vocation.

TO DO

This is a very simple suggestion. In the next two or three days, do one or two things you've always wanted to do but have considered too risky. Stay close to your feelings about the experience and try to figure out what you learned about yourself that you didn't know before.

Be aware of your use of defense mechanisms. Although we are not always aware of it, each of us uses certain "defense" mechanisms to help us preserve and protect the integrity of our self-systems. Indeed, our ability to mobilize certain defensive processes is to some extent related to how successful we are in handling the daily stresses and strains of living. Regardless of how necessary defense mechanisms may be, they nonetheless can prove to be a serious roadblock to greater self-understanding and self-awareness if one uses them, however consciously or unconsciously, to avoid assuming responsibility, to abstain from taking periodic risks, or to manufacture excuses for persisting in behavior that may be immature and self-destructive.

Defense mechanisms can be described both positively and negatively. Positively, they seek to maintain or enhance self-esteem; negatively, they seek to avoid feelings of anxiety and self-doubt.   However, all defense mechanisms are fundamentally alike in the sense that *each serves as a defense against real or imagined personal failures and inadequacies.*

Defense mechanisms can be self-defeating.   On the whole, the use of defense mechanisms is a normal human reaction, unless they are used to such an extreme and with such obviousness to their presence that they begin to interfere with the maintenance of self-esteem rather than aiding it. Progress toward greater self-awareness can very easily stagger to a standstill under the weight of extensive practices of self-deception.   This is an important point to understand.   A defense mechanism is successful only if there is a certain amount of self-deception and reality-distortion built into the process.   For example, the student who fails an exam but then blames his poor performance on either "an unfair test" or a "lousy teacher" never has to look at his own inadequacies as a possible contributing factor.

So, defense mechanisms are perfectly normal processes, but they can be self-defeating if one persists in inventing excuses for his shortcomings rather than facing them for what they are.

With this small cautionary note of introduction, let's turn now to a brief consideration of some of the more frequently used defense mechanisms along with a brief discussion of how each functions.

Rationalization (excuses, excuses).   This is probably the most common mechanism of all.   Typically, it involves thinking up logical, socially acceptable reasons for our past, present, or future behavior.   Rationalization has two primary objectives: (1) it helps us invent excuses for doing what we don't think we should do but want to do anyway, and (2) it aids us in reducing the disappointment connected to not reaching a goal we had set for ourselves.   You may recall the fox in Aesop's fable who rejected the grapes he could not reach "because they were sour."   Not only did he invent an excuse to soften his disappointment, but he also escaped acknowledging his inability to reach the grapes by asserting that he did not really want them.

There are many other examples of rationalization.   With not too much effort we can soon think of a reason for not going to class ("It'll probably be a dull lecture anyway"), for goofing-off instead of studying ("There really isn't *that* much to do and besides I can do it tomorrow"), for eating more than we need ("A little snack won't hurt and besides I'll be dieting soon anyway).

Although a certain amount of rationalization is normal in our day-to-day behavior, excessive use of this process can be damaging.   How can we be sensitive to its excessive use?   There are two good symptoms to which we can be alert: (1) hunting for reasons to justify our behavior and beliefs, and (2) getting emotional (angry, tense, guarded) when someone questions the reasons we offer.   If we find these reactions occurring with any frequency, it usually means that we should stop and examine how factual our reasons really are.

Psychologists are pretty much agreed that excessive rationalization can be highly damaging to personal integrity and good adjustment. As one psychologist describes it:

> Rationalizing probably does more harm than any of the other methods of ego-defense because it is used more extensively and because it is *so subtle a force to the life of reason*. Two very damaging effects of rationalization may be cited, by way of evaluation.
>
> First, using our wits to excuse our mistakes is to sacrifice the value of intelligence as an instrument for planning action in a rational manner. . . . Rationalization involves a costly waste of one's mental resources.
>
> Second, rationalizing is harmful because it *undermines the rationalizer's integrity*. Being dishonest with oneself is one of the subtlest ways of disintegrating, since the personality must dissociate to some extent in order for one part to fool another part. . . . Putting something over on oneself requires some degree of disintegration; in so far as the hoodwinking succeeds, the individual goes that much further to pieces. Kidding oneself is fun but it is fraught with psychological danger.[32]

As you can see, the price of excessive rationalization is self-deception for if we accept invalid reasons for our behavior, we are less likely to profit from our errors.

Denial of reality (the old head-in-the-sand trick). This is a common, everyday mechanism and one we put into gear everytime we turn away from disagreeable realities by ignoring or refusing to acknowledge them. This inclination is reflected in a great many of our day-to-day behaviors. We turn our attention from unpleasant happenings (a women screams for help but six people within hearing distance claim not to have heard her); we refuse to discuss unpleasant topics (a student receives a low grade on a test but turns down an opportunity to meet with the instructor and a small group of students to find out how to improve); we ignore or disclaim criticism ("The professor who flunked me doesn't know what he's talking about"); and we sometimes refuse to face our real problems ("I don't need counseling help—this depression will go away").

The old sayings, "Love is blind," and "None is so blind as he who will not see," are probably fairly accurate illustrations of the inclination to look away from those things that are incompatible with our wishes, desires, and needs. Denial of reality can, indeed, protect us from painful experiences. However, like the proverbial ostrich who buries his head in the sand, denial may also keep us from perceiving things that might otherwise facilitate progress toward greater self-understanding.

Projection (not my fault—it's yours). Projection is a means by which we: (1) relegate the blame for our shortcomings, mistakes, and transgressions to others, and (2) attribute to others our own unacceptable impulses, thoughts, and desires.   This process is usually apparent in our tendency to blame others for mistakes that rightfully are our own.   The teacher who fails to get tenure may feel certain the principal was unfair; the athlete who didn't make the team may accuse the coach of playing favorites; an angry spouse may cry, "You're always starting fights"; a bruised eight year old may exclaim, "Well, Joey hit me first"; the baseball player called out on strikes may suggest that the umpire not delay in consulting an ophthalmologist; and so it goes.

Through the process of projecting threatening qualities or behaviors within ourselves onto other people, we're able to achieve several goals. First, we allow ourselves to believe that we really don't own any of the feelings or behavior in question.   A person may be fearful of his sexual feelings.   ("I think there are more important things to be concerned about than sex.")   Second, we can attack these behaviors, thereby keeping a safe distance from them while at the same time casting ourselves in a self-righteous mold.   ("I can't stand being around people who think about sex all the time.")   Third, we may not feel so badly after all since these behaviors are so widely shared.   ("So what if I think about sex now and then. Everyone else does.")   And fourth, there may be some vicarious satisfaction gained from seeing these behaviors indulged in by others.   ("I'd better keep my eye on these sex-starved people to find out just how far they go with such talk.")

Such projections help maintain our feelings of adequacy and self-esteem when we behave in ways that are inconsistent with how we see ourselves. Placing the blame on others for behavior and/or feelings that originally belonged to us may help us avoid social rejection and disapproval, but over the long haul it is a self-defeating process.   If we are so engaged in looking for faults and shortcomings in other people, we may never get around to expanding our awareness of our own shortcomings.

Reaction formation (behavior different than feelings).   Reaction formation is a process of doing or thinking pretty much the exact opposite of what one really wants to do or think.   Why do some people behave in this contradictory manner?   Primarily because they feel their real impulses or desires would get them into trouble if they were actually carried out.   For example, a teacher may intensely dislike a certain student in his class, yet go out of his way to be nice to that student for fear of saying something that he fears might be unethical or unprofessional.   This may seem desirable on the surface of it.   Unfortunately, repressed negative feelings usually find expression in more devious and less direct ways, and which frequently are more damaging.   For example, I recall a fifth-grade teacher who, as it turned out, thoroughly disliked a certain boy in her room. She always spoke to him and of him kindly enough — thereby avoiding her real feelings — but not once over a six-month period did she call on him in class, even when he

355

vigorously volunteered. Consciously, she was being "nice" to him. At a less conscious level, when it came to deciding who would be called on in class, her true feelings were expressed.

Reaction-formation behavior is frequently recognizable by its extreme and intolerant attitudes, which are usually out of proportion to the importance of the situation. Not uncommonly, self-appointed guardians of the public's morals who voluntarily give their time to censoring books and movies are frequently found to have rather high sexual impulses themselves. Indeed, the most dedicated crusaders are very often fighting their own suppressed impulses as well as condemning the expression of such impulses in others.

Let us be quick to add that the presence of reaction-formation in some people does not mean that motives can never be taken at their face values. Not all reformers are moved to action by veiled impulses. Real abuses need to be corrected. If polluted water is spreading disease, rational men seek to solve the problem. It would be a silly exaggeration, for example, to suggest that those looking for a solution are reflecting reaction-formation behavior against their own unconscious desires to poison someone.

Reaction-formation behavior can be an effective way for helping us maintain socially approved behavior and to control unacceptable impulses. However, it can also hinder knowing our true feelings better if we too quickly convert unpleasant impulses to more congenial ones without finding out why the unpleasant ones exist in the first place.

Fantasy (personality's Walt Disney). Not only are we inclined to convert an unpleasant feeling into something more palliative, but we are also disposed to "embellish" out perceptions so that the world is seen more as we would like it to be. Fantasy is nourished by frustrated desires and fed by a need to make the existing reality different. In a world of fantasy, it is possible to make one's real or imagined inferiorities and inadequacies vanish in a wink of the mind's eye.

> In all societies, one of the most inexhaustible sources of compensatory substitution is that of covert fantasy—the fleeting thought, the dream, the daydream. What one cannot have to eat one can talk of eating, silently imagine oneself enjoying, or realize to the point of fulfillment in a dream at night . . . in thinking, dream and daydream, one can enjoy all manner of forbidden fruit, achieve every imaginable satisfaction, witness pageants of triumph and parades of disaster, turn light into darkness and night into day, bring contradictions together side by side, violate the arrangements of time and space and make an unlikely beginning lead irresistibly to an impossible end.[33]

Fantasy can be either productive or nonproductive. That is, it can be used constructively in solving problems, as in creative imagination, or it can be a kind of nonproductive wish-fulfilling process aimed at compensating for *lack* of achievement rather than stimulating or promoting achievement. James Thurber's Walter Mitty creation is a classic example of how one can achieve wished-for status by imagining that he is rich, powerful, and respected. Einstein, on the other hand, had cognitive pictures of "fantasies" that led to productive hunches, formulas, and solutions.

As each of us can no doubt testify to, the capacity to detach ourselves temporarily from an unfriendly reality into a more affable world of fantasy has considerable therapeutic value. Sometimes, for example, a bit of fantasy is just what the doctor ordered to add the dash of excitement and interest we need to spur us to greater efforts toward our goals in real life. However, the individual who *consistently* turns to fantasy as a solution to a troublesome reality is in danger psychologically. No problem ever disappeared by imagining it would.

All in all, there is good evidence to suggest that fantasizing and daydreaming is not only normal, but an almost universal activity among people of both sexes.[34] It is when a person uses it as a permanent and not a temporary escape that he is apt to get himself into trouble. It is one thing to build a castle in the sky; it is another to try to live in it.

Displacement (someone safer gets it). Displacement refers to a shift of an impulse, usually hostile and/or aggressive, away from the person or object toward which it was originally intended to a more neutral or less dangerous person or object. If, for example, I am afraid of you (afraid of the loss of your love or respect or friendship or fearful of your retaliation) then I may displace or direct to someone else, any angry feelings I may have for you. There are many illustrations of how displacement works. A student who suppresses the anger he feels toward his professor may take it out on his unsuspecting (but safer) roommates. A teacher upbraided by her principal for not having lesson plans in may keep her anger to herself but then be grouchy with her students for the remainder of the day.

Displacement is a process whereby one can vent dangerous emotional impulses without loss of love and possible retaliation, and without even the necessity of recognizing the person for whom such feelings were originally intended. By displacing his anger toward the professor, the student maintains an air of cordiality in his relationship to his professor. The teacher who grouched at her students all day can more easily avoid showing her hurt and angry feelings to a principal who demands she gets lesson plans in on time. Although displacement may serve the needs of the displacer, it obviously places a heavy, not to mention unfair, burden on its misdirected targets.

Over the long pull, displacement behavior usually becomes increasingly more deviant and more often than not results in continual avoidance of situations that could be more efficiently handled by a more direct approach. On the whole, one is psychologically better off when he learns to express and discuss his feeling with the person to whom the feelings are intended in the first place, rather than direct them at someone who does not even know what they're all about. One very specific advantage to a more direct approach is that it offers the possibility for feedback from the original source of our frustrations, which is a much better way to enhance understanding not only of ourselves, but the other person as well.

Compensation (emphasizing the positive). This is a process that involves an attempt to disguise the existence of a weak or undesirable characteristic by stressing a more positive one. We can distinguish between several types of compensatory behavior. *Direct action* is one kind and occurs when an individual persistently attacks the *source* of an actual shortcoming and attempts to remove it. The heroic and successful efforts of the fine actress, Patricia Neal, following her stroke is an example of what sheer effort and persistence can accomplish. Demosthenes, so the story goes, not only overcame his stammer to become a normal speaker, but a great orator.

We speak of *substitute* compensation when a person cannot overcome or remove the original shortcoming but develops other satisfactions. The unattractive girl may develop a winning personality, the uncoordinated boy may turn from athletics to scholastics, a Helen Keller may make up for her lack of sight and hearing through extraordinary development of tactile and intellectual ability. The point is that, in every walk of life, there are personal opportunities that do not involve setting up unreachable goals or the cessation of effort and hope. There are legitimate, wholesome compensations that can add zest and meaning to anyone's life.

Unfortunately, not all compensatory behaviors are desirable or useful. For example, a girl who feels unloved may become sexually promiscuous; the insecure teacher may turn into an authoritarian despot; the lonely person may eat or drink too much; the inadequate feeling soul may brag too much.

It seems a fact of life that we constantly compare ourselves with others and frequently gauge our worth in relation to other people's status, achievements, and possessions. Living in a social world as we do, comparison of self with others should not be surprising. In fact, it can lead to strong motivation toward at least average and, if possible, superior achievement. In meeting these conditions, compensating behaviors may help, but where they become exaggerated or take antisocial forms, they can hinder rather than assist a person in understanding and expressing the potential within himself.

Defense mechanisms in summary. This has by no means been an exhaustive discussion of all the possible defense mechanisms, but it has been a brief overview of some of the more commonly exployed practices designed to protect the image that one has of himself. The primary functions of defense mechanisms are to reduce anxiety, diminish conflict, and lessen frustration. Defense mechanisms are learned adjustive behaviors, they function at a relatively unconscious level, and they involve a fair amount of reality-distortion and self-deception. All in all, defense mechanisms are normal and even desirable, except when they are used so excessively as to blind a person to his deeper feelings and to his more authentic self. Sometimes, if a person lies to others long enough, he begins to believe the lies himself. That is when it becomes very difficult to know where the truth really is.

Having an awareness of how defense mechanisms work is part of the total effort toward self-understanding. There are several other possibilities. Let's turn to them.

Take a personal inventory. William Menninger of the famous Menninger Foundation in Topeka, Kansas, has suggested that one of the steps a person can take in understanding himself is to try to see the source of problem areas in his life. In order to encourage the sort of "personal inventoring," which may lead to greater self-discovery and peace of mind, Menninger suggests the following self-inventory questions:

1. Are you always unhappy and dissatisfied?
2. Do you frequently have vague physical complaints for which the doctor can find no physical cause?
3. Do you feel more or less lonesome and discouraged all the time?
4. Do you have a continuing feeling that people don't like you?
5. Are you always in friction with children or other adults—always arguing about one thing or another?
6. Do you complain a lot? Are most things—your work, your social life, your friends—unsatisfactory to you?

. . . There are three methods for working out solutions to problems: (1) you can change yourself; (2) you can change your environment; (3) you can change both. The third method . . . usually works best. . . . Many times, of course, a good hard look at a problem is all that's needed to make it disappear. By thinking it through carefully, you may find a solution or get the problem down to a manageable size.

. . . The most important factor in your personal happiness and effectiveness is your ability to get along well with other people. This ability really depends on whether you *can love* and *are loved* more than you hate. . . . Difficulties and unhappiness almost always are related to the fact that one does not give and receive enough love to balance the hate.[35]

TO THINK ABOUT

Which of Menninger's personal inventory questions best fits you? If you find that one or two (or more) do fit, jot down the major reasons why you feel they (it) do (does) fit.

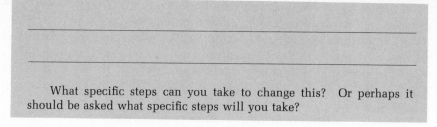

What specific steps can you take to change this? Or perhaps it should be asked what specific steps will you take?

I think it would not be inaccurate to suggest that the better we know ourselves, the more able we will be to forget ourselves for it is usually those things we do *not* know about ourselves, in terms of personal dynamics, that bog us down from time to time. It takes a certain courage to look at oneself—to look at one's shortcomings and limitations without denying their presence, and to examine one's possibilities and strengths without either fearing their existence or brushing them aside with something on the order of "Anybody could do it." (Or "have it" or "be it," whatever the case may be.) This latter point may be something worth thinking about because the fact is that some persons are inclined to discount their potential strengths as essential neutral possessions. Consider an example. A teacher says to a low self-concept student, "Joe, you've written an exceptional paper and I'm just delighted to have had the opportunity to read it." And Joe replies, "Well gosh, it really isn't that good and besides anyone could have done a good job with the topic I chose." Unless a person views himself as a basically worth-while and capable individual to begin with, then it is extremely difficult for him to incorporate the idea of having done some things worthwhile or, of all things, better than someone else could have done it. The point is that some individuals feel that if they, of *all* persons, can do something—which to an outside observer may be perceived as extraordinary or very well done—then this must mean that anyone can do it.

Each individual, no matter who he is or what he does, has his strengths and limitations. One of the outcomes typically associated with getting to know oneself better is the discovery of strengths, talents, and healthy personal qualities that frequently have lain dormant in the shadow of overwhelming feelings of worthlessness and inadequacy.

There is still another step one can take toward understanding himself better.

Avail yourself to therapy. This is by no means a last-resort measure. One does not have to be a thoroughly messed up neurotic or a helpless schizophrenic in order to seek the assistance of a professional person. In fact, much of a psychologist's or psychiatrist's time is spent with normal people with normal problems who need someone with an objective ear to help them sort through their difficulties.

Do therapy experiences help? Evidence would suggest that they do. For example, in an investigation involving 302 prospective teachers, Padgett and Gazda[36] found that group guidance and group counseling procedures produced significant positive changes in the self-concept and professional attitudes of prospective teachers.

Jersild[37] reported another study that located 200 teachers who had received at least two years of psychotherapy. It was discovered that for most teachers, the decision to undergo therapy was a struggle. The final decision was motivated either by intense personal problems or by the desire to live more fully. Some of the major benefits these teachers said they derived from therapy include the following:

1. Deeper insight into own anger (90 percent of group).
2. First realization that own anger was a problem (66 percent).
3. Deeper insight into nature of anxiety (90 percent).
4. Less disturbance over the problem of handling anxiety (90 percent).
5. Ability to engage in competition with better grace (many of the group).
6. Less need of approval or adulation from others (many of the group).
7. Less distress when confronted with personal problems of students:
   Can offer help with assurance when that seems wise (90 percent) or can be comfortable in refusing to "treat" the problem when it seems to be one for the specialist (92 percent).
8. Considerable change in women's attitude toward their femininity. (Less change in men's attitude toward their masculinity).
9. More candid in reporting sex problems.
10. Concern about sex shifted from physical to emotional aspects.
    A control group, not experiencing therapy, reported similar types of improvement over the same period of time, but not to the same extent.

In still a different study by Jersild,[38] 90 percent of a different group of teachers (68 high school teachers) said that they believed that unconscious factors play a large part in life. About 45 percent thought it would be a good idea if more teachers experienced therapy and over two-thirds said they would be willing for a therapeutic experience themselves if the time and money were available.

One of the advantages of a therapeutic experience, whether in a one-to-one setting or with a group is that it helps to make unconscious sources of irritation more available to awareness so they can be dealt with. Sometimes, if we're not careful, trouble spots that remain buried in the unconscious seek other outlets. For example, while discussing one of his teacher self-understanding studies, Jersild[39] reported that all but one of a representative group of teachers admitted to a variety of personal problems. This

361

lone and sturdy soul replied that he was not a bit anxious. In fact, he was never troubled by his anger, his love life, and furthermore his social life and work life were okay, too. He had no personal problems. He did, however, have ulcers.

Therapy experiences provide no magic cures, and there is even evidence to suggest that one gets out of an experience of that sort pretty much what he *expects* to get out of it.[40] Suffice it to say, if one desires to come closer to being "that self which one truly is," as Rogers[41] would say, then a carefully selected therapy experience can greatly enhance that possibility. Among other things, therapy can lead to greater self-acceptance, a state of mind which has been found to be highly related to teaching effectiveness.[42,43]

Now that we have looked at some possible avenues for increasing self-understanding, let's turn our attention briefly to what seems to be a logical question to raise at this point.

How Can Self-understanding Help?

The more an individual understands himself the less likely he falls victim to unconsciously motivated whims, selfish desires, or unnecessarily defensive behavior. In the case of a teacher, self-understanding can help one put the interpersonal dynamics of a classroom into their proper perspective. Sometimes, however, a teacher is less effective than he or she could be because transference and countertransference interactions are unconsciously triggered in both the student and the teacher.

It helps to understand transference phenomena. First, let's look at what these processes involve. Transference is the label given to describe the process that occurs when one person unconsciously responds to a person or experience in a way that is similar to how he originally felt or responded toward some other individual or experience in his life. For example, sometimes a client in therapy will behave toward the therapist as if he were her father. Or a second grader will behave toward his teacher as if she were his mother. In other words, the client and the second grader literally "transfer" feelings for one person in their lives to another. This can be a conscious process; that is, we can say, "I like this person (or dislike him, as the case may be) because he reminds me of so and so." When the transference phenomenon is conscious, one is more able to control its effect and expression. It is when it happens without our awareness that we can run into difficulty.

It helps to understand countertransference. Countertransference has all the attributes of transference and is the term given to what happens when individual A *responds in kind* to individual B's original transference behavior. If, let's say, our therapist friend above responded to his client as if she were his daughter, then this would be what is called *countertransference*. In varying degrees, both transference and countertransference are processes that go on all the time with all people. And they surely go on between students and teachers.

There are many examples of how these phenomena work detrimentally in teacher-student interactions. A high school teacher, for instance, finds herself constantly "picking on" girls in her class who are popular and attractive. "My sister was the glamorous one, I wasn't," said in a sneering sort of way, shed some light on her motives when it slipped out one day. In another instance, an elementary teacher, who was the oldest of six children and who spent much of her growing years caring for younger siblings, continuously complained that "the children in my class seem like such a burden at times." As still another example, I knew a male high school teacher who had the reputation for being unduly and even unfairly harsh on boys in his class who excelled in athletics. Although most of the fellows who were athletically gifted avoided his history class like a plague, many had to take it out of sheer necessity. His favorite threat at the beginning of each new term was to warn the varsity participating boys in his class, whom he sarcastically referred to as "jocks," not to "expect any special favors." Every now and then he would drop a tidbit or two about his two-year-older brother "who thought he was a big chief in school just because he was captain of the football team and a star pitcher and basketball player." This helps explain much of this teacher's behavior, especially when one also knows that he tried out for football and could make only third string and was equally unsuccessful (at least as he saw it) in other sports he tried. The point is that he felt terribly resentful toward his older brother, whom he thought was overloaded with recognition and special favors because of his athletic talents, and he literally lived out (transferred) his resentment toward boys in his class who reminded him of that brother.

> ### TO THINK ABOUT
>
> Reflect for a moment. Think of someone you simply do not like—you can't (or won't) relate to him/her in any way. Who does that person remind you of that you've known before? How are your feelings toward the two people similar? Different? To the extent that they are similar, either positively or negatively, this is transference.

It can reduce unhealthy transference transactions. Transference-countertransference interactions are by no means always injurious to healthy teacher-student relationships. Indeed, the transference phenomenon can be an asset to both the teacher and the student *provided that the teacher is aware of what is happening.* If the teacher is aware of the transference-countertransference dynamics, then he or she can use this insight as a stepping stone to understanding and acceptance—feeling "with" a student because within oneself one knows how he feels. It enables a teacher to react in a positive fashion to transferences from the student.

It also helps to make the countertransference positive when the teacher can see that students sometimes use the teacher as a target for their misplaced projections. For instance, if a teacher recognizes that students frequently transfer onto him their negative and hostile feelings toward their parents, this can help relieve him of unnecessary guilt, self-condemnation, and needless sense of falure.

It helps avoid unnecessary personalization. An example of how one very aware and self-understanding teacher behaved in the face of a class' transference behavior is cited by Solomon. Consider the constructive use the teacher in question made of his knowledge about himself and his students' behavior:

> In a (high school) history class . . . the subject of freedom was being discussed. There were muttered swear words, throwing of erasers, shy passing of notes, general disorder. These the teacher recognized, to quote his own words, "not as an affront to me, as I might have formerly thought. But I knew they were mad." And I thought: Better get it out legitimately. So I said, "You seem bothered and mad at me or at somebody in connection with this business of freedom. Suppose you write anything you feel. Anything goes in writing. But no more swearing, etc. Here is a way to get out your anger." To give just a simple sample of the transference evidence, I quote in part from one boy's paper: "There is supposed to be freedom in the U.S. but teachers tell me what to do. The principal tells me what to do. We can't talk. We can't be late. We can't chew gum. We can't do anything but our own schoolwork which is terrible. It's the same at home. The old lady tells me to mow the lawn, sweep the patio, do this, do that. The old man comes home. 'You forgot to do this. You forgot to do that. Leave your car in the garage and walk to school.' And there it starts all over."[44]

This was a wise teacher. He recognized that the students were not angry at him, but at the adults in their lives who they saw depriving them of their freedom. A less sensitive teacher may have personalized it by erroneously concluding that the students were mad at him or the assignment. He could have then gotten angry back at them by assuming a defensive and reactive posture ("How dare you act that way" or "I'll teach you for acting up like that"), and the whole happening might've been blown out of proportion.

As another example, I recall an incident that occurred on a school playground involving a third-grade boy and his teacher. What he did was to take a ball, place it in front of his teacher, and kick it as hard as he could.

Then he'd say something on the order of, "Na, na, Ms. Jones, I just kicked your brother." Ms. Jones was also a wise, non-defensive teacher. The second time the boy did that she said, "Tom, you know, I bet you're really mad at somebody else's brother—yours, maybe?" He said, "Yes." He went on to add that he was mad at his mother, too, "just like you." Ms. Jones replied that "all little boys get angry at their mothers and brothers sometimes—even their sisters and fathers—and feel like they want to hit them, or the teacher instead." So, rather than berating the boy for expressing his honest feelings or acting as if he really wanted to kick her brother as he said he did, she offered the more constructive suggestion that he either kick the ball again as hard as he could or play with the tether ball hanging loose nearby.

The transference-countertransference idea comes not only from sound clinical observations, but it is also a phenomenon supported by empirical research as well. For example, research shows that just as it is possible that students react to how teachers behave, there is also evidence to suggest that teachers behave in a manner that is more or less consistent with how they perceive their students behaving toward them. A case in point is Klein's[45] research related to student influence on teacher behavior and her general conclusion that "when students behaved positively, the teachers were positive, and when the students behaved negatively, the teachers were negative." This conclusion is supported by Elkind,[46] who observed that inner-city children may influence a teacher to become more defensive, critical, and rigid, all of which are self-defeating behaviors because they encourage the very student behavior that triggered them in the first place. These findings and observations are consistent with those of Turner,[47] who had earlier hypothesized that an important locus of control for a teacher's behavior may lie in the behavior of the students. Perhaps we should add here that a student's behavior is an important locus of *possible* control for a teacher's behavior. Again, we want to emphasize that if a teacher is aware of what is happening he or she is in a much better position to control his own behavior or, to put it a bit differently, to be an *actor* not just a *reactor*.

It helps one to be at peace with oneself. One of the best ways to feel good about oneself is to know with reasonable certainty what one wants and what it will take to get there. When a person knows himself, he is less apt to delude himself into believing that he is happy when he is not. Along with self-understanding comes a certain amount of self-acceptance. That is, we not only know our strengths, but are aware of our limitations and prepared to make the best of them.

Understanding yourself or "becoming what you are" means two things at once: accepting one's basic nature and limitations, and at the same time struggling to realize one's full potentialities. A creative and developing life is a continual "tension" between these two.

INSTITUTES THAT STRESS
SELF-UNDERSTANDING

There are any number of institutes across the country that offer programs throughout the year designed to assist people to greater self-awareness and self-understanding. I have listed four well-known institutes below in the event you would be interested in exploring the possibilities of taking part in those programs at some time.

1. *Esalen Institute* — This is the well-known growth center located in the Big Sur in California. Since its inception a little over a decade ago, about 200 similar centers have sprung up in North America. There is a heavy emphasis on encounter groups, body therapies, meditation, and dance as a vehicle for personal expression. An Esalen catalog can be obtained through: Esalen Institute, 1776 Union Street, San Francisco, Calif. 94123
2. *National Training Laboratory Institute* — This was organized in 1947 to apply what behavioral scientists have learned in the last half century about man, organizations, and cultural systems to the problems of individuals, families and schools. It helps educate men and women to recognize and develop their potentials, and understand themselves better in a variety of group and educational programs. Further information can be obtained by writing: NTL Institute, 1201 Sixteenth Street, N.W., Washington, D.C. 20036
3. *Human Development Institute* — The primary aims are to acquaint people with interpersonal programs that usually involve a set of sequenced, structured occasions that allow two or more people to experience and explore behavioral situations together. More information can be obtained by writing: The Human Development Institute, 166 E. Superior Street, Chicago, Ill. 60611
4. *The Adirondack Mountain Humanistic Education Center* — This is a living-learning educational retreat and conference center based on the hypothesis that people tend to thrive and grow and change and pursue self-actualizing goals when placed in a warm, accepting, encouraging atmosphere. More information can be obtained by writing: Adirondack Mountain Humanistic Education Center, Upper Joy, N.Y. 12987

There are many more institutes, schools, and growth centers throughout the United States that stress personal growth and self-understanding. There is an interesting little paperback available in most bookstores which, among its other offerings, includes a directory of growth centers and their addresses. The title is: *Growth Games,* by Howard R. Lewis and Harold S. Streitfeld (New York: Bantam Books, 1971). A fascinating book. If the idea of personal growth and some ways to achieve it intrigue you, this volume will be worth your time.

EPILOGUE

Self-understanding does not come in a single burst of sudden insight, but rather is more on the order of a continual summation of empathic observations, experience, introspection, and honest interactions. The statistics concerning the effects of teacher maladjustment on students is frightening, and there is evidence to suggest that the problem is serious enough to warrant increasing discussion among an increasingly concerned lay public.[48,49]

Understanding oneself is hard work. It is also challenging and exciting and can open doors to one's upper limits and hidden potentials, which might otherwise remain locked away forever. One of the nice things about knowing more about oneself is that its benefits extend far beyond the classroom to include all the arenas of one's active life space.

Write your own chapter summary (major points, ideas, and concepts that had meaning for you).

_____

_____

_____

_____

_____

_____

_____

_____

REFERENCES

1. Jersild, A. T. *When Teachers Face Themselves.* Bureau of Publications, Teachers College, Columbia University, 1955, pp. 13–14.

2. Ringness, T. A. *Mental Health in the Schools.* New York: Random House, 1968, pp. 65–93

3. United Nations Educational, Scientific, and Cultural Organization. "Highest Neurosis Found in Teachers." *UNESCO Courier* 5(May 1954):25.

4. Randall, H. B. *Twenty-Year Report on Teacher Absences.* Presented at the annual meeting of the American School Health Association and the American Public Health Association, Chicago, Ill.: October, 1965.

5. Stirdivant, L. E. "Teacher Turnover Due to Ill Health." *California Teachers Association Journal* 53(November 1957):20–22.

6. National Education Association Research Division. "A Teacher Looks at Personnel Administration." *Research Bulletin* 23(December 1945).

7. U.S. Department of Health, Education and Welfare. *Projections of Educational Statistics to 1975–76.* Washington, D.C., U.S. Government Printing Office, 1966, pp. 42–43.

8. National Education Association. "Characteristics of Teachers." *Research Bulletin* 45(1967):87–89.

9. Davis, M. "Profile of the American Public School Teachers." *NEA Journal* 56(May 1967):12–15.

10. Adams, C. R. "Classroom Practice and the Personality Adjustment of Children." *Understanding the Child* 13(June, 1944):10–15.

11. Brenton, M. "Troubled Teachers Whose Behavior Disturbs Our Kids." *Today's Health* (November 1971):17–19, 56–60.

12. Altman, E. "Our Mentally Unbalanced Teachers." *The American Mercury* 52(April 1941):401

13. Mason, F. V. "Study of 700 Maladjusted Teachers." *Mental Hygiene* 15(July 1931):576–599.

14. Peck, L. "A Study of the Adjustment Difficulties of a Group of Women Teachers." *Journal of Educational Psychology* 27(September 1936):401–416.

15. Ryans, D. G. "A Study of the Extent of Association of Certain Professional and Personal Data with Judged Effectiveness of Teacher Behavior." *Journal of Experimental Education* 20(1951):67–77.

16. Boynton, P., H. Dugger, and M. Turner. "The Emotional Stability of Teachers and Pupils." *Journal of Juvenile Research* 18(1934):223–232.

17. Nichols, M., J. Worthington, and H. Witner. "The Influence of the Teacher on the Adjustment of Children in Kindergarten." *Smith College Studies Social Work* 9(1939):360–402.

18. Baxter, B. *Teacher-Pupil Relationships.* New York: Macmillan, 1941.

19. Bard, B. "Mentally Unfit Teachers." In *The Psychology of School Adjustment,* edited by B. D. Starr. New York: Random House, 1970, pp. 402–413.

20. National Education Association, American Association of Classroom Teachers. *Health in Schools,* 20th Yearbook, Washington, D.C., 1942, p. 21.

21. Wallin, J. E. W. *Personality Maladjustments and Mental Hygiene,* 2nd ed. New York: McGraw Hill, 1949, p. 105.

22. Snyder, W. U. "Do Teachers Cause Maladjustment." *Journal of Exceptional Children* 14(December 1947):76–77.

23. Laycock, S. R. "Effect of the Teacher's Personality on the Behavior of Pupils." *Understanding the Child* 19(April 1950):50–55.

24. Branden, N. *The Disowned Self.* Los Angeles: Nash, 1971, p. 171.

25. Adler, A. *The Individual Psychology of Alfred Adler.* New York: Basic Books, 1956, pp. 135–136.

26. Fromm, E. *Beyond the Chains of Illusion.* New York: Pocket Books, 1962, p. 186.

27. Buber, M. *I and Thou,* New York: Charles Scribners Sons, 1958.

28. Jourard, S. M. "Healthy Personality and Self-Disclosure." *Mental Hygiene* 43(1963):499–507.

29. Coleman, J. C. *Abnormal Psychology and Modern Life,* 3rd ed. Glenview, Ill.: Scott-Foresman, 1964, pp. 248–261.

30. Alexander, F. *Psychosomatic Medicine.* New York: Norton, 1950.

31. Cartwright, D., and A. Zander. *Group Dynamics: Research and Theory.* New York: Harper and Row, 1968, pp. 45–62.

32. Vaughn, W. F. *Personal and Social Adjustment.* New York: Odyssey, 1952, pp. 356–357.

33. Cameron, N., and A. Margaret. *Behavior Pathology.* Boston: Houghton Mifflin, 1951, p. 378.

34. Ruch, F. L. *Psychology and Life,* brief 6th ed. Glenview, Ill.: Scott, Foresman, 1963, p. 203.

35. Menninger, W. C. "Self-Understanding for Teachers." *National Education Association Journal* 42(1953):332–333.

36. Padgett, H. G., and G. M. Gazda. "Effects of Group Guidance and Group Counseling on the Self-Concept and Professional Attitudes of Prospective Teachers." *SPATE Journal* (Winter 1968):42–49.

37. Jersild, A. T., E. A. Lazer, and A. M. Brodkin. *The Meaning of Psychotherapy in a Teacher's Life and Work.* New York: Teachers College, Columbia University, 1962.

38. Jersild, A. T. "What Teachers Say About Psychotherapy." *Phi Delta Kappan* 44(1963):313–317.

39. Jersild, A. T. "The Voice of the Self." *NEA Journal* 54(October 1965):23–25.

40. Bednar, R. L. "Persuasibility and the Power of Belief." *The Personnel and Guidance Journal* 48(April 1970):647–652.

41. Rogers, C. R. *On Becoming a Person.* Boston: Houghton Mifflin, 1961, pp. 163–182.

42. Combs, A. W. *The Professional Education of Teachers*, 2nd ed. Boston: Allyn and Bacon, 1974, pp. 80–98.

43. Foster, S. F. "Self-Acceptance and Two Criteria of Elementary Student Teacher Effectiveness." Paper presented at the American Educational Research Association Convention, Minneapolis, Minn., March, 1970.

44. Solomon, J. C. "Neuroses of School Teachers." *Mental Hygiene* 44(January 1960):87–90.

45. Klein, S. S. "Student Influence on Teacher Behavior." *American Educational Research Journal* 8(May 1971):403–421.

46. Elkind, D. "Letter to the Editor." *Saturday Review* 51(20 January 1968):46.

47. Turner, R. L. "Pupil Influence on Teacher Behavior." *Classroom Interaction Newsletter* 3(1967).

48. Ringwald, B. E., et al. "Conflict and Style in the College Classroom—An Intimate Study." *Psychology Today* (February 1971):45–47, 75–76.

49. Brenton, M. "Troubled Teachers Whose Behavior Disturbs Our Kids." *Today's Health* (November 1971):17–19, 56–59.

REFERENCES OF RELATED INTEREST

Bennis, W. G., et al. (eds.). *Interpersonal Dynamics* rev. ed. Homewood, Ill.: The Dorsey Press, 1968.

Berne, E. *Games People Play*. New York: Grove Press, 1964.

Boy, A. V., and G. J. Pine. *Expanding the Self: Personal Growth for Teachers*, Dubuque, Iowa: Brown, 1971.

Bugental, J. F. T. *The Search for Authenticity*. New York, Holt, Rinehart and Winston, 1965.

Chiang, H. M., and A. H. Maslow, (eds.). *The Healthy Personality*. New York: Van Nostrand Reinhold, 1969.

Clarizio, H. (ed.). *Mental Health and the Educative Process*. Chicago: Rand McNally, 1969, Chapter 8.

Egan, G. *Face to Face*. Monterey, Calif.: Brooks/Cole, 1973.

Erb, E. D., and D. Hooker, *The Psychology of the Emerging Self*, 2nd ed. Philadelphia, Pa.: Davis Co., 1971.

Fast, J. *Body Language*. New York: Pocket Books, 1971.

Fromme, A. *Our Troubled Selves: A New and Positive Approach*. New York: Farrar, Straus and Giroux, 1967.

Goldberg, C. *Encounter: Group Sensitivity Through Training Experience*. New York: Science House, 1970.

Haas, K. *Understanding Ourselves and Others*. Englewood Cliffs, N.J.: Prentice-Hall, 1965.

Hamachek, D. E. (ed.). *Human Dynamics in Psychology and Education*, 2nd ed. Boston: Allyn and Bacon, 1972, chapters 2, 13, 14.

_____. *Encounters with the Self.* New York: Holt, Rinehart and Winston, 1971, chapters 1, 7.

_____. *The Self in Growth, Teaching, and Learning.* Englewood Cliffs, N.J.: Prentice-Hall, 1965, Part IX.

Harris, T. A. *I'm OK—You're OK.* New York: Harper and Row, 1967.

Hunter, E. *Encounter in the Classroom.* New York: Holt, Rinehart and Winston, 1971.

James, M., and D. Jongeward, *Born to Win.* Reading, Mass.: Addison-Wesley, 1971.

Jenkins, J. R., and S. L. Deno. "Influence of Student Behavior on Teacher's Self-Evaluation." *Journal of Educational Psychology* 60(1969):439–442.

Johnson, D. W. *Reaching Out: Interpersonal Effectiveness and Self-Actualization.* Englewood Cliffs, N.J.: Prentice-Hall, 1972.

Jourard, S. M. *Personal Adjustment.* 2nd ed. New York: Macmillan, 1963.

Khleif, B. B. "Sociocultural Framework for Training Teachers in a School Mental Health Program." *School Review* 73(1965):102–113.

Major, J. (ed.). *The Search for Self.* New York: Macmillan, 1968.

Maslow, A. H. *The Further Reaches of Human Nature.* New York: Viking Press, 1971.

_____. *Toward a Psychology of Being,* 2nd ed. Princeton, N.J.: D. Van Nostrand, 1968.

May, R. *Man's Search for Himself.* New York: W. W. Norton, 1953.

Murphy, G. "Experiments in Overcoming Self-Deception." In *Biofeedback and Self-Control,* edited by J. Barber et al. Chicago: Aldine, 1971.

Peterson, S. *A Catalog of the Ways People Grow.* New York: Ballantine, 1971.

Rogers, C. *Carl Rogers on Encounter Groups.* New York: Harper and Row, 1970.

Samler, J. "School and Self-Understanding." *Harvard Educational Review* 35(1965):55–70.

Schneiders, A. A. *Personality Dynamics and Mental Health,* rev. ed. New York: Holt, Rinehart and Winston, 1965.

Schutz, W. C. *Elements of Encounter.* Big Sur, Calif.: Joy Press, 1973.

Severin, F. T. *Discovering Man in Psychology: A Humanistic Approach.* New York: McGraw-Hill, 1973.

Simon, S. B., L. W. Howe, and H. Kirschenbaum. *Values Clarification.* New York: Hart, 1972.

Strecker, E. A., K. E. Appel, J. W. Appel. *Discovering Ourselves,* 3rd ed. New York: Macmillan, 1958.

Weiner, M. L. *Personality: The Human Potential.* New York: Pergamon Press, 1973.

Whitehall, J. "Mental Health in the Classroom." *Journal of Teacher Education,* 15(1964):193–199.

Wrenn, R. L., and R. A. Ruiz (eds.). *The Normal Personality: Issues to Insights.* Belmont, Calif.: Brooks/Cole, 1970.

NINE

Toward Making Teaching Meaningful, Relevant, and Lasting

CHAPTER OUTLINE

PROLOGUE

Students Expect More from Their Formal Education

Today's Student Is Brighter than Ever Before

STRATEGIES FOR MAKING TEACHING RELEVANT AND MEANINGFUL

Teach for Transfer of Learning

Positive and negative aspects of transfer

Some misconceptions about transfer

the mind is a muscle: misconception one / only specific facts transfer: misconception two / transfer occurs automatically: misconception three

Suggestions for Maximizing Transfer

Strive for similarity between in-school learning and out-of-school experiences

Teach for greater understanding of the "whys"

Encourage the intent to learn and remember

372

Provide opportunities for students to experience early success

Provide opportunities for sequential, cumulative learning

Learn How to Ask Divergent Questions

Differences between divergent and convergent questions

Relate Teaching to Students' Backgrounds and Experiences

Help students discover personal meaning

A poor scholar's soliloquy

Exploit the Psychological Content Of the Curriculum

Design courses around the concerns of students

Some possibilities for social studies

Some possibilities for history and English

Some of the best experiences are unplanned

Biographies and autobiographies can be useful

Possibilities in physical education

Ways To Enhance Freedom and Authentic Learning (C. Rogers)

Build upon problems perceived as real

Provide resources

Use contracts

Divide a group when necessary

Form learning groups

Pose problems

Use programmed instruction

Create encounter groups

STRATEGIES FOR MAKING THE RESULTS OF TEACHING MORE LASTING

Provide the Appropriate Mental Set

Different directions produce different results

Utilize the Advantages of "Part" and "Whole" Teaching and Learning

The whole approach is usually best

A school's organization makes a difference

When to use the whole method

When to use the part method

Consider the character of the material

Distribute Work and Study Activities

Variables to consider before distributing work and study activities

complexity of the material / similarity of the material / monotony and fatigue factors / level of motivation

Encourage Overlearning When Appropriate

When overlearning is most efficient

When to encourage overlearning

When not to encourage overlearning

Provide Knowledge of Results and Progress

Why knowledge of results is important

Teaching machines give instant feedback

Motivation is enhanced

Provide Ample Review Time

Review complex material more frequently

TAKE A STUDENT'S READINESS TO LEARN INTO ACCOUNT

Differences in Reading Readiness

Mental Age as an Index to Readiness

Look for Those "Teachable" Moments

Use the Developmental Task Model to Assess Readiness

Use Piaget's Intellectual Developmental Model to Assess Readiness

Opposing Views About the Nature and Expression of Readiness

The "natural" view

The "guided-experience" view

TEACHING STUDENTS OF DIFFERING SOCIAL AND ETHNIC BACKGROUNDS

Factors to Consider When Teaching Students from Different Social and Ethnic Backgrounds

Be realistic about your perceptions

Understand a student's background

Realize the effects of intellectual impoverishment

Be aware of the effects of stressful family conditions

Be sensitive to how ethnic group membership influences self-image

Allow for language differences

Interpret results of intelligence tests cautiously

Establish firm boundaries that are consistently enforced

Use honest praise—avoid harsh criticism

EPILOGUE

REFERENCES

REFERENCES OF RELATED INTEREST

IMPORTANT CHAPTER IDEAS

1. An interesting, competent teacher and relevant school experiences are educational strategies against which students have not devised a defense.

2. One of the major aims of schooling is to encourage desirable modifications in behavior that will apply (transfer) to new situations.

3. In-school learning is more likely to transfer to out-of-school settings to the extent that teachers build creative bridges between the academia of school and the realities of everyday living.

4. Divergent and convergent questions both have a place in the classroom and good teaching involves a skillful blend of both kinds.

5. Most students in most grades do not seem to do much real thinking on the basis of abstractions alone.

6. Any curricular area has many psychological possibilities for meaningful, relevant learning when viewed in terms of what it might do to help students find themselves, realize their potentialities, and use their personal resources in productive ways.

7. The approaches a teacher can use to enhance freedom and authentic learning in the classroom range all the way from using programmed instruction to creating encounter groups.

8. There are research-proven and time-tested strategies that all teachers can use for making the results of their teaching more lasting.

9. School experiences should be geared to the natural unfolding of each student's developmental pattern (Havighurst and Piaget).

10. There is little sense in waiting for a child to "naturally" unfold because the intellectual development of the child grows in spurts that are not clearly linked to age (Bruner).

11. Students from different social and ethnic backgrounds may not have either the readiness or experience for accepting traditional middle-class values about education.

12. When relevance, meaning, purpose, and hope are absent from the curriculum, increasing numbers of students lose their motivation to learn.

PROLOGUE

There is a simple and stubborn myth about teaching that tenaciously lingers on in spite of what personal experience, research evidence, and common sense tell us to the contrary. It has to do with the idea that the chief, if not the only, function of teaching is to impart information. Sounds simple enough on the surface of it—a teacher gives and a student gets; unfortunately, it doesn't work out so neatly as this in practice. Teachers still "give" all right, but *what* they give and *how* they give it are making a greater and greater difference as far as the extent to which a student's level of curiosity and motivation are affected and his ultimate learning is influenced.

It used to be that a student's mind was perceived to be something on the order of a blank slate and all a teacher had to do was to write the wisdom of the ages across it and the student learned. There may have been a time when this concept of teaching was more or less true. However, in our contemporary society few students come to school with entirely "blank" slates. Indeed, education for increasing numbers of children begins from the time they're old enough to look at a Dr. Seuss book and/or turn on the television set. Through the increased efforts of various mass communications media, which includes among other things, cleverly written and attractively produced books, countless hours of uniquely prepared television programs, not to mention "specials," designed to capture the minds and imaginations of a youthful audience, students are going through elementary school and entering high school better prepared, better read, and more broadly exposed to the language and events of our culture and the world generally than ever before. Curriculum planners and teachers no longer have exclusive rights to what a student learns. Both educational television produced for the general public and commercial television, even with its somewhat consistent level of mediocrity, compete heavily with the schools for portions of a school age child's time and energy.

Students Expect More from Their Formal Education

There was a time when students had little with which to compare their schooling. The elementary student could compare this year's teacher to last year's, or the high school student could compare his English teacher to his science teacher, but these comparisons were usually limited to personal preferences between two personalities with little thought given to the content or relevancy of one teacher over the other.   Such is not the case for teachers of today's youths. By and large, young people expect more of their *formal* education because they are accustomed to more from their *informal* education. The standards of comparison are not only more available, but higher and more demanding.   For example, if a student watches an informative, interesting, and even entertaining science presentation over his classroom television set, he cannot help but compare his real-life teacher with what he sees on Channel 18.   Or, as a wide-eyed five year old sits for an hour thoroughly involved and motivated by the antics and shenanigans of the assorted characters and happenings in a program such as "Sesame Street," he probably cannot help but be turned off a bit to a kindergarten or first-grade experience that may be notable for its lack of life, color, zest, or enthusiastic teaching.

Today's Student Is Brighter than Ever Before

The fact is that schools are no longer dealing with the student of 1900 whose sources of information were limited to parents, preachers, teachers,

"NOW THEN, JUST WHICH PART OF THE KINDERGARTEN CURRICULUM NEEDS TO BE MORE RELEVANT?"

A student's need for relevancy and meaningful school experiences starts early. (Crenshaw, reprinted by permission of Masters Agency)

and the neighborhood gang. Today's student comes equipped with a vast storehouse of facts and vicarious experiences gleaned from the new media of an expanding electronic age. On the whole, today's youths are brighter, more sophisticated, and have higher expectations for their teachers than at any time before in history. The demands for teaching that is relevant and for content that is meaningful are not the wailings of indulged youths throwing a kind of collective tantrum of protest, but rather they are the voices of aware youths disenchanted with teaching and curriculums that bear little, if any, relationship to either their interests or concerns. Like it or not, today's teacher is in competition with a host of rival communicators, most of whom are as smart, certainly richer, and considerably more efficient. However true this may be, the fact remains that an interesting, competent teacher and relevant school experiences are educational strategies against which students have not devised a defense. Nor would they want to.

Our task in this chapter, then, will be to consider some of the basic teacher strategies for enhancing relevancy, meaningfulness, long-term remembering, and some ideas for teaching students from different social and ethnic backgrounds.

STRATEGIES FOR MAKING TEACHING RELEVANT AND MEANINGFUL

William Glasser, psychiatrist and author of *Schools Without Failure*, has spent many years studying educational processes and children's learning. In his experience he has observed that there are really two parts to the relevance question. In the first place, he notes that "too much taught in school is not relevant to the world of child. When it is relevant, the relevance is too often not taught, thus its value is missed when it does exist." He goes on to suggest that the second part of the relevancy question is that "the children do not consider that what they learn in their world is relevant to the school."[1] There is considerable truth to Glasser's observations. If we are going to teach for greater relevance, then we must think of ways to help students relate their school learning to their life outside of school. Another way of looking at this is from the point of view of assisting students to *transfer* their in-school learnings to their out-of-school experiences, an idea to which we now turn.

Teach for Transfer of Learning

One of the major goals of schooling is to encourage desirable modifications in behavior that will apply (transfer) to new situations. Mathematics

Teachers don't have to do all the work.   Students—at any age—have their own ideas about how to make school meaningful and relevant to their needs. (Allyn and Bacon)

teachers want to enable their students to be better able to solve problems, English teachers hope that their courses in composition prepare their students to write coherently, and teachers of American government no doubt

380

hope that their students will be prepared to participate as responsible citizens. Worthwhile goals all, and at first glance it may seem that their
achievement depends primarily on providing sufficient education so that
what is learned is remembered. Were it that simple, the fact is that not
only must a person remember, but he must be able to select from his experiences those responses that seem most appropriate in a new setting.
When learning thus carries over into new situations, it is known as *transfer
of learning.*

Positive and negative aspects of transfer. Transfer can be either negative or positive. In the case of positive transfer, the previous learning is
likely to facilitate and enhance subsequent learning. For example:

A student learns	$5 \times 4 = 20$
This should help him learn	$4 \times 5 = 20$
And, further	$50 \times 40 = 2,000$

Another illustration of positive transfer is reflected in the considerable success experienced by driver education students as they make the transition
from the driver education car to the family car.

Negative transfer occurs when previous learning interferes with
learning something new. For example, the T-formation high school quarterback may have trouble adapting to the wishbone formation of his college
team; parents who learned to do math the "old" way invariably experience
trouble with their children's "new" math; learning the rules for driving on
the right-hand side of the road in the United States presents trouble for the
sightseeing American who rents a car in a country where driving is on the
left side of the road, and so on.

More generally, transfer from one activity to another contains both negative and positive aspects. For example, many of the skills of handball are
sufficiently similar to those in paddleball that a person learning to play
paddleball may be helped by his previous experience with handball. At
the same time, there are also skills involved in each that are sufficiently incompatible to make it necessary for him to readjust his old skills
(learnings) before he can get on with the new one.

Some misconceptions about transfer. Inasmuch as positive transfer is
a major goal of meaningful and relevant teaching, it is imperative that we
understand not only what transfer is, but what it is not.

The mind is a muscle: misconception one. One of the most common
misconceptions about transfer of learning stems from a late nineteenth century belief that the "mind is like a muscle." This was derived from a point
of view called *faculty psychology,* a now outmoded idea of education that
asserted the mind was divided into separate "faculties" such as will,

memory, and cognition.   Related to this was the doctrine of *formal discipline*, which advocated that any one or all of these faculties could be trained or sharpened through rigorous mental exercise.   The reasoning was that just as a boy who did 100 chin-ups would develop strong arms, so, too, would a boy who memorized 50 lines of Poe develop a strong memory.

The "mind is a muscle" view was first challenged by the brilliant philosopher-psychologist, William James,[2] who discovered that a month's practice in memorizing *Victor Satyr* did not result in improving his ability to memorize.   More elaborate studies of more or less the same type concerned with memory,[3] perception,[4] and reasoning[5] were performed by other psychologists with the same results.

The research *coup de grace* was conducted by E. L. Thorndike[6] in a mammoth experimental study designed to measure the growth in general reasoning ability of over 8,500 high school students over a period of a year's enrollment in various curricula.   Comparisons were set up to determine whether the study of Latin, or any other subject, seemed to have any pervasive effect on reasoning ability.   The results rather conclusively demonstrated that the superiority of any particular subject in improving reasoning ability had been grossly exaggerated.   If mathematics or science or Latin appeared to produce "better thinkers," this is an artifact very likely caused by the fact that better students *take* these courses in the first place.   Other studies[7,8] similar to Thorndike's have been carried out, and although the results have not been entirely consistent with each other, they do indicate that the relative contribution of specific courses to the improvement of reasoning ability is not appreciably different.

Although empirical research evidence has long since laid to rest the misconception that one's mental "muscle" can be improved by exposure to certain subject matter, we still hear rumblings now and then from those who advocate hard courses to "toughen the mind" and who feel that what we need is a return to the classics, logic, the great books, and that other such courses allegedly contain the intellectual protein necessary for undernourished mental faculties.   Perhaps whatever controversy remains about whether one subject or another is better for the development of intellectual competence is best answered by Andrews et al.,[9] whose review of transfer of learning research led them to conclude that "there is no superior subject matter for transfer, there are only superior learning experiences." Maybe we should add to that "and also superior teachers."

Only specific facts transfer; misconception two.   A second misconception about transfer is just the opposite of the first and probably grew up as a reaction to it.   This is the idea that nothing learned in one situation gets transferred to another except very specific facts and information.   Early applications of this view led to curriculums that were supposed to provide practice for "real-life" situations.   Unfortunately, subject-matter specialists found it difficult to agree which "real-life" skills most young Americans would need and as a consequence the basic needs of students were sometimes lost sight of amid the confusion of internal power struggles around whose curriculum was most important. The fact is: *All* curriculums are important to different students for different reasons and at different times in their development. One author wisely noted that if we view transfer of learning too narrowly we could very well do a disservice to students by not preparing them to shift from one vocation to another or one job to another because we had not helped them to see relationships or look for similarities among jobs.[10]

Transfer occurs automatically: misconception three. A third common misconception about transfer of learning is that it occurs automatically. It doesn't. Just because there is teaching does not mean that meaningful learning follows as a natural consequence. This is not to say that in-school learning does not transfer to out-of-school settings. Empirical research shows that it can and does. As an example of this, Webb[11] reviewed 167 investigations related to transfer and found that 28 percent concluded that there was considerable transfer between what was taught in school and used outside of school, while another 48 percent concluded that there was appreciable transfer. More recent evidence to support the validity of transfer of learning has been documented by Klausmeier.[12]

TO THINK ABOUT

The idea of transfer of learning may be more meaningful if you can think of three or four instances where things you've learned in a formal school setting have been useful to your in- and out-of-school experiences. Jot down the ones that stand out for you.

_____

_____

_____

_____

The point we want to stress is that although transfer does not occur automatically, it is more likely to occur, and with more positive consequences, to the extent that we teachers develop skills in building creative bridges between the academia of school and the realities of everyday living. The question remains, "How can we make positive transfer more possible?" Let's look at some ways.

Suggestions for Maximizing Transfer

There are at least five interrelated ideas and suggestions you can consider using to facilitate the possibility of in-school learning transferring to out-of-school experiences.

Strive for similarity between in-school learning and out-of-school experiences. This is a principle that coaches are very skilled in applying. A football coach, for example, knows that the best play diagramming in the world is practically useless information until his players have an opportunity to execute those plays on the practice field. He knows, further, that those plays are even more likely to transfer from the board to the actual game as the players have an opportunity to execute them in scrimmage under game-like conditions. So, too, does the wise band director recognize that his intricate marching patterns are more likely to be performed correctly by his high-stepping musicians if they have had a chance to practice them on a marked field prior to the half-time show.

A first-grade teacher I know uses this principle to help her students apply the basic skills of addition and subtraction she teaches them in class. Like the good teacher she is, she goes beyond the lesson itself. She appoints four children, different ones each day, to help her manage the milk money for which she is responsible during the lunch program. Thus, in a simple but meaningful way she is able to create a bridge between abstraction and real-life practice by having them adding and subtracting real money for a real reason. It is surely a greater bother for her to have the children involved in counting the money and making change and such, but she recognizes that this is a chance to put classroom learning into a reality context. And, I might add, each committee of four eagerly awaits its turn.

Sometimes what a student learns in school is left in school because the teacher did not help him to see that it was relevant to other settings than the classroom. Several years ago, while doing some research related to high school dropouts,[13] I interviewed a young man who had been out of school for nine years and asked him, among other things, what he thought he got out of school. His answer:

> I think I could've got more out of it than I did. Partly it was my fault and partly it was my teachers'. I mean I think I probably needed more help than some other kids. Sometimes when I'd be in school working on stuff like verb tenses or writing complete sentences or learning the multiplication tables or stuff like that I would wonder what it was all for. Finally, at the end of tenth grade, I dropped out. Now I'm sorry I did. I just wish that I had been smart enough to know better or a teacher could've shown me—knocked it through my thick skull—I guess that lots of stuff we get in school really is useful in more places than the classroom. Hell, the job I have now isn't great [gas station attendant], but even here I need to know how to multiply, add, subtract, divide and all that in making change, figuring out how much gas we pumped

in a given period of time, and how much more to order. In school I hated math, but now I use it all the time and wish I knew more. I even use English on this job. I used to hate English in school. But now I write up simple order forms for backroom equipment and of course there's a certain amount of writing with all those credit cards customers use. I don't think that all kids need it, but I sure was one who could've used some help in understanding how English courses were related to life outside of school.

One thing that this young man was apparently lacking—at least as he remembers it—in his school experiences were opportunities to apply his multiplication tables or arithmetic concepts or complete sentences to a greater variety of settings than just the classroom.

> ### TO DO
>
> It would be an interesting experience for you to interview several high school dropouts in order to learn more about their motivations in the first place. Explore with them their perceptions of school, teachers, and schoolwork. What did they like most? Least? What was most painful and frustrating for them? How is their school performance linked to home background and social environment? (A good place to find dropouts, by the way, is at employment bureaus.)

The point is that either *lateral transfer* (ability to perform a different but similar task of about the same level of complexity as that which was initially learned) or *vertical transfer* (ability to learn similar but more advanced or more complex outcomes)[14] is enhanced to the extent to which there is a similarity between what a student learns in class and the experiences he has outside of it.

Teach for greater understanding of the "whys". Retention and transfer are more apt to occur if the content a student is learning is meaningful to him or if he can understand the basic principles involved. It is one thing to know that $4 + 4 = 8$, but it is another to know *why* it does.

As an illustration of this, one study[15] found that a group of young elementary age children learned more and remembered longer the basic principles of subtraction when it was taught in a meaningful (rational) way than did another group of children who were taught by a mechanical (rote) method. Students taught in such a way so that the material had meaning for them were given a variety of suggestions to help them understand the process of borrowing in subtraction. The second group was taught one mechanical method and then drilled. Although the second group used exercises that required borrowing, no attempt was made to help them understand the meaning of the exercises or the basic principle involved in borrowing. It's interesting to note that although those taught by the rote method made more rapid progress in the *first few* days, *at the end of fifteen days* they begin to drop behind those taught by the meaningful method.   In addition, when a transfer situation was arranged, those who had been taught *understanding* of subtraction performed far better than those who had not.

In another experiment,[16] problem-solving tasks were presented to sixty students, with one group memorizing the solution without understanding how it worked and the other group seeking to understand the solution before applying it.   Although, as in the study mentioned above, more time was required to teach the understanding group, this group did significantly better than the memorizing group on all three problems used in measuring transfer.

Teaching for understanding takes longer, but the learning lasts longer and can be applied to more different situations.

Encourage the intent to learn and remember.   Research[17] and common sense have both taught us that the intention to achieve or complete something can be a source of great energy in getting started at a task and staying with it until it's completed.   There is good evidence to show that an *intention* to learn well and to remember has a positive effect on retention.   As an illustration of this, Ausubel et al.,[18] asked two groups of undergraduate educational psychology students to read a passage of about 1,400 words on the history of drug addiction.   One group (the control) was instructed to read the material at normal speed, to use the remainder of the class to study facts and ideas, and to be prepared for a test that would immediately follow their reading and study.   Fourteen days later they were given a second test, similar to the first, but this one wasn't announced in advance.   This same procedure was used with a second group (the experimental), the only difference being that they were told immediately after completing the first test they would get another fourteen days later.   The scores for the two groups were about the same on the first test.   However, the second group scored *lower* than the first group on the fourteen day later retention test.   These results suggest that encouraging the intent to learn can facilitate retention, but that encouraging the intent to remember *after* learning apparently has little effect on remembering.

The implication here for teachers is that the intent both to learn and to remember should be encouraged *before students start a new learning task,* rather than after the teaching is completed.

Provide opportunities for students to experience early success.   There is a simple truism about learning: The pleasant effects of success and reward facilitate learning, whereas the unpleasant effects of failure and punishment inhibit it.   Clinical evidence as far back as Freud indicates that we tend to repress (forget) unpleasant emotional experiences, and experimental evidence[19] shows that a feeling of being threatened interferes with recalling previously learned material. For example, there is evidence to show that remembering factual information in a competitive atmosphere under an authoritarian leader is more difficult than in a pleasant, cooperative atmosphere managed by a democratic leader.[20]

The message here is clear. The more opportunities there are for a student to experience early success, the more likely it is that his initial learning will be confirmed, trusted, and recalled. It is also more likely that it will be used.

TO THINK ABOUT

How about in your own experiences? Do you recall some instances in your life when a lack of early success caused you to give up learning something you might otherwise have enjoyed? What happened? How did you feel at the time? Why was success important to you? What have you learned from it?

Provide opportunities for sequential, cumulative learning. A fundamental truism in learning is that most concepts, skills, attitudes, and abilities are not totally mastered in one day, week, or month but cumulatively, through distributed practice and study over a period of time. Hence, it is important that we pay particular attention to the sequence of instruction in order to insure continuity in learning. For example, to attempt to make full-fledged mathematicians out of eleventh- and twelfth-grade students would be unrealistic. Instead, what we have to do is organize the various fields of mathematics into appropriate and realistic segments that can be mastered in stages. In this way, a student not only learns more mathematics at each step along the way, but he also experiences the feelings of success and competency so necessary for him to go on to more advanced stages. Eventually, he may study advanced mathematics in college. Only then will he become a mathematician.

Basically, the principle here is that one must learn to crawl before he walks, walk before he runs, and so on. Once again, it is a skill we see a good coach or good music teacher, for that matter, use as each instructs his other charges first of all in the fundamentals and then adds increasingly more complex skills to those learned initially. This idea contains the basic ingredients of Bruner's "spiral curriculum,"[21] which consists basically of two ideas. First of all, the basic concepts or principles of a discipline, such as, say, physics, mathematics, or chemistry, are identified. Second, these concepts or principles are taught at recurring times and at increasing levels of difficulty to attain ultimate deep understanding. Over time, the emphasis in this approach to instruction is both sequential and cumulative.

The fact is that today's learning is apt to be both more meaningful and generalizable when it is based on yesterday's understandings and aimed toward tomorrow's goals.

Learn How to Ask Divergent Questions

When a student, whining, says to the teacher something like, "Are you going to make us *think* today?" it is usually memory thinking that he has in mind. Sometimes, in the frantic quest for the "right answers," teachers fall into the trap of asking only one kind of question—the memory kind. Guilford[22,23] a psychologist who has done a great deal of research related to intelligence and creativity, has distinguished among five different kinds of thinking, any one of which could be prompted by its counterpart in question form. One kind is *cognition*, which involves immediate discovery, comprehension, or recognition of information in various forms. Another kind of thinking is simply *memory*, or a rote recall of facts. A third kind is what Guilford calls *convergent*, and it demands the sort of mental activity in which data, or "facts," are assembled, shifted, and in some way synthesized in order to come up with a logical conclusion. A fourth kind of thinking is called *divergent*, and in this process one is invited to create something new. A fifth kind of thinking is *evaluative*, and here the task is to make a moral or aesthetic judgment about something.

Differences between divergent and convergent questions. No doubt we can all remember answering our share of memory or convergent questions as we progressed through our formal education years. The problem is that there can be only one kind of answer to these kinds of questions, and it is usually a response that sorts through, synthesizes, and integrates answers from existing data. Divergent questions, on the other hand, invite answers that are original, novel, and creative. To ask a divergent question is to ask not only "What do you *know* about this?" but also "What do you *think* or how do you *feel* about this?"

Perhaps a few examples of convergent and divergent questions will help delineate clearly between them. Let's say, while teaching a social studies unit related to the Vietnam conflict, the teacher asks, "How many American troops were lost in action in Vietnam and what percentage of our total budget was allocated for military purposes over the last five years of the war?" In this case, only memory thinking is involved: The student either knows the answer (from reading the assignment, or John's notes) or he does not know. This is convergent thinking. However, when the teacher asks, "What alternative solutions short of our actual fighting involvement do you think the U.S. government should have considered?" The student is invited to think divergently, to think of other ways to handle the problem based on his own views. Finally, if the teacher asks, "Should the United States have entered the Vietnam conflict at all?" he is attempting to encourage some sort of moral judgment, which is an open invitation to all sorts of divergent thinking.

Convergent, memory-time questions do have a place in the classroom, but we may seriously interfere with the possibility of teaching being more meaningful and relevant if we encourage only convergent thinking. For example, a convergent question about a literature assignment forces the student to come to terms with the book as it is given, a collection of information to be analyzed in some logical way. Divergent questions, however, make it more possible for a student to participate in the book, to become a character in it, to shape its plot to fit his own needs. If, for instance, while teaching *Macbeth*, the teacher asks, "Who killed Duncan?" then only convergent thinking is involved. If, on the other hand, the teacher asks questions like "Why did Macbeth kill Duncan?" or "What would you have done if you were Lady Macbeth?" then students can begin to think along more divergent lines. Generally speaking, divergent questions are likely to encourage more meaningful and relevant thinking because the student is freer to move around in his imagination and to draw more freely from his experiences, either one of which contain intrinsic relevancy for him. Happily, a teacher can make it possible for a student to create his own meaning and relevancy by simply asking the right questions.

> ### TO DO
>
> Consider the material you've just read on convergent and divergent questions. Using this material as your information base, write two convergent questions over the material and then two divergent questions. You might want to check your efforts out with a friend to see if they're really different questions.

Relate Teaching to Students' Backgrounds and Experiences

To be most meaningful, school work should be related to pupils' backgrounds. The fact is that most students in most grades do not seem to do much real thinking on the basis of abstractions alone. As has been pointed out by those who do research with words and their meanings, ". . . the difficulty is that the higher-order abstractions go farther and farther from the realities of concrete experiences."[24]

Let's say, for example, that you ask someone how to ride a bike. One answer might be, "You first try to get a sense of balance and then go

In order to maximize learning, we have to take into account that different students come from different socioeconomic or ethnic backgrounds. (Allyn and Bacon)

straight ahead fast enough so you won't fall sideways." This seems a direct enough answer and in fact even draws on our experience and knowledge of balance and forward movement so we can convert an abstraction to a more personal understanding. Let's say, however, that we ask another person about how to ride a bike and the advice we get is, "Well, the most important thing is to adjust the curvature of the bike's trajectory in proportion to the ratio of your sense of unbalance over the square of your probable speed." I think you might agree that although the advice is essentially the same as in the first instance, we are not likely to learn to ride if we have only the offering of the second person. We may understand the individual words but find very little in our own experience that give them meaning.

Consider the following definition from a high school geometry text: "The word *area* conveys the idea of space on a plane surface." Each one of the words in the above definition is listed in Thorndike's[25] most common 4,000 words in the English language, yet the definition remains an enigma to many high school students because the idea is not connected to any real-life experience that students have had in dealing with the concept of area.[26]

Help students discover personal meaning. More and more, research is beginning to show us that learning is a problem of the discovery of personal meaning. Necessarily, then, teaching becomes a process of helping people *discover* personal meaning. To put this in somewhat more technical terms, we could say that the effect of any bit of information will depend upon its psychological distance from one's *self*. The problem of teaching then becomes a problem of moving information from the not-self

390

end of the continuum to the self end. Arthur Combs, a prominent psychologist from the University of Florida, has made some observations that speak eloquently to this point.

> "In our zeal to be scientific and objective, we have sometimes taught children that personal meanings are things you leave at the schoolhouse door. Sometimes, I fear, in our desire to help people learn, we have said to the child, "Alice, I am not interested in what you think or what you believe. What are the facts?" As a consequence, we may have taught children that personal meanings have no place in the classroom, which is another way of saying that school is concerned only with things that do not matter! If learning, however, is a discovery of personal meaning, then the facts with which we must be concerned are the beliefs, feelings, understandings, convictions, doubts, fears, likes and dislikes of the pupil—those personal ways of perceiving himself and the world he lives in.[27]

TO THINK ABOUT

Reflect for a moment. What was the most meaningful course you've ever had? Why was it meaningful? What did the instructor do to help make it that way? What did *you* do to help make it that way? What implications do you see here for your own teaching behavior?

A poor scholar's soliloquy. Thirty years ago Stephen Corey wrote a short piece that he titled, "A Poor Scholar's Soliloquy." It doesn't seem to have aged a bit and in fact seems to fit very nicely in this section where we've talked about relating what we do as teachers to students' backgrounds and experiences. As a teacher, you, too, may eventually have some "poor scholars" as students. Hopefully, school will mean more to our contemporary "poor" scholars than the one about whom you are to read. As you will see, sometimes a student does poorly not because he's "dumb" or unmotivated, but because a teacher either fails to ask the right questions or to tap into experiences that are really meaningful to him.

As expressed by our poor scholar:

> No, I'm not very good in school. This is my second year in the seventh grade and I'm bigger and taller than the other kids. They like me all right, though, even if I don't say much in the schoolroom, because outside I can tell them how to do a lot of things. They tag me around and that sort of makes up for what goes on in school.
>
> I don't know why the teachers don't like me. They never have very much. Seems like they don't think you know anything unless you can read the book it comes out of. I've got a lot of books in my own room at home—books like Popular Science, Mechanical Encyclopedia, and the Sears'

and Wards' catalogues, but I don't very often just sit down and read them through like they make us do in school. I use my books when I want to find something out, like whenever Mom buys anything secondhand I look it up in Sears' or Ward's first and tell her if she's getting stung or not. I can use the index in a hurry to find the things I want.

In school, though, we've got to learn whatever is in the book and I just can't memorize the stuff. Last year I stayed after school every night for two weeks trying to learn the names of the Presidents. Of course I knew some of them like Washington and Jefferson and Lincoln, but there must have been thirty altogether and I never did get them straight.

I'm not too sorry though because the kids who learned the Presidents had to turn right around and learn all the Vice-Presidents. I'm taking the seventh grade over but our teacher this year isn't so interested in the names of Presidents. She had us trying to learn the names of all the great American inventors.

I guess I just can't remember names in history. Anyway, I've been trying to learn about trucks because my uncle owns three and he says I can drive one when I'm sixteen. I already know the horsepower and number of forward and backward speeds of twenty-six American trucks, some of them Diesels, and I can spot each make a long way off. It's funny how the Diesel works. I started to tell my teacher about it last Wednesday in science class when the pump we were using to make a vacuum in a bell jar got hot, but she said she didn't see what a Diesel engine had to do with our experiment on air pressure so I just kept still. The kids seemed interested, though. I took four of them around to my uncle's garage after school and we saw the mechanic, Gus, tearing a big truck Diesel down. Boy, does he know his stuff!

I'm not very good in geography either. They call it economic geography this year. We've been studying the imports and exports of Chile all week but I couldn't tell you what they are. Maybe the reason is I had to miss school yesterday because my uncle took me and his big trailer truck down state about two hundred miles and we brought almost ten tons of stock to the Chicago market.

He had told me where we were going and I had to figure out the highways to take and the mileage. He didn't do anything but drive and turn where I told him to. Was that fun! I sat with a map in my lap and told him to turn south or southeast or some other direction. We made seven stops and drove over five hundred miles round trip. I'm figuring now what his oil cost and also the wear and tear on the truck—he calls it depreciation—so we'll know how much we made.

I even write out all the bills and send letters to the farmers about what their pigs and beef cattle brought at the stockyards. I only made three mistakes in 17 letters last time, my aunt said—all commas. She's been through high school and reads them over. I wish I could write school themes that way. The last one I had to write was on, "What a Daffodil Thinks of Spring," and I just couldn't get going.

I don't do very well in school in arithmetic either. Seems I just can't keep my mind on the problems. We had one the other day like this: If a 57 foot telephone pole falls across a cement highway so that $17\frac{3}{8}$ feet extend from one side and $14\frac{9}{17}$ feet from the other, how wide is the highway? I don't even try to answer it because it didn't say whether the pole had fallen straight across or not.

Even in shop I don't get very good grades. All of us kids make a broom holder and a book end this term and mine were sloppy. I just couldn't get interested. Mom doesn't use a broom anymore with her new vacuum cleaner, and our books are in a bookcase with glass doors in the parlor. Anyway, I wanted to make an end gate for my uncle's trailer but the shop teacher said that meant using metal and wood both and I'd have to learn to work with wood first. I didn't see why, but I kept still and made a tie rack at school and the tail gate after school at my uncle's garage. He said I saved him $10.

Civics is hard for me, too. I've been staying after school trying to learn the "Articles of Confederation" for almost a week because the teacher said we couldn't be good citizens unless we did. I really tried, because I want to be a good citizen. I did hate to stay after school, though, because a bunch of us boys from the south end of town have been cleaning up the old lot across from Taylor's Machine Shop to make a playground out of it for the little kids from the Methodist Home. I made the jungle gym from old pipe and the guys made me Grand Mogul to keep the playground going. We raised enough money collecting scrap this month to build a wire fence clear around the lot.

Dad says I can quit school when I'm fifteen and I'm sort of anxious to because there are lots of things I want to learn how to do, and as my uncle says, I'm not getting any younger.[28]

Exploit the Psychological Content of the Curriculum

Nearly everything in a curriculum teams with psychological possibilities for meaningful, relevant learning when viewed in terms of what it might do to help students find themselves, realize their potentialities, use their personal resources in productive ways, and enter into relationships that have a bearing on their ideas about school and attitudes towards themselves.

Design courses around the concerns of students. Weinstein and Fantani,[29] of the Ford Foundation's fund for the Advancement of Education, developed an interesting theoretical model for designing courses around the basic concerns of students. They made a particularly important distinction between the progressive education clichés about student interests and what they defined as concerns. They pointed out, for instance, that a student might be *interested* in cars because he was *concerned* with his feelings of powerlessness and that the sensible approach to such a student was not necessarily *Hot Rod Magazine,* but rather a more direct way of helping him explore his understanding of power. They were also careful to emphasize that they did not envisage the classroom as a place for solving the emotional problems of individuals; rather they wanted to find a way to direct lessons toward the general, yet personal, concerns of an entire class. Now this is not to suggest that simply because a student is interested in something that he's troubled by deep underlying concerns. This may or may not be the case; all a teacher can try to do is to make his teaching and presentation style as interesting, personal, and relevant as possible so that if there are deeper concerns these, too, can be explored as legitimate school-related activities. Consider some examples of what is meant here.

Some possibilities for social studies.   In social studies, why not encourage more inquiries into human values, needs, human aspiration, and the competitive tendencies involved in economic affairs? Unfortunately, our social study offerings frequently do not make much of an impact on the students who take them. For example, a recent study done at the University of Michigan's Survey Research Center found that civics courses, as presently conducted, had little immediate positive effect on over 1,600 seniors in 97 high schools across the country.[30] Indeed, the study noted that students who had not been exposed to civics courses received almost identical scores on a government knowledge test as did students who had taken the courses. On other factors, such as interest in politics, keeping up with political news, and developing a sense of political effectiveness, there was even less effect from taking civics courses. Do the consequences of teaching have to be so dismal? What would happen in civics, for instance, if rather than simply *talk* about and memorize the different forms of city and state government, the class could actually set them up in the classroom? Students could run for office, conduct campaigns, debate issues — in short *live* the government, the election, the victory, and the defeat.

Some possibilities for history and English.   Take history as another case in point. Wouldn't it be better to teach history in terms of people and their experiences rather than just in terms of events, institutions, and movements? We all know something about significant historical dates, but what do we know about the motivations of the men behind them? Or, as another example, is it possible that high school students might get more out of Shakespeare's works by reading them not only as great literary masterpieces, but as unfolding dramas of human greed, love, and hate? How many students actually "see" *Julius Caesar* as an example of what untamed, selfish ambition can do to a man? Think a moment. How many contemporary men can you think of who reflect the personal qualities that led to Caesar's downfall? Could they be used as examples in class?

I know of a class of slow learning ninth graders who not only read *Romeo and Juliet*, but enjoyed it! A wise, sensitive teacher first exposed them to something they already knew about — *West Side Story*. They listened to the music in class, and since the movie was playing at a local theater, most of the students saw the film, too.   True, the characters were Tony and Maria, not Romeo and Juliet; the scene was a fire escape, not a balcony; but they were in love, there were two feuding families, and it did not end tragically.   Thus, through the simple process of exposing students to something they already knew about and liked, the teacher made a study of *Romeo and Juliet* not only possible, but, of all things, fun!   What could easily have been a laborious, nonmeaningful English assignment was converted into an exciting adventure as the students puzzled through the similarities and differences between the two stories.

Some of the best experiences are unplanned.   As another illustration, I recall an incident involving a sixth-grade teacher in a Kentucky school who converted one girl's anger, another boy's enthusiasm, and the entire class's anxiety into an exciting simulated courtroom trial.   This is what happened. As the teacher walked along the side of the room during a class lesson, she accidentally stepped on a cockroach.   One of her little eleven-year-old girls, sitting in an aisle seat, saw this happen and in dismay and anger blurted out, "Oh, Ms. Criswell, look at what you've done.   How cruel!"   This girl—a very sensitive individual—had on previous occasions defended the right to live of all living things, including "bugs and even spiders."   One of the boys, also sitting in an aisle seat, immediately responded to the girl by asserting that "All cockroaches should be killed anyway" and that what Ms. Criswell had done was not only all right but "her obligation!"   The rest of the class stirred somewhat restlessly, and a few of the youngsters even went so far as to line themselves up on either one side or the other.   Within the span of sixty seconds or so, several important issues were spontaneously aroused in a class of twenty-seven sixth-grade students.

In the first place, there was the "moral" question of whether the teacher did something that was good or bad.   And secondly there was the "legal" question of whether the teacher did something that was right or wrong. Although, at the moment of its happening, Ms. Criswell was not consciously aware of turning this incident into a kind of object lesson, she was wise enough to know that a great deal of feeling was being expressed by her students.   So, what she did was to suggest that this whole incident needed to be explored from as many different points of view as possible and proposed a courtroom trial to settle the issue.   The eleven-year-old girl, naturally enough, was appointed prosecuting attorney.   The boy who originally defended the teacher was appointed the defense counsel.   Ms. Criswell's lesson plan was abandoned for the remainder of the afternoon, and each of the "attorneys" talked to witnesses and gathered evidence for their side. Among the first things that happened, by the way, was the scraping of exhibit "A" off the bottom of Ms. Criswell's shoe.   A portion of each morning for the next week was set aside for the children to plan the trial, and several students whose fathers were lawyers assumed the responsibility for seeing to it that the correct legal procedures were followed. A judge was chosen via a general class election. On the day of the "trial" a jury was picked from another sixth-grade class in the same school and for the better part of one entire morning the evidence for and against Ms. Criswell was weighed and debated.

When it was all done and over with, the teacher was "acquitted." Actually, the outcome was not nearly so important as the process. The children were able to be meaningfully involved with the concept "justice" along with some of the social, legal, and moral implications that are attached to it. Later on in the semester the class visited a downtown courthouse and even talked to a real judge (all of which had been planned before this incident happened). When they did go, it was more than just a class trip but an experience with personal meaning.

Biographies and autobiographies can be useful. Biographies and autobiographies offer mirrors in which students can study, among other things, their own self-reflections. Drama and fiction are filled with conflicts such as occur in our daily lives—it only remains for the teacher to point these things out, to help students see the similarities to their lives, and to utilize the feelings that exist in all of us.

Possibilities in physical education. Physical education abounds in psychological possibilities. It can be more than basketball, swimming, and push-ups. It can be that part of a curriculum where students can learn to discover and accept their own bodies. They can be introduced to a human laboratory in which they can see acts of madness, cruelty, and hostility on the one hand, or behavior that reflects good sportsmanship and dignity in the face of defeat on the other. More than that, they can learn to recognize the healthy as well as the morbid features of competition. Some students may discover that winning is not so impossible after all. Others may find that being first is not so important as they thought. Still others may find that to do anything well, whether in the classroom or on the game field, takes persistence, effort, hard work, and discipline.

Exploiting the psychological possibilities of a curriculum offers exciting new avenues for enhancing motivation and learning. This doesn't mean that we negate the importance of content—not at all. In fact, our concern about how to teach in more meaningful ways may be less of a problem if we can teach in a more self-related rather than a less self-related manner. In the final analysis, none of us is highly motivated to learn about those things that appear to be disengaged from and unconnected to his own personal life.

TO THINK ABOUT

Consider the subject matter and age level you plan to teach. What ideas do you have for making your teaching more meaningful and self-related? Or, as another way for looking at this, what do you wish your teachers had done to make your learning more meaningful? Jot down your ideas in the space below.

_____

_____

_____

_____

_____

Ways to Enhance Freedom and Authentic Learning (C. Rogers)

In his book, *Freedom to Learn*,[31] Carl Rogers discusses a number of approaches a teacher can use to enhance freedom and authentic learning in the classroom. Some of his suggestions, in modified form, are included in the eight approaches discussed briefly below.

Build upon problems perceived as real. Confronting a real problem is an essential condition of genuine learning. This is true whether it applies to a small child wanting to build a sand castle, a young person struggling to build a stereo set, a college student formulating his views on racial problems, a young teacher's anxiety about student teaching, or an adult dealing with marital problems.

Provide resources. The teacher brings to the classroom all those resources that are believed to contribute to important learning in reading, science, literature, art, music, and dance.

Use contracts. The teacher and the student agree on a timetable of lessons, projects, and activities. Some of these are initiated, sponsored, or derived by the teacher, and some by the student. Both enter the contract in good faith and are expected to fulfill the terms.

Divide a group when necessary. When a group is offered freedom, some provision should be made for those who, for any reason, do not wish this freedom, but prefer to be instructed or guided. For example, students who want or need to learn sequentially, step by step, can be worked with by the teacher in more traditional ways.

Form learning groups. Here students are divided into interest groups or groups pursuing specific issues and problems in learning. These groups are formed to set up projects aimed at expanding knowledge and skill. The teacher serves more in the role of facilitator or resource person.

Pose problems. Possession of a body of knowledge *about* a subject area is not adequate achievement today. The student must get away from the image of a subject area as an absolute, permanent system. In order to encourage this, the teacher sets the stage by posing problems, creating a learner-responsive environment, and giving assistance in investigative operations. In this way, students become scientists on a simple level, seeking answers to real questions.

Use programmed instruction. Sometimes in the process of learning, the student becomes aware of gaps in his knowledge or of information needed to solve a problem. In these instances, programmed instruction is often a more efficient guide than the classroom teacher. There are programmed instruction texts for practically everything under the sun, and the student who likes a step-by-step approach will usually do well with this kind of teaching device.

Create encounter groups. In these groups, little structure is imposed and members of the group are encouraged to make decisions and create their own experiences. The focus is usually on issues and problems in relationships and communication. Spontaneous feedback is given by group members. Eventually, there is greater freedom of expression of each individual, and the group as a whole develops a sense of community.

STRATEGIES FOR MAKING THE RESULTS OF TEACHING MORE LASTING

Exploiting the psychological content of a curriculum, asking divergent questions, relating subject matter to students' backgrounds, and so on are all legitimate methods to help students learn; what we need now are some strategies to help students *remember* what they learn. We should be clear at the outset that the methods for aiding retention we're about to discuss do not work with the simple flick of a magic wand. They are not mere gimmicks pulled randomly from an instructional bag of tricks, but they are, rather, research-proven and time-tested strategies that can assist to make the results of teaching more lasting. Each is so basic as to be among those things that every good teacher does:

1. Provide the appropriate "mental set"
2. Utilize the advantages of "part" and "whole" teaching and learning
3. Distribute work and study activities
4. Encourage overlearning when appropriate
5. Provide knowledge of results and progress
6. Provide ample review time

Now, then, let's look at the meaning, implications, and practice of each of the above retention strategies or "aids."

Provide the Appropriate Mental Set

When we talk about providing the proper mental set, we're also talking about the importance of being as clear as possible when giving a class directions or assignments. Research is very clear in showing us that students tend to remember best those things they *intend to remember*.[32] A psychologist by the name of Sanford[33] gives an excellent illustration of this fact. He reported that even though he had repeated the prayers of the Episcopal service over 5,000 times in a twenty-five year period he was unable to recall them unaided. He very likely did not *intend* to remember them (they'll be in the same book next Sunday, why bother?), which is why he forgot. This "lack of intent" phenomenon is demonstrated daily in our everyday living. We forget the name of a person we just met, we forget to do an unpleasant task or assignment, we forget to write a letter we've been meaning to write for weeks, and, in fact, we can take the stairs from the first to the second floor of the Arts and Science Building 500 times in a term and have no idea at all of how many steps there are. It all depends on our intent or "mental set" to remember.

TO EXPERIMENT WITH

Here's a little trick demonstrating the effects of mental "set" you can try on a friend. Ask him or her to do it very quickly. You say, "Spell stop." Your friend does. And then quickly add, "What do you do in front of a green light?" Two out of three will say, "Stop" because of the "mind set" they're in. Try it and see what happens.

Different directions produce different results. An interesting experiment conducted by Torrance and Harmon shows the importance of giving students an *appropriate* mental set. What they did was to give three groups of students three different instructions: (1) to *apply creatively* the content of assigned readings; (2) to *evaluate* the content critically; and (3) to *remember* the content. Then the students were given tests to measure their recall of information, as well as their ability to creatively and critically apply the substance of the content to problems. For each type of test item, the group receiving the related "mental set" scored highest. That is, the group that had previously been instructed to "think creatively" scored highest on the creative items, the group that had been instructed to concentrate on remembering did better on overall recall, and so on. The investigators also found that the memory set was apparently easier to maintain over the three-week period of the experiment. They attribute this effect to the subjects' extended exposure to this kind of mental set, the one most likely to be induced in many classes and from many teachers. The subjects' reactions to the various mental sets used in this study are also interesting. For instance, memory set evoked descriptions such as "old," "boring," "dull"; creative sets, descriptions like "rash," "new," and "interesting." Although committing new information to memory can be a pretty dull process, we might all agree that there are times when it is both necessary and advisable.

All in all, the evidence suggests that a student's mental set can have a powerful influence on his ability to solve problems and/or remember newly acquired material for long periods of time. The evidence also shows that teachers can play a very important role in helping to modify or determine the direction of a student's mental set.

If we want students to remember something, then we should tell them that memory is important; if we want them to be creative, "look for new ways," then we should let them know that these are our expectations; if we want them to simply skim the material and get the general idea, then we should let them know that, too.

TO EXPERIMENT WITH

You can verify what you've just read with another little experiment. Choose any seven or eight words such as *recommend, physiology, ecology, psychology, occasion,* etc., and tell another person that you're trying to find out how well people can spell. Give that person the list of words one at a time. When finished, have that person try to *recall* the words he spelled. Most will have trouble because they were concentrating on spelling, not remembering. Try the same list with two or three others, but tell them you want them to *remember* the words as well as spell them. Compare the results. Do the directions you give make a difference?

Utilize the Advantages of "Part" and "Whole" Teaching and Learning

All content areas, even in a core curriculum, contain elements of various size and complexity. In biology, for instance, there are cells, tissues, systems, and members; in addition there are organisms that are grouped into categories such as species, orders, and phyla. In reading, there are letters, groups of letters having certain sounds, words, sentences, paragraphs, chapters, punctuation meanings, and so on. The question is: In what sequence and in what sized units should this material be taught? Should new material or a new skill be approached a step at a time, taking each of the parts in their separate order until some level of overall mastery is accomplished? Or would a better approach be to present the "big picture" so that students are not bogged down with too many details? You may not like what may seem like a fuzzy answer, but the fact is that it depends. And it depends basically on two considerations: (1) the nature of the student (his intelligence, background and readiness for learning, motivation, need for feedback), and (2) the nature of the material or task (its length, meaningfulness, complexity, organization, intellectual and/or physical skill demands).

The whole approach is usually best. Although there are advantages to both whole and part teaching, research efforts have been fairly consistent in giving the edge to approaches falling under the whole method of teaching and learning.[35-38] A major criticism of the part approach to teaching is that it tends to overlook a student's need to develop some kind of a frame of reference that will help him relate one aspect of what is being taught to its other aspects. Good teachers have, among other things, a knack for showing, telling, or demonstrating how smaller units of material fit into larger wholes. A good piano teacher, for example, is not likely to send her budding virtuoso home to practice only finger exercises and the C and F scales, but she would also be certain that he had an opportunity to actually *use* his scales in a simple composition. The wise piano teacher knows that a piano student takes up the study of music because he wants to play real songs, not practice scales and finger exercises. The point is that unless some whole experiences are introduced into the instructional sequence rather early, students, of the piano or anything else, are inclined to lose interest.

By way of illustration, I recall a neighbor of mine—a teen-age boy—who quit taking tennis lessons after just two weeks because, as he put it, "I've been hitting forehand shots off a wall for ten days and have yet to play an actual game." He didn't lose his motivation for playing tennis, but he did lose it for taking lessons. Whether it is learning to play the piano or to paint or to play tennis, or whether it is learning new words or the basic principles of addition and subtraction, it is important that students see how what they are doing fits into a larger context.

401

A school's organization makes a difference. One practical matter that relates to the whole-part procedure is school organization. Schools emphasizing a subject-matter philosophy are inclined to have one period devoted to arithmetic, one to science, one to spelling, and so on. This may provide convenient scheduling, but the day is broken into too many short periods. High schools are probably dominated more by such schedules than are elementary schools, but the growing popularity of "double periods" and flexible scheduling seem indicative of a growing resistance to traditional block scheduling. Larger units of time allow for field trips, excursions, longer audio-visual presentations, discussions that have more opportunity to expand the breadth and depth of a subject and, in general, make the whole approach both more feasible and possible. Actually, the core-curriculum approach goes a step further, grouping together the learning experiences that are designed to help students live more effectively in a democratic society. In fact, a review of evaluative studies indicates a slight but consistent superiority of the core-curriculum approach over subject organization when it comes to assessing students' knowledge, critical thinking, work habits, and social skills.[39]

When to use the whole method. In sum, the whole method of teaching is probably better when

1. You want to give a global picture of something without paying particular attention to details. Encouraging students to scan a book, read only chapter summaries and occasional paragraphs, is an illustration of this process.
2. Your students have above-average IQs.
3. The material is meaningful and more concrete than abstract.
4. The material is closely knit together, on one theme, and not too long.

When to use the part method. The part method of teaching is better when

1. A student is not very capable intellectually. For example, slow learners need to learn new material a step at a time because of the intellectual difficulty they may have in seeing the "whole" picture. Students need the reward and encouragement they can receive more frequently when learning smaller subunits of material. The whole method can be more discouraging because some students have to work too long before they see any return for their efforts.
2. The material is long, complicated, and lacking a central theme running through it.

Consider the character of the material. As you can see, the *character of the material* has much to do with the relative advantages of these two methods. For best motivational and learning results, a combination of the two methods is probably the best idea. For example, whatever you teach, it would be good practice to begin by helping your students see the "whole" picture. Then divide the whole picture into suitable subsections and approach it by the part method. Finally, review the whole to secure adequate organization of the parts into a total associative train.

Distribute Work and Study Activities

Even though teaching and learning can be meaningful and relevant, and the material is presented or studied in the form of comprehensible problems or units, there still is the question of spacing and pacing the activity. Teaching and learning new material may be concentrated into relatively long unbroken periods of work or spread over several short sessions. Research is clear in showing that learning efficiency varies with the length of study or practice periods, with the spacing of such periods, and with the pace with which the material is presented.[40]

There are probably very few among us who have not learned from firsthand experience that complex and abstract material requires more time for assimilation and comprehension than does simple material that has immediate meaning. Nothing is more frustrating and defeating for a student than to have new material presented more rapidly than he can understand it. Of course this varies from student to student and from subject to subject, which means that teachers have to remain alert to both content and student in order to decide on an appropriate teaching pace. Almost without exception, research concerned with the relative effectiveness of spacing new learning over a period of time or cramming it into a shorter time span indicates that learning should be spaced over longer periods of time in order to facilitate and sustain high motivation and retention.[41-44] For example, a few words in spelling each day for a week will be mastered better than a large number bunched into one lesson.

Variables to consider before distributing work and study activities. Although the complex interplay of human and subject-matter variables makes it difficult to determine the optimal temporal distribution of practice or study time in a given school subject, there are, nonetheless, some general guidelines that can be used to determine the appropriate spacing of work and study activities in school subjects. Four variables that should be considered in determining the distribution of work and study activities include the following:

403

Complexity of the material.   The type of material to be learned is an important consideration.   For instance, complex perceptual motor learning (e.g., learning to write or dive or drive a car) and difficult memorization requires short, frequent (more than once a week) practice sessions.   On the other hand, well-integrated and interesting tasks (e.g., learning to play Monopoly, reading an exciting book even though some words are not recognized) may be pursued for longer periods of time without a great loss in motivation.

Similarity of the material. The similarity in the materials to be learned is another consideration.   That is, in order to reduce the possibility of what was previously learned interfering with what is currently being learned, it is better to have the practice or study periods more widely spaced.   For example, rather than spend one hour, let's say, learning fifty new foreign language words, it would be wiser to spend twenty minutes with ten words and then come back and spend another twenty minutes with ten different words, and so on.   In other words, the more similar the material the more chance there is of it *interfering* with itself if pursued for long periods of time.   Hence, the value of making practice periods short and more widely spaced.

Monotony and fatigue factors.   Other variables to consider are monotony, boredom, and fatigue.   As any of us can testify to, these conditions are most apt to occur when we find ourselves doing the same thing over and over again for long periods of time.   The more variety we can introduce into our learning, teaching, and study activities, the less likely it is that this will occur.

Level of motivation.   Since motivation is a key to achievement and learning, encouraging students to map out their own study schedules is a goal worth working toward.   Predetermined schedules rigorously imposed on students in an effort to make learning more efficient may serve the reverse purpose of stifling interest and initiative.   We probably have to go no further than our own study habits to know that students who work at meaningful tasks matched with their interests and needs frequently work long and arduously without any apparent detrimental effects.

TO EXPERIMENT WITH

Distribution of work and study activities is something you can actually experiment with yourself.   For example, in one of your current courses make a deliberate effort to space your study time according to the principles discussed above.   In another course, cram your study time into shorter periods.   Let this go on for several or more weeks or so.   Do you notice any difference in your retention of material? Do you *feel* any differently about your study one way or the other? It would be interesting to do this with a friend so you can "compare notes," as it were.

Encourage Overlearning When Appropriate

Forgetting is generally reduced by overlearning. That is, retention of new materials can be increased if practice or review continues beyond the point of the first errorless reproduction of the new information. That we can drive a car after years of not driving, type after years of not typing, play the piano after months of not playing, or remember portions of our high school fight song are all examples of things we have "overlearned."

Experimental evidence indicates that overlearning results in more accurate retention over longer periods of time than practice that ceases at the point of original learning.[45]

For instance, the skills of driving a car or swimming or skating or remembering the multiplication tables are not readily forgotten because we have continued to use these skills on a more or less consistent basis after their original acquisition. However, it is important to keep in mind that the gain from overlearning decreases as additional practice continues. Although 100 to 200 percent overlearning is better than 50 percent overlearning, the additional gain is usually not proportional to the extended effort.[46]

When overlearning is most efficient. As a general rule, overlearning is most efficient when confined to from half to double the number of repetitions required for original learning. If you were trying to commit a list of names or dates or formulae to memory and it took you ten trials to do so, then you could probably succeed in overlearning this material and thereby reduce the possibility of forgetting if you repeated what you had just learned another fifteen or twenty times. (Somehow this seems like such an effort, probably because it is so easy to delude ourselves into believing we "really know it" after just one errorless trial.)

When to encourage overlearning. As a technique for increasing motivation and retention, encouraging students to overlearn new material is most advisable when (1) they are learning specific, concrete material such as grammar rules, multiplication tables, names, dates, the periodic table, or even football plays, or (2) there is a long interval between learning new material and its recall. Overlearning is not enhanced through elongated study sessions but rather is best accomplished through the use of spaced review periods.

When not to encourage overlearning. Encouraging students to over-learn abstract principles or concepts that they do not understand is *not* wise because it may invite them to simply memorize new material without first understanding it. What's worse, meaningless repetition may encourage a student to respond mechanically. There is an old, but classic, story illustrating this about an elementary school boy who persisted in saying, "I have went." After correcting him dozens of times, his teacher finally could take it no longer and sentenced him to write "I have gone" 100 times on the board after school. As he wearily reached the ninety-first repetition, the teacher left the room momentarily. When she returned, she discovered that the hapless student had finished his task and departed. On the board were 100 progressively sloppier "I have gone's" concluded by this note: "Dear teacher, I have wrote 'I have gone' 100 times and I have went home."

The moral of this tale is, of course, that repetition does little good unless a student *understands what he is doing.* For example, it would be much better for a student who can't remember how to spell *principal* to write the word five times and utilize a mnemonic aid such as "The principal is a pal," than to write it fifty times and think his teacher is a louse.

Provide Knowledge of Results and Progress

The principle we're talking about can be simply stated: We are more likely to avoid mistakes and improve performance if we know what our mistakes are in the first place. Hence, it is important to students that we indicate to them not only *what* was wrong, but *why.* In addition, the time span should be as short as possible between, for example, handing in a paper or writing an exam and feedback about the results. Nothing stifles motivation and encourages loss of retention more effectively than to have to wait two or three weeks to get an exam or a paper back. Even worse is the experience of having to wait two or three weeks and receive no more feedback than a cold, impersonal grade in the upper–right hand corner. Along these lines, you may recall that Page's[47] study, which was discussed in Chapter 6, showed rather clearly that when students' received exams back with personalized comments from their teachers, along with the grade, they were more apt to improve on subsequent exams than students who received just grades, but no personalized comments.

Why knowledge of results is important. Knowledge of results leads to improved achievement and greater retention for at least five reasons: (1) it tends to encourage repetition of those things we're successful at, (2) it helps us correct or improve incorrect or unsuccessful responses, (3) it provides an incentive to perform as accurately as possible, while lack of such knowledge reduces the incentive, (4) it helps to capitalize on what has been called the "law of increasing energy," which states that the closer one gets to his goal, the greater the effort he puts forth.[48]   Thus, it is usually easier, as most of us have discovered, to write the last two pages of a term report, than the first five. (5) Knowledge of results also has the effect of introducing intermediate, short-term goals in addition to the ultimate and final goal—thus providing a more frequent resurgence of new energy.

Teaching machines give instant feedback. We might add here that a very basic feature of programmed learning and teaching machines is the instant feedback provided.   Theoretically, this immediate feedback provides much of the motivational power that gives psychological support to programmed approaches to learning.   In one type of program (linear), the material is so constructed that few errors occur, but the student knows how accurately he is responding almost sentence by sentence.   In another type of programming (branching), an error of a specific type leads the student immediately to the kind of content that will correct the wrong impression.[49]

Motivation is enhanced. All in all, providing knowledge of results can be an excellent way of motivating students to apply themselves to the task at hand.   Not only is it a fairly safe method, but it is an honest, intrinsic form of motivation.   Knowledge of our previous performance tends to make us compete against ourselves.   And for most of us, this is a contest in which we can hope for considerable success.

Provide Ample Review Time

One of the best means of maintaining retention above a given level is through the systematic use of review.   Research bears out this supposition.

Television and teaching machines are practical aids that can be used to enhance learning.   (Allyn and Bacon)

For example, Spitzer[50] found that when several thousand grade school children read a selection and were given four-minute review tests afterward, the amount remembered was directly related to the time of the review test. Immediate recall after reading the material proved the best way to facilitate retention. For instance, groups that took immediate review tests had over 60 percent better retention of material read than those who took their first recall test a week later. Furthermore, a group that took an immediate recall test and another one the next day did better on retention tests than a second group that took an immediate recall test, and a second a week later. Gagné,[51] in his review of research related to retention in learning, also observed that "periodic and spaced reviews . . . have an important role to play in retention." He goes on to note that "when a review is given, the student has to exercise his strategies of retrieval."

Review complex material more frequently. In general, the more abstract or complicated the new material, the more frequent the reviews should be. If one has thoroughly *overlearned* the original material, then reviews can be less frequent. However, from the standpoint of economy and time, reviews are generally more effective than overlearning. This is especially true inasmuch as effective review is more than just bringing the material up to the original level, but it can be an important stepping stone to more advanced work. As you may have discovered yourself, reviews often reveal new meanings, deeper understandings, and relationships that were not apparent the first time through.

TAKE A STUDENT'S READINESS TO LEARN INTO ACCOUNT

There are enormous differences among students when it comes to what is called "readiness" to learn. Indeed, if we were to select any class at random, we would soon find that there is no single or standard series of lessons and work materials that would be equally effective for all pupils. The fact is that different students are "ready" to learn different materials at different times. This is particularly true during the school years when there can be incredibly large differences among and between growing youngsters as far as physiological, psychological, and experiential readiness factors are concerned.

Differences in Reading Readiness

Let's take reading as an example of a single expression of readiness in one area. Consider Table 9–1, which indicates the approximate percentage

TABLE 9–1.   *The Percentage of Children in Each Grade Ready for Each Book Level*

Book level		Grade level					
Grade	Age	I	II	III	IV	V	VI
Nursery School	5	2	2	2			
Kindergarten	6	23	8	5	7		
1	7	50	24	11	9	7	
2	8	23	33	20	10	9	7
3	9	2	24	24	16	10	9
4	10		8	20	17	16	10
5	11		2	11	16	17	16
6	12			5	10	16	17
7	13			2	9	10	16
8	14				7	9	10
9	15					7	9
10	16						7

(From Willard C. Olson. "Seeking Self-Selection and Pacing in the Use of Books by Children." *The Packet*, vol. 7. Boston: D. C. Heath, Spring 1952, p. 7. Used by permission.)

of students in each grade who might be expected to be reading at or below their grade level.

In the second grade, roughly 33 percent are reading at grade level (grade level referring to the level of development of the average or middle student in designated grades), while 24 percent are reading one grade above and 24 percent are reading one grade below. Eight percent are reading as high as the fourth-grade level. The differences are even more striking at the sixth-grade level where we find approximately 17 percent reading at grade level, while another 42 percent are *below* grade level!

Research evidence also indicates that there are vast differences in intellectual ability readiness at different ages. By way of summarizing these differences, Cook has written:

> When a random group of six-year-olds enters the first grade, two percent of them will be below the average four-year-olds in general mental development and two percent will be above the average eight-year-olds. Disregarding the extreme two percent at eight end, there is a four-year range in general intelligence.[52]

Mental Age as an Index to Readiness

Perhaps you can get a better idea of the wide range of differences in mental ages at various chronological ages by examining the information in Table 9–2.

TABLE 9–2. *Theoretical Distribution of Mental Ages for Groups of 100 Children with Given Chronological Ages (Based on a Theoretical Standard Deviation of IQ of 16.6)*

Mental age	Chronological age										
	4	5	6	7	8	9	10	11	12	13	14
11											
11											
20											1
19										1	2
16										1	4
17									1	4	8
10								1	3	7	12
14								2	7	13	15
14							2	6	12	16	16
13						1	5	12	17	17	15
12					1	4	12	18	19	16	12
11					3	11	19	21	17	13	8
10				2	11	21	23	18	12	7	4
9			1	9	22	25	19	12	7	4	2
8			7	23	28	21	12	6	3	1	1
7		5	24	31	22	11	5	2	1	1	
6	2	24	36	23	11	4	2	1			
5	23	41	24	9	3	1					
4	50	24	7	2	1						
3	23	5	1								
2	2										
Totals	100	99	100	99	102	99	99	99	99	101	100

(From P. M. Symonds. "Case Study and Testing Methods." In *Handbook of Child Guidance*, edited by Ernest Harms. New York: Child Care Publications, 1947, p. 311.

As you can see, the range in mental age increases as children grow older. For example, at age twelve one could expect to find some children with mental ages as high as sixteen or seventeen and some as low as seven or eight. Extensive mental ability differences persist on into high school and college, although an increasing number of students from the lower mental ability levels drop out when school attendance becomes voluntary.

The evidence related to differences in mental ability or in reading skills among students of the same ages points to the same general conclusion; namely, that not all students are ready at the same time to learn, much less comprehend, the same material. For example, in a typical sixth-grade class, a range of about eight school years will be reflected on tests in reading comprehension, vocabulary, arithmetic reasoning, and arithmetic computation. In other words, in almost any sixth-grade class you are likely to find a student or two with average *second grade* reading and arithmetic ability and a student or two with average tenth-grade abilities in these areas.

TO COMPREHEND

Remember: Mental age (MA) is not the same as chronological age. MA is simply an expression of where a student ranks intellectually in comparison with others his age. For example, to say that a twelve-year-old youngster has a mental age of thirteen years and seven months means that he has passed the same number of items on an IQ test as the average youngster of thirteen years and seven months.

Look for Those "Teachable Moments"

Understanding and appreciating this readiness concept is important because if a student is forced to try to learn a skill before he has the necessary maturational and experiential equipment, he could easily grow frustrated, feel defeated, and end up with a negative attitude not only toward that particular skill but school generally. What can a teacher do to minimize this possibility? For one thing, we can be on the lookout for our students' "teachable moments." Since youngsters mature at different rates, and since the curriculum of the schools must be geared to the average child, we would be confronted with an impossible task if we hoped to assess the readiness of every single student for every subject. It just couldn't be done. At best, we can only try to recognize as many teachable moments as possible for the age groups we teach.

There are two frames of reference we can use to assess the readiness of students. One is the developmental task idea that was discussed in Chapter 2. The other has reference to Piaget's stages, or periods, of intellectual development.

Use the Developmental Task Model to Assess Readiness

Inasmuch as this concept has already been discussed in Chapter 2, we'll do nothing more with it at this point except remind you that developmental tasks refer to specific behavioral expectations which, according to Havighurst, "arise at or about a certain period in the life of an individual, successful achievement of which leads to happiness and success with later tasks, while failure leads to unhappiness of the individual, disapproval of society, and difficulty with later tasks."[53]

411

It might be a good idea to review Table 2–1 (Chapter 2) in order to reacquaint yourself with the assorted behavioral tasks you can expect at different age levels. In particular you will want to familiarize yourself with the age level you anticipate teaching. Remember, Havighurst's developmental tasks are not intended as absolute expectations for what all growing youngsters are all supposed to achieve at the same time. Rather, they are general guidelines to help us predict what we might reasonably expect, within broad limits, as behavioral tendencies at different stages of growth. Knowing, for example, that developing fundamental skills in reading, writing, and calculating are major tasks normally included in the six- to twelve-year age group enables us to begin developing an educational program to help growing youngsters acquire these skills when they are "ready."

Use Piaget's Intellectual Development Model to Assess Readiness

Jean Piaget is a Swiss psychologist. (Actually, he has been described as a "zoologist by training, an epistemologist by vocation, and a logician by method.")[54] He is regarded as the authority on the general intellectual development of children.[55] Specifically, what Piaget has done is to map an elaborate series of periods and subperiods, which start at birth and progress through adolescence. Since the idea of intellectual readiness is so intimately linked with Piaget's research on the intellectual development of children, it is important at this point for you to become at least generally familiar with the major periods of intellectual development and the age ranges associated with each. Although Table 9–3 is a somewhat simplified representation of Piaget's conception of the stages, or periods, of intellectual development, it does provide a broad overview of the sorts of mental operations most children will be "ready" for at different ages.

As you can see, a child progresses from a more primitive level of sensory learning during his first two years of life to a more complex level of abstraction in his adolescent years. What we have to keep in mind is that there are vast expressions of individual differences within each of these age ranges. For example, even though two second graders may be ready to function in the concrete operations stage does not mean that they will be equally skilled in learning, say, the basic principles involved in addition and subtraction. Though their readiness for learning arithmetic principles may be the same, this does not necessarily mean that either their rate or capacity for learning are the same.

A framework such as Piaget's is designed to provide us with some general notions about the probable intellectual skills that children of different ages bring to specific learning situations so we have some idea about

412

TABLE 9–3. *Stages, or Periods, of Intellectual Development Conceptualized by Piaget*

Stage	Age range	Basic characteristics
1. Sensorimotor period	Birth to 2 yrs.	Infant learns that he is different from other objects and learns primarily through his senses and manipulations. Child both wants and needs as much stimulation as possible.
2. Preoperational thought period a. preoperational phase	2–4	An essentially egocentric period insofar as the child is unable to see things from another person's point of view; tends to classify in very simple ways—e.g., if A is like B in one respect, it must be like B in other respects, too.
b. intuitive phase	4–7	Child slowly begins to think in terms of classes, to handle number concepts, and to see simple relationships. Child is "intuitive" because even though he is capable of making classifications, he doesn't really understand why or how. He develops a gradual awareness of conservation of mass, weight, and volume—i.e., he can see that the amount may remain the same even if transferred to different size container.
3. Concrete operations period	7–11	Child grows in ability to consciously use and understand logical operations such as *reversibility* (in arithmetic), *classification* (putting objects into heirarchies of classes), and *seriation* (organizing objects into a specified series, such as increasing size).
4. Formal operations period	11–15	Youngster further develops the ability to comprehend abstract concepts—e.g., the ability to think about "ideals," to understand cause-effect relationships, to think about the future, and to develop and test hypotheses.

(Table developed from R. M. Beard. *An Outline of Piaget's Developmental Psychology for Students and Teachers.* New York: Basic Books, Inc., 1969.)

his readiness to cope with this or that task. This framework does not allow us to assess either how quickly or how slowly the learning will occur. A teacher's job is to assess a student's readiness, by whatever tools and information are available, and then go on from there making whatever adjustments seem necessary in light of each student's performance. Along these lines, Piaget himself has observed that:

It is a great mistake to suppose that a child acquires . . . concepts just from teaching . . . when adults try to impose . . . concepts on a child prematurely, his learning is merely verbal; true understanding of them comes only with his own mental growth.[56]

Opposing Views About the Nature and Expression of Readiness

You should be aware that not all psychologists and educators share a common agreement about the nature and expression of readiness. Tyler,[57] for instance, while documenting a large body of research related to readiness, noted that "the idea of readiness has been and still is inherent in our thinking about education, although there is considerable diversity of opinion about both practice and theory."

The "natural" view. Indeed there is. On the one hand, there are those who advocate the "natural" view of development and who feel that school experiences should be geared to the natural unfolding of each student's developmental pattern. Piaget and Havighurst would fall into this camp and so, too, would Hilgard,[58] whose series of studies during the thirties demonstrated that older, more mature children were able to learn more rapidly and easily than younger children. Out of these studies grew the conclusion that practically all children would develop the general skills for readiness if time was simply allowed for them to "grow up."

In addition to the Hilgard studies, investigations that reinforced the philosophy of natural readiness were conducted by Gesell[59] and Olson,[60] both of whom emphasized the idea that development and behavior at all age levels, up to and including the teen years, are controlled by inner maturational forces.

The "guided-experience" view. On the other hand, there is an opposing camp—sometimes referred to as the "guided-experience" point of view—which is favored by those who see little sense in waiting for a child to "naturally unfold" and prefer to speed up this process a bit. This is a position advocated by those suggesting that education for all children begin by age four, by those who want to teach two year olds to read and three year olds to do algebra.

A major spokesman for this view of readiness has been Jerome Bruner, who differs from Piaget by arguing that the intellectual development of the child grows in spurts that are not clearly linked to age. In addition, Bruner maintains that some environments can impede the sequence while others can move it along faster. Bruner does admit that "Some capacities must be matured and nurtured before they can be called into being."[61] He does not, however, believe that readiness should be left to chance and goes on to state that:

> . . . the idea of "readiness is a mischievous half-truth. It is a half-truth largely because it turns out that one *teaches* readiness or provides opportunities for its nurture; one does not simply wait for it. Readiness, in these terms, consists of mastery of those simple skills that permit one to reach higher skills[62]

All in all, readiness is a complex phenomenon influenced by both genetic and social factors. One thing that is more certain today than ever before is that readiness for schooling is being built long before a child enters school. It is certainly true that today's children come to school exposed to a great deal more intellectual and quasi-intellectual stimulation than was true of children a generation ago. Research shows that television, for instance, has had an enormous impact — most of it for the better, by the way — on the language readiness of children.[63-66] In fact, even the greater availability of 25-cent paperback children's books in local supermarkets has played a small part in helping a growing child's readiness for school.[67]

Making teaching meaningful, relevant, and lasting is no easy task. Not only does it involve taking a student's readiness to learn into account, but it means that we must also consider a student's ethnic and social background.

TEACHING STUDENTS OF DIFFERING SOCIAL AND ETHNIC BACKGROUNDS

It is very likely that the teacher who is successful with any group of students is the one who respects them and they, in turn, respect him. As a teacher of students who come from differing ethnic and social backgrounds, you may see many who are discouraged, disgruntled, and defeated. You may see still others who act out their alienation from the school and the society it represents by aggressive, hostile behavior or by tuned-out lethargy and listlessness. As a teacher, you may feel sorry for them or angered by their apparent laziness or you may even feel a strong urge to write them off as hopeless, too dumb to learn, and victims of genetic influences too powerful for the environment to overcome. Any one or all of these views are possible for a teacher to possess and any one could seriously hinder successfully teaching students of differing social and ethnic backgrounds.

TO THINK ABOUT

How do you feel about teaching students from differing social and ethnic backgrounds? Does it sound challenging to you? Scary? What do you perceive as your greatest difficulty when it comes to teaching youths whose social and ethnic backgrounds are different than yours? Something you might do to prepare yourself is to get to know classmates who represent backgrounds that are socially and ethnically different than yours. In the process, you may make some interesting discoveries about yourself.

415

Factors to Consider When Teaching Students from Different Social and Ethnic Backgrounds

In a sensitive article discussing the idea of adapting teacher style to pupil differences, Miriam Goldberg, drawing on her wide experience of working with teachers, described nine teacher behaviors most likely to be associated with those who are most likely to be successful with students whose educational background may be limited. She provides us with some excellent clues about the sort of person who, how shall we say, "makes it" with students who come from differing social and ethnic backgrounds.

Be realistic about your perceptions. In the first place, the successful teacher sees his students realistically. He does not, for example, see "beauty" or "strength" where others see poverty and emptiness. He sees them as youths who are different, yet like all youths, coping in their own way with the trials and frustrations of growing up. And he also sees them, unlike middle-class youths, struggling to survive in the dog-eat-dog world of their peers, confused by the conflicting pull of the two cultures in which they live—the one of the home, street, and neighborhood, the other of the school and society that supports it.

Understand a student's background. The successful teacher understands the backgrounds from which his students come, the values placed on various achievements, and the reasons for their reluctance to strive toward future goals, where such labor provides limited payoff in the present.

Realize the effects of intellectual impoverishment. He knows many of his students bear the scars of the intellectual impoverishment of their early years. He realizes that they rarely are helped to name the things they see and feel and hear or to recognize similarities and differences, to categorize and classify perceptions, or even to learn the word for an object.

Be aware of the effects of stressful family conditions. The successful teacher is aware of the array of family structures from which the students come: the father-absent matriarchal family; the home in which both parents are working; where one or both parents are out of work, perhaps on relief; where the extended family—grandparents, aunts, uncles, and other relatives—live together. In a word, the successful teacher is aware of the physical conditions in which his students live: their lack of privacy, the poor facilities, and the absence of basic amenities.

Be sensitive to how ethnic group membership influences self-image. The effective teacher is cognizant of the ethnic group membership of his students and the extent to which such membership shapes a person's image of himself. In addition, he knows something about the history, traditions, and social expectations of the various ethnic groups, their status in American society, the blocks and frustrations that they confront, and their perceptions of what life has in store for them.

Allow for language differences. He recognizes that the language of his pupils is closely tied to the life they lead. Although it may be a distortion of "acceptable English," a good teacher will know and accept the idea that it represents the only known and acceptable medium of exchange in the homes and neighborhoods from which his students come.

Interpret results of intelligence tests cautiously. The successful teacher takes the results of a student's intelligence test with a grain of salt. He is aware that native potential intelligence is, thus far at least, not measureable; that what tests measure is learned behavior; and that the learning results not only from a student's native ability but also from his total experience.

He is also aware that the tests provide a fairly accurate description of a student's present ability to handle academic material and, unless there are significant changes in his life experiences, the tests will predict with fair reliability how a child will function academically in the future. The successful teacher accepts the test scores as reasonably valid measures of a student's present academic ability but tends to reject them as measures of native intelligence.

Establish firm boundaries that are consistently enforced. The successful teacher of the disadvantaged is able to meet his students on equal terms, as person to person, individual to individual. While he accepts, he doesn't condone. That is, he sets very clearly defined limits and tolerates few transgressions. Unlike middle-class youths, he recognizes that he cannot control them through appeals to their sense of shame and/or guilt. So, he sets rules and establishes the boundaries with a minimum of discussion. Here he is impersonal, undeviating, strict but not punitive. Within firmly established boundaries, which are consistently and fairly enforced, the teacher knows where he's going and the students know what to expect. Perhaps most importantly, he is freed from having to spend undue time coping with his students because they don't know what the rules are and able to spend more time relating to them within a clearly defined framework that allows him to be friendly and outgoing rather than punitive and restrictive.[68]

Use honest praise — avoid harsh criticism. Successful teachers of culturally abused youths seem to have a deep understanding of the danger of the "self-fulfilling prophecy" of expecting only so much from their students and consequently finding a low level of achievement. Rather than expecting less, successful teachers set their standards high, but not so lofty as to be unattainable. In addition, the effective teacher rewards each tiny step, is alert to opportunities for honest praise, and, as much as possible, withholds harsh criticism when progress is slow or lacking. Above all, and this is important, he is honest. He doesn't pretend that a student's work is good when it clearly is not, and he doesn't condone unacceptable behavior.

In many ways, the successful teacher of the disadvantaged student is not unlike the successful teacher of any kind of student. My own experiences with teachers who have taught students from differing social and ethnic backgrounds suggest to me that those who sometimes have difficulty are the same ones who have an unusually strong "identification with the underdog." Wanting to help (or to teach) the less fortunate is a noble enough motive, but sometimes it may leave one so immersed in self-righteous altruism that he can be neither firm when firmness is called for nor challenging when the work is too easy. Arthur Pearl, a psychologist who has worked extensively with disadvantaged youth, makes a point that is relevant here:

Not long ago I heard the dean of a school of education say that the one thing disadvantaged children need is love. If we could only give them enough love, we could solve all our problems, he implied. He became furious with me, however, when I tried to explain to him that love given so promiscuously is known in the streets as prostitution.

By trying to give universal love, the teacher actually punishes the disadvantaged student. In effect, the teacher is asking him to feel guilty for anything he does to displease her because he is hurting or disappointing one who loves him.

For example, take the fifth grade teacher in a Chicago slum school who . . . found some salacious comments scrawled on her record book. Turning to the class, she said, "After all I've done for you, why are you being so mean to me?"

After a long silence, one of the boys finally answered, "Because you're white."

. . . with tears in her eyes, she told the class that she could not teach them anymore that morning; she was too upset. Her self-righteousness was the most excruciating punishment that she could have used against the boy. He presented himself honestly and courageously and, if anything, should have been rewarded for his contribution. Instead, he was humiliated. Not surprisingly, at the end of the class he walked up to the teacher and stamped as hard as he could on her feet.

The object lesson here is quite clear. The teacher had established a love relationship that no one had asked for. By failing to acknowledge the boy's honesty and by humiliating him, she drove him to the only kind of face-saving action he knew how to express. If she had handled the situation honestly, say by discussing this particular problem with the class, she could have built up this boy's self-respect and her own effectiveness as a teacher.

It is not love that disadvantaged children need so much as honest respect. Anything phoney will force them to lash out against the teacher and whatever else the school imposes upon them.[69]

There is ample research to indicate that youths from differing social and ethnic backgrounds do suffer from multiple intellectual handicaps.[70] However, research also shows that the academic performance of ethnically different students can be improved to the extent that these students feel they are welcome partners in an educational enterprise that they experience as friendly, empathic, stimulating, and basically supportive.[71]

When it comes right down to it, teachers are the ones who contribute most to the educational enterprise. That's why we need as many good ones as we can get.

EPILOGUE

This chapter has considered some of the possible ways for making teaching more meaningful, relevant, and lasting. It probably goes without saying that no "strategy" we can consider for doing these things is more important than the teacher using them. However, if those of us who teach are reasonably sensitive individuals and well-versed in our content areas, then there is no reason why our students cannot both enjoy school more and get more out of it.

When relevance, meaning, purpose, and hope are absent from the curriculum, increasing numbers of students lose their motivation to learn. We cannot depend upon the idyllic belief that the natural curiosity of growing children will bridge the relevance gap and automatically make their learning and our teaching meaningful and personal.

Just as Madison Avenue psychologists create new needs in the consumer to buy this or that product, so too is it possible for teachers to create new needs or rekindle existing needs in their students to learn, discover, solve problems, or persist in seeing a puzzling, difficult task through to its completion.

For one thing, we can help students to see that what goes on in school is not unrelated to what goes on outside of school. School and life outside of school do not have to be unconnected experiences left only for the very bright to discern their common components. We can help to make school more meaningful and relevant for more students if we show them how to transfer their learning and provide opportunities for doing so; if we consider our students' readiness to learn so we avoid starting out ahead of them; if we relate our teaching to students' backgrounds and experiences; and if we exploit the psychological content available to us in the curriculum. It may help, too, if we ceased putting so much emphasis on getting the right answer and put a bit more stress on asking the right questions.

As a good friend of mine, Dr. Wayne Joosse, puts it, "Teaching can be one of the easiest jobs in the world but not when it's done right."

The next question is, how does learning occur and what can we do to facilitate learning? Part IV, coming up, will help us with these questions.

Write your own chapter summary (major points, ideas, and concepts that had meaning for you).

_____

_____

_____

_____

_____

_____

_____

_____

_____

_____

REFERENCES

1. Glasser, W. *Schools Without Failure*. New York: Harper and Row, 1969, pp. 52–53.

2. James, W. *Principles of Psychology*, vol. I. New York: Holt, Rinehart, and Winston, 1890.

3. Sleight, W. "Memory and Formal Training." *British Journal of Psychology* 4(1911):386–457.

4. Thorndike, E. L., and R. S. Woodworth. "The Influence of the Improvement in One Mental Function upon the Efficiency of Other Functions." *Psychological Review* 8(1901):247–261, 384–395, 553–564.

5. Briggs, T. H. "Formal English Grammar as a Discipline." *Teachers College Record* 14(1913):251–343.

6. Thorndike, E. L. "Mental Discipline in High School Studies." *Journal of Educational Psychology* 15(1924):1–22, 83–98.

7. Broyler, C. R., et al. "A Second Study of Mental Discipline in High School Studies." *Journal of Educational Psychology* 18(1927):377–404.

8. Wesman, A. G. "A Study of Transfer of Training from High School Subjects to Intelligence." *Journal of Educational Research* 39(1945):254–264.

9. Andrews, T. G., L. J. Cronbach, and P. Saniford. "Transfer of Training." *Encyclopedia of Educational Research*, edited by W. S. Morrow. New York: Crowell-Collier and Macmillan, 1950, pp. 1483–1489.

10. Spaulding, F. T. *High School and Life.* New York: McGraw-Hill, 1939.

11. Webb, L. W. "The Transfer of Training." In *Educational Psychology*, edited by C. E. Skinner. Englewood Cliffs, N. J.: Prentice-Hall, 1936.

12. Klausmeier, H. J. "Transfer of Learning." In *Encyclopedia of Educational Research*, 4th ed., edited by R. L. Ebel and V. H. Noll. London: Collier-Macmillan Ltd., 1969, pp. 1483–1493.

13. Hamachek, D. "A Counseling Approach for Enhancing Achievement Motivation Among Potential High School Dropouts." Paper presented at the American Educational Research Association Program, (Division E), New York City, 4 February 1971.

14. Gagné, R. M. *The Conditions of Learning*, 2nd ed. New York: Holt, Rinehart, and Winston, 1970.

15. Brownell, W. A., and Moser, H. E. "Meaningful versus Mechanical Learning: A Study in Grade II Subtraction." *Duke University Studies in Education*, no. 8. Durham, N. C.: Duke University Press, 1949.

16. Hilgard, E. R., R. P. Irvine, and J. E. Whipple. "Rote Memorization, Understanding, and Transfer: An Extension of Katona's Card-Trick Experiments." *Journal of Experimental Psychology* 46(1953):288–292.

17. Miller, G. A., E. Galanter, and K. Pribram. *Plans and the Structure of Behavior.* New York: Holt, Rinehart, and Winston, 1960.

18. Ausubel, D. P., S. H. Schpoont, and L. Cukier. "The Influence of Intention on the Retention of School Materials." *Journal of Educational Psychology* 48(1957):87–92.

19. Aborn, M. "The Influence of Experimentally Induced Failure on the Retention of Material Acquired Through Set and Incidental Learning." *Journal of Experimental Psychology* 45(1953):225–231.

20. Yuker, H. E. "Group Atmosphere and Memory." *Journal of Abnormal and Social Psychology* 51(1955):17–23.

21. Bruner, J. S. *The Process of Education.* Cambridge, Mass.: Harvard University Press, 1960.

22. Guilford, J. P. "Three Faces of Intellect." *American Psychologist* 14(1959):267–293.

23. Guilford, J. P. "The Structure of Intellect." *Psychological Bulletin* 53(1956):267–293.

421

24. Semmelmeyer, M. "Extentional Methods in Dealing with Abstractions in Reading." *Elementary School Journal* 50(1949):28.

25. Thorndike, E. L., and I. Lorge. *The Teacher's Word Book of 30,000 Words.* Bureau of Publications, Teachers College, Columbia University, 1944.

26. Semmelmeyer, M. Op. cit., 1949, pp. 30–31.

27. Combs, A. W. "Personality Theory and Its Implications for Curriculum Development." In *Learning More About Learning*, edited by A. Frazier. Washington, D. C.: Association for Supervision and Curriculum Development, 1959, p. 11.

28. Corey, M. S. "The Poor Scholar's Soliloquy." *Childhood Education* 20(January 1944):7–8.

29. Weinstein, G., and M. Fantini. *A Model for Developing Relevant Content for Disadvantaged Children.* Ford Foundation Fund for the Advancement of Education, 1966.

30. "Education Briefs." *Education Digest* (November 1967):61.

31. Rogers, C. R. *Freedom to Learn.* Columbus, Ohio: Merrill, 1969, pp. 129–145.

32. Ausubel, D. D., S. H. Schpoont, and L. Cukier. "Influence of Intention on Retention of School Materials." *Journal of Educational Psychology* 48(1957):87–92.

33. Sanford, E. C. "A Letter to Dr. Titchner." In *Psychology of Human Learning*, edited by J. A. McGeoch. New York, Longmans, Green and Co., 1942, p. 276.

34. Torrance, E. P., and J. Harmon. "Effects of Memory, Evaluative, and Creative Reading Sets on Test Performance." *Journal of Educational Psychology* 52(1961):207–214.

35. Seagoe, M. V. "Qualitative Wholes: Classroom Experiments." *Journal of Educational Psychology* 27(1936):612–620.

36. Symonds, P. M. "What Education Has to Learn from Psychology, IV, Whole versus Part Learning." *Teachers College Record* 58(1957):329–339.

37. McGuigan, F. J. "Variations of Whole-Part Methods of Learning." *Journal of Educational Psychology* 51(1960):213–216.

38. Jensen, M. B., and A. Lemaire. "Ten Experiments on Whole and Part Learning." *Journal of Educational Psychology* 28(1937):37–54.

39. Capehart, B. E. "Illustrative Courses and Programs in Selected Secondary Schools." *The Integration of Educational Experiences*, Fifty-seventh Yearbook of the National Society for the Study of Education. Chicago: University of Chicago Press, 1958, Part III.

40. Underwood, B. J. "Ten Years of Massed Practice on Distributed Practice." *Psychological Review* 68(1961)229–247.

41. Glaser, R. "Learning." In *Encyclopedia of Educational Research*, 4th ed., edited by R. L. Ebel and V. H. Noll. London: Collier-Macmillan Ltd., 1969, pp. 706–726.

42. Travers, R. M. *Essentials of Learning*, 3rd ed. New York: Macmillan, 1972, pp. 119–122.

43. Leith, G. O., L. A. Biran, and J. A. Oppollot. "The Place of Review in Meaningful Verbal Learning." *Canadian Journal of the Behavioral Sciences* 1(1970):113–118.

44. Reynolds, J. H., and R. Glaser. "Effects of Repetition and Spaced Reviews upon Retention of a Complex Learning Task." *Journal of Educational Psychology* (October 1964):297–308.

45. Holland, J. G., and D. Porter. "The Influence of Repetition of Incorrectly Answered Items in a Teaching-Machine Program." Paper presented to the American Psychological Association, Harvard University, Cambridge, Mass., 1960.

46. Travers, R. M. Essentials of Learning, 3rd ed. Op. cit., pp. 50–53.

47. Page, E. B. "Teacher Comment and Student Performance: A Seventy-four Classroom Experiment in School Motivation." *Journal of Educational Psychology* 49(1958):173–181.

48. Wheeler, R. H. *The Science of Psychology*, 2nd ed. New York: Thomas Y. Crowell, 1940, p. 139.

49. Crowder, N. A. "On the Differences Between Linear and Intrinsic Programming." *Phi Delta Kappan* 44(1963):250–254.

50. Spitzer, H. F. "Studies in Retention." *Journal of Educational Psychology* 30(1939):641–656.

51. Gagné, R. M. "Some New Views of Learning and Instruction." *Phi Delta Kappan* (May 1970):471.

52. Cook, W. W. "Individual Differences and Curriculum Practice." *Journal of Educational Psychology* 39(1948):141.

53. Havighurst, R. *Developmental Tasks and Education.* New York: Longmans, Green, 1952, p. 2.

54. Inhelder, B. "Criteria of the Stages of Mental Development." *Discussions on Child Development*, edited by J. M. Tanner and B. Inhelder. New York: International Universities Press, 1953, p. 75.

55. Piaget, J. *Origins of Intelligence in Children.* New York: Norton, 1963.

56. Piaget, J. "How Children Form Mathematical Concepts." *Scientific American* 189(1953):76.

57. Tyler, F. T. "Readiness." In *Encyclopedia of Educational Research*, 4th ed., edited by R. L. Ebel and V. H. Noll. London: Collier-Macmillan Ltd., 1969, p. 1062.

58. Hilgard, J. R. "Learning and Maturation in Preschool Children." *Journal of Genetic Psychology* 41(1932):40–53.

59. Gesell, A., et al. *The First Five Years of Life: A Guide to the Study of the Preschool Child.* New York: McGraw-Hill, 1934.

60. Olson, W. C. *Child Development*, 2nd ed. Boston: D. C. Heath, 1959.

61. Bruner, J. S. *Toward a Theory of Instruction.* Cambridge, Mass.: Harvard University Press, 1966, p. 27.

62. Bruner, J. S. Op. cit., 1966, p. 29.

63. Ball, S., and G. A. Bogatz. "A Summary of the Major Findings in the First Year of Sesame Street: An Evaluation." *Congressional Record—Senate* (23 November 1970):18684–18689.

64. Harrison, A., Jr., and E. G. Seriven. "TV and Youth: Literature and Research Reviewed." Clearing House 44(October 1969):82–90.

65. Mason, G. E. "Children Learn Words from Commercial TV." *Elementary School Journal* 65(March 1965):12–15.

66. Witty, P. A. "Children of a Television Era." *Elementary English* 44(May 1967):528–535.

67. Russell, D. H., and H. R. Fea. "Research on Teaching Reading." In *Handbook of Research in Teaching,* edited by N. L. Gage. Chicago: Rand McNally, 1963, pp. 865–928.

68. Goldberg, M. "Adapting Teacher Style to Pupil Differences: Teachers for Disadvantaged Children." *Merrill-Palmer Quarterly of Behavior and Development* 10(1964):161–178.

69. Pearl, A. "As a Psychologist Sees Pressures on Disadvantaged Teen-agers." *Today's Education* 19(February 1965):21.

70. Osler, S. F. "Concept Studies in Disadvantaged Children." In *Cognitive Studies,* vol. I, edited by J. Hellmuth. New York: Brunner/Mazel, 1970, pp. 258–274.

71. Spears, M. J. "Improving Educational Opportunities for Minority Groups." *The Bulletin* 55(May 1971):98–105.

REFERENCES OF RELATED INTEREST

Alloway, D. N., and F. Cordasco. *Minorities and the American City.* New York: McKay, 1970.

Bandt, P. L. *A Time to Learn.* New York: Holt, Rinehart and Winston, 1974.

Banks, J. A., and J. D. Grambs (eds.). *Black Self-Concept.* New York: McGraw-Hill, 1972.

Baughman, E. E. *Black Americans: A Psychological Analysis.* New York: Academic Press, 1971, Chapter 3.

Bergeson, J. B., and G. S. Miller (eds.). *Learning Activities for Disadvantaged Children.* New York: Macmillan, 1971.

Borton, T. "What Turns Kids ON?" *Saturday Review* (15 April 1972).

———. *Reach, Touch, and Feel (Student Concerns and Process Education).* New York: McGraw-Hill, 1970.

Bremer, J., and M. vonMoschzisker. *The School without Walls.* New York: Holt, Rinehart, and Winston, 1971.

Bruner, J. S. *Toward a Theory of Instruction.* New York: W. W. Norton, 1966.

———. "The Functions of Teaching." *Rhode Island College Journal* 2(March 1960):35–42.

Clark, D. H., A Goldsmith, and C. Pugh. *Those Children: Case Studies from the Inner-City School.* Belmont, Calif.: Wadsworth, 1970.

Crary, R. W. *Humanizing the School: Curriculum Development and Theory.* New York: Harper and Row, 1969.

Cuban, L. *To Make a Difference: Teaching in the Inner City.* New York: The Free Press, 1970.

Dillon, J. C. *Personal Teaching.* Columbus, Ohio: Merrill, 1971.

Dreikurs, R., M. D. *Psychology in the Classroom, A Manual for Teachers.* New York: Harper and Row, 1968.

Emmer, E. T., and G. B. Millet. *Improving Teaching Through Experimentation.* Englewood Cliffs, N.J.: Prentice-Hall, 1970.

Engelmann, S. "Relationship Between Psychological Theories and the Act of Teaching." *Journal of School Psychology* 5 (Winter 1967):93–100.

Frost, J. L., and G. R. Hawkes (eds.). *The Disadvantaged Child.* 2nd ed. Boston: Houghton Mifflin, 1970.

Gagné, R. M. and L. J. Briggs. *Principles of Instructional Design.* New York: Holt, Rinehart and Winston, 1974.

Galloway, C. M. *Teaching Is Communicating.* Washington D.C.: The Association for Student Teaching, National Education Association, 1970.

Ginsburg, H. *The Myth of the Deprived Child.* Englewood Cliffs, N. J.: Prentice-Hall, 1972.

Gnagey, W. J., P. A. Chesebro, and J. J. Johnson (eds.). *Learning Environments: Readings in Educational Psychology.* New York: Holt, Rinehart and Winston, 1972.

Good, T. L. and J. E. Brophy. *Looking in Classrooms.* New York: Harper and Row, 1973.

Goodlad, J. I. "The Schools vs. Education." *Saturday Review* (19 April 1969).

Greenberg, H. M. *Teaching with Feeling.* New York: Macmillan, 1969.

Greenberg, S. *Selected Studies of Classroom Teaching: A Comparative Analysis.* Scranton, Pa.: International Textbook Company, 1970.

Haddan, E. E. *Evolving Instruction.* New York: Macmillan, 1970.

Holt, J. *How Children Learn.* New York: Pitman, 1967.

Horn, T. D. (ed.). *Reading for the Disadvantaged: Problems of Linguistically Different Learners.* New York: Harcourt, Brace and World, 1970.

Joyce, W. W., and J. A. Banks (eds.). *Teaching the Language Arts to Culturally Different Children.* Reading, Mass.: Addison-Wesley, 1971.

Kleinjans, E. K. "What Do You Mean—'Relevance'?" *Educational Perspectives* 10(October 1971):3–12.

Kuethe, J. L., *The Teaching-Learning Process,* Glenview, Ill.: Scott-Foresman, 1968.

Lembo, J. M. *Why Teachers Fail.* Columbus, Ohio: Merrill, 1971.

Lyon, H. C., Jr. *Learning to Feel, Feeling to Learn.* Columbus, Ohio: Merrill, 1971.

McClosky, M. G. (eds.). *Teaching Strategies and Classroom Realities.* Englewood Cliffs, N. J.: Prentice-Hall, 1971.

Mosston, M. *Teaching: From Command to Discovery.* Belmont, Calif.: Wadsworth, 1972.

Moustakes, C. *The Authentic Teacher.* Cambridge, Mass.: Doyle, 1966.

Noar, G. *Individualized Instruction: Every Child a Winner.* New York: Wiley, 1972.

Postman, N., and G. Weingartner. *Teaching as a Subversive Activity.* New York: Delacorte Press, 1969.

Rogers, C. R. *Freedom to Learn.* Columbus, Ohio: Merrill, 1969.

Rohwer, W. D., Jr. "Learning, Race, and School Success." *Review of Educational Research* 41(June 1971):191–210.

Schmuck, R. A., and P. A. Schmuck. *A Humanistic Psychology of Education.* Palo Alto, Calif.: National Press Books, 1974.

Silberman, M. L. (ed.). *The Experience of Schooling.* New York: Holt, Rinehart, and Winston, 1971.

————. J. S. Allender, and J. M. Yanoff (eds.). *The Psychology of Open Teaching and Learning.* Boston: Little, Brown, 1972.

Simon, S. B., L. W. Howe, and H. Kirschenbaum. *Values Clarification.* New York: Hart, 1972.

Skinner, B. F. *The Technology of Teaching.* New York: Appleton-Century-Crofts, 1968.

Stanley, J. *Preschool Programs for the Disadvantaged.* Baltimore: Johns Hopkins University Press, 1972.

Stone, J. C., and F. W. Schneider (eds.). *Teaching in the Inner City.* New York: Crowell, 1970.

Weigand, J. E. (ed.). *Developing Teacher Competencies.* Englewood Cliffs, N. J.: Prentice-Hall, 1971.

Wright, N., Jr. (ed.). *What Black Educators Are Saying.* New York: Hawthorn, 1970.

Zohorik, J. A., and D. L. Brubaker. *Toward More Humanistic Instruction.* Dubuque, Iowa: Brown, 1972.

IV

Learning Dynamics, Motivation Inputs, Self-concept Variables, and Evaluation Processes

Having looked now at the dynamics of good teaching in Part III, a natural next step is to examine the variables and processes related to learning, motivation, and evaluation procedures that can be used to assess the extent of, or degree of, learning.

Chapter 10 will acquaint you with several important and major points of view about how learning goes on. We will see that there are different "styles" of learning and their implications for teachers, and we will also examine some of the remarkable advances in our knowledge of relationships between brain biochemistry and learning.

Chapter 11 will discuss the operation, place, and importance of motivation in human learning. We'll consider some of the important ways in which motivation can be affected — for better or for worse — by praise and criticism, and by success and failure. We'll also look at why and how one's level of self-esteem influences the manner in which a person responds to success and failure experiences.

Chapter 12 will expose you to a system-atic examination of the ways in which self-concept variables can influence learning to achievement outcomes. More and more we are finding that how a student "feels" about his ability to learn can dramatically influence how much, in fact, he actually learns. Teacher expectancies play a part in this, and we'll take a careful look at the "psychology of expectations" and why they work the way they do.

In Chapter 13 we'll take up the matter of measurement and evaluation of learning, some ways for doing this, and some specific suggestions for constructing good examinations.

Does learning lead to a change in behavior? Are reinforcement and discovery methods of learning mutually exclusive? Can learning experiences lead to quantitative changes in the brain? Are "memory pills" in the future? What kind of testing is best — norm-references or criterion-referenced?

The next four chapters will address themselves to these and related questions.

TEN

Dynamics of Learning, Learning Processes, and Biochemical Developments

CHAPTER OUTLINE

PROLOGUE

WHAT IS LEARNING?

Learning Can Result in Many Different Kinds of Behavior Changes

Learning Leads to Improvement in Behavior

IMPORTANT VARIABLES IN LEARNING SETTING

The Stimulus (S) Variables

The Organism (O) Variables

Influence of needs

Influence of values

Influence of beliefs

Influence of self-concept

Influence of intelligence

Influence of previous learnings

The Response (R) Variables

TWENTY-FIVE IMPORTANT PRINCIPLES OF LEARNING

DIFFERENT POINTS OF VIEW ABOUT THE NATURE AND NURTURE OF LEARNING

Discovery Methods of Learning

Learning by doing is emphasized

Intuitive thinking is important

A certain amount of structure is needed

Examples of discovery learning in practice

Discovering one's own errors is important

Strategies for encouraging discovery learning

Cognitive autonomy an outgrowth of discovery learning

Evidence supporting discovery learning

Criticisms of Discovery Methods

Students sometimes mistake wrong answers for "right" ones

Discovery learning too seriously negates teaching

Discovery learning is inappropriate for some students

Discovery learning is time-consuming

Discovery learning may encourage a jump to hasty conclusions

Reinforcement Methods of Learning √

Emphasis on reinforcing desired responses

Reinforcing operant behavior is stressed

how operant conditioning works

Programmed instruction is frequently used

The effects of punishment are unpredictable

punishment and negative reinforcement are not the same

Some students may need more than verbal reinforcement

Intermittent reinforcement works best

Criticisms of Reinforcement Methods

Extrinsic learning is overemphasized

The teacher exerts too much control

Reinforcement methods produce different results on different students

Reinforcement and Discovery Methods Are not Mutually Exclusive

DIFFERENT STYLES OF LEARNING

Three Learning Styles: Visual, Aural, Physical (Riessman)

Reasons for Identifying a Student's Style Early

Four Characteristic Learning Patterns (Rosenberg)

The rigid-inhibited pattern

The undisciplined pattern

The acceptance-anxious pattern

The creative pattern

Some Students Are Impulsive Thinkers—Others Are Reflective

Some Students Conceptualize Analytically—Others Thematically

THE BIOCHEMISTRY OF LEARNING

Nature's Remarkable Computer: The Brain

Biochemical Factors Related to Long-term and Short-term Memory

The two-stage memory storage process theory

Brain Protein Synthesis Necessary for Long-term Memory

Protein Synthesis not Necessary for Short-term Memory

Biochemical Explanation for How We Remember

Memory Facilitators

Ribonucleic Acid (RNA) May Be the Physical Basis for Memory

McConnell's research

A note of caution

Changing the Environment Can Change the Brain

An enriched environment does make a difference

Experience changes the brain

The "kind" of experience makes a difference

Implications for Teachers

EPILOGUE

REFERENCES

REFERENCES OF RELATED INTEREST

IMPORTANT CHAPTER IDEAS

1. Learning is a process by which behavior is either modified or changed through experience or training.

2. The nature of the stimulus conditions acting on a student, his own internal state of mind, and the responses he makes are all part of the total learning experience.

3. Although there are different points of view about how to best encourage learning, there are at least twenty-five principles of learning with which different theoretical camps would consistently agree.

4. Those who emphasize discovery methods of learning believe that learning is more apt to occur when students are encouraged to think intuitively, make their own errors, and find their own answers to tasks that have a certain amount of structure built in.

5. Discovery methods consider knowing a process, not a product.

6. Discovery methods encourage the development of cognitive autonomy.

7. A major disadvantage of discovery methods of learning, say the critics, is that students may jump to premature conclusions or overgeneralize with too little support.

8. Reinforcement methods applied to learning stress the importance of both the quality and quantity of extrinsic rewards.

9. Positive reinforcement is a major strategy behind reinforcement methods.

10. Critics of reinforcement methods say that reinforcement approaches give the teacher too much power and control over the student.

11. Reinforcement and discovery methods are not mutually exclusive; good teachers use both to facilitate learning.

12. Research evidence indicates that there is no one best way to solve problems, think, or conceptualize; rather, there are many "best" ways and it behooves the teacher to recognize and accept these different ways among students.

13. Brain research indicates that there are certain biochemical changes that go on in the brain as learning takes place.

14. Research has shown that rats raised in an enriched environment have brain weights 4 to 6 percent higher than those coming from restricted environments.

15. Research indicates that manipulating the educational and psychological environment is a more effective way of inducing long-lasting brain changes than direct administration of drugs.

PROLOGUE

Learning is a complex mix of intelligence, motivation, sociopsychological factors, and biochemistry. Its processes and consequences can be as simple and direct as in the instance of a child who touches a hot stove and "learns" not to do it again or as intricate and prolonged as in the case of a physics student struggling to understand the basic principles of relativity. Learning is a continual, ongoing process of assimilating, integrating, re-integrating, and differentiating new experiences and information so that it makes a difference either in behavior or attitudes or both. In this chapter we will take a look at some of the human dynamics involved in learning, briefly overview several major theories of learning, examine the different types and styles of learning, and, finally, consider some of the remarkable new discoveries showing up in laboratories exploring relationships between brain chemistry and learning.

Let's turn our attention to what seems to be a logical first question.

WHAT IS LEARNING?

Although there is no one definition universally accepted by all psychologists, most would generally agree that *learning is a process by which behavior is either modified or changed through experience or training.* Ernest Hilgard,[1] an eminent American learning theorist, has emphasized that it is important to recognize the existence of both overt and covert behavioral changes by distinguishing between *learning* (covert) and *performance* (overt). We can only tell if learning has occurred by observing whether or not there is some change in behavior (performance) following the alleged learning. Let's say, for example, that a heavy smoker reads for the first time that there may be a causal relationship between smoking and lung cancer. If he either reduces his smoking or gives it up, we can assuredly say that learning has occurred. If, on the other hand, he persists in smoking as much as before we cannot so confidently conclude that learning has occurred. That is, his behavior is the same as it always was—at least his overt physical behavior. We note, however, that his intellectual behavior (the way he thinks about smoking) and his emotional behavior (the way he feels about smoking) are different. We may hear him deny the evidence ("The research isn't conclusive") or rationalize his smoking ("If I didn't smoke, I'd gain weight and that would be worse"). In addition, we also note that he seems generally more nervous, uncertain, ambivalent, and even a bit guilty when he does smoke. Even though one's overt behavior (performance) may remain the same after being exposed to something new, there may be more subtle behavior changes going on behind the scenes.

Learning Can Result in Many Different Kinds of Behavior Changes

Behavior, as we are using it in our definition, refers not only to that which is manifestly physical and therefore more observable, but also to attitudes, feeling states, and intellectual processes, any one of which may be more difficult to "see" at first glance. The point is that not all behavioral changes following learning are easily seen. On the other hand, not every experience we are a part of results in learning. Indeed, there probably is not one among us who cannot remember saying to himself or herself, after botching a task for the third or fourth time, "When will I ever learn?"

We might also note that the sort of change we're talking about here is specifically related to learning and changes in behavior that take place as a result of special stimulation. A man whose leg has been amputated will surely experience a change in his walking behavior, but this direct change cannot be called learning. However, as a consequence of his physical status the man will undoubtedly be a changed individual in changed circumstances, all of which will cause him to engage in much new learning and relearning as a result of the physical change. He will have to learn to adapt to the changes. This we can call *learning*. Learning, as it is defined here, also excludes any changes directly associated with maturation of inherited structure and predispositions or any changes in behavior that might be associated with fatigue or drugs. If, let's say, a shy student comes to class high on a dose of amphetamines and participates vigorously in class discussion, his behavior change is not the consequence of insight into his shyness but the result of biochemical changes over which he has no control. He is, literally, the prisoner of his change, not the master of it. His behavioral change reflects not learning, but bondage.

Learning Leads to Improvement in Behavior

Learning can also be defined as *improvement* in behavior in the sense that one usually becomes more proficient at whatever he is learning. This

Learning about new things, new places, and new ideas can be an exciting process.

does not, however, mean that one's behavior gets necessarily better from the standpoint of desirability. A student could, for example, learn to be a clever con artist, a superb apple-polisher, or a crafty cheater. On the other hand, he could learn to be honest, straightforward, and confident in his ability.

IMPORTANT VARIABLES IN A LEARNING SETTING

There are at least three important variables to consider in relation to the dynamics of learning. One, there are the external *stimuli* that we call the S variables; two, there are the internal factors characteristic of the *organism* itself, the O variables; and three, there are the responses—the R variables—which the organism (the student) gives to conditions of stimulation. Although in actual practice it is almost impossible to separate these variables in any absolute way, we will look at each variable one at a time in order to make the distinction among them as clear as possible.

The Stimulus (S) Variables

Any stimulus of which a student is aware can become part of the learning situation. In fact, each of us is continually surrounded by a myriad of stimuli that are capable of affecting us. For example, as I sit here in my office writing, I am surrounded by both active and latent stimulus inputs. At the moment, my books, journals, assorted notes, and a cup of coffee are stimuli occupying most of my attention. These represent the active stimuli of my immediate sensory world because my behavior is most affected by them at the moment. My phone, which at this time nestles quietly in its cradle, shifts from its role as a latent stimulus to a more active one each time it buzzes for my attention. The point is that whether it is in the classroom or anyplace else, every setting contains both active and latent stimuli that can affect the sensorium of touch, taste, sight, hearing, smell, and kinesthesia. A stimulus condition can arise either inside or outside a person. For instance, the exam you find yourself cramming for is an example of a stimulus working on you from the outside; the novel you read entirely for its own sake is an example of a stimulus working on you from the inside. That is, the novel is not *making* you read it—you do so for your own inner reasons.

All in all, the stimuli to which we attend in our sensory world are those that are intense, novel, and contrasting (e.g., a sharp noise, a new musical sound, a red lamp in a white room), and those which offer the greatest possibility for personal gratification.

The implications here for teachers would suggest frequent changes of pace in the presentation of both self and academic material. Nothing loses its stimulus potential (arousal ability, motivational capacity) more quickly than a predictable teacher who does more or less the same old dreary things day after day.

The Organism (*O*) Variables

In any complex classroom situation, a student must interpret stimuli, differentiate and combine them, and give them some meaning. There is no simple way for describing how the complex organism known as the human learner does this, but there are certain aspects of his total personality that enter the picture everytime he responds to and interprets his sensory world. Let's consider some of the more prominent influences on behavior.

Influence of needs. Out of all the stimuli we might perceive, we usually perceive what is consistent with the needs we feel at the moment. This has been demonstrated under rigorous laboratory conditions. For example, Levine and his associates[2] presented food-deprived subjects with pictures of various objects distorted behind a ground-glass screen and found that those who had gone three to nine hours without eating "saw" more food objects than those who had eaten within two hours of the experiment.

In classes you may have had that lasted into the lunch hour, have you noted how your thoughts turn increasingly to food images? And of course we're all familiar with the desert scene of the parched, dehydrated man pulling himself across the hot sands toward a watery illusion created in answer to his desperate need for body fluid.

> **TO THINK ABOUT**
>
> Consider your own needs at this very moment. Which need are you most aware of? A body need? An emotional need? An intellectual need? A social need? If a need does exist (don't try to invent one if it isn't there), how is it influencing your concentration and learning?

Influence of values. As a general rule, we more readily perceive those things, experiences, and people we value, prize, and esteem. For instance, Postman and others[3] have shown that personal values can be the determinants of an individual's perceptual selectivity. First they measured the value orientation of twenty-five students with a value scale. They flashed words representing six values one at a time on a screen with increasingly longer exposures until they were recognized by each student. Their general finding was that the more closely a given word reflected a value already held by the student, the more rapidly he was able to recognize it. As an illustration of this, students with dominant religious values tended to recognize on very brief exposure such words as *church* or *minister*, while taking longer to perceive economic words such as *cost*, *prices*, or *bonds*. In other words, there seems to be a predisposition, or readiness, to see more quickly words reflecting one's personal values.

Influence of beliefs. By and large, people are inclined to behave in a manner that is consistent with what they believe to be true and this principle strongly influences the O variables in a learning setting. In this sense, seeing is not only believing; seeing is behaving! A fact is not necessarily what is; a fact is what one believes to be true. When man believed that the earth was flat he avoided (or at least thought he did) its edges; when he believed that phrenology (the study of "bumps" on one's head) could help him, he had his head examined (literally). There is even evidence to suggest that when a researcher believes his hypothesis is true, he is more apt to find evidence supporting that hypothesis is true, than if he didn't believe it was true.[4] And so it goes.

A research effort a bit closer to home as far as teaching and learning are concerned was conducted by Bills and McGehee,[5] who found that students who learned and retained the most in a psychology experiment were inclined to believe such views as, "Psychology experiments are useful and

437

will eventually help us to completely understand people," and "Psychology, in general, is a valuable, quantitative science with many practical aspects." On the other hand, students who quickly forgot the material were those who held beliefs such as "Psychological experiments are a total waste of time," and "Psychology, in general, is nothing but a witch hunt."

Influence of self-concept. How a student sees himself has a strong influence on his behavior both inside and outside a classroom setting. Depending on how one sees himself, an exam is perceived as either something to avoid failing or something to pass with as high a grade as possible; a class discussion is viewed as either something to actively engage in or something to sit quietly through for fear of saying the wrong thing; front seats of classrooms are seen as either vantage points for better seeing and hearing or as potentially dangerous spots where one could be more easily seen and, heaven forbid, called on! It depends on how one perceives himself. The point is that the student who sees himself as essentially adequate and successful will respond to classroom experiences differently from one who anticipates failure. All in all, self-concept can have a powerful influence on a student's behavior. (This idea is developed more completely in Chapter 11.)

TO THINK ABOUT

How about your own self-concept? To what extent do your self-perceptions influence how you behave in a classroom? If your self-concept as a student was the complete reverse of what it is now, how do you suppose you would behave differently in classes you're taking? Write down the three things you would probably change right away.

_____

_____

_____

Influence of intelligence. Intelligence is an important O variable because, at any given time, a student's reaction to a learning situation will be affected by his ability to give meaning to the situation. Just as one person can be biologically superior to another in the sense of being physically more adept at more things, so, too, is it possible for one person to be intellectually superior to another when it comes to conceptual thinking, abstract thought, and problem solving.[6] The fact is that a student's ability to think and the way he thinks are important determinants of his behavior in a classroom setting.

Influence of previous learnings. Finally, all of these factors we're considering under the *O* variables are modified by the present status of the student's life history. His recognition of similarities and differences between current and past situations helps to determine his present reactions. The child who has a whore for a mother, a drunk for a father, and a floor for his bed will very likely interpret school experiences in a far different way than a child with a mother who cares, a father who works, and a bed he knows for sure will be there tonight to sleep in.

Let's turn now to another important variable found in every learning setting.

The Response (R) Variables

Learning depends on what a student does. It is his *response* to the situation that makes either change or modification of behavior possible. Perhaps we can illustrate the major idea here best by example.

Suppose I were to ask you to select five major principles of learning and then write a five-page essay explaining how these principles are interrelated and function in a classroom. Let's also assume that you were not only willing to do so, but that your *O* variables today are in a condition such that the assignment is an attractive and possible one. What would you do? Different students would approach the task in different ways. Some would go to the library, others would talk among themselves, and still others would hope for a glimpse at someone else's paper in order to find out how to get started.

As we have discussed the major components that are a part of every classroom setting, it is evident that learning takes place anytime a student reacts in a situation that affects him. *That* a student responds depends on the S variables; *how* a student responds depends on the O variables; the consequences of one's responses provide the feedback that govern probable future behavior.

TWENTY-FIVE IMPORTANT PRINCIPLES OF LEARNING

Arriving at what we can call "major" principles of learning is not an easy matter because of disagreement among psychologists and educators as to what these principles are. However, there are certain principles of learning with which psychologists representing various theoretical camps would probably consistently agree. Burton,[7] Symonds,[8] and Watson[9] have examined this issue in some depth and what follows is a summarized listing of twenty-five major learning principles that can enhance learning if we understand and practice them.

1. The learning process is experiencing, doing, reacting, and undergoing.

2. Active participation and acceptance by the student is superior to the type of passive reception often accompanying a lecture or motion picture. This is less likely to be true if lecturing (sometimes a sophisticated form of telling) and motion pictures are among a variety of approaches used.

3. Behaviors that are reinforced (rewarded) are more likely to recur. Most normal children, youths, and adults enjoy doing those things that are pleasurable to themselves and/or others.

4. Sheer repetition of a learning task without either any indication of how to improve or change inhibits progress in learning.

5. Threat and punishment have generally unpredictable effects upon learning. That is, punished responses may or may not occur again.

6. A learning task that is set or accepted by the student is likely to lead to socially and intellectually acceptable outcomes.

7. The learning process, initiated by need and purpose, is likely to be motivated by its own incompleteness, though extrinsic (outside) motives or encouragement may sometimes be necessary.

8. The learning situation, to be of maximum value, must be perceived by the learner as realistic, meaningful, and useful.

9. The type of reward that has the greatest possibility of applying to other life situations is the kind one gives oneself — the sense of satisfaction found in meeting a challenge or accomplishing a personal goal. We sometimes refer to these as ego-rewards.

10. Reward, to be most effective in encouraging learning and continued motivation to learn, should follow as soon after the successful completion of a task as possible.

11. The learning process proceeds most effectively when the experiences, materials, and desired results are adjusted to the maturity and experiential background of the student.

12. Learning proceeds best when the student can see the results, has knowledge of his status and progress, and reaches a personally meaningful level of insight and understanding. All of this contributes to the development of a desirable self-concept, which in turn affects how and what he learns.

13. Most students progress in any area of learning only as far as they need to go in order to achieve their progress. Often they do only enough to "get by"; with increased motivation they improve.

14. The learning process and achievement are materially affected by a student's level of aspiration.

15. Most students will persist through difficulties, over obstacles, and through unpleasant situations to the extent that they see the objectives as worthwhile and the goal attainable.

16. The learning process is stimulated to best effort when it operates within a rich and varied environment. Sameness, either in the teacher or in learning setting, dulls attention and stifles motivation.

17. Forgetting proceeds most rapidly at first—then more slowly. Deliberate recall immediately after learning reduces the possibility of forgetting new material.

18. The experience of learning by sudden insight into previously puzzling situations arises when: (a) the student has sufficient background and preparation; (b) attention is given to relationships operative in the whole situation; and (c) the task is meaningful and within the range of ability of the student.

19. The most effective learning effort is offered by students when they attempt tasks that fall in the "range of challenge"—not too easy and not too hard—where success seems possible but not certain.

20. Learning from reading is enhanced more by time spent recalling what has been read than by rereading.

21. The best way to help students form a general concept is to present the concept in numerous and varied specific situations, and then to encourage formulations of the general idea and its applications in situations different from those in which the concept was learned.

22. No school subjects are markedly superior to others for "strengthening mental powers." General improvement as a result of study of any subject depends on instruction that encourages generalizations about principles, concept formation, and improvements of techniques of study, thinking, and communication.

23. Students vary not only in their present learning but in their rate of growth and the "ceiling" that represents their potential level of achievement. Some slow growing students may eventually surpass students who seemed far ahead of them in grade school.

24. Ability to learn increases with age up to adult years.

25. The learning process is stimulated to best effort when it encourages a diversity of learning opportunities and experiences.

With these major learning principles as a backdrop, let's turn our attention to two important theoretical views about the nature of learning and how it occurs.

DIFFERENT POINTS OF VIEW ABOUT THE NATURE AND NURTURE OF LEARNING

Just as there is no one "best" kind of student or one "best" kind of teacher, it is also true that there is no one "best" approach to learning.

This is the case because there is no single, systematic, inclusive theory as yet available, no final set of "laws" of learning. Indeed, the very complexity of human behavior makes it difficult for a single point of view to account for all the variables involved in human learning. Research indicates that every person develops his own unique cognitive style, a unique way in which he tackles intellectual problems and in which he organizes his experience. Ausubel,[10] for instance, has outlined three dimensions on which people differ: (1) tendency toward progressive differention, (2) tendency toward cognitive simplification, and (3) tendency toward consistency of information. In actual practice, it's difficult to compartmentalize these three factors. For example, complex experience may be scaled to more easily managed levels because it is cognitively simpler to handle it or because in doing so discrepant data can be filtered out and greater consistency achieved.

However, in spite of the vast differences among people when it comes to how they learn best, there are two broad strategies for learning enhancement that are part of every classroom. One approach falls under the general title of *discovery methods,* which grow out of cognitive-file theory, and the other falls under the label of reinforcement methods, which grows out of that branch of psychology known as *behaviorism.* What we will try to do is present the essential ingredients of each of these methods and then discuss their respective strengths and weaknesses.

Discovery Methods of Learning

Psychologists who advocate approaches to learning called *learning by discovery* believe that students learn best when they are given a wide variety of examples of a certain phenomenon and then encouraged to find the underlying rule that ties them together.[11]

Those who favor this point of view contend that principles learned by discovery are remembered better and are more accessible to transfer to another learning situation because the search-out-and-selection process is an active one.

Learning by doing is emphasized. The idea behind this approach goes back as far as John Dewey's early notions about the importance of "learning by doing" and of the vital necessity of encouraging students to solve their own problems within a broad "field of possible solutions" and arrive at their own answers. As Dewey put it:

The child cannot get power of judgment excepting as he is continually exercised in forming and testing judgment. He must have an opportunity to select for himself, and then to attempt to put his own selections into execution that he may submit them to the only final test, that of action. Only thus can he

Learning by doing is the major thrust behind the "discovery approach." (SSSP)

learn to discriminate that which promises success from that which promises failure; only thus can he form the habit of relating his otherwise isolated ideas to the conditions which determine their value.[12]

Intuitive thinking is important. In recent years, Jerome Bruner has been among the most articulate spokesmen for the discovery method. Like Dewey, Bruner thinks it important for students to discover—to intuit, actually—for themselves what they didn't know before.[13] He maintains that discovery learning leads to a type of understanding that is not only more exciting to students but also very likely to increase their self-confidence and self-reliance. The reason Bruner feels this way is because the student is literally encouraged to "discover" on his own, which is diametrically opposed to "telling" a student the answer or giving him the solution in the more traditional expository fashion.

The intuitive thinking involved in discovery learning is not the same as analytical thinking, which is more methodical, precise, and planned. As Bruner describes it:

. . . intuitive thinking characteristically does not advance in careful, well-defined steps. . . . Usually intuitive thinking rests on familiarity with the domain of knowledge involved and with its structure, which makes it possible for the thinker to leap about, skipping steps and employing shortcuts in a manner that requires a later rechecking of conclusions by more analytic means, whether deductive or inductive.[14]

A certain amount of structure is needed. With the discovery method, learning is regarded primarily as a rearrangement of thought patterns and perception of new relationships. This being the case, proponents of this approach emphasize the importance of a certain amount of structure as important in order for discovery learning to go on. From Bruner's point of view, structure is important for at least four reasons:

1. Understanding the fundamentals makes a subject more comprehensible. . . .
2. Unless detail is organized in a structured pattern, it is rapidly forgotten. Detailed material is conserved in memory by representing it in simplified ways. . . .
3. An understanding of fundamental principles and ideas appears to be the main road to adequate transfer. . . .
4. Structure permits a person to narrow the gap between elementary and advanced knowledge.[15]

The point is: A certain amount of structure gives a student a framework within which he can integrate and comprehend new information and ideas. For example, a falling body can be viewed only as a discrete event or as an organization of gravitational forces. When one assimilates knowledge of the first sort, one has to learn each new fact anew. On the other hand, when one comprehends the principle of gravitation, one has hold of a more dynamic knowledge that provides the necessary framework or structure to explain new phenomena and predict the consequences of events. Teaching, then, is directed to helping the student establish a relationship between his existing information and the new information so that which we call "knowledge" can be reintegrated and updated. In this way, content is seen not only as an array of facts to be absorbed, but as something that has structure, namely, a way of organizing detailed facts in the light of some concepts and principles.

Examples of discovery learning in practice. To illustrate how someone like Bruner would convert these various ideas about structure and intuition into classroom practice, here is an illustration from a social studies unit for fifth graders as described in his book, *Toward a Theory of Instruction*.

Bruner writes, "The content of the course is man"—his nature as a species, the forces that shaped and continue to shape humanity. Three questions recur throughout: "What is human about human beings? How did they get that way? How can they be made more so?"[16]

In their search for answers, students study five topics considered significant in man's humanization: tool making, language, social organization, man's management of prolonged childhood, and man's urge to explain his world.

To give you a feeling of how these topics are studied, here is a brief account of the subunit on language.

To begin with, there are opening discussions on the question of what communication is and the various ways it can occur. One focus of attention is the contrast between the ways in which human beings and animals send and receive messages. Each new topic includes a presentation by the teacher (e.g., explanations of how dogs communicate anger by growling; or wolves, passion by howling; or bees, direction by dancing) to provide some structure. This can be followed by class activities that demonstrate how pictures, diagrams, and words refer to objects and experiences; and games in which columns of words are arranged and rearranged into an endless variety of sentences. Eventually, the process of language acquisition is explored as much as it can be and is concluded with a section on the origins and functions of human language and the role it plays in molding the final product, species homo sapiens.

In another example, a fifth-grade geography class was given simple outline maps showing rivers, lakes, and simple notes about natural resources. The student's task was to predict where the major cities were likely to be found, where the railroads would be located, and where the highways would probably be. As Bruner himself has said, this was presenting geography "not as a set of knowns, but as a set of unknowns." As you can see, it was not the purpose of this assignment to transmit "facts" about geography. Indeed, for the duration of this experiment, students were not even permitted to consult books and maps for information. Instead, they were encouraged to exercise their analytic powers to draw inferences from the data they had. The emphasis was on thinking and analysis rather than on memory and regurgitation.

Understandably enough, these students made some errors in drawing conclusions. However, Bruner is careful to point out that such errors, far from being fatal, may be highly instructive. If a student is to avoid making the same mistake again, he needs to know where his logic was faulty, not simply to memorize a different answer. But he also needs a classroom climate that tolerates *wrong* hypotheses and incorrect answers—where he is not rewarded for correct answers only.[17]

TO THINK ABOUT

Consider the subject(s) you will one day teach. If you wanted to encourage learning by discovery methods, how would you do it? How would you set it up so that discovery learning might occur? Briefly describe the steps you would take.

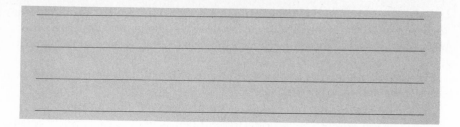

Discovering one's own errors is important. As in all learning, the idea of feedback to the learner is an important consideration in the discovery approach. You may recall from our discussion in Chapter 1 that within a stimulus-response or behavioristic view of behavior and learning, immediate feedback or reinforcement is important. Indeed, the basic principle behind the use of a teaching machine or a programmed textbook is that of immediate feedback so the student knows right away whether or not his answer is correct. Within the discovery method, however, the idea of instant feedback is not so crucial. There is feedback all right, but it is not necessarily given by an outside source, nor does it occur immediately after the student makes a response. Rather, feedback is a process whereby the learner makes corrections and adjustments in his problem-solving strategy as a *result of the errors he perceives.* Discovery of one's own errors, according to Bruner, is an important part of effective problem solving. In Bruner's words:

> Knowledge of results . . . should come at that point in a problem-solving episode when the person is comparing the results of his try-out with some criterion of what he seeks to achieve. Knowledge of results given before this point either cannot be understood or must be carried as extra freight in immediate memory.[18]

Strategies for encouraging discovery learning. Bruner suggests four specific approaches for making discovery learning more possible in a classroom:

1. *Emphasize contrast* (e.g., contrasting man with animals, modern man with prehistoric man, man with child)

2. *Stimulate informed guessing* (e.g., asking students to develop hunches about how Eskimo hunters decide which breathing holes in the ice to stake out in hunting seals and then showing a film to demonstrate how they actually do decide)

3. *Encourage participation* (e.g., having students develop a social system within their classroom along with a hierarchy of authority in order to better understand how and why early man's social system developed)

446

4. *Stimulate awareness* (e.g., having students think about the consequences of being given adult status at, say, age seven or eight to make them conscious of the need for, and perhaps even the importance of, a prolonged childhood)[19]

Teaching by the discovery method is not a matter of getting students to commit facts to mind. As Bruner sees it:

> . . . it is to teach him to participate in the process that makes possible the establishment of knowledge. We teach a subject not to produce living libraries on the subject, but rather to get a student to think mathematically for himself, to consider matters as an historian does, to take part in the process of knowledge-getting. Knowing is a process, not a product.[20]

Cognitive autonomy an outgrowth of discovery learning. A major strength of learning by discovery is that it offers a student a certain degree of what has been called "cognitive autonomy."[21] That is, when a student has developed an organizing scheme for his own learning, he is presumably in a position to harvest a greater amount of knowledge as well as to grow increasingly autonomous and independent of external forms of authority. Further, when a student learns to rely on his own intellectual processes, when he is conscious of the relationships between what he is learning and his own experience, and when he has developed a search strategy and discovery method under his own steam, he is in a much better position to continue these processes on his own.

Evidence supporting discovery learning. It seems likely that learning by discovery, being an active process, has a significant potential for not only encouraging what White[22] has called the "competency motive," but also for helping a student to actually *feel* more competent through the exhilaration that follows from actually discovering or finding out something for himself. Indeed, these conclusions about the effectiveness of this strategy of learning are generally verified by Suchman's[23,24] research with "inquiry training," an approach that generally follows the discovery method model. He found that not only do students show increased autonomy, but also increased productivity and increased discipline in the sense of reflecting a greater understanding of the rules of logical inference and a greater precision and control in asking their questions.

After a critical review of studies of discovery learning, Hermann[25] arrived at the following tentative findings:

1. Retention is much improved by discovery learning.
2. Discovery learning results in better transfer.
3. With increased difficulty of the transfer task, discovery learning is relatively more effective.
4. With the increase of time between learning and testing of a transfer task, discovery learning is relatively more effective.

5. The task of learning, when involved with school-like materials, results in more effective learning with the discovery method.
6. Discovery learning may have a tendency to be more effective when there is limited background knowledge of the subject matter.
7. Discovery learning is relatively more effective for those in lower ability groups than in the higher ability groups.
8. After learning by the discovery method, immediate verbalization of the material tends to affect adversely original learning.
9. In discovery learning a reasonable degree of guidance is more desirable than little guidance.

TO THINK ABOUT

Learning by discovery for yourself has distinct advantages. But is it always the best way? When, for example, do you prefer to be "told" the answer as opposed to finding it for yourself? You may find it interesting to check out your response to this question with other students in class. Do you find overlaps and differences?

Criticisms of Discovery Methods

Discovery methods are by no means a panacea to learning. They have strengths, but shortcomings as well. Let's turn our attention now to what some of the leading antagonists of the discovery approach have had to say about its weakness as a learning model.

Students sometimes mistake wrong answers for "right" ones. Bernard Friedlander feels that there are too many possibilities for a student to discover the "wrong" answer. He cites the case of a boy who, without any apparent basis, "discovered" that the difference between the phonetic value of the soft "c" in "cent," compared with the hard "c" in "cat," was due to the fact that the "c" in "cent" was a capital letter, while the "c" in "cat" was a lowercase letter, which was the way the two words happened to appear in the material the boy was reading. According to Friedlander, this discovery was accompanied by "the full Brunerian glow of satisfaction at having scaled a great peak of learning." Apparently the boy clung stubbornly to the propriety of his discovery, and it was only through a tactful explanation by the teacher that the boy finally accepted a correct differentiation of the two "c's." Friedlander went on to observe:

> . . . I soon found that it does not take many hours of classroom observing to see frequent mistakes of this kind, mistakes that often go uncorrected. . . . I also found that when, as often occurs, the teacher has understandable difficulty identifying the seemingly inscrutable logical or psychological juncture where the students' thoughts have jumped the rails, the consequence is likely

to be quite justified discomfiture on the teacher's part and useless disruption of the lesson for the rest of the class. Such failures may be the price of progress, but we should not close our eyes to how high that price should be.[26]

Discovery learning too seriously negates teaching. B. F. Skinner is another psychologist who has taken issue with discovery learning. As Skinner sees it:

> . . . discovery is no solution to the problems of education. A culture is no stronger than its capacity to transmit itself. It must impart an accumulation of skills, knowledge, and social and ethical practices to its new members. The institution of education is designed to serve this purpose. It is quite impossible for the student to discover for himself any substantial part of the wisdom of his culture, and no philosophy of education really proposes that he should. Great thinkers build upon the past, they do not waste time in rediscovering it. It is dangerous to suggest to the student that it is beneath his dignity to learn what others already know, that there is something ignoble (and even destructive of "rational powers") in memorizing facts, codes, formulae, or passages from literary works, and that to be admired he must think in original ways. It is equally dangerous to forego teaching important facts and principles in order to give the student a chance to discover them for himself. Only a teacher who is unaware of his effects on his students can believe that children actually discover mathematics, that (as one teacher has written) in group discussions they "can and do figure out all the relationships, facts, and procedures that comprise a full program in math."
>
> There are other difficulties. The position of the teacher who encourages discovery is ambiguous. Is he to pretend that he himself does not know. . . . Or, for the sake of encouraging a joint venture in discovery, is the teacher to choose to teach only those things which he himself has not yet learned? Or is he frankly to say, "I know, but you must find out" and accept the consequences for his relations with his students?
>
> Still another difficulty arises when it is necessary to teach a whole class. How are a few good students to be prevented from making all the discoveries?[27]

Discovery learning is inappropriate for some students. We must also acknowledge the possibility of interpersonal difficulties occurring when the discovery method is used. For one thing, students could become frustrated and even angry if a teacher refuses to tell them what he obviously knows. This is particularly apt to be the case for highly anxious and highly compulsive students, who, research shows, do their best work in the more structured teacher-directed classes.[28]

Discovery learning is time-consuming. Another flaw that some teachers see in the discovery method is that it is a time-consuming process. That is, it takes longer for students to discover their own answers than it does for a teacher to tell them or to at least be more direct and forceful in leading them to the desired solutions or information. The argument proceeds on the grounds that since mastery of minimum amounts of information is a prerequisite for higher education in the United States, students who are exposed only to discovery methods may not learn enough to meet the admission standards for entrance into most colleges and universities. It may not be as drastic as that, but it seems reasonable to question whether students would learn as much as they could through the *exclusive* use of discovery approaches. Besides, is there really anything wrong with having an enthusiastic teacher, skilled in the art of communication, telling his students what he has learned?

Discovery learning may encourage a jump to hasty conclusions. Ausubel has been a persistent critic of discovery methods for learning. One of the major disadvantages he sees in this approach is that it feeds into a child's exaggerated tendency to jump to conclusions, to overgeneralize with too little evidence, and to consider only one aspect of the problem at a time. As observed by Ausubel:

> It is true that one objective of [school] is to educate [students] out of these tendencies. But it is one thing to do so as part of a [total] program, and quite another to struggle full-time with this handicap as children are required to self-discover everything they have to learn.[29]

The discovery method is one way of learning. Let's turn our attention now to a second broad approach to learning that is favored by many psychologists and educators.

Reinforcement Methods of Learning

Reinforcement methods applied to human learning are those which stress outer experience, overt behavior, action and reaction. Essentially, the idea is to reinforce (reward) the correct answers or proper behavior to increase the likelihood of it being repeated again.

Emphasis on reinforcing desired responses. The foremost contemporary exponent of learning within a reinforcement framework is B. F. Skinner, who, like Bruner, is a Harvard University psychologist. Starting with the intention of describing learning and behavior from the observer's point of view, Skinner has concentrated almost exclusively on how learning can be shaped, controlled, and manipulated by reinforcing or rewarding certain desired behaviors or "responses." As Skinner sees it, there are two kinds of responses—the usual response "elicited" by known stimuli and the "emitted" response, which occurs without known stimuli. The first type is known as "respondant" behavior; the second type, as "operant" behavior.

Reinforcing operant behavior is stressed. Skinner has been more concerned with operant behavior, which is associated more with the responses than with stimuli. What this means in a school situation is that the learner emits responses to his environment, and these responses, if reinforced, tend to be repeated. Thus, an *operant* is behavior that has been reinforced. As Skinner puts it, "if the occurrence of an operant is followed by presentation of a reinforcing stimulus, the strength of the operant is increased."[30] In other words, when a desired response is given, a reinforcing stimulus is presented. This tends to condition that response and make it more likely to appear again under similar circumstances. At the same time, failure to reinforce will result in the extinction of that response.

How operant conditioning works. O'Leary and Becker[31] are two psychologists who have attempted to extend the idea of operant conditioning in a classroom in practical ways. For example, they have shown that the indiscriminate methods now in use often work against the teacher's good intentions and the student's best interests because the reinforcement is associated with a perverse response. To correct this, teachers are advised to ignore—insofar as possible—all improper behavior and to reward instead whatever proper behavior may be present. Thus, if one student is misbehaving, the teacher praises the student next to him who is attending to his lesson. The thinking behind this approach is that student A, who sees student B being praised (rewarded), will want to behave more like student B. This may or may not work, but if it does, the teacher must be sure to praise, acknowledge, or otherwise reward student A's improved behavior.

TO THINK ABOUT

Sometimes, teacher behavior such as described above is seen as manipulative—and in a negative sort of way. That is, it is sometimes seen designed, contrived, and therefore insincere. How do you feel about the use of operant conditioning to change or modify behavior?

Skinner has shown little concern about a theory of motivation or about a need to infer internal processes. The reinforcement of behavior seems to be taken for granted in a common sense sort of way. Food is reinforcing to a rat or a pigeon. Knowledge of correctness is reinforcing to a learner in school. The whole idea behind operant learning is to elicit the correct responses so they can be rewarded in a positive manner.

Programmed instruction is frequently used. Reinforcing correct responses is the basic principle in programmed instruction. That is, each correct answer is supposed to provide the learner with the immediate gratification of "I'm right" and this, then, is the impetus to go on to the next step. Table 10–1 shows a sample page from a programmed learning textbook. You can see that the student gets instant feedback about how he is doing, which makes it possible for him to change erroneous responses to the more gratifying correct responses.

Teaching machines are constructed with the same principle in mind. That is, the teaching machine provides reinforcement for every correct response; the learner proceeds as quickly or as slowly as he wants. As Skinner describes it, " . . . the machine helps the student come up with the correct answer. The student is helped by the orderly construction of the program and in part by the hints and suggestions which may be derived from the verbal material."[32]

The effects of punishment are unpredictable. The use of punishment to discourage the possibility that a given response will occur is also possible. This can lead to problems, however, since punishment is apt to be associated with the given rather than with the response that is supposed to be extinguished. In addition, punishment does not necessarily tell the student what the right response is or make him want to make it. On the whole, operant conditioning in the classroom is most effective where rewards are emphasized.[33,34] Students' reactions to punishment (teacher sarcasm or ridicule, public disapproval by the teacher, negative teacher comments written on an exam or paper, and so on) are typically more variable, less predictable, and more likely to arouse anger and resentment.

Punishment and negative reinforcement are not the same. Punishment is not the same as negative reinforcement. Negative reinforcement occurs when an aversive stimulus is turned off, and punishment has its effect when an aversive stimulus is turned on. What usually happens in practice is that punishment and positive reinforcement are used together. For example, if a student persists in interrupting other students when they're talking, a teacher may express mild annoyance about the interruptions. Most students would likely interpret signs of teacher annoyance as a form of punishment and discover that when they didn't interrupt, the teacher ceased being annoyed. The cessation of the teacher's expression of annoyance has the effect of strengthening the response that accompanies it. In this case, the response associated with the cessation of the aversive stimulus is that of not interrupting other students and hence this response is strengthened by negative reinforcement. According to Travers, a learning theory expert, "a negative reinforcer is a stimulus the removal of which increases the strength of the response."[35]

TABLE 10–1.

Only an _____ can modify a verb.	adverb
Many adverbs end in _____.	ly
When they modify the verb, these adverbs usually tell us something about the _____ of the verb.	action
Adverbs ending in _____ seldom modify linking verbs.	ly
Do they often modify verbs of action?	yes
Some of the following sentences contain linking verbs. The others contain verbs of action.	
The linking verbs are followed by objectives which modify the _____ of the sentence.	subject
The verbs of action are followed by adverbs ending in *ly* which modify the _____.	verb
In each sentence select the correct form of the adjective or adverb:	
A rose smells – sweet/sweetly.	sweet
This food tastes – bad/badly.	bad
The professor speaks – rapid/rapidly.	rapidly
You sing – good/well.	well
He felt – quick/quickly/ – for the door knob.	quickly
He polished – vigorous/vigorously.	vigorously
The play ended – happy/happily.	happily
The snake struck – vicious/viciously.	viciously

A programmed learning text looks something like this. A student covers the right-hand side of the page and looks at it only when he wants to check his answers for the exercises on the left.

Another learning theorist has distinguished between punishment learning and negative reinforcement learning in the following way: "It is proposed that so-called punishment be termed passive avoidance learning (learning to avoid by *not* doing something—e.g., not interrupting) and that the contrasting form of avoidance learning (learning to *do* something as a means of avoidance—e.g., keeping quiet while others are talking) be termed active avoidance learning."[36]

Punishment, then, is what one person experiences from another as a consequence of engaging in inappropriate behavior. Negative reinforcement is the label given to the phenomenon that happens when, as a consequence of a change to appropriate behavior, an individual no longer experiences the punishment.

Some students may need more than verbal reinforcement. Teachers are usually quick to recognize the value of reward once they pay more attention to the learner than to themselves as a stimulus presenter. Many teachers stress praise, recognition of good work, and the like, on the assumption that these are rewarding—which, in fact, they are most of the time. On the other hand, there is evidence from the reinforcement methods to suggest that we may overestimate the power that traditional praise has for many students. Social reinforcers ("Good work, Bill" "Fine paper, Sally") are not always enough. The fact is that some students work best when there is a more tangible, materialistic payoff they can look forward to receiving. Green and Stacknik have suggested that we even go as far as paying certain students to go to school and learn:

> The challenge, then, so long as the schools accept and promote middle-class values, is to find appropriate ways of reinforcing middle-class behavior in disadvantaged children. One possibility is that we pay them in cold, hard cash for acquiring academic skills.[37]

O'Leary and Becker have used trinkets, candy, and money as reinforcers and found that these material rewards can gradually be spaced at longer intervals, given proportionately for greater accomplishments, and eventually replaced by social reinforcers such as praise from the teacher.

There is other research to support this idea. For example, Benowitz and Busse[38] reviewed numerous laboratory studies and found that reinforcements involving small trinkets, toys, and other attractive items desired by children led to greater learning than was produced by verbal reinforcements.

Intermittent reinforcement works best. We might also note that it is not necessary to reinforce every satisfactory response or correct answer in order to get positive results. Skinner,[39] for example, has demonstrated rather conclusively that whether it is pigeons or people, both seem to work harder if they are reinforced only intermittently. If, let's say, you were praised for having made a fine contribution every time you opened your mouth in class, you very likely would grow insensitive or at least indifferent to subsequent compliments because they were too easily won and too indiscriminately given. Praise from a teacher usually means more and has greater impact if it is not too easily won and not given every time more or less indiscriminately.

> ### TO EXPERIMENT WITH
>
> You can do a little research yourself to see how this works. For the next several days make it a point to praise practically everything that several of your friends do. Let nothing pass. And then at some appropriate point, ask them how they feel about all the positive reinforcement they've been getting from you. Were they comfortable? Uncomfortable? Why?

In summary, the use of reinforcement methods to encourage learning is one which stresses the importance of both the quantity and quality of extrinsic rewards. It is a viewpoint that assumes that the primary motive power for learning lies outside the student. Learning occurs and teaching succeeds, according to reinforcement theory, when desired behavior has been adequately rewarded. Learning is retarded when undesirable behavior is reinforced. A teacher can control and manipulate learning by providing reinforcement (usually approval or praise) when the student's behavior is consistent with the objectives the teacher is seeking to accomplish. On the other hand, sometimes a teacher may undermine his or her own efforts by inadvertently reinforcing (through giving attention, sympathy, or whatever) when a student engages in behavior contrary to the teacher's goals. As you may sense, reinforcement methods to learning makes the teacher a central figure in the classroom. A high school chemistry teacher, himself a rather devout advocate of reinforcement principles in teaching and learning, answered me this way when asked why he thought reinforcement theory was a good or helpful frame of reference from which teachers could operate:

> Well, for one thing reinforcement principles are specific. What I mean by that is that I can concentrate more fully on what a student *does*. This, I think, puts the emphasis where it should be, namely, on academic performance and ways to maximize that performance. In addition, adhering to reinforcement principles means that I must be very specific about what my objectives are for my students. If I am clear at the very beginning about what I want them to learn, then I can be more certain about what to reward in my student's behavior that will increase the likelihood of them learning what I want them to learn.

455

This very likely comes close to capturing the basic spirit behind why some teachers value and identify with the reinforcement methods in learning. It is precise, exact, and, more importantly, research done with both animals and humans strongly suggests that positive reinforcement works. Let's turn now to the other side of the coin.

Criticisms of Reinforcement Methods

A major criticism leveled at reinforcement methods is that it gives the teacher an enormous amount of power and control over both the student and the student's curriculum. The teacher establishes the objectives, determines which student behaviors to reinforce, and then evaluates students to see how well they have met these predetermined objectives. While there are those who say that this is exactly the way teaching and learning should be, there are others who fear that reinforcement strategies encourage students into a kind of blind obedience, an obedience that is conditional on the presence of the authority of the teacher.

Extrinsic learning is overemphasized. Maslow has been as straightforward as anyone in pointing to the dangers of reinforcement methods. As he has expressed it:

> [Reinforcement methods encourage] extrinsic learning, i.e., learning of one outside, learning of the impersonal, of arbitrary associations, of arbitrary conditioning . . . of arbitrary meanings and responses. In this kind of learning, most often it is not the person himself who decides, but rather a teacher . . . who says, "I will use a buzzer," "I will use a bell," "I will use a red light," and most important, "I will reinforce this but not that." In this sense the learning is extrinsic to the learner, extrinsic to the personality, and is extrinsic also in the sense of *collecting* associations, conditionings, habits or modes of action. It is as if they were *possessions* which the learner accumulates in the same way that he accumulates keys or coins and puts them in his pocket. They have little or nothing to do with the actualization or growth of the peculiar, idiosyncratic kind of person he is.[40]

The teacher exerts too much control. Any system that proposes to induce learning and control behavior through the subtle use of reinforcement principles has strong implications for what a teacher does in a classroom and how he or she teaches. A criticism shared by many psychologists and educators has to do with the teacher being too central a figure and of exerting too much control. The criticism leveled at the reinforcement position about this is not entirely unwarranted. Consider, for example, the following passage taken from Skinner's novel, *Walden Two*, which is about a fictional utopia wherein the basic ideas of reinforcement theory are operationalized with a system which Skinner calls "behavioral engineering." The person talking here is the book's hero, Frazier:

> Now that we know how positive reinforcement works . . . we can achieve a sort of control under which the controlled, though they are following a code much more scrupulously than was the case under the old system, nevertheless feel free. By careful cultural design, we control not the final behavior, but the inclination to behave—the motives, the desires, the wishes. The curious thing is that the question of freedom never arises.[41]

As you can see, a basic theme within reinforcement theory is the idea of control, which is the point with which most people take issue. The battle rages on, for example, in Skinner's recent and very controversial book, *Beyond Freedom and Dignity*,[42] which is really a nonfiction version of *Walden Two*. In this, he offers the passionless hypothesis that each man and woman is a unique collection of behaviors determined by environment; that, and nothing more. Through evolution the environment selected the behaviors that survive in our genes, and environmental conditioning shapes each of us in this life. Skinner maintains that individual freedom is an illusion because we are all controlled by our environment and suggests, further, that man would do well to surrender the last vestiges of freedom and dignity that are regarded as indispensable to a meaningful existence. Richard Rubenstein, professor of religion at the Florida State University, has observed that "in spite of Skinner's assurances to the contrary, his utopia projection is less likely to be a blueprint for the Golden Age than for the theory and practice of Hell."[43]

TO THINK ABOUT

How do you feel about Skinner's position? Is freedom an illusion? Are we controlled by the environment? Jot down the two or three ideas that best represent your views about these questions.

_____

_____

_____

Reinforcement methods produce different effects on different students. Another criticism of the reinforcement approach is that neither positive nor negative reinforcement have the same effects on all students. To put it another way, different kinds of reinforcement have different effects on different students. For instances one investigator found that some students showed greater gains in learning when they were praised, others learned better when criticized, and still others learned better when given only neutral feedback.[44] Years ago another researcher found that, although positive reinforcement generally spurred the greatest improvement, bright students tended to perform better when criticized.[45] Hans van de Riet[46] discovered that praise resulted in faster learning among a group of normal achievers in grades five, six, and seven, but was followed by slower learning among a group of very low achievers from the same grades.

Brookshire's[47] interesting discussions about learning pointed out some other complications associated with the application of reinforcement principles to human learning. For example, in a task in which an animal or a human is confronted with a problem involving two levers or two buttons to press, the experimenter may arrange conditions so that pressing the right-hand lever is reinforced at random 70 percent of the time, while the left-hand is rewarded at random only 30 percent of the time. The reinforcement could be food or a toy in the case of a child or money in the case of an adult. Under these circumstances, the rational approach that would deliver the maximum number of reinforcements would be to press the right-hand lever, which is exactly what animals other than man do. When a human is faced with such a problem, he'll usually settle into pushing the right-hand lever 70 percent of the time and the left-hand 30 percent of the time, even though he gets fewer reinforcements than he would have received if he had stayed with the right-hand lever. Brookshire points out that man's behavior is different because man persists in the belief that the problem is solvable and that, if he can only find out the right system, then he could get a reinforcement every time he pushed the lever. ˙Other animals do better than man because they do not try to outfox a random system. They simply make the correct response and, in the majority of cases, get rewarded, which is the basis of any successful reinforcement method.

The point is that the application of reinforcement principles is not so neat as it may sound. A human being is a vastly complex organism whose responses to his environment are more than a series of conditioned responses. In the first place, man has a will—also variously referred to as determination, stubbornness—he can say, "I *will not* do it your way, no matter what you do." He also has a brain that is capable of seeing beyond the response and into the act itself. He can say, "Yes, I can see you want me to do it that way, but I see other alternatives."

Reinforcement approaches are compact, neat, and orderly. As our high school chemistry teacher said a few pages back, "it puts the emphasis where it should be, namely, on academic performance and ways to maximize that performance." Programmed textbooks and teaching machines are very likely the epitome of reinforcement principles inasmuch as the whole idea behind them is the immediate feedback (reinforcement) for each response made.   H. T. Fitzgerald captured the essence of a good many criticisms to the various applications of reinforcement theory when he said:

> This approach assumes that our knowledge of the world is a fixed and orderly body of facts and conclusions. It implies a concept of reality wrapped up in separate little packages and tied with string, stacked neatly on the shelves of a vast warehouse. But the task of intelligence is more than that of a warehouse employee picking stock down the aisles, more than that of a novitiate reciting a long catechism of correct answers. Education is also inquiry, insight, emergence, the development of a critical faculty and an intuition of the web of interdependent hypotheses and inferences, the structure of abstractions about the seen and the unseen that comprise our understanding of the physical world. Learning is also exploring, conceptualizing, experimenting, interacting, valuing. Reality is also process, flow, a great running together, a barely intelligible, absurd, endless poem, a brilliant light at the entrance to our cave.[48]

Such criticisms and studies of reinforcement approaches to teaching and learning suggest that before teachers decide whether to use praise or reproof, they should ask themselves questions like, praise or reproof for what kind of student and under what circumstances? In order to answer questions of this sort, teachers must have some understanding of the emotional and cognitive backgrounds of the students they teach. Since students respond in such different ways to rewards and punishments, it would appear that a standard approach would serve to produce highly variable and unpredictable results.

Reinforcement and Discovery Methods Are Not Mutually Exclusive

As you've read the pros and cons of each of these ways to "emphasize" (enhance, encourage, facilitate) learning, you may still be left with the "Well, which should I use as a teacher?" feeling. I don't think we have to look at it as an either/or choice. Both have merits and strengths, and we can use the best that both have to offer.

Discovering something new about one's world or about oneself by oneself can be an exciting adventure. Indeed, finding out for oneself can be among those happy events that enables any person, at any age, to feel more competent, more actualized, and more fully functioning. I remember an incident involving a fourth-grade class in which the teacher told her students to try to figure out why multiplying was a quick way of adding. As she said, "Take what you know about adding and multiplying and try to discover it for yourself." About fifteen minutes later a little girl jumped from her seat and said, "I've got it, I've got—now I know why!"

459

The teacher was not a passive figure to this girl's discovery, but she made an active effort to praise and reinforce her for a job well done. Both the teacher's face and words said, "Good work, I'm so pleased." It made the teacher feel good, and it surely helped make a little seven-year-old girl feel warm all over.

Discovery and reinforcement methods are by no means mutually exclusive. They can work side by side in the same classroom and be used by the same teacher. Discovery methods stress learning by doing, intuitive thinking, and cognitive antonomy—goals that any reasonable teacher would value. Reinforcement methods focus our attention on the need for and importance of reinforcement, praise ("positive strokes"), and the value of feedback from significant others, such as teachers.

TO DO

The way to really learn about these methods is to talk to teachers, watch them at work. If possible, it would be a really worthwhile experience for you to actually get into a classroom to see learning go on and to observe how different teachers encourage it. Ask teachers about the methods they use, why they use the ones they do. Good teachers are able to encourage different kinds of learning for different kinds of students. Will you?

There are different ways to emphasize learning because there are different styles of learning. Let's turn our attention to this.

DIFFERENT STYLES OF LEARNING

In any given classroom, it is not very likely that any two students learn the same things in the same way at the same pace. We are finally beginning to realize that in order to assist each pupil and capitalize on his natural inclination to understand we must first be able to not only diagnose his style of learning but accept it. John Holt, a champion for students' classroom rights in recent years, puts it this way:

> Children have a style of learning that fits their condition, and which they use naturally and well until we train them out of it. We like to say that we send children to school to teach them to think. What we do, all too often, is to teach them to think badly, to give up a natural and powerful way of thinking, in favor of a method that does not work well for them and that we rarely use ourselves.[49]

Individual differences in learning are apparent even among pre-schoolers. Consider the variety of intellectual and motor activities that are apparent among four year olds.

Judy still needs to smear with her hands and makes endless finger paintings. Joe, Bob, and Ed strengthen large muscles by working with large hollow blocks, but they also learn social and intellectual skills as they pool ideas to construct their houses and garages. Sally is dainty, quiet, and sedentary, preferring to activate her tiny fingers through taking puzzles apart and putting them together again. Keith takes a moment to quickly thumb the pages of a book, but he drops it readily when Jim invites him to play on the indoor climber.[50]

Three Learning Styles: Visual, Aural, Physical (Riessman)

The point is that each student, like each of us, has a distinct style of learning, as individual as his personality. Riessman,[51] for example, has suggested that these styles may be categorized principally as *visual* (reading), *aural* (listening), or *physical* (actively doing things), although it is certainly possible that any one person may use more than one depending on the circumstances. Some persons may find that working on an assignment is much more tolerable while, say, pacing the floor than sitting perfectly still at a desk. Their style may be more physical. To take myself as an example, I find that I learn best and am able to absorb more when I can work and study for extended periods confined to my desk. Riessman has correctly observed that:

> Each classroom is likely to include students whose styles of learning vary widely. Although the teacher cannot cater completely to each student's particular style, he can attempt to utilize the strengths and reduce or modify the weaknesses of those in his classes.
>
> An individual's basic style of learning is probably laid down early in life and is not subject to fundamental change. For example, a pupil who likes to learn by listening and speaking (aural style) is unlikely to change completely and become an outstanding reader. I am not suggesting that such a pupil will not learn to read and write fluently but rather that his best, most permanent learning is likely to continue to come from listening and speaking.
>
> Since the student is the person most vitally concerned, the first step is to help him discover his particular style of learning and recognize its strengths and limitations.[52]

Reasons for Identifying a Student's Style Early

In the interests of effective motivation, it is important to identify each student's learning style as quickly as possible. If, for example, some students seem to learn best by reading, you may want not only to suggest books to them, but also to call on them more often in class to encourage them to experience more physical or verbal learning encounters. (Some students even *hope* to be called on because they lack the confidence to raise their hands.) On the other hand, you may find it beneficial to encourage the more physical and aural students to read more. The point is: Once we identify and become aware of each student's particular style for learning, we can encourage his best use of that style and help him experience other modes of learning as well.

TO THINK ABOUT

What is your preferred style for learning? Are you actively involved in class? Or do you prefer listening and reading? How do you feel when an instructor calls on you? If you could change your learning style, in what ways would you change?

Four Characteristic Learning Patterns (Rosenberg)

When we talk about learning style, we're referring specifically to a person's characteristic pattern of behavior when confronted with a problem. After reviewing the work of many investigators who had studied learning, Rosenberg[53] found that most of them were more or less in agreement on the existence and description of four general learning patterns. Rosenberg was struck by the consistency of these four patterns and labeled them the "rigid-inhibited," the "undisciplined," the "acceptance-anxious," and the "creative." He is quick to point out that these four learning patterns do not necessarily represent an exhaustive list of all possible learning styles. What we're dealing with are general categories rather than with individuals. With this caution in mind, let us turn our attention now to a brief examination of the four categories discussed by Rosenberg to get a better understanding of how varied different learning patterns can be.

The rigid-inhibited pattern. Students with this style of learning do best when given very precise directions and rules to follow. They tend to be among those in class who are tense, nervous, and generally on edge about one thing or another. The rigid-inhibited student learns best in an authority relationship. That is, he does better when directed by the teacher. I have observed, for example, that students who seem to fall into this category are likely to be rather uncertain about their own decisions. If students are given an open-ended assignment as broad as writing a paper on any course-related topic that interests them, the rigid-inhibited ones are typically the first to ask questions like: "What kind of paper do you want me to write?" "How long should it be?" "Should I typewrite or can I handwrite?" "Can you give me an idea for a topic?" And so on. You can probably sense the anxiety in those questions, not to mention the need for structure and direction.

The undisciplined pattern. Students reflecting this pattern, particularly younger ones, are pretty much what the label indicates—undisciplined. Their behavioral characteristics include refusal to do what is asked; an inclination to throw tantrums; a tendency to be wildly destructive; to lie, steal, get into fights; and to speak to the teacher with disrespect. They frequently do not finish their work and have very low tolerance for frustration. Like the rigid-inhibited student, they do better when their work is structured and they know exactly what is expected of them. In addition, they usually function best when the teacher is firm. Lacking inner controls, they must rely more on the teacher for help in that area.

The acceptance-anxious pattern. The need for approval and acceptance dominates the acceptance-anxious learner. This is the type of student who is more concerned about what others think of his school performance than he is with the school work itself. Most of all, he is fearful of being judged negatively. Holt observed this phenomenon in his book, *How Children Fail:*

> When they get a problem, I can read their thoughts on their faces, I can almost hear them, "Am I going to get this right? Probably not; what'll happen to me when I get it wrong? Will the teacher get mad? Will the other kids laugh at me? Will my mother and father hear about it?"[54]

The acceptance-anxious student cannot easily incorporate the idea of being wrong, and he is inclined to worry excessively about whether or not he is pleasing others. This kind of student does best with teachers who are warm and accepting and feels his greatest tension and frustration with teachers who manipulate their classes through anxiety, distance, and fear.

Since dependency comes easily for acceptance-anxious students, it is important for teachers to emphasize the importance of self-evaluation over the evaluation of others. Rather than say, "I think you have done a fine job" it would be wise to, from time to time, say things like, "You have done a fine job, *don't you think?* or "You must really feel pleased with that effort." It is particularly important for this kind of student to feel free to make mistakes without fear of ridicule, derision, or embarrassment.

The creative pattern. A student with this pattern is typically confident, capable of objectively evaluating his performance, and inclined to think divergently. Anxiety, rather than immobilizing him, spurs him to even greater achievement. He enjoys competition, likes solving his own problems, and, particularly, he jumps at opportunities to use his imagination. This is the kind of student who very much likes the opportunity of doing the sort of open-ended paper described earlier in which students write on any topic that interests them.

Whereas students fitting the first three learning patterns we considered learn best by authority, the creative student learns best by exploring, testing the limits, searching, manipulating, and playing. This kind of learning is best done in an environment that encourages this kind of activity. E. P. Torrance, a psychologist noted for his work with creative students, has made the following observation about the need for a special kind of environment to encourage students with creative learning patterns:

> The cat and the creative child both need a responsive environment more than a stimulating one. Many teachers and parents ask, "What can we do to stimulate creativity?" It is not necessary to stimulate the creative child to think creatively, although it may be necessary to provide a stimulating environment for the child who prefers to learn by authority and the child whose creativity has been suppressed for a long time. With the creative child, adults need largely to avoid throwing off course the child's thinking processes, guiding him by providing a responsive environment. It is my belief that this approach will lead to the controlled kind of freedom that seems to be necessary for productive, creative behavior. In defending the possible consequences of this approach, I point to the fact that the dogs in our neighborhood are kept on leashes so that they will remain under control. No one would think of placing a leash on any of the cats in this same neighborhood.
>
> A responsive environment is something quite different from what is commonly termed a "permissive atmosphere" or a "laissez-faire" environment. A responsive environment requires the most alert and sensitive kind of guidance and direction. It involves absorbed listening, fighting off criticism and ridicule, stirring the unresponsive and deepening the superficial. It requires that each honest effort to learn meet with enough reward to ensure continued effort. The focus is on potential rather than on norms.[55]

While we might all agree that the creative style seems to hold the most promise as far as learning that is exciting, lively, and vivid, we have to remember that not all students are capable of learning this way. Some students do, in fact, learn best in a more rigid-inhibited way or in a more acceptance-anxious style. A teacher's job is not to force students to change, but to accept their strengths as they exist and to show them alternative ways so they can change if so inclined. The fact is: Different students *do* learn in different ways and we must guard against pushing one kind of learning to the exclusion of all others.

A case in point is the discovery method of learning. Its most fervent advocates sometimes forget that, because of differences in learning styles, some students can learn more effectively in other ways. As noted by Shulman:

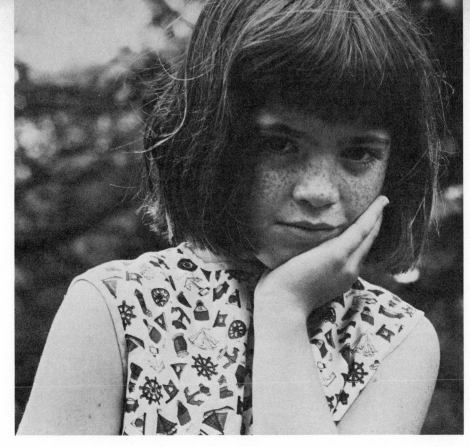

Some students are reflective thinkers and learn best when they can thought-fully weigh the problem confronting them.

All things being equal, there are some kinds of children who cannot tolerate the ambiguity of a discovery experience. . . . Individual differences in learning styles are major determinants of the kinds of approaches that work best with different children.[56]

Some Students Are Impulsive Thinkers—
Others Are Reflective

Just as there are differences among people in learning patterns and styles, so, too, are there differences in how people think and conceptualize. Jerome Kagan's[57,58] research, for instance, has shown that some students are characteristically impulsive thinkers while others are characteristically reflective. Impulsive students operate in a fast conceptual tempo in the sense of being among the first to respond to a question, even if their response is wrong. Reading difficulties, notes Kagan, are not infrequently the consequence of an impulsive conceptual tempo that moves so rapidly that the learner skips words, overlooks letters, and, as a result, fails to grasp either the meaning or sounds of words as quickly as other students.

Reflective students, on the other hand, are slower to respond, preferring to evaluate alternative answers and to give correct responses rather than quick, erroneous ones. Indeed, Kagan found that when tests of reading and inductive reasoning were administered in the first and second grades, impulsive students made more errors than reflective students. Interestingly, he also discovered that impulsiveness appears early in one's life, is reflected in a wide variety of situations, and is a relatively permanent and general trait.

Impulsivity could be psychologically harmful to a student if he is punished and made to feel badly by peers and teachers. If this happens over a long enough span of time, Kagan warns that:

> . . . he will become alienated from the educational process. I have seen too many teachers respond with harsh sarcasm to the child who offers incorrect answers quickly, but praise the child who offers correct answers quickly. This attitude communicates to the child the value that teacher places upon speed of response and handicaps the impulsive child with average ability.[59]

Some Students Conceptualize Analytically— Others Thematically

Kagan has also found that some students conceptualize analytically and others thematically. Whereas analytic students tend to pay greater attention to the smaller details of a problem, thematic students respond to the problem as a whole, to the big picture, as it were. It has also been found that these styles are just as permanent and generalized as impulsiveness and reflectivity.

Awareness of these various styles of conceptualization may assist us in comprehending the wide range of individual differences in the way students think about problems and conceptualize new material. This, in turn, may help us understand why different students respond in different ways to different approaches to teaching.

Implications for teachers. This does not mean that a teacher's job is a hopeless one. Recognizing, for example, that some students blurt out the first thing that comes to their minds, thereby frustrating the more reflective students who may still be in the process of formulating careful answers, a teacher may require that everyone just think about the question for two or three minutes before responding. Or, the teacher may suggest a kind of informal rotation plan for recitation. Understanding that some students flourish best within the global framework of the discovery approach but are frustrated by the step-by-step method of programmed instruction enables a teacher to design learning experiences that are best suited for each student.

Analytic students, for instance, may feel uncomfortable working for extended periods within a discovery framework, but they do nicely with a teaching machine or programmed textbook. Thematic students, on the other hand, maybe get easily bored with a programmed textbook or teaching machine but work enthusiastically to solve an open-ended problem that encourages divergent, "way-out" thinking.

TO THINK ABOUT

At least one way to understand how learning occurs, even *why* it occurs, is to know more about your own learning processes. In the past few pages we've talked about different styles and patterns of thinking along with a look at some different ways for thinking. All considered, how would you describe your *own* learning style and thinking patterns? Why do you suppose you approach learning the way you do?

_____

_____

_____

_____

So far we've looked at what might be called the psychology of learning. Let's turn now to its biochemistry—an exciting, fresh frontier in the field of learning.

THE BIOCHEMISTRY OF LEARNING

At first glance, a discussion about biochemistry and learning may seem out of place for a volume that claims to be people-oriented and humanistically inclined. I can only tell you that for me it does not seem out of place. Each one of us is a total person in the fullest sense of the word. We not only have, how shall I say, a "psychology," but a biochemistry, both of which contribute to our total functioning as human beings.

In a very real sense of the word, this portion of the chapter is futuristic insofar as it discusses where we are heading rather than where we are. As teachers, we have an obligation to not only help our students understand "what is" and "what was," but to help prepare them for "what might be." It is hard to know at this writing just how much of what we're to discuss "might be," but it is clear from the exciting findings emerging from brain research laboratories that a more complete grasp of the dynamics of learning will occur as we are able to integrate our understanding of the psychology of learning with our comprehension of its biochemistry.

We are a long way from such things as enzyme-assisted instruction, biochemical memory transmitters, synaptic transmission drugs, antibiotic memory repellers, and the like, but these are possibilities that are currently being researched. Although this may sound a bit more like science fiction than education, the advances made in the past fifteen years or so regarding the biochemical and physiological changes that occur in the brain during and following learning are beginning to open up what David Krech,[60] an eminent University of California psychologist, has referred to as *psychoneurobiochemeducation*. With these remarks as an introduction to the pages that follow, let's turn our attention now to what research is beginning to tell us about the biochemistry of learning.

Nature's Remarkable Computer: The Brain

The human brain has always staggered the imagination of man. A relatively small three and one-half pound mass of convoluted pinkish-gray tissue that you can hold in the palm of your hand, it contains over ten billion (10,000,000,000) cells, each of which may have 60,000 junction points, whose interplay still eludes our understanding. Some have estimated that the brain, in a lifetime, absorbs as many as one quadrillion — 1,000,000,000,000,000 — separate bits of information. Much of what the brain absorbs is irrelevant, meaningless trivia that is quickly forgotten. On the other hand, there is a good deal the brain absorbs that is not irrelevant trivia and that, in spite of our best efforts to remember, we still forget it.

How much and how long one remembers a particular experience or some new information varies from person to person. At least part of this variance may have a physiological base caused by biochemical factors. Let's look at the evidence.

Biochemical Factors Related to Long-term and Short-term Memory

Most normal adults can repeat a series of seven numbers — 5, 7, 9, 6, 3, 1, 4 — immediately after hearing them stated as a series. However, if these same normal adults were asked to repeat these same numbers twenty minutes later, most would not be able to do so. In the first instance, we are dealing with the immediate memory span and in the second, with long-term memory. These are primary behavioral observations that are basic to what is called the *two-stage memory storage process theory*.

The two-stage memory storage process theory. According to this view, a process that will be the mechanism of "short-term memory" begins within the nervous system immediately after a learning trial. This is a short-lived process and fades quickly away, but it is crucial in producing a second nervous system change, one that will be more permanent and serve as the basis for "long-term memory." However, in order for this to happen, the short-term memory must have an opportunity to be *consolidated* into a long-term memory. This second process involves the production of ribonucleic acids (RNA's) and the stimulation of higher enzymatic activities in the brain cells.

One approach to testing this theory has been to use white rats (rats, not only because they are readily available and easy to train, but also because, from a neurochemical point of view at least, they are not totally unlike man) in an experimental technique devised by Jarvik and Essman[61] known as the *step-down procedure*. This is based on the fact that it happens to be quite natural for a rat placed on a small platform several inches off the floor to hop down to the floor within seconds. And he will do this consistently day after day. One day, however, it steps to the floor only to be greeted by a painful shock when it does. When the rat is put back on the platform, even as long as twenty-four hours later, it *remains* on the platform. It has learned from the earlier experience that stepping onto the floor is painful, and it remembers it to the next day. He thus demonstrates that he has a long-term memory for that experience.

Now, if we take another rat and interfere with his short-term memory immediately after his first experience with the electric floor, his short-term memory will not have had a chance to become consolidated into long-term memory. The way Jarvik does this, by the way, is to pass a mild electric shock across the animal's brain, which is not strong enough to harm the brain cells, but intense enough to activate brain neurons and disrupt the short-term memory process. If this procedure follows closely enough after the animal's first experience with the foot shock, and the rat is tested a day later, it promptly steps down from the platform with no apparent expectation of shock.

When there is a longer interval between the foot shock and the brain shock, the rat *does* remember the foot shock, and it remains on the platform when tested the next day. What apparently happens is that the short-term electrochemical process has now had time to set up the long-term chemical memory process before it was disrupted. The length of interval necessary to interfere with long-term memory varies widely, depending upon the nature of the task and the disrupting agent.

Some long-known facts about the effects of accidental head injury in humans seem to parallel the findings of these animal experiments. For example, in head injuries severe enough to produce unconsciousness but not causing permanent damage to brain tissue, it is not uncommon for the patient to experience a loss of memory for those events immediately preceding the accident. He may wonder, "Where am I?" not only because he doesn't recognize where he is, but also because he can't remember how the injury happened in the first place. It is as if the events that had just occurred were still in short-term memory at the moment of the injury and the interruption of the neural activity triggered by the accident were sufficient to prevent the induction of long-term processes.

Brain Protein Synthesis Necessary for Long-term Memory

There is evidence to suggest that a synthesis of new brain proteins is necessary for the establishment of long-term memory processes. Agranoff[62] has done some interesting research that suggests that if the formation of new proteins in the brain is prevented, then—although the short-term electrochemical memory process is not interfered with—the long-term memory process could never complete its cycle.

Agranoff has done most of his work with goldfish. He placed the fish at one end of a small rectangular tank, which was divided into two halves by a barrier extending from the bottom to just below the surface of the water. When a light was turned on, the fish had to learn to swim from one end of the tank to the other within a twenty-second period or receive an electric shock. It doesn't take long for a goldfish to learn this shock-avoidance behavior and remember it for several days. Immediately before—and in other experiments, immediately after—training, the antibiotic puromycin or actinomycin-D was injected into the goldfish's brain. (These are both antibiotics that prevent the formation of new proteins or nuclear RNA in the brain's neurons.) What were the results of this? Interestingly, it was noted that the goldfish—even those injected prior to training—were not impaired in their ability to learn the necessary shock-avoidance behavior. However, when tested a day or so later, they showed no memory at all for what had been previously learned.

Protein Synthesis not Necessary for Short-term Memory

These findings mean that the *short-term* memory process is not dependent upon the formation of new proteins, but that the long-term process, which permits the animal to retain what he has learned, is dependent upon the production of new proteins. We might also note here that, as in the instance of Jarvik's rats, if the puromycin injection occurs at a longer interval after learning—in this case about one hour—it has no effect on long-term memory development.   That is, the long-term memory has presumably been completed and inhibition of protein synthesis can no longer affect memory.   Thus, we have our first chemical long-term memory preventative.   Krech[63] notes that somewhat similar findings are being reported by psychologists working in other laboratories with such animals as mice and rats, which have far more complex nervous systems than goldfish.

Biochemical Explanation for How We Remember

From the research that has been cited, it seems reasonable to assume that immediately following every experience a relatively short reverberatory process (continuous, self-exciting neural discharges in an unending circuit of connections) is started in the brain.   This is a process that permits us to remember events that occurred moments or minutes ago.   However, it very quickly dissipates and disappears, and so, too, does the related memory.   Under certain conditions this short-term reverberatory process triggers off a second and different series of events in the brain, which involves the production of new RNA's and new proteins.   It is these chemical changes that serve as the basis for our long-term memories.

Memory Facilitators

You will recall from our discussion in Chapter 9 (assuming your long-term memory processes are working) that there are many strategies a teacher can use to enhance the possibility of newly learned material being remembered for long periods.   One way of increasing the possibility is through the use of repetition, which, in schools at least, is known as "drill" or "practice" or "review."   Overlearning is still another activity that can be used to encourage long-term memory.   Apparently, when one repeats the same task over a long enough period of time, one presumably prolongs or reinforces the reverberatory process that induces permanent chemical changes in the brain.

James McGaugh[64] came up with the bright idea that perhaps the same results could be achieved chemically.   His major thesis was that a drug that increased the neural and chemical activity of the brain might either increase the intensity of the reverberatory process or facilitate the conversion of short-term memories into longer ones by making the process easier.   As it turned out, the idea was a sound one.   With the use of central nervous stimulants such as strychinne and metrazol he has been highly successful in raising the intellectual performance of the hundreds of mice used in his experiments.

In an experiment that teems with social implications and forebodings for the future, McGaugh tested two different strains of mice in their ability to maneuver through complicated six-unit mazes. One of the strains was, by heredity, adept at maze learning, while the other strain was particularly stupid at this task. Some of the mice from each group were injected with varying dosages of metrazol after each daily learning trial to see if this would have an effect on their ability to remember what they had learned on that trial. Other mice from each group were not given the metrazol. What were the results? Those animals that received the optimal dosage of metrazol were 40 percent better in remembering their daily lessons than were their untreated brothers. Another interesting finding was that, with metrazol treatment, the hereditarily dull mice were able to turn in better performances than their hereditarily superior but untreated cohorts. Here we have a chemical memory injection that serves to improve not only memory and learning, but is also able to reduce the intellectual differences between genetically unequal mice!

TO THINK ABOUT

We have pills to relieve headaches, calm nerves, and even some to assist with weight production. Someday we may have a pill to help us remember a passage we read only lightly or retain the essence of a book we skimmed through but once. How do you feel about the use of chemical memory facilitators? How do you suppose you'd feel if your entire class of students took a memory pill at the beginning of each school day? Would you support such an idea? Why? Or, why not?

Ribonucleic Acid (RNA) May Be the Physical Basis for Memory

RNA (ribonucleic acid) is receiving increasing attention as a substance related to memory and learning. Although DNA (deoxyribonucleic acid) is a very stable molecule whose structure provides the genetic code for the synthesis of proteins in the nerve cells, RNA is relatively unstable. That is, the RNA can be altered, as a result of experience, to form the biochemical storage unit for information about how new proteins are produced and how the brain responds to new stimulation.

The most influential evidence of how RNA influences memory comes from the work of the Swedish biochemist Holgar Hyden,[65] who demonstrated that stimulation of the brain tissues of rats and rabbits in learning increased the amount of RNA in the neurons, a change that does *not* take place if the stimulation is unrelated to learning.

Inasmuch as RNA influences the synthesis of proteins that determine

"OF COURSE, I WOULDN'T HAVE RECEIVED THOSE TWO D'S IF MY RIBONUCLEIC MEMORY FACILATOR PILLS HADN'T RUN OUT RIGHT BEFORE EXAMS."

Biochemical applications to learning have not come to this point yet, but they may be in the not too distant future.

the sensitivity of nerve cells to stimulation, and because experience seems to alter the structure of the RNA molecule itself, RNA has been proposed as the physical basis to memory, just as DNA is the biochemical basis of genetic information.[66]

McConnell's research.   McConnell's work with planaria — a fairly primitive type of flatworm — provides evidence for the relationship between RNA and memory.   What he did was to teach a group of flatworms, via simple conditioning procedures, to associate a bright light with an electric shock.   That is, whenever a light came on, the worms suffered a shock; after some 500 trials they simply responded to the light without the shock. Then the worms were cut in half, since in this species of planaria, each half eventually regenerates itself into a full worm.   After the regeneration, *both* *halves showed nearly perfect retention* of the original learned connection between the light and the shock! In McConnell's words:

> . . . when we chopped off the worm's head and it grew a new one, the functional blueprint for constructing the new brain had somehow been altered such that what was once a conditioned response was now "built in" as a prototypical innate response.[67]

In still another McConnell[68] study, remarkable for both its methods and results, he had untrained worms dine on the tissues of their trained counterparts. Astonishingly, the uneducated flatworms ended up with the *memories* of the late-lamented and digested "donor" worms. That is, the newly fed worms could, without any training, perform the response of their cannabalized friends!

A note of caution. A note of caution may be appropriate here. Some of McConnell's work on the chemical transfer of learning has been repeated by other researchers with rats and mice performing more complex tasks. Some psychologists report positive findings, while others have been unable to replicate them. Nonetheless, as a result of the work done so far, the number of steadfast disbelievers has reduced in number. Now the attitude seems to be more one of, "Well, maybe . . ."

Some people have looked upon the results of planaria research with skepticism because they fear that the neurochemical jump from flatworm to man is too great. This is certainly a reasonable skepticism. On the other hand, many of the structural elements are the same in both, and biochemical processes are biochemical processes wherever they occur. RNA is present in the neuronal cells of man as well as in the flatworm, suggesting that, to some extent at least, some of the same biochemical processes may occur in both species. As time and research move on, so, too, will progress up the evolutionary ladder. This is only the beginning.

Changing the Environment Can Change the Brain

So far, the research we've looked at has involved various techniques for physiologically or chemically interfering with cerebral activity in order to observe the effects of such intervention upon memory storage and subsequent learning. Four researchers, who include Dr. E. Bennett, M. Diamond, M. Rosenzweig, and Dr. Krech,[69–71] a biochemist, anatomist, and two psychologists, respectively, have approached the intriguing problem of relationships between brain chemistry and learning from a somewhat different slant. Rather than directly intervene in the natural chemical processes of the brain during learning, they chose, instead, to specifically manipulate the *environments* in which different groups of rats were raised. Their thinking was that *if the establishment of long-term memory processes involves increased RNA activity in the synthesis of proteins in brain nerve cells, then animals that have had more opportunities for learning and remembering should wind up with a different brain chemistry than those animals not similarly challenged by a stimulating environment.*

An enriched environment does make a difference. Consider one of their standard experiments. At weaning time, one rat from each of a dozen pairs of male twins is randomly chosen and housed in educationally and innovative environments, which include an attractive (to rats, at least) array of tunnels to explore, shelves to hop on, ladders to climb, levers to press, and so on. It is, you might say, an "educationally enriched" setting in which all twelve rats live in a well-lighted, bustling, busy laboratory. In addition, for thirty minutes each day, the rats are taken out of their cages and allowed to explore new surroundings. As they grow older, they are given a variety of new learning tasks to master and then rewarded for their efforts with bits of sugar. These happy circumstances are continued for eighty days.

Meanwhile, each of their twelve less fortunate brothers lives out his time in an "educationally impoverished" environment, which consists of a small cage situated in a dimly lit, quiet room. He is rarely handled, never allowed to explore outside his cage, or to interact with other rats. Both groups of rats, however, have free access to the same standard food and can eat whenever moved to do so.

When the rats are 105 days old, both groups are sacrificed, their brains dissected out and various chemical and histological analyses performed.

Experience changes the brain. Research done over the years along the lines of that described above has shown that differential living environments do, indeed, influence the composition and chemistry of the brain. Rosenzweig's[72] summary of the research, for example, reports that, of the total number of 130 pairs of rats studied, 115 pairs of rats exposed to the enriched environment showed superiority of cortical brain weight as contrasted to only 15 pairs from the impoverished environment. Physiologists have generally assumed the brain to be relatively stable in weight, but it was apparent that brain weights were being significantly altered, presumably by manipulating environmental conditions. For instance, the *animals that had had the enriched environments showed brain weights 4 to 6 percent higher than those coming from the more restricted environments.*

The "kind" of experience makes a difference. Not only did the cortex vary in weight as a consequence of differential experience, but it was also noted that parts of the cortex could be modified in differing degrees according to the *kind* of environmental experience. When the experimenters raised the rats in the dark and offered very little other stimulation, there was a measurable weight deficit in that portion of the cerebral cortex that handles visual perception. On the other hand, if the environment was dark but complex, rats raised in them developed heavier somesthetic cortical regions, which function to serve kinesthesis and touch. In general, it appears that greater exercise of functions controlled by specific areas of the cerebral cortex will lead to an enlargement of the tissue of those areas.

All in all, the evidence indicates that raising the young rat in an educationally and experientially restricted environment is likely to produce an animal with a relatively deteriorated brain. It seems clear that a lack of adequate educationally and psychologically enhancing experiences for the young animal—no matter how sufficient the food supply or how good his heritage—results in palpable, measurable, growth-impaired changes in the brain's chemistry and anatomy.

Krech has suggested that "for each species there exists a set of species-specific experiences which are maximally enriching and which are maximally efficient in developing the brain." He goes on to observe that it may well be in the language arts that we find a sort of species-specific experience necessary for humans inasmuch as verbal-written language is probably the clearest instance of behavior to human beings. He adds, "if we ever achieve an understanding of language development, and if we learn how to push the *human* brain with this *human* experience, then will we indeed be on our way."[73]

Implications for Teachers

The role of biochemical factors in learning is beginning to open new vistas to our understanding of how learning occurs and the internal changes that may result when it does. The role of the teacher and the school is not at all diminished by advances in this arena of learning. In fact, Krech's work in the area of relationships between environmental stimulation and brain chemistry has led him to the following conclusion:

> . . . —as we have just seen—if the chemical and anatomical status of the individual's brain is determined by his educational experience, then the effectiveness of the biochemist's "get smart pill" will depend upon how the educator has prepared the brain in the first instance. Indeed, a review of all the data indicates that manipulating the educational and psychological environment is a more effective way of inducing long-lasting brain changes than direct administration of drugs. Educators probably change brain structure and chemistry to a greater degree than any biochemist in the business.[74]

It is clear from research done so far that, just as biochemical factors are important inhibitors or facilitators of learning, so, too, is environment.

Both the biochemist and the teacher of the future will likely combine their skills and insights toward furthering the educational and intellectual development of students. Debbie needs a bit more of a memory stimulant; Greg would function better with a chemical attention-span stretcher; Dan maybe needs an anticholinesterase to slow down his racing mental processes; Valarie could use a little puromycin—she remembers too many details and gets confused.

All the brain stimulants and memory pills in the world are not going to help much unless a student first of all has the proper environment in which to learn. Good teachers can help provide that.

EPILOGUE

Learning is a complex phenomenon that usually leads to some kind of modification or change in behavior as a result of experience. The changes are not always in overt behavior but may be in attitudes, beliefs, or values. The major variables in a learning setting include: (1) the stimulus components (teacher, book, puzzle, problem, lighting, etc.), which in various ways influence a student's total behavior; (2) the organism components, which are comprised of the more personal and psychological considerations of the student; and (3) the response variables, which include the myriad ways a student can respond to both external conditions and internal feelings.

Although there are more than two approaches to learning, both discovery and reinforcement strategies stand out as major theoretical camps. In very broad terms, the discovery approach focuses more on what the student does and reinforcement approach, more on what the teacher does. From discovery methods we learn that it is best for a student to uncover, as it were, basic principles for himself. From reinforcement methods we learn how and when to accentuate the positive.

Just as there are different approaches to learning, there are also different styles. Some students, by virtue of their experience, background, personal inclination, and perhaps a bit of heredity, too, are rigid learners. Others are more accepting but anxious, while still others are creative divergent thinking souls who seem so caught up in their own thing that routine assignments bore them. People learn in different ways. Good teachers not only know that, but allow it.

Research related to biochemical changes within brain tissue during learning promises to offer new understandings of the physiological conditions necessary for maximum learning and memory. Although we are nowhere near developing a memory facilitating pill capable of turning an average Joe into a super intellect, we are nonetheless at the point of being able to identify drugs that can either inhibit or enhance learning, at least in lower animals such as flatworms and mice.   In addition, we are beginning to see that an enriched environment can produce objective, measurable changes in cortical tissue.   Chemistry alone will not solve our learning problems.   Better teachers and more stimulating environments will always be top priority items when ways to facilitate learning are considered.

One of the ways to facilitate learning is to put into action all that we know about motivation, an idea we turn to in Chapter 11.

Write your own chapter summary (major points, ideas, and concepts that had meaning for you).

_____

_____

_____

_____

_____

_____

_____

_____

_____

REFERENCES

1. Hilgard, E. R., and G. H. Bowers. *Theories of Learning*, 3rd ed. New York: Appleton-Century-Crofts, 1966, p. 5.

2. Levine, R., I. Chein, and G. Murphy. "The Relation of the Intensity of the Need to the Amount of Perceptual Distortion, a Preliminary Report." *Journal of Psychology* 13(1942): 283–293.

3. Postman, L., J. S. Bruner, and E. McGinnis. "Personal Values as Selective Factors in Perception." *Psychological Review* 55(1948):314–324.

4. Rosenthal, R. *Experimenter Effects in Behavioral Research.* New York: Appleton-Century-Crofts, 1966.

5. Bills, R. E., and B. R. McGehee. "The Effect of Attitude Toward Psychology in a Learning Experiment." *Journal of Personality* 23(1955):499–500.

6. Eysenck, H. J. *The IQ Argument.* New York: The Library Press, 1971.

7. Burton, W. H. "Basic Principles in a Good Teaching-Learning Situation," *Phi Delta Kappan* 39(March 1958):242–248.

8. Symonds, P. M. *What Education Has to Learn from Psychology,* 2nd ed. New York: Bureau of Publications, Teachers College, Columbia University, 1960.

9. Watson, G. "What Psychology Can We Be Sure About?" *Teachers College Record* 61(1960):253–257.

10. Ausubel, D. P. *Educational Psychology: A Cognitive View.* New York: Holt, Rinehart and Winston, 1968.

11. Shulman, L., and E. Keislar (eds.). *Learning By Discovery: A Critical Appraisal.* Chicago: Rand McNally, 1966.

12. Dewey, John. *Ethical Principles Underlying Education.* Chicago: University of Chicago Press, 1903, p. 27.

13. Bruner, J. S. *The Relevance of Education.* New York: Norton, 1973, pp. 82–97.

14. Bruner, J. S. *The Process of Education.* New York: Vintage Books, 1960, pp. 55–56.

15. Bruner, J. S. *The Process of Education.* Op. cit., pp. 23–26.

16. Bruner, J. S. *Toward a Theory of Instruction.* Cambridge, Mass.: Belknap Press of Harvard University Press, 1966, p. 74.

17. Auglin, J. M. (ed.). *J. S. Bruner: Beyond the Information Given.* New York: Norton, 1973, pp. 416–421.

18. Bruner, J. S. "Some Theorems on Instruction Illustrated with References to Mathematics." In *Theories of Learning and Instruction,* edited by E. R. Hilgard, 63rd Yearbook, National Society for the Study of Education, Part I. Chicago: University of Chicago Press, 1964, p. 315.

19. Bruner, J. S. *The Relevance of Education.* Op. cit., pp. 68–80.

20. Bruner, J. S. *Toward a Theory of Instruction.* Op. cit., 1966, p. 72.

21. Taba, Hilda. "Learning by Discovery: Psychological and Educational Rationale." *Elementary School Journal* 63(1963):308–316.

22. White, R. W. "Motivation Reconsidered: The Concept of Competence." *Psychological Review* 66(September 1959):297–333.

23. Suchman, J. R. "Inquiry Training in the Elementary School." *Science Teacher* 27(1960):42–47.

24. Suchman, J. R. "Inquiry Training: Building Skills to Autonomous Discovery," *Merrill-Palmer Quarterly* 7(1961):147–169.

25. Hermann, G. "Learning by Discovery: A Critical Review of the Studies." *The Journal of Experimental Education* 38(Fall 1969):57–72.

26. Friedlander, B. Z. "A Psychologist's Second Thoughts on Concepts, Curiosity, and Discovery in Teaching and Learning." *Harvard Educational Review* 35(Winter 1965):26.

27. Skinner, B. F. *The Technology of Teaching.* New York: Appleton-Century-Crofts, 1968, pp. 109–111.

28. Hamachek, D. E. "Motivation in Teaching and Learning." *What Research Says to the Teacher,* no. 34. Washington, D.C.: National Education Association, 1968, pp. 16–17.

29. Ausubel, D. P. *Educational Psychology: A Cognitive View.* Op. cit., 1968, p. 483.

30. Skinner, B. F. *The Behavior of Organisms.* New York: Appleton-Century-Crofts, 1938, p. 21.

31. O'Leary, K. D., and W. C. Becker. "Behavior Modification of an Adjustment Class: A Token Reinforcement Program." *Exceptional Children* 33(1967): 637–642.

32. Skinner, B. F. "Teaching Machines." *Science* 128(24 October 1958):975.

33. Howe, M. J. A. "Positive Reinforcement: A Humanizing Approach to Teacher Control in the Classroom." *The National Elementary School Principal* 46(April 1970):31–34.

34. Ward, M. H., and B. L. Becker. "Reinforcement Therapy in the Classroom." *Journal of Applied Behavior Analysis* 1(1968):323–328.

35. Travers, R. M. W. *Essentials of Learning,* 3rd ed. New York: Macmillan, 1972, p. 69.

36. Mowrer, O. H. *Learning Theory and Behavior.* New York: Wiley, 1960, p. 28.

37. Green, R. L., and T. J. Stacknik. "Money, Motivation, and Academic Achievement." *Phi Delta Kappan* 50(1968):228.

38. Benowitz, M. L., and T. V. Busse. "Material Incentives and the Learning of Spelling Words in a Typical School Situation." *Journal of Educational Psychology* 61(1970):24–26.

39. Skinner, B. F. "The Experimental Analysis of Behavior." *American Scientist* 45(1957):347–371.

40. Maslow, A. H. "Some Educational Implications of the Humanistic Psychologies." *Harvard Educational Review* 38(Fall 1968):p. 685.

41. Skinner, B. F. *Walden Two.* New York: Macmillan, 1948, p. 218.

42. Skinner, B. F. *Beyond Freedom and Dignity.* New York: Knopf, 1971.

43. Rubenstein, R. L. "Review of Beyond Freedom and Dignity." *Psychology Today* (September 1971):96.

44. Grace, G. L. "The Relation of Personality Characteristics and Response to Verbal Approval in a Learning Task." *Genetic Psychological Monographs* 37(1948):73–103.

45. Hurlock, E. B. "Evaluation of Certain Incentives Used in School Work." *Journal of Educational Psychology* 16(1925):145–159.

46. van de Reit, H. "Effects of Praise and Reproof on Paired-Associate Learning in Educationally Retarded Children." *Journal of Educational Psychology* 55(1964):139–143.

47. Brookshire, K. H. "Quantitative Differences in Learning Ability and Function." In *Learning Interactions,* edited by M. H. Marx. New York: Macmillan, 1970, pp. 299–347.

48. Fitzgerald, H. T. "Teaching Machines: A Demurer." *School Review* 70(Autumn 1962):251.

49. Holt, J. *How Children Learn.* New York: Pitman, 1967, p. 9.

50. Berson, M. P. "Individual Differences Among Preschool Children: Four-Year-Olds." *Individualizing Instruction,* Yearbook of the National Society for the Study of Education. Chicago: National Society for the Study of Education, 1962, p. 117.

51. Riessman, F. "Styles of Learning." *NEA Journal* (March 1966):15–17.

52. Riessman, F. "Styles of Learning." Op. cit., p. 16.

53. Rosenberg, M. G. *Diagnostic Teaching.* Seattle: Special Child Publications, 1968.

54. Holt, J. *How Children Fail.* New York: Pitman, 1964, p. 48.

55. Torrance, E. P. "Different Ways of Learning for Different Kinds of Children." In *Mental Health and Achievement,* edited by E. P. Torrance and R. D. Strom. New York: Wiley, 1965, pp. 261–262.

56. Shulman, L. S. "Psychological Controversies in the Teaching of Science and Mathematics." *The Science Teacher* 35(September 1968):34–38.

57. Kagan, J. *Developmental Studies of Reflection and Analysis.* Cambridge, Mass.: Harvard University Press, 1964.

58. Kagan, J. "Impulsive and Reflective Children: Significance of Conceptual Tempo." In *Learning and the Educational Process,* edited by J. D. Krumboltz. Chicago: Rand McNally, 1965, pp. 133–161.

59. Kagan, J. "Impulsive and Reflective Children." Op. cit., 1965, p. 159.

60. Krech, D. "Psychoneurochemeducation." *Phi Delta Kappan* (March 1969): 370–375.

61. Jarvik, M. E., and W. B. Essman. "A Simple One Trial Learning Situation for Mice." *Psychological Report* 6(1960):290.

62. Agranoff, B. W., B. E. Davis, and J. J. Brink. "Memory Fixation in Goldfish." *Proceedings of the National Academy of Science, U.S.* 54(1965):788–793.

63. Krech, D. "The Chemistry of Learning." *Saturday Review* 20(January 1968):48–50, 68.

64. J. L. McGaugh, and Westbrook, W. H. "Drug Facilitation of Latent Learning." *Psychopharmacologia* 3(1964):440–446.

65. Hyden, H. "Biochemical Changes in Glial Cells and Nerve Cells at Varying Activity." In *Biochemistry of the Nervous System,* vol. III, edited by O. Hoffman-Ostenhoff, Proceedings of the Fourth International Congress of Biochemistry. London: Pergamon Press, 1959, pp. 64–89.

66. Ferguson, M. *The Brain Revolution.* New York: Taplinger Publishing Co., 1973, pp. 277–280.

67. McConnell, J. V. "A Tape Recorder Theory of Memory." *The Worm Runner's Digest* 7(1965):6.

68. McConnell, J. V. "Memory Transfer viz Cannibalism in Planaria." *Journal of Neuropsychiatry* 3(1962):1–42.

69. Krech, D., et al. "Enzyme Concentrations in the Brain and Adjustive Behavior Patterns." *Science* 120(1954):994–996.

70. Rosenzweig, M. R., D. Krech, and E. L. Bennett. "A Search for Relations Between Brain Chemistry and Behavior." *Psychological Bulletin* 57(1960):476–492.

71. Bennett, E. L., et al. "Chemical and Anatomical Plasticity of the Brain." *Science* 146(1964):610–619.

72. Rosenzweig, M. R. "Environmental Complexity, Cerebral Change, and Behavior." *American Psychologist* 21(1966):321–332.

73. Krech, D. "Psychoneurochemeducation." Op. cit., 1969, p. 374.

74. Krech, D. "Psychoneurochemeducation." Op. cit., 1969, p. 373.

REFERENCES OF RELATED INTEREST

Bandt, P. L., N. M. Meara, and L. D. Schmidt (eds.). *A Time to Learn: A Guide to Academic and Personal Effectiveness.* New York: Holt, Rinehart and Winston, 1974.

Bigge, M. L. *Learning Theories for Teachers.* New York: Harper & Row, 1964.

Corning, W. C., and M. Balaban (eds.). *The Mind: Biological Approaches to Its Functions.* New York, Wiley, 1968.

Craig, R. C. *The Psychology of Learning in the Classroom.* New York: Macmillan, 1966.

Davis, R. A. *Learning in the Schools.* Belmont, Calif.: Wadsworth, 1966.

Deutsch, J. A. "Neural Basis of Memory." *Psychology Today* (May 1968):56–61.

Ellis, H. C. *Fundamentals of Human Learning and Cognition.* Dubuque, Iowa: Brown, 1972.

Gagné, R. M. *Essentials of Learning for Instruction.* New York: Holt, Rinehart and Winston, 1974.

––––––. *The Conditions of Learning.* 2nd ed. New York: Holt, Rinehart and Winston, 1970.

Garry, R., and H. L. Kingsley. *The Nature and Conditions of Learning* 3rd ed. Englewood Cliffs, N. J.: Prentice-Hall, 1970.

Glock, M. L. (ed.). *Guiding Learning.* New York: Wiley, 1971.

Gnager, W. J., P. A. Chesebro, and J. J. Johnson (eds.). *Learning Environments.* New York: Holt, Rinehart and Winston, 1972.

Hilgard, E. R. "The Psychological Heuristics of Learning." *Processes of the National Academy of Science.* 63(1969):580–587.

––––––, and G. H. Bower. *Theories of Learning* 3rd ed. New York: Appleton-Century-Crofts, 1966.

Hill, W. F. *Learning: A Survey of Psychological Interpretations.* San Francisco: Chandler, 1963.

Ilg, F. L. and L. B. Ames. *School Readiness.* New York: Harper & Row, 1965.

Kimble, D. P. *The Organization of Recall.* New York: The New York Academy of Sciences, 1967.

_____. (ed.). *The Anatomy of Memory, vol. I.* Palo Alto, Calif.: Science and Behavior Books, Inc., 1965.

Klemm, W. R. *Science, the Brain, and Our Future.* New York: Pegasus, 1972.

Kumar, V. K. "The Structure of Human Memory and Some Educational Implications." *Review of Educational Research* 41(December 1971):379–418.

Maddox, H. *How to Study.* New York: Crest Books, 1963.

McGaugh, J. L. "Some Changing Concepts About Learning and Memory." *NEA Journal* (April 1968):8–9, 51–54.

Rogers, C. R. *Freedom to Learn.* Columbus, Ohio: Merrill, 1969.

Seagoe, M. V. *The Learning Process and School Practice.* Scranton, Pa.: Chandler, 1970.

Shulman, L. S., and Keislar, E. R. (eds.). *Learning by Discovery.* Chicago: Rand McNally, 1966.

Silberman, M. L., J. S. Allender, and J. M. Yanoff (eds.). *The Psychology of Open Teaching and Learning.* Boston: Little, Brown, 1972.

Sperry, L. *Learning Performance and Individual Differences.* Glenview, Ill.: Scott, Foresman, 1972.

Travers, R. M. *Essentials of Learning,* 3rd ed. New York: Macmillan, 1972.

ELEVEN

Motivational Processes
and Human Learning

CHAPTER OUTLINE

PROLOGUE

WHAT IS MOTIVATION?

    Relationship Between Motives and Motivation

    We Are Never Unmotivated

    Motivation Can Either Be Towards Something or Away from It

    Maslow's "Grumble" Theory

    Differences Between Extrinsic and Intrinsic Motivation

    Dangers to Overstressing Extrinsic Motivators

    A Blend of Extrinsic and Intrinsic Motivators Is Best

MOTIVATIONAL EFFECTS OF PRAISE AND CRITICISM

    Effects of Praise and Criticism Related to Personality Differences

    Why Introverts and Extroverts Respond Differently

    Praise Given Indiscriminately Is not Very Meaningful

How Praise and Criticism Are Given Makes a Difference

As a General Rule, Praise Is Best

MOTIVATIONAL CONSEQUENCES OF SUCCESS AND FAILURE

Success Enhances Learning—Failure Depresses It

Excessive Failure Can Lead to Unrealistic Levels of Aspiration

Risk-taking Behavior Is Related to Our Calculations of Success

Fear of Failure and Hope for Success Can Exist Simultaneously

Self-esteem Certainty As Related to Success and Failure

How Self-esteem Certainty Influences Motivation

Implications for Teachers

High self-esteem students need to be challenged

Offer a variety of ways to achieve success

Short-circuit the "I can't" cycle with ample praise over time

MOTIVATIONAL EFFECTS OF COMPETITION AND COOPERATION

What Research Says

Some advantages to cooperative efforts

A certain degree of competition may increase desire

Too much competition has adverse effects

A cooperative mood increases good feelings

Implications for Teachers

Examples of destructive competition in the classroom

Examples of constructive competition in the classroom

PROS AND CONS ABOUT CLASSROOM FREEDOM AS A MOTIVATOR

Summerhill School: An Example of Total Freedom

Summerhill: nay

Summerhill: yea

The Summerhill Experience as Former Students See It

What Can We Learn from Summerhill?

A Balance Between Too Much Freedom and Too Much Control

A Flaw in Classroom Freedom Overextended

A Flaw in Classroom Control Overdone

Implications for Teachers: Distinguish Between Authoritarian and
Authoritative Control

EPILOGUE

REFERENCES

REFERENCES OF RELATED INTEREST

IMPORTANT CHAPTER IDEAS

1. Motivation is related to what a person wants to do but is not necessarily related to ability.

2. Motivation can either be positive or negative; away from something or towards it.

3. Extrinsic motivation is outside the student; intrinsic motivation is inside.

4. As a general rule, praise is a more powerful motivator than either criticism or reproof on the work performance of students.

5. Praise that is universally and indiscriminately given, no matter what the effort, is not very meaningful.

6. Success experiences tend to enhance learning while failure experiences impair it.

7. The motivation for achievement of students with histories of academic failure tends to be both unpredictable and immature.

8. Whether or not a student "believes" a success or failure experience depends on how certain he is of his self-esteem.

9. Confident, high self-esteem, high need-achieving students not only want a higher level of intellectual and personal challenge, but they may *need* it as well.

10. Competitive conditions are not universally bad—some students do their best work under these circumstances.

11. Cooperative classrooms are usually associated with greater group cohesiveness and more pleasant feelings than competitive classrooms.

12. Those who advocate that there should be as much classroom freedom as possible for students say that learning occurs best when it is a function of *wanting* to learn, rather than *having* to.

13. The best way to encourage motivation and learning is to blend a student's choices and interests with a teacher's guidance, direction, and experience.

14. When a student assumes responsibility for his own choices, it encourages greater intrinsic motivation because he then has something inside himself (his choice) to live up to.

15. The ability to motivate students is not a gift given to a chosen few; it is the result of hard work and careful planning.

PROLOGUE

To consider the subject of motivation is, in the end, to ask ourselves the meaning of man, and how and why he does the things he does. Indeed, there probably isn't a single teacher who hasn't at one time or other asked, "How do you motivate students to work, to study, to learn?" However, when inquiring about motivation we sometimes fall into the trap of looking for a single technique, or gimmick, that will motivate. Although it might be nice if there was a single best technique, we had better admit at the outset that there is no one formula, or strategy, or set of devices that will motivate all students in the same way or in the same degree. Rather, we must understand that what turns some students on is the very thing that may turn others off; that what motivates Sam may discourage Robert; that what excites Barbra may bore Valerie. Furthermore, the same individual may be motivated by different factors at different times. If we can begin by agreeing that motivation to learn is a complex blend of different environments, attitudes, aspirations, and self-concepts, then we are a step closer to effectively using what research tells us about how to improve both our teaching and learning practices. This brings us to a logical question.

WHAT IS MOTIVATION?

One psychologist[1] has called motivation the "go" of personality, an apt description since the absence of motivation usually reduces most normal people to a state of listless boredom. Although motivation cannot be seen directly, it can be inferred from behavior, which, in relation to motivation, is ordinarily referred to as "ability." While our observation of another person's ability (or lack of it) denotes what an individual *can do* or *is able to do*, "motivation" (or lack of it) tends to summarize our observations as to what a person *wants to do*. As you know from personal experience, motivation and ability are not necessarily related. For example, a low grade on an exam may not be so much of a reflection of low ability as it is of low motiva-

488

Sometimes when students learn something new, they're motivated to share it with someone else. (Allyn and Bacon)

tion. Or, as another instance, a highly motivated student could compensate for his low ability in a particular subject through increased study, effort, and plain hard work and do very well as far as learning and measured achievement is concerned. All in all, what a person—whether in first grade or college—*wants to do* can be a powerful factor in helping him achieve his goals.

Relationship Between Motives and Motivation

Motives are related to motivation in the sense that they refer to the needs or desires that cause us to act and, hence, feel motivated, in the first place. Motives serve three important and overlapping functions that include: (1) energizing a person—i.e., getting him started, (2) *directing* a person—i.e., pointing him the right way, and (3) *helping him select* the behavior most appropriate to help him achieve his goals. The feeling of being motivated, then, is a psychological state of mind that is the consequence of a person activating his motives. The question of how motivation is expressed in behavior involves not only psychological factors, but ethical considerations as well. For example, one student, motivated by a need to do as well as possible in all his courses, puts in long, hard hours of diligent study, while another student with a similar motivation buys his term papers from the local "creative writing" outfit; one man motivated to earn extra money, works overtime, while another man with a similar motivation robs a gas station.

The point is that human motivation is a complex issue that involves not only what one wants to do but its appropriateness as well. In spite of the complexity of the motivation question, one fact remains certain.

We Are Never Unmotivated

If we view motivation from the point of view of the behaver himself, he is never unmotivated. That is to say, each of us, no matter who he is or what he does, is motivated by a continuous endeavor to maintain and enhance his personal feelings of self-esteem. We already talked about this in greater length in chapters 1 and 2, and you may recall that this same idea has been expressed, in different ways, by different psychologists and educators. For White,[2] motivation grows from a need to be competent; for Maslow,[3] it springs from a need for self-actualization; for Rogers,[4] motivation is derived from a need to become more fully functioning; and for Combs and Syngg,[5] it comes from a deep need for personal adequacy. It would not be inaccurate to say that the most basic human motivation starts with the need for *some satisfactory level of self-realization,* which can also be expressed as the need to do something for and with oneself; to be, in a word, somebody!

Motivation Can Either Be Towards Something or Away from It

Unfortunately, not all students find that they can feel personally adequate or realize their potential for growth and development in the elementary grades or in high school. If a student does fairly well in school—at least has some successes that matter to him—he is more likely to be motivated toward selecting school-related activities than a student who constantly experiences failure. Like anyone else, students—at any level—do not long stay motivated by things in which they experience more failure than success. Dropouts, for example, do not leave school because of either too many success experiences or too many opportunities for enhancing personal adequacy. I suppose all we have to do is closely examine the things we have "dropped out" of, such as a club, a job, a class, a friendship, an engagement, a marriage, or whatever, to get an idea of the reasons behind why we are sometimes motivated to move *away from,* rather than *toward* certain experiences.

TO THINK ABOUT

How would you describe the "feeling states" you associate with classes you really enjoy attending as opposed to those you would just as soon cut? Try to get close to the basic feelings you have when going to a class you like. Why do you like it? What does it do for you? How are you changed? Or, to put it differently, what motivates you to come to some classes and not others?

_____

_____

_____

Maslow's "Grumble" Theory

Maslow[6] has added an interesting note to why people are never unmotivated in what he called the *Grumble Theory,* which we mentioned briefly in Chapter 2. The essence of this theory is that we may function best when we're striving for something we lack, when we wish for something we do not have, and when we organize our energies in the service of striving toward the fulfillment of that wish. Thus, for some individuals, motivation may begin by grumbling about something they don't have or haven't attained and then striving to attain it or achieve it. In some respects, it is the student who gets an exam back that he had hoped (prayed, even) would be at least a C only to discover that he had achieved a B and then grumbles about it not being an A.

Motivation, then, is an ongoing process. We are motivated in different ways, at different times, and for different reasons. Sometimes those reasons are intrinsic and sometimes they are extrinsic, an idea to which we turn next.

Differences Between Extrinsic and Intrinsic Motivation

If a student works hard to win his parents' favor or gain the teachers' praise or earn a high grade, we can rightly conclude that his motivation is primarily extrinsic; that is, his reasons for work and study lie primarily *outside* of himself. If, on the other hand, a student studies because he enjoys the subject and desires to learn it irrespective of the praise he wins or grade he earns, this is an example of intrinsic motivation inasmuch as his reasons for learning reside primarily *inside* of himself. A simple test of whether a person is intrinsically or extrinsically motivated when he performs some task is the extent to which he feels independent or dependent on the need for someone's approval at the completion of the task. Extrinsically motivated effort relies more on another person's praise and approval.

491

Dangers to Overstressing Extrinsic Motivators

Extrinsic motivation is the model of education that most people have in the back of their minds and that is not very often made explicit. In this model the teacher is the assertive one who teaches a passive person, who gets shaped and molded, and who is given rewards of some sort, which he then accumulates in the same way he accumulates keys or coins and puts them in his pocket. It is likely that some 80 percent of "learning theory" is constructed primarily around the implicit power of extrinsic motivation. If carried to extremes, this kind of learning too often reflects the goals of the teacher and ignores the values and goals of the student himself. Indeed, one of the most frequent criticism students make of teachers who believe whole-heartedly in extrinsic motivation is that they offer too few opportunities for students to learn what they're really interested in.

A student who is intrinsically motivated is difficult to spot because even when he does do class-related work for its own sake and as an end in itself, he frequently winds up with some kind of payoff in the form of a grade or teacher approval or recognition by peers. Thus, the myth of "only extrinsically motivated students work" is perpetuated. This is not only an erroneous conclusion but one which could lead us down the path of overstressing extrinsic motivators and unwittingly discourage intrinsic motivation. There is, for example, research to indicate that external rewards or "payoffs" can affect one's intrinsic motivation. As an illustration of this, one psychologist has observed that:

> . . . money is frequently used as means of "buying" services which would probably not otherwise be rendered. Perhaps, then, the presence of money as an external reward suggests to [some persons] that they "should probably not render this activity without pay," that is, they should not be so intrinsically motivated to do the activity.
>
> This could lead [a person] to a process of cognitive reevaluation of the activity from one which is intrinsically motivated to one which is motivated by the anticipation of money.[7]

There seems little question that money is a powerful motivator, either as an end in itself or for what it can purchase. This is fine except for the fact that when a person receives money he could easily come to accept the money as the reason for his behavior. That is, when an intrinsically motivated student does something for money ("A dollar for every A," says Dad), his perception of the reason for doing it shifts from "it is intrinsically motivated" to "it is motivated by money." Since the student is then performing for money (and therefore has less intrinsic motivation), he is apt to stop performing or working once the money stops.

On the other hand, there is evidence to suggest that when verbal reinforcements are given as external rewards ("This is certainly a fine job," or

"I'm very pleased with this effort," or "That's excellent, keep up the good work"), these rewards apparently are not so easily distinguishable from the intrinsic feelings of satisfaction one may get from doing a certain task.[8,9]   If, let's say, you complete a difficult and demanding project in which you were deeply involved for one of your classes and your instructor says, "You have done a superb job with this—excellent work!", the chances are good that the instructor's positive external evaluation would blend nicely with your own intrinsic feelings of satisfaction.   When this occurs, the inclination to perform a similar activity in the absence of external rewards will be strengthened, which means that one's intrinsic motivation will be increased.   A recent study by Deci involving intrinsic motivation and extrinsic reinforcement supports this conclusion.   In Deci's words

> . . . one who is interested in developing and enhancing intrinsic motivation in children, employees, students, etc., should not concentrate on external-control systems such as monetary rewards, which are linked directly to performance, but, rather, he should concentrate on structuring situations that are intrinsically interesting and then be interpersonally supportive and rewarding to the persons in the situation.   While large payments can lead to increased performance [they can also make] people dependent on the money, thereby decreasing intrinsic motivation.[10]

A Blend of Extrinsic and Intrinsic Motivators Is Best

There can be no mistaking the fact that extrinsic motivators do work, which is why many students suddenly increase the tempo of their study activities when parents promise them a given amount of money for each high grade they earn.   It is also why some of these same students cease to put as much effort into their studies when parents find (1) they can no longer afford to pay a dollar for every A, or (2) that they have grown weary (as most do) of having to bribe their children to do well in school.   I suppose we might all agree that intrinsic motivation is really the best kind inasmuch as it is born from within, is fed internally, and is sustained by the results of its own best efforts.   It is a nice feeling to be able to say, "I am pleased with what I have done" and to know that this feeling is reward enough for one's toil.   However ideal intrinsic motivation may be, a fact of life we acknowledge is that it varies from student to student and from subject to subject.   Our task is not to eliminate extrinsic motivators but to use them wisely and to be aware of their differing impacts on different students.   A teacher's use of praise and blame or approval and disapproval are common examples of extrinsic motivators that can have different effects on different students, a topic to which we now turn.

Students are motivated by many different kinds of activities.

TO RESEARCH

An interesting and worthwhile investigation you could do yourself (maybe as a term or semester project?) would be to locate ten students who are experiencing a kind of free, "do your own thing in your own way class" and ten who are experiencing a class where the instructor assigns papers, gives tests, and stresses grades, and then conduct in-depth interviews about how each person feels about the experience. Does one group work harder than the other? Enjoy class more? Less? How about anxiety levels between the two? What are the advantages of extrinsic and intrinsic motivation? Disadvantages?

MOTIVATIONAL EFFECTS OF PRAISE AND CRITICISM

We've all been the recipients of praise and criticism at one time or other. Sometimes we work harder when praised and other times we maximize our efforts when reproved or criticized in some way. How one responds when either praised or reproved depends on his own personality dynamics, the nature of the task at hand, and the person doing the praising or reproving.

As a general rule, praise is a more powerful motivator than either criticism or reproof on the work performance of students. For example, in a classic experiment to determine the relative effectiveness of praise and reproof, 100 fourth- and fifth-grade children were divided into 4 groups matched on the basis of intelligence and arithmetic skill.[11] A 15-minute daily practice period in addition problems, which included tests, was given to the groups for five consecutive days. Members of group one were regularly praised for the quality of their work, called by name, and en-

494

couraged to improve. Those in group two were scolded for their errors, carelessness, and failure to improve. The third group was literally ignored; that is, these students heard some of their classmates praised and others reproved, but they themselves were apparently unnoticed. A fourth group, which acted as a control, was placed in a separate room and given no special motivation.

At first both the rewarded and punished groups were stimulated to greater effort than either the ignored or control groups. But, then after the second day the reproved group declined markedly in achievement, while the praised group steadily and consistently continued to improve. The reproved group, however, made greater gains than the ignored group throughout the experiment. Apparently, being scolded or even admonished are signs of recognition and are better than no recognition at all! Although the experiment did not address itself to this point, it would not be unfair to speculate that some members of the reproved groups were probably motivated to avoid further teacher harrassment, which, we must admit, is hardly the healthiest kind of incentive.

Effects of Praise and Criticism Related to Personality Differences

However, the effects of praise and criticism on motivation and learning are not so simple and clear-cut as Hurlock's study may indicate. Other research has indicated that the effects of praise or blame are related to personality differences as well. For instance, studies by Forlano and Axelrod[12] and Thompson and Hunnicutt[13] both found that extroverted and introverted students respond differently to approval or disapproval. The major conclusions growing out of these studies indicate that:

1. When introverts and extroverts are grouped together (as is the case in most classrooms), either praise or blame is more effective in increasing the work output of fifth-grade pupils than no external incentives.
2. If repeated often enough, praise increases the work output of introverts until it is significantly higher than that of introverts who are blamed or extroverts who are praised.
3. If repeated often enough, blame increases the work output of extroverts until it is significantly higher than that of extroverts who are praised or introverts who are blamed.

Why Introverts and Extroverts Respond Differently

As you can see, the general trend of evidence suggests that introverts achieve a higher level of performance when praised, and extroverts responded best when reproved or criticized. The question is, "Why?" One reason may have to do with the different relationship styles of introverts and extroverts. That is, since the more introverted student relates best to his own inner world of feelings and reflections, praise may be the very thing that helps him to relax his inhibitions and to encourage the necessary confidence to engage more open risk-taking behavior. An extroverted student, on the other hand, relates best to the outer world of people and events and apparently is inclined to work harder when he feels that his relationship with the outside world is threatened by his subpar performance. When criticized or reproved the extrovert student might think, "Wow, I'd better get busy and win back this approval." A criticized introvert may think, "Well, I blew it again. I guess the thing to do is for me to be quiet and take as few risks as possible." Introverted students are not the only ones who are likely to feel this way. Other research shows that anxious and dependent students have similar feelings of insecurity and, although they may or may not be introverted, they also respond favorably to the use of a teacher's praise.[14]

TO THINK ABOUT

Do you respond best to praise or criticism from an instructor? Under which conditions have you found yourself really digging in? What is it about you as you know yourself that makes you want to either work harder or give up when praised or criticized? What implications can you see here for your own role as a teacher?

_____

_____

_____

Praise Given Indiscriminately Is not Very Meaningful

The message is clear. In order to use praise and criticism wisely, we must take careful note of its effects on individual students. Some, you will find, can be commended and praised for relatively minor accomplishments because of either their limited ability or shy, withdrawn nature, while others can be motivated — spurred on, as it were — only by praise for genuinely noteworthy accomplishments related to their high ability. We might also note that just because the more extroverted, secure students rise to the challenge of criticism, this does not mean that praise and approval of their efforts is ineffective. It is just that secure, confident, and highly motivated students are more apt to reject praise that is designed to make them "feel good" rather than having as its end the simple acknowledgement of a job well done. During a group discussion I had recently with high school students about the sorts of things that motivate them in school, one student, who had a history of above-average work, expressed his thoughts about teacher praise in the following manner:

> I think I like hearing a teacher say good things about my work as well as anybody, but the thing that really turns me off is when a teacher is constantly being goody-goody with students. I mean I'm talking about teachers who are always approving you or saying nice things no matter what you do. I know when my work is good. What I need to know is when it's not and how to improve it. I have the feeling that some teachers are too afraid of being disliked if they were more critical and so that's why they're always approving everything.

This was a wise young man. He intuitively knew that praise universally given, no matter what the effort, was impotent and meaningless. In order for praise or approval to mean something to its recipient, he's first of all got to have the feeling that (1) he really deserves it, and (2) there is the possibility of not getting it to begin with.

How Praise and Criticism Are Given Make a Difference

Research also shows that praise or criticism given by a teacher with one type of personality does not have the same effect as praise or criticism given by another.[15] That is, a distinction should be made between constructive criticism given by a friendly teacher in a spirit of helpfulness ("That's an interesting idea, John, and one that is different. I wonder if you can think of some practical ways to fit it into the framework of our discussion?") and the vicious abuse—under the guise of constructive criticism—sometimes hurled at students by frustrated teachers who satisfy neurotic cravings for power and recognition in their role as superjudge ("John, you may think your idea is a good one, but I frankly don't see how it is relevant to our concerns"). Constructive criticism is essential for enhancing student growth, but little good is likely to grow from a situation in which the student, because of insecurity or the way criticism is given or the person giving the criticism, feels compelled to close himself off from attack in order to protect his self-image.

Not only does the ratio, kind, and quality of praise and criticism affect a student's academic performance, but there is evidence to suggest that it can influence his overall adjustment as well. For example, de Groat and Thompson[16] found that male and female students who received a combination of high amount of approval with only small or moderate degrees of disapproval exhibited better self-adjustment than groups who received large amounts of disapproval and only little or moderate approval. It was concluded that a student's evaluation of himself and his self-confidence were significantly influenced by the degree of teacher approval or disapproval he received.

Along this line I am reminded of an experience in a class I had while a freshman in college. Although it may not seem a particularly significant event, at the time it happened it was to me and I remember it to this day. I was not altogether confident of either myself or my abilities in this class and the instructor was a man I admired immensely. He was a sensitive yet a no-nonsense type person who praised and criticized, approved and disapproved as the situation and case warranted it. I was not one of the more vocal students in class, but I did contribute from time to time, although, I must admit, not fearlessly. I remember one class period in particular when after having made a contribution to the discussion, the instructor commented on the appropriateness of my comment and patted my shoulder approvingly as he said it. I felt enormously good about that incident and I distinctly remember feeling generally more confident about contributing from that point on. Praise or approval can be communicated in many ways and not all of them are verbal. The instructor's hand briefly on my shoulder is an example of how nonverbal approval can underscore and strengthen what words alone may not be able to accomplish. There are other ways — a nod, a smile, or merely stopping long enough to take a good look at what is being done may express the sentiment. Unfortunately, there is evidence to suggest that the use of nonverbal techniques begins to decline by the third grade or so,[17] which is in the face of other evidence that stresses that nonverbal messages can be a powerful means for positively influencing behavior.[18-20] If this decline is general, it may mean that teachers may be overlooking an important "other" way for communicating with students and enhancing motivation. A smile or a frown can be every bit as communicative as verbal discourse, and we would do well to pay more attention to how we convey our approval and disapproval through messages of this sort.

TO EXPERIMENT WITH

Are nonverbal cues really that important? Find out for yourself. For one whole day do nothing but smile at people, whether you're talking to them or not. The next day frown at people. Try to keep track of three things: (1) how you feel under each condition, (2) how others appear to feel in response to you, and (3) how you feel in response to other's responses. It could be quite a learning experience.

As a General Rule, Praise Is Best

In sum, it appears that the successful use of praise and criticism depends both upon the student and his needs and prior experiences and on the teacher who uses praise and criticism. Being ignored is less motivating than either praise or criticism; and, as a general statement, praise that is not indiscriminately given helps most students feel more personally adequate and confident. Indeed, recent research not only shows that more learning goes on under praise conditions than reproof conditions but that praise and reproof in one subject-matter area in the classroom may well transfer, in terms of effects on academic performance, to other classroom behavior that is entirely distinct and independent.[21] We should not be surprised if the student harshly criticized in math class does less than his best in English. Feelings are like that—they follow one around.

A fact of school life is that not all students are motivated *before* they learn. This does not mean that they cannot become motivated *while* they learn. The judicious and appropriate use of praise and criticism can facilitate the process of becoming motivated during learning as well as before it.

Two other important variables related to motivational processes are the experiences of success and failure, which, like praise and criticism, can affect different students in different ways. Let's turn our attention to why and how.

MOTIVATIONAL CONSEQUENCES OF SUCCESS AND FAILURE

If we were to ask a random sampling of 100 students why they were studying for that test tomorrow, we very likely would find that some would say, "I'm studying to get as high a grade as possible," while others would say, "I'm studying so I won't fail, that's why!" The first of these statements is success-oriented and the second is failure-oriented. The first represents an *approach* response because of the anticipation and preoccupation with being successful in reaching a goal, while the second represents an *avoidance* response because of the anticipation and preoccupation with the consequences of failure. The approach response reflects the effects of success experiences, and the avoidance tendency, the effects of failure experiences. There seems little question that failure and success experiences each leave their own particular mark on both the direction and intensity of subsequent motivation. A student may feel what we can call "achievement motivation," or if he's concerned about failure, he may feel "achievement anxiety." There are two different behavioral consequences growing out of these different basic motivational states and Figure 11–1 is designed to give you an overall view of the major distinctions between the two.

Success Enhances Learning—Failure Depresses It

Research has rather consistently demonstrated that success in mastering worthwhile concepts and skills leaves most students feeling more adequate,

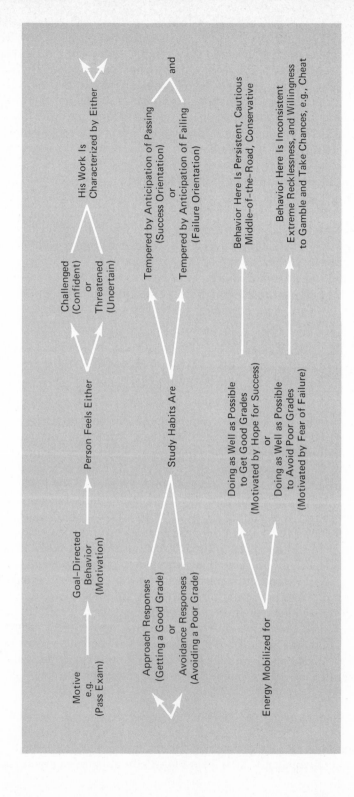

FIGURE 11–1. Differential Effects of Achievement Motivation and Achievement Anxiety on Behavior

confident, and self-enhanced. Frequent failure experiences, particularly during the early years (we'll talk about this more in the next chapter), can leave a student feeling anxious, defensively uninterested, and generally reluctant to establish realistic goals for himself. For example, Rhine,[22] working with college students, Lantz,[23] with nine year olds, and Steigman and Stevenson,[24] with four to five year olds, as their subjects, all compared the learning efficiency, and the latter two, the attitudes, of their subjects before and after specially contrived success and failure experiences. Each of these investigations verified the idea that success tends to enhance learning and, even to a greater degree, failure impairs it. It also depresses self-confidence and eagerness for further academic learning.

Excessive Failure Can Lead to Unrealistic Levels of Aspiration

Perhaps one of the most troublesome motivational consequences of excessive failure is that it produces students who are sometimes unwilling and sometimes unable to establish realistic levels of aspiration. Reasonably successful students, for instance, usually aspire to do better the next time around on learning tasks that are more or less within the same range of difficulty as ones they had been exposed to previously. As an illustration of this, Sears,[25] working with elementary school children, and Gruen,[26] with adolescents, both found that students who in the past had consistently experienced success — subjectively in their day-to-day school work and objectively in tests and school marks — continue aspiration or accomplishment levels just beyond their past achievement. Inasmuch as aspirations are continually reinforced by success, they become a self-perpetuating aspect of further motivation for achievement. However, when students are continually frustrated in their day-to-day school efforts and disappointed in their marks, they set aspiration levels that are either too high or too low. Consider it this way. People who have little money will sometimes engage in wild, risk-taking ventures to get more or become uncommonly conservative in order to reduce the risk of losing what they have. Students with histories of academic failure do somewhat the same thing. They set goals either so low that no hazard is involved or so high that success is impossible. Their motivation for achievement is both unpredictable and immature. If they set unrealistically high aspirations, they enjoy temporary, fantasied approval for their good intentions. If they set their goals unjustifiably low, they derive a certain naive satisfaction from overreaching them.

TO THINK ABOUT

In light of what has been discussed so far, would you say that, on the whole, you're a failure-oriented or success-oriented person? If you

view yourself as failure-oriented, what could teachers do to help you
change that?

_____

_____

_____

If you view yourself as success-oriented, how would you suggest that
teachers enhance that?

_____

_____

_____

Risk-taking Behavior Is Related to
Our Calculations of Success

Fear of failure and expectation of success are two aspects of school motivation that have distinctive roles in what is called risk-taking behavior.
Generally speaking, the risks we take are related to our perceptions of possible success. Atkinson,[27] for example, has shown that when a person's
success-orientation exceeds his failure-orientation, he is more likely to
choose tasks in which he has at least a fifty-fifty chance of being successful.
A failure-oriented person, or "avoidance-oriented," as Atkinson calls him,
tends to select learning tasks in which the probability of success is as far
away from the fifty-fifty range as possible, thus selecting tasks from either the
easy or difficult categories.

Recent research by Moulton[28] confirms the idea that persons high in fear
of failure tend to raise their level of aspiration following failure and lower it
after success. On the face of it, it would appear that individuals who are
motivated by a fear of failure take the greater risks, at least when they raise
their levels of aspiration. Not so. What actually happens is that they lower
the risks by increasing the possibilities of excusing their poor performance
due to the fact that what they chose to do tends to be exceptionally difficult.
If a failure-oriented student chooses a goal that is clearly over his head (a
tough course, a vocational possibility far beyond his grasp, etc.), he can
always say to himself, "The task was so hard or so difficult that anybody
might have failed." In doing this he is asserting that his inability to reach
the goal cannot be considered a failure for nobody could really be expected

to succeed. Of course, his fear of failure also explains why he frequently chooses situations in which he has a high expectation of success. The success-oriented person, on the other hand, tends to choose experiences in which the chances for success are in the middle range of those ordinarily encountered, and he avoids either very high- or low-risk situations. Middle range experiences provide him with sufficient challenge to satisfy his need for achievement while at the same time offering him reasonable chance for success. In a very real sense, risk taking is greater for the student choosing middle-range experiences because it would be more difficult to excuse away or rationalize poor performance if that should happen. He cannot say, for example, "The task was so hard that anyone might have failed."

We might add here that the risk taking we're talking about does not refer to situations involving games of chance, but rather risk taking where success or failure is dependent upon one's own skill and know-how. For most adults, games of chance do not stimulate a strong motivation for achievement primarily because neither success nor failure can be attributed to the individual's competency and capability. On the other hand, it is important to recognize that children below the age of ten have considerable difficulty in discriminating between a situation in which they're successful because of their own skill and situations in which success is more dependent on the luck of the draw, as it were. When a young child wins at a game of chance (as in some games involving dice, for instance), he is likely to credit himself for winning, as if in some magical way he controlled the situation.

Fear of Failure and Hope for Success Can Exist Simultaneously

Another consideration is worth noting about failure- and success-oriented motivation, and this has to do with the fact that a person can experience both the fear of failure and hope for success in the same situation. It would not be unlike what most of us have experienced from time to time as we struggled silently with the conflict of whether or not to raise our hands and contribute to class discussion. One part of us says "Go ahead, do it" and another part of us cautions, "Be careful, better not." Fear of failure or saying the wrong thing urges us to withdraw and be quiet, but the possibility of the successful offering of a brilliant insight urges us to get involved. Thus, the approach and avoidance aspects of success-failure aspects of motivation come into conflict. Typically this kind of conflict is reflected in vacillating behavior full of the go-aheads and stops of ambivalent behavior. I remember once during a discussion in one of my undergraduate classes when a fellow near the back of the room (by the way, students who participate less do tend to sit toward the back of a room if given a choice—check this out in your own classes) raised his hand abruptly once, twice, three times within about a fifteen-second span of time. I finally said to him, "Bill, did you have something you wanted to say?" His reply, "Well yes—no, not really—yes, I do but . . . well maybe . . . oh hell, forget it, I forgot what I was gonna say." This is fairly typical of approach-avoidance behavior. The closer an ambivalent person comes to doing what a part of him wants to do, the more the fear of failure looms heavy on his mind and so he withdraws. But then as he withdraws the possibility of failure begins to seem more remote, and he decides that maybe he should go ahead after all. And so the vacillation continues. Most of us resolve approach-avoidance conflicts in one of two ways. One, we decide that the task is not really worth doing anyway, which serves as a convenient rationalization for escaping. Or two, we can conclude that, if we fail, it won't really be our fault because the task was unreasonably difficult to begin with. Thus, we have a built-in excuse for failing, in the event that that should happen. A sensitive teacher can help students over their ambivalences by being supporting and encouraging in moments like this.

Self-esteem is an important variable to consider in our examination of how and why success and failure experiences motivate different people in different ways, an idea to which we turn next.

Self-esteem Certainty as Related to Success and Failure

There is a considerable body of clinical and experimental research literature to suggest that each individual strives to behave in a manner that is more or less consistent with how he views himself as a person.[29-31] Indeed, there is evidence to support the idea that just as some individuals develop "success-type" personalities and look for ways to succeed, there are others who develop "failure-type" personalities and look for ways to fail in order to be consistent with their respective self-images.[32-34] According to theories of self-consistency, persons who view themselves as failure types will tend to reject their successes because success experiences "just don't fit" how they see themselves. In a similar way, persons who view themselves as success types will tend to reject their failures because, as in the case above, failure experiences "just don't fit" how they see themselves. There are, however, some instances when the positive effects of an *unexpected* success (a smile of approval, a good grade, a pat on the back, etc.) can make even a failure-type person feel good. There are other instances, however, when no matter how good or unexpected the success, certain failure-expectancy persons still reject outcomes that are inconsistent with their negative self-pictures.

The question is: What determines which of these experiences—success or failure—will be dominant over the other? In an effort to answer this question, psychologists have begun looking at how an individual's feelings about himself influence his readiness to incorporate or "believe" his success or failures.

In one study a team of researchers found that low self-esteem subjects who resisted the induction of low self-esteem proceeded to participate even more vigorously in the experimental task. These were subjects who could not easily be induced to feel more negative about themselves. At the same time another group of low self-esteem subjects easily accepted the induction of low self-esteem and behaved in a listless manner consistent with their low self-esteem.[35] Coopersmith[36] found somewhat similar results when he delineated two distinct behavior patterns among low self-esteem boys. In one group there were boys who had low self-esteem but who were nonetheless held in high esteem by their peers and teachers. The overt behavior of these boys reflected high achievement and a strong desire for improvement. It was almost as if their low self-appraisal had put them in a state of hyper-readiness for praise and success. On the other hand, there was another group of boys who did not strive to achieve and, in fact, seemed to be locked into a self-perception of failure. They were, apparently, boys who had all but given up hope for improvement.

Self-esteem, then, appears to be related to the extent to which a person "believes" a success or failure experience. The question remains: What determines whether an individual believes one way or the other? An interesting study by Marecek and Mattee[37] may provide some answers for us. In this investigation it was hypothesized that low self-esteem persons may differ as to the certainty of their self-appraisal and that perhaps certainty about a low self-appraisal is a crucial factor in determining whether a low self-esteem individual allows himself to be buoyed by success or rejects it in favor of remaining consistent with his failure image. The thinking was that if a person is *certain* about his self-esteem he would be more likely to maintain the status quo. On the other hand, the individual who is *uncertain* about his low self-appraisal may be more open to success experiences. If a person is uncertain, it indicates that he doesn't believe that his negative self-feelings stem from intrinsic, immutable qualities. Further, this state of uncertain self-appraisal may leave the success-deprived low self-esteem individual "hungry" for success experiences that will help him reject his past failure experiences.

This is all well and good because it leaves the uncertain low self-esteem person free to seek out and accept his success experiences for whatever growth potential they may offer. But what of the low self-esteem person who is *convinced* of his lowly status? Are there conditions under which he can accept success? Mattee[38] discovered just such a condition when he found that "failure" persons are more likely to accept success if it was associated with a "lucky break" or "windfall" over which they had no control. In this instance, the person is not responsible for the success, and hence it does not refer to his self-evaluation any more than having one's unoccupied,

505

properly parked car banged in the rear reflects upon his driving skills. Inasmuch as the person himself has nothing to do with the success, it has the net effect of leaving a low self-esteem individual free to react to the success without regard to his low self-appraisal and hence under no pressure to behave in a manner consistent with his low self-esteem. I have frequently seen this happen among low self-esteem, "failure"-motivated students who disclaim any credit for unexpected success on an exam with comments to the effect that "Anyone could have done it — it was so easy."

How Self-esteem Certainty Influences Motivation

In order to explore the relationships between self-esteem and certainty, the study by Marecek and Mattee examined the interplay between high and low self-esteem and high and low certainty of self-esteem in a study involving seventy-two college age subjects. Those with high and low self-esteem were psychologically evaluated to determine the amount of certainty attached to their self-appraisal, and then they performed a task in which the outcome was either produced by their own effort or determined by chance. Half-way through the task, all individuals were led to believe that their performance to that point was highly successful. It was predicted that the subjects' reactions to the success would depend not only on their self-appraisal, but also on the amount of certainty invested in that appraisal and the perceived self-responsibility for the success outcome. All in all, there were four groups, which consisted of those who were (1) high in self-esteem and certain of it, (2) high in self-esteem and uncertain of it, (3) low in self-esteem and certain of it, and (4) low in self-esteem and uncertain of it. How did each of these groups respond to success experiences? Here's what the data showed:

1. Persons with high self-esteem and certain of it were inclined to accept their successes no matter whether the successes were self-determined or obtained by luck. In fact, they were even a bit blasé about it, probably because success experiences were neither strange to them nor inconsistent with their expectations. Their motivation for achievement, which was high to begin with, remained the same.

2. Persons with high self-esteem and uncertain of it were positively affected by success whether it was by luck or self-determined effort. In other words, they welcomed success since it enabled them to fortify their tenuous hold on a high-status position and substantiated their precarious high self-appraisal.

3. Persons with low self-esteem and certain of it tended to reject their success experiences (in order to be consistent with their failure image), but were inclined to be positively affected and motivated by successes they saw as determined by luck or fate. Indeed, one of the interesting results of the study was that this group made the greatest improvement in their performance in the second half of the experimental condition. This verifies Mattee's

earlier study that indicated that even persons with deeply rooted chronic low self-esteem will enthusiastically embrace a successful outcome if they believe it had more to do with luck than with skill.

4. Persons with low self-esteem and uncertain of it tend to accept success no matter what form it comes in, particularly since they are unconvinced of their low self-appraisals and are eager for any evidence to the contrary.

TO DO

Getting feedback from others and comparing it with our own self-perceptions is a way that helps us grow. You can do that here. Choose the one research finding of the four discussed above that you think best fits you. Have two or three friends who know you also choose the one which each thinks fits you. How do they compare? If your friends see you differently, ask why they do. What can you do to enhance your motivation for learning to make it more positive?

Implications for Teachers

It seems fairly clear that neither a success nor a failure experience *by itself* can explain the motivational consequences that follow either of these occurrences. We also have to consider the level and certainty of a student's self-esteem in order to encourage high motivation and greater risk-taking behavior. I see at least three implications for teaching practices that may be of some value in enhancing student motivation.

High self-esteem students need to be challenged. Confident, high self-esteem, high need-achieving students not only want and can stand a higher level of intellectual and personal challenge, but in fact that may *need* to be more critically challenged and pushed in order for them to test the upper limits of their abilities and capacities to perform. Just as the average, and surely the below-average student, needs a teacher who will not push him too fast too soon, so does the above-average student need a teacher who does not indiscriminately praise everything he does. Sometimes one of the finest compliments a teacher can give a student, is to say something along the lines of "You know Richard, I really think you can do better work than this." This is not something one would want to say to a student who has tried his hardest and given you his best effort, but it might be an observation appropriately shared with a student who is giving you less than his best and both you and he know it. Suggesting to a student that he can probably improve his performance communicates two things: (1) that you have faith in his capacity to do better and, (2) that he has the ability to do better, both of which can serve as strong motivators.

507

Offer a variety of ways to achieve success. Both low self-esteem and high self-esteem students who are uncertain about their self-appraisals are inclined to respond favorably and eagerly to success experiences whether they are gained through one's own efforts or through a lucky break. In either case, a teacher can hardly go wrong by making success experiences with different degrees of difficulty as available and as varied as possible for all students. For example, a high school English teacher of mine was fond of giving short daily quizzes on the homework assignments. Some of these quizzes were exceptionally difficult and only the very best students did well on them, while other quizzes were fairly simple and most students did well on them. He admits to me now that he used to do this on purpose so that students on both ends of the ability continuum could feel some success. Since practically all students had an opportunity to sample the fruits of success in his class, it will come as no surprise to you for me to report that practically all the students who took his class enjoyed being there and learned quite a bit about English.

Short-circuit the "I can't" cycle with ample praise over time. Probably one of the most important findings growing out of research dealing with the certainty of self-esteem lies in the implications for at least interrupting the vicious cycle, whereby a low self-esteem student confirms his low self-image by (1) avoiding experiences that might otherwise help him view himself more positively, and (2) disbelieving his successes when he does have them so he can maintain his consistency. Remember that even an individual certain of his low self-esteem responds favorably to success if he can believe his own ability didn't have too much to do with it. Although a "lucky" success should be irrelevant to a person's self-appraisal, it is still possible that over time enough "lucky" successes will subtly draw a low self-esteem person toward a somewhat more positive view of himself. This may happen in the following manner: Even though a low self-esteem student may attribute a good score on an objective test to "luck," he may still take partial credit for the success and thereby gently raise his self-esteem. This may gradually help a low self-esteem student subtly toward a more positive self-evaluation.

A teacher can encourage this in many ways. He can praise the low self-esteem student publicly, but being careful not to overdo it and thereby reduce his credibility. ("That's an interesting idea, Betty; I hadn't thought of it that way before.") He can look for strengths to comment on in papers handed in or examinations. ("This is a well-expressed paragraph, Joe" or "You did well on this part of the exam, Sue.") He can also be sensitive to experiences that the low self-esteem student may have outside the classroom, whether it happens to be on the playground or in extracurricular activities. ("You can really sock that ball, Billy" or "I hear you had an interesting idea for the Science Club fair, Bob. I'm sure you must be pleased.")

Who cares that a low self-esteem student may initially deny any credit for a successful effort? The point is that over a long enough period, positive feedback might encourage his self-appraisal to be slightly more positive so that slightly greater degrees of credit for success would be defined as acceptable.

Once such a positive escalating cycle is initiated, we can, I think, reasonably assume that self-esteem could gradually be enhanced until eventually a student would be able to evaluate himself at least a bit more positively. There is, in fact, research evidence to suggest that this really is possible,[39,40] an idea developed more fully in the next chapter. Suffice it to say, nothing, as the saying goes, succeeds like success, and once we understand the subtle dynamics between one's self-esteem and the acceptance of success experiences we are in a position to help a student both maintain and enhance his motivation for learning and achievement.

Knowing something about the effects of competition and cooperation are also important. Let's see how they work.

MOTIVATIONAL EFFECTS OF COMPETITION AND COOPERATION

By definition competition refers to a contest between rivals engaged in the process of vying with each other, as Webster says, "for or as if for a prize." Cooperation, on the other hand, refers to an association with another or others for a mutual or common benefit. Just as, for many persons, there is a certain thrill and self-satisfaction connected to beating a worthy opponent in a race or getting the highest grade on a test, there is, for still others, a certain depression and self-devaluation connected to *being* beat or *receiving* the lowest grade on a test. As you might suspect, there are some wide differences of opinion among educators and psychologists about the worth and merit of competition in the classroom. John Holt, for instance, asserts that we stifle students' motivation by:

> . . . encouraging and compelling them to work for petty and contemptible rewards—gold stars, or papers marked 100 and tacked on the wall, or A's on report cards, or honor rolls, or dean's lists, or Phi Beta Kappa Keys—in short, for the ignoble satisfaction of feeling that they are better than someone else.[41]

Strong words, these, but they echo the sentiments of many who believe that competitive classrooms are breeding grounds for anxiety, despair, and defeat. Arthur Combs,[42] a psychologist very much identified with humanistic trends in education, is equally antagonistic to the use of competition in the classroom. From his point of view, there are three major disadvantages to competition as a motivating device:

1. Competition is a motivation force only to those who feel they have a chance of winning.

2. Persons who are forced to compete when they see little chance of success are not motivated by the experience; they are threatened by it. The idea here is that if one is forced to compete against his will, he may simply "go through the motions" in a somewhat dispirited, listless manner.

3. When competition becomes too important, any means become justified to achieve the ends. Combs, like many others, feels that since the aim of competition is to win, the temptation may be to win at any cost. The fear is that this may encourage students to cheat on exams, athletes to "play dirty" when they can get away with it, and, in general, cause otherwise virtuous persons to behave dishonestly.

TO THINK ABOUT

Competitive versus cooperative efforts bring out different qualities in each of us. I, for example, like competitive circumstances. I also know that too much of an emphasis on "winning" or "being first" makes me anxious and tense. Under which conditions do you function best? My parent messages were: "Do well." "Get high grades." "You can do better than that," and so on. Hence, I learned to compete. What were your parent messages? How have they influenced your attitudes toward cooperation and competition? Jot down the two or three most powerful parent messages you recall.

_____

_____

_____

The points made by Holt and Combs have merit. Competition may bring out the best in people, but sometimes it may also bring out the worst. The relative effects of cooperative versus competitive conditions on performance is something that has been examined by various research strategies and this may be a good time to lay the rhetoric aside and look at the data.

What Research Says

Interpersonal relationships, ways of dealing with conflict, and learning activity can and do occur in either cooperative or competitive situations and are all likely to be influenced strongly by the context within which they appear. In addition, competitive and cooperative processes tend to be self-confirming, so that cooperative experiences produce a spiral of increasing cooperation and competitive experiences induce a spiral of increasing competition. The question is: Do either one of these conditions work best or better as motivators in the classroom?

Some advantages to cooperative efforts. We should first of all recognize that cooperative and competitive conditions involve at least two aspects: (1) the motivational factor, or the individual's need to achieve under the two conditions, and (2) the procedural factor, which refers to the relative effectiveness of either one or the other in the attainment of goals. In addition, the nature of the task to be accomplished will often determine whether competition or cooperation will be most effective. Cooperative efforts are particularly appropriate for tasks in which collective effort is an important prerequisite to solving a particular problem. For example, one investigation found that cooperative groups were much more successful than competitive groups in a task requiring them to withdraw from the narrow neck of a jar as many cones as possible attached to strings before water flowing in from the bottom of the jar made them wet. In this task, which of necessity required an orderly sequence of movements, individuals within groups competing for prizes invariably ended up in "traffic jams" in the necks of the jars and, more often than not, none was able to win.[43]

A certain degree of competition may increase desire. Another experiment involved a tracking task that required flexible, carefully timed adjustments in the operation of a handwheel in order to keep a pointer on a rotation white-painted target. Three groups of ten college students in each worked under three motivational conditions: as individuals, in cooperating pairs, and in competing pairs. In terms of performance, the cooperative pairs did better than either those working as individuals or as competing pairs, but in terms of motivation, or, you might say, the *desire* to do well, those in the competitive groups were higher.[44] This is consistent with another study that asked both high school and college students to list those procedures most motivating to them and found that competitive conditions were ranked number one.[45] Not only do competitive conditions make some students feel more motivated to give their best efforts, but there is evidence that competitive circumstances *do* produce the best results. Maller,[46] for instance, compared the effects of three different conditions of motivation on learning computations by groups of fifth- and eighth-grade students. Group I was given no special motivation. Group II competed for a class prize. The students in Group III competed individually for a personal prize. The average scores for computations successfully completed by groups I, II, and III were 41.4, 43.9, and 46.6, which, as we see, favors the competitive condition. An early review of literature related to learning experiments led Vaughn and Diserens[47] to conclude that rivalry does indeed tend to increase learning efficiency. Torrance[48] reports that competition is also effective in the stimulation of creative thinking. He noted, for example, a "fairly consistent tendency" for children performing creative thinking tasks under competitive conditions to excel those who worked in a noncompetitive situation, with the former producing a much larger number and a greater flexibility of responses. This is further supported by the research of Julian and Perry,[49] who found that group members were more highly motivated and more productive under both individual and intergroup competition than in a purely cooperative condition in which individual group members cooperated without their group competing with other groups.

Too much competition has adverse effects. Although competitive conditions may motivate students to produce at a higher level, there is evidence to suggest the possibility of undesirable side effects as far as social and interpersonal consequences are concerned.

Phillips and D'Amico[50] investigated the effects of cooperation and competition upon the cohesiveness of groups of fourth graders and arrived at two significant findings. First, groups that operated under cooperative conditions during the experiment increased in cohesiveness, which suggests that individuals who worked together under cooperative conditions liked each other better (according to a questionnaire filled out by the students) at the end of the experiment than they did at the beginning of the experiment. Secondly, although groups that operated under competitive conditions did not necessarily decrease in cohesiveness, they did not increase a great deal either.

A further examination of the data for the competitive groups revealed that rewards were fairly evenly distributed in the groups in which there was either no change or an increase in cohesiveness during the experiment. This implies that the effect of competition on group cohesiveness may be dependent on the effect that competition has on the distribution of the group's rewards. Thus, if competition results in a reasonably uniform distribution of the group's rewards, the effect of competition on the group's cohesiveness may be similar to the effect that cooperation has on the group's cohesiveness. However, if one or two of the group's members receive most of the rewards the effect of competition may be to decrease the group's cohesiveness by increasing the rivalry. The significance of this study is that the effect of competition on a classroom group's interpersonal relationships seems to be influenced by its effects on the distribution of the group's rewards. If the members are well matched and rewards are evenly divided among them, competition appears to have fewer undesirable effects on interpersonal relationships than if members are poorly matched and rewards are not evenly divided.

A cooperative mood increases good feelings. A similar study performed by Stendler and her co-workers[51] was designed to investigate the effects of working under cooperative and competitive conditions and involved the participation of three groups of eight second graders consisting of four boys and four girls. Each group was asked to paint two murals. For the first one, they were told that if everyone painted and the mural was a good one, everyone in the group would receive a prize. For the second mural, they were told that only the best painter in each group would receive a prize. Observers found that the effects of cooperation and competition were practically the same, but they noted more sharing of materials, friendly conversation, and mutual help among the children while they were cooperating and more selfishness, unfriendly conversation, and obstruction while they were competing.

Along the same lines, Deutsch[52] grouped college students in ten sections of five members each. Five of the sections were told they would receive a common grade, determined by how well the members worked together, while students in the remaining sections were told they would be graded competitively against the four other members of the group each was in. Although there was no difference in learning between the cooperative and competitive groups, it was noted that the competitive groups were generally more insecure and anxious, while the cooperative groups were distinguished by their greater willingness to exchange ideas. Also, students in both groups seemed equally and strongly motivated to do well in the course. A number of other studies have replicated Deutsch's findings in both actual classroom and laboratory situations.[53,54] That is, given a task that generates tension, students working in cooperatively functioning groups will feel less tense and those working in competitive groups will feel more tense.

Although research conclusions do not paint an entirely consistent picture, the general trend of results seems to indicate that although competitive conditions are more motivating, cooperative conditions are more pleasant. I think we have to keep in mind that this is not an either-or situation and that what is "motivating" and "pleasant" will vary from student to student. This brings us to our next point.

Implications for Teachers

When it comes right down to it, our feelings about the effects of competitive and cooperative classroom practices on student learning are probably very much related to our own successes or lack of them in competitive situations. This is both inevitable and normal, but either the pursuit of competitive experiences or their avoidance could be harmful if carried to extremes. There are some students who need and want a competitive atmosphere in order to do their best. There are still others who need the more relaxed climate that cooperative activities provide. In any classroom there rightfully should be a place and opportunity for both of these activities. But not one to the exclusion of the other. Both have a place and just because we may not have had the experience of performing very well under competitive circumstances is no reason to attack all competitive activities as bad. On the other hand, just because we may have had the experience of doing well under competitive conditions and, in fact, reaching peak performances doesn't mean that competition does that for all people. It can be good or bad depending on how it is used. Competition can be destructive or constructive. Let's look at examples of each.

Examples of destructive competition in the classroom. Dealing wisely with individual differences means, first of all, recognizing the destructive effects of competition when it is misused. Examples of destructive competition are endless (unfortunate, this), and what follows are three actual examples to give you a better feel for what we mean by this kind of competition.

1. A fifth-grade science teacher had each of her thirty-one students read his most recent test score aloud in class so that she could record that score and its corresponding grade in her grading book. On top of that, she announced out loud the grade equivalent of each score. Very rewarding for the top students. Very sad (and punishing) for the bottom students. Destructive competition at its worst—if you don't do well, the whole class knows.

2. A high school history teacher posts the grades of his exams by *name*, *score*, and *letter grade* on his classroom door, which, as he says, "lets the kids know how they're doing and gets the low scorers off their fannys." This may be fine in some cases, but what of the low scorers who did the best they could? Besides, why should one's performance in history class become a topic of invidious comparison and idle social conversation, particularly among high school students who are not particularly noted for merciful judgments of each other?

3. A junior high English instructor hands back both exams and term papers in chronological grade order, announces the grade associated with each new grade category, and then calls students one at a time to retrieve their papers. Again, a primitive reward-punishment system in action.

Approaches such as the above are destructive for the following reasons (you may think of others):

1. Learning gets de-emphasized because the primary goal is to be better than others. Thus, learning is seen as a means to an end, not as an end in itself. (Who cares about learning when survival is at stake?)

2. Only a few students can feel satisfied and rewarded. Public disapproval or failure is many times worse than that experienced privately because now one has to be concerned not only about his lack of performance, but his possible loss of approval and acceptance as well. It's difficult enough to improve one's effort without having his social image to worry about, too.

3. When performance is consistently reported in terms of relative position, what frequently happens is that for many students quality deteriorates, experimentation and risk taking decrease because of the fear of failure, and general improvement is discouraged. *Remember, there can be little, if any, improvement if one does not try and experience some success in doing those things he thought he couldn't do.*

Now then, how can we make competition more positive and constructive?

Examples of constructive competition in the classroom. The very nature of competition means someone wins and someone loses. There are, however, some ways of reducing the sting of losing without diluting the healthy features of competition. For example:

1. Encourage each student to compete against himself as much as possible. On a term paper a teacher may write, "Pretty good work here, Dan, perhaps next time you can write a stronger concluding statement." Or another teacher may write on a C+ exam, "This is not at all bad, Alice. I'm pleased with your effort. Let's see if you can top this next time." In these instances we're not requested to match the record of the brightest student in class, but challenged only to beat our own previous performance. True, both the term paper and exam were graded competitively against the whole class, but *the emphasis is on how the student can top himself* — that's the difference.

2. Keep grades confidential. The implications of this should be self-evident. How a student does — at any level — is his own business. It should be his choice to divulge his grades, not the teacher's.

3. Try to give every student a chance for success by arranging situations and recognizing experiences in which different students of different abilities can be acknowledged for their best efforts. Ways for doing this might include putting up examples of not just the best idea or content papers but the *neatest* papers and the best *organized* papers. In addition, a teacher could make a special effort to recognize behavior such as punctuality and dependability and by giving special acknowledgement for skill in arts and crafts, special interests, music, and hobbies. If a student knows for sure that there are some things he can do pretty well and that are appreciated, the things he *can't* do so well may not be so devastating to his ego.

One fourth-grade teacher I know has a knack for turning otherwise dull class activities into interesting games in which all students have a chance of experiencing success. One such game is called *Spelling Baseball*, which is done very simply by dividing the class into two approximately equal teams and "pitching" each player a spelling word. Each time a player spells a word correctly his team is awarded a base. Four bases equal one run and each misspelled word is an out. No team member is ever eliminated, and the pressure is reduced considerably. If a particular student makes too many outs, the teacher simply feeds him a slow ball in the form of an easy word his next time at bat. Also, she uses a different arrangement of players for each game to minimize the possibility of intense team rivalries building up. There are no prizes or anything like that for winning—just the score and whatever naturally good feeling might accompany it. The students love it and the teacher has fun, too. Another thing she does is to arrange simulated quiz programs, which are usually conducted during those times when material is being reviewed for, say, an examination. Again, equal sides are chosen and each side gets so many points for a right answer to the teacher or the "quizmaster," as she is called. Students who may be a bit slower are asked somewhat easier questions so that, again, everyone has an opportunity for success. A variation of both of these games is to have groups of at least three students work together so that each "team" is actually composed of perhaps four groups of three students. Thus, within a modified competitive framework, students can also have the experience of cooperating together.

PROS AND CONS ABOUT CLASSROOM FREEDOM AS A MOTIVATOR

What with the advent of free schools, open classrooms, flexible scheduling, and the like, the idea of maximizing a student's freedom so he can make more of his own educational decisions has received renewed emphasis in recent years. Many people, for example, believe as John Holt[55,56] does, namely, that the best sort of education is that which is "natural" to the student, unstructured and determined by his own needs and interests at that time. What a student learns should be a function of *wanting* to learn and not *having* to learn, or so say those advocating larger degrees of student freedom.

Summerhill School: An Example of Total Freedom

Probably the most dramatic example of the classroom freedom concept in action is a school known as Summerhill, founded by Alexander S. Neill and located in the village of Leiston, in Suffolk, England. Some students come to Summerhill when they are five years old, others as late as fifteen. Generally, there are about twenty-five boys and twenty girls. In many ways Summerhill is a unique educational experience. In the first place, students live right at the school. The philosophy of the school is that students should be allowed the freedom to be themselves. In order to ac-

516

complish this noble end, Summerhill renounces all discipline, all direction, all suggestion, all moral training, all religious instruction. Education at Summerhill begins with a complete and uncompromising belief in the child as a good, not an evil, being. Going to class is optional. Students can go or stay away—for years if they want to. There is a timetable, but only for teachers. Summerhill is entirely self-governing. Every child, no matter how young, has one vote, and his vote counts as much as anyone else's. The students have an equal say with adults in making rules and fixing penalties. It is, as you can see, a very permissive school with flexible rules. It is the best example of total freedom in education to be found anywhere. In Neill's words, the merits of Summerhill "will be the merits of healthy, free children whose lives are unspoiled by fear and hate." He goes on to observe that "a school that makes active children sit at desks studying mostly useless subjects is a bad school. It is a school for only those who believe in such a school, for those uncreative citizens who want docile, uncreative children who will fit into a civilization whose standard of success is money."[57]

Summerhill: nay. Needless to say, the Summerhill approach to child rearing and education has not gone unnoticed. Both Neill's critics and supporters have voiced their opposition and favor with equal intensity and enthusiasm. On one side of the fence is Dr. Max Rafferty, author of the 1962 bestseller, *Suffer, Little Children*, who writes:

> . . . Summerhill is a dirty joke. It degrades true learning to the status of a disorganized orgy. It turns a teacher into a sniggering projectionist of a stag movie. It transforms a school into a cross between a beer garden and a boiler factory. It is a caricature of education.
> I would as soon enroll a child of mine in a brothel as in Summerhill.[58]

Summerhill: yea. On the other side of the fence we have Reverend John M. Culkin, whose articles and ideas on film study, instructional television, and educational innovation have appeared in scores of periodicals. He writes:

> Although I never visited Summerhill, I know that it is a holy place.
> The wisdom of Summerhill is exquisitely suited to the needs of the child of the electronic age. It begins with respect for and love for the child. All good communication does.[59]

Yes, views about the Summerhill concept of student freedom do vary. The question remains: Does the Summerhill concept work? How effective *is* student freedom as a motivator for growth and learning of the mind and spirit? Although research related to this question is somewhat limited, Bernstein[60,61] conducted in-depth interviews with fifty former Summerhill students that provide some interesting insights regarding the impact of a totally free learning environment. Let's take a look at what Bernstein learned from those interviews.

The Summerhill Experience as Former Students See It

To begin with, Summerhill is not so free as it may appear. As one boy remarked to Bernstein, "There are more rules in a free school than anywhere else, even though we make them all for ourselves." So there *are* rules and restrictions; it's just that the students and not the adults make them. Secondly, Summerhill by no means affects all students in the same way. For example, Bernstein found that the gregarious, aggressive people (both as children and as adults) seemed to benefit the most, while the school seemed to have a somewhat negative effect on the more withdrawn, quiet ones. If the students are to take active, assertive roles in managing their own lives and learning, it is not difficult to see that the shy, quiet students would have more difficulty coping with the total freedom concept. Former students said many positive things about Summerhill, but five items were mentioned more frequently than any others. These included, (1) fostering a healthy attitude towards sex and relationship with the opposite sex (students of all ages frequently swim in the nude together), (2) enabling one to be more comfortable and at ease with authority figures, (3) providing a free environment in which children could develop naturally and within the boundaries of their own interests and abilities, (4) allowing children to grow out of the need to play continuously and then to settle into academic pursuits of their own choosing, and (5) helping them to understand their own children better and develop healthy relationships with them. That's on the plus side.

On the negative side, the majority of Summerhillians had one major complaint about the school and that had to do with the lack of academic opportunity, along with the lack of inspired teachers. Bernstein found that Summerhill attracted a variety of teachers. Some apparently were available but not inspired in any dynamic sense, and were content to pad about in sandals and grow long beards, content that nobody was coming to their classes. Others were active and vigorous to the point of plucking children out of trees and trying to lure them to their classes. One student, who had attended Summerhill for ten years, confessed that classes were rather "humdrum" and that it was rather easy to be led astray by new students who did little or no studying. In fact, he went on to say that procrastination was an attitude one could easily pick up at Summerhill. The disenchantment with the lack of academic emphasis was further evidenced in the fact that only three of eleven parents—all former Summerhill students—sent their own children to Summerhill. The three parents who did send their children to Summerhill took them out before the age of thirteen, almost wholly due to their convictions that not enough emphasis was placed upon the academic side and that there should be more fine teaching and good equipment than Summerhill provided.

However, in spite of the complaints that Summerhill was academically weak, there is no compelling evidence to suggest that those who attended were either any stronger, in the academic sense of the word, or, for that matter, any weaker. The occupations that Summerhillians go into seem as varied and as broad as may be chosen by a group of graduates from a more traditional school. For example, of the fifty persons interviewed, the only occupations they represented that included more than two of them were housewife and secretary.

What Can We Learn from Summerhill?

All in all, Bernstein found the feelings of the fifty former students he interviewed to be mainly positive. Almost all were working, raising responsive children, and enjoying life. Their main reservation was about Summerhill's academic emphasis and strength, which, on the basis of their experience, was lacking. Those who had attended Summerhill ten years or longer were more apt to have adjustment problems after leaving than those who were there for shorter periods. In particular, those who attended Summerhill during their elementary years and then finished in a regular school were inclined to be the most enthusiastic about learning. There is no clear-cut reason for this, but one possibility is that a Summerhill type experience, where a growing child has maximum opportunities to experience success in his own time, in his own way, and on his own terms, is more conducive to nurturing the seeds of adequacy and confidence so necessary for the development of a robust, healthy self-image. I am not at all sure that schools need go as far as adopting a Summerhill philosophy in order to provide opportunities for growing children to develop their confidence and competence, but it does not seem unreasonable to think that more of our elementary age youngsters would be more motivated to take more risks, and feel better about themselves for doing it, if they were not so fearful of failing. One of the nice things about a Summerhill philosophy, particularly for elementary age youths, is that it allows them to learn at their own pace and *when they're ready to learn*, which is the best kind of motivation of all. Not infrequently elementary age students in our more traditional schools are forced to learn arithmetic concepts or reading skills before they're developmentally ready to handle tasks of that sort. This cuts into their sense of adequacy and as that dwindles, so, too, does their self-esteem and motivation.

A Balance Between Too Much Freedom and Too Much Control

Somewhere between too much freedom and too much control there is a fulcrum point that allows us to balance and weigh the advantages of student choice and teacher guidance. Although John Holt, A. S. Neill, and Carl Rogers have made impassioned defenses for allowing as much freedom as possible, the fact remains that it does not work equally well for all students. On the other hand, neither does a totally structured approach where the student is told exactly what he must learn, how he should behave, and what is expected of him. Nonetheless, the fact is that some students do indeed flourish and grow in an atmosphere of uncompromised freedom. So, too, do some students develop and learn best under totally controlled conditions. There is research to support both of these ends of the continuum.[62] Still, the bulk of related research, not to mention good old common sense, suggests that the best way to encourage motivation and learning is to blend a student's choices, interests, whims even, with a teacher's guidance, direction, and experience. There is little question that Neill's Summerhill philosophy is appealing. It can hardly be anything else. It does, after all, make a great deal of sense to allow students to study only those topics and subjects that have intrinsic value because then the problem of extrinsic motivation is eliminated altogether. However, it is a rare and fortunate student who is able and willing to put together fragmented bits of information if left entirely to his own cunning and devices. This may explain why so few Summerhill graduates send their children to Neill's school.

A Flaw in Classroom Freedom Overextended

There seems to be another flaw in the idea that classrooms should be totally free. In the absence of imposed standards and expectations, a student (or anyone else for that matter) has fewer opportunities to experience the very good, and rewarding, and very self-satisfying feelings that typically follow on the heels of having pleased someone who is significant to him. Characteristically, a growing youngster not only wants to please adults (parents and teachers for sure), but he needs their expectations as guidelines against which he can measure his developing skills and abilities. Being exposed to caring, but firm, adults who establish reasonable expectations and firm rules that are consistently enforced can be a growth enhancing experience. Coopersmith's research,[63] which will be discussed more completely in the next chapter, has demonstrated rather convincingly that high self-esteem children are more apt to come from homes where parental expectations for both behavior and performance are high. Why

Good teachers *are* open-minded and liberal, but the question always remains: How "open" is open-minded; how "libral" is liberal? Effective teachers seek a reasonable balance.

should this be? Well, for one thing, when a student has expectations to live up to and does it, this has immediate input into his feelings of competency and adequacy.

A Flaw in Classroom Control Overdone

The major argument against a controlled curriculum, however, remains a formidable one. At its worst, it very likely contradicts all the positive arguments. That is, students who are forced to study too many subjects that stimulate little or no interest may grow so frustrated and resistive that further learning is impossible. Kohl, another articulate spokesman for an educational system that releases rather than closes students to their own natural potential for growth, puts it even more strongly.

> Our schools are crazy. They do not serve the interests of adults, and they do not serve the interests of young people. They teach "objective" knowledge and its corollary, obedience to authority. They teach avoidance of conflict and obeisance to tradition in the guise of history. They teach equality and democracy while castrating students and controlling teachers. Most of all they teach people to be silent about what they think and feel, and worst of all, they teach people to pretend that they are saying what they think and feel. To try to break away from stupid schooling is no easy matter for teacher or student. It is a lonely and long fight to escape from believing that one needs to do what people say one should do and that one ought to be the person one is expected to be. Yet to make such an escape is a step toward beginning again and becoming the teachers we never knew we could be.[64]

Worse yet, students could become apathetic, if not negative, about school and learning in general. What, then, can a teacher do to reduce the possibility of that happening while at the same time bringing some kind of balance between freedom and control?

Implications for Teachers: Distinguish Between Authoritarian and Authoritative Control

Perhaps one of the first things we can appreciate is that the vast majority of students want not only elbow room to explore their individual interests and curiosities, but they also want and need guidance and direction from the teacher as well. Sometimes a teacher is hesitant to offer too much advice or direction for fear of being viewed as a dictatorial monster. (Unfortunately, those who *are* dictatorial monsters never worry about that possibility. There is, you know, some truth to the statement that "No one is so blind as he who will not see.") There is, however, a distinction between being *authoritative* and *authoritarian*. Authoritative refers to what one knows, while authoritarian refers more to what one does. An authoritative statement tends to focus more on problems and solutions ("John, you may want to try inverting the fraction before dividing to see how that affects your answer"), while an authoritarian statement focuses more on personal views and mandates ("John, I don't see how you can possibly work the problem that way — now invert the fraction first!"). Although the content of each of the statements is essentially the same, you can see that the second is judgmental in tone and emphasis — e.g., "I don't see how . . ." The authoritative statement, "You may want to try inverting . . ." is suggestive rather than directive. Not only that, but it concentrates on the process rather than the person, which, in the long run, is more apt to produce more change because it arouses less resistance. You may have learned from your own experience that the times you find yourself most resistive to change are when someone *demands* you do this or that. Most children and adults feel this way.

The point is that it is possible for a teacher to give guidance and direction — so important for enhancing and maintaining motivation — without totally eliminating students' opportunities for making choices and decisions. For example, rather than assigning one or two books that all students *have* to read, are there five or six in the same general area they could choose from? Rather than assigning seats, allow students to sit where they please. Rather than assign one kind of paper to write, allow a choice of four or five or more possibilities to choose from. Rather than there being only one grading plan, how about three or four? For instance, some teachers have found that students not only feel better about the evaluation process when they feel some personal investment in the grade plan they've had an opportunity to choose for themselves, but they also put more effort into class. One possibility for this are grade options that give different or equal weights to different class activities. It may look something like Table 11-1.

With the grading options any number of combinations of plans are possible, the important point being that both the teacher and the student participate in a process in which they are both involved. What typically happens is that students who have the time and talent for doing good "projects," whatever they might be, choose the plan that puts most of the weight on that activity. On the other hand, there are students who don't care for projects or papers but who prefer reading, outlining, taking notes, and so on, who are inclined to choose to put most of their weight on examination performance. Each student makes his own individual choice. Once a student has made a choice, he is committed to that choice — a fact he knows beforehand, so *that he becomes responsible for his own decision.* When a student assumes responsibility for his own choices, it encourages greater intrinsic motivation because he then has something inside himself (his choice) to live up to. It is usually wise for a teacher to keep a small percentage for his own purely "subjective" evaluation (which includes assessment of a student's contributions in class, attendance, extra efforts, and so on), which he may want to use for borderline cases. Of course, another variation is to allow students the option of putting all their weight on the

TABLE 11-1.

	Plan A	Plan B	Plan C
Exam 1	20%	10%	22%
Exam 2	20%	20%	22%
Project 1	25%	20%	22%
Project 2	25%	35%	22%
Teacher's subjective evaluation	10%	15%	12%
	100%	100%	100%

project(s) or all of it on the exam(s). My own recommendation would be to divide it up in some way so they can sample both kinds of learning experiences but with their own choice of weightings. A fact of life seems to be that a person—whether child or adult—does not always choose what is good for him, but rather what is easiest at the time or most expedient at the moment. If a teacher plans the available options wisely, with the learning in mind and the student at heart, he is in a position to assist students in making not just the easiest choice, but the one which is good for them as well. As one student said to me at the end of a term:

> You know, I'm really sorta glad your options all included taking the exams. Knowing me, I would've chosen the no-exam option if there had been one and I also know I probably would've goofed off more. Funny thing about me— even though I know it's probably best to be motivated to work and study for my own reasons, there are still lots of times when the only time I do anything is when I know I have to. Anyway, I knew I had to here, but I'm kinda glad because I think I learned some things I never would have thought about. I wonder if most students are like me?

Although there is no precise answer to this query, both research evidence and common sense suggest that a fair and reasonable response to this question is that *some* students are *not* like him, but that *most* students are.

TO THINK ABOUT

I had the feeling that the student quoted above spoke for a lot of other students. But I know not all. Try to really *feel* what that student said and felt as a way of getting close to your own feelings about the issue—i.e., choices, but there was still an exam. What might you have said in his place at the end of the term? (I mean other than "Whoopee!")

_____

_____

_____

EPILOGUE

Just as there is more than one way for learning to occur, there is more than one way to stimulate and enhance student motivation. Some students, we know, are driven by strong inner drives to learn and achieve, while others function best when working for reasons or goals that are outside or extrinsic to their inner states. Some students are spurred on by praise and other expressions of positive reinforcement, while others work hardest when their work is more critically appraised.

Self-esteem is an important personal variable to take into account when considering the relative impact of a success or failure experience on a student's motivation. Not only is self-esteem important, but so, too, is the "certainty" of a student's beliefs about his high or low self-esteem.

The merits of a competitive versus cooperative classroom is an ongoing debate by proponents of each who see value and worth in each approach. Since learning does occur in so many different ways for so many different students, there is a place and purpose for each of these processes in the classroom at every level.

It is not easy to assess the extent to which students are motivated or not. Unfortunately, classrooms are not neatly divided into the sleepers and hand-wavers. Sometimes the most involved student is the one who says hardly a word, but who, in actuality, is deeply caught up in ideas and thoughts related to what is happening. He or she is not unmotivated, but merely quiet. Or what about the student who is constantly waving an eager hand in the air? Is he deeply involved and highly motivated to learn or is he a highly insecure soul less anxious for knowledge than for attention? Be assured that involvement and detachment are not permanent conditions. More accurately, they are fleeting psychological states that can, and often do, come and go in a twinkling of an eye. The girl who was furiously waving her hand a few minutes ago is now daydreaming out the window. The bored-looking boy is now the one actively engaged in the class discussion. The ceiling-gazer is now looking directly at the teacher with a look of interest. And so it goes. The kaleidoscope of motivational postures is in constant flux. Motivation is not a permanent state, but one that varies in kind and degree depending on the moment, the content, the student, and the teacher. It would very likely be a lesson in futility to think that all students can be motivated in the same way to the same degree all the time. More likely, the case for any given classroom at any given point in time is that the existing level of motivation is an uneven mental state that varies from student to student.

All in all, classroom motivation and human learning is a three-dimensional process that includes the content at hand, the student, and the teacher. Each plays a part. Motivating students is not a gift reserved only for the super teacher with built-in charisma, but it is, rather, the consequence of hard work, careful planning, and a deep concern for the ultimate expression of growth potential in each student.

You may agree that most students, at any level, don't want or need "lots of laughs" to keep them motivated, but they don't want a perpetual atmosphere of sour staleness either; what they do want and need is authority, humor, insight, personal attention, and a lot of justice tempered by a bit of mercy; when they get this, just watch them work!

Write your own chapter summary (major points, ideas, and concepts that had meaning for you).

_____

_____

_____

_____

_____

_____

_____

_____

_____

_____

REFERENCES

1. Allport, G. W. *Personality and Social Encounter.* Boston: Beacon Press, 1960, p. 218.
2. White, R. W. "Motivation Reconsidered: The Concept of Competence." *Psychological Review* 66(1959):297–333.
3. Maslow, A. H. *Motivation and Personality,* 2nd ed. New York: Harper & Row, 1970.
4. Rogers, C. R. "Toward Becoming a Fully Functioning Person." In *Perceiving, Behaving, Becoming,* edited by A. W. Combs. Washington, D.C.: Association for Supervision and Curriculum Development, 1962, pp. 21–33.
5. Combs, A. W., and D. Snygg. *Individual Behavior* rev. ed. Harper & Row, 1959.
6. Maslow, A. H. *Eupsychian Management: A Journal.* Homewood, Ill.: Irwin-Dorsey, 1965.
7. Deci, E. L. "Effects of Externally Mediated Rewards on Intrinsic Motivation." *Journal of Personality and Social Psychology* 18(1971):107.

8. Koch, S. "Behavior as 'Intrinsically' Regulated: Work Notes Towards a Pretheory of Phenomena Called Motivational." *Nebraska Symposium on Motivation*" 4(1956):42–87.

9. de Charms, R. *Personal Causation: The Internal Affective Determinants of Behavior.* New York: Academic Press, 1968.

10. Deci, E. L. "Intrinsic Motivation, Extrinsic Reinforcement, and Inequity." *Journal of Personality and Social Psychology* 22(1972):119–120.

11. Hurlock, E. B. "An Evaluation of Certain Incentives Used in School Work." *Journal of Educational Psychology* 16(1925):145–159.

12. Forlano, G., and H. C. Axelrod. "The Effect of Repeated Praise or Blame on the Performance of Introverts and Extroverts." *Journal of Educational Psychology* 28(1937):92–100.

13. Thompson, G. G., and C. W. Hunnicutt. "The Effect of Praise or Blame on the Work Achievement of 'Introverts' or 'Extroverts'". *Journal of Educational Psychology* 35(1944):257–266.

14. Marx, M. H., and T. N. Tombaugh. *Motivation.* San Francisco: Chandler, 1967, p. 214.

15. Schmidt, H. O. "The Effects of Praise and Blame as Incentives to Learning." *Psychological Monograph* 53(1941).

16. de Groat, A. F., and G. G. Thompson. "A Study of the Distribution of Teacher Approval and Disapproval Among Sixth-Grade Pupils." *Journal of Experimental Education* 18(1949):57–75.

17. Sechrest, L. B. "The Motivation in School of Young Children: Some Interview Data." *Journal of Experimental Education* 30(1962):327–335.

18. Davidson, H. H., and G. Lang. "Children's Perceptions of Teachers' Feelings Toward Them Related to Self-Perception, School Achievement, and Behavior." *Journal of Experimental Education* 24(December 1960):107–118.

19. Galloway, C. M. *Teaching Is Communicating: Nonverbal Language in the Classroom,* Bulletin no. 29. Washington, D.C.: Association for Student Teaching, NEA, 1970.

20. Galloway, C. M. "Teacher Nonverbal Communication." *Educational Leadership* 24(October 1966):55–63.

21. Anderson, H. E., W. F. White, and J. A. Wash. "Generalized Effects of Praise and Reproof." *Journal of Educational Psychology* 57(1966):169–173.

22. Rhine, R. J. "The Effect on Problem Solving of Success or Failure as a Function of Cue Specificity." *Journal of Experimental Psychology* 53(1957):121–125.

23. Lantz, B. "Some Dynamic Aspects of Success and Failure." *Psychological Monographs* 59(1945):1–40.

24. Steigman, M. J., and H. W. Stevenson. "The Effect of Pre-training Reinforcement Schedules on Children's Learning." *Child Development* 31(1960):53–58.

25. Sears, P. S. "Levels of Aspiration in Academically Successful and Unsuccessful Children." *Journal of Abnormal Psychology* 35(1940):498–536.

26. Gruen, E. W. "Level of Aspiration in Relation to Personality Factors of Adolescents." *Child Development* 16(1945):181–188.

27. Atkinson, J. W. "Motivational Determinants of Risk-Taking Behavior." *Psychological Review* 64(1957):359–372.

28. Moulton, R. W. "Effects of Success and Failure on Level of Aspiration as Related to Achievement Motives." *Journal of Personality and Social Psychology* 1(1965):399–406.

29. Gergen, K. J. "Personal Consistency and the Presentation of Self." In *The Self in Social Interaction,* edited by G. Gordon and K. J. Gergen. New York: Wiley 1968, pp. 299–308.

30. Lecky, P. *Self-Consistency: A Theory of Personality.* New York: Island Press, 1945.

31. Hamachek, D. E. *Encounters with the Self.* New York: Holt, Rinehart & Winston, 1971, Chapter 3.

32. Maltz, M. *Psycho-Cybernetics.* Englewood Cliffs, N.J.: Prentice-Hall, 1960.

33. Lowin, A., and G. F. Epstein. "Does Expectancy Determine Performance?" *Journal of Experimental and Social Psychology* 1(1965):248–255.

34. Aronson, E., and J. M. Carlsmith. "Performance Expectancy as a Determinant of Actual Performance." *Journal of Abnormal and Social Psychology* 65(1962):178–182.

35. Pepitone, A., et al. *The Role of Self-Esteem in Competitive Behavior.* Unpublished manuscript. University of Pennsylvania, 1969.

36. Coopersmith, S. *The Antecedents of Self-Esteem.* San Francisco: Calif.: Freeman, 1967.

37. Marecek, J., and D. R. Mattee. "Avoidance of Continued Success as a Function of Self-Esteem, Level of Esteem Certainty, and Responsibility for Success." *Journal of Personality and Social Psychology* 22(1972):98–107.

38. Mattee, D. R. "Rejection of Unexpected Success as a Function of Negative Consequences of Accepting Success." *Journal of Personality and Social Psychology* 17(1971):332–341.

39. Rosenthal, R., and L. Jacobson. *Pygmalion in the Classroom.* New York: Holt, Rinehart and Winston, 1968.

40. Staines, J. W. "The Self-Picture as a Factor in the Classroom." *British Journal of Educational Psychology* 28(1958):97–111.

41. Holt, J. *How Children Fail.* New York: Dell Publishing Co., 1964, p. 168.

42. Combs, A. W. "The Myth of Competition." *Childhood Education* 33(1957):264–269.

43. Mintz, A. "Non-adoptive Group Behavior." *Journal of Abnormal and Social Psychology* 46(1951):150–159.

44. Shaw, M. E. "Some Motivational Factors in Cooperation and Competition." *Journal of Personality* 26(1958):155–169.

45. Park, J. "How They Thought They Were Motivated." *Journal of Educational Research* 39(1945):193–200.

46. Maller, J. B. "Cooperation and Competition, an Experimental Study of Motivation." In *Recent Experiments in Psychology,* edited by L. W. Crafts. New York: McGraw-Hill, 1938, pp. 60–69.

47. Vaughn, J., and C. M. Diserens. "The Experimental Psychology of Competition." *Journal of Experimental Education* 7(1938):76–97.

48. Torrance, E. P. *Rewarding Creative Behavior.* Englewood Cliffs, N.J.: Prentice-Hall, 1965.

49. Julian, J. W., and F. A. Perry. "Cooperation Contrasted with Intra-Group and Inter-Group Competition." *Sociometry* 5(1967):9–24.

50. Phillips, B. N., and L. A. D'Amico. "Effects of Cooperation and Competition on the Cohesiveness of Small Face-to-Face Groups." *The Journal of Educational Psychology* 47(February 1960):65–70.

51. Stendler, C. B., D. Damrin, and A. C. Haines. "Studies in Cooperation and Competition: I. The Effects of Working for Group and Individual Rewards on the Social Climate of Children's Groups." *Journal of Genetic Psychology* 79(1951):173–197.

52. Deutsch, M. "Social Relations in the Classroom and Grading Procedures." *Journal of Educational Research* 45(1951):145–152.

53. Haines, D. B., and W. J. McKeachie. "Cooperative versus Competitive Discussion Methods in Teaching Introductory Psychology." *Journal of Educational Psychology* 58(1967):386–390.

54. Naught, G. M., and S. E. Newman. "The Effect of Anxiety on Motor Steadiness in Competitive and Non-Competitive Conditions." *Psychonomic Science* 6(1966):519–520.

55. Holt, J. *How Children Fail.* Op. cit., 1964.

56. Holt, J. *How Children Learn.* New York: Dell Publishing Co., 1967.

57. Neill, A. S. *Summerhill: A Radical Approach to Child Rearing.* New York: Hart Publishing Co., 1960, pp. 3–4.

58. Rafferty, M. "Argument Against Summerhill." In *Summerhill: For and Against,* edited by H. H. Hart. New York: Hart Publishing Co., 1970 pp. 17, 24.

59. Culkin, J. M. "Argument for Summerhill." In *Summerhill: For and Against,* edited by H. H. Hart. New York: Hart Publishing Co., 1970, pp. 28, 31.

60. Bernstein, E. "Summerhill After 50 Years, The First Follow-Up." *The New Era* 48(1967).

61. Bernstein, E. "Summerhill: A Follow-Up Study of Its Students." *Journal of Humanistic Psychology* (Fall 1968):123–136.

62. Hamachek, D. E. *Motivation in Teaching and Learning.* Washington, D.C.: Association of Classroom Teachers of the National Education Association, "What Research Says to the Teacher," series no. 34, 1968, pp. 15–21.

63. Coopersmith, S. *Antecedents of Self-Esteem.* San Francisco: Freeman, 1967.

64. Kohl, H. R. *The Open Classroom.* New York: Vintage Books, 1969, p. 116.

REFERENCES OF RELATED INTEREST

Atkinson, J. W., and N. T. Feather (eds.). *A Theory of Achievement Motivation.* New York: Wiley, 1966.

Bigge, M. L. "What Does Motivation Mean to S-R Associationists and Gestalt-Field Theorists?" In *Learning Theories for Teachers,* by M. L. Bigge. New York: Harper and Row, 1964, pp. 79–83.

Bremer, J., and M. vonMoschzisker. *The School without Walls.* New York: Holt, Rinehart & Winston, 1971.

Brown, J. S. *The Motivation of Behavior.* New York: McGraw-Hill, 1961.

Clark, P. M. "Psychology, Education, and the Concept of Motivation." *Theory into Practice* (February 1970):16–22.

Cofer, C. N., and M. H. Appley. *Motivation: Theory and Research.* New York: Wiley, 1967.

Flanagan, J. C. "Motivation and Achievement." In *Encyclopedia of Educational Research,* 4th ed., edited by R. L. Ebel and V. H. Noll. New York: Macmillan, 1969, pp. 1333–1339.

Fuller, J. L. *Motivation: A Biological Perspective.* New York: Random House, 1962.

Gagné, R. M. *The Conditions of Learning,* 2nd ed. New York: Holt, Rinehart & Winston, 1970.

Gnagey, W. J., P. A. Chesebro, and J. J. Johnson (eds.). *Learning Environments: Readings in Educational Psychology.* New York: Holt, Rinehart & Winston, 1972.

Haber, R. N. *Current Research in Motivation.* New York: Holt, Rinehart & Winston, 1966.

Hall, J. F. *Psychology of Motivation.* Philadelphia: Lippincott, 1961.

Hamachek, D. E. (ed.). *Human Dynamics in Psychology and Education,* 2nd ed. Boston: Allyn and Bacon, 1972, Chapter four.

Heckhausen, H. *The Anatomy of Achievement Motivation.* New York: Academic Press, 1967.

Madsen, K. B. *Theories of Motivation.* Cleveland: Howard Allen, 1961.

Marx, M. H., and T. N. Tombaugh. *Motivation: Psychological Principles and Educational Implications.* San Francisco: Chandler, 1967.

Maslow, A. H. *Motivation and Personality,* 2nd ed. New York: Harper & Row, 1970, Chapter four.

McClosky, M. G. (ed.). *Teaching Strategies and Classroom Realities.* Englewood Cliffs, N.J.: Prentice-Hall, 1971.

Murray, E. J. *Motivation and Emotion.* Englewood Cliffs, N.J.: Prentice-Hall, 1964.

O'Kelly, L. I. "Motivation: The Concept." In the *International Encylopedia of the Social Sciences.* New York: Crowell Collier and Macmillan, 1968.

Rethlingshafer, D. *Motivation as Related to Personality.* New York: McGraw-Hill, 1963.

Rogers, C. R. *Freedom to Learn.* Columbus, Ohio: Charles E. Merrill, 1969.

———. "The Facilitation of Significant Learning." In *Instruction: Some Contemporary Viewpoints,* by L. Siegel. San Francisco: Chandler, 1967.

Skinner, B. F. "Why Teachers Fail." *Saturday Review* (16 October 1965).

Sperry, L. (ed.). *Learning and Individual Differences.* Glenview, Ill.: Scott, Foresman, 1972.

Trabasso, T., and G. H. Bower. *Attention in Learning.* New York: Wiley, 1968.

Travers, R. M. W. *Essentials of Learning,* 3rd ed.   New York: Macmillan, 1972, Chapter 10.

Waetjen, W. B. "The Teacher and Motivation."   *Theory into Practice* 9(February 1970):10–15.

Weiner, B. "Motivation."   In *Encyclopedia of Educational Research,* 4th ed., edited by R. L. Ebel and V. H. Noll.   New York: Macmillan, 1969, pp. 878–888.

TWELVE

Self-concept Variables and Achievement Outcomes

CHAPTER OUTLINE

PROLOGUE

WHAT IS THE SELF?

The Self Is Expressed in Different Ways by Different People

Level of Aspiration and Self-esteem Are Interrelated

Self-esteem Is Influenced By Past Successes and Failures

EFFECT OF EARLY SCHOOL FAILURE ON SELF-IMAGE DEVELOPMENT

Too Much Failure to Low Self-esteem and Possible Dropping Out

Not All Drop Out—Some Stay, but Suffer

Why Elementary School Success Is So Crucial

The elementary child's self-system is incomplete and impressionable

The elementary child has immature defenses—he is vulnerable

The elementary child is still in the "industry versus inferiority" stage

Three reasons why elementary school success is important

Effects of Elementary School Letter Grades on Self-concept Development

   Not all students are ready for the same learning at the same time

Effects of Elementary School Nonpromotion Practices

Constructive Steps to Take if Nonpromotion Is Inevitable

Long-term Consequences of Early School Failure Experiences

   Juvenile delinquency and crime may be one of the consequences

   Maladjustment in adulthood may be another consequence

Stabilization of School Achievement Begins Early

SELF-CONSISTENCY AND ITS RELATIONSHIP TO SCHOOL PERFORMANCE

We Behave in Terms of What We Believe to Be True

New Perceptions May Lead to New and Improved Behavior

Behavior Reinforced Early Tends to Remain Stable Over Time

The Chicken or the Egg Question

SELF-CONCEPT AND RELATIONSHIPS TO ACADEMIC ACHIEVEMENT

Reading Skills Adversely Affected by a Low Self-image

A Low Self-image May Lead to Underachievement

The Underachievement Syndrome Is More Common Among Boys

Low-achievers and Underachievers Express More Negative Self-feelings

It's True — Nothing Succeeds like Success

Significant Others Make a Difference

A Positive Self-concept Is Necessary but not Enough

A Positive Self-concept Does not Cause High Achievement

SELF-CONCEPT AS IT IS AFFECTED BY ANXIETY

Low Anxiety Is Associated with High Self-esteem

Effects of Anxiety on School Performance

   A certain amount of anxiety has its advantages

STRATEGIES FOR ENHANCING SELF-CONCEPT AND ACHIEVEMENT

What a Teacher Says Makes a Difference

Teacher Expectations May Influence Performance

Why teacher expectations work the way they do

Do Teacher Expectations Really Make That Much Difference?

The Psychology of Expectations

A Note of Caution About Expectations

EPILOGUE

REFERENCES

REFERENCES OF RELATED INTEREST

IMPORTANT CHAPTER IDEAS

1. What a person has by way of personal qualities is less important than how he *feels* about those qualities.

2. Failure is more tolerable if it is preceded by success experiences.

3. The problems that result in a dropout begin way back in the elementary grades.

4. Success experiences during the elementary years are crucial in helping a child develop a healthy, positive self-concept.

5. Nonpromotion practices are generally not helpful as a way of promoting learning.

6. Research concerned with mental health and adjustment shows that adults who fail were usually children who failed.

7. Factors that contribute to school achievement other than intelligence are to a considerable extent stabilized during the first three grades.

8. A person tends to behave in ways that are consistent with the sort of person he conceives himself to be.

9. Low academic achievement may be related to a student's conception of himself as being unable to learn academic material.

10. Although it is not possible to say which comes first, good school work or a positive self-concept, each is mutually reinforcing to the other to the extent that a positive change in one facilitates a positive change in the other.

11. If persons who are "significant" to a student think highly of him, he is apt to think highly of himself.

12. A positive self-concept is a necessary but not a sufficient condition for achievement.

13. Too much anxiety can adversely affect school achievement.

14. Students have a better chance of doing well academically if a teacher "expects" or believes that they can and are able to do well.

15. Expectations not only represent a belief in a student's adequacy, but they also relay the message that he has the ability to do what is required of him.

PROLOGUE

Psychologists and teachers are becoming more and more aware of the fact that a person's view of himself, or self-concept, is closely related to how he behaves and learns. Indeed, there is increasing evidence to indicate that low achievement in basic school subjects, as well as the misguided motivation and lack of academic involvement so characteristic of the underachiever, the dropout, and the chronic failure, may be due at least in part to negative perceptions of the self. Some students, for example, have trouble with school work, not because of low intelligence or poor hearing, but because they have learned to consider themselves as unable and inadequate. For instance, if a student says, "I'll *never* pass that test, I just know it," he is telling us something rather significant about his inner feelings of powerlessness and intellectual impotency. All things being equal, chances are good that a student with this attitude probably *will not* do well on the test. We are beginning to understand that how a student performs in school depends not only on how bright he *actually* is, but also on how bright he *feels* he is.

Basically, the self has two essential aspects—concepts and feeling. That is, each person knows that he has particular qualities, but, more importantly, he has certain feelings about those qualities. For example, a student may "know" that his measured IQ is, say, 120, but unless he has the self-confidence and necessary belief in himself to act on his intelligence, his 120 IQ is a practically useless possession. The fact is that what a person has by way of personal qualities is far less important than how he feels about those qualities. Before we go furthur, let us address ourselves to an important first question.

WHAT IS THE SELF?

As the *self* has evolved in psychological thought and research, it has
come to have two rather distinct meanings. One approach is to define it as

a person's attitudes and feelings about himself, while the other is to regard it as a group of psychological processes that influence behavior and adjustment. The first meaning can be viewed as a self-as-object definition, in as much as it conveys a person's attitudes, feelings, and perceptions of himself as an object. It is almost as if we could stand outside of ourselves to evaluate what we see in a more or less detached sort of way. In this sense, it is what a person thinks of himself. The second meaning is more in line with what can be called a self-as-process definition. In other words, the self is a doer, in the sense that it includes an active group of processes such as thinking, remembering, and perceiving.

Acquiring a self-concept involves a slow process of differentiation as a growing child's individuality gradually emerges into focus out of his total world of awareness and gets progressively defined with greater and sharper clarity. Jersild is probably as clear as anyone about what the self is when he says:

> A person's self is the sum total of all he can call his. The self includes, among other things, a system of ideas, attitudes, values, and commitments. The self is a person's total subjective environment; it is the distinctive center of experience and significance. The self constitutes a person's inner world as distinguished from the outer world consisting of all other people and things.[1]

The Self Is Expressed in Different Ways by Different People

Ultimately, it is through the door of the self that one's personality is expressed. How the self is expressed is a complex phenomena done in different ways by different people. It is one person's assertiveness and another person's timidity; it is one person's need for social approval and another person's lofty independence; it is one person's sympathetic nature and another person's lack of empathy or caring; in the classroom it may be one student's confident interaction and another student's guarded quietness; it is one student's determined-to-succeed behavior and another student's resigned-to-failure attitude, and so it goes. Each individual's image of himself is constructed from his conception of the "sort of person I am," which is then acted out in behavior.

To a very large extent, how one sees himself is influenced by what he *backs* himself to be and do. William James, who was a very wise, sensitive psychologist, has illustrated this idea nicely in the following passage:

> I am not often confronted by the necessity of standing by one of my empirical selves and relinquishing the rest. Not that I would not, if I could, be both handsome and fat and well-dressed, and a great athlete, and make a million a year, be a wit, a bon-vivant, and lady-killer, as well as a philosopher, a philanthropist, statesman, warrior, and African explorer, as well as a "tone-

poet" and saint. But the thing is simply impossible. The millionaire's work would run counter to the saint's; the bon-vivant and the philanthropist would trip each other up; the philosopher and lady-killer could not keep house in the same tenement of clay . . . to make any one of them actual, the rest must more or less be suppressed . . . So the seeker of his truest, strongest, deepest self must review the list carefully, and pick out the one on which to stake his salvation. All other selves thereupon become unreal, but the fortunes of this self are real. It's failures are real failures, its triumphs real triumphs, carrying shame and gladness with them . . . I, who for the time have staked my all on being a psychologist, am mortified if others know more psychology than I. But I am contented to wallow in the grossest ignorance of Greek. My deficiencies there give me no sense of personal humiliation at all.[2]

It should be clear from the above quotation that how James felt about himself depended, in large measure, on how he viewed his own efforts in relation to others *who also backed themselves to be psychologists*. In other words, our feelings of self-worth and self-esteem grow in part from our perceptions of where we see ourselves in comparison to others whose skills, abilities, talents, and aptitudes are similar to our own. For example, if a psychology major "backs" himself to be an above-average student of psychology, but gets mostly C's in his psychology courses, or if an athlete "backs" himself to be an excellent football player but can only make third team, then each will either have to find acceptable excuses for their subpar performances or lower their expectations for themselves or move on to other endeavors where success is more possible. As soon as one's performance in what he backs himself to be good in is less than his minimum level of self-imposed expectations, then he typically begins to lose a certain measure of self-esteem. Inasmuch as self-esteem usually comes from being able to do one or two things at least as good as, if not a trifle better than, most other people it would be difficult to maintain self-esteem, not to mention enhancing it, if we see ourselves consistently falling somewhere behind that with which we were comparing ourselves.

TO THINK ABOUT

What two or three things do you "back" yourself to be good at?

_____

_____

_____

Would you rank yourself as high, medium, or low in comparison with others you know who may back themselves to be good in the same areas? Think about your ranking in relation to how you feel about yourself. Do you have good feelings? Bad ones? If they're negative, what can you do to change that?

Level of Aspiration and Self-esteem Are Interrelated

Self-imposed expectations refer to our personal levels of aspirations and these expectations are related to our feelings of self-esteem because they help establish what we interpret as either success or failure. What is a success or enhancing experience for one person can be a failure or deflating experience for another. For instance, I recall a C I received in an undergraduate course that I regarded as particularly difficult. That C, however, was consistent with my personal expectations and level of aspiration, and I felt that it was a minor, if not a major success. At the same time, a friend, who also received a C in that course, regarded this as a failure because his expectations and level of aspiration were not lower than a B. By getting that C I maintained my self-esteem, because it was an even money return on my personal investment. My friend, however, lost a measure of self-esteem, *because the return was less than his personal investment.* By starting out with different amounts of personal investment, we had different expectations for a personal return in order to maintain our original investments. In a similar vein, both of us could have enhanced our self-esteem if we had received grades that *exceeded* our original levels of aspiration.

Self-esteem Is Influenced by Past Successes and Failures

Although each person's level of aspiration determines to a large extent what he interprets as failure or success, and hence what either adds to or takes from his self-esteem, another factor worth considering is one's history of successes and failures. For example, to fail at something is more tolerable and less apt to threaten our self-esteem if we have had a history of success in that particular endeavor. Some cases in point: a girl who has had many boyfriends is not likely to sour on boys if she loses one, but a girl with few boyfriends could; a team with a 10-0 record is not apt to give up after losing the eleventh game, but a 0-10 team might; a .350 baseball player is not particularly discouraged when he strikes out, but a .150 player is; a student with a long string of above average grades is not likely to quit

Students usually start school with good feelings about themselves. We can leave them that way, too. (Allyn and Bacon)

school if he fails his first course, but a below average student who fails his tenth course might. In other words, the impact of falling short of one's personal aspirations stands to be a less self-deflating experience, if one's list of successes in that endeavor exceeds his tally of failures.

Unfortunately, not all students are able to taste the fruits of success and, in fact, are so dominated by the idea of failure that their entire lives are altered by the fear of failure and its consequences. This brings us to a topic worthy of our extended consideration.

EFFECT OF EARLY SCHOOL FAILURE ON SELF-IMAGE DEVELOPMENT

In a land where education is so highly valued and so much the key to one's personal advancement and society's total growth, it is a curious and sad paradox to note that approximately one-third of those students who start first grade this year will drop out before reaching the eleventh grade. If history repeats itself, as it has a knack for doing, these students will drop out not because of a sudden whim or capricious impulse, but because of more or less continous exposure to failure experiences that reinforce feelings of worthlessness and inadequacy. On the average, over one million young people leave school each year. One of the first explanations for this staggering number is that those who drop out are ones who cannot benefit from educational experiences anyway. Were it that simple. The fact is that well over half those who drop out have average mental ability. For example, in a U.S. Department of Labor study of seven widely dispersed, middle-sized cities, 6 percent of the dropouts were found to have IQ's over 110 and 55 percent had IQ's over 90.[3] This means that the majority of those who dropped out had the necessary intellectual equipment to complete high school.

Too Much Failure Leads to Low Self-esteem and Possible Dropping Out

The question is: Why do so many young people drop out of school? Some, we know, leave because they're bored. Others leave because they're angry or emotionally disturbed or both, and it is doubtful whether any school program—no matter how good—could hold them. The great majority, however, drop out because they simply cannot tolerate more failure and the commensurate feelings of low self-worth and self-esteem. This being the case, it should come as no surprise to note that one of the major findings of a four-year study of dropouts was that dropouts' self-esteem *got higher* once they were out of school.[4] In fact, measures of self-esteem of those who graduated were not much higher than those who dropped out. What a sorry commentary it is to think that a student must leave school in order to feel better about himself! And what a tragedy it is to find, as several studies have, that almost half of those who drop out cite adverse school experiences and negative feelings about themselves as their reasons for leaving the educational fold.[5,6]

Not All Drop Out—Some Stay, but Suffer

I have stressed the dropout and the dropout problem to this point because it is one very explicit and dramatic consequence of failure experiences that occur too early and too frequently among those who leave school. What we haven't mentioned are those hundreds of thosands of children who are victimized by excessive early school failure experiences, but who do not choose so dramatic an exit as dropping out. Rather, they persist on through school, suffering quietly and inwardly, and eventually graduate into a competitive society that demands not only a reasonable level of competence in some kind of work, but also a certain degree of confidence in one's ability to do the work. Unfortunately, thousands of young people graduate after thirteen years of school feeling somewhat helpless, hopeless, and defeated. Feelings like these, whether among those

"YOUNG MAN, UNLESS YOU RETURN TO SCHOOL IMMEDIATELY, WE'LL EXPELL YOU!"

Sometimes students avoid school because their experience with failure is overwhelming. Threatening them with more hardly helps.

who drop out because they can't tolerate more failure or among those who stay in and suffer through it, start during the elementary school years.

TO DO

If you could make the necessary arrangements, it would be an eye-opening experience for you to go into an elementary school and personally talk to youngsters who are not doing well, who have tasted the fruits of failure. How do they feel about themselves? About school? About their future?

How about your own elementary school years? Did you experience some failure experiences? If so, how were you affected?

For example, although studies indicate that approximately 70 percent of all dropouts complete at least a ninth-grade education, there is increasing evidence to show that the negative attitudes about school and thoughts about leaving it begin early in a child's school experiences. Wolfbein concluded from a series of dropout studies that

> . . . the problems which finally result in a dropout begin, and are quite overt, way back in elementary grades. In fact, it is quite early in grade school that many of the potential dropouts begin to fall behind in their scholastic achievements . . .[7]

In an intensive study of forty-five girls and sixty boys who were about to dropout of school, Lichter,[8] found that the reason was not the result of any specific learning failure, but rather a broad educational disability that, for boys in particular, started in elementary school.

As we stressed in Chapter 2, early school failure experiences simply do not encourage the early sense of competency so necessary for the growth of a positive self-image. Let's turn our attention next to why this is so.

Why Elementary School Success Is So Crucial

Success experiences for elementary school youngsters are important because they can be numbered among those positive early happenings upon which an increasingly more complex psychological superstructure can be built. In order to build a firm house, we give it a firm foundation that rests squarely on solid ground. The same is true for the human psyche. In order for it to be strong, it must begin with a firm foundation. Some adults, as we all know, have very shaky foundations and these must be repaired before further growth is possible. The point I'm trying to make is that what happens to a child during his elementary school years is critical because these are his foundation laying years. Everything that happens to him is simply incorporated as part of the basic personality foundation pour that occurs, as far as school is concerned at least, during the years from five to twelve, or grades one through six. These are the years when the footings of a child's personality are either firmly established in experiences of success, accomplishment, and pride in himself or flimsily planted in shifting sands of self-doubt, failure, and feelings of worthlessness.

The elementary child's self-system is incomplete and impressionable.
An elementary age child is in the early phases of forming his concept of
self. This is not to say that he has no sense of identity whatsoever, but it is
to suggest that *his sense of who he is and what he can do is incompletely
formed.* Characteristically, an elementary age youngster is malleable and
impressionable. He is not only ready to please adults, but to *believe* them
as well. Indeed, what adults say about him or how they evaluate either his
person or performance is incorporated more readily, more easily, and more
uncritically than at any other stage during his developmental years. This
means that the feedback a child receives from peers and adults — particularly significant adults like parents and teachers — is more likely to have
a greater impact because it is more readily absorbed into a developing self-
system, which, precisely because it *is* still developing and incomplete, is
more open to input and more available to change.

The elementary child has immature defenses — he is vulnerable. An
elementary school age child is not well defended psychologically. In the
absense of a consolidated and reasonably well-integrated self-image, he is
less likely to use active and assertive mechanisms such as denial or projection in order to protect himself from ego-damaging experiences and more
likely to use the passive and more primitive mechanisms of regression,
which allow him to stay at a safer and more dependent level of development. (Indeed, whether in children or adults, regressive behavior is not an
uncommon phenomenon following failure experiences.) In order to use a
defense mechanism, one first of all has to have a reasonably well-defined
self to begin with. This is not to suggest that the elementary age child is
totally incapable of compensating for his failure or displacing his anger or
projecting blame for poor work on the teacher. It is a matter of degree. If a
second grader fails a spelling test, he is more likely to "believe" that mark
(that is, incorporate it, internalize it) than a twelfth-grade boy with a positive view of himself and a history of doing well in school, who fails a
geometry test. The twelfth grader can blame his performance on a fluke,
deny its importance, rationalize his lack of study, or project it on his
teacher. As long as his performance is inconsistent with his concept of
self, he can defend himself against the loss of self-esteem. The second
grader, on the other hand, does not yet have a well-defined self with which
he can or has to be consistent. Hence, whether it is a failure or success
experience, the elementary age child can offer far less resistance to its impact and will be a much less critical recipient of its place in his evolving
sense of self.

Perhaps another way of stating this would be to suggest that an elementary age child does not yet have a consolidated self-system to serve as
the framework within which he can evaluate another person's evaluations

of him. For example, if you say something negative about me, I must first of all have some idea of who I am (a consolidated self-system) in order to evaluate what the meaning of your comment is for me.

The elementary child is still in the "industry versus inferiority" stage. As noted in greater detail in Chapter 2, the six- to twelve-year-old age group represents a growth phase that psychiatrist Erik Erikson[9] refers to as the "industry versus inferiority" stage. In other words, this is a natural time in a child's growth and development when he learns either to be industrious, productive, and autonomous, or inferior-feeling, withdrawn, and dependent. The major danger of this period, as Erikson sees it, is the development of a sense of inadequacy and inferiority in a child who does not receive recognition for his efforts. Again we are reminded of how incredibly important a teacher's feedback is to a child at this point in his development.

TO DO

You might find it particularly interesting to get hold of your old elementary school report cards to see how you fared academically and review the sorts of comments teachers made about you. Be especially sensitive to the comments that teachers wrote on your report cards. Do you find consistencies? Were teachers responding to the same things? Try to remember how teacher feedback (positive or negative) made you feel. What implications do you see for your own teaching behavior?

Three reasons why elementary school success is important. Early school success is crucial for three basic reasons: (1) subsequent success is not only easier to build onto early success, but it also seems more possible to the student; (2) early success gives him not only a sense of competence and accomplishment, but also establishes a precedent with which he can strive to be consistent; (3) early school success makes any later school failures more bearable because they are more likely to occur within a consolidated self-system buttressed by achievement and fortified by personal accomplishment.

As noble or as worthy as early school success may be, it unfortunately is not available to all children. Two widely used practices, letter grading and nonpromotion, doom thousands of children to failure at a very time in their lives when they are apt to be most lastingly influenced by it. Both of these practices are notorious for their negative effects on a young child's self-concept development, motivation, and subsequent achievement. Let's examine more closely why.

Effects of Elementary School Letter Grades
on Self-concept Development

Letter grades enter into many aspects of the mental health and self-concept development of elementary pupils. For bright children with high achievement needs, letter grades are no problem. They usually receive high marks and enjoy the challenge of competing for them. For many other children, however, letter grades are continual reminders to them that they are not doing as well as the others and that they are slow learners. As one second grader expressed it after receiving four D's and one F on his report card, "I must really be dumb." In ways like this, a child's *performance* gets translated into *feeling* and over a long enough period of time the perception of "dumbness" is converted into a *conception* of "dumbness," which is far more difficult to change.

Alexander[10] has correctly noted that low marks function more as a threat of failure than as motivation for improvement. More often than not they are actually punishment for previous failure, poor past environment or emotional problems. As a young elementary school child continues to experience failure, he begins to perceive himself as a poor achiever. Once a negative self-perception sets in, he will, in all likelihood, continue to perform at a low level no matter what his ability.

Not all students are ready for the same learning at the same time. In spite of a certain amount of lip service to the documented evidence that supports the concept of wide individual differences in growth among elementary age youngsters, some schools doggedly persist in behaving as if all children were ready for the same curriculum at the same time. Nothing could be further from the truth. As one small example of the wide disparities in academic readiness among elementary children, a typical fifth-grade class may reflect a range of reading skills all the way from those who are still at the second-grade level to those who are reading at the high school level. In fact, reading test data indicated that we might expect to find as many as 42 percent of a fifth grade reading below grade level.[11] This does not necessarily mean that students in this 42 percent group are less smart than their fellows; it may only mean that developmentally they still have some growing to do and have not yet completed the business of putting it all together in order to cognitively handle the symbol manipulation necessary for reading at grade level.

All in all, the letter-grade system in elementary schools, particularly if it is based on norm-referenced measurement,* is an almost certain method of guaranteeing that up to 40 percent of all elementary age children will be exposed to failure, and thus encouraged to incorporate a failure attitude as

---

* The idea of norm-referenced measurement, along with other kinds of measurement, will be discussed more fully in Chapter 13.

a part of their self-image during the most impressionable years of their development.

Effects of Elementary School
Nonpromotion Practices

A popular education assumption underlying the practice of nonpromotion is that the retained student, is re-covering material, is better able to overcome his deficits in subject-matter savvy than he would be were he passed on and exposed to new material.   Research has consistently shown that such an assumption is built more on myth than fact.   Some of the evidence:

1. The average repeater learns no more in two years than does the average nonrepeater of the same mental age in one year.[12]
2. Nonpromotion does not reduce the range of abilities within a particular grade level; that is, grades with a high proportion of repeaters are as apt to have as wide a range of ability differences as grades with a low proportion of repeaters.[13]
3. Failed students during two years following failure do not progress significantly greater than promoted matchees during the single year spent in the next grade.[14]
4. A policy of "achieve or fail" seems to have a more negative effect on students who are being retained than those who are not.   Although there is a trend toward increased achievement in the school with an "achieve or fail" policy, the increase is limited largely to those who are in no real danger of being retained anyway.[15]
5. Achievement does not decrease when students cease to be threatened by the possibility of nonpromotion; e.g.,
    a. No difference in reading ability was found over a ten-year period when a school changed to a 100 percent promotion policy.[16]
    b. Children who were told at the beginning of a school year that all would be promoted did as well on comprehensive achievement tests as those who were reminded throughout the year that they would not be promoted if they didn't do good work.[17]
6. Retention of students because of their inability to achieve academically can have undesirable effects on their personal-social adjustment.[18,19]
7. Teachers and peers tend to develop unfavorable attitudes toward nonpromoted students, which encourages nonpromoted students to develop increasingly more negative attitudes toward school and even an eager anticipation towards dropping out.[20]
8. Of those who repeat beyond the first grade, about 35 percent show some improvement, about 53 percent show little or no improvement, and about 12 percent do poorer work.[21]

9. Lack of motivation and subsequent poor school achievement is positively related to a student's experience with nonpromotion; e.g.,

   a. Of those students dropping out between grades eight and nine, all had experienced nonpromotion at least once and over four-fifths had experienced nonpromotion twice.[22]

   b. Out of 2,000 children who began first grade at the same time in the same school system, 643 dropped out before completing high school. All but five of these dropouts, 638, or 99 percent, had been retained in the first grade. As a combined total, these 643 students failed a total of more than 1,800 grades during their first six years of school. This averages out for each dropout failing every other year for six years![23]

   c. Over 74 percent of the dropouts in one school system repeated at least one grade as compared to only 18 percent among students who graduated from high school.[24]

   d. More than 1,200 students in grades 6 and 7 from 14 representative schools in a North Carolina study were investigated to differentiate between repeaters and nonrepeaters. Results showed that those who had been retained were reading a 6.8 grade level; those repeating one grade scored a 5.2 level, and those who had repeated two or more grades dropped to a 4.5 grade level. On mathematics achievement, nonrepeaters averaged in the 27th percentile; those repeating one grade in the 10th percentile; and those repeating two or more grades dropped to the 5th percentile. All in all, the data do not indicate that retention helps a student "catch up" academically—the usual justification for having students repeat. Failing was also found to have a strong influence on a student's feeling of self-worth. For example, on all the subscales of the *Tennessee Self-Concept Scale,* students who repeated grades scored lower than those who had not. Students repeating two or more grades scored far below the mean on each subscale.[25]

Constructive Steps to Take if Nonpromotion Is Inevitable

The list of indictments against nonpromotion practices in elementary school are long and convincing. Whether nonpromotion is looked at on the basis of subsequent academic achievement or emotional-social consequences, the general view leads to a rather dismal picture of grade retention as a means for enhancing a child's self-image development or academic achievement. Repeating a grade is an event of enormous import to a youngster. It is a failure experience that lasts not just a day or week, but one which persists for an entire academic year and can be remembered for a lifetime. It can be a particularly bad experience for those children who must return to the same school, the same curriculum, and the same teacher. For the student who fails to master the work of an academic year with his classmates Symonds has correctly observed:

> Something must be changed. He must be given a chance to learn from fresh, unfamiliar material, or the methods of instruction must be changed. Perhaps he would learn better with a different teacher. Probably he needs more detailed explanation or closer guidance. Somewhere he failed to comprehend and as a result made an inappropriate response. The emphasis should be on remedial instruction rather than nonpromotion.[26]

Research supports Symonds' observation; that is, if a nonpromoted student repeats a more or less identical program his second year, the evidence indicates that under these conditions he generally makes no more progress than he would had he been promoted.[27] On the other hand, there is evidence to indicate that the nonpromoted pupil has a better chance of improving when exposed to a different kind of program the second year.[28] There is also evidence to suggest that deleterious social and emotional effects of repeating a grade can be lessened for the child when the reason for school failure is based primarily on his immaturity for the grade in which he has been placed.[29] That is, if a child understands that he is repeating because "he has got some growing to do," then the overall negative impact of grade repetition can be reduced. If repeating a grade is considered, it is absolutely essential that the child in question be appraised of this possibility and the matter discussed with him or her. Probably one of the worst things that can happen to a youngster is to be forced to repeat a grade when (1) he has had neither voice nor choice in the decision, and (2) he believes his nonpromotion is because he is "too dumb."

Long-term Consequences of Early School Failure Experiences

With mind-boggling consistency, research concerned with mental health and adjustment shows that adults who fail were usually children who failed. For example, Robins[30] studied 500 guidance patients thirty years after they had been brought to attention as children for deviant behavior and reported that the more severe the maladjustment in childhood, the more disturbed was the adult adjustment. Clinic children, as opposed to a matched normal population, experienced more arrests, were more alienated from family and friends, had more occupational problems, and were hospitalized more frequently for mental problems. The children referred for antisocial behavior had a very low level of school achievement and many failed to make it even through elementary school.

549

Juvenile delinquency and crime may be one of the consequences. These conclusions are similar to Powell's[31] findings that indicated that failure in school is also likely to contribute to a rejection of norms of the larger society, and normlessness appears to be related to crime. This is not to say that all crime or even most of it is due to low educational achievement. Rather, the evidence suggests that since there is a limited range of life alternatives for individuals with failure-studded histories, they may be more tempted to fill their ego needs and status aspirations through such illegal activities as gambling, prostitution, robbery, dealing in narcotics, and so forth.

There is also evidence to relate school failure experiences to juvenile delinquency. For example, Spiegelman[32] found a high negative correlation between educational attainment and the probability of being arrested for committing a major juvenile crime. Even when differences in the probability of being arrested due to other factors (e.g., race, family income, family size, presence of both parents at home, IQ scores) were considered it was found that high school dropouts were three to five times more likely to be arrested for committing a juvenile crime. Since delinquents do not seem to be any less intelligent than the general population, but are more likely to fail in school, the potential role of the schools in preventing delinquency is strongly implied.[33]

Maladjustment in adulthood may be another consequence. Kolberg's et al.[34] monumental review of literature related to the predictability of adult mental health from childhood behavior, noted that research rather consistently found a moderate association between early low school achievement and almost every obvious expression of adult maladjustment except suicide and neurosis. However, it is not the low school achievement itself that is related to later adult maladjustment, but rather those behavioral factors that most likely *cause* low school achievement, as, for instance, low IQ, lack of attention, difficulty with authority figures, and general rule-defying behavior. In other words, early school failure is not a cause of later adult maladjustment, but, rather, symptomatic of personal and interpersonal problems that could lead to it. However, Kolberg makes the excellent point that "because underachievement is associated with defects in these ego-strength variables (trouble with authority figures, lack of attention, etc.), underachievement is a statistical predictor of all major forms of adult maladjustment (and) it seems likely that early school failure is itself an environmental cause of later low status . . . ."[35]

Stabilization of School Achievement Begins Early

Sometimes those children who have many failure experiences in elementary school are difficult *not* to fail precisely because of their general slowness or recalcitrant behavior. On the other hand, they are precisely the children who should not fail, particularly at a time in their lives when they are most susceptible to its effects. Longitudinal research findings indicate that there is something like a critical period for the formation of abilities and attitudes for school learning that occurs in or is set or stabilized sometime between the ages of five and nine. For example, Bloom's[36] surveys of longitudinal research suggest that adolescent or adult intelligence is about 50 percent stabilized or predictable by the first grade, whereas adolescent school *achievement* is predictable to the same extent only at age nine or about the end of grade three. This means that factors that contribute to school achievement other than intelligence are to a considerable extent stabilized during the first three grades. In large measure, these factors are sheer skill factors, which are cumulative in nature. That is, if a child has more skills in the first grade, he accumulated further skills in the second, and more in the third, and so on. Again Kolberg makes an observation that needs to be stressed at this juncture:

> In large part, however, this stabilization of school achievement is based on the stabilization of factors of interest in learning, attention, and *sense of competence*.[37] [Italics mine.]

What this all points to is the establishment during the early school years of an attitudinal set that can have either a positive or negative valence and that can influence, for good or evil, subsequent school achievement. Apparently, a child's feelings about his ability to do school work are rooted in his early school experiences and these determine, to a great extent, both the intensity and direction of his emerging self-image as a student.

TO DO

You can explore for yourself how elementary school experiences are related to later school performance and current self-attitudes by talking about this with your friends. Are a person's feelings about his ability to do school work rooted in early school experiences? What experiences have made the most difference? Can you see patterns of consistency emerge in yourself and others as you link the past with the present? What implications do you see in this for teachers?

When it comes to assessing the importance of early success experiences for later adult behavior, Bower has observed:

> . . . there is an increasing clinical research and evidence to support the hypothesis that children who find healthful satisfactions in relationships with family, neighborhood, and school will as adults find these same satisfactions;

and that the children who find frustration and defeat in these primary institutions also tend to be defeated as adults.[38]

There is, in other words, a certain consistency in behavior that persists over time, an idea worth our brief consideration.

SELF-CONSISTENCY AND ITS RELATIONSHIP TO SCHOOL PERFORMANCE

Whether conscious of it or not, every person carries about with him a mental blueprint of the kind of person he is. This blueprint is made up of a system of interrelated ideas, attitudes, values, and commitments that are influenced by our past experiences, our successes and failures, our humiliations, our triumphs, and the way other people responded to us, particularly during our formative years. Eventually, each person develops a consolidated framework of beliefs about himself and proceeds to live and perform in a manner that is more or less consistent with that framework. In short, an individual "acts like" the sort of person he conceives himself to be. Indeed, it is extremely difficult to act otherwise, in spite of a strong conscious effort and exercise of will power. The boy, for example, who conceives himself to be a "failure-type student" can find all sorts of excuses to avoid studying, doing homework, or participating in class. Frequently, he ends up with the low grade he predicted he would get in the first place. His report card bears him out. Now he has "proof" that he's less able! Or, as another example, the socially isolated boy who has an image of himself as the sort of person nobody likes may find that he is indeed avoided by others. What he does not understand is that he may behave in a style that literally invites rejection. His sour expression, his hangdog manner, his own overzestfulness to please, or perhaps his unconscious hostility towards those he anticipates will affront him may all act to drive away those who might otherwise be friendly.

We Behave in Terms of What We Believe to Be True

Because of this objective "proof," it seldom occurs to a person that his trouble lies in his own evaluation of himself. If you tell a student that he only "thinks" he cannot grasp algebra, or English, or reading, or whatever, he may very well give you that "Who are you trying to kid?" look. In his own way, he may have tried again and again, but still his report card tells the story. A request (more often a demand or admonishment) destined to fall on deaf ears is the one parents and teachers frequently make of some students to "study harder." This is fine if the student already has a high self-concept and high need for achievement, because he is likely to respond to the challenge in order to produce at a level consistent with his self-image. However, for a student whose self-picture is that of being a poor student, the impact is lost. As a low-concept, low-achieving ninth-grade girl once told me, "Study? Ha! Why should I study to fail?"

Although we may not like this girl's flip answer, it is important to understand that from her point of view it was a perfectly logical conclusion. She saw herself as fairly dumb and of course dumb people don't do well. So why study? She was expressing a need that all of us have, namely, the need to maintain an intact self-structure so that the person we are today can be counted on as being pretty much the same person tomorrow. Again, we should remind ourselves that this consistency is not always voluntary or deliberate, but compulsive, and generally unconsciously motivated.

It is important to keep the self-consistency idea in mind because it will help us understand better the relationship between school performance and self-concept. Once a student "locks in" on a perception of what he is and is not able to do, it is difficult to shake him from it, particularly if the perception has time to root itself into a firmly established belief. Again, it is a reminder to us of why success in elementary school is so important for healthy self-image development.

TO THINK ABOUT

What perception of yourself as a student are you "locked in on?" If you could change that perception, how would it be different? How would you be different?

_____

_____

_____

New Perceptions May Lead to New and Improved Behavior

A pioneer in the area of relating self-consistency to school performance was Prescott Lecky,[39] who was one of the first to point out *that low aca-*

demic achievement may be related to a student's conception of himself as being unable to learn academic material. He observed, for example, that some children made the same number of errors in spelling per page no matter how difficult or easy the material. These children spelled as though they were responding to a built-in upper limit beyond which they could not go. It occurred to Lecky that they were responding more in terms of how they *thought* they could spell than in terms of their *actual* spelling abilities. He arranged to have a group of these children spend some time with the counselor who helped them explore their feelings about their spelling abilities. As a consequence of these discussions and despite the fact that these children had no additional work in spelling whatever, there was a notable improvement in their spelling! There was less improvement for some children than for others, but the general trend was in the direction of better spelling. One can only speculate about the dynamics at work here, but it does not seem unreasonable to suggest that as the childrens' spelling *confidence* increased, so, too, did their spelling *skills*. In other words, as they acquired new perceptions of their spelling abilities, they also acquired new consistencies, which is to say that as a child moves from believing he is a poor speller to believing he is at least a better speller than he thought he was, his performance changes in the direction of being consistent with his new perception.

Behavior Reinforced Early Tends to Remain Stable Over Time

The purpose for understanding something about the nature and expressions of self-consistency is not merely an academic one. Psychological research and developmental evidence suggests that basic personality styles begin early in life, which means that whether we are teachers or other professional people or parents we can be alert to signs indicating the possible direction of a child's growth. Too often we wait for a child to "grow out of" his shyness, or aggressiveness, or lack of motivation, or speech problem, or whatever without realizing that we are confusing the symptom of a possible personality defect for what is frequently called "just a stage he's going through." Behavior that is established early and reinforced while the child is young is likely to remain stable over time and serve as the seedbed in which one's basic ideas about himself are nurtured. The fact that a child's personality structure is established early and tends to remain stable over time would suggest that, if we are to have a positive effect on a child's self-image development, then we must do this while he is going through his formative years. Sensitive parents and psychologically tuned elementary level teachers working in conjunction with extended guidance and counseling programs in elementary schools would surely be a constructive step in the right direction.

The Chicken or the Egg Question

An inevitable question that always seems to come up in any discussion related to self-concept and achievement is the one which asks what comes first, a positive self-concept or high achievement? It is not possible to give a definitive answer to this question because the fact is that we just don't know for sure. Although one could argue that a student would first have to have a positive self-image in order to do well in school, the flip side of that argument is that doing well must precede a positive self-concept rather than follow it. In fact, there's some evidence to support the argument's flip side from research done by Shore, Massimo, and Ricks,[40] who found that, among delinquents at least, changes in competence preceded changes in self-concept. They further noted that this change was then followed by improvement in social behavior and adjustment.

Even though it is not possible to specify exactly which came first, good school work or high self-regard, *it does not seem unreasonable to suggest that each is mutually reinforcing to the other to the extent that a positive change in one facilitates a positive change in the other.* That is, if a child begins school with a low level of self-confidence and self-regard but experiences success almost in spite of himself, we could reasonably expect that his concept of self as far as school ability is concerned will be elevated. In fact, there is research evidence to suggest that persons who initially are the least confident in their ability to do well or to even complete a particular task end up feeling the most satisfied upon completing something they didn't think they could do in the first place.[41] In other words, unexpected success can do great things for a student's ego, whether he is in first grade, high school or college, and this in turn makes him feel more confident, which then gets translated into higher self-imposed expectations that he strives harder to live up to. On the other hand, an equally plausible possibility is that if a youngster begins school with high confidence in his ability to do school work and experiences excessive failure his concept of self may be lowered. When this happens, he will either have to shift this attention to other areas, usually nonacademic, to maintain his self-esteem, or continue to lose self-confidence and self-esteem.

Fortunately, the chicken or the egg question is more academic than practical. If we get too caught up in deciding which comes first, we may miss the real issue — namely, the student, who he is and where he is. The important fact is that self-concept and achievement do seem to be interrelated, an idea to which we now turn our attention.

TO THINK ABOUT

Consider the courses you avoided taking in high school and college. You may also want to consider those courses you've taken but have felt shaky about taking in the first place. As you think about it, what do you suppose came first for you? Low ability or a low self-concept? As you think about your feelings related to this question, how does the one (high or low ability) interact with the other (high or low self-concept) in your behavior? What can you do as a teacher to help make this a positive interaction in your students?

SELF-CONCEPT AND RELATIONSHIP TO ACADEMIC ACHIEVEMENT

The self is a complicated subjective system that a student brings with him to school. A student perceives, interprets, accepts, resists, or rejects what he encounters at school in the light of the way he sees himself as a person generally and as a student specifically. Indeed, there is a mounting body of evidence to suggest that a student's performance in an academic setting is influenced in both subtle and obvious ways by his concept of self. For example, Roth, investigating the role of self-concept in achievement observed: " . . . in terms of their conception of self, individuals have a definite investment to perform as they do. With all things being equal, those who do not achieve, *choose* not to do so, while those who do achieve, *choose* to do so."[42]

Reading Skills Adversely Affected by a Low Self-Image

Although, as noted earlier, an elementary school child's self-image is incompletely formed, there is research data to suggest that the beginnings of a negative self-concept can have adverse affects on a child's school performance even at a very young age. For example, Wattenberg and Clifford[43] found that an unfavorable view of self and poor achievement is already established in many children before they enter first grade. The investigators studied the relationship of kindergarten children's self-attitudes to subsequent school achievement in elementary school. Their method was to study 128 kindergarten students in two schools, one serving lower-class, the other middle-class neighborhoods. They measured intelligence, self-concept, ego-strength, and reading ability of all the students when they were in kindergarten, and then measured these same variables again when these same students finished second grade. They found that measures of self-concept and ego-strength made at the beginning of kindergarten were more predictive of reading achievement two and one-half years later than were measures of intelligence. In other words, the self-attitudes of the kindergarten student were a more accurate indication of his potential reading skills than his intelligence test scores. We cannot, however, assume from this finding that there is no relationship between mental ability and reading achievement. All we can safely conclude is that a measure of a kindergarten student's self-concept and ego-strength is a better predictor of how he might fare in his reading skills by the third grade than is a measure of his intelligence. In addition, we should also keep in mind that a five year old's verbal skills are usually not sufficiently developed to be measured with great accuracy, which may be one reason why Wattenberg and Clifford found a low relationship between intelligence and later reading achievement.

A Low Self-image May Lead to Underachievement

If a child starts with a negative self-image about his ability to do school work, we might expect to find explicit signs of low or poor academic achievement during the early elementary years. For instance, Shaw and McCuen[44] reasoned that if it is true that academic underachievement is related to basic personality structure, then such behavior is, indeed, likely to occur during the early school years. To check this out they took a group of eleventh- and twelfth-grade students who had been in the same school system since the first grade and who scored in the upper quarter of an intelligence test administered in the eighth grade and divided them into achiever and underachiever groups, which were separated for males and females: thirty-six male achievers, thirty-six male underachievers, forty-five female achievers, and seventeen female underachievers. The mean grade point averages were computed for each group at each grade level. They found that there were significant differences between male achievers' and underachievers' grade point averages at the first grade. The grade point difference between the two groups increased at each grade level from grade three up to grade ten, where there was a slight decrease. There were no significant differences between female achievers and underachievers before grade nine, although nonsignificant differences were apparent in grade six. These differences between the two groups of girls continued to increase through grade eleven. So, as you can see, underachievement for boys can begin as early as the first grade, is definitely present by third grade, and becomes increasingly more serious into the high school years. For girls the problem may exist as early as grade six and is definitely present and of increasing importance from grades nine to eleven.

The Underachievement Syndrome Is More
Common Among Boys

In an investigation to explore possible relationships between academic underachievement and self-concept, Fink[45] studied a group of ninth-grade students, which included twenty pairs of boys and twenty-four pairs of girls. They were matched for IQ's (all in the 90 to 110 range), and each individual student was judged as underachiever or achiever depending on whether his grade point average fell below or above the class median. One achiever and one underachiever made up each pair. The self-image of each student was rated as adequate or inadequate by three separate psychologists, based on data from three personality tests, a personal data sheet, and a student essay: "What I Will Be in Twenty Years." The combined ratings of the three psychologists showed significant differences between achievers and underachievers, with achievers being rated as far more adequate in their concepts of self. Fink concluded that there was a strong significant relationship between self-concept and academic underachievement and, further, that this relationship was stronger for boys than for girls. In view of the fact that boys are more likely than girls to acquire negative perceptions of themselves and school, Fink's conclusion does not seem surprising.

Later research by Campbell[46] supports the conclusions reached in the study cited above, but this time with fourth-, fifth-, and sixth-grade children. Among other things, the author found a direct relationship between self-concept and academic achievement and also noted that girls were more inclined to have higher self-concepts than boys.

Low-achievers and Underachievers Express
More Negative Self-Feelings

Walsh[47] conducted a study involving twenty elementary school boys with IQ's over 120 who were "underachievers" and who were matched with twenty other boys who had similar IQ's but who were high-achievers. She found that bright boys who were low-achievers had more negative feelings about themselves than did high-achievers. In addition, she noted that low-achievers differed reliably from high-achievers in (1) feelings of being criticized, rejected, or isolated; (2) acting defensively through compliance, evasion, or negativism; and (3) being unable to express themselves appropriately in actions and feelings.

In another investigation, the personality characteristics and attitudes toward achievement of two groups of fourth- and fifth-grade children differentiated in reading ability were analyzed. Subjects in this study consisted of seventy-one "poor" readers and eighty-two "good" readers equated as nearly as possible for age, sex, ethnic composition, and intelligence. As compared to the poor reader, the good reader was found to be more apt to describe himself as "well-adjusted and motivated by internalized drives which result in effortful and persistent striving for success." This is in contrast to the picture presented by poor readers, who, according to the investigators, ". . . willingly admit to feelings of discouragement, inadequacy, and nervousness, and whose proclaimed goals are often ephemeral or immediate—especially in avoiding achievements."[48] The results of this study are consistent with Bodwin's[49] who found a significant positive relationship between immature, low self-concepts and reading disabilities among students in the third and sixth grades.

In a study involving junior high students, Nash[50] developed a set of one hundred items that included three dimensions of self-perceptions assumed to be important, which included: (1) the importance of peer relationships, (2) nonconformity, and (3) satisfaction with self. Interestingly, the items that were found to be best in differentiating between high- and low-achievers were those concerned with the student's perception of the quality of his performance in school work, such as, "My grades are good" and "I am accurate in my school work."

It's True—Nothing Succeeds like Success

In a significant investigation by Dyson dealing with the relationships between self-concept and ability grouping among seventh graders, it was found that high-achieving students reported significantly higher self-concepts than did low-achieving students and that this was true regardless of the type of grouping procedures utilized in the academic program. Noteworthy is the author's final observation in which he states:

> If there is one particularly significant result growing out of this research, it is that "nothing succeed like success." This is not a new understanding, as the old cliché indicates. The work reported here does, however, re-emphasize the importance of success in the learning situation as a contribution to positive psychological growth and it indicates that this feeling of success is probably more crucial in its effect on the student's self-concept than how an individual is grouped for instruction.[51]

The results of the above study are consistent with one of the conclusions reached by Borislow[52] in his investigation of relationships between self-evaluation and academic achievement among 197 college freshman. He observed that students who underachieve scholastically have a poorer concept of themselves as students than do achievers subsequent to their scholastic performance, *regardless of initial intention to strive for scho-*

lastic achievement as a goal. In other words, though an underachiever may say something like "I don't care if I do well or not," indicating that he isn't motivated anyway, doing poorly still leaves a mark on him. Just as success is likely to breed a "success feeling," so, too, does failure, in spite of the assertion "I don't care whether or not I fail," breed a "failure feeling." Indeed, it would not be reasonable to speculate that low academic performance may make a student even more defensive and willing to claim "I don't care whether I fail or pass." Funny thing about people— sometimes those who holler loudest about *not* caring, care the most.

Significant Others Make a Difference

A monumental research effort by Brookover and his colleagues[53] involving over 1,000 seventh-grade students focused specifically on self-concept of ability in school and academic achievement. They found a significant and positive relationship between self-concept and academic performance and, in addition, observed that self-concept was significantly and positively related to the perceived evaluations that significant others held of the student. This literally means that if persons "significant" (valued, prized, important) to a student think highly of him, then he is apt to think highly of himself.

TO DO

Identify three "significant others" in your life who have made a difference to you in terms of how you feel about yourself as a student. What "messages" about your intellectual ability do you recall hearing most frequently from them?

_____

_____

How have those messages made you feel about your academic ability.

A Positive Self-concept Is Necessary but not Enough

In the second phase of a longitudinal investigation of the relationship between self-concept of ability and school achievement that began with the study cited above, Brookover and his associates[54] found that self-concept of ability was a significant factor in achievement at all levels, seventh through tenth grade.

In the third and final phase of this longitudinal project, which studied the same students from the time they were seventh graders through grade twelve, the following observation regarding the relation of the self-concept of ability to achievement was made:

> The correlation between self-concept of ability and grade point average ranges from .48 to .63 over the six years. It falls below .50 only among boys in the 12th grade . . . In addition, the higher correlation between perceived evaluations and self-concepts tends to support the theory that perceived evaluations are a necessary and sufficient condition for [the growth of a positive or high] self-concept of ability, but [a positive] self-concept of ability is only a necessary, but *not* a sufficient condition for achievement. The latter is further supported by the analysis of the achievement of students with high and low self-concept of ability. This revealed that although a significant proportion of students with high self-concepts of ability achieved at a relatively lower level, practically none of the students with lower (less positive) self-concepts of ability achieved at a high level.[55]

The research reported by Brookover and his associates is important for several reasons. One, it points out the important impact that "significant" people can have on the self-concept of a growing child. Since the self begins early in life and is nurtured in a framework of social interaction, a substantial dimension of any person's feelings about himself is derived from his incorporation of the attributes he perceives other people assigning to him. It is through an individual's long immersion in an interpersonal stream of reflected appraisals from people important to him that he gradually develops a view of himself that he strives to maintain. And number two, the Brookover research serves to remind us that it takes more than a positive self-concept in order for there to be high academic achievement. Why should this be? Why do some students with high, positive self-concepts fail to achieve at commensurately high levels?

A Positive Self-concept Does not Cause High Achievement

We have to understand that the possession of a high, positive self-concept does not *cause* high academic achievement. It appears to be a necessary and vital personal quality for one to have *prior to* achievement, but it is no guarantee that high achievement will naturally follow. A person could have a positive self-concept that is sustained and nurtured by success in nonacademic pursuits—athletics, extracurricular participation, popularity with the opposite sex, creative expression in the various arts, and so on. If a student is motivated to do well in a nonacademic area and *does* well, he is less likely to be deflated by failure experiences encountered in

561

the scholastic arena.   Indeed, some students work very hard and diligently in nonacademic areas in order to compensate for any deficits tallied in their academic work.   For example, an artist friend in graduate school always tried to save as much face as possible in the wake of his sometimes mediocre academic work by reminding his friends of the "long hours he had to spend on his best paintings, and, after all, one can't be good in all things at once."   The fact was that he couldn't care less about his academic performance.   He did, however, care considerably about his painting skills, and it was on canvas, and not in the classroom, that he was motivated "to be somebody" and to enhance and maintain his positive concept of self.

SELF-CONCEPT AS IT IS AFFECTED BY ANXIETY

Anxiety is a chronic, complex emotional state with apprehension or fear as its most prominent component.   The fear of bringing on anxiety is usually generated by dread of the past or apprehension of the future rather than a specific fear-provoking situation in the present.   For example, if a person is walking across a narrow board high over deep water and hears the board begin to crack and he starts to sweat—that's fear!   If a person walks across a well-constructed reinforced bridge and worries about the whole thing crashing down—that's anxiety.

As any one of us who has ever panicked or "clutched" the moment an exam was put before him knows, anxiety, self-concept, and the ability to engage in deliberate thinking are closely interrelated.   A student in school constantly faces situations whose demands he must compare with his own resources.   And whenever a person's assessment of the situational demands leads him to conclude that they are greater than his own resources, he is ripe for the various consequences of anxiety.   How much anxiety two given individuals feel when confronted with a similar situation depends partly on their overall concept of personal adequacy and self-esteem and partly on their specific feelings about being able to cope with the circumstances at hand. Experimental evidence, for example, shows that low self-esteem persons, when faced with anxiety-provoking situations, are inclined to make hasty, impulsive judgements—behavior not unlike that of a student who feels overwhelmed (either for real or imagined reasons) by an exam and answers questions without really knowing what he's doing just so he can hand the test in and relieve the anxiety.   On the other hand, high self-esteem persons when faced with anxiety-provoking situations (at least as judged by an outside observer) are more deliberate and careful in making judgments.

Low Anxiety Is Associated with High Self-Esteem

Studies involving both children and college students indicate a relation between self-rejection or negative self-concept and measures of anxiety. In one of these, Lipsitt[56] obtained an overall index of the "good-bad" dimension of the self-concepts of about 300 fourth-, fifth- and sixth-grade boys and girls with good self-concepts. Other research has shown that high-anxious children, when compared to low-anxious children, are less popular;[57] have greater difficulty with conceptually complex learning tasks;[58] and in at least some cases do less well in the more complicated school subjects.[59]

Coopersmith[60] measured the anxiety level of 102 fifth- and sixth-grade students and found that children who had high self-esteem were significantly less anxious than those with low self-esteem. In addition, high self-esteem youngsters were also more popular. In a later research report, Coopersmith[61] noted that fifth and sixth graders who had positive self-concepts were better able to recall (presumably to correct) their failures than are children with negative self-concepts, who apparently repress and deny their poor performances.

Such relations between self-concept and anxiety are not limited to children. For example, Mitchell[62] measured the self-concepts and anxiety levels of 100 freshman and sophomore women students and found that the better the self-concept the less the anxiety.

Anxiety and self-concept do, indeed, seem to be related. How, then, does anxiety affect academic achievement?

Effects of Anxiety on School Performance

According to conventional wisdom, things are either "good" or "bad" for a person, and since anxiety may have negative effects on behavior, it therefore must be "bad." Part of the difficulty here lies in the *degree* of anxiety that is desirable, particularly as it is related to school learning. In regard to this question of degree," a number of research efforts suggest that some, but not too much, anxiety is helpful. For instance, Sarason and his co-workers[63] presented a group of high-anxious and low-anxious college students with a specific task and found that low-anxious students did better in general than high-anxious students, and that pressure to finish the task (from the experimenters) resulted in improved performances for low-anxious students, but not for high-anxious students. As another example of the effect of anxiety on performance, Cox[64] found that fifth-grade boys scoring in the *middle range* of two measures of anxiety tended to have better school marks than those scoring at the high or low ends of the scale.

A certain amount of anxiety has its advantages. What we call *anxiety* is actually a form of activation or tension. When a person is too relaxed and too free from anxiety, he is not likely to be very attentive to the kind of stimuli that might otherwise result in problem-solving activity and other forms of learning. On the other hand, when anxiety is too high, he is likewise unable to attend to stimuli that might lead to learning-related activity because of his overwhelming fear of failure. The optimum level of anxiety is thus somewhere between the two extremes. In general, research indicates that the differences in performance between high-, medium-, and low-anxious students are evidently due to tendencies of people to maintain anxiety at rather consistent levels. In other words, a student who is consistently relaxed and who has a relatively low level of anxiety tends to be somewhat unresponsive and consequently a rather poor learner. Other students are characteristically over-tense and over-anxious and experience difficulty in coping with new learning situations.

The best classrooms, as far as learning is concerned, are probably those that combine a happy blend of tension and acceptance—not so tense that students are afraid to speak out and not so accepting that they never feel challenged.

TO THINK ABOUT

What sorts of classroom situations make you feel most anxious? How do you behave when you feel anxious in a classroom? As a teacher, what will you do to help students feel less anxious (or at least not so anxious as to be immobilized)?

_____

_____

_____

STRATEGIES FOR ENHANCING
SELF-CONCEPT AND ACHIEVEMENT

Both our own personal experience and empirical research evidence tell us that students come to school with all sorts of ideas about themselves and their abilities. A host of studies have shown that successful students are typically characterized by self-confidence, self-acceptance, feelings of adequacy and personal competence, and generally more stable feelings of positive self-regard.[65–68]   On the other hand, research shows that unsuccessful students are characterized by feelings of uncertainty, low self-regard, self-derogatory attitudes, and strong inferiority feelings.[69–71]   The question remains: Are there specific things a teacher can do to enhance a student's self-image as part of an overall effort to raise achievement?   Let's turn our attention now to some investigations that have addressed themselves to that question.

What a Teacher Says Makes a Difference

A psychologist by the name of Staines[72] got interested in the question of what teachers do and say in a classroom that influence students to feel either good or badly about themselves and set up a research design to find out more about this.   He began by asking the following questions:

1. What part do teachers play in the development of the child's self?
2. Can teachers change a student's self-picture if they try to do so?
3. If they can, what methods of teaching produce what kinds of self-picture?
4. Is it possible to distinguish between teachers in the frequency and kind of comment that they make about a student's self?

The basic assumption of the study was that since a teacher is an important aspect of a student's emotional world, it is likely that he can have an important influence on a student's self-concept.

In order to test this assumption, two elementary classes were matched for age, intelligence, and socioeconomic class.   In one class, Teacher A deliberately set out to actively assist students to view themselves as planning, purposing, choosing, responsible, and accountable individuals.   It was considered important that the student should test his purposes by carrying them through, see himself as adequate and causal (i.e., one who can *make* things happen) and, at the same time, differentiate between his strengths and weaknesses.   In order to facilitate these goals, Teacher A made it a point to get to know each student and also to familiarize himself with the general area of self-concept dynamics and how these dynamics were related to behavior.   In class, the teacher was likely to make comments such as the following, all designed to help students toward a more positive view of themselves, while at the same time assisting them to be realistic about their abilities:

1. "Randy, you're tall.   Help me with this."
2. "Barbara, you know, you're very good at solving addition problems."
3. "Good boy!   Look at this everyone!"

In part, how students feel about themselves and their abilities depends not only on *what* a teacher says, but *how* she says it.   (Allyn and Bacon)

4. "Sally, you seem to do better in arithmetic than English."
5. "You're a fine one, you are."

Note the emphasis on highlighting specific strengths, assets, and skills; on helping the student sort out his strengths and weaknesses; and, as in the last statement, on commenting on his value as a total or "whole" person.

Teacher B was judged to be an equally effective teacher, but his techniques were more along the lines of traditional teaching and not adapted to fit within a framework that explicitly considered self-concept enhancement variables.

When the twelve-week experimental period was concluded, data from Teacher B's class indicated that traditional high-pressure teaching, with vigorous personal emphasis, with great stress on correctness and on the serious consequences of failure, and with the constant emphasis on passing examinations, leads to greater insecurity. As far as achievement was concerned, the students of Teacher A reflected slightly higher average improvement than the students of Teacher B in standardized reading and number tests. If it is objected to that a teacher cannot spend time assisting students toward a more positive, healthy attitude for fear of shortchanging them in the way of content, here is some evidence to suggest that at least equally good academic results may be obtained while helping students to see themselves in a more positive light.

Teacher Expectations May Influence Performance

In still another investigation, Rosenthal and Jacobson[73] have shown that a teacher's *expectations* for his students' performance can be a significant determinant of how the students actually respond. For example, within each of the six grades in a particular school were three classrooms, one each of children performing at above average, average, and below average levels of scholastic achievement. In each of these classes, an average of 20 percent of the children were identified to the teachers as having scores on the *Test for Intellectual Blooming* which suggested that they would show unusual academic gains during the academic year. Actually, the children had been picked at random from the total population of children taking the test. Eight months after the experimental conditions were instituted, all children were retested with the same IQ test. What were the results?

The major finding was that the experimental children on the average increased 12.2 points in IQ during the year, while the control group children increased only 8.4 IQ points. That is, those children from whom teachers had been led to expect greater intellectual gain showed significantly greater gain in IQ score than did other children in the school! In fact, the lower the grade level the greater the IQ gain, particularly in grades one and two. Apparently teachers interacted with "brighter" children more positively and more favorably and the children responded in kind by showing greater gains in IQ, which very likely resulted from a more enthusiastic attitude about school and enhanced feelings about themselves. Why should there be more change in the lower grades? One reason may be due to the fact that younger children are generally more malleable, less fixed, and more capable of change. A second possibility may be related to the fact that younger elementary school children do not yet have firmly established "reputations" that can be passed on from one teacher to the next. Indeed, it may well be that as a student gets older, teachers' interaction with that student is increasingly determined by the kind of "reputation" (good student or poor, delinquent or well-behaved, "Better watch him—he can't be trusted," or "He's a good student; he'll work hard for you") that has been established.

Why teacher expectations work the way they do. A great many studies related to effect of teacher expectations on student performance have been done since the original research by Rosenthal and Jacobson and although not all have supported Rosenthal's conclusions, many of them have. In an effort to explain why teacher expectations work the way they do, Rosenthal[74] has proposed a four-factor "theory" of the influences that are likely to encourage students to do well when teachers expect them to do well. As Rosenthal sees it, people who have been led to expect good things from their students, children, clients, or what-have-you appear to:

1. Create a warmer social-emotional mood around their "special students" (climate).
2. Give more positive feedback to those students about their performance (feedback).
3. Teach more material and more difficult material to their special students (input).
4. Give their special students more opportunities to respond to questions (output).

Do Teacher Expectations Really Make That Much Difference?

Neither Rosenthal's research design nor his conclusions have been universally accepted by all psychologists. In fact, the results of this study have been severely criticized by measurement specialists who have questioned the validity of the tests used and also the validity of the pretest data.[75-77] Although not all studies[78,79] have been able to replicate Rosenthal's findings (replication is always the best way to verify or refute the results of an initial research effort), other investigations have found that teacher expectations do indeed influence student performance. For example, Rosenthal,[80] himself, has reported three replications of the study in the Midwest and the East, which corroborated the original results. More recently, Rosenthal[81] reviewed 242 studies and found 84 of them reported that experimenters or teachers' expectations made a significant difference in how subjects performed in various situations. Eighty-four studies supporting the expectation theory may not seem like very many. However, if we apply the rules of statistical significance to the number, we could expect that only about 5 percent of those 242 studies (about 12) have come out as predicted just by chance. The fact that we have 84, 7 times more than chance would dictate, suggests that expectations do indeed affect performance in certain circumstances.

On a more objective note, Gumpert and Gumpert[82] went as far as to reanalyze Rosenthal's original data and after a thorough study concluded that the teacher-expectation effects hypothesized do indeed take place. Additional support for the power of teacher expectations comes from an investigation by Palardy[83] who found that if first-grade teachers believed boys would achieve as well as girls in reading, the boys did, in fact, perform better than boys with teachers who believed them to be less successful in reading than girls.

There is still other support for the expectancy idea, and it comes from research done with parents who raise children with high self-esteem. For example, Coopersmith[84] has found that families that produced high self-esteem children also had high expectations for academic performance and excellence. That is, parents who *expected* their children to live up to the standards they established were more likely to facilitate healthy growth than parents who did *not* have these expectancies.

Do teacher expectations make a difference? On the basis of the evidence, I think they definitely do. There is no magic in this. A student will not do better or work as hard as he is able just because the teacher "expects" or "believes" that he can do good work. A teacher's expectations or beliefs in a student's adequacy probably wouldn't make a whit of difference unless those beliefs were explicitly expressed in teacher behavior that was supportive, encouraging, and functionally helpful. All in all, it appears that teachers see what they expect to see, and the pupil sees what the teacher sees.

The Psychology of Expectations

How do expectations work and how do they influence another person's behavior? Specifically, how and why do a teacher's expectations influence a student's behavior and performance? In the first place, expectations make it clear to a student that he cannot, willy-nilly, do what he wants just because he wants to do it. Having the opportunity to do what he wants just because that is what he wants to do is an important right that every student should have opportunities to exercise. However, if that's all there is, he may seldom be stretched beyond the safety of his own choices.

I say "safety" of his own choices because there is evidence to indicate that when one does only what he chooses to do, he feels less successful and competent, even if he succeeds at what he chooses to do, than one who accomplishes a task that he did not choose and that represents another person's expectations. Luginbuhl[85] has noted, for example, that if a person succeeds at a problem that he chose from a number of problems, his feelings of success may be blunted by the knowledge that he influenced the situation to make success more possible. This suggests that it may not be wise for a teacher to permit the student to have his own way (e.g., choose the number or kind of books to read or the kind of paper to write, etc.) *all the time*. Living up to a teacher's expectations (e.g., writing a report on an assigned topic, getting it done and in on time) can be another way a student can feel successful and thereby add to his feelings of competence and self-esteem.

Clearly defined teacher expectations can serve as an important framework for student self-evaluation. For instance, if an elementary school child is supposed to keep quiet when someone else is talking and does it, he *knows* he's successful. If a high school student knows he's expected to participate in class discussion and he does it, he *knows* he tried his best. If he's supposed to have a book report in by Friday noon and he does it, he *knows* he successfully lived up to an expectation. In other words, the existence of teacher expectations can leave a student with the feeling that a definition of his school environment *is* possible and that the world does impose restrictions and make demands that he can learn to handle on an everyday basis.

Teachers who are less certain and more permissive about their expectations may unwittingly encourage students to be more dependent on them (not knowing exactly what's expected, they may wait around longer to be told). Another consideration is that if a student has no expectations to live up to, he is apt to be left with the omnipotent feeling that everything he does is all right, which, in the long pull, robs him of important practice opportunities in dealing with situations and circumstances—both inside and outside of school—when everything is *not* all right.

Expectations perform another important function. They not only represent a belief in a student's adequacy, but they also relay the message that he has the ability to do what is required of him. When set at reasonable levels, expectations represent the strongest vote of confidence possible. Positive self-esteem grows out of successfully doing those things we weren't too sure of being able to do in the first place, and if we have someone who believes in us, "expects that we can," then taking that first step is at least a bit easier.

TO EXPERIMENT WITH

You can try out this "expectation" idea the next time you have an opportunity to interact with school age youths. Make a specific effort to give a youngster positive feedback, to let him know that you really believe in his ability to accomplish some task. (Be sure, however, it is within reason, "reachable.") See for yourself whether your encouragement and "expectations" make a difference in your performance. You could even try this on your roommate or boyfriend or girlfriend.

A Note of Caution About Expectations

There is nothing mystical about how a teacher's expectations work and the influence these expectations can have on student behavior and performance. If a student strives to live up to a teacher's expectations, it will not only be because the expectations are reasonable, but also because of the existence of an interpersonal relationship in which the teacher is viewed as a person who is basically trustworthy, friendly, warm, and sure of himself. (It is difficult for an uncertain person to have expectations for another person if for no other reason than he is doubtful about what his expectations are for *himself*.)

It is entirely possible that one teacher's reasonable expectations can become another teacher's unfair demands. If a teacher is viewed as harsh, authoritarian, and competitive, it may become a matter of face-saving principle and personal strength *not* to do what the teacher expects. We do not easily live up to the expectations of a dictator whose primary aim is to control us or hurt us. We do, however, strive harder to cooperate with a person we see as having our best interests at heart.

There is one final note of caution. No matter how benign, trustworthy, or friendly a teacher is, that teacher's expectations will still have different effects on different students. The teacher is not the only variable; the student is too. For example, students who are adult-oriented, who have a high need for approval from adults, or who are "other-directed" will probably be more affected by teacher expectations than will students who are peer-oriented, independent, and "inner-directed." A wise teacher will take these student differences into account by encouraging the adult-oriented student to be less dependent and by working a bit harder with the peer-oriented student to help him see that adult values aren't so bad after all.

EPILOGUE

There is probably no thirteen-year span in a person's life that is more crucial in shaping one's attitudes about himself—particularly his feelings of adequacy and competency—than those which occur between five and eighteen. These are the years—the formative years—when a growing child and developing adolescent incorporates and refines the attitude that says "I can" or the one that says "I can't." When you think about it, the role of the school in the development and change of self-concept is enormous. It dispenses praise and reproof, acceptance and rejection on a colossal scale. Indeed, school provides not only the stage upon which much of the drama of a young person's formative years is played, but it houses the most critical audience in the world—peers and teachers. And it is here, in the face of his severest critics, that a student is likely to be reminded again and again of either his failings and shortcomings or of his strengths and possibilities.

If we were to pick out a time in a child's life that is probably the most crucial in shaping his feelings of academic competency and intellectual adequacy, it would have to be the elementary school years. These are the years when he is most susceptible to the emotional consequences of success or failure precisely because his sense of who he is and what he can do is incompletely formed. This means that if a child experiences more failure than success in elementary school he very likely will develop the sort of negative self-attitudes that lead to defeatism, despair, and hopelessness, none of which are good predictors of later academic success or healthy adjustment during the adult years.

Research evidence does not permit us to say that a high self-concept will automatically lead to high achievement, but it does allow us to conclude that high achievement rarely occurs in the absence of a reasonably high self-concept. Although we cannot say with definitiveness which comes first, good school work or high self-regard, we can say that each is mutually reinforcing to the other to the extent that a positive change in one encourages a positive change in the other.

Although a child's self-concept is formed during his elementary years, it is important to keep in mind that it can be re-shaped, re-directed, and modified for better or for worse during his junior high and high school years. No matter what the grade level—kindergarten or college—teachers are a potent source of feedback when it comes to a student's feelings about himself. A child ridiculed at the blackboard by an insensitive teacher in front of all his buddies may learn that it's better not to raise his hand, that maybe he's not as able as other kids. Or a quiet, uncertain adolescent praised in the presence of his classmates for a contribution he made may learn that speaking out, that taking a risk now and then, is not so dangerous after all.

All in all, what happens to a youngster as he goes through school must certainly rank as one of the most important experiences in his life. Depending on what happens at school, a student learns that he is able or unable, adequate or inadequate. One's concept of self is learned and what is learned can be taught. The question is not whether we approve of teaching for a positive sense of self in school settings, but whether the effects of schooling are positive or negative. School is likely to be a positive experience that encourages healthy self-attitudes to the extent that we concentrate on a student's strengths, praise his best efforts, and establish fair and consistent expectations for performance.

Write your own chapter summary (major points, ideas, and concepts that had meaning for you).

_____

_____

_____

_____

_____

_____

_____

_____

_____

REFERENCES

1. Jerslid, A. T. *In Search of Self.* New York: Teachers College Press, Columbia University, 1952, p. 9.
2. James, W. *Principles of Psychology,* vol. 1. New York: Holt, 1890, p. 91.
3. Schreiber, D. "The School Dropout—A Profile." In *Guidance and the School Dropout.* Washington, D.C.: National Education Association and the American Personnel and Guidance Association, 1964, pp. 1–16.
4. Bachman, J., S. Green, and I. Wirtanen. *Dropping Out—Problem or Symptom?* Youth in Transition Series, vol. III. Ann Arbor, Mich.: Institute for Social Research, 1971, pp. 169–183.
5. Wolfbein, S. L. "Transition from School to Work: A Study of the School Leaver." *Personnel and Guidance Journal* (October 1959):98–105.

6. Harding, K. L. *A Comparative Study of Caucasian Male High-School Students Who Stay in School and Those Who Drop Out.* Unpublished Ph.D. Dissertation. E. Lansing, Mich.: Michigan State University, 1966.

7. Wolfbein, S. L. Op.cit., 1959, p. 103.

8. Lichter, S. O. *The Drop-Outs.* Chicago: Free Press, 1962.

9. Erikson, E. H. *Childhood and Society.* New York: Norton, 1950, pp. 219–234.

10. Alexander, E. D. "The Marking System and Poor Achievement." *The Teachers College Journal* 36(1964):110–113.

11. Olson, W. C. "Seeking, Self-Selection, and Pacing in the Use of Books by Children." *The Packet* 7(Spring 1952):7. Boston: D. C. Heath.

12. Arthur, G. "A Study of the Achievement of Sixty Grade 1 Repeaters as Compared with that of Non-Repeaters of the Same Mental Age." *Journal of Experimental Education* 5(1936):203–205.

13. Cook, W. W. "Some Effects of the Maintenance of High Standards of Promotion." *Elementary School Journal* 41(1941):430–437.

14. Coffield, W. H., and P. Blommers. "Effects of Non-Promotion on Educational Achievement in the Elementary School." *Journal of Educational Psychology* 47(1956):235–250.

15. Kowitz, G. T., and C. M. Armstrong. "The Effect of Promotion Policy on Academic Achievement." *Elementary School Journal* 61(1961):435–443.

16. Hall, W. F., and R. Demarest. "Effect on Achievement Scores of a Change in Promotion Policy." *Elementary School Journal* 58(1958):204–207.

17. Otto, H. J., and E. O. Melby. "An Attempt to Evaluate the Threat of Failure as a Factor in Achievement." *Elementary School Journal* 35(1935):588–596.

18. Morrison, I. E., and I. F. Perry "Acceptance of Overage Children by Their Classmates." *Elementary School Journal* 56(1956):217–220.

19. Goodlad, J. I. "Some Effects of Promotion and Nonpromotion upon the Social and Personal Adjustment of Children." *Journal of Expermintal Education* 22(1954):301–328.

20. Sandin, A. A. "Social and Emotional Adjustments of Regularly Promoted and Nonpromoted Pupils." *Child Development Monographs*, no. 32, 1944.

21. McKinney, B. T. *Promotion of Pupils a Problem of Educational Administration.* Unpublished Ph.D. Dissertation. Urban, Ill.: University of Illinois, 1928.

22. Livingston, A. H. "Key to the Dropout Problem: The Elementary School." *Elementary School Journal* 59(1959):267–270

23. Dillon, H. A. *A Major Educational Problem.* New York: National Child Labor Committee, 1949, pp. 35–40.

24. Hall, J. *A Study of Dropouts.* Miami, Florida: Dade County Public Schools, Department of Research and Information, 1964, p. 21.

25. Godfrey, E. *North Carolina Education.* 2(October 1971):10–11, 29.

26. Symonds, P. M. *What Education Has to Learn from Psychology,* 2nd ed. New York: Teachers College, Columbia University, Bureau of Publications, 1959, p. 102.

27. Coffield, W. H., and P. Blommers. Op.cit., 1956.

28. Goodlad, J. I., and R. H. Anderson. *The Non-Graded Elementary School,* rev. ed. New York: Harcourt, Brace and World, 1963.

29. Chase, J. A. "A Study of the Impact of Grade Retention on Primary School Children." *Journal of Psychology* 70(1968):169–177.

30. Robins, L. N. *Deviant Children Grown Up.* Baltimore: Williams and Wilkins, 1966.

31. Powell, E. H. "Crime as a Function of Anomie." *The Journal of Criminal Law, Criminology, and Police Science* 57(1966):161–171.

32. Spiegelman, R. *A Benefit/Cost Model to Evaluate Educational Programs.* Menlo Park, Calif.: Stanford Research Institute, 1968.

33. Prentice, N. M., and F. J. Kelly. "Intelligence and Deliquency: A Reconsideration." *The Journal of Social Psychology* 60(1963):327–337.

34. Kolberg, L., J. LaCrosse, and D. Ricks. "The Predictability of Adult Mental Health from Childhood Behavior." In *Manual of Child Psychopathology,* edited by B. B. Wolman. New York: McGraw-Hill, 1972, p. 1240.

35. Kolberg, L., et al. Op. cit., 1972, p. 1242.

36. Bloom, B. S. *Stability and Change in Human Characteristics.* New York: Wiley, 1964.

37. Kolberg, L., et al. Op.cit., p. 1242.

38. Bower, E. M. "Primary Prevention of Mental and Emotional Disorders: A Frame of Reference." *The Protection and Promotion of Mental Health in the Schools.* Bethesda, Md.: U. S. Department of Health, Education and Welfare, 1965, p. 3.

39. Lecky, P. *Self-Consistency—A Theory of Personality.* New York: Island Press, 1945.

40. Shore, M. F., J. L. Massimo, and D. F. Ricks. "A Factor Analytic Study of Psycho Therapeutic Change in Delinquent Boys." *Journal of Clinical Psychology* 21(1965):208–212.

41. Feather, N. T. "Attribution of Responsibility and Valence of Success and Failure in Relation to Initial Confidence and Task Performance." *Journal of Personality and Social Psychology* 13(1969):129–144.

42. Roth, R. M. "Role of Self-Concept in Achievement." *Journal of Experimental Education* 27(1959):265–281.

43. Wattenberg, W. W., and C. Clifford. "Relation of Self-Concepts to Beginning Achievement in Reading." *Child Development* 35(1964):461–467.

44. Shaw, M. C., and J. T. McCuen. "The Onset of Academic Underachievement in Bright Children." *Journal of Educational Psychology* 51(1960):103–108.

45. Fink, M. B. "Self-Concept as It Related to Academic Achievement." *California Journal of Educational Research* 13(1962):57–62.

46. Campbell, P. B. "Self-Concept and Academic Achievement in Middle Grade Public School Children." *Dissertation Abstracts* 27(1966):1535–1536.

47. Walsh, A. M. *Self-Concepts of Bright Boys with Learning Difficulties.* New York: Bureau of Publications, Teachers College, Columbia University, 1956.

48. Zimmerman, I. L., and G. N. Allebrand. "Personality Characteristics and Attitudes Toward Achievement of Good and Poor Readers." *Journal of Educational Research* 59(1965):28–30.

49. Bodwin, F. B. "The Relationship Between Immature Self-Concept and Certain Educational Disabilities." Unpublished Doctoral Dissertation. E. Lansing Mich.: Michigan State University, 1957.

50. Nash, R. J. "A Study of Particular Self-Perceptions as Related to Scholastic Achievement of Junior High School Age Pupils in a Middle Class Community." *Dissertation Abstracts* 14(1964):3837–3838.

51. Dyson, E. "A Study of Ability Grouping and the Self-Concept." *Journal of Educational Research* 60(1967):403–405.

52. Borislow, B. "Self-Evaluation and Academic Achievement." *Journal of Counseling Psychology* 9(1962):246–254.

53. Brookover, W. B., S. Thomas, and A. Patterson. "Self-Concept of Ability and Academic Achievement." *Sociology of Education* 37(1964):271–278.

54. Brookover, W. B., et al. "Self-Concept of Ability and School Achievement, II." Final Report of *Cooperative Research Project #1636*, U. S. Office of Education. E. Lansing, Mich.: Bureau of Educational Research Services, Michigan State University, 1965.

55. Brookover, W. B., E. L. Erickson, and L. M. Joiner. "Self-Concept of Ability and School Achievement, III." Final Report of *Coperative Research Project #2831*, U. S. Office of Education. E. Lansing, Mich.: Human Learning Research Institute, Michigan State University, 1967, pp. 142–143.

56. Lipsitt, L. P. "A Self-Concept Scale for Children and Its Relationship to the Children's Form of the Manifest Anxiety Scale." *Child Development* 29(1958):463–472.

57. McCandless, B. R., A. Castaneda, and D. S. Palermo. "Anxiety in Children and Social Status." *Child Development* 27(1956):385–392.

58. Castaneda, A., D. S. Palermo, and B. R. McCandless. "Complex Learning and Performance as a Function of Anxiety in Children and Task Difficulty." *Child Development* 27(1956): 327–332.

59. McCandless, B. R., and A. Castaneda. "Anxiety in Children, School Achievement, and Intelligence." *Child Development* 27(1956):379–382.

60. Coopersmith, S. A. "A Method for Determining Types of Self-Esteem." *Journal of Educational Psychology* 59(1959):87–94.

61. Coopersmith, S. A. "Self-Esteem and Need Achievement as Determinents of Selective Recall and Repetition." *Journal of Abnormal and Social Psychology* 60(1960):310–317.

62. Mitchell, J. V., Jr. "Goal-Setting Behavior as a Function of Self-Acceptance, Over- and Under-Achievement, and Related Personality Variables." *Journal of Educational Psychology* 50(1959):93–104.

63. Sarason, S. B., G. Mandler, and P. G. Graighill. "The Effect of Differential Instructions on Anxiety and Learning." *Journal of Abnormal and Social Psychology* 47(1952):561–565.

64. Cox, F. N. "Correlates of General and Test Anxiety in Children." *Australian Journal of Psychology* 12(1960):169–177.

65. Gowan, J. C. "Factors of Achievement in High School and College." *Journal of Counseling Psychology* 7(1960):91–95.

66. Brunkan, R. J., and Sheni, F. "Personality Characteristics of Ineffective, Effective and Efficient Readers." *Personnel and Guidance Journal* 44 (1966):837–844.

67. Farls, R. J. "High and Low Achievement of Intellectually Average Intermediate Grade Students Related to Self-Concept and Social Approval." *Dissertation Abstracts* 28(1967):1205.

68. Farquhar, W. W. *A Comprehensive Study of the Motivational Factors Underlying Achievement of Eleventh-Grade High School Students.* U. S. Office of Education, Cooperative Research Report No. 846. E. Lansing, Mich.: Office of Research and Publications, Michigan State University, 1968.

69. Combs, A. W. *The Relationship of Child Perceptions to Achievement and Behavior in the Early School Years.* U. S. Office of Education, Cooperative Research Project No. 814. Washington, D. C.: Department of Health, Education and Welfare, 1963.

70. Durr, W. K., and R. R. Schmatz. "Personality Differences Between High-Achieving and Low-Achieving Gifted Children." *Reading Teacher* 17(1964):251–254.

71. Taylor, R. G. "Personality Traits and Discrepant Achievement: A Review." *Journal of Counseling Psychology* 11(1964):76–81.

72. Staines, J. W. "The Self-Picture as a Factor in the Classroom." *British Journal of Educational Psychology* 28(1958):97–111.

73. Rosenthal, R., and L. Jacobson. *Pygmalion in the Classroom.* New York: Holt, Rinehart and Winston, 1968, pp. 72–97.

74. Rosenthal, R. "The Pygmalion Effect Lives." *Psychology Today* (September 1973):60.

75. Thorndike, R. L. "Review of Pygmalion in the Classroom." *American Educational Research Journal* 5(1968):708–711.

76. Gephart, W. J. "Will the Real Pygmalion Please Stand Up?" *American Educational Research Journal* 7(May 1970):473–475.

77. Elashoff, J. D., and R. E. Snow. *A Case Study in Statistical Inference: Reconsideration of the Rosenthal-Jacobson Data on Teacher Expectancy* (Tech. Rep. No. 15). Stanford, Calif.: Stanford Center for Research and Development in Teaching, Stanford University, 1970.

78. Clairborn, W. L. "Expectancy Effects in the Classroom: A Failure to Replicate." *Journal of Educational Psychology* 60(1969):377–383.

79. Jose, J., and J. J. Cody. "Teacher-Pupil Interaction as it Relates to Attempted Changes in Teacher Expectancy of Academic Ability and Achievement." *American Educational Research Journal* 8(January 1971):39–49.

80. Rosenthal, R. *The Social Psychology of the Behavioral Scientist: On Self-fulfilling Prophecies in Behavior Research and Everyday Life.* Paper presented at the 4th Annual Research Conference of the New Directions in Social Science Research, North Dakota University, November, 1967.

81. Rosenthal, R. "The Pygmalion Effect Lives." Op.cit., 1973, p. 59.

82. Gumpert, P., and C. Gumpert. "On the Psychology of Expectations in the Classroom." *The Urban Review* 3(1968):21–26.

83. Palardy, M. J. "What Teachers Believe, What Children Achieve." *Elementary School Journal* 69(1969):370–374.

84. Coopersmith, S. *The Antecedents of Self-Esteem.* San Francisco: W. H. Freeman, 1967.

85. Luginbuhl, J. E. R. "Role of Choice and Outcome on Feelings of Success and Estimates of Ability." *Journal of Personality and Social Psychology* 22(1972):121–127.

REFERENCES OF RELATED INTEREST

Banks, J. A., and J. Brambs (eds.). *Black Self-Concept.* New York: McGraw-Hill, 1972.

Birney, R. C., H. Burdick, and R. C. Teevan. *Fear of Failure.* Princeton, N. J.: D. Van Nostrand, 1969.

Brophy, J. E., and T. L. Good. *Teacher-Student Relationships.* New York: Holt, Rinehart and Winston, 1974.

Cabianca, W. A. *The Effects of a T-Group Laboratory Experience on Self-Esteem, Need, and Attitudes of Student Teachers.* (Doctoral Dissertation, Washington State University.) Ann Arbor, Michigan: University Microfilms, 1967, no. 68–688.

Campbell, P. B. "School and Self-Concept." *Educational Leadership* 27(1967):510–515.

Felker, D. W. *Building Positive Self-Concepts.* Minneapolis, Minn.: Burgess, 1974.

Fitts, W. H. *The Self-Concept and Performance.* Research Monograph no. 5. Acklen Station, Nashville, Tenn.: Counselor Recordings and Tests, 1972.

————, et al. *The Self-Concept and Self-Actualization.* Research Monograph no. 3. Acklen Station, Nashville, Tenn.: Counselor Recordings and Tests, 1971.

Fleming, E. S., and R. G. Anttonen. "Teacher Expectancy as Related to the Academic and Personal Growth of Primary-Age Children." *Monographs of the Society for Research in Child Development* 36(1971), Serial no. 145.

Gergen, K. J. *The Concept of Self.* New York: Holt, Rinehart and Winston, 1971.

Hamachek, D. E. (ed.). *The Self in Growth, Teaching and Learning.* Englewood Cliffs, N. J.: Prentice-Hall, 1965, parts VII and VIII.

Harris, T. A. *I'm OK—You're OK.* New York: Harper & Row, 1967.

Hawk, T. L. "Self-Concepts of the Socially Disadvantaged." *Elementary School Journal* 67(1967):196–206.

Jenkins, G. G. *Helping Children Reach Their Potential.* Glenview, Ill. Scott, Foresman, 1961.

Johnson, D. W. *The Social Psychology of Education.* New York: Holt, Rinehart, and Winston, 1970, Chapter 3.

Kubiniec, C. M. "The Relative Efficacy of Various Dimensions of the Self-Concept in Predicting Academic Achievement." *American Educational Research Journal* 7(May 1970):321–336.

Kvaraceus, W. C., et al. *Negro Self-Concept.* New York: McGraw-Hill, 1965.

LaBenne, W. D., and B. I. Greene. *Educational Implications of Self-Concept Theory.* Pacific Palisades, Calif.: Goodyear, 1969.

Lefebvre, A. *The Relationship Between Self-Concept and Level of Aspiration with Negro and White Children.* (Doctoral Dissertation, Loyola University of Chicago.) Ann Arbor, Mich.: University Microfilms, 1970, no. 71–28, 128.

Morse, W. C. "Self-Concept in the School Setting." *Childhood Education* 41(1964):195–198.

Peters, D. M. *The Self-Concept as a Factor in Over- and Under-Achievement.* (Doctoral Dissertation, Indiana University.) Ann Arbor, Mich.: University Microfilms, 1968, no. 68–17, 289.

Purkey, W. W. *Self-Concept and School Achievement.* Englewood Cliffs, N. J.: Prentice-Hall, 1970.

Soffen, F. *Teaching for Improvement of Self-Concept.* (Doctoral Dissertation, Temple University.) Ann Arbor, Mich.: University Microfilms, 1968, no. 68–14, 472.

Taylor, T. D. *Effects of Group Counseling on Self-Concept and Academic Achievement of Selected High School Health Classes.* (Doctoral Dissertation, Oregon State University.) Ann Arbor, Mich.: University Microfilms, 1970, no. 70–18, 066.

Thompson, W. *Correlates of the Self-Concept.* Research Monograph no. 6. Acklen Station, Nashville, Tenn.: Counselor Recordings and Tests, 1972.

Weldon, F. A. *The Effects of a Value Seminar Group Experience in Relation to Selected Student Teacher Needs, Level of Self-Esteem, and Attitudes.* (Doctoral Dissertation, University of Montana.) Ann Arbor, Mich.: University Microfilms, 1971, no. 71–28, 071.

Wylie, R. C. *The Self-Concept.* Lincoln, Neb.: University of Nebraska Press, 1961.

Yamamoto, K. (ed.). *The Child and His Image.* Boston: Houghton Mifflin, 1972.

Ziller, R. C. *The Social Self.* New York: Pergamon, 1973.

THIRTEEN

Measurement and Evaluation of Learning: Concepts and Issues

CHAPTER OUTLINE

PROLOGUE

ASSESSMENT OF STUDENT PERFORMANCE IS A PERSONAL MATTER

Generalizing Too Broadly from Personal Experience Can Be Dangerous

Ideas About the "Best" Evaluation System Vary Widely

MEASUREMENT AND EVALUATION: THEIR MEANING AND FUNCTION

ESTABLISHING OBJECTIVES AND GOALS IS IMPORTANT

The Value of Behavioral Objectives: Pros and Cons

BASIC CONCEPTS AND APPROACHES RELATED TO SOUND MEASUREMENT PRACTICES

A Good Test Must Be Valid

Construct validity reflects content coverage

Construct validity reflects adherence to objectives

A Good Test Must Be Reliable

Three Common Indices of Central Tendency

  The arithmetic mean

  The median

  The mode

Use of Mean, Median, or Mode Depends on Score Distribution

Range, Percentile Rank, and Standard Deviation Can Be Helpful Interpreters

The Standard Error of a Test Should Be Taken into Account

CRITERION-REFERENCED TESTING—EVERY STUDENT CAN PASS

What Is Criterion-Referenced Testing?

Criterion-Referenced Measurement Is Related to Mastery Learning

Arguments For and Against the Mastery Approach and Criterion-Referenced Testing

NORM-REFERENCED TESTING—THERE ARE DEGREES OF SUCCESS

NORM-REFERENCED VERSUS CRITERION-REFERENCED TESTING: WHICH TO USE?

WAYS TO PLAN AND CONSTRUCT GOOD CLASSROOM TESTS

Determine the Kind of Exam You Want to Use

Factors to Consider When Preparing and Using Essay Exams

  Suggestions for scoring essay exams

  A final word about essay exams

Factors to Consider When Preparing and Using Objective Exams

Four Commonly Used Types of Objective Exams

  Multiple-choice tests

  True-false tests

  Matching tests

  Completion tests

Which Kind of Test Is Best—Essay or Objective?

Suggestions for Creating A Positive Examination Climate

ISSUES AND PROBLEMS RELATED TO GRADING AND REPORTING

Varieties of Reporting Systems

Elementary School Report Cards

Let's Stress What Is "Right" and De-emphasize What Is "Wrong"

To Grade or not to Grade

Some Alternative Grading Systems

  Use written evaluations

  Use self-evaluation procedures

  Give grades, but don't tell students

  Use the contract system

  Use the mastery approach or performance curriculum

  Use pass/fail grading

  Credit/no credit grading

  Blanket grading

Some Kind of Grading System Is Necessary

EPILOGUE

REFERENCES

REFERENCES OF RELATED INTEREST

IMPORTANT CHAPTER IDEAS

1. There is no universal agreement among measurement specialists about what constitutes the "best" or most appropriate assessment procedure.

2. Measuring a student's progress is a way of asking "How much does he know" or "how high is his achievement."

3. Evaluation asks "how good" or "how satisfactorily" has a student performed?

4. Measuring and evaluating student progress can only be done in relation to the learning objectives.

5. There is disagreement among teachers and measurement experts about how specific the objectives should be.

6. A teacher's testing procedures must be both valid and reliable in order for a grade to accurately and fairly reflect a student's performance.

7. Measures of central tendency are used to determine where scores tend to pile up or center in a distribution.

8. Use of the range, percentile rank, and standard deviation help to understand test scores in relation to how they are dispersed in a total distribution.

9. The standard error of a test helps us understand the variability of test scores.

10. Criterion-referenced testing is an approach to measurement in which each student is tested against an objective criterion.

11. Mastery learning and teaching is associated with criterion-referenced measurement and is built on the assumption that most students can master what they're taught if given enough time to do so.

12. Norm-referenced testing is a way of assessing whether students have accomplished specified objectives in a specified period of time.

13. The specific kind of test a teacher uses is determined to some extent by what he or she wishes to measure.

14. Either essay tests or objective tests can be used to measure educational achievement and to assess a student's understanding of principles and integration of ideas.

15. Letter grades are used in the large majority of schools, although alternative methods of grading and reporting are being explored.

PROLOGUE

So far we've looked at some of the dynamics of learning and processes involved, we've examined some of the ways in which motivation is related to learning, and we've overviewed how self-concept variables are related to achievement outcomes. We're going to turn our attention now to one of the more sensitive issues related to the business of teaching and learning—issues that have to do with testing, grading, deciding who gets the A's or the C's, and problems associated with reporting a student's performance to others.

Like it or not, evaluation is part of everyday living. It helps us understand who we are, what we can do, and where we have to improve to do better if we choose. Making up exams, grading papers, assigning grades, and the like by no means have to be passionless, mechanical, and dehumanizing teacher activities. They can, to the contrary, be honest, humane efforts to help students accept their limitations and appreciate their strengths. Like most everything else in life, there are good ways and bad ways to do this. But in order for us to select the "good" ways, there are some basic concepts and issues related to classroom measurement and evaluation to which we must first address ourselves.

Let's first of all turn over our attention to a very basic issue.

ASSESSMENT OF STUDENT PERFORMANCE IS A PERSONAL MATTER

The issue of student assessment is not an easy one to resolve. Each teacher has his or her own private "philosophy" about what grades mean, how they should be interpreted, and how a student's learning should be assessed. It is an issue that involves not just administrative policies and procedures, but personal beliefs and values. For example, your own experience as a student will have (indeed, is having) a great influence on your

"YOU HAVE TO KEEP AN EYE ON HIM.
I HEAR HE CAN BE DR. JEKYLL UNTIL RIGHT BEFORE
REPORT CARDS, AND THEN HE TURNS INTO MR. HYDE !"

Inconsistencies between a teacher's daily behavior and his or her grading practices are not only picked up quickly by students, but cause much needless anxiety.

attitudes toward grading and testing procedures and the manner in which you will handle measurement and evaluation in your own classroom. This, naturally enough, is to be expected. It is impossible to be a student for some sixteen years or more and on the receiving end of testing and grading

585

without developing some personal ideas about how measurement and evaluation should be done.

Generalizing Too Broadly from Personal Experience Can Be Dangerous

A major pitfall to watch for is the inclination to generalize too broadly from our personal experiences and behaving as if everyone felt and thought the way we did about testing and grading. For example, Teacher A, who had always done well in highly competitive academic tasks—maybe because she was exceptionally bright or had a good memory or studied extra hard or some combination of these characteristics—thinks that rigorous exams and high academic standards are important for all students at all levels because they were important to her. Teacher B, on the other hand, has done only average work throughout his school career, and he has a strong suspicion that examinations didn't really allow him to express what he knew, so his grades cannot, he feels, be "accurate assessments of what I've learned." This teacher may be among those who minimize the importance of testing and who downplay the idea that grades reflect real learning.

This is not to suggest that all teachers who were high-achieving students end up as rigorous graders championing the cause of lofty academic standards, or that teachers who were only average students are included among those who may feel that grades are relatively unimportant. In fact, it sometimes happens that the teacher who received consistently high grades in high school and college winds up being the most vigorous and active supporter of proposals that would abolish grades altogether. I have seen this happen, for example, among some teachers who excelled academically during their school days, but who in retrospect wish that they had not been so slavishly addicted to getting high grades. On the other hand, I have seen teachers who received only average grades in school end up ranking among those who extoll the virtues of high academic standards. I have the feeling this is sometimes an effort to construct a public image that is higher and more positive than that of the extoller.

TO DO

You may find it both interesting and revealing to do a little first-hand research on this issue of relationships between attitudes about grades and grading and success (or lack of it) in school. Talk to some of your peers who you know have done exceptionally well grade-wise and ask them about their attitudes toward grading. Do the same with some others who have done about average (or even below) and wonder about their attitudes toward grading. What are the differences and similarities? What are your attitudes about grading?

Ideas About the "Best" Evaluation System
Vary Widely

The fact is that there is no universal agreement among teachers, or, for that matter, among measurement specialists about what constitutes the "best" or most appropriate kind of assessment procedure. The problem of measurement and evaluation is as much an emotional issue as it is an academic one and as such it involves not only ideas and strategies, but feelings and personal preferences.

We can talk all we want about self-realization and personal adequacy as educational goals, about the psychology of effective teaching, about ways to make teaching and learning meaningful, relevant, and lasting, about the dynamics of learning, and so on, but in the final analysis every student's achievement—or lack of it—must in some way be measured, evaluated, and reported in some manner that is palatable to students, parents, and school administrators.

Before we go further, let's first of all turn our attention to what "measurement" and "evaluation" mean.

MEASUREMENT AND EVALUATION:
THEIR MEANING AND FUNCTION

Although the terms measurement and evaluation are used loosely and frequently interchangeably, they actually refer to different processes. The term *measurement* refers to a process of determining the extent, dimensions, or quantity of something. In daily living, it implies the assignment of an exact and quantitative number such as three pounds, ten yards, four amperes, or sixty miles an hour. In education, measurement procedures refer to the use of objective tests that yield quantitative data. A measurement is relatively objective and impersonal and addresses itself to the question of "how much does a student know" or "how high is his achievement." The last multiple-choice test you took is an example of an instrument designed to "measure" your learning. Customarily in the measurement process students are ranked along a scale from high to low, or, in measurement terminology, they are "ordered along a scale from high to low." Thus in a spelling test consisting of fifty words, the range of scores in a class of twenty-five might vary from seven to forty-eight words spelled correctly. This range of scores then affords a teacher a basis for differentiating levels of spelling ability.

Evaluation is a different process in the sense that it involves a qualitative judgment of "how good" or "how satisfactorily" a student has performed. Evaluations are usually subjective, personal, and difficult to define with a high degree of precision. Thus the term "evaluation" consists of placing a value on something, on the basis of previously determined standards. To return to our fifty-word spelling test: The teacher, after examining the range and distribution of scores, might decide that students with more than forty-three points did very well on the test, that students falling between thirty-five and forty-two points were somewhat above average, and that students with scores between nineteen and thirty-four points were about average. Those students achieving scores between twelve and eighteen points might be judged as a bit below average, while those with eleven points or lower could be considered as having done rather poorly. Once a decision or judgment concerning the value or degree of excellence or goodness is made—then evaluation exists. To put it another way, the score from the test represents a measurement; the interpretation concerning the meaning and value of that score represents an evaluation.

Evaluation, then, can be viewed in a much broader framework than measurement. Whereas a measurement tool, like a classroom test, allows us to quantify a student's performance, evaluation procedures allow us to be concerned with how effective or how useful or how meaningful a student's performance has been, whether it is reflected in achievement in language arts, geometry, science, music, spelling, or manifested in personal adjustment or any other experience included as an essential part of the school program. Evaluation can be a significant dimension of the total learning process when: (1) it encourages a student to see how he can improve his performance; (2) it permits a teacher to assimilate and interrelate as much evidence as he can about student learning; (3) it encourages a teacher to do a bit of soul-searching regarding his teaching effectiveness. In short, evaluation is concerned with the total student—with all forms of learning experience that may contribute to his intellectual, physical, emotional, social, and aesthetic development and thus to enhancing his possibilities for self-realization and personal adequacy. Let's turn now to a more extended look at some of the basic concepts related to sound evaluation and measurement procedures.

ESTABLISHING OBJECTIVES AND GOALS IS IMPORTANT

A good teacher should be able to answer at least two basic questions before considering what sort of evaluation would be most appropriate. One question is "Why is the course or subject matter being offered in the first place?" And the second, "What would I like my students to learn because of it?" Once a teacher is able to answer these questions in at least a general sort of way, then he can begin to be more specific about what the objectives and goals should be. Usually these goals and objectives can be broken down into three major classes, which include:

1. *Informational goals and objectives*
   a. This would include learning and mastering such things as names, dates, technical terms, rules, definitions, principles, concepts, formulas, and so on.
2. *Proficiency goals and objectives*
   a. Some examples of proficiencies or skills here might include things such as learning to write legibly, using the school library, presenting a reasonably clear, coherent oral report in class, or even swimming 100 yards without stopping.
3. *Attitudinal goals and objectives*
   a. This is a more difficult arena of evaluation because it involves matters of aesthetic values, personal preferences, and individual tastes. It would include such objectives as, for example, encouraging an appreciation for reading, or for the contributions of political and scientific figures, or pride in one's social heritage, or loyalty to certain democratic ideals, and so on.

TO DO

Consider the subject area(s) you'll be teaching one day. For the sake of a little practice, write down two or three objectives you would want to achieve under each of the three categories described above.

Informational objectives _____

_____

_____

Proficiency objectives _____

_____

_____

Attitudinal objectives _____

_____

_____

The Value of Behavioral Objectives: Pros and Cons

The purpose of classroom evaluation is to find out how well students are accomplishing what they are supposed to accomplish, or the objectives that have been established. Objectives can be determined in one of three ways: (1) the teacher can establish them, (2) the students can determine them, or (3) the teacher and students can both have a voice in this process. My own preference is route three. This is a more cumbersome process, it takes more time, but the long-term gains of students having some voice and choice in their destinies more than offset the time and trouble involved. No matter who determines the objectives, however, the person constructing a test should know what they are.

Almost all educational psychologists and teachers agree that objectives are important. There is, however, disagreement about how specific they should be. It has been argued by some educational psychologists — Mager,[1] McDonald,[2] Tyler,[3] and DeCecco,[4] to name a few — that there are many advantages to formulating and stating very explicit objectives that are based on observable performance. Some examples of objectives of this sort would be the following:

1. The student should be able to add and subtract fractions associated with three-digit numbers.
2. The student should be able to discuss four major political-social causes of the Civil War.
3. The student should be able to park a regular-sized sedan in a space of fourteen feet, no more than six to eight inches from the curb. He should do this in thirty seconds, using no more than four changes of gear.

Objectives described in terms similar to those above are called *behavioral objectives*. They describe the desired outcomes in terms of specific acts or behavior. They indicate the *conditions* or *context* (e.g., *three*-digit fractions, *four* political-social causes, *regular*-sized sedan in a *fourteen* foot space, and so on) under which the behavior should occur.

Those who argue for the establishment of specific behavioral objectives maintain that: (1) teachers will know more clearly what to teach for to achieve those objectives; (2) objectives can serve as neon-bulbed guidelines to assist students directly toward their mastery; and (3) behavioral objectives can be utilized as the basis for constructing examinations to evaluate how well and to what extent the objectives have been accomplished.

Not all, however, agree that behavioral objectives are a good idea. According to Atkin,[5] the fundamental problem with behavioral objectives "lies in the easy assumption that we either know or can readily identify the educational objectives for which we strive, and thereafter the educational outcomes that result from our programs." Ojemann[6] points out two other frequently heard criticisms: (1) the construction and use of behavioral objectives requires a great deal of time and detail and (2) the use of the objectives stifles creativity and leads to teacher frustration.

Robert Ebel, a noted educational measurement specialist, has summarized the hazards of explicit behavioral objectives in the following way:

> Defining educational objectives in terms of desired behavior . . . appears to assume that despite the highly complex and rapidly changing world in which we live, a teacher can know ahead of time how the scholar ought to behave in a given set of circumstances. It also seems to assume that the teacher is entitled to prescribe his behavior for him. . . . It seems important to suggest strongly that the proper starting point of educational planning in a democracy is not the kind of behaviors present adults desire future adults to exhibit, but rather the kind of equipment that will enable them to choose their own behaviors intelligently.[7]

The debate about the need for and specificity of behavioral objectives very likely will continue for a long time. I think there is little question that objectives are an important part of the total evaluation process. I personally feel somewhat restricted by specific behavioral objectives—I prefer more general objectives that offer—in my view at least—both me and my students more latitude. On the other hand, I have colleagues who give their students extensive and lengthy outlines detailing very specifically the behaviors they will demonstrate by the end of the course and they feel not at all restricted. The degree of specificity is a matter of personal preference, and I think it would be erroneous to believe that there is just one best way for stating the objectives of the course. Some curriculum areas such as math, science, or physics may demand more specific objectives to reflect the more exact nature of the content. Other curriculum areas, such as social science, art, literature, and English composition may tolerate more general objectives because of the more relative nature of the content.

When you stop to think about it, there are a number of valuable educational aims (e.g., developing responsible behavior, encouraging greater self-confidence) that may be difficult to translate into behavior that is altogether apparent while a student is still enrolled in your course.[8,9] One educational psychologist has suggested that we use terms like *aims*, or *goals*, to describe the long-range, ultimate outcomes we have in mind and reserve the term *objectives* for the more immediate, proximate outcomes that might develop during a course or other school experience.[10] (Whether a teacher goes the route of very specific behavior objectives or that of more general objectives, *The Taxonomy of Educational Objectives*, I, II, edited and compiled by Bloom, Krathwohl, and Masia,[11,12] can be extremely useful references to use as guidelines for establishing useful and worthwhile goals.)

BASIC CONCEPTS AND APPROACHES
RELATED TO SOUND MEASUREMENT
PRACTICES

Whether we want to measure the distance to the moon or our weight or school achievement, we must first of all be certain that the measuring instruments we use can be depended on for reasonably accurate results. In order to check this out, we have to ask two basic questions:

1. Is the measuring instrument valid? That is, does it measure what it is supposed to measure?
2. Is the instrument reliable? That is, does it give consistent results?

A Good Test Must Be Valid

In order to determine whether a test measures what it is supposed to measure, we must first have some idea of what it is we want to measure in the first place. Hence, the value of having goals and objectives toward which we are teaching. If our goals and objectives are clear, then it is more possible to not only guide students' learning more effectively, but to assess their learning with greater validity. When students complain—and many times justifiably so—that an exam covers material that they were unprepared for, this may suggest that the test is not valid for the purpose for which it was intended. As you undoubtedly know from personal experience, students do not assess an exam in terms of the more abstract concept of validity, but they do react to a more personally sensed feeling of fairness. Although there very likely are some students who constantly accuse exams as being unfair in order to rationalize their own poor performance, there are others who protest from time to time because, in fact, the exam did *not* measure what they had been led to believe it would. A wise teacher knows that if too many students take issue with an exam's "fairness," this probably means that either the exam was inappropriate for the goals and objectives it sought to measure or that the goals were not clearly spelled out to begin with.

Content validity reflects content coverage. There are several aspects or ways of looking at validity. One of these is content validity—the extent to which a test "covers" the content. When testing for achievement in a particular subject area, you can get some idea of the validity of a test by carefully examining its content and comparing that content with the things you want to test. If, for example, you wished to measure skill in solving mathematical problems, you would want to stay away from items that dealt primarily with number manipulation.

It is possible that a test may have content validity for one teacher but not for another. If you're interested primarily in problem solving, you may want a test in which the numerical computations were relatively easy, and you would regard this test as valid for your purposes. Another teacher, or even you at a different time, may be searching for a test that will determine skill in numeral computation. If the test was limited to easy computation items, it would not be valid for this objective.

All in all, a good test provides for measurement of a good sampling of content and is balanced with respect to coverage of the various parts of the subject.

Construct validity reflects adherence to objectives. This is a second aspect of validity, and it refers to the kinds of learning specified or implied in the objectives. For example, a test that measures *only* memory of certain facts would lack validity if the objectives specify other learning goals. Knowledge of facts, for instance, is not the same as understanding of ideas and if all a test did was measure a student's memory of factual material without giving that student a chance to synthesize and integrate ideas, then we would have to say that the test lacked construct validity. Think of it this way: the definition of the noun form of *construct* is something "constructed" by mental synthesis. If a test allows a student to "construct" his responses in a manner that is consistent with what the objectives had prepared him for we would say it had "construct validity."

Thus, test validity is specific to purpose, to subject matter, to objectives, and to students; it is not a general quality. Actually, validity is a relative term; there are degrees of goodness, as there are degrees of badness. Validity is taken into consideration by designing a test that will cover the subject adequately, will measure the kinds of learning indicated by objectives, and will be suitable for a particular group of students.

A Good Test Must Be Reliable

A characteristic of a reliable test is that it gives consistent results. This means that with repeated testing, each student would be likely to maintain about the same relative rank in his group each time he takes the test.

Actually, it is nearly impossible to construct a totally reliable test. That is, it is not too probable that students' performance on the same examination taken two days apart would be identical. There are at least three factors that could contribute to this variability in examination performance. One is that exams that are too easy or too difficult or that encourage students to make widely divergent interpretations of the questions are not likely to yield highly reliable scores. Another is the stability of a student's ability to respond to the items on the examination. The fact is that most of us vary from hour to hour and from day to day in our intellectual alertness, physical energy, and emotional balance. Any one of these personal considerations can affect test performance appreciably and thereby influence the reliability of the test results. A third factor is the consistency and objectivity of the teacher who scores the test. If the scores he assigns depend largely on his personal whims of the moment rather than on standards applied equally to all papers he reads, then it is not likely that his scores will be reliable ones.

We might also note that a test may be reliable without being valid. For example, a 100 item multiple-choice mathematics test would very likely be an invalid test for measuring, say, English proficiency. Nonetheless, if similar test forms of this test were to be administered on two occasions to a group of students and yielded identical results for these students, we would conclude that the test was reliable, although not necessarily valid. On the other hand, if a test is to be valid, it must also be reliable. That is, unless a test consistently measures what it is supposed to measure, we can never be certain that the results are accurate indications of what a student knows or has mastered.

TO THINK ABOUT

A test can be reliable even if it's not valid, but it can't be valid if it's not reliable. Think about that. Try to explain in your own words why this is so.

_____

_____

_____

Generally speaking, the reliability of a test can be increased by increasing its length. For example, a student's performance, relative to other students, can be expected to fluctuate much less on a 100-item test than on a 10-item test and less on a 10-item test than one made up of 5 items. The operation of chance factors in a student's response to questions is much greater when there are 10 items than when 100 items are involved. Thus the possibility of ending up with a low score because of several very difficult questions or a high score because of some lucky guesses tends to be balanced out, as it were, on longer tests.

Other factors that can influence the reliability of tests include such considerations as: (1) failure of the student to understand or follow directions, (2) variations of attention span, (3) emotional disturbance or physical illness, (4) the threatening presence (as perceived by some students) of the teacher, (5) mistakes in scoring, and (6) environmental distractions such as noise, a hot room, poor ventilation, and the like.

Devising tests that are valid and reliable is an important first step. Let us turn our attention now to ways in which we can interpret and understand what test scores mean.

Three Common Indices of Central Tendency

A measure of central tendency is a single value that describes average performance on a test. Measures of central tendency show us the score or point about which a group of scores tend to pile up or center. Those used most frequently are the *arithmetic mean*, the *median*, and the *mode*. Let's briefly examine these one at a time.

The arithmetic mean. The arithmetic average of the mean score is obtained by adding all the scores together and dividing by the number of tests. Thus the mean for six test scores of 40, 50, 65, 70, 75, and 80 would be 380/6, or 63.3. When the word *average* is used without further definition, it is generally synonymous with mean.

The median. The *median* is defined as a point in a distribution that has an equal number of cases on both sides of it. It is the midpoint in a distribution above which and below which 50 percent of the scores lie. For example, given test scores of 11, 13, 19, 20, and 21, the median would be 19. This is easy enough to figure out when there are an odd number of test scores, as in the preceding example. However, when there are an even number of test scores, the average of the two middle numbers is taken. Thus, given test scores of 15, 16, 18, 19, 23, 25, 25, and 30, the median would be 21 (19 + 23 = 42 ÷ 2 = 21).

The mode. A third measure of central tendency, and one used rather infrequently, is the mode. Quite simply, the mode is that score in a group of scores that occurs most often. The mode of 80, 83, 83, 87, 92, and 97 is 83 because there are more 83's than any other score.

Use of Mean, Median, or Mode Depends on Score Distribution

For the most part, test scores tend to be distributed around the average in a characteristic manner. That is, there is a tendency for more students to get average or near-average scores than either very high or very low scores on most tests. Often, but by no means always, the test scores of large groups of students are distributed in a manner which, in mathematics, approximates a normal curve or forms a *normal distribution*. What this amounts to is a rough kind of probability distribution one might get by noting the number of times heads and tails would come up if you tossed a coin twenty times in succession. The most common combination of results would be ten heads and ten tails. Somewhat less often, nine heads and eleven tails or nine tails and eleven heads would come up. It would be highly unusual to get twenty heads or twenty tails in a row. If the frequency with which each possible combination of heads and tails were plotted on a line graph, a rough approximation of the normal distribution would be obtained.

TO DO

You may find this kind of interesting to try out for yourself. Take a coin and flip it twenty times. Keep track of the heads/tails ratio. How close does it come to approximating the normal curve distribution?

In Figure 13–1, note that when scores are normally distributed the mean, median, and mode all fall at about the same point and bisect the distribution into two equal parts. (If you want to see what a normal distribution or normal curve looks like in a real-life situation, take note of how an audience naturally distributes itself the next time you go to a movie that is about half full. There will be many bunched up in the center, and then they will tail away at both sides. Check it yourself.)

Although there is reason to believe that in the total population many skills and abilities tend to be distributed in a form similar to the normal curve, in actual practice this is not always the case. The reason for this is that the distribution of scores is dependent not only on the characteristic being measured, but also on (1) how it is measured, (2) the individuals being measured, and (3) a number of chance factors — e.g., mood, external factors, luck, and so on.

When scores are not normally distributed, they sometimes form a "skewed" distribution. What this means is that the high scores or low scores tend to be more bunched together than in a normal distribution, with the remaining scores piled up at one end. Figure 13–2 will give you an idea of skewness.

When a distribution is skewed toward one end or the other, the mean, and the median will not be identical. The mean is likely to be pulled in the direction of the skewness or toward the "tail" of the distribution. When this happens, extremely high scores will tend to raise the mean and extremely low scores will tend to lower it. A very difficult test is likely to

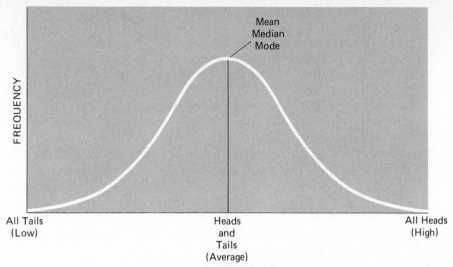

FIGURE 13–1. A Normal Distribution Curve

have a positively skewed distribution of scores, whereas a very easy one is likely to have a negatively skewed distribution.

Whenever a distribution of scores approximates the shape of a normal curve, the *mean* is our best indication of the "central tendency" of the scores. However, if the distribution is skewed in one direction or the other,

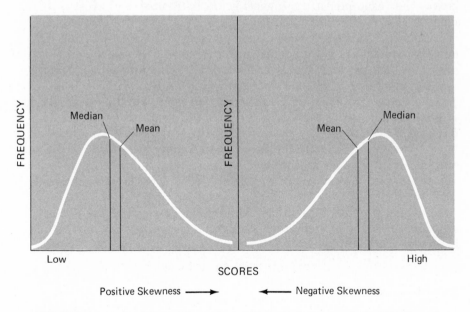

FIGURE 13–2. Positively Skewed and Negatively Skewed Distribution of Test Scores

597

the *median* is probably our indication of central tendency. The reason that the median is the preferable statistic to use in the case of distribution skewness is because extreme scores are counted over, and it makes no difference how far out they are from the center. The mean, on the other hand, is of such a nature that every score in a distribution affects it, and it is easily pulled in the direction of scores that severely deviate from center.

The mode is, at best, only a gross and quickly calculated measure of central tendency. It satisfies our curiosity about which score was repeated most frequently but little more. In summary, then, the mean gives us the "average" score, the median provides us the midpoint score, and the mode is the score appearing most frequently.

Range, Percentile Rank, and Standard Deviation Can Be Helpful Interpreters

In describing and interpreting a group of test scores, it is often useful to indicate not only an average score, but also how widely the test scores are spread out and how a particular score can be understood in relation to others.

The most simple measure of spread or dispersion is the *range*, which indicates the difference between the lowest score and the highest score in a group. For example, if the highest score is 95 and the lowest is 40, the range is 55.

Probably the easiest way of making sense of scores and one that is quickly understood by students and parents, is to establish percentile norms for the class and convert each student's score into an equivalent percentile rank. By definition a percentile rank refers to the percentage of cases falling below a certain given score. To figure out the percentile rank of particular scores, what we do is divide the total number of students in the class by the number who rank below each raw score *plus* one-half of those who receive exactly the score in question. The formula for computing percentile ranks is as follows: (N equals the total number of students) percentile rank + number of persons below score + ½ of persons at score × 100.

To give you an idea of how this formula works, assume that the numbers shown below represent scores on a certain test for thirty students in a given class.

71	65	61	60	57	52
69	64	61	60	57	50
67	63	61	59	56	47
66	63	60	59	55	46
65	62	60	58	54	43

In order to determine the percentile rank of a score of 57, we would note that eight students have scores lower than this and two students have scores at 57. So, substituting 30 for N in our formula, we would have

$$\text{percentile rank} = \frac{8 + 1}{30} \times 100 = 30$$

Thus, 30 would be the percentile rank of a raw score of 57. What this means is that 43 percent of all students taking the test scored higher than 57.

Let's take another example, this time a raw score of 62. We note that twenty students have scores lower than 62 and that only one student has a score at 62. The percentile rank of 62 then figures out to be

$$\text{percentile rank} = \frac{20 + 0.5}{30} \times 100 = 68.3$$

Note that when only one person obtains the raw score for which the percentile rank is being determined, we add one-half of one, or 0.5, to the number of persons below the score.

Another common method of translating scores into equivalents that indicate where a student stands in a group utilizes the *mean* and the *standard deviation* as a basis for norms. The mean is simply the average of a group of scores. The standard deviation is a measure of the amount of variability in a group of scores, which in a normal distribution of scores indicates how far one needs to go above and below the *mean* to include approximately 68 percent of all the scores on the test. This technique is not very often used in the classroom. It is, however, frequently used to report standardized achievement, personality, aptitude, and interest test results, which means that as a teacher you need at least a reading, if not a functional, understanding of its use. (If you are curious about the statistical procedures for working out the standard deviation of a group of scores, Ebel[13] and Mehrens and Lehmann[14] would be useful references.)

In any normal distribution, about two-thirds of the cases (or 68 percent) fall within one standard deviation above or below the mean, which suggests that there is a fixed relationship between where a score falls in a normal distribution and its distance from the mean. In Figure 13–3 you can see the approximate percent of cases that correspond to each standard deviation unit. You can also see the corresponding percentile equivalents for each of the standard deviation units.

Regardless of how large or small the standard deviation is in any particular group of scores, it can be used as a meaningful unit of distance along the base line. For instance, in a normal distribution of scores, if we look at those that are one standard-deviation unit from the mean, we find ourselves directly at that point where the curve changes from convex to concave. If we go three standard-deviation units from the mean, we reach

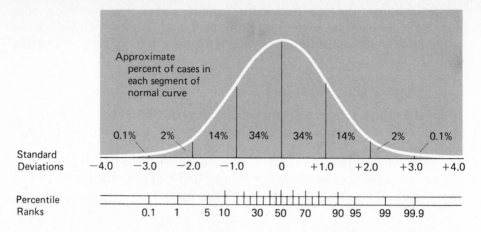

FIGURE 13–3. Normal Curve Distribution Showing Standard Deviations and Percentile Equivalents

a point in the distribution in which we find less than 1 percent of the scores. Thus, it is possible to state in standard-deviation units how far each score is from the mean and also to indicate where each one fits in the total distribution.

The Standard Error of a Test Should Be Taken into Account

A very difficult or a very easy test will tend to "bunch" the scores near the all-wrong or the all-right end of the scale. Whenever the assessment of student performance is important, as it is in marking, the spread is important. This is particularly true in non-referenced measurement, which is an expression of the quantity of a student's achievement in relation to those who did less well on the same test. (More will be said about norm-referenced and criterion-referenced measurement shortly.)

As mentioned earlier, a score on a single test, whether an IQ test or a classroom achievement test, is subject to variation due to both chance and personal factors. This variation is known as the "standard error" of a score. (Despite its name, the term does not refer to mistakes, but to the degree to which a person's score may vary if he took the same test or a similar test over.)

Research has shown that on a typical classroom test anywhere from twenty-five to fifty objective items can be expected to have a standard error of three score points. What this means is that on another like test the student might score as many as three points higher or lower. A test of fifty to seventy-five items, on the other hand, will have a standard error of about four points.[15–17] Thus, a score of 55 (as an illustration) may be interpreted as "probably between 52 and 58."

The standard error of the difference between two scores is somewhat greater than the standard error of a single score. In the above example, the standard error of the difference between 55 and some other score is about four points. The score of 55 probably represents a performance difference from scores of 59 and above or 51 and below. When trying to decide whether there is a real difference between two scores, they must be separated twice by the standard error of difference. So, to be reasonably certain of a difference from 55, scores must be 63 and above, or 48 and below. Scores that fall between 48 and 63 are said to be "overlapping" scores and do not indicate strong differences in performance. This is particularly important when it comes to determining what grades to give which students.

The factors we've examined so far—validity, reliability, measures of central tendency, standard error of measurement, and so on are all very important to consider when setting up a testing program. A basic question still remains and it is one you will one day have to answer: What kind of testing is most appropriate for my purposes? Let's turn our attention now to some of the options from which you can choose.

CRITERION-REFERENCED TESTING—EVERY STUDENT CAN PASS

The quantity of a student's learning can be expressed in one or both of two ways (1) as the amount or extent of learning in relation to what he could (or should) have learned, or (2) as the amount he learned in relation to those who learned less than he did. The first way gives us what has been called criterion-referenced measurements. The second method give us what are called norm-referenced measurements.

What Is Criterion-Referenced Testing?

This is a method of testing in which each person is measured against an objective *criterion*. Since there is no predetermined number of passes or failures, every student in class has a chance of passing. In this kind of test we do not ask where a student stands in relation to other students, but rather where he stands on a scale representing zero mastery of a subject to perfect mastery. In driver education, for example, we could decide that in order to pass the course a student must be able to park a car within so many inches of a curb, between two other cars so many feet apart, and be allowed so many minutes or so many gear changes. How a student performs in relation to other driver-education students does not matter. How he performs in relation to an objective and predetermined criterion does. If all students met the criterion, they would pass. Those that didn't would re-practice and re-take the test until they did.

Criterion-Referenced Measurement Is Related to Mastery Learning

The recent encouragement for criterion-referenced measurement stems in large part from the emphasis in some quarters on behavioral objectives, the sequencing and individualization of instruction, the development of programmed materials, and a learning theory that strongly suggests that most students can learn (master) most anything if just given enough time. The core of the argument for criterion-referenced measurement is that if we can state our objectives in behavioral terms, then the important consideration is to assess whether a student has in fact achieved these objectives rather than to be concerned about his position relative to other students. This is where "mastery test" comes into the picture, which is nothing more than a particular kind of criterion-referenced test.

Although the idea for mastery learning and testing goes back as far as 1922,[18] it wasn't until 1963 that the approach was rekindled by the publication of a paper by Carroll[19] entitled "A Model of School Learning." The essence of the model suggests that the degree of learning should be a function of the time a student spends on the material, divided by the student's aptitude for the task, his comprehension of the instruction, and the quality of instruction.

Bloom has been a major proponent of the mastery learning model and has gone as far as to boldly suggest that "Most students (perhaps over 90 percent) can master what we have to teach them."[20] Within a mastery learning model, each individual is required to work on a particular learning unit until he has achieved a specified minimum level of achievement. When he does this, he is considered to have "mastered" the material. If he does not perform at a minimum specified level, then he is required to re-study the material covered in the test until he performs adequately — in other words, "masters" the material.

Does mastery testing work? Tentative evidence indicates that in many subject-matter areas all students can achieve some (often arbitrarily) established level of mastery.[21] Carroll,[22] however, has pointed out that if a task is very difficult or depends upon special aptitudes, there may be a number of students who will never make it. For example, no matter how highly motivated some persons are or how much time they put into it, they may never run 100 yards in 9.5 seconds or become concert violinists or brain surgeons.

Arguments For and Against the Mastery Approach
and Criterion-Referenced Testing

A major argument presented in the case for mastery testing is that it allows all students to demonstrate the same level of learning if given enough time to do so. In this way, so say the mastery proponents, failure is virtually eliminated and self-concept enhanced. Bloom et al. put it this way:

> Mastery learning can be one of the more powerful sources of mental health. We are convinced that many of the neurotic symptoms displayed by high school and college students are exacerbated by painful and frustrating experiences in school learning. If 90 percent of the students are given positive indications of adequacy in learning, one might expect them to need less and less in the way of emotional therapy and psychological help. Conversely, frequent indications of failure and learning inadequacy are bound to be accompanied by increased self-doubt in the student.[23]

An idea basic to mastery testing is that the learning of any behavior, no matter how complex, rests upon the learning of a sequence of less-complex component behaviors. Mastery advocates maintain it is then theoretically possible to break complex behavior down into a chain of component behaviors and thereby make it possible for any student to master even the most complex skills by first of all mastering each link of the chain.

What are some arguments *against* the use of criterion-referenced testing? Focusing as it does on a mastery approach the emphasis is necessarily on a "part" rather than a "whole" method for learning. This is fine, but a major drawback, as you may remember from our discussion of "whole" versus "part" learning in Chapter 10 is that not all students learn best or quickest when subject-matter is broken down into a lengthy chain of component parts. Some students learn best by seeing the big picture and integrating its various parts for themselves. Criterion-referenced testing does not encourage this sort of learning.

Ebel sees several other problems in relation to criterion-referenced testing:

> Where the emphasis is on knowledge and understanding, effective use of criterion-referenced measurements seem less likely, for knowledge and understanding consist of a complex fabric that owes its strength and beauty to an infinity of tiny fibers of relationship. Knowledge does not come in discrete chunks that can be defined and identified separately.
>
> Another difficulty in the way of establishing meaningful criteria of achievement is that to be generally meaningful they must not represent the interests, values, and standards of just one teacher. Making them generally acceptable calls for committees, meetings, and long struggles to reach at least verbal consensus, which in some cases serves only to conceal unresolved

603

disagreements over perceptions, values, and standards. These processes involve so much time and trouble that most criterion-referenced type measurements are idiosyncratic.[24]

Those favoring criterion-referenced testing tend to agree with Bloom's observation that up to 90 percent of the students in a mastery framework will experience positive indications of adequacy in learning. Two measurement specialists, Mehrens and Lehmann, do not agree:

> We are inclined to think that the student who is forced to spend ten weeks on a unit that another student finished in two weeks will perceive that experience to be more painful and that he will have experienced more indications of failure and inadequacy than if we had assigned him a grade of C or D after the first two weeks.[25]

Should you use criterion-referenced testing procedures? As you have seen, there are two sides to that question. Before we address ourselves more specifically to it, let's first of all take a brief look at another major approach to testing and then contrast the two in our search for guidelines to help determine what testing procedure to use when.

NORM-REFERENCED TESTING – THERE ARE DEGREES OF SUCCESS

There are basically two different goals or objectives in testing for a student's achievement: (1) to find out where a person ranks among other individuals according to their levels of achievement on a similar task and (2) to determine whether a person has achieved a specified set of objectives. Criterion-referenced testing is interested in number two and norm-referenced testing in number one. For example, in criterion-referencing we might say that "Sam got 75 percent of the items correct on a test for multiplying fractions." In norm-referencing, however, we might say "Cindy did better than 75 percent of other students in the class on a test for multiplying fractions."

Norm-referenced testing is the kind that most of us are familiar with because it is the one most commonly used by teachers. It is a way of discriminating among individuals at all points along a continuum, and it is deliberately devised so that persons who have more aptitude or who have learned more will score higher on a test than those who have less aptitude or who have learned less. The interpretation, then, of "how much" aptitude a person possesses or "how much" he has learned is a normative one.

A primary difference between norm-referenced and criterion-referenced measurements is in the quantitative scales used to express how much or how well a person can do. In norm-referenced testing, it is appropriate to use our various measures of central tendency so we can locate the middle or average level of performance for a specified group of students. Our scale is then anchored somewhere in the middle of the distribution, and we report a student's performance in relation to how he ranks relative to others. We might say, "Your score is about average in relation to others in class" or "You excelled 70 percent of your class." Such group *norms* are typically used when we need to give meaning to scores on intelligence tests and standardized tests of achievement. They are also used in teacher-made tests whenever the instructor "marks on the curve."

NORM-REFERENCED VERSUS
CRITERION-REFERENCED TESTING:
WHICH TO USE?

Both kinds of measurements are useful. Each has its place and each can serve a particular purpose depending on what a teacher's objectives are for testing in the first place. If you want to discriminate degrees of excellence or deficiency, or differentiate levels of proficiency in a given task, then norm-referenced testing is most appropriate. It tells us how good or poor a student is performing in relation to others.

If, on the other hand, you are less concerned with differential levels of ability or skill and more concerned with each student reaching a predetermined level of performance no matter how much time it takes, then criterion-referenced testing is appropriate.

One way to decide when to use norm-referenced or criterion-referenced tests is to make a distinction between what Grondlund[26] describes as objectives that are considered *minimum essentials* and those that encourage *maximum development*. If we want our students to achieve certain minimum essentials, then the amount of time he takes to "master" them is probably less important than the fact that he does it. Here, criterion-referenced testing is most appropriate. If you want to encourage maximum development (and you would need to discriminate among those who achieve beyond a certain minimal level of mastery), then norm-referenced testing is probably most appropriate.

I, for one, do not see the argument of norm-referenced versus criterion-referenced measurement as an either-or issue. It is more a question of which is most *appropriate* in light of the goals and purposes a teacher has in mind. The way most schools are currently organized, with the time of instruction constant and the degree of learning variable, norm-referenced testing is most prevalent. This does not mean, however, that it is most *appropriate* in all instances. In Chapter 12, for example, we looked at some of the disasterous consequences that can follow on the heels of early school failure experiences. I can't think of a better time and place to use a mastery approach and criterion-referenced testing than during the elementary years when it is as critical and as important as it ever will be for students to get the "minimum essentials" so necessary for later "maximal development."

TO THINK ABOUT

If you had your choice, would you rather be in a class that used criterion-referenced or norm-referenced evaluation procedures? Why? What is it about you that makes you feel you would do better under one system rather than the other? Compare your views on this with someone who is on the other side of the fence.

Whether one uses a criterion- or norm-referenced format, there is still the problem of writing good exams—either essay or objective—to help us achieve our goals. To this we turn next.

WAYS TO PLAN AND CONSTRUCT
GOOD CLASSROOM TESTS

No matter what kind of measurement format you use—norm-referenced or criterion-referenced—or what kind of test you choose—essay or objective—it should be related to your course objectives. This will enable you to more accurately assess how well your students are progressing in relation to what the course or unit is supposed to cover.

A good way to begin thinking about the kind of test you want to use and what sorts of things you want the test to cover is to do a content analysis of the course or unit material. This can be simply done by making an overview outline of (1) the major ideas, (2) the general concepts, and (3) the specific knowledge that are associated with the objectives. *Major ideas* might include a list of complex ideas, principles, relationships, generalizations, laws, and the like, which students should be able to explain in a page or more. *General concepts* might include lists of terms and simple ideas, which students should be able to explain in a sentence or two. *Specific knowledge* might include a list of facts, dates, names, and the like, which students should be able to recall or recognize. This is your starting point and it brings you to a logical next step.

Determine the Kind of Exam You Want to Use

The question of what type of test to use is determined to some extent by what it is you wish to measure. If one of your objectives was to have students understand major ideas and general concepts, it may be more appropriate to construct an essay test, or a short-answer test, or some combination of the two. If, on the other hand, your objectives involved more in the way of having students come to grips with specific knowledge, it may seem more appropriate to construct some kind of objective test. There are advantages and disadvantages to both essay and objective tests, and, as you no doubt know from personal experience, there are both good and bad tests of each type. What you have to do as a teacher is to take advantage of the advantages by constructing tests that are fair, valid, and reliable. Easier said than done, but there are guidelines to follow. Let's turn our attention now to what these guidelines are.

Factors to Consider When Preparing and Using Essay Exams

In the first place, there are at least seven advantages to using essay questions:

1. It is relatively easy to construct and administer.
2. It is adaptable to nearly all types of subject matter.
3. It offers a way to find out how well a student can express himself in writing.
4. It serves as a natural test of a student's ability to synthesize, integrate, and organize his ideas.
5. It permits a student to make subtle distinctions inasmuch as he has no need to be satisfied with short one- or two-word responses or flat-footed "Yes" or "No" or "True" or "False" answers.
6. It offers less opportunity to guess inasmuch as alternative responses are not neatly lined up asking for an eeny-miney-moh approach.
7. It encourages students to prepare in such a way that stresses synthesis and organization. Many students report that, with essay test preparation, they are more likely to look for broad, general concepts, and relations between concepts rather than memorizing specific facts and isolated components.

There are also disadvantages, and you should know about those as well. Consider five of the more prominent ones:

607

1. The subjectivity of scoring can adversely affect the reliability and validity of the test.
2. It can sample only a limited amount of subject matter.
3. It is laborious and time-consuming to grade.
4. The scoring of an essay exam can be influenced by irrelevant factors such as handwriting and neatness, length, organization, and bluffing.
5. The scoring can also be influenced for better or for worse—by the scorer's frame of mind, his physical state, and time factors.

Gorow[27] has suggested that a "good" essay question is characterized by at least six virtues:

1. It requires one or more of the higher mental processes, rather than memory alone.
2. It is so clearly stated that students have no difficulty in determining what is required.
3. It is valid in that it measures abstractions or processes that are important in the subject.
4. It is sufficiently limited so that students can demonstrate their abilities in a reasonable length of time.
5. It requires originality of thought, of organization, and of expression.
6. It challenges the student with an interesting and worthwhile problem.

A virtue not mentioned by Gorow, but suggested by Mehrens and Lehmann[28] is that, in order for an essay question to approach being "good," it should establish the framework within which the student operates when answering the question. There are three ways for doing this:

1. *Be specific about the area covered by the question.* That is, give the student an idea of what it is you're looking for. For example, the question "Discuss criterion-referenced testing" is so nonspecific and open-ended that thirty different students could give thirty different responses. When specificity is lacking, so too, is validity. A better question would be "Discuss and explain why criterion-referenced testing may be a fairer procedure to use in elementary schools than norm-referenced testing."

2. *Use descriptive words.* Words such as "outline, select, define, classify, illustrate, and summarize" are fairly clear in their meaning. They describe for the student what he has to do and thereby reduce ambiguity. Words such as "discuss, compare, explain, and contrast" are less clear and may need to be defined further in order for the student to be certain what is meant by their usage. For example, the question "Explain what is meant by validity and reliability" is fairly vague as it stands. We can tap a student's knowledge about validity and reliability by being more descriptive about what we want him to explain. An example of a better question, then, might be: "Explain how the validity and reliability of a test can affect the results and the interpretation of the results."

3. *Indicate the value of the question and the approximate time to be spent in answering it.* This is fairly self-explanatory. It simply helps the student gauge his time on each question in relation to the total time allotted for the test, and it also helps him to decide where he should place his emphasis in responding to the various essay questions.

Suggestions for scoring essay exams. There is no question that scoring an essay exam is a very subjective process. Students don't expect perfection in a teacher, but they do look for fairness. What follows are five suggestions that may help make the task of grading essay exams as precise and as fair as possible.

1. It is useful to prepare at least a broad outline of the major points, ideas, or concepts that you feel should be included in the answer. This outline should reflect the objectives of the course or unit studied.

2. Strive for consistency in grading. A teacher is human and therefore fallible. It is possible to be influenced by the first few papers read and grade either too permissively or too harshly, depending upon your initial mind set. To minimize this possibility, it is wise to check your scoring criteria against the actual responses to be certain that the standards are being applied consistently.

3. Grade only one question at a time for all papers. This is a good idea because it reduces the possibility of the reader being unduly influenced—for better or for worse—by the quality of response to one question as he reads another on the same exam. It also makes it more possible to concentrate on one set of scoring criteria without being distracted by moving from one question to another.

4. Make an effort to judge the mechanics of expression separately from what the student writes. This is not to say that grammar and syntax are of no importance. They are. If you feel that the mechanics of expression are very important, then it is best to assign a certain percentage of a question's total value to such factors as legibility, punctuation, spelling, and grammar usage. In addition, make it clear to students that you are going to do this. As we've talked about in previous chapters, once a student knows what a teacher's expectations are, he is more apt to live up to them—or at least try.

5. Avoid scoring essay papers while you're feeling angry, depressed, or down. Inner feelings tend to get projected "out there" some place and if one is feeling angry or down-in-the-mouth while attempting to read essay exams, those feelings could be unconsciously projected into the scoring of them. I, for example, have found myself to be a far sterner judge of a student's effort—whatever it might be—when feeling a bit upset or angry about something than when I'm in a more tranquil frame of mind. The best advice here is to put the papers aside and come back to them when your spirits are up.

A final word about essay exams. Speaking from a more personal, rather than technical, point of view about the merits and demerits of essay exams, I tend to favor them because they encourage a student to demonstrate what he knows and understands in a way that is uniquely his own. From a strictly selfish stance, I find that my own learning is enhanced when I read essay exams. Students many times offer remarkable answers to even the simplest question. One teacher, for instance, relates the following episode as an example of student ingenuity far beyond the call of duty.

Some time ago, I received a call from a colleague who asked if I would be the referee on the grading of an examination question.

It seemed that he was about to give a student a zero for his answer to a physics question, while the student claimed he should receive a perfect score and would do so if the system were not set up against the student. The instructor and the student agreed to submit this to an impartial arbiter and I was selected.

I went to my colleague's office and read the examination question which was, "Show how it is possible to determine the height of a tall building with the aid of a barometer."

The student's answer was, "Take the barometer to the top of the building, attach a long rope to it, lower the barometer to the street, and then bring it up, measuring the length of the rope. The length of the rope is the height of the building."

Now this is a very interesting answer but should the student get credit for it?

I pointed out that the student really had a strong case for full credit, since he had answered the question completely and correctly.

On the other hand, if full credit were given, it could well contribute to a high grade for the student in his physics course. A high grade is supposed to certify that the student knows some physics, but the answer to the question did not confirm this.

With this in mind, I suggested that the student have another try at answering the question.

Acting in terms of the agreement, I gave the student six minutes to answer the question, with the warning that the answer should show some knowledge of physics. At the end of five minutes, he had not written anything.

I asked if he wished to give up, since I had another class to take care of, but he said no, he was not giving up. He had many answers to this problem; he was just thinking of the best one. I excused myself for interrupting him, and asked him to please go on.

In the next minute, he dashed off his answer which was:

"Take the barometer to the top of the building and lean over the edge of the roof. Drop the barometer, timing its fall with a stopwatch. Then using the formula, $S = \frac{1}{2} AT$ squared, calulate the height of the building."

At this point, I asked my colleague if he would give up. He conceded.

In leaving my colleague's office, I recalled that the student had said he had other answers to the problem, so I asked him what they were.

"Oh yes," said the student "There are many ways of getting the height of a tall building with the aid of a barometer. For example, you could take the barometer out on a sunny day and measure the height of the barometer, the length of its shadow, and the length of the shadow of the building, and by the use of simple proportion, determine the height of the building."

"Fine," I said, "And the others?"

"Yes," said the student. "There is a very basic measurement method that you will like. In this method, you take the barometer and begin to walk up the stairs. As you climb the stairs, you mark off the length of the barometer along the wall. You then count the number of marks and this will give you the height of the building in barometer units. A very direct method.

"Of course, if you want a more sophisticated method, you can tie the barometer to the end of a string, swing it as a pendulum, and determine the value of g at the street level and at the top of the building.

"From the difference between the two values of g, the height of the building can, in principle, be calculated."

Finally he concluded, "If you don't limit me to physics solutions to this problem, there are many other answers, such as taking the barometer to the basement and knocking on the superintendent's door. When the superintendent answers, you speak to him as follows": "Dear Mr. Superintendent, here I have a very fine barometer. If you will tell me the height of this building, I will give you this barometer."[29]

Factors to Consider When Preparing and Using Objective Exams

As with essay tests, there are both advantages and disadvantages associated with objective tests. Major advantages that stand out include at least five factors:

1. It allows for a more comprehensive sampling of a broader range of subject matter.
2. It offers a greater economy of time in answering and scoring.
3. Its objectivity in scoring improves test reliability and insures agreement regardless of who scores it.
4. The test items can be stated in simple language and easily read.
5. It eliminates external influences on scoring such as how the scorer feels and the student's skill at bluffing.

On the other hand, frequently cited disadvantages of an objective test include the following:

1. Test construction is generally tedious and time-consuming.
2. It may tend to overemphasize factual knowledge.
3. It may place undue emphasis on rote memorization.
4. It may encourage guessing rather than thinking through and problem solving.

611

5. It may be difficult or even impossible to adapt to some forms of subject matter.

Four Commonly Used Types of Objective Exams

An objective test is "objective" insofar as different scorers can arrive at the same score. The answers are short, consisting of a single word, number, or phrase, which is precisely predetermined by the person constructing the test. Typical examples of this kind of test are multiple-choice tests, true-false tests, matching tests, and completion-type tests. Let's briefly examine each of these to get an idea about how they're used and constructed.

Multiple-choice tests. This type of exam is probably the most highly regarded and widely used form of objective testing. According to Ebel, it is the kind of objective test that is:

> . . . adaptable to the measurement of most important educational outcomes — knowledge, understanding, and judgment; ability to solve problems, to recommend appropriate action, to make predictions. Almost any understanding or ability that can be tested by means of any other form — short answer, completion, true-false, matching, or essay — can also be tested by means of multiple-choice items.[30]

The following suggestions may be useful in writing effective multiple-choice items.

1. Write as many items as possible in question form. Not only does this reduce the possibility of copying the item directly from the textbook, but it encourages specific wording and focuses on one important idea. An example:

When is a test considered valid?
   a. when it is reliable
   b. when it does what it says it does
   c. when the scoring can be done objectively
   d. when it measures knowledge that is indirectly related to the objectives

2. Include three or more alternatives for every stem. (The stem is the question or initial statement.) Four alternatives to choose from are preferable to three because it reduces the possibility of correctness by guess. For example, if a student tries to guess his way through an exam, his chances of guessing correctly with a four-choice item would be 25 percent and with a five-choice item, 20 percent.

3. Make certain that all the incorrect alternatives (the *distractors*) are credible and logical enough not to be dismissed as absurd by a student who does not know the correct answer. An example of non-plausible distractors:

What is an important factor in New York City's development as an important seat of commerce?
  a. its population of industrious citizens
  b. its ready access to a large foreign-born population
  c. its excellent harbor facilities
  d. its scenic setting, considered worth visiting

4. If the item stem is a statement, be sure that each distractor can fit as a grammatically correct ending. An example of distractors that don't fit grammatically:

A biologist who studies the relationships between an organism and its environment is *an*:
  a. structuralists
  b. taxonomist
  c. ecologist
  d. ethnologist

The appearance of the indefinite article *an* automatically rules out a and b as possible answers. This situation could be remedied by using a combination a (an) at the end of the stem or by having each of the distractors begin with a vowel.

5. Try to make all the responses approximately the same length. Sometimes beginners in test construction unwittingly make their correct answer longer than the rest and thereby provide an irrelevant clue to the correct answer.

6. Be sure that the distractors and correct responses have some homogeneity—that is, they should be fairly similar in content or location. In the following example about the eye, other sense organs are brought in and this reduces the effectiveness of the item:

What is the term for that part of the eye most sensitive to light waves?
  a. retina
  b. iris
  c. cochlea
  d. stapes
  e. septum

This could be improved by using only parts of the eye and thereby calling for finer discrimination:

What is the term for that part of the eye most sensitive to light waves?
a. retina
b. choroid layer
c. iris
d. fovea centralis
e. lens

7. The responses "none of the above" or "all of the above" may be useful in items with only one possible answer, as in problems involving spelling or mathematical computation, but they should not be used in a "best answer" type of item.   The reason for this is direct and simple—they're difficult to construct, particularly the "all of the above" variety, and take more time than measurement experts think is worthwhile.

8. If it's impossible to invent more than three plausible responses, don't waste time trying to create others.

True-false tests.   Linus, that blanket-loving little rogue in *Peanuts*, once observed: "Taking a true-false test is like having the wind at your back." There is by no means 100 percent agreement that true-false tests are all that easy or even desirable, but the fact remains that they are widely used as another kind of objective measure.   This being the case, let us turn our attention to some practical ways to make *good* true-false tests if we do use them.

1. Minimize the possibility of confusion by writing each item so that it contains only one idea.

> A poor item: A valid test is one that measures what it is supposed to measure and a reliable one gives similar results with repeated administrations.
> A better item: A valid test is one that measures what it is supposed to measure.

2. Avoid the inclination to lift items directly from the text.   This favors the student who has slavishly memorized the actual words of the assignment.   It is better to create an item that calls for the sense of a paragraph or larger unit.

3. Take care not to use certain words that make it possible for the student to respond correctly to the item, even when he knows nothing about the material.   The words *all* and *always* call for a "false" response, *sometimes* or *usually* a "true" response, *no* or *never* a "false" response, and so on.   If, however, you're careful to distribute words of this nature equally among true and false items, the problem is eliminated.

4. Don't emphasize the trivial.   To do so only encourages rote memorization.

A poor item: Charles Darwin was born February 12, 1809.

A better item: Charles Darwin was born early in the nineteenth century.

5. Avoid negative statements. Suppose, for instance, we say, "True-false tests are not limited to the testing of factual material." Since true-false tests do not have this limitation, the general idea is false. However, because of the wording, the statement is true. It would be clearer and more direct to say, "True-false tests are limited to testing factual material." Here the statement is false both generally and in its technical phrasing.

6. Attribute opinions or attitudes used as item content to some particular source so that the students know you are not asking for a personal opinion.

A poor item: All dreams are expressions of our repressed desires and frustrations.

A better item: According to Freud, all dreams are expressions of our repressed desires and frustrations.

7. Construct the test so there are an equal number of true and false statements. These should be arranged so there is no particular pattern of response.

Matching tests. As the name implies, this is the kind of test that measures a student's ability to match or associate related objects or ideas. A student is asked to match an item in one column with an item in a second column. For example:

In the left-hand column below are some basic "discoveries" associated with different psychologists and educators of our time. For each discovery, choose a name from the right-hand column and place the letter identifying it on the line preceding the number of the title. Each item may be used once, more than once, or not at all.

1. __ self-actualization	a. C. Rogers
2. __ the fully functioning person	b. R. Cattell
3. __ the urge for competency	c. D. Wechsler
4. __ mastery learning	d. A. Maslow
5. __ crystallized and fluid intelligence	e. S. Freud
	f. R. White
	g. B. Bloom

Some general suggestions for constructing good matching tests include the following:

1. Make each matching exercise *homogeneous* in the sense that all premises and all responses refer to the same type of thing. In the example

above, all the names are of psychologists and/or educators and each is associated with some sort of psychological and/or educational endeavor.

2. Be able to give a full and logical basis for your matching.

3. Avoid the "perfect matching" situation in which the number of premises on the left is equal to the number of responses on the right. If a student knows all the associations except one, he'll automatically get this by elimination, thus diminishing the discriminating ability and the accuracy of the test as a measuring device.

4. Be sure that all responses are plausible distractors for each premise. If I had included, say, Henry Kissinger in the right-hand column of our example, he would not have been a very plausible distractor.

Completion tests. Completion items are statements with one or more missing words that must be provided by the student. The following items are simple examples of this form:

a. The process of determining the extent, dimensions, or quantity of something is called _____.

b. The normal curve is used in conjunction with _____ -referenced measurement. _____

c. What is the term for that group of scores that occurs most frequently in a distribution? _____.

Whatever form a completion item takes, its essential features are that the answers consist of only one or two words and that these words are supplied by the student rather than selected from a list of possible alternatives. It is the kind of item that is relatively easy to construct, particularly when contrasted to multiple-choice and matching items, since it does not require a list of plausible distractors. Another of its strengths (although not from a student's point of view) is that it offers little opportunity for guessing. A student either knows the answer or he doesn't.

An inherent weakness of this type of testing is that the teacher can never possibly anticipate all the possible correct answers that students might insert. Another weakness is that too much reliance on it may lead to an overemphasis on memorization of factual information.

Which Kind of Test Is Best—Essay or Objective?

This may seem an evasive answer to you, but the fact is that research does not point to a consistent answer. It appears that both essay tests and objective tests have value. Ebel, for instance, has concluded that:

1. Either an essay or an objective test can be used to measure almost any important educational achievement that any written test can measure.

2. Either an essay or an objective test can be used to encourage students to study for understanding of principles, organization and integration of ideas, and application of knowledge to the solution of problems.[31]

Perhaps the question should not address itself to which is best, but, rather to the more complex issues of which type of test is best for this teacher, for this class, for this material, and under these conditions?

Probably the best strategy for testing, as with other classroom activities, is to go with a variety of approaches. Some students feel more comfortable with objective tests, while others are more at home with the essay type. If the class is not so large as to make essay testing impractical, there can be no harm in using both kinds of examinations. No matter what you do, you can be sure that although you may please some of the students some of the time, you will never please all of the students all of the time. If a teacher gives an objective test, some students say, "It doesn't let you express yourself." If an essay is administered, some students complain, "It's so vague—how can we know what's expected?" If a teacher gives many smaller tests some students wonder, "Why not have a few big ones? These keep you on edge all the time." On the other hand, when given a few major tests, students not infrequently respond with, "This isn't fair. Too much depends on each one." And when a teacher gives no tests at all some students are heard to say, "This is ridiculous. How can he possibly judge what we know?" The lot of a teacher is not an easy one.

Suggestions for Creating a Positive Examination Climate

No one has ever said that giving examinations and grading students was a pleasant task, but there are at least eight basic principles we can follow to make it less unpleasant and more fair to more students. The psychological climate that exists during an examination period is only one more part of a teacher's total relationship to a class. These are steps that a teacher can take to enhance the possibilities of that relationship being a positive one.

1. *Be certain that students are clear about what material will be covered by and included in the examination.* Your own experience has probably taught you that bitter, angry feelings follow easily on the heels of of taking an exam that includes material that you had no idea would be covered.

2. *Specify the kind of test that will be given.* As discussed earlier, students prepare differently for different kinds of exams.

3. *Specify when the exams will be given.* Although some teachers like the idea of unannounced quizzes to "keep students on their toes," this approach typically arouses more anxiety and resentment than is productive for the vast majority of students.

4. *Tell students how much each test will count toward their final grade.* This gives students an opportunity to make decisions and take responsibility for how to budget their time.

5. *Avoid extremely easy or extremely difficult items or questions.* Actually, it is best to develop test items with a range of difficulty levels from relatively easy to relatively hard. (Difficulty level is indicated by the proportion or percentage of students answering the item correctly—the smaller the proportion of examinees responding correctly, the more difficult the item.) Although many measurement specialists would argue that items should be approximately at the 50 percent level of difficulty (i.e., one-half of the students should be able to answer a given item correctly), a slight loss in reliability can be tolerated by varying this difficulty level in order to enhance student motivation. For example, many times teachers will deliberately include some easy items or questions on a test if for no other reason than to give every student a chance to experience some success.

6. *Allow enough time to complete the exam.* Inasmuch as most teacher-made tests are administered to find out how much students know rather than how fast they can tell you what they know, time is an important consideration. How much time is enough is an open question, but one to which every teacher must be sensitive. As a general rule, it is better to have a bit too much time rather than not enough.

7. *Give students the results of their performance as quickly as possible.* Probably nothing is more frustrating and de-motivating to a student than to have to wait weeks or longer for his test results. Again, your own experience can no doubt tell you what this is like. The importance of quick feedback is not idle speculation. Two separate research efforts showed, for example, that college students who learned the correct and incorrect answers soon after taking their hour quizzes did significantly better on the final examination than matched students who had to wait for longer periods to get their results.[32,33]

8. *Give students an opportunity to go over their test results and to check any incorrect responses against the correct answers.* Time and again research has demonstrated the value of this procedure. For instance, Stone,[34] and Plowman and Stroud[35] have shown that the more feedback information provided when objective tests were returned, in terms of why incorrect choices were wrong and why keyed choices were correct, the better students performed when retested.

Closely connected to testing are the matters of grading and reporting, issues to which we turn our attention next.

ISSUES AND PROBLEMS RELATED TO
GRADING AND REPORTING

Just as there are problems and differences of opinion regarding measurement and evaluation procedures, so too are there problems and differing viewpoints when it comes to the purpose, place, and expression of grading and reporting procedures. In a very real sense of the word, grading and reporting are more human problems than they are measurement problems. Whether it is a first-grade teacher or a high school chemistry instructor or a college professor, the task of sitting in judgment—of placing a value on another person's performance, if you will—is an awesome responsibility. We can talk about "objectifying" our examinations and scoring procedures all we want, but in the final analysis every teacher has to be in some way involved in the very personal process of assessing, grading, and reporting how well or how poorly a student has done over a given period of time. As we shall see, there is a notable lack of universal agreement about how to do these things.

TO THINK ABOUT

If you plan to teach, you will soon be in a position that asks for your judgments and evaluations of someone else's performance. Jot down (quickly) three adjectives which describe your feelings about that.

_____,   _____,   _____

Why do you suppose you've chosen the ones you have? What do they suggest about your attitude toward grading?

Varieties of Reporting Systems

The matter of how a student's performance is reported varies from school system to school system. The most common form of reporting is via some kind of report card and this sometimes supplemented by parent-teacher conferences, particularly at the elementary school level. Umstattd[36] reported a summary of grade reporting systems found in 258 school systems and as you can see in Table 13-1, letters or other symbols, such as numbers, 1, 2, 3, 4, 5, were used in 81 percent of the schools. Percentages were still used in 26 percent of the schools; some schools used both plans. More recent evidence suggests that the relative frequency of the various kinds of grade reporting systems is still about the same.[37]

Report cards come in a wide range of assorted shapes, sizes, types, and even colors. They vary from a semiannual letter to parents to a three-page

TABLE 13–1.

| | Frequency | |
Types of grade reporting systems	Number	Percent
Letters or other symbols	210	81
Percentages	67	26
Class ranks	25	9
Percentile ranks	7	3
Written records or logs of pupil's progress	4	2
Accomplishment quotients	2	1
Standard deviation scores	7	1

inventory to a simple card covering every possible academic and nonacademic pursuit. Most, however, fall into a similar pattern.

Elementary School Report Cards

Report cards for the elementary level typically have two major sections, one for academic achievement and the other for social growth or, as it is commonly called, "citizenship." Ordinarily a teacher is required to assess each student on his ability in reading, language skills, arithmetic, handwriting, science, art, physical education, and so on. As we have already noted, grading is usually done on a five-step "A" to "F" scale. This is more common at the junior high and high school level. In elementary school, either a three-step system is used such as "above average," "satisfactory," "needs improvement" or a two-step method such as "satisfactory-unsatisfactory." In addition, many elementary school systems make a distinction between academic performance and estimates of social adjustment under the heading of "citizenship." Unfortunately, more and more elementary schools are using the "A" to "F" scale, which is a sad trend to note because, as discussed in detail in Chapter 12, it dooms thousands upon thousands of children to explicit failure experiences at that very time in life when success experiences are most important.

Let's Stress What Is "Right" and De-emphasize What Is "Wrong"

Although it is surely important for elementary age youngsters to have as many success experiences as possible during their formative years, the importance of success is no less crucial for students at other levels as well.

"ABOUT THIS REPORT CARD... I JUST MAY SUE FOR DEFAMATION OF CHARACTER!"

No one need suffer "defamation of character" if we search diligently for ways for all students to experience success. (Zeis, reprinted by permission of Masters Agency)

I wonder what would happen if teachers—at all levels—began stressing and reporting those things students did that were "right" or "correct" rather than focusing so intently on those things that were "wrong" or "incorrect." Rather than a teacher saying something like "John, you got fifteen wrong and that's not very good," perhaps it would be better if he said something along the lines of "John, you got ten *right* and I bet you can improve the next time." In the first instance, the emphasis is on John's errors and what is past, while in the second the emphasis is on John's accuracy and what is possible for the future. John Holt[38] has suggested that a teacher might accomplish a whole lot more if he helped students to evaluate their responses not just in terms of "Is it right?" or "Is it wrong?" but more in terms of "Is it sensible?"

Generally speaking, the best kind of reporting system is one that summarizes the progress a student is making, what might reasonably be expected of him, and the nature of any learning difficulties he may be having. Parent-teacher conferences are usually the most desirable means for communicating this kind of information and Mahler and Smallenberg[39] have made some suggestions that can make these conferences more meaningful:

1. Report to the parents in terms of the student's achievement in relation to his capacity—how he is developing in relation to his strengths and limitations.
2. Report on the student's attainments in any learning situation in relation to the others in his group.
3. Report also on the student's aptitudes and achievements in relation to the larger numbers of children beyond his particular school and community—by reference to published norms.
4. Make certain that parents and teachers share observations about the student. The teacher should listen rather than lecture.
5. Differences in points of view should be respected.
6. Avoid comparison of the student with individual classmates.
7. End conference on a constructive note of confidence in each student and his development. Consider all aspects of his growth—not just intellectual.

Where there is a system of measurement and evaluation of a student's achievement and progress, there is reporting, and where there is reporting there is the question of grading—a controversial issue to which we now turn our attention.

To Grade or not to Grade

The business of grading is a touchy, emotional issue. Some assert that grades represent an important cog in the wheel of educational pursuit, while others advocate abolishing grades altogether. For example, Ernest Melby, who has served as a high school principal, school superintendent, college professor, college dean, and university president, has observed that:

The marking system is irrelevant and mischievous. It is destructive. It destroys the self-concepts of millions of children every year. Note the plight of the deprived child. He often enters school at six with few of the preschool experiences that the middle-class children bring to school. We ask him to learn to read. He is not ready to read. We give him a low mark—we repeat the low mark for each marking period—often for as long as the child remains in school. At the end of perhaps the ninth grade, the child drops out of school. What has he learned? He has learned he cannot learn. We have told him so several dozen times. Why should he think otherwise?[40]

That's one side of the issue. The other side is expressed by Robert Ebel, a widely respected measurement expert, who says:

> The source of anxiety, dislike of schooling, and the decision to drop out of school is low achievement, which marks do not cause but simply report. In the essential process of adjusting education to individual pupils and individual pupils to education, marks are far more helpful than harmful.[41]

I can tell you that the literature is replete with passionate articles for and against grades and with research reports, some of which support the traditional use of grades and public reporting of same, and some which conclude that grading will surely lead us into an educational wasteland studded with school failures. What can we do about the grading issue? Well, we can continue as we have with our varied public reporting systems, or we can look for alternatives. A group that calls itself, appropriately enough, *The Center for Grading Alternatives*, is doing just that. (In the event you wish to be in touch with them, their address is: 2100 E. Genessee St., Syracuse, N.Y., 13210; phone 315–472–6777.)

Some Alternative Grading Systems

The organization mentioned above published a book not long ago that is titled: *Wad-Ja-Get: The Grading Game in American Education.*[42] In this book they proposed some ideas for alternative grading systems that are worth our consideration.

In the first place, they make a distinction between *private* evaluation, which involves teachers, students, and parents working together in identifying strengths and weaknesses and planning steps toward improved performance, and *public* evaluation, which is the summary data about the student made available to parties outside the school and home. Since it is the information about a student that is made public that can be most damaging (or most helpful, I would think, if the student has done well) as far as future opportunities are concerned, eight alternatives to traditional grading practices are offered. Let's look briefly at each of them.

Use written evaluations. The purpose of this is to allow the teacher to spell out in greater detail strengths and weaknesses and to discuss recommendations for improvement. The thinking is that these will be more meaningful to parents, admission officers, and potential employers.

Use self-evaluation procedures. Here, the student evaluates his own progress, either in writing or in a conference with the teacher. These

623

evaluations are then sent to parents and included in the permanent records. There are no grades.

Give grades, but don't tell students. Students get grades as usual but aren't told. Rather a strong, personalized advising system keeps students appraised of how they're doing and gives them a clear perspective of where they stand in relation to peers.

Use the contract system. There are two ways to do this. One is to make a "contract" with the whole class as to the type, quantity, and, ideally, quality of work they will do and then assign a blanket grade to the whole class, which could be anywhere from A to F, depending on how well the contract was met. The other way is to make contracts with individual students that would include the student's own agreement as to how his grade would be determined.

Use the mastery approach or performance curriculum. Since we've already discussed this in relation to criterion-referenced testing, there's no need for a lengthy repeat here. The teacher establishes the behavioral objectives, a student works at his own pace in what amounts to an individualized course of study, and when a prescribed level of mastery has been reached, he passes with at least a C. If he chooses, he can earn a B or A by going on for a higher level of mastery in whatever the subject area happens to be.

Use pass/fail grading. At the beginning of a course, a teacher states his criteria for a passing grade, or else the teacher and students together decide on the criteria for a passing grade. Students who meet the criteria pass. Those who don't fail. Students who fail can redo the work if they desire.

Credit/no credit grading. This works exactly the same way as the pass/fail system does, except that the categories are called "credit" and "no credit." The major difference is that "no credit" does *not* connote failing work and is noted as such in the transcripts.

Blanket grading. The teacher announces at the beginning that anyone in the class who does the work will receive a blanket grade, which would be anywhere from C to an A. The teacher says, in effect, anyone who achieves this minimum level of mastery will receive this blanket grade.

Some Kind of Grading System Is Necessary

It is surely true that our assorted grading systems are something less than perfect or 100 percent reliable. Those who would toss out grades altogether are confronted with what Ebel sees as a logical dilemma:

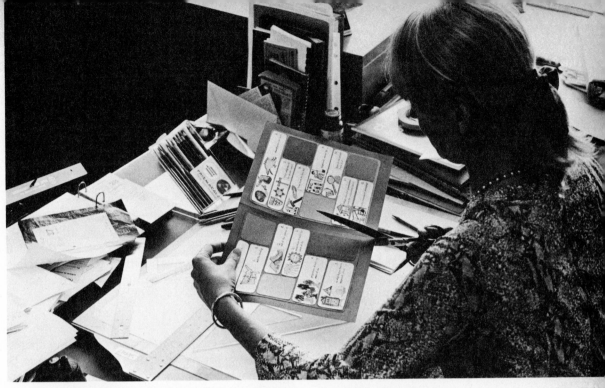

Figuring out ways to assess student performance is a problem that every teacher must face. (Allyn and Bacon)

Those who claim that learning proceeds better in the absence than in the presence of systematic determinations of achievement encounter an interesting logical problem. They cannot provide evidence to support the claim without doing what they say ought not to be done. They must measure achievement to prove that learning is facilitated by not measuring achievement. It is impossible in principle to show that more will be learned when no attempt is made to determine how much has been learned. And there is something patently absurd in the assertion that the best progress will be made when no attention is paid to progress.[43]

Grades that are fair, free from negative teacher bias, and based on observable performance related to the learning objectives are necessary. Grades that are unfair, distorted by negative teacher attitudes, and that have little, if any, relationship to the learning objectives are not necessary.

Students not only have a right to know, but *want* to know how they are progressing academically in relation to their previous effort and in relation to their peers. Comparing oneself with his past performance — in whatever it might be — and with others who have performed in the same area is an important way for reality-testing the limits of one's talents and abilities.

Eliminating grades does not seem to be either a rational or constructive possibility. Perhaps what we need to do is spend more attention to improve the validity and precision of the marks we give, while at the same time experimenting with alternative approaches to assessing and reporting

625

student achievement. A student doesn't mind being graded. He does, however, mind being graded unjustly and unfairly.

EPILOGUE

Measuring student achievement and evaluating learning are difficult, demanding tasks. Although I frequently hear the idea expressed that tests and grades destroy, or at least interfere, with healthy, positive teacher-student relationships, I have yet to see any good evidence to verify that assertion. I think it is the nature of the teacher who makes a difference in the quality of student-teacher relationships and not the nature of the grading system.

In order for classroom measurement and evaluation to have any chance at all for working fairly and equitably for all students, you will have to be as clear as possible about your goals and objectives. It is impossible to construct a valid measurement instrument unless you're clear about what it is supposed to measure in the first place. Hence, the importance of objectives. Not only that, but objectives help define the content boundaries and answer anxious questions like: "What is this course or unit all about anyway?"

Two major approaches to measurement are criterion-referenced testing and norm-referenced testing. With the former, the major variable is time, with each student taking as much of it as necessary to reach a predetermined level of "mastery." There seems little question that this takes the heat off students who, because of lack of development or lack of previous experience, do not learn as quickly as some others in class. Criterion-referenced measurement is ideally suited to measure achievement at the elementary school level inasmuch as it automatically takes into account the fact that differential growth rates cause vast differences in learning readiness.

Norm-referenced measurement, on the other hand, pits students against each other along a performance continuum from high to low. That is, students are assessed according to an established norm of what is high achievement or low achievement. In this system, there will always be some who fail. It is a system still too frequently used in elementary schools and one that encourages at a very young, impressionable age the "I'm-a-failure" attitude discussed in Chapter 12.

Both objective tests and essay tests have a place and purpose in classroom measurement. Which kind is used should, again, relate back to what your objectives are. Generally, an approach to student evaluation that includes a variety of measurement procedures is most likely to satisfy both you and your students in your mutual quest for a productive and satisfying learning experience.

It is not enough to simply motivate students and measure their learning. You must also have a basic understanding of group dynamics and develop strategies for managing a class in positive ways. More about this in Part V around the corner.

Write your own chapter summary (major points, ideas, and concepts that had meaning for you).

_____

_____

_____

_____

_____

_____

_____

_____

_____

REFERENCES

1. Mager, R. F. *Developing Attitude Toward Learning.* Palo Alto, Calif.: Fearon, 1968.

2. McDonald, F. J. *Educational Psychology,* 2nd ed. Belmont, Calif.: Wadsworth, 1965.

3. Tyler, R. W. "Some Persistent Questions in Defining Educational Objectives." *In Defining Educational Objectives,* edited by C. M. Lindvall. Pittsburgh: University of Pittsburgh Press, 1964.

4. DeCecco, J. P. *The Psychology of Learning and Instruction.* Englewood Cliffs, N.J.: Prentice-Hall, 1968.

5. Atkin, M. J. "Behavioral Objectives in Curriculum Design: A Cautionary Note." *The Science Teacher* (May 1968):27–30.

6. Ojemann, R. H. "Should Educational Objectives Be Stated in Behavioral Terms?", Part II. *The Elementary School Journal* (February 1969):229–235.

7. Ebel, R. L. *Essentials of Educational Measurement.* Englewood Cliffs, N.J.: Prentice-Hall, 1972, pp. 62–64.

8. Broudy, H. S. "Can Research Escape the Dogma of Behavioral Objectives?" *School Review* 79(1970):43–56.

9. Eisner, E. W. "Educational Objectives: Help or Hindrance?" *School Review* 75(1967):250–260.

10. Payne, D. A. *The Specification and Measurement of Learning Outcomes* Waltham, Mass.: Blaisdell, 1968.

11. Bloom, B. S. (ed.). *Taxonomy of Educational Objectives, Handbook I: Cognitive Domain.* New York: McKay, 1956.

12. Krathwohl, D. R., B. S. Bloom, and B. B. Masia. *Taxonomy of Educational Objectives, Handbook II: Affective Domain.* New York: McKay, 1964.

13. Ebel, R. L. *Essentials of Educational Measurement.* Op. cit., 1972, pp. 279–281.

14. Mehrens, W. A., and I. J. Lehmann. *Measurement and Evaluation in Education and Psychology.* New York: Holt, Rinehart and Winston, 1973, pp. 90–93.

15. Lord, F. M. "Do Tests of the Same Length Have the Same Standard Error of Measurement?" *Educational and Psychological Measurement* 17(Winter 1957):510–521.

16. Lord, F. M. "Tests of the Same Length Do Have the Same Standard Error of Measurement." *Educational and Psychological Measurement* 19(Summer 1959):233–239.

17. Gorow, F. F. *Better Classroom Testing.* San Francisco, Calif.: Chandler, 1966, p. 75.

18. Washburn, C. W. "Educational Measurements as a Key to Individualizing Instruction and Promotions." *Journal of Educational Research* 5(1922):195–206.

19. Carroll, J. B. "A Model of School Learning." *Teachers College Record* 64(1963):723–733.

20. Bloom, B. S. "Learning for Mastery." *Evaluation Comment* (May 1968):1. UCLA, CSEIP.

21. Block, J. H. (ed.). *Mastery Learning: Theory and Practice.* New York: Holt, Rinehart and Winston, 1971.

22. Carroll, J. B. "Problems of Measurement Related to the Concept of Learning for Mastery." In *Mastery Learning: Theory and Practice,* edited by J. H. Block. New York: Holt, Rinehart and Winston, P. 152.

23. Bloom, B. S., J. T. Hastings, and G. F. Madaus. *Handbook on Formative and Summative Evaluation of Student Learning.* New York: McGraw-Hill, 1971, p. 56.

24. Ebel, R. L. *Essentials of Educational Measurement.* Op. cit., 1972, pp. 84–85.

25. Mehrens, W. A., and I. J. Lehmann. *Measurement and Evaluation in Education and Psychology.* Op. cit., 1973, p. 68.

26. Grondlund, H. E. *Stating Behavioral Objectives for Classroom Instruction.* Toronto, Ontario: Macmillan, 1970, p. 32.

27. Gorow, F. F. *Better Classroom Testing.* Op. cit., 1966, p.87.

28. Mehrens, W. A., and I. J. Lehmann. *Measurement and Evaluation in Education and Psychology.* Op. cit., 1973, pp. 217–218.

29. Calandra, A. "A Barometer Measures Critical Thinking." St. Louis, Mo.: Washington University, Mimeograph (no date).

30. Ebel, R. L. *Essentials of Educational Measurement.* Op. cit., 1972, p. 187.

31. Ebel, R. L. *Essentials of Educational Measurement.* Op. cit., 1972, pp. 138–139.

32. Spitzer, H. F. "Studies in Retention." *Journal of Educational Psychology* 30(1939):641–656.

33. Angell, G. W. "The Effect of Immediate Knowledge of Quiz Results on Final Examination Scores in Freshman Chemistry." *Journal of Educational Research* 42(1949):391–394.

34. Stone, G. R. *The Training Function of Examinations: Retest Performance as a Function of the Amount and Kind of Critique Information.* Research Report No. AFPTRC-TN-55-8. San Antonio: USAF Personnel Training Research Center, Lackland Air Force Base, 1955.

35. Plowman, L., and J. B. Stroud. "Effect of Informing Pupils of the Correctness of their Responses to Objective Test Questions." *Journal of Educational Research* 36(1942):166–179.

36. Umstattd, J. G. *Secondary School Teaching.* Lexington, Mass.: Ginn, 1953, pp. 417–418.

37. National Educational Association. "School Marks and Reporting to Parents." *National Education Research Bulletin,* 48(1970):76–81.

38. Holt, J. *How Children Fail.* New York: Dell, 1964, p. 108.

39. Mahler, D., and H. Smallenburg. "Effect of Testing Programs on the Attitudes of Students, Teachers, Parents, and the Community." In *The Impact and Improvement of School Testing Programs,* 62nd Yearbook of National Society for the Study of Education, Part II, edited by N. B. Henry, and H. G. Richey. Chicago: University of Illinois Press, 1963.

40. Melby, E. O. "It's Time for Schools to Abolish the Marking System." *Nation's Schools* 77(1966):104.

41. Ebel, R. L. *Essentials of Educational Measurement.* Op. cit., 1972 p. 312.

42. Kirschenbaum, H., S. B. Simon, and Rodney W. Napier. *Wad-Ja-Get? The Grading Game in American Education.* New York: Hart, 1971.

43. Ebel, R. L. "Should School Marks Be Abolished?" *Michigan Journal of Secondary Education* 6(Fall 1964):14–15.

REFERENCES OF RELATED INTEREST

Ames, L. B., C. Gillespie, and J. W. Streff. *Stop School Failure.* New York: Harper and Row, 1972.

Brown, F. G. *Measurement and Evaluation.* Itasca, Ill.: Peacock, 1971.

Chansky, N. M. "The X-Ray of the School Mark." *The Educational Forum* (March 1962):347–352.

Davis, F. B. *Educational Measurements and Their Interpretation.* Belmont, Calif.: Wadsworth, 1964.

Dizney, H. *Classroom Evaluation for Teachers.* Dubuque, Iowa: Brown, 1971.

Downie, N. M. *Fundamentals of Measurement: Techniques and Practices.* New York: Oxford University Press, 1958.

Gorow, F. F. *Better Classroom Testing.* San Francisco, Calif.: Chandler, 1966.

Grunlund, N. E. *Constructing Achievement Tests.* Englewood Cliffs, N.J.: Prentice-Hall, 1968.

Hoffman, B., and J. Barzun. *The Tyranny of Testing.* New York: Collier Books, 1962.

Interpretation of Test Results. Washington, D.C.: U.S. Department of Health, Education and Welfare, 1964.

Jarrett, C. D. "Marking and Reporting Practices in the American Secondary School." *Peabody Journal of Education* 41(July 1963):36–48.

Karmel, L. J. *Measurement and Evaluation in the Schools.* Toronto, Ontario: Macmillan, 1966.

Kingston, A. J., and J. A. Wash, Jr. "Research on Reporting Systems." *National Elementary School Principal* 45(1966):36–40.

Kryspin, W. J., and J. F. Feldhusen. *Developing Classroom Tests.* Minneapolis, Minn.: Burgess, 1974.

Lien, A. S. *Measurement of Learning,* 2nd ed. Dubuque, Iowa: Brown, 1971.

Lindeman, R. H. *Educational Measurement.* Glenview, Ill.: Scott, Foresman, 1967.

Lindvall, C. M. *Measuring Pupil Achievement.* New York: Harcourt, Brace and World, 1967.

"Marking and Reporting Pupil Progress." *Today's Education* (November 1970):56–57.

Marshall, J. C., and L. W. Hales. *Classroom Test Construction.* Reading, Mass.: Addison-Wesley, 1971.

Marshall, M. *Teaching without Grades.* Portland: Oregon State University Press, 1969.

McLaughlin, K. F. *Interpretation of Test Results,* no. 7. Washington, D.C.: U.S. Department of Health, Education and Welfare, 1964.

Mehrens, W. A., and I. J. Lehmann. *Measurement and Evaluation in Education and Psychology.* New York: Holt, Rinehart and Winston, 1973.

———. *Standardized Tests in Education.* New York: Holt, Rinehart and Winston, 1969.

Payne, D. A. *The Specification and Measurement of Learning Outcomes.* Waltham, Mass.: Ginn/Blaisdell, 1968.

Phillips, R. C. *Evaluation in Education.* Columbus, Ohio: Merrill, 1968.

Robertson, D., and M. Steele. "To Grade Is to Degrade." In *The Halls of Yearning,* by Donald Robertson and Marion Steele. Lakewood, Calif.: Andrews Printing Co., 1969, pp. 41–67.

Sanders, N. J. *Classroom Questions: What Kinds?* New York: Harper & Row, 1966.

Terwilliger, J. S. *Assigning Grades to Students.* Glenview, Ill.: Scott, Foresman, 1972.

Thorndike, R. L. "Marks and Marking Systems." In *Encylopedia of Educational Research,* 4th ed., edited by R. L. Ebel and V. H. Noll. Toronto, Ontario: Collier-Macmillan, 1969, pp. 759–766.

Tyler, L. E. *Tests and Measurements.* Englewood Cliffs, N.J.: Prentice-Hall, 1963.

Wrinkle, W. L. *Improving Marking and Reporting Practices in Elementary and Secondary Schools.* New York: Holt, 1947.

Wood, D. A. *Test Construction.* Columbus, Ohio: Merrill, 1960.

V

The Psychology of Group Behavior, Classroom Dynamics, and Management Strategies

If you have read and studied the material up to this point, you must surely have the feeling that being a teacher or youth-worker—a good one—is not only exciting and challenging, but a taxing and complex activity. It demands a background in psychology in order to help understand behavior, an exposure to theories and processes of learning in order to help you encourage achievement, an understanding of yourself in order to help you maximize your effectiveness as a person and an exposure to concepts and facts of growth to help you understand the developmental dynamics of the age group with whom you are or will be working.

This seems quite enough, but one more thing is needed. You must not only be a bit of a behavioral and developmental psychologist, and a learning facilitator, but you have to be something of a social psychologist and management strategist as well.

Chapters 14 and 15 in this last part of the book are included to help give you an understanding of the psychology of group dynamics and how to encourage "healthy" group dynamics, along with some suggestions that may be helpful to you in "managing" a class in positive, constructive ways.

How does a classroom's social-emotional climate influence individual and group behavior? What can you do to help build constructive group norms? What is sociometry and how can you use it to understand individuals within the group? How does a teacher's response style influence behavior? Is classroom discipline a serious problem? What are some strategies for handling discipline problems when they occur? Do behavior modification approaches work? Should physical restraint ever be used?

All of these questions and others, too, are discussed in chapters 14 and 15.

FOURTEEN

Psychology and Development of Healthy Classroom Group Dynamics

CHAPTER OUTLINE

PROLOGUE

INFLUENCE OF A CLASSROOM'S SOCIAL-EMOTIONAL CLIMATE ON INDIVIDUAL AND GROUP BEHAVIOR

A Classroom's Social-Emotional Climate Can Influence Learning

A Teacher's Personal Style Makes a Big Difference

Outcomes of Authoritarian, Democratic, and Laissez-faire Classrooms

Authoritarian Classrooms May Produce More, But . . .

A Share in Decision-making Processes Is Important

Ways to Create a Positive Classroom Climate

INTERPERSONAL ATTRACTIONS AND GROUP PROCESSES

Factors Influencing Classroom Liking Patterns

Intelligence: being perceived as either too stupid or too smart is risky

Physical characteristics: caution — what is beautiful may not be good

Mental health characteristics: psychological health related to social acceptance

Social behavior: friendliness is accepted everywhere
social-class structure influences social behavior

Teacher behavior: who a teacher likes influences who others like

DEVELOPMENT AND EXPRESSION OF GROUP NORMS

Varieties of Norm Structures

Necessary Building Blocks for the Development of Classroom Norms

Perceptual norms: how students see things

group discussion can influence perceptual norms / trust can be a perceptual norm—it's up to the teacher

Cognitive norms: how students think about things
cognitive norms are best developed by teachers and students working together

Evaluative norms: how students feel about things
flexible evaluative norms work best

Behavioral norms: how students act
behavioral norms best arrived at through open discussion

DEVELOPMENT AND EXPRESSION OF GROUP COHESIVENESS

What Group Cohesiveness Means

Antecedents of High Group Cohesiveness

Widely Dispersed Friendship and Power Associated with High Cohesiveness

How Teachers Can Influence Classroom Cohesiveness

High need-for-affiliation teachers discourage cohesiveness

High need-for-autonomy teachers encourage cohesiveness

Group-centered teachers encourage cohesiveness

Varieties of Classroom Cohesiveness

SOCIOMETRY AS A WAY FOR UNDERSTANDING CLASSROOM GROUPS

Examples of Sociometric Testing

Categories of peer acceptance

The "Guess Who" test

The "Class Play" technique

Using drawings as sociometric devices

Sociometric Patterns Keep Changing

Are Sociometric Approaches Really Necessary?

COMMUNICATION SKILLS FOR ENHANCING GROUP PROCESSES

Classroom Communication Problems

Toward Creating a Climate for Open Communication

A supportive atmosphere helps

Your response style makes a difference: five from which to choose

How to make appropriate use of those response patterns

Why being able to trust a teacher is so important

Use immediate reinforcement: it facilitates good feelings

Make your feedback constructive

EPILOGUE

REFERENCES

REFERENCES OF RELATED INTEREST

IMPORTANT CHAPTER IDEAS

1. The social-emotional climate of a classroom can influence, for better or for worse, how a student performs academically and adjusts socially.

2. The manner in which a teacher interacts with students is another factor that influences the psychological climate of a classroom.

3. Students are most receptive to, and productive in, classroom climates in which they feel they can influence decision-making and operating policies.

4. Teachers with positive classroom climates include many, rather than few, students in class discussions.

5. Students who are socially rejected tend to do less well academically than students of comparable intelligence who are socially accepted.

6. The prevailing social-class structure of a school makes a big difference in the kinds of social behavior that are acceptable or unacceptable to students.

7. Who the teacher likes or dislikes tends to influence who students like or dislike.

8. The existence of group norms is important because they are the guides used to control or regulate proper or acceptable behavior.

9. Being able to trust the teacher is an important part of a psychologically healthy classroom climate.

10. Highly cohesive classrooms usually have a large number of overlapping friendship patterns.

11. Group-centered teachers tend to encourage high classroom cohesiveness.

12. Sociometric techniques are useful in helping a teacher to better understand the interpersonal dynamics of a class.

13. Friendship patterns, particularly at the elementary level, are constantly shifting.

14. The need for a supportive (as opposed to rejecting) classroom climate is essential for healthy psychosocial growth and maximum intellectual development.

15. Immediate positive reinforcement and constructive feedback enhances the possibility of open, free communication among students and between students and teacher.

PROLOGUE

In a very real sense, each classroom is a miniature society with its own members, rules, organizational structure, social stratification, and hierarchy of authority. Just as each person develops his own unique characteristics, so, too, does each classroom. Indeed, it would not be going too far to say that each classroom develops its own "personality," which, for better or for worse, is the collective blend of the individual personalities within it. One classroom, for example, is somewhat quiet and withdrawn, while a second is outgoing and assertive; a third classroom is cold and detached, while a fourth is warm and receptive. The kind of personality a class group develops is not a chance happening. It is, rather, the outgrowth of student-student and teacher-student interactions that, together, give a classroom's evolving personality both form and substance.

Perhaps the most useful insight we can begin with is that all members of a classroom—no matter what age—are at the same time different and similar. That is to say, all persons, whether students or teachers, have certain interpersonal needs that must be satisfied in order for healthy growth to occur. Each individual needs to feel included, influential, respected, and cared about. Each person wants, in a word, to *matter* and to be *significant*.

Handling a class of twenty or more students is no easy matter. It takes skill, patience, tact, a genuine concern for individuals within the group, and a conceptual framework for understanding group processes. The basic purpose of this chapter, then, is to examine the related roles of both students and teachers as they interact in a group setting to create a classroom's unique social-emotional climate.

INFLUENCE OF A CLASSROOM'S SOCIAL-EMOTIONAL CLIMATE ON INDIVIDUAL AND GROUP BEHAVIOR

One of the two most important and influential environments for a student—whether in kindergarten or twelfth grade—is the classroom in

A positive social-emotional "atmosphere" usually results in a productive and highly interactive classroom. (Allyn and Bacon)

which he lives for five days a week. A student can have an enormous number of interpersonal transactions in a single day. For example, an intensive study of a single boy's day from the time he got up in the morning to the time he went to bed in the evening showed that about one-fourth of the 712 episodes in his day occurred in the classroom. Of the 166 schoolroom episodes, 70 percent involved an interaction of some kind or other with one or more persons.[1] This may not seem like such a large number of schoolroom interactions until you have some idea of their cumulative total over time, which at an average of, say, 120 per day, would be in the neighborhood of 600 interactions in a week, about 2400 interactions in a month, and over 21,000 interactions in a nine-month school year. Although a single classroom day in a student's life will probably not make much difference in his total development as a social intellectual person, the cumulative effect of many days undoubtedly will.

A Classroom's Social-Emotional Climate Can Influence Learning

As you can imagine, the social-emotional climate of a classroom can make a big difference in how a student performs academically and adjusts socially within a school environment. Research strongly indicates that classroom climate influences not only how much is learned, but also how long the learning lasts and future learning.[2-4] Hostile, sullen, or passive, emotional climates usually dampen enthusiasm for current learning and decrease ambition for future learning. On the other hand, warm, stimulating, interpersonal classroom relations not only facilitate current learning, but they also foster positive attitudes toward future learning.

A Teacher's Personal Style Makes a Big Difference

However, a classroom is composed or whatever climate it possesses, it is still an involuntary enterprise. That is, the students have to come, they have to accept the teacher, and they have to be together some of the time. When you think about it, student and teacher have quite a lot to make the best of! Some students and teachers do make the best of it, while others have a hard time developing even a neutral social climate, not to mention one that is a happy blend of excitement, warmth, and facilitation. How a class functions and the kind of "personality" it reflects depends not only on the students and how well their particular mix of backgrounds and experiences blend together, but it also depends very much on the teacher and the kind of personal style he projects in his everyday behavior.

Whatever way we look at it, the teacher occupies a central position as the leader of the class. How a class behaves as a group or feels about itself depends on how the teacher handles his role. For example, in a very detailed series of classroom observations, Anderson and his co-workers[5,6] found that emotional chain reactions can be set in motion by certain teacher behaviors. Where a teacher relied largely on dominating techniques, there were more signs of interpersonal conflict. On the other hand, where more cooperation evoking methods were used, spontaneity and social contributions were more frequent. Moreover, the longer a class was with a teacher, the greater was the effect. In addition, it was found that when a class changed teachers, the conditions disappeared, only to be replaced by those found in classes where the new teacher had been before.

Outcomes of Authoritarian, Democratic, and Laissez-faire Classrooms

Since the classic White and Lippitt[7,8] study was discussed in some detail in Chapter 7, when we examined the behavior and psychology of effective teachers, we need highlight only the major conclusions of that investigation here. The major purpose of this study was to investigate the effects of three different social climates (authoritarian, democratic, and laissez faire) on individual and group of four clubs of eleven-year-old boys. A major finding of this study was that different social-emotional climates do, indeed, produce different group and individual behavior. In the authoritarian climate, the boys were frustrated and reacted with greater hostility, aggression, and a nearly unanimous disliking of their autocratic leader. A good many scapegoats emerged in authoritarian groups and aggression increased when the leader left the room. In the more democratic climate, in contrast, the boys were responsive, spontaneous, and a great deal friendlier to each other. In addition, they continued working when the leader left the room, showed higher levels of frustration tolerance, and were less aggressive and hostile toward each other and the leader. Quite simply, they had less to be mad about. The laissez-faire group floundered a good deal, engaged in desultory activity, and appeared to be frustrated, discontented, and demoralized.

Authoritarian Classrooms May Produce More, But . . .

Although the fact is often overlooked in discussions of this experiment, it should be pointed out that the boys who experienced the authoritarian climate produced the greatest number of masks, which was one of each club's major activities. This fact is sometimes cited by those who favor a more authoritarian approach to teaching. "See, the way to get results is to be tough" is the way one teacher I know expressed it. What this teacher overlooked was another significant finding; namely, even though the boys from the authoritarian climate produced more, they still had negative attitudes about the total experience. Students in authoritarian classrooms may produce more, but they don't necessarily like it more, an important consideration for any teacher to consider when deciding what kind of social climate to foster. We might also mention that although the boys in the democratic climate were "out-produced," they were judged by the experimenters to have shown a much greater degree of creativity in their finished products. A tough, autocratic climate may encourage (demand even) greater productivity in terms of the number of completed tasks, but apparently a more democratic "we"-spirited climate is the most conducive for encouraging one to feel safe and accepted enough to take the personal risks necessary to do things that are creative and different.

An important implication of this study is that the teacher or leader is a very important variable in determining the social-emotional climate of the group or classroom. We should not, however, overgeneralize the results of this study.

For example, not all authoritarian classroom climates are destructive and harmful. It is possible to lean toward a more authoritarian teaching style in terms of firmness strict discipline, and careful structure, without necessarily being an angry despot for power and alienated from students. I have seen some fine teachers who were authoritarian in their methods, but warm and interpersonally responsive in their styles. The authoritarian classroom climate that is vindictive, rejecting, and punitive and that reflects the exercise of power for its own sake the one that is frequently destructive to its members. A successful class, in terms of attitudes and accomplishments, can exist within an authoritarian framework, but only if the emotional tone of the class includes such qualities as acceptance, caring, and mutual respect between teacher and student.

A Share in Decision-making Processes Is Important

Students are most receptive to, and productive in, classroom climates in which they feel they can influence decision-making and operating policies. Research has shown that the satisfaction of group members in other organizations, such as industry, business, and voluntary enterprises, is also related to the degree to which they can influence decision making.[9] Teachers, too, are found to report their greatest satisfaction with their principal and the school district when they perceived that they and their principal were mutually influential.[10]

A major finding that grows from these studies is that a positive classroom climate is one in which the leadership functions are well distributed and where there are opportunities for all participants to feel some sense of power and self-worth in accomplishing tasks and working together.

> ### To Think About
>
> Do you see yourself as the kind of person who is able to allow others to share in decisions that have to be made? Or are you accustomed to making decisions pretty much on your own without much consultation? Can you picture yourself talking comfortably and easily with your students about, say, disciplinary policies and allowing them to have a voice in the making of those policies? Or do you see yourself sitting quietly in the background with students making all of the decisions? In what ways is your picture of yourself consistent with how you know yourself at this point in time? What do you feel would be desirable to change in your own behavior that could make you a better teacher when it comes to decision making?

Ways to Create a Positive Classroom Climate

A positive climate is one that involves many opportunities for participation and involvement of students. Schmuck,[11] for example, studied twenty-seven different classrooms and found that the teachers with the most positive social climates tended to mention cooperative classroom work more and grading less than other teachers. Indeed, teachers who created the more positive classroom climates were more inclined than those with less positive classroom climates to view sound teaching practices as including both academic learning and personality growth and development. Consistent with this attitude, teachers with more positive classroom climates mentioned almost twice as many health conditions important to their teaching as the other teachers. They also showed more sensitivity to the conditions they felt were necessary for positive classroom functioning.

Teachers with less positive climates tended to emphasize the physical conditions of a classroom much more than other teachers. One such teacher listed as necessary conditions for good mental health such items as "bright colors in the room," "good lighting," "fresh air," and "cleanliness of the room." Teachers with more positive climates, on the other hand,

"YOU KNOW, WE'RE IN A SPOT. HOW CAN WE BREAK THE RULES IF WE'VE MADE THE RULES ?"

Students usually think twice about misbehaving if they've had a voice in shaping the ground rules for acceptable class behavior.

more frequently mentioned the quality of interpersonal relations that existed in their classrooms. For example, one teacher with a high positive group climate mentioned such things as "mutual respect for ideas of others," "relaxed relations," "kindly attitudes towards each other," and "ability to plan and work in groups and not always with the same people" as being most conducive to a positive and constructive teaching-learning setting. Still another teacher with a positive social climate said that "tolerance for individual differences is perhaps the most important condition for positive mental health in the classroom."

It is also worth noting that teachers with more positive climates attended to and talked with a larger number of students compared with the other teachers. Many of the teachers with less positive climates tended to call on fewer students for classroom participation and, in addition, paid

643

little attention to the slower, less involved students. Moreover, the teachers with positive classroom climates frequently rewarded individual students with such statements as, "Dan, you've done a very nice job." They also tended to control class disruptions by making general statements aimed at the total group such as, "Class, it's really very difficult for us to concentrate on what we have to do when there is all this noise." Teachers with less positive social climates, on the other hand, tended not only to reward less, but they were inclined to pubicly punish individual students for deviant behavior. This particular strategy may accomplish some peace and quiet, but the cost is usually high in student hostility and alienation toward the teacher. All in all, teachers with more positive classroom climates enumerated a higher number of relationships between mental health and academic learning than other teachers.

The social climate of a classroom is affected by at least three variables, which include interpersonal attraction dynamics, the development of group norms, and the cohesiveness of a group. We'll look at these one at a time to better understand how each influences a group's functioning.

INTERPERSONAL ATTRACTIONS AND GROUP PROCESSES

No matter what kind of group we talk about there is ample evidence to suggest that how the group members feel about each other influences their performance on tasks. Baseball players perform more poorly in games when interpersonal relations are upsupportive; industrial workers produce more when their co-workers relate positively to each other; and a popular person's contributions in a problem-solving or brainstorming group are accepted more readily than those of a less popular person. And so it goes. The dynamics of classroom groups are basically the same as any other group in terms of there being fluid undercurrent of attraction and/or hostility among peers that influences group behavior.

The friendship patterns of a classroom are an important part of the social and psychological realities of the classroom. Teaching and learning involve interpersonal processes, sometimes of a very intense sort, and when these processes occur they are affected by the relationships among students, and between students and teachers. How students and teachers feel about each other, how students handle their own peer relations, and who is attracted to whom are all cogs in the machinery of a dynamic teaching-learning environment. Let's look at this more closely.

Factors Influencing Classroom Liking Patterns

Friendship patterns in classrooms develop in systematic ways and are influenced by at least five specific factors, which include: (1) intelligence,

(2) physical characteristics, (3) mental health characteristics, (4) social behavior, and (5) teacher behavior.   Let's see how each of these work.

Intelligence: being perceived as either too stupid or too smart is risky. Research shows that one's intelligence, or lack of it, makes a difference as far as acceptance or rejection by peers is concerned.   This is particularly true at the extreme ends of the intelligence range.   Mentally retarded students, if they are in a normal classroom, are usually the ones most severely rejected by the peer group.[12]   At the other end of the continuum, Torrance[13] has shown that highly intelligent conforming students rank high among those who are socially accepted.   This was not, however, as likely to be true for intelligent students who were creative but not conforming. What this seems to suggest is that there is a heavy social risk involved in being perceived as either too stupid and different or too smart and different.   Nonconformity, especially when it is unexplained and not well understood, is usually an uncomfortable and threatening experience to others. It is worth noting that teachers, too, were among those who ranked intelligent, creative students low on the social acceptance scale.

> **TO DO**
>
>   You may find it particularly meaningful to do some "in head" research.   Make it a point to carefully observe peers who you consider to be unusually bright and then do several things: (1) note whether they are generally "conformers" or "nonconformers"; (2) note how people in each of these categories are accepted by others; (3) what are your *own* feelings toward persons in the "bright conforming" and bright nonconforming" categories?   What implications can you see here for you as a teacher?

There is little relationship between intelligence and peer acceptance in the early primary grades.   This does, however, begin to change by about the fifth grade when the more intelligent students are found to experience greater social acceptance than less intelligent students.[14]   This relationship continues to grow even stronger as a student moves into his high school years.   Children in their early elementary years are not particularly sensitive to intellectual differences.   At that age, a child is more concerned about whether his friends are good playmates with whom he can have fun. He could care less about their intellectual skills and problem-solving capacities.

Research also shows that, among students who are rejected, there is likely to be a significant discrepancy between intelligence and performance.[15,16]   What this means is that average or above-average students who are, for one reason or other, socially rejected, tend to do less well academically than students of comparable intelligence who are socially accepted. Rejection lowers self-esteem, which in turn lowers one's confidence, and this, in turn, can leave a student with a feeling of inadequacy and worthlessness that may generalize to his school work. Actually, it is difficult to know which comes first, the low performance or low social acceptance. The best we can say is that there is an interaction effect that results in lowered self-esteem and increased feelings of alienation toward school.

Intelligence, then, is one factor that influences group processes and interpersonal attractiveness in the classroom. Physical appearance is another.

Physical characteristics: caution — what is beautiful may not be good.

Most of us don't have to go any further than our own personal experiences to know that different body types and physical characteristics elicit different feelings, attitudes, and stereotypes in us. Although physical appearance is often considered to be a superficial variable, it is an initial factor in making friends, choosing dating partners, and in selecting marital partners. For example, Brodsky[17] found that different body builds elicit different social reactions from people. Endomorphic body types (heavy, obese) were judged by others to be least aggressive, least preferred as a personal friend, least skilled athletically, and least likely to be a good leader. Ectomorphic body types (thin, tall) were generally viewed as likely to have emotional-social problems, to be least self-sufficient, to have the fewest friends, and, like the endomorph, to make a poor leader. Perceptions of the mesomorphic body type (athletic, muscular) were in vivid contrast to the first two. They were judged to be the best leaders, the most coordinated, the most self-sufficient, and the most preferred as a friend.

Although Brodsky's research was done with college age males, there is evidence to suggest that body build stereotypes are apparent even in young children. A case in point is research by Staffieri,[18] who found that boys as young as six or ten years of age are already in close agreement when it comes to assigning certain personality characteristics to particular body types. For instance, there was a remarkably similar tendency for endomorphic types to be described as socially offensive and delinquent; the mesomorphic types as aggressive, outgoing, active, and having leadership skills; and the ectomorphic types as retiring, nervous, shy, and introverted. It was also found that ectomorphs and mesomorphs were chosen as the most popular by their peers and endomorphs as the least popular.

Startling as it may seem, there is also research to suggest that even nursery school age children are responsive to the physical attractiveness of their peers.[19] The clearest results emerging from this research is that physically attractive boys are liked better than physically unattractive boys. Moreover, unattractive boys were judged to be more aggressive (not getting much in the way of peer acceptance, they were more aggressive in seeking after it?) than their more attractive counterparts. In addition, when the children were asked to name classmates who "scared them," they tended to nominate the unattractive children.

Physical attractiveness, or lack of it, can also influence an adult's judgment about the seriousness a particular child's misbehavior. In an interesting study by Dion,[20] a group of over 200 women were asked to examine reports of rather severe classroom disturbances written by teachers. Attached to each report was a photo of the child who was said to have initiated the disturbance. In some instances, the picture was that of an unattractive boy or girl, while in others it was that of an attractive boy or girl. What happened was that attractive children were evaluated less harshly than the unattractive children. For example, when children were pictured as physically attractive, adults tended to downplay or make excuses for their behavior. As one woman put it, " . . . she plays well with everyone but, like anyone else, a bad day can occur. Her cruelty need not be taken too seriously." However, when a physically unattractive girl was portrayed as the culprit in exactly the same situation described in exactly the same way, a typical response was: "I think the child would be bratty and would probably be a problem to teachers. She would probably try to pick a fight with other children her own age . . . all in all she would be a real problem."

It would come as no surprise to you to learn that what is true for younger age children and youths is also true for adults. Research shows, for example, that we are more affected by physically attractive people than by physically unattractive people, and unless we are specifically abused by them, we tend to like them better.[21,22] In addition, research shows that, as a general rule, attractive people tend to receive more favorable treatment than less attractive people. This is an interpersonal process that begins at a very young age. The disquieting aspect of this evidence is that there is a strong possibility that such preferential treatment is the beginning of a cycle of a self-fulfilling prophecy. That is if people are treated poorly (or well, as the case may be), it affects how they perceive themselves and how they feel about their personal qualities. Thus, unattractive children may come to think of themselves as unloveable or at least as undesirable, if they are continually treated in negative, rejecting ways. Ultimately, they may begin to behave in a style that is consistent with this self-concept, a way that is consistent with how they were treated in the first place.

As teachers, we need to keep an eye on our own student preferences so that we aren't caught in the trap of believing, either consciously or unconsciously, that only that which is beautiful is good.

There is still another factor that influences classroom liking patterns, and this one goes beyond the "skin deepness" of physical attraction.

Mental health characteristics: psychological health related to social acceptance. Another important variable that influences peer-group acceptance is the psychological adjustment of the individual student. This is an area that has been pretty thoroughly researched, and the results point to rather significant relationships between being rejected by peers on the one hand and poor interpersonal adjustment on the other. For example, anxious, tense students are more likely to be socially rejected.[23-25] In addition, it has also been noted that rejected students tend to use more primitive defense mechanisms, such as denial and regression.[26] Along similar lines, it has also been demonstrated that rejected youths tend to exhibit more of the behavior symptoms typically associated with poor mental health. For example, they are more likely to be overly aggressive and withdrawn or listless and in poor physical health, or emotionally unstable, or some combination of these characteristics.[27-29]

All in all, it appears that the relationship between liking in the peer group and mental health is monotonic; that is, the greater the degree of psychological imbalance, the more likely that such a student will be rejected. Teachers can help reduce the intensity of the rejection process, if not reverse it altogether, by giving public emotional support to those students who need it most. One way of doing this is to make an extra effort to praise the uncertain and emotionally wavering student when he does something of note in class, even though that student says no more than three words in a group discussion. Another way is to appoint that student to certain groups or committees and see to it that he has specific responsibilities or tasks to carry out. An objective here would be to make it very apparent that the student is *valued*, so that not only he knows it, but others in the class could see it too. Students tend to value and appreciate those persons and activities that they perceive the teacher as valuing and appreciating.

Mental health characteristics are closely related to one's social behavior, another interpersonal attribute that is related to classroom liking patterns.

Social behavior: friendliness is accepted everywhere. When we talk about social behavior, we're referring specifically to acts carried out in relation to other people. As it turns out, a student's social behavior is indeed related to the extent to which he is either accepted or rejected by his peers.

Lippitt and Gold[30] have done extensive research on the social behavior of liked and disliked students, and a major finding that emerges from their efforts is that students who are most liked by their peers are seen as enhancing, supportive, and helpful to others, rather than threatening or hostile. I suppose another way of saying it is that best-liked students are not only nice to their male and female peers, but genuine about it. Least-liked students, on the other hand, expressed more negative feelings toward others and were generally more hostile in both aggressive and passive ways.

The Lippitt and Gold research also pointed to some interesting sex differences in regard to social behavior and liking. For instance, boys who were disliked by their peers were more apt to be aggressive, physically abusive, openly defiant. On the other hand, girls who were disliked were passively dependent and less socially mature. I suppose you could say that they were likely to be girls who didn't come right out and directly ask for help or attention but, rather, did something more along the lines of whining for it. Both acted out aggression on the part of boys and passive dependency on the part of girls tend to make others in the class feel uncomfortable.

There are, however, interesting social-class differences that need to be taken into account. Aggression, physical fighting, and high amounts of dependency run counter to middle-class values and expectations. This is not so likely to be true in lower-class settings. Pope,[31,32] for example, found that, in predominately low-socioeconomic settings, the students who were esteemed most highly by their peers were the ones who were belligerent and nonconforming. Although these students were not always liked, they were respected. It was an attitude that said, "I may not like who you are but I value what you are able to do." At the same time, low-socioeconomic students who minded their manners and behaved themselves were more likely to be rejected by their peers.

Social-class structure influences social behavior. The prevailing social-class structure of a school makes a big difference in the kinds of social behavior that is acceptable or unacceptable to students. The lower socioeconomic boys in Pope's study valued strength, loyalty, physical prowess, and friendliness. Whereas the middle-class boys in the Lippitt and Gold study valued coordinated skills, activity, and competition. Actually, boys in both class settings valued friendliness (a rather universally accepted quality of positive worth, it seems), but its expression was more physical among lower-class youths than middle-class youths. Interestingly enough, no such striking differences between the social classes were apparent for girls. Among both middle- and lower-class girls, social skills (talking, making friends, being friendly, etc.) and cooperation were equally valued. Middle-class girls did, however, place a greater value on buoyancy of activity. The greater similarity between lower- and middle-class girls is due to the greater similarity of the two social classes when it comes to socializing girls.

Where it happens that about equal numbers of lower- and middle-class students are mixed in the same school system, the norms of the middle class typically prevail. The social behaviors of middle-class students are usually more appropriate for the demands of the school and consistent with the expectations of teachers and, as a consequence, middle–class oriented students experience more success more easily than do lower-class students. The power of middle-class values was reflected in a study by Cook,[33] which indicated that middle-class students, in a school with both a middle- and lower-class population, received more nominations from their peers on such considerations as best dressed, best liked, most fun to be with, and leadership potential. Even after an intense effort to change students' attitudes by increasing the possibility for social interaction among students, it was found that a social-class stratification of friendships still prevailed. That is, higher social-class students were still being chosen more frequently for a variety of attractive attributes than were lower social-class students.

We should keep in mind that middle-class criteria for what is considered "attractive" or appropriate social behavior are evident only in schools where middle-class students are in a clear majority, or when middle- and lower-class students are about equal in number. In schools, for example, which contain mostly lower-class students, research shows that middle-class students in those schools will tend toward lower-class values and standards for what is and what is not appropriate social behavior.[34]

TO DO

Make a deliberate effort to visit a school that is as much the opposite from what you came from as possible. With your own school experience as your reference base, try to answer the following questions: (1) What differences (if any) do you see in interpersonal behavior in class, in the hallways, during recess, after school? (2) How do the values and attitudes of those students differ from your own? (3) How would you feel teaching those students? (4) What would be hardest for you?

Social-class differences increase in importance as the child grows older. By the time a student reaches high school he's generally well aware of these differences, and his preference for relating to others is influenced heavily by those perceived differences. It is important for a teacher to know both himself and the psychology of social-class differences well enough to be better able to accept those students who are different from his own background and experiences.

There is at least one other factor that influences friendship patterns in the classroom and it more directly involves the teacher. Let's see how this works.

Teacher behavior: who a teacher likes influences who others like. A few pages back it suggested that teachers can help reduce the intensity of peer rejections, if not reverse it altogether, by giving public emotional support to those students who need it most. The possibility of this happening has been demonstrated experimentally. Flanders and Havumaki[35] showed how this works by having teachers respond positively and consistently to selected students and not to others. The way this was done was to have teachers interact with and praise only those students in odd-numbered seats, while in comparison groups all students were encouraged to speak and the teachers' praise was directed to the whole class. In the first situation, students in the odd-numbered seats, who received most teacher recognition, later received more "liking" votes from their peers than did students in even-numbered seats. This was not true in the comparison groups, where the teachers made an effort to encourage and praise all students. In these groups, positive peer choices were spread around more evenly, indicating greater general acceptance no matter where one sat.

Other research indicates that teachers of more diffusely structured classrooms (less centralized) attended to and talked with a greater number of students per hour. On the other hand, teachers with centrally structured peer groups were inclined to neglect the slower, less involved students. In addition, they called on fewer students for class participation, which is, in fact, why their classes were more centralized in terms of the number of people involved. A clear implication from research is that the more specifically a classroom group, with the teacher's help, identifies and designates its popular and unpopular members, the less likely the group will be to function as a unit, work cooperatively under stress (as in preparation for an exam), and be friendly to one another.[36,37]

How a teacher treats students in his class, then, is an important factor influencing classroom liking patterns. A teacher is a model, and, as such, students will identify not only with his general problem-solving approach to course material, but with his general attitudes toward, and specific treatment of, students in class. One of the best ways to help an unpopular student to be treated more positively by his peers is to treat him in more friendly ways yourself. Students who experience continual rejections (for what ever reasons) by classroom peers and/or teachers were dandy candidates for the self-defeating cycle or low self-esteem, unfriendly overtures to others, and poor performance in academic work. Teachers can be helpful in seeing to it that this doesn't happen.

Thus, how students perform and behave is influenced strongly by the sort of "group life" that exists in the classroom. In order for a group—classroom or other—to function it first of all needs some guidelines or norms for helping it to do so, a topic to which we now turn.

DEVELOPMENT AND EXPRESSION OF GROUP NORMS

By definition, group norms are principles of right or appropriate behavior that members of a group agree to use as guides to control or regulate proper and acceptable behavior. Or, to be more succinct, norms help group members know what is right and wrong. Without such guideposts, group processes can be both confusing and chaotic. When classroom groups behave predictably it is largely because of their adherence to group norms. The existence of norms is also important because once the students know what the rules are, so to speak, they can help monitor one another's behaviors and in this way the whole group contributes to the class's stability.

When talking about a definition of norms, we must also emphasize the idea of sharing. The psychological counterpart of a norm is an attitude, which is a predisposition to think, feel, and act in specific ways in particular circumstances. Thus, norms are individuals' attitudes that are shared in a group.

Varieties of Norm Structures

Norms can be labeled as either *static* or *dynamic,* depending on the degree of active interpersonal exchanges, and as either *formal* or *informal,* depending on how codified or traditional they were.

Static norms are made up of the basic, unconscious culture of groups. These are the norms that people respond to as a matter of course and take more or less for granted. For example, the shared expectations that every student shall have his own tennis shoes for physical education or his own textbook for class are formal, static norms in most schools. These are not questioned by students or anyone else and they remain unchanged over time.

Norms of greater interest to the teacher are the dynamic and informal ones. These are norms that can, indeed, do, change; they usually depend less on tradition for their existence and more on the personal style of the teacher and the particular class he instructs. In most classrooms, for instance, the existing norm for test-taking is each man for himself. Looking on another's paper or talking are definite no-no's. If a student tells the teacher someone is cheating or if the teacher intercepts a note passed from one student to the next, they are actively supporting the maintenance of a shared norm through their interpersonal influence. In other classrooms, however, talking is not discouraged during examination periods but encouraged as a valuable learning activity. For instance, during the exam periods of a ninth-grade English teacher I know, students and teacher have agreed that not only is talking all right, but so, too is looking at notes and books. It has all the elements of a take-home exam except that the exams are written in class. This procedure would obviously not work if either the teacher or the majority of students were opposed to it.

Generally speaking, norms develop first as dynamic and informal, and become either static, informal, or dynamic and formal. If the teacher described above gave open-book, talk-as-much-as-you-want exams all the time with no change in format or procedure, what started out as dynamic and informal norms for exam-taking, could soon become static and formal.

Necessary Building Blocks for the Development of Classroom Norms

Norms are group agreements that help direct the course of group processes. They influence how people view things—their *perceptions;* how they think about things—their *cognitions;* how they feel about things—their *evaluations;* and how they act—their *behavior.* Each of these factors plays a part in building the overall norm structure of a classroom. Let's briefly examine how each functions.

Perceptual norms: how students see things. Through our perceptual processes we derive meaning from our sensory experiences. Perception research tells us pretty convincingly that people tend to behave in a manner consistent with what they believe to be true, irrespective of what the facts may be.[38] Now it sometimes happens in a group that perception is a straightforward process where most persons agree with what they see. Many times, however, individual group members differ widely on the meaning they attach to a particular experience. Furthermore, groups, classroom groups in our case, can have a decided effect on the way in which individual student members interpret their perceptions.

For instance, if a tenth-grade student who has positive views about a particular teacher hears large numbers of other students describe that teacher negatively, he may begin to question his initial perceptions. Evidence from group dynamics research indicates that when an individual's personal perceptions deviate from those held by the group as a whole, he will tend to change his perceptions in the direction of the existing group norms.[39, 40] Thus, through a process of interpersonal influence, perceptual norms are established and students are affected psychologically. Indeed, research also shows that the more stable and cohesive a group is, and the more attached the members are to it, the more influential it will be in forming the perceptual standards for how events or people will be perceived.[41]

Group discussion can influence perceptual norms. Sherif[42] carried out an interesting experiment to describe the processes and dynamics of perceptual norms in which he used the "autokinetic phenomenon"—a stationary pinpoint of light that, in a totally darkened room, looks as if it is moving about. What he did was to have a group of subjects estimate the light's movement for 100 separate trials at two-second exposures. Initially one-half of the subjects worked alone and established personal, but private, standards of perceptual judgment.   The range of movement settled on was usually between two and ten inches.   Then, the participants worked in small groups in which one-half of the group members had established a perceptual standard and one-half had had no experience whatsoever with the autokinetic phenomenon.   After discussion in their groups, each participant was asked to publicly state his estimate of movement.   As it happened, all subjects developed group agreements, even though agreement was not stressed by the experimenter.   Interestingly, if the group norm ranged from eight to ten inches of movement, those who previously saw the light moving two or three inches changed in the direction of the group, and vice versa.

As a second part of the experiment, Sherif again asked the participants to judge the light's movement this time working alone.   Significantly, most of them persisted to conform (with no pressure to do so) to the estimates established in their small groups.   Sherif's findings are consistent with other research,[43] which suggests that the ambiguity of sensory data, along with small-group discussion, encourages the formation of shared group perceptual norms.   When a perceptual norm is developed within a group context it usually has a greater potential for becoming an internalized attitude, which is why, even when alone, participants continued to refer to it.

Trust can be a perceptual norm — it's up to the teacher.   The typical classroom, with its vast array of sensory experiences, has many ambiguous and unclear events.   At the beginning of a school year particularly, the teacher figures prominently among the many unknowns of the classroom. It is precisely because a teacher has so much power — at least from students' point of view — that he is an especially important figure in the development of perceptual norms.   What is the teacher like?   Will he be tough?   Can she be trusted?   Will he be consistent?   Will she be fair?   Beginning with the first day of class, students consciously and unconsciously attach meanings to their perceptions of a teacher's behavior.   Not infrequently, students bring from previous experiences negative attitudes toward active participation in class.   If a teacher says that he really values participation and hopes that everyone will feel free to speak openly, this is likely to be met with a great deal of initial suspicion.   Is he for real?   Can I *really* speak my mind? If the teacher, in fact, does allow different and even hostile points of view to be expressed and behaves in a nondefensive manner toward offerings clearly different from his own leanings, he will go a long ways toward encouraging a perceptual norm that says, "He can be trusted; he does mean what he says."

Cognitive norms: how students think about things.   The overall academic and intellectual tone of a classroom is determined to a large extent by the sort of cognitive norms a group abides by.   It is no coincidence that intellectual and social development of students occurs more effectively when the expressed educational goals of the school and the basic cognitive norms of the peer group are reasonably consistent. One situation that has always created conflict is where a school places such a strong emphasis on academic achievement and preparing students for the future that it forgets that students need immediate relevance and satisfaction. During a group discussion related to the "goals of education," a high school student expressed one of the existing conflicts in cognitive norms in the following way:

> Look, I think a basic disagreement my friends and I have with the educational system (specifically he was referring to his high school) is that it talks about where we're supposed to be before we're even done with understanding what where we are now all means. I mean we keep talking about all the things we have to know to get along in tomorrow's world. How about today's world? There are a lot of things we don't understand completely about that, you know. Our social studies teacher is a good example. He keeps talking about how important it is to know about our social system so we can survive in it and make a good living. Heck, I'd like to know a little more about the social system of our own city so I can find a job this summer.

This student was saying what many students say: "Recognize my needs for what they are and acknowledge their existence. Point me toward the future and encourage my awareness of it, but don't push me out of the relevancy of my own time and needs."

Of course, the conflict in cognitive norms can occur in the other direction, too. For example, a recent article in a major metropolitan newspaper[44] revealed that the principal of a large school system was about to be ousted from his job because he was "too lax in stressing academic goals" as important educational objectives. Even the president of the senior class, acting as a spokesman for his peers, suggested that the principal was "too permissive in his academic philosophy." As with most other extreme positions in life, radical stances regarding the importance of this or that educational philosophy run the heavy risk of conflicting with either more moderate or extreme positions.

Cognitive norms are best developed by teachers and students working together. One of the most serious contemporary conflicts between peer norms and school goals is that which relates to the students' role in decision making. More and more, educational technology allows for individualization of instruction. With the assistance of the computer, class schedules can be aligned to individual interests, and curriculum materials can be made more diversified and individualized than ever. Indeed, schools from the elementary level through high school are finding that students themselves can be used to tutor and to learn from each other.

However, it is often the case that cognitive norms in the peer group to support this kind of instructional design are not present. All sorts of questions arise: Should students work separately or with adults? To what extent should students and teachers work together in establishing new instructional procedures and curriculum innovations? When new ways evolve, old expectations and rules do not work. Only through ongoing, open discussions and arriving at public, group agreements can such cognitive norms be established.

Evaluative norms: how students feel about things. Evaluative norms ordinarily involve high levels of positive or negative feelings. Whereas cognitive norms grow primarily from intellectual expressions, evaluative norms develop essentially from emotional expressions. For example, the fact that students jostle through the hallways faster than they should or rush pell-mell out of the classroom at the final bell may not be liked by the teacher, but after a time it comes to be expected and is taken more or less for granted. These are cognitive norms. That is, there are no active attempts to embarrass those who rush out or who jostle too vigorously in the halls. Evaluative norms, however, are those you see when a student sasses the teacher or refuses to pay attention, and then he is criticized by the teacher or is given looks of disgust and rejection (or looks or praise and support, as the case may be) by his peers.

Flexible evaluative norms work best. Especially with evaluative norms, teachers should make an effort to develop those that encourage individual diversity and uniqueness. This is important not only because it's valuable in itself, but also because it is healthier for individual group members when they know they are supported by the group. Group dynamics research shows rather clearly that the closer an individual conforms to the accepted norms of the group, the better liked he will be; the better liked he is, the closer he conforms; the less he conforms, the more disliked he will be.[45-47] We should also note that evaluative norms are not entirely rigid when it comes to conformity. Although it is true that a certain amount of group conformity reduces negative evaluations, it has also been found that:

> Very high ranking members . . . who have a secure social position, do not conform as strictly to some group norms as do individuals of middle rank [and are not] subjected to serious pressure to conform. Rather, a certain tolerance of "eccentricity" among high-ranking members is the rule in many groups.[48]

All in all, overly rigid evaluations about dress, hair length, appearance, and behavior by the teacher or peer group can cause certain students to have a great deal of alienation and feelings of low self-worth. As with cognitive norms, it is important—even more so perhaps—that evaluative norms be shared and discussed throughout the school year so that both teachers and students are clear about what constitutes the basic framework for positive self-other feelings and healthy interpersonal relationships. There is little that cannot be discussed by the group as far as its evaluations of behavior are concerned. These can range all the way from gum chewing, to decisions about whether talking during study period is allowed, to whether or not it's okay to interrupt when the teacher is talking. Once students know what the evaluation norms are, then they themselves can be responsible for consequences of their behavior.

Behavioral norms: how students act. Behavioral norms serve two functions: (1) they serve as a guide for a person's actions through a complex psychological network that simultaneously involves perceptual, cognitive, and evaluative norms, and (2) they serve as a barometer indicating the degree of conformity demanded by those in one's immediate social environment.

Interesting work has been done to show how group pressure operates to influence an individual's behavior by making him aware of the group's norms for appropriate or inappropriate behavior. In one famous experiment, Asch[49] assembled fifty groups, each consisting of eight male college students, and asked them to match the length of a line presented on the board, with one of three other lines of varying lengths, and to declare their judgments on twelve different trials. The experimental catch was that all members of each group, except one participant, were instructed to give the wrong answer. Thus, one person in each group was confronted by a situation in which his eyes told him one thing while other group members were telling him another. As it turned out, one-third of the subjects, called, in this instance, *yielders,* conformed to the groups' wrong answers about one-half of the time. Information from post-experiment interviews suggested that very few of the yielders distorted their perceptions; almost all gave in to avoid standing out and being different. As one yielder expressed it, "I knew I was probably right and the others wrong, but I just didn't want to run the risk of being wrong myself."

TO DO

You could easily replicate the Asch experiment by doing a small-scale experiment of your own along the same lines. If you could arrange it, an interesting variation of this experiment would be to do it with a group of elementary age youngsters and a group of high school youths. Do you suppose there would be any differences in the results? What are your hunches? This may be an interesting project to work on with one or two others.

This experiment helps us understand some of the dynamics of behavioral conformity in schools. As it sometimes happens, students do not completely internalize peer-group norms to the extent that perceptions, cognitions, or feelings get modified. The consequence of this is that they may conform to group standards in order not to appear different and risk being rejected. Even defiant students can conform in ways that do not involve a deep personal commitment. As a ninth-grade boy with something less than a positive attitude toward school expressed it: "The teacher wants me to get my homework in—I'll get it in. She wants me to do a paper by Friday—I'll do it. But that doesn't mean I'm going to learn anything."

Behavioral norms best arrived at through open discussion. As with other dimensions of the norm structure of a classroom, about the only viable way to arrive at behavioral norms which includes the best thinking of both students and teacher is through open, public communication involving the entire class. Under conditions like this, the teacher can encourage students to discuss circumstances in which superficial allegiance to behavioral pressures keeps them from being effective. As an example of how this works, consider the following excerpt taken from a paper written for a graduate class by a tenth-grade English teacher:

> I had developed the idea that at least one book report per week would be a good idea to help my students develop their writing skills. They all did it, although some grumbled a lot. As you might suspect, some reports were better or worse than others, but I guess I expected that. The thing that really got me was when I got wind of what five of my best students were doing. Apparently, each of them took turns being responsible for reading the short story assigned for the week and then wrote a brief outline of it which the other four used as a basis for writing their report. Well, I felt pretty angry at first, but then I got to thinking that maybe my assignment wasn't as interesting as I thought it might be to all students. So, rather than confront the five with what I knew they were doing (and also keeping in mind that there were probably others who were fudging on the assignment while leading me to believe they were digging it), I asked the whole class during one of our open discussion periods to share ideas about projects which could either supplement or replace our weekly book reports.
>
> I never got so many ideas in my life. Some students really enjoyed reading the short stories and writing reports, but others—including the five I originally heard about—had other suggestions that went all the way from writing their own short stories and having others review them, to volunteer oral reports in class (rather than written).
>
> When the discussion was over it was clear that the students would still be reading and writing, which is what I wanted them to do in the first place, but now the standards for what was acceptable were sufficiently broad and encompassing enough to include every student in class.[50]

This is a fine example of how a teacher can, through open discussion, use the natural differences that exist in students' perceptions, cognitions, and evaluations in order to arrive at behavioral norms more satisfying and more real for more students. The teacher intuitively recognized that sharedness is the essence of normativeness and rather than indignantly confronting the five fudging students, whose behavior was only superficially satisfying the goals of the assignment, he wisely utilized the best of not only his ideas, but the whole class's as well. Our teacher friend put into practice what group dynamics research has been saying for a long time; namely, when group members participate in the establishment of group norms and are helped to feel important and valued by the group, then they are willing to support both its structure and goals.[51, 52] Out of the norm structure of a classroom emerges still another dimension — cohesiveness, a topic to which we now turn.

DEVELOPMENT AND EXPRESSION OF GROUP COHESIVENESS

Our own experiences have taught us that class groups can vary enormously with respect to the unity and the amount of togetherness and friendliness exhibited by the students and teacher. Why, for example, do the members of one sixth-grade class work better together, seem happier, and show more enthusiasm for doing their school work than do the members of a sixth grade who come along the following year? What underlying dynamics are responsible for effecting enormous group spirit among hundreds of high school youths who, in spite of only casual, sometimes indifferent, and even distant relationships, are nonetheless capable of behaving as a spirited, coordinated unit at a Friday night basketball game?

What Group Cohesiveness Means

There are many group dynamics phenomena working in each of the above instances and one that makes a very large difference in whether a classroom group, or any other group for that matter, comes together, "meshes," is its cohesiveness. Specifically, cohesiveness has to do with the feelings that class members hold about the classroom group as a group. It differs from the topic of attraction because of its emphasis on each student's relationship to the group rather than on his relationships with specific members, subgroups, or the teacher. Whereas norms refer to shared attitudes about objects and behaviors important to the classroom

659

group, cohesiveness has more to do with the relations to group members.

A literal definition of *cohesiveness* is "the tendency to stick together and be in accord."[53]   A cohesive classroom group is characterized by students who are actively involved with one another, who care about one another, and who help one another. Some typical responses of students from a cohesive classroom are: "I really enjoy going to the class," "I know my contributions count when I make them," and "The kids in that class are really fun to be with." The question is: What determines the degree of cohesiveness in a classroom group? Let's turn to what research says about this.

TO DO

Before reading further, stop a moment and explore your own ideas about what makes for a cohesive, "together" group. Write down four or five factors that you think make a significant difference in a classroom's cohesiveness.

_____

_____

_____

_____

_____

Antecedents of High Group Cohesiveness

Signs of classroom cohesiveness are sometimes obvious and easy to observe, while at other times they are confusing and misleading. Some of the more obvious signs of high cohesiveness are class members hanging around together after class is over, a large proportion of students using the pronoun "we" in contrast to "I" or "me" during class discussions, and active, ongoing involvement among students during group interaction times. Of course, there may be high negative cohesiveness, too. For example, if a group of students have hostile feelings toward school, they may reflect their cohesiveness about this in high rates of tardiness, absenteeism, and even vandalism. In other words, cohesiveness is not related only to student behaviors that are positively valued by adults. Indeed, delinquent gangs and defiant classroom subgroups are evidence enough for the existence of highly cohesive groups motivated primarily by anti-school or antisocial goals.

Widely Dispersed Friendship and Power
Associated with High Cohesiveness

One of the basic antecedents to high positive classroom cohesiveness is a relatively wide dispersion of friendship relations among class members. Schmuck,[54] for example, found that classrooms with diffusely structured friendship patterns were more cohesive than classes in which friendship structures were more centralized. What this means is that the closer and more cohesive classes were those in which most students had at least one or two friends. The less cohesive classes, on the other hand, were those in which only a few students were highly liked, a few others strongly rejected, and most not chosen at all as friends by other students.

These results are consistent with Muldoon's[55] findings, which indicated that the more clearly a group recognized and designated its popular and unpopular members, the *less* the group functioned as a unit, worked cooperatively under stress (as in preparation for an exam), and behaved in friendly ways toward each other. Both Schmuck and Muldoon's research strongly suggest that when there is a wide dispersion of influence, power, and friends a classroom is likely to be more attractive to students and, as a natural outgrowth, more cohesive.

How Teachers Can Influence Classroom
Cohesiveness

You may recall from an earlier discussion in this chapter, that teachers who were most skilled in encouraging the sort of friendship dispersion that enhances group cohesiveness were those who responded to their students out of a psychological frame of reference, as opposed to a purely academic one. In other words, teachers good at building group cohesiveness were sensitive to their students' anxieties, personal perceptions, and feelings of self-worth. Students, at any level, commonly reflect the basic personality characteristics of their teachers in their own behavior, and it would not be going too far to say that if the teacher is a psychologically sensitive person to the needs and concerns of his students, then the students will be more likely to behave that way toward each other, too.

High need-for-affiliation teachers discourage cohesiveness. A teacher can influence the cohesiveness of a class in still another way. Walberg,[56] for example, found that teachers with a high need for affiliation (that is a high need to have friends, to make as many friends as possible, to be around people) tended to have classes with low internal cohesiveness among students. Why should high-need-affiliation teachers have low student cohesiveness? One possible explanation for this has to do with the amount of time a high-need-affiliation teacher spends with students. That is, this is the sort of teacher who may so monopolize the affective behavior of a class that the students spend more time relating to the teacher than to each other. If this is true, then this means that students' opportunities for interacting with each other and developing into a more cohesive "together" class are minimized.

High need-for-autonomy teachers encourage cohesiveness. The findings of the Walberg study do not stand alone. Two other investigations, for instance, have found that teachers high on the need for autonomy (that is, the need to be somewhat independent of others, to avoid situations where conformity is demanded, and to feel relatively free to be one's own person without excessive concern about what others are thinking), and lower on the need for affiliation, were more likely to have classes that reflected greater intimacy and cohesiveness among students.[57,58] What this suggests is that the more personally secure and independent teachers were able to allow, and very likely encourage, more interpersonal transactions among the students themselves, which, as we've noted, is a necessary and important condition for the development of classroom cohesiveness.

Group-centered teachers encourage cohesiveness. Classroom communication is another antecedent to high group cohesiveness. Frequent interactions among students allow for possibilities of greater cohesiveness to emerge, while minimal interaction generally succeeds in keeping students from getting too highly involved with one another. An interesting study by Bovard[59] may help us better understand how different communication patterns influence classroom cohesiveness. In one part of the study, characterized by "group-centered" discussions, students sat in a circle and the teacher participated as a member of the discussion group. In another classroom, called "leader-centered," the teacher sat in the front of the classroom as the focus for discussion, and most of the interaction consisted of the teacher talking to one student at a time. Interactions in the group-centered discussions were more open and spontaneous; the students were more involved and active, and they became more cohesive. Communication channels in the leader-centered group were primarily through the teacher. What happened was that students seldom talked to one another; they were more formal when they did talk; and they felt less free to express their ideas and feelings directly. Needless to say, there was little sense of cohesiveness among students in the leader-centered class.

Bovard's investigation gives us a nice overview of the way in which some of the antecedent conditions such as leadership dynamics, attraction variables, norm structure, and communication processes interrelate in a cohesive classroom. The informal, supportive leadership style used by the teacher in the group-centered discussion enhanced the possibilities for open communication among all members of the class. In this manner, influence is more widely dispersed, a greater number of friendships occur, supportive norms evolve, two-way communication is enhanced, and, from it all, a stronger sense of group unity and cohesiveness emerge as natural by-products of a group working together.

Varieties of Classroom Cohesiveness

Classroom groups can be described as being cohesive for different reasons. It has been observed, for example, that different groups have different "pulls" for individuals. Back's[60] research nicely illustrates this idea. Subjects participating in his study worked in pairs cooperatively on a task. The pairs were formed to be cohesive or noncohesive, and the cohesive pairs were arranged in one of three ways: (1) attraction to the group because of a liking for the other member; (2) attraction to the group because of a mutually high interest in the task; (3) attraction to the group because of its prestige for the members. A major finding was that even though the three types of cohesiveness were different, the cohesive groups were more productive and worked more effectively than the noncohesive groups.

These three different kinds of cohesiveness are also apparent in school settings. For instance, common interest in an activity or a task is frequently the motivation behind the school's football team or theater group. Liking for other students often serves as the primary cohesion bond for extracurricular clubs, informal get-togethers after school, and, certainly, for parties. Prestige is often a powerful motive for the cohesiveness of the basketball squad, the math team, the cheerleader's club, and certain advanced honor's classes. Indeed, it is possible that any group in the school can possess one or more of these motives for cohesiveness, and each gains strength as it incorporates one or more of them. Groups that have fewer bases of cohesiveness work less effectively as a unit.

The sources of attraction for any one group are not necessarily the same for individual students. As an example of this, Schmuck and Schmuck[61] asked a group of junior high school students, who were very enthusiastic about their local government class, the question, "What do you like most about this government class?" Some of the answers: "It's interesting to find out how this town operates," "I get to study with my two best friends," "I'm thinking about politics as a career," and "The work is fun to do." Although each of these responses revealed a different individual need and several different motivations for cohesiveness, together they added up to a very cohesive class.

The research findings are clear. Students who have the best chances for achieving high self-esteem and for working up to their intellectual potential are usually accepted members of a cohesive, reasonably high morale class with a dispersed friendship structure.

SOCIOMETRY AS A WAY
FOR UNDERSTANDING
CLASSROOM GROUPS

A classroom group is something like a jigsaw puzzle, consisting as it does of interlocking parts forming an analyzable pattern. In an effort to better understand this jigsaw, a sociologist by the name of Moreno[62,63] administered what he called a *sociometric test* (from Latin meaning social or companion measurement) to all the students from kindergarten through eighth grade in a Brooklyn school system. In this test, they were requested to choose the two classmates they preferred to have sit near them. Some students received a large number of choices as seating companions, some received no choices at all, and others ranged in between those two extremes. A deeper analysis of the choices revealed an underlying social structure of which the teachers were only partly aware. It was found, for example, that mutual friendships, small student cliques, a sexual cleavage between boys and girls, and other facets of interpersonal relations existed among students that were not readily apparent even to the teachers who worked with these youngsters on a day-to-day basis. Thus was born the sociometric test as a means for determining the internal social structure of a group.

Since its discovery over forty years ago, use of the sociometric test has spread to prisons, industry, summer camps, large organizations, and other places where interpersonal relations are considered important. Indeed, entire communities have been studied by means of sociometric techniques. Although sociometry has been widely used, it's most extensive utilization has been in the classroom.[64]

Examples of Sociometric Testing

A sociometric approach will allow you to supplement your own personal observations of the interaction patterns and friendship groupings in the classroom. Basically, a sociometric approach is a means of exploring students' perceptions and preferences for other members of the class under a variety of conditions. It is a way to encourage students to be explicit about their interpersonal choices. For instance, students can be asked to identify their preferences for other members of the class by responding to such questions as the following:

1. Who would you like to sit next to in class? _____

2. With whom do you want to work in the chemistry laboratory?

_____

3. Which three students in this class would you like to have spend the weekend at your house? _____ , _____ , _____

4. Which two boys do you like the least? _____ , _____

5. Which two girls do you like least? _____ , _____

6. Which two boys do you like the most? _____ , _____

7. Which two girls do you like the most? _____ , _____

8. Which two students in this class are the most popular? _____ ,

_____

These are a few examples of the kinds of questions that can be asked to get at the social relationships and interpersonal feelings that exist among students. On the basis of the responses, a simple diagram, known as a *sociogram*, can be constructed that allows a quick visual overview of the sorts of friendship patterns that exist among students. Although a larger class would result in a much more complex sociogram, the interaction patterns of a small group of students in Figure 14–1 will give you an idea of how a sociogram looks. A major advantage of actually drawing the sociogram out is that you can actually *see* the direction and intensity (or lack of it) of existing interaction patterns.

Categories of peer acceptance. As you can see in Figure 14–1, students differ widely in the extent to which they are part of a group and in the frequency with which they are chosen by their classmates. In one of the pioneering studies in which sociograms have been used, Bronfenbrenner[65] observed that there seemed to be two types of students among those who were not chosen. Some, who he called *isolates*, were so colorless and inconspicuous as to be simply overlooked or neglected. Others, who he called *rejects*, manifested undesirable or offensive behavior and were consciously and actively disliked by others. You can see examples of both of these types of students in Figure 14–1. Gronlund and Anderson[66] have identified three major categories of pupil acceptance, which pretty well cover the range of social interaction patterns found in most classrooms:

1. The *socially accepted*, who are characterized as attractive, friendly, likable, neat, and outgoing.
2. The *socially neglected*, who receive neither positive nor negative mention; they are simply neutral personalities lacking in stimulus value; they tend to be overlooked rather than disliked.
3. The *socially rejected*, who are usually rated as unlikable, restless, and talkative, untidy, and not very attractive. They attempt to make social contacts but lack the necessary social skills.

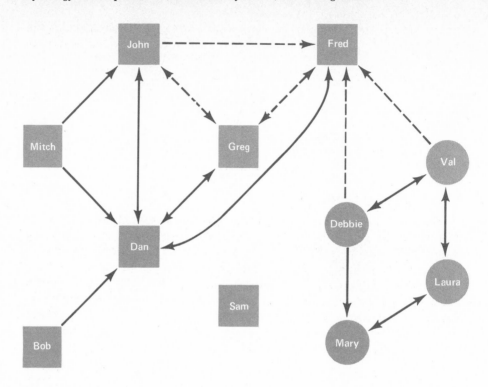

SYMBOLS

A ◄────── B	B chooses A, but A does not mention B
A ◄─────► B	A and B choose each other
A ▪▪▪▪► B	A dislikes B
A ◄▪▪▪► B	A and B dislike each other

There is a clique centering around Dan, as leader.
John is a fringer in this group; only Mitch has chosen him.
Bob and Sam are both isolates; neither has been chosen by other youngsters.
There are two pairs of mutually chosen girlfriends: Debbie and Val, and Mary and Laura.

FIGURE 14–1. Example of a Sociogram (Friendship Patterns of a Small Group)

The "Guess Who" test. For further understanding of students' social relationships, you may wish to explore more deeply why certain students are accepted or rejected. There are several approaches for doing this. One way is through what is known as the *Guess Who* test or game, which involves asking students for the names of peers who they think fit certain patterns of behavior.[67]   A series of behavior descriptions is listed and the students are asked to identify the person who best fits each description. The behavioral descriptions are prepared on the basis of tentative hunches regarding the acceptance or rejection of certain pupils. For instance, if it is suspected that certain elementary age children are being rejected because of their immaturity, questions such as the following could be asked:

1. Who never likes to play rough games? _____

2. Who always wants his own way? _____

3. Who is always crying about something? _____

4. Who is always the quietest one in class? _____

5. Who always plays with younger kids? _____

Replies to such questions will either confirm your suspicions or suggest other avenues for study. With junior high and high school age students, the questions might take the form of asking the class to name the student whom they would rate as most dependable, most mature, most responsible in assuming leadership positions, most popular with boys and/or girls, and similar characteristics that are significant in preadolescent and adolescent friendship choices.

The "Class Play" technique. An instrument called *A Class Play* is another technique to stimulate the interest of children in making sociometric selections.[68] With this approach, students are asked to imagine that the class was going to put on a play and that different students in the class would play the various parts. Fifteen parts are suggested and each child asked to name an appropriate male or female student to fit it. They're also asked to indicate which parts they would like to play themselves. Some of the characters needed to fill the various roles include the following:

1. Someone to play the part of a cruel, mean boss. _____

2. Someone who could play the part of a true friend. _____
3. Someone who is a sore loser and gets mad when things go wrong.

_____

4. Someone who seems unhappy and seems to have little fun. _____

5. Someone who is snobbish, conceited, and acts superior. _____

6. Someone who is very shy and prefers to work alone. _____

These are only a few examples of a vast range of questions a teacher could ask. You could ask practically any kind of question, depending on the kind of information you wanted. It is a simple way to get information about how students in class perceive each other, and it allows them the safety of a game-like situation to express their personal feelings about how certain class members fit different behavioral ciriteria. Most of all, it is a way for a teacher to get valuable information about the interpersonal perceptions of his students, which in turn should help him know his class better and select student combinations that stand the best chance of working effectively together.

Using drawings as sociometric devices. A particularly interesting sociometric study done by Lott and Lott[69] involved not only asking a group of first-grade children to name the classmates whom they liked, disliked, or felt neutral about, but to draw them as well. Drawings and art work have been shown to project a great deal about a child's inner feelings and clinical psychologists frequently use a child's art productions as another avenue to understanding him better.[70-73] Evidently they can also be used as sociometric devices to indicate how children feel toward each other. For example, when a group of psychologists in the Lotts' study was asked to interpret the drawings in terms of the feelings each "artist" had for the child he was drawing, their predictions were close to the answers children gave on sociometric questionnaires.

Consider the drawings in Figure 14-2 and see whether you can determine what attitudes were being expressed by the first-grade boy who drew them. By examining the three pictures, can you tell which classmate was liked, which was disliked, and which one evoked neutral feelings? (Make a mental note of your predictions before reading further.)

If you predicted that Boy A was disliked, that Boy B was viewed neutrally, and that Boy C was liked, give yourself a perfect score. Actually, you may have gotten them all right without fully understanding why they were all right. Look at the pictures again. Even though each is smiling, the smile belonging to Boy A is on the face of what must surely be a less attractive boy. More than that, he is smaller in relation to the other two boys. Both of these characteristics are very likely unconscious projections on the part of the first grader who drew Boy A indicating that he didn't like him very well. The differences between the drawings of boys B and C are not so easy to discern. It is interesting, however, to note that Boy B, while as attractive as Boy C, was not drawn to be as fully developed through the body. It may be that this was the first-grade boy's unconscious projection of the more neutral regard he had for Boy B. (A word of caution: It takes a great deal of skill and savvy to interpret drawings. This is not something one can do after reading only what is offered here. If you're interested in understanding this at a deeper level, the references[70-73] cited above will be of great help.)

Sociometric Patterns Keep Changing

There are, as you can see, a variety of sociometric approaches to understanding both group dynamics and individual behavior within a classroom.

(From A. J. Lott and B. E. Lott. "Some Indirect Measures of Interpersonal Attraction Among Children." Journal of Educational Psychology (1970) 61:133. Copyright 1970 by the American Psychological Association. Reprinted by permission.)

FIGURE 14–2. First-Grade Boy's Drawings of Three Classmates

A little inventiveness on the part of the teacher can go a long way toward devising a simple questionnaire that allows students to express their friendship choices and personal perceptions of classmates. It is important to remember that friendship patterns among students, particularly at the elementary level, are constantly shifting. Thus, it would be a mistake to think that a sociometric study made at the beginning of a school year would be the same three months later. The very label, "group dynamics," implies a fluid, changing pattern of interpersonal relationships, which suggests that a teacher take sociometric glimpses of the class throughout the school year.

Are Sociometric Approaches Really Necessary?

Not infrequently, teachers and teacher candidates raise the question of whether sociometric techniques are worth the time and effort because they feel that they can tell pretty much where students are in the social matrix of their classrooms without the help of such approaches. There are, however, a number of research studies that indicate that teachers may not know their students as well as they think they do. For instance, several investigators found that there was a tendency for teachers to overestimate the popularity of students who adjust well to adults and to underestimate the influence of children with low academic ability. In addition, it was noted that teachers are prone to misjudge the importance of the noisey child who is in a number of groups, but not accepted by any of them, or the leadership exercised by the quiet child.[74,75]

In another investigation, it was found that teachers were only 18 percent accurate in predicting who the most and least popular children would be among their fourth, fifth, and sixth graders. An earlier study by Gronlund[76] also showed that teachers were not very accurate in judging the popularity of students. One of the major findings was the tendency for teachers to overrate the peer acceptance of the students they themselves preferred and to underestimate the status of children they least preferred. Perhaps the most significant finding to emerge from Gronlund's study is that there was *no* relationship between a teacher's ability to accurately judge a child's acceptance on any of the following factors: teaching experience, age, years of college training, credits earned in education courses, size of class, and length of time the teacher had been with the class. The only thing that separated the best teacher-judges from the poorest was whether they had taken an in-service, child development course set up for the purpose of helping teachers to understand the "whole child," with particular reference to his social adjustment. As it turned out, teachers who had taken this course were better judges of a student's social position in a group than those who had not. We have to be cautious with how far we extend this finding because it may be that those teachers who were interested enough to take such a course would also be the teachers best able to judge the social acceptance of students more accurately.

One possible reason why teachers fail to identify children who are accepted or rejected is that they are not fully aware of the criteria that students use to make choices regarding who is most popular, least popular, and so on. The difficulty could be one of low empathy; that is, the inability of a teacher to put himself in the same perceptual frame of reference as students and see things as students see them.

Are sociometric approaches really necessary? There is no hard and fast answer to this. Some teachers find them a very useful source of supplemental information. Others find them time-consuming and not worth the trouble. However, there seems little question but that the sociometric patterns of a classroom can be more accurately evaluated when sociometric approaches are used.

As discussed in greater detail in chapters 6 and 8, good teachers are good because, among other things, they know a great deal about the students they teach. Sociometry is just one more tool at your disposal to help you do just that.

COMMUNICATION SKILLS FOR ENHANCING GROUP PROCESSES

Unless there is open communication among and between students and teacher, the whole process of acquiring, growing, and changing is short-circuited and deadened. Indeed, experiments conducted with various combinations and conditions of group interaction have found that the

There is a continual flow of activities and good feelings in classrooms marked by healthy group dynamics. (Allyn and Bacon)

more accessible group members are to one another's communications, the more effective they are at solving problems.[77] Another study found that the achievement of students studying and interacting in groups was superior to students who studied alone.[78]

A very sensitive educational psychologist, Alice Keliher, once made the following observation on a finding that a three-year-old child used as many as 11,000 running words per day and a four year old as many as 15,000:

> Think how the formal teacher of five- and six-year-old children stems this flood by raising her hand against speech! I marvel that young children are actually able to inhibit speech as much as they do for four or five hours a day; but I marvel more at the continuing stupidity of schools which thus cut off the very life-blood of the intellectual development of children.[79]

What Keliher was referring to was the fact that speech—oral communication— is a vehicle for learning. When a student's opportunities for communication within a classroom are minimized, it reduces his chances for learning both as much or as effectively as he otherwise might. It is that simple.

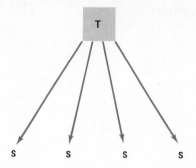

1. LEAST EFFECTIVE. The teacher attempts to maintain one-way communication with students in the class.

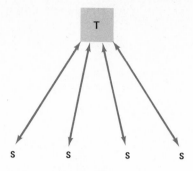

2. MORE EFFECTIVE. The teacher tries to develop two-way communication with students in the class.

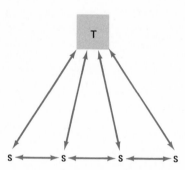

2. EVEN MORE EFFECTIVE. The teacher maintains two-way communication with students and also permits some communication among students on a rather formal basis.

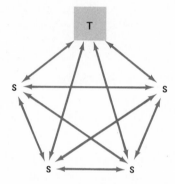

4. MOST EFFECTIVE. The teacher becomes a co-participant in the group and encourages two-way communication among all members of the group, including himself.

(From H. C. Lindgren. Educational Psychology in the Classroom, 4th ed. New York: Wiley, 1972, p. 258. Used by permission.)

FIGURE 14–3. Communication Patterns Between Teachers and Students, in Order of Their Effectiveness

Classroom Communication Problems

There are at least four different communication networks that can be observed in different classrooms. Consider the four basic patterns of classroom interaction depicted in Figure 14–3.

You will recognize Type 1 as the most traditional and associated with classrooms in which the communication flow is usually from teacher to student in the form of lectures, orders, or even exhortations. Type 2 is an improvement because at least there is mutual exchange between teacher and students. Here, at least, a teacher can correct errors of misunderstanding. Type 3 communication is improved even further because there is now some communication among students as well. Type 4 communication is theoretically the best because all possible channels among and between students and teacher are opened up.

Having open channels is one thing; creating the sort of atmosphere conducive to a productive use of those channels is another. Let's look at some ways for doing this.

Toward Creating a Climate for Open Communication

There is a rather universal recognition that some degree of acceptance and warmth in interpersonal relationships is absolutely essential for psychosocial and intellectual growth in a classroom. The need for acceptance is one that begins at birth and, though it might change in how it expresses itself throughout the maturational process, is a need we all have throughout life. When our need for acceptance, which is closely linked to the need to feel adequate or competent, is threatened, the natural tendency is to withdraw, or at least to take some kind of defensive action to parry the threat. In a classroom, this defensive posture is variously reflected in such behaviors as sitting near the back of the room, not participating in class discussions, skipping class, or, as a more extreme reaction, dropping out of school altogether.

As teachers, what can we do to reduce the possibility of these things happening?

TO DO

Once again, before reading further, jot down the three to four things you would do to create a climate for open communication. Or, as another way of looking at this, what are some techniques used by teachers you've had yourself who have created an "open climate"?

_____

_____

A supportive atmosphere helps. The need for a supportive classroom climate is a crucial one if open communication is to exist. The fear of nonsupport and rejection is, by far, one of the greatest anxieties typically experienced by class members. Each of us knows from personal experience that some classroom climates make us feel defensive and on guard, while others help us feel safer and more supported. After an intensive study of recordings of discussions occurring in various groups, Gibb[80] was able to

TABLE 14–1. *Categories of Behavior Character-istic of Defensive and Supportive Climates*

Defensive climates	Supportive climates
1. Evaluation	1. Description
2. Control	2. Problem orientation
3. Strategy	3. Spontaneity
4. Neutrality	4. Empathy
5. Superiority	5. Equality
6. Certainty	6. Provisionalism

define six pairs of psychological conditions or categories that were most frequently associated with defensive or supportive group climates. Behavior that a person perceives as possessing any of the characteristics listed in the left-hand column in Table 14–1 causes one to feel closed and defensive, whereas that which he interprets as having any of the qualities designated as supportive helps him to be more open and available to his ideas and feelings.

As you can see, supportive climates are less judgmental and more accepting in nature. Speech or other behavior that appears evaluative increases defensiveness. If by expression, manner of speech, tone of voice, or verbal content, the sender seems to be evaluating or judging the listener, then the receiver is likely to go on guard. Of course it doesn't have to happen that way. If, for example, the listener thought that the speaker perceived him as an equal and was simply being open and spontaneous, then the possibility of the message being evaluative might not even occur. This same principle is also true of the other five categories of potentially defense-producing climates. The six sets are, in this way, interactive.

Your response style makes a difference: five from which to choose. Porter[81] has been able to identify five primary response styles that individuals most frequently tend to use with each other in face-to-face situations. In the order of the frequency with which they are used, they are listed below.

Five Most Frequently Used Response Patterns

1. *Evaluative:* This is a response that reflects a judgmental, "evaluative" assessment of the relative goodness, appropriateness, effectiveness, or rightness of another person's behavior. One person implies to another how he (the receiver) should or ought to behave. Examples: "I don't know why you're dating him; he just uses women. And besides you should be able to do better than that." "Not only is the format for this paper wrong, but it's not even related to our unit of study."

2. *Interpretative:* This is a response that reflects an intent to teach, to tell another person what his problem "really" means, or to tell him how he (the other person) "really" feels about the situation. An interpretative response either obviously or subtly tells another person what his behavior means at a deeper level. Examples: "I think the reason you date him is because he's older and this makes you feel more like you're going out with a protecting father." "You probably wrote this paper the way you did because underneath you feel pretty angry at me and the students in this course."

3. *Supportive:* This is the sort of response that reflects an intent to reassure, to pacify, to reduce another person's intensity of feeling. It is the sort of response that helps a person to feel more comfortable and less anxious about his current circumstances. Examples: "You seem to be concerned about the fact that John's older than you, yet you seem to have a nice time when you're together, don't you?" "I know that writing papers is difficult for you, but, as you get into it, it may not seem so bad after all."

4. *Probing:* This is a response that indicates a person's intent to seek further information and to provoke further discussion along a certain line. The speaker implies to the other person that there is something that can be developed further. Examples: "Did you ever think about why it is that the fellows you date always seem so much older than you?" "Students are motivated for different reasons to choose the topics they do to write about—I wonder what yours was for this paper?"

5. *Understanding:* The multiple purposes of this response are to: (1) be sure that the listener correctly understands what the sender is saying; (2) find out how the sender feels about the problem or circumstance; and (3) find out how the sender sees the problem. Examples: "You feel pretty ambivalent about dating older men, is that it?" You've worried about this paper for so long, you're almost afraid to hand it in, right?"

Several years ago, C. Rogers and F. Roethlisberger[82] conducted a series of studies on how individuals communicate with each other in face-to-face situations. What they found was that the categories of evaluative, interpretative, supportive, probing, and understanding statements encompass about 80 percent of all communications between individuals. Once again, please note that evaluative and interpretative responses rank number one and two in frequency of use, neither of which are very conducive for creating climate for open communication. We might also note that Rogers and Roethlisberger found that if a person uses one category of response as much as 40 percent of the time, then other people see him as *always* responding that way.

Actually, the response patterns are in themselves neither good nor bad. It is the *overuse* or *underuse* of any one of the response patterns that may cause communication handicaps.

How to make appropriate use of those response patterns. Research is pretty clear in telling us that evaluative, interpretive responses are counterproductive in the early phases of a relationship because they tend to leave a person with the feeling of being judged and weighed rather than accepted and valued for whom he is as an individual.[83,84]

On the other hand, the understanding response is particularly useful in building a positive climate for open communication because it is an open invitation for the other person to say what he wants to say and to elaborate and further explore whatever his idea or feeling is at the moment. The understanding response is also the most helpful for seeing the other person's problem or position from his point of view. Saying to a young lady something very evaluative like, "I don't know why you're dating him; he just uses women. And besides you can do better than that," is hardly an invitation for her to explore the motivations that may be behind her dating patterns. The person talking to her seems to know all the answers. It's difficult to be open with another person, be that person's friend, teacher, or spouse if he or she comes across as an omnipotent, clairvoyant know-it-all. The usual attitude is, "What's the use? He doesn't listen anyway." However, if the response to that same young lady is something on the order of, "You feel pretty ambivalent about dating older men, is that it?" then this is an invitation for her to explore further as much as she wants.

Of course, we have to also understand that tone of voice, along with body and facial cues also communicate acceptance or rejection. Sometimes our voice says one thing, while our nonverbal messages say another. I remember a sixth-grade boy who approached his teacher (a noted grouch, by the way) one day and said, "Mr. Brown, do you like teaching?" Mr. Brown, sweetly, "Why of course I do," to which the boy replied, "Well your face doesn't look like it."

There will be many times when a student tries to discuss something with you that you do not understand. Probing responses may be helpful at this time to assist you in getting a clear definition of the problem before trying to answer. Supportive responses are useful when another person needs to feel accepted or when he needs enough support to try out something in the way of new behavior to solve his problem. Interpretative responses are sometimes valuable in confronting another person with the impact of his behavior on you. Indeed, both evaluative and interpretative responses, if conveyed with empathy, integrity, and self-other sensitivity, can be powerful stimulants to growth. If done in a non-hostile manner, both interpretation and evaluation can lead to insight, and insight is a key to fuller cognitive understanding and better psychological living.

Why being able to trust a teacher is so important. As a teacher, you will probably find yourself having to evaluate and interpret more than most people in their interpersonal transactions. The very nature of a teacher's job involves a certain amount of evaluative ("That's good," "This could be better," "We can improve here") and interpretative ("This paragraph seems to suggest that . . .'') feedback. In order for evaluative and interpretative feedback to be nondefensively accepted by a student (insofar as it is possible in individual cases), a teacher first of all must be perceived as supportive and caring. If, for example, your close friend or loved one criticizes your hair style or dress habits, and you know for certain that he or she genuinely values you as an individual and cares for you as a person, you will be less likely to get defensive about that sort of feedback. You would, in effect, be more open to the constructive aspects of evaluations regarding your dress habits if you were certain that it was motivated by a sincere desire to be helpful rather than destructive to you.

The same is true in a classroom between teachers and students. When a student can trust a teacher, when he knows the teacher is really ''for him,'' then the doors to honest, open communication are opened wider than ever. One of the most difficult conditions to establish in human relationships inside and outside the classroom is a basic sense of trust. A teacher who is himself, authentically and fully, and who is available to all types of experiences and feelings without being defensive and retreating into safe roles, will go a long way in establishing the groundwork for bringing about the sort of prerequisite trust necessary for open communication. The idea here was nicely expressed by an eleventh-grade boy, who, when I asked a group of high school students why they seemed to like a certain chemistry teacher so well, answered this way:

> It's hard to explain, but I know he likes me. I think he likes all of us. I mean he does things for us and with us; like, for example, he stays after school to help us in the lab. If we don't like something, we can tell him and he won't get mad. He doesn't always change, but he does always listen. Another thing I like is that we know where we stand with him. I mean he's not afraid to tell us about the good, the bad, or the indifferent. I like that—it makes him seem, well, more real.

Use immediate reinforcement: it facilitates good feelings. Sometimes it happens that a student will make a significant contribution to class discussion and not even receive a nod of approval from the instructor. As you may know from personal experience, nothing is more demoralizing. The principle we're talking about here is a simple one and comes directly from the behavioristic position discussed in Chapter 1. It goes like this: Rewards or reinforcements are most effective when they follow the desired behavior almost immediately.[85,86] If, for instance, a student makes an effort to participate in class and is greeted by either no response from the teacher or a negative one (''That statement doesn't even make sense, John''), it is not likely that he will feel greatly moved to participate in the future.

A major value of immediate reinforcement—particularly if it is positive—is that a student can feel immediately good about himself. Success experiences typically lead to feelings of pride and a sense of competency, which, in turn, create a new urgency to want to get more of those immediately felt good feelings.

677

Another important function of immediate reinforcement is that it lets the student know not only where he stands, but where the teacher stands as well. It lets him know that the teacher cares enough to listen and respond to him, both of which are important conditions for open communication.

Make your feedback constructive. Immediate reinforcement can't always be positive, but it can still be offered in constructive ways. For example, saying to a student, "Paul, I don't know where you ever got an idea like that—it doesn't even make sense," is a devasting negative remark and offers no constructive help to the student. It would be more constructive to say something like, "Paul, that's an idea that I hadn't thought of before. I'd like to understand it better; do you suppose you could rephrase it?" The teacher gets the same message across, namely, he (the teacher) doesn't understand it, and he also communicates to the student that it is an idea with merit. Perhaps the idea doesn't make sense, but if this is so it may have more to do with how it was phrased rather than a flaw inherent in the idea itself. Whatever the case, it should be clearer to both the teacher and student when it is reconsidered and put into fresh words.

These, then, are some ideas, research findings, and strategies for creating a classroom climate for more open communication, which, in the final analysis, is what positive classroom group dynamics is all about anyway.

EPILOGUE

There is all the difference in the world between dealing with people (young or old) one at a time and working with them in groups of thirty or forty. One-to-one relationships are not only easier to predict, but easier to control. Not so with a class of twenty to forty first graders or twelfth-grade high school students. Just as it is important to understand personality dynamics in order to establish healthy interpersonal relationships on a one-to-one basis, so, too, is it important to have a grasp of the basic processes involved in group dynamics in order to facilitate a healthy relationship with an entire class.

There is little question that the social-emotional climate of a classroom influences both individual and group behavior. And there is also little question that the teacher plays a strong part in determining the tone, intensity, and force of that classroom climate. A teacher, by virtue of his behavior, can decidedly affect whether a classroom is warm and supportive or cold and rejecting. The test is not how he handles the best behavior of the healthiest students, but in how effectively he deals with the most troublesome behavior of aggressive, angry, and even the highly passive students. A teacher who works at combining fairness and gentleness with firmness and strength will go a long way toward helping students to trust his capacity to not only encourage an atmosphere of freedom, but to control a class when control is necessary. Students not only need to know that they are valued by the teacher, but they need to know for sure of the teacher's personal strength—that he has the capacity to say "No," and mean it. For most students, it is a scary feeling to be in a classroom where there is the possibility that the strongest (most vocal, assertive, aggressive) classmates could take over and dominate a class if they so choose.

What are healthy group dynamics? Perhaps we can summarize them. Considerations that stand out would be such factors as: (1) a wide dispersion of friendship choices, as opposed to small clusters of friends; (2) a dispersion of power so that portions of the authority and responsibility for decision making is shared by as many students as possible; (3) a psychological atmosphere that is more supporting and democratic than rejecting and authoritarian; (4) a norm structure in which the whole class has participated in developing; (5) response styles by both teacher and students that are geared more to probing and understanding than to evaluating and interpreting; and (6) a general spirit of unification and "we-ness"—a spirit that is usually the natural outgrowth of the five preceding factors.

Write your own chapter summary (major points, ideas, and concepts that had meaning for you).

REFERENCES

1. Wright, H. F., et al. "Toward a Psychological Ecology of the Classroom." *Journal of Educational Research* 45(1951):187–200.

2. Johnson, D. W. *The Social Psychology of Education.* New York: Holt, Rinehart & Winston, 1970, pp. 238–240.

3. Anderson, G. J., and H. J. Walberg. "Classroom Climate and Group Learning." *International Journal of Educational Sciences* 2 (1968):175–180.

4. Anderson, G. J. "Effects of Classroom Social Climate on Individual Learning." *American Educational Research Journal* 2(1970):135–152.

5. Anderson, H. H., and J. E. Brewer. "Studies of Teachers' Classroom Personalities, II." *Applied Psychology Monographs* no. 8 (1946).

6. Anderson, H. H., J. E. Brewer, and M. R. Reed. "Studies of Teachers' Classroom Personalities, III." *Applied Psychology Monographs* no. 46 (1946).

7. White, R., and R. Lippitt. "Leader Behavior and Member Reaction in Three 'Social Climates.'" In *Group Dynamics*, 3rd ed., edited by D. Cartwright and A. Zander. New York: Harper & Row, 1968, pp. 318–335.

8. White, R. K., and R. Lippitt. *Autocracy & Democracy: An Experimental Inquiry.* New York: Harper, 1960.

9. Tannenbaum, A. S. *Control in Organizations.* New York: McGraw-Hill, 1968.

10. Hornstein, H., et al. "Influence and Satisfaction in Organizations: A Replication." Unpublished paper. New York: Teachers College, 1967.

11. Schmuck, R. "Some Aspects of Classroom Social Climate." *Psychology in the Schools* 3(1966):59–65.

12. Jordan, T. E. *The Mentally Retarded.* Columbus, Ohio: Merrill, 1961.

13. Torrance, E. P. *Education and the Creative Potential.* Minneapolis: University of Minnesota Press, 1963.

14. Bonney, M. E. "The Relative Stability of Social, Intellectual, and Academic Status in Grades II to IV, and the Inter-relationships Between These Various Forms of Growth." *Journal of Educational Psychology* 34(1943):88–102.

15. Schmuck, R. A., and E. Van Egmond. "Sex Differences in the Relationship of Interpersonal Perceptions to Academic Performance." *Psychology in the Schools* 2(1965):32–40.

16. Schmuck, R. A. "Sociometric Status and Utilization of Academic Abilities." *Merrill-Palmer Quarterly* 8(1962):165–172.

17. Brodsky, C. M. *A Study of Norms for Body Form-Behavior Relationships.* Washington, D.C.: Catholic University of America Press, 1954.

18. Staffieri, J. "A Study of Social Stereotype of Body Image in Children." *Journal of Personality and Social Psychology* 7(1957):101–104.

19. Dion, K., and E. Berscheid. *Physical Attractiveness and Sociometric Choice in Nursery School Children.* Mimeographed. Minneapolis: University of Minnesota, 1971.

20. Dion, K. K. "Physical Attractiveness and Evaluation of Children's Transgressions." *Journal of Personality and Social Psychology* 24(1972):207–213.

21. Sigall, H., and E. Aronson. "Liking for an Evaluator as a Function of the Physical Attractiveness and Nature of the Evaluations." *Journal of Experimental Social Psychology* 5(1969):93–100.

22. Dion, K., E. Berscheid, and E. Walster. "What Is Beautiful Is Good." *Journal of Personality and Social Psychology* 24(1972):285–290.

23. Horowitz, F. D. "The Relationship of Anxiety, Self-Concept, and Sociometric Status Among 4th, 5th, and 6th Grade Children." *Journal of Abnormal and Social Psychology* 65(1962):212–214.

24. Feldhusen, J. F., and J. R. Thurston. "Personality and Adjustment of High and Low Anxious Children." *Journal of Educational Research* 56(1964):265–267.

25. Coopersmith, S. A. "A Method of Determining Types of Self-Esteem." *Journal of Abnormal and Social Psychology* 59(1959):87–94.

26. Douglas, V. "The Development of Two Families of Defense." *Dissertation Abstracts* 20(1959):1438.

27. Kerr, A. "A Study of Social Acceptability." *Elementary School Journal* 45(1944–45):257–265.

28. Bonney, M. E. "Popular and Unpopular Children: A Sociometric Study." *Sociometry Monographs* no. 9(1947).

29. Commoss, H. H. "Some Characteristics Related to Social Isolation of Second Grade Children." *Journal of Educational Psychology* 53(1962):38–42.

30. Lippitt, R., and M. Gold. "Classroom Social Structure as a Mental Health Problem." *Journal of Social Issues* 15(1959):40–58.

31. Pope, B. "Socioeconomic Contrasts in Children's Peer Culture Prestige Valances." *Genetic Psychology Monograph* 48(1953):157–220.

32. Pope, B. "Prestige Values in Contrasting Socioeconomic Groups of Children." *Psychiatry* 16(1953):381–385.

33. Cook, L. A. "An Experimental Sociographic Study of a Stratified 10th Grade Class." *American Sociological Review* 10(1945):250–261.

34. Wilson, A. B. "Residential Segregation of Social Classes and Aspirations of High School Boys." *American Sociological Review* 24(1959):836–845.

35. Flanders, N. A., and S. Havumaki. "The Effect of Teacher-Pupil Contacts Involving Praise on the Sociometric Choices of Students." *Journal of Educational Psychology* 51(1960):65–68.

36. Schmuck, R. R. "Some Relationships of Peer Liking Patterns in the Classroom to Pupil Attitudes and Achievement." *School Review* 71(1963):337–359.

37. Muldoon, J. F. "The Concentration of Liked and Disliked Members in a Group and the Relationship of the Concentration of Group Cohesiveness." *Sociometry* 18(1955):73–81.

38. Hamachek, D. E. *Encounters with the Self.* New York: Holt, Rinehart & Winston, 1971, pp. 32–45.

39. Sherif, M., and C. W. Sherif. *Social Psychology.* New York: Harper & Row, 1969, pp. 232–242.

40. Cartwright, P., and A. Zander (eds.). *Group Dynamics: Research and Theory,* 3rd ed. New York: Harper & Row, 1968, pp. 139–181.

41. Festinger, L. "Informal Social Communication." *Psychological Review* 57(1950):271–292.

42. Sherif, M. "A Study of Some Social Factors in Perception." *Archives of Psychology* no. 187 (1935).

43. Berelson, B., and G. A. Steiner. *Human Behavior: An Inventory of Scientific Findings.* New York: Harcourt, Brace and World, 1964, pp. 334–335.

44. *The Detroit Free Press* (25 March 1973):3,15.

45. Homans, G. C. *Social Behavior: Its Elementary Forms.* New York: Harcourt, Brace and World, 1961, p. 163.

46. Argyle, M. *The Scientific Study of Social Behavior.* London: Methuen, 1957, p. 155.

47. Johnstone, J., and E. Katz. "Youth and Popular Music: A Study in the Sociology of Taste." *American Journal of Sociology* 62(1957):563–568.

48. Rieken, H. W., and G. C. Homans. "Psychological Aspects of Social Structure," In *Handbook of Social Psychology*, vol. II, edited by G. Lindzey. Reading, Mass.: Addison-Wesley, 1954, p. 793.

49. Asch, S. E. "Studies of Independence and Conformity: I A Minority of One Against a Unanimous Majority." *Psychological Monographs* no. 9 70(1956).

50. Graham, Robert. *Group Dynamics at Work.* Term paper excerpt. E. Lansing, Mich.: Michigan State University, 1973.

51. McGrath, J. E., and I. Altman. *Small Group Research.* New York: Holt, Rinehart and Winston, 1966, pp. 103–189.

52. Mann, R. D. *Interpersonal Styles and Group Development.* New York: Wiley, pp. 120–195.

53. Bany, M. A., and L. V. Johnson. *Classroom Group Behavior.* New York: MacMillan, 1964, pp. 52–53.

54. Schmuck, R. "Some Aspects of Classroom Social Climate." *Psychology in the Schools* 3(1966):59–65.

55. Muldoon, J. F. "The Concentration of Liked and Disliked Members in Groups and the Relationship of the Concentration to Group Cohesiveness." *Sociometry* 18(1955):73–81.

56. Walberg, H. J. "Teacher Personality and Classroom Climate." *Psychology in the Schools* 5(April 1968):163–169.

57. Walberg, H. J., and W. W. Welch. "Personality Characteristics of Innovative Physics Teachers." *Journal of Creative Behavior* 1(Spring 1967):163–171.

58. Anderson, G. J., H. J. Walberg, and W. W. Welch. "Curriculum Effects on the Social Climate of Learning: A New Representation of Discriminant Functions." *American Educational Research Journal* 6(May 1969):315–328.

59. Bovard, E. "Interaction and Attraction to the Group." *Human Relations* 9(1956):481–489.

60. Back, K. "Influence Through Social Communication." *Journal of Abnormal and Normal Psychology* 46(1951):9–23.

61. Schmuck, R. A., and P. A. Schmuck. *Group Processes in the Classroom.* Dubuque, Iowa: Brown, 1971, pp. 108–109.

62. Moreno, J. L., H. H. Jennings, and R. Stockton. "Sociometry in the Classroom." *Sociometry* 6(1943):425–428.

63. Moreno, J. L. *Who Shall Survive?* New York: Beacon House, 1953.

64. Gronlund, N. E. *Sociometry in the Classroom.* New York: Harper & Row, 1959, pp. 1–2.

65. Bronfenbrenner, U. *Social Status, Structure and Development in Classroom Groups.* Unpublished Ph.D. dissertation. Ann Arbor, Mich.: University of Michigan, 1942.

66. Gronlund, N. E., and L. Anderson. "Personality Characteristics of Socially Accepted, Socially Neglected and Socially Rejected High School Pupils." *Education and Administrative Supervision* 43(1957):329–338.

67. Rogers, C. R. *Measuring Personality Adjustment in Children Nine to Thirteen Years of Age.* New York: Bureau of Publications, Teachers College, Columbia University, 1931.

68. Lambert, N. M., and E. M. Bowser. *A Process for In-School Screening of Children with Emotional Handicaps.* Sacramento: California State Department of Education, 1961.

69. Lott, A. J., and B. E. Lott. "Some Indirect Measures of Interpersonal Attraction Among Children." *Journal of Educational Psychology* 61(1970):124–135.

70. Brick, M. "Mental Hygiene Value of Children's Art Work." *American Journal of Orthopsychiatry* 14(1944):136–147.

71. Alschler, R. H., and L. W. Hattwick. *Painting and Personality: A Study of Young Children.* Chicago: University of Chicago Press, 1947.

72. Goodenough, F. L., and D. B. Harris. "Studies in the Psychology of Children's Drawings." *Psychological Bulletin* 47(1950):369–433.

73. Swensen, C. H. "Empirical Evaluations of Human Figure Drawings, 1957–1966." *Psychological Bulletin* 70(1968):20–44.

74. Barclay, J. R. "Variability in Sociometric Scores and Teachers' Ratings as Related to Teacher Age and Sex." *Journal of School Psychology* 5(1966):52–59.

75. Bonney, M. E. "Sociometric Study of Agreement Between Teacher Judgments and Student Choices." *Sociometry* 10(1947):133–146.

76. Gronlund, N. E. *The Accuracy of Teachers' Judgments Concerning the Sociometric Status of Sixth-Grade Students.* New York: Beacon House, 1951.

77. Heise, G. A., and G. A. Miller. "Problem Solving by Small Groups Using Various Communication Nets." *Journal of Abnormal and Social Psychology* 46(1951):327–335.

78. Blue, J. T., Jr. "The Effect of Group Study on Grade Achievement." *Journal of Educational Psychology* 49(1958):118–123.

79. Keliher, A. V. "Some Developmental Factors in Children . . . Two to Eight." In *Growth and Development: The Basis for Educational Programs.* New York: Progressive Education Association, 1936, p. 6.

80. Gibb, J. R. "Defensive Communication." *ETC: A Review of General Semantics* 22(1965):14–24.

81. Porter, E. H., Jr. *Therapeutic Counseling,* Boston: Mass.: Houghton Mifflin, 1956, pp. 10–24.

82. Rogers, C. R., and F. J. Roethlisberger. "Barriers and Gateways to Communication." *Harvard Business Review* (July-August 1952):28–35.

83. Johnson, D. W. *Reaching Out: Interpersonal Effectiveness and Self-Actualization.* Englewood Cliffs, N.J.: Prentice-Hall, 1972, pp. 117–139.

84. McCroskey, J. C., C. E. Larson, and M. L. Knapp. *An Introduction to Interpersonal Communication.* Englewood Cliffs, N.J.: Prentice-Hall, 1971, pp. 77–167.

85. White, W. W. *Psychosocial Principles Applied to Classroom Teaching.* New York: McGraw-Hill, 1969, pp. 47–54.

86. Travers, R. M. W. *Essentials of Learning.* New York: Macmillan, 1972, pp. 41–99.

REFERENCES OF RELATED INTEREST

Barker, R., and P. Gump. *Big School, Small School: High School Size and Student Behavior.* Stanford, Calif.: Stanford University Press, 1964.

Bigelow. R. C. *The Effect of Organizational Development on Classroom Climate.* Eugene, Ore.: Center for the Advanced Study of Educational Administration, 1969.

Bion, W. R. *Experiences in Groups.* New York: Basic Books, 1961.

Egan, G. *Face to Face: The Small Group Experience and Interpersonal Growth.* Monterey, Calif.: Brooks/Cole, 1973.

———. *Encounter: Group Processes for Interpersonal Growth.* Monterey, Calif.: Brooks/Cole, 1970.

Eisenstadt, J. W. *Personality Style and Sociometric Choice.* Washington, D.C.: NTL Institute for Applied Behavioral Science, 1969, no. 3.

Hamachek, D. E. *How to Get Your Child to Listen to You and How to Listen to Your Child.* Washington, D.C.: National Education Association, 1971.

Jackson, P. W. *Life in Classrooms.* New York: Holt, Rinehart & Winston, 1968.

Kaplan, L. *Education and Mental Health.* New York: Harper & Row, 1971, pp. 297–399.

Katz, D., and R. Kahn. *The Social Psychology of Organizations.* New York: Wiley, 1966.

Kemp, C. G. (ed.). *Perspectives on the Group Process.* Boston, Mass.: Houghton Mifflin, 1964.

McCroskey, J. C., C. E. Larson, and M. L. Knapp. *Introduction to Interpersonal Communication.* Englewood Cliffs, N. J.: Prentice-Hall, 1971.

Schmuck, R. A., and P. A. Schmuck. *A Humanistic Psychology of Education.* Palo Alto, Calif.: National Press Books, 1974,

Schmuck, R., M. Chesler, and R. Lippitt. *Problem-Solving to Improve Classroom Learning.* Chicago: Science Research Associates, 1966.

Stanford, G., and A. E. Roark. *Human Interaction in Education.* Boston: Allyn and Bacon, 1974.

White, R., and Lippitt, R. *Autocracy and Democracy.* New York: Harper & Row, 1960.

FIFTEEN

Understandings and Strategies for Achieving Positive Classroom Management

CHAPTER OUTLINE

PROLOGUE

HOW SERIOUS AN ISSUE IS CLASSROOM DISCIPLINE?

Most Students Are Well Behaved

Teachers Differ About What Constitutes a Discipline Problem

How Elementary School Teachers View Discipline

Are the Youths of Today Really That Much Different?

FIVE FACTORS THAT INFLUENCE CLASSROOM DISCIPLINE

Situational and Environmental Factors

Size of the school system is an important consideration

Class size and composition can affect behavior

Administration and school organization are strong forces

Teacher-Related Factors

Lack of experience and a generation gap may cause problems

Too much emphasis on control and punishment is detrimental

Academic and Curriculum Factors

Students' Personality and Growth Factors

Problem behavior and normal growth consequences sometimes confused

Not all "defiant" behavior means the same thing

Group Factors

Dynamics of group contagion

Three reasons why individuals behave differently in groups

Student participation in rule making is important

DIAGNOSTIC THINKING AS A METHOD FOR SOLVING CLASSROOM PROBLEMS

A Classroom Incident: Diagnostic Thinking in Action

Alternative solutions to a complex problem—what to do?

Five Steps Involved in Diagnostic Thinking

Listen to your first hunch

Look for hidden factors

Use behavior as a guide to action

Test hunches by action

Try new approaches when old ones fail

STRATEGIES FOR HANDLING WOULD-BE AND ACTUAL DISCIPLINE PROBLEMS

When Are Disciplinary Measures Necessary?

Coping Techniques a Teacher Can Use

Deliberately ignore the misbehavior—to a point

Intervene with nonverbal signals

Reduce the distance between the offender and you

Make an effort to rekindle lost interest

Use humor to defuse tension

Give functional assistance to perplexed students

Do things differently now and then

Give support through routine—some students need it more than others

Use nonpunitive exile

Physical restraint is sometimes necessary

Use behavior-modification approaches—emphasize the positive

humanness need not be lost using behavior modification

Put-Down Messages That Cause Trouble

Teacher Behavior and Classroom Procedures That Make a Difference

POINTS TO REMEMBER ABOUT CONSTRUCTIVE CLASSROOM MANAGEMENT

EPILOGUE

REFERENCES

REFERENCES OF RELATED INTEREST

IMPORTANT CHAPTER IDEAS

1. What constitutes a disciplinary problem may vary from teacher to teacher.

2. Only a small percentage of students are discipline problems, but it only takes one or two out of a class of thirty or so to occupy up to 50 percent of a teacher's management time.

3. Problems of recalcitrant youths and classroom discipline have always been with us, and there is no reason that these problems will suddenly disappear in the future.

4. Personal, social, and environmental factors all interact to influence a student's classroom behavior.

5. Classroom misbehavior is sometimes the consequence of a teacher's personality characteristics and manner of relating to students.

6. Sometimes a student's "misbehavior" is more the by-product of a particular growth stage than it is a consequence of angry feelings toward either the teacher or school.

7. A student may behave differently when in a classroom group than he does when by himself.

8. Student participation in rule making is an important step toward encouraging self-discipline.

9. "Diagnostic thinking" is a way of defining, locating, and solving immediate classroom discipline problems.

10. Limits for appropriate classroom behavior should be established early and consistently enforced.

11. Behavior modification is an approach to classroom management that stresses the value of positively reinforcing desired student behavior.

12. A wise teacher knows that not only does *what* he say influence behavior for better or for worse, but *how* he says it makes a difference.

PROLOGUE

Classroom management means different things to different teachers. To a low self-confident, insecure teacher it may mean letting students do pretty much as they please because to do it any differently is to run the risk of not being liked and, hence, feeling even more insecure. To a domineering, authoritarian teacher, it may mean controlling the class through an elaborate system of controls, fiats, and punishments because to do it any differently is to run the risk of having his power usurped by recalcitrant students. To an anxious, nervous teacher it may mean resolving conflict and reducing tension as quickly as possible and by any means possible because to do it any differently is to run the risk of increasing the anxiety and inner tension. To a secure, democratic teacher it may mean working as much as possible within a group-oriented framework in order to consider both the students' feelings and his or her own when it comes to determining the management policies of the classroom.

When we talk about "managing" a classroom, we're referring to more than just controlling it; this is part of the picture, but it is not all. In a broader sense, classroom management has reference to the overall coordination of a classroom's activities, being responsible for the flow of learning, and seeing to it that there is a reasonable semblance of order.

With a definition this broad, it may occur to you that a good deal of what we've discussed so far in this volume fits under the label of classroom management. For example, motivating a class, using a variety of teaching strategies, evaluating learning, and being sensitive to the group dynamics of a class are all classroom management techniques in a more general sense of the word. What we haven't really looked at is how the management concept is related to problems of discipline in the classroom and approaches to handling these problems when they occur.

Let's turn our attention to this now, but before we do there is an important question we need to ask.

HOW SERIOUS AN ISSUE IS
CLASSROOM DISCIPLINE?

Every classroom has its share of discipline problems. Some, to be sure, are less serious than others, but they are, nonetheless, problems. Indeed, after salary complaints and lack of facilities, discipline is the concern most frequently cited by teachers as a source of major irritation and trouble.[1,2] As you might imagine, discipline problems are an even greater source of concern among beginning teachers, with as many as 70 percent of them noting that discipline was one of their major worries.[3,4]

Most Students Are Well Behaved

The majority of students, in both high school and elementary school, are well-behaved youngsters who respond favorably to rules and verbal control. For example, one teacher opinion survey found that more than 60 percent of the 4,270 teachers questioned stated that less than 1 percent of their students were troublemakers. In addition, 38 percent of the elementary school teachers, 12 percent of the junior high school teachers, and 17 percent of the high school teachers felt that they had no troublemakers at all in their classes. And when the students were asked, "What is the last thing you did in your last school that your teacher thought you shouldn't have done?" many answered with one word, "Nothing." A seventh grader elaborated: "I enjoyed everything I did. The teacher asked if we liked what we were doing and let us make a few suggestions of what we would like to do. I felt it was a good idea, what the teacher did."[5]

Teachers Differ About What Constitutes
a Discipline Problem

There is a problem, however, we must face when teachers are asked for their views about discipline and how much in the way of discipline they must contend with in their classrooms. Not all teachers judge similar behavior in the same way. I recall, for example, a time when I was talking to three elementary school teachers on the playground of their school during recess when all of a sudden two fifth-grade boys started fighting. It wasn't an all-out bloody war, but rather some mutual pushing, shoving, and exchanges of verbal threats. Teacher A commented, "It's about time those two got their anger out in the open" and seemed prepared to let the

"THIS IS RADIGAN. TELL THE PRINCIPAL WE WANT TEN DOLLARS IN UNMARKED BILLS, A SCHOOL BUS WAITING OUTSIDE, AND 29 TICKETS TO THE ZOO!"

Discipline problems aren't really all this bad, but sometimes to harrassed teachers they seem to be.

boys go at it. Teacher B muttered something about "They know better than that" and rushed out to hold them apart. Not only did she hold them apart, but, as soon as one of the boys took a half-hearted swiping kick at the other, she marched them off to the principal's office.

A discipline problem, like beauty, seems to be in the eye of the beholder. Whether one kind of acting-out behavior or another constitutes a discipline problem or not seems to have as much to do with a particular teacher's mood, patience, and tolerance for misbehavior as it does with the behavior itself. Teachers A and B obviously had different ideas about what was and was not a discipline problem. For some teachers, chewing gum, passing notes, and whispering are disciplinary issues to be dealt with on the spot. Other teachers could care less about offenses of that sort and exercise their disciplinary powers only in more serious offenses. As one of my more liberal junior high teacher friends expressed it, "Why should I get upset over notes being passed? At least they're practicing their writing."

So, when we see statistics noting that 38 percent of the elementary school teachers and 17 percent of the high school teachers report no discipline problems, we have to interpret those percentages cautiously. It may well be that those teachers who say they have no troublemakers in class are simply those who have a higher level of tolerance for minor infractions and a more flexible concept of what a discipline problem is in the first place.

TO DO

On a scale from 1 to 5 (1 very serious and 5 not serious at all) how would you rate the following classroom incidents?

a. chewing gum _____

b. whispering during class _____

c. punching and hitting _____

d. passing notes during study period _____

e. calling names, e.g., "You bastard" _____

f. sassing the teacher, e.g., "Go jump in the lake" _____

What do your ratings suggest about your expectations and values regarding student behavior? Were you ever guilty of any of the above? What happened to you? How have your own experiences as a student influenced your attitudes toward what is and what isn't a discipline problem in the classroom? Do you see yourself as being pretty liberal with regard to disciplinary issues or fairly conservative? Why?

How Elementary School Teachers View Discipline

However few the number of troublemakers in any given class, the fact remains that every teacher, at one time or another, is confronted with disciplinary issues that must be solved. Research by Cutts and Moseley[6] suggests that almost every teacher has in his class one or more students whom he has difficulty controlling. Elementary school teachers are somewhat divided about whether or not discipline is more difficult today than it used to be. As one elementary teacher remarked, "I certainly feel that some of the problems I face are more serious than any I used to have, but this may be because I'm more aware of the implications. I know more than I did about how emotional maladjustment originates and how hard it can be to overcome."

How Secondary School Teachers View Discipline

Secondary school teachers are more of one voice in their opinion that discipline is a greater problem today than it ever was and that the problem grows more burdensome every year. That secondary teachers should feel the crunch of the disciplinary problem is not surprising, particularly when we consider that their students are bigger, more conflicted about authority figures to begin with, and more involved in significant social issues, which tend to solidify their ranks more than ever before. One fifty-year-old mathematics teacher, who had just retired on a minimum pension, expressed his feelings in the following way: "I felt guilty when the superintendent begged me to stay. I agree that I perhaps owe the system a debt of loyalty after thirty years, but I just can't take it any more. I'm sorry. But I really can't."

Are the Youths of Today Really That Much Different?

A committee of New York City high school principals, meeting with their board of education, said, "We were shocked and depressed by the general failure of the authorities to understand the sorry deterioration in our high schools. More insolence and indignities are being perpetuated than ever before. These are not the high schools of the good old days. . . ."

If that sounds familiar, there is good reason for it. Twenty-five hundred years ago, Socrates said, "Children now love luxury. They have bad manners and contempt for authority. They show disrespect for their elders and love chatter in the place of exercise. Children are not tyrants, not the servants of their households." Not much difference between a committee of New York City high school principals and Socrates, is there?

The late Professor Earl Kelley, a sensitive, wise psychologist and educator, once observed that the complaint about today's youths going to the dogs is a wail recorded in the literature going back almost as far as the written language goes. He went on to note:

> In Boston in 1850, it took sixty-five beatings a day to keep a school of four hundred going. About 1875, an uncle of mine decided on teaching as a career and started with a country one-room school. His professional career ended when the pupils tipped the outhouse over, door down, with him in it. I never heard how he got out, but by the time I knew he was an aging farmer.[7]

In one way or another, problems related to recalcitrant youths and classroom discipline have always been with us, and there is no reason to believe that these problems will suddenly disappear in the future. Indeed, there are at least five factors that practically guarantee the existence of ongoing management problems, and it may help us minimize these problems if we understand how they start in the first place.

FIVE FACTORS THAT INFLUENCE CLASSROOM BEHAVIOR

A healthy approach to discipline is one that is more comprehensive than merely maintaining order in the classroom. It is more comprehensive because it includes considerations that also involve personal, social, and environmental factors that influence a student's behavior. The five factors that we'll consider briefly in the pages to follow include: (1) situational and environmental factors, (2) teacher-related factors, (3) academic and curriculum factors, (4) students' personality and growth factors, and (5) group factors.

Situational and Environmental Factors

Social-class conflicts, irresponsible parents, and bad family conditions are among those obvious influences that trigger emotional problems that may be reflected in classroom misbehavior. These are conditions that are external to the immediate school situation and that, unfortunately, the school cannot directly change. There are, however, at least three conditions that are more intrinsic to the school itself and that, as research shows, can have a powerful influence on school behavior.

Size of the school system is an important consideration. Size of the school system is one of those important intrinsic conditions. For example, research indicates that the typical teacher in a large school system copes with almost twice as many severe behavior problems as a teacher in a small or medium size school system.[8] The frustrations of crowded living conditions, racial conflicts, heterogeneity of class membership, and limited dollar resources for upgrading the instructional program are all factors that have been identified by sociologists as affecting the behavior of students in large city schools.

Class size and composition can affect behavior. Class size and composition is another situational condition influencing classroom behavior. Research data clearly shows that as the size of the class increases, discipline problems multiply.[9] Group interaction research indicates that as a group grows larger it becomes less able to satisfy the demands of all its members for recognition, affection, and social interaction. This in turn makes it necessary for the teacher to impose more rigid controls, while at the same time reducing the opportunities for responding positively to any one student.[10]

Administration and school organization are strong forces. Administration and school organization is a third situational factor affecting the behavior of students. For example, if the school administration and parents stress the importance of routine, order, and quiet, and rate teachers in terms of how well these objectives are achieved, then many teachers, for the sake of their own survival, may feel forced to bypass psychologically healthier methods of student management and use more punitive and coercive techniques to maintain control. The net effect of this approach is twofold: (1) it drains a teacher's emotional energy, and (2) students start behaving in counter-aggressive and impulsive ways.[11]

Teacher-Related Factors

Classroom misbehavior is sometimes the consequence of a teacher's personality characteristics and manner of relating to students. Some teachers, for example, are so rigidly locked in to doing things a certain way that they unwittingly establish a climate for misbehavior by establishing rules that violate the conditions of growth. They may insist upon total subservience to authority, long periods of enforced concentration, and other patterns of behavior inconsistent with the natural exuberance and energy level of growing children. When restrictive requirements exceed the limits of a youngster's tolerance, they may trigger reactions that are more a rebellion against unreasonable constraints rather than an expression of personal problems unrelated to school.

695

TO THINK ABOUT

Reflect back over the teachers you've had over the years. Were there any particular kinds or "types" you had more trouble with (or who gave you more trouble) than others? IF so, what was it about the teacher or you, or the two of you in combination, that seemed to be at the root of the problem? What are the implications here for your own teaching behavior?

_____

_____

_____

_____

Lack of experience and a generation gap may cause problems. A teacher's capacity to tolerate or accept or handle misbehavior is influenced by a number of personal factors, which may be interesting for you to know about. For instance, it has been found that teachers who are in good physical health seem to be better able to cope with misbehavior than those who are in poor health. In addition, it has been noted that teachers under twenty-five and over sixty years of age seem to have the most difficulty with discipline problems.[12] Lack of experience is very often associated with the disciplinary problems of younger teachers, while with older teachers it seems to have more to do with greater rigidity and loss of touch with the values and behavior standards of the younger generation. Although it doesn't have to be this way, it does seem to be true that once a teacher reaches his fifties or so he may have to make a special effort not to allow his memories of the "way things used to be" to cloud his perceptions of how young people change from generation to generation.

Too much emphasis on control and punishment is detrimental. Research also shows that some teachers' insistence on control and order in their classes occur at the sacrifice of qualities of personal warmth. In one investigation, for example, observers sat in on the classes of 118 teachers and wrote down the first remark these teachers made at the start of each minute of a 25 minute period.[13] Altogether there were 4 observation periods, and a total of 100 statements was collected for each teacher. These statements were then rated by other researchers in terms of whether they indicated a concern with achievement, control, management, or affiliation. The ratings

TABLE 15–1. *Classroom Behaviors That Tend to Be Related to Certain Teacher Types*

Type of Teacher			
A	B	C	D
Cold and controlling (as contrasted with warm and permissive)	Vigorous and dynamic (as contrasted with dull and quiet)	Insecure and anxious (as contrasted with confident)	Much academic activity (as contrasted with little academic emphasis)
Type of Classroom Behavior Associated with Each Teacher			
Activities very orderly Much direct control Delegates little authority to students Low affiliation motivation Frequently punishes Aloof Harsh Inflexible Hostile Dull Much evidence of emotional frustration Negativistic Neuroticism	Stimulating Excitable Gives support Vigorous Functions often as a source of knowledge. Very verbal	Uncertain Disorganized Much evidence of emotional frustration Dull Excitable Frequently punishes Negativistic	Systematic Much direct control Emphasized learning Functions often as a source of knowledge High achievement motivation

(From N. E. Wallen et al. "Relationships Between Teacher Needs and Teacher Behavior in the Classroom." *Journal of Educational Psychology* 54(1963):23–32. Copyright 1963 by the American Psychological Association. Reprinted by permission.)

were in turn related to other measures of teacher behavior, including the general impression teachers made on observers. The results of this study are shown in Table 15–1.

Note that the teachers who were perceived as cold and controlling tended to behave toward students in ways that were perceived as punitive and rigid. Their classes were dull and monotonous, and there appeared to be little concern for students' academic achievement. This does not mean that a concern about control is a negative quality, but it does raise the issue about how control is used. Notice that Teacher A maintains order more or less for its own sake, or because he finds disorder personally upsetting. Teacher B, on the other hand, uses control procedures to support a systematic program of classroom learning. The insecure and anxious teacher exercises rather little direct control and punishes often (probably out of frustration), whereas the vigorous and dynamic teacher controls less by threat and punishment and more by the intrinsic holding power of an interesting class and stimulating presentations.

However we look at it, teacher-related factors play a significant part in the sort of discipline problems that occur in a classroom. Wise teachers realize this and make a point of being as aware of themselves as possible in order to minimize the possibility of being the instigator of unnecessary problems. As one teacher expressed it, "It's difficult to cure a problem if you've caused it in the first place."

Academic and Curriculum Factors

Many discipline problems may be traced to an academic curriculum that imposes learning tasks that are unchallenging, unstimulating, and unrelated to students' needs. When coupled with an educational organization that literally forces youngsters to achieve at a certain level before they are either physically or psychologically prepared to do so is an open invitation for the development of discipline problems.

Compulsory education laws that keep youngsters in the classroom many years after they have reached the limit of either their academic educability or interest have created some unhappy problems for teachers. Without judging the merits of compulsory attendance laws, it is evident that we need to acknowledge the futility of trying to cram additional academic learning of the traditional kind into youngsters, who are either unwilling or unable to learn, and instead teach them skills that will contribute to their usefulness as citizens in everyday life.

These observations are not meant to imply that all teachers should be indicted for bad teaching or that all schools are insensitive to the needs of the youths. The fact is that many children and adolescents pursue school-related activities with eagerness and enthusiasm, and many teachers are challenging and stimulating individuals. Yet we cannot deny that significant numbers of children experience feelings of repeated frustration and failure (remember, over one million youngsters drop out of school each year[14]), which generalize into negative attitudes toward the school and are acted out in classroom misbehavior.

Students' Personality and Growth Factors

Even when the curriculum offerings are suitable and varied, the teachers skillful artists, and the administrative organization satisfactory, there will be classroom disciplinary problems because of certain personality and growth characteristics of students. We know, for example, that a youngster's physical condition may be responsible for his misbehavior in school. Lack of sleep, a poor diet, parent conflicts, or an incipient illness may make a child nervous, irritable, unable to concentrate, or difficult to manage in a classroom.

Problem behavior and normal growth consequences sometimes confused. We would do well to keep in mind that there are some aspects of perfectly normal behavior that can lead to problems of control and management if they are not properly understood. Take, for example, the following account of behavior commonly observed among preadolescent youngsters:

> With the onset of puberty there is an increasing tendency to withdraw from the parents, to exaggerate friendship with peers, and to idealize adults other than parents. Affective restraint and personal habits that had been acquired and maintained for the parents' sake begin to deteriorate. Unaccountable giggling, laughing, and crying fits, and unexpected coarseness in behavior contrast sharply with the composure of latency.[15]

Sometimes teachers overreact to youngsters who behave this way, forgetting that the behavior may be motivated more by the natural consequences of growth than by angry feelings toward either the teacher or school. What we have to do is learn how to temper control with flexibility, and we have to remember that not all misbehavior is abnormal but merely symptomatic of a particular growth period. There are many times when youngsters have difficult growing experiences that may be reflected as an inability to sit still, lack of attention, irritability, or other reactions that can be annoying. The solution to problems created by growth is not to be found through an attack upon behavior but, rather, through a better understanding of the psychological growth pains that a youngster is experiencing.

Fritz Redl, a clinical psychologist with over forty years experience with problem children, has made the point that teachers and youth workers create unnecessary problems for themselves because they fail to understand that much of the so-called "defiant" behavior of children and adolescents is both appropriate and normal. There is what Redl calls "developmental defiance," which, rather than being in any sense abnormal, is a youngster's healthy inclination to defend his own integrity against the wrong demands made by others. In Redl's words:

> We want Johnny to be respectful to his teacher but we don't want him to run after the first designing bum that offers him candy just because the man is an adult and looks like a mixture of Abe Lincoln and Santa Claus. On the contrary, we want our children to retain the capacity for *intelligent rebellion* — courage to stick to what they believe in even against strong-armed pressure and the fear of becoming unpopular with the mob.[16]

Actually, a lot of behavior usually termed *defiance* is exactly the opposite. The fifteen year old who participates in smashing the school's windows because he is afraid of being called a sissy is not a *defiant* youngster. He's a coward, an overconformist, a frightened adolescent with no convictions of his own. The fact that he is a sucker for the wrong sort of acclaim does not change the fact that submission rather than defiance is the problem at hand.

Not all "defiant" behavior means the same thing. From a clinical point of view, then, we have to look deeper than surface behavior to know what the problems really are in any specific "defiant act." Where behavior falls into the category of "developmental defiance," we are presented with an educational challenge, and we must be cautious not to be lulled into too hastily diagnosing it "delinquent" or "abnormal."

Then there is what can be termed *reactive defiance*. If you pour a foul-tasting substance down someone's throat, his organism will likely rebel by choking sensations to ward off the unpleasant intrusion. Vomiting under such conditions is not symptomatic of illness but, rather, a healthy defense against hurt from the outside.

A lot of youthful "defiant" behavior falls into the same category. That is, rather than being the outgrowth of a corrupt personality, it is more a defense used by a healthy person against the kind of treatment that shouldn't happen to a snake, but often it does happen to school age youths. For example, in a classroom of normal students bored out of their heads by inane teaching methods, the intelligent ones will be the first to become "hard to handle." Their misbehavior is a defense against the devitalizing impact of excessive boredom. If a child with deep-rooted fear of adult violence (perhaps he sees so much of it at home) gets hit by a teacher, the resulting outburst will not be the consequence of a "warped personality" but his frantic defense against the possibility of being overwhelmed by a frightening adult. This sort of "reactive defiance" calls for a consideration of not only what is wrong with the youngster, but also of what is wrong with what we're doing to him.

To be sure, there are many occasions when a student misbehaves that he is, in fact, disturbed or sick or delinquent and what he needs are strict, firm controls or an immediate referral to the school system's mental health personnel. To know the difference between normal reactiveness and abnormal coping, we must first of all be empathic, sensitive observers of child-adolescent behavior, thoroughly grounded in the basic dynamics of each growth stage. We must also recognize that a classroom group can influence behavior, an idea to which we now turn.

Group Factors

There is little doubt that individual behavior is influenced by the complex, shifting tides of interpersonal relations within the classroom group. Inasmuch as group forces may make a student a bully or a scapegoat, a leader or an isolate, the effects of group climate and the psychological forces operating within a group are matters that have specific implications for the management of child behavior.

Dynamics of group contagion. As discussed in greater detail in Chapter 14, a group develops distinctive attitudes and patterns of behavior that make its members act as a collective unit. This force is so strong that individuals tend to bow to majority opinion, even when the majority is wrong. This is an important insight into group life because it means that a teacher must be skillful in handling a group's behavior if he hopes to control the behavior of particular individuals within it. The idea behind this insight is that group contagion, or the spread of behavior through a group, can radically alter the behavior of individual group members. We have all seen how the behavior of normally restrained individuals can change dramatically at, say, a football game or pep rally or even an out-of-town convention. Redl[17] has referred to this phenomenon as a form of group psychological intoxication. It is the sort of group contagion that can cause a group of students to lose their sense of proportion, move them to enthusiasm or hostility, spread unrest or irritation through a group, or weld them solidly together for a joint purpose.

Three reasons why individuals behave differently in groups. Why should an individual in a group behave in a more brazen, risk-taking way than he might if he was not either a group member or subjected to group pressures? There are at least three reasons for this. One has to do with the sort of peer pressure that individuals within a group begin to feel from others to behave as they do. If you have ever tried to study while four or five of your friends pestered you to join them at the local pub or go to a movie with them, you have a good idea of how peer pressure can work and how easy it is to submit to it. A second reason is related to the fact that there is a certain safety in numbers—or at least it appears that way to group members. When a fourth-grade boy, kept after school because he had zapped another boy in the eye with a paper wad, was asked why he was shooting paper wads in the first place, he replied, "Well, everyone else was." Somehow in his mind, the fact that "everyone else was" made it safe (or safer) for him to go ahead and do it, too. A third reason why an individual in a group behaves differently than he might outside the group has to do with the anonymity and camouflage a group offers. That is, not only can one conclude that "everybody else is doing it" (the safety aspect), but since everyone is doing it, no one will really see me while I do it. You may, for example, feel very comfortable dancing on a crowded dance floor, but very conspicuous and uncomfortable if suddenly everyone sat down and you and your partner were left alone.

Student participation in rule making is important. Thus, because of the inevitable peer pressures, the safety in numbers, and the anonimity of group camouflage, you can predictably expect groups of students (or groups of any sort, for that matter) will generally take higher social risks and will be more difficult to control. The risk of losing control can, however, be reduced by sharing authority for decision making with the class so that students have opportunities for setting their own standards of behavior and rules of conduct. It is more difficult to break a rule or violate a code of conduct that you have had a part in making. It then becomes a matter of conscience. I saw this nicely illustrated during an elementary school fire drill. While a vast majority of the children were running around once they were outside and generally raising all sorts of havoc, one class of fourth graders remained quietly together as a total group waiting for the all-clear bell. I asked the teacher how she managed to keep twenty-nine healthy and potentially vigorous nine year olds so restrained and she replied, "It wasn't anything I did directly. We spent one whole morning talking about some rules for *appropriate* (note that she did not say "good" or "bad") behavior, and we came up with what we call our 'ten rules for appropriate conduct.' One of those rules is that we stay together during fire drills. All the children agreed to it and it is as simple as that." A major advantage in having all the students participate in setting up the regulations of a classroom is that it helps each of them to feel more personally responsible not for only their own behavior, but the behavior of others as well.

TO DO

A project well worth your time would be to interview four or five teachers at both elementary and high school levels to get some first-hand ideas about their views regarding student participation in rule making. Not all teachers buy this as a worthwhile activity, but many do. Find out for yourself why some teachers reject the idea and why others accept it. Which direction do you lean in? Why?

The sharing of authority with students is typically a hot issue at the secondary school level. Teachers and administrators acting unilaterally to establish arbitrarily and contradictory regulations without involving students in the decision-making machinery deserve all the trouble this invariably brings. Hair length, skirt length, holding hands in the halls, chewing gum, etc., are issues about which there are deep feelings, particularly when students consider demands for conformity in these matters as violations of their individual rights. Both experience and research indicate that there is practically no issue that cannot be discussed and agreement reached about what is reasonable and acceptable behavior.[18,19] Although it is admittedly difficult, time-consuming, and cumbersome, open discussion and a bit of give and take on both sides is probably one of the best ways to reduce the destructive effects of negative group contagion. A high school sophomore expressed the issue nicely when he observed:

Students shouldn't be forced to conform to dress standards and then told not to follow the pack, to be an individual. Forced conformity to anything, save essential laws, is backward and actually does more to hinder the growth process than aid its forward progress. Such forced participation only breeds resentment and rebellion, whereas by the use of simple discussion and logic I really gained understanding and learned what is best for myself. Shouldn't high schools teach and allow understanding rather than today's forced conformity in all aspects of the curriculum?[20]

DIAGNOSTIC THINKING AS A METHOD FOR SOLVING CLASSROOM PROBLEMS

It may seem to you by now that the interaction patterns and disciplinary problems involved in the everyday operation of a normal classroom are so complex that the sanity of even the most balanced teacher is taxed to the limit. Actually, a teacher's life is not so harried as it may seem, although there are surely times in every teacher's life when he or she wonders whether it is all worth it. Discipline problems can be a burden, but they can usually be constructively dealt with by using an approach that Redl and Wattenberg[21] have called *diagnostic thinking*.

What this has reference to is a general problem-solving attitude that prepares one for "sizing up a situation" and then experimenting with various measures to cope with it. Although no one solution can help a teacher solve all the highly specific situations that can arise, it is possible to outline general approaches within a diagnostic thinking framework that can be used to handle difficult management problems; with practice, this sort of approach can become second nature.

A Classroom Incident: Diagnostic Thinking in Action

In order to better understand the processes involved in the diagnostic thinking approach, let's take a look at an incident that occurs in an ordinary classroom setting and how the teacher handles it.

As her fourth-grade class worked in their spelling workbooks, Ms. Rinehart noticed that Billy was looking very anxious and worried and making no effort at all to get into his workbook. He was a quiet, frail boy but well liked by the others. Her first thought was that he couldn't do the assignment. She asked him if that was the case, but he said that it wasn't. She then wondered whether he was feeling sick. He answered that he was feeling fine and sounded as though he really meant it. During this exchange, Ms. Rinehart noted that Billy kept glancing at Sam, who had been watching this exchange with a scowl on his face. When Ms. Rinehart looked around the class, Sam began working in his spelling book with what seemed to be uncommon vigor and enthusiasm.

703

Her hunch was that there had been something going on between the two boys, but, recognizing the juvenile code against tattling, she kept the hunch to herself. However, she did want more information, and so pressed Billy to tell her what was wrong. As she did so, she sensed that the rest of the class was more quiet than it usually was. She suspected that the rest of the students knew something. Billy finally relented and allowed that he had lost his arithmetic homework assignment, which was due during the arithmetic period after lunch. Ms. Rinehart was sure that Sam had something to do with the assignment being lost, but she couldn't be certain.

Alternative solutions to a complex problem—what to do? Her conclusions felt right to her, but the question was: What should she do? Tell Billy to forget about it? That wouldn't do because the very fact that he was so upset suggested that he couldn't easily forget it. Give him time to do the assignment over? It didn't seem fair that he should have to do it over again, and, besides, the issue seemed more deeply related to *how* it was lost, as opposed to it being a simple matter of accidentally losing something. Should she force him to tell the whole story? That wouldn't be a good idea because she felt it would turn the class against Billy and give Sam social reinforcement outside of school. Browbeat Sam or some other youngster into telling the truth? They may still blame Billy. She decided she had to show that Billy was not a ratfink tattletale and yet let Sam discover that the actions she suspected had social consequences. She recognized that Sam was average for the class and was using his greater size to feel powerful by bullying other students but that was a problem that could be handled later. A vivid lesson now might make him more ready to accept her intervention later, especially if she did not confront him directly.

> **TO DO**
>
> Before reading any further, what would you do if in Ms. Rinehart's shoes?

All of these possibilities for action flashed through her mind as she was talking to Billy. She decided to take a chance on one of the possibilities that occurred to her. What she did was to tell the class that Bill had lost his completed arithmetic assignment and then she good naturedly admonished him to be more careful in the future. She then said she had to go to the office and asked the class to see if they could help Billy find his missing homework while she was gone. To make the request a bit more striking, she dwelt a little on how frustrating it feels to complete a homework assignment only to lose it before it's handed in.

As she hoped, no sooner was the door closed behind her than there was a noisy chattering. Although she couldn't be sure, she thought she heard several loud voices saying, "Come on, Sam, give it back to him." At any rate, when she returned after ten minutes or so the class was quiet. Billy had "found" his completed arithmetic assignment, and Sam was busily working in his spelling book. All she said was, "You found your paper, Billy? That's good. I'm sure you must be pleased."

Five Steps Involved in Diagnostic Thinking

In this simple classroom incident, Ms. Rinehart illustrated five steps usually involved in diagnostic thinking. Essentially, it is the same sort of thinking a lawyer, physician, auto mechanic, or plumber might use to define and locate the problem and then work out an appropriate action plan for taking care of it. Redl and Wattenburg have identified five basic components of diagnostic thinking, which, in somewhat modified form, include: (1) listening to the first hunch; (2) looking for hidden factors; (3) using behavior as a guide to action; (4) testing the hunches by action; and (5) trying new approaches when original ones fail. Let's briefly examine each of these.

Listen to your first hunch. In the face of any new problem situation, we almost invariably form a hunch as to what it means and what we should do to solve it. These are not carefully thought through and reasoned hunches, but more on the order of an unconscious reflex as to what the problem is all about based on our past experiences. Ms. Rinehart, for example, had no doubt seen many students look anxious and worried when they couldn't do an assignment and so her first hunch had to do with the possibility that Billy couldn't handle the classwork.

It makes no difference whether this first hunch is correct or not. What is important is that it is an essential first step to working out a solution. It helps focus observations and reduces aimless thinking. In the best sense of the word, first hunches can be used to act out an empathic response to a troublesome situation. When Ms. Rinehart, for instance, asked Billy if he was having trouble with the assignment or feeling sick, it was as much a response to how he was feeling as it was a search for a solution. Sometimes just hearing the teacher ask if anything is wrong or if there's something she can do has a certain calming effect for a student. Note, too, that Ms. Rinehart had to drop her first two guesses before she hit upon a promising lead. A first hunch is a point of departure, not a final destination.

Look for hidden factors. Here we use our information concerning psychological dynamics by bringing to bear the facts we already know with those we can gather by observation. One of the hidden factors Ms. Rinehart paid attention to was the natural aversion most children have to tattling. Other hidden factors that she took into account included the idea that Billy was liked by most of the class members (which meant she could probably count on them to not be destructive if she left the problem, as she did, for the group to solve), and the fact that Sam was giving Billy harsh scowls.

As another illustration, I recall an incident involving a sixteen-year-old high school girl who complained to her teacher that Tom, one of the more aggressive and troublesome boys in class, was always trying to "feel her up" as she changed classes during the course of a day. An obvious first hunch would be that this was just another incident of Tom's troublesome nature and low impulse control. A deeper investigation into the matter found that that wasn't entirely the case. He had been trying to "feel her up," as she put it, but what the girl failed to mention is that she deliberately taunted not only Tom, but other boys as well with her seductive miniskirts and tight-fitting blouses or T-shirts. In addition, she would say suggestive things such as, "You can look, but I dare you to touch." As you can see, we're dealing with a somewhat different situation than was at first suspected. Tom was as much a victim as an aggressor, and the solution involved helping the girl to better understand her seductive inclinations as well as helping Tom to control his impulses.

Use behavior as a guide to action. Even when we cannot see the cause of behavior, we can still see some meaning in it. Consider a few illustrations. During the course of a discussion in an eighth-grade social studies class about the importance of the family unit and some different styles of parent-child relationships, a girl in the back of the room began crying very softly to herself. A brief while later, a boy walked to the door with quick, tense strides, and slammed the door as he left. Now we cannot know on the basis of so few facts the cause of the crying or the slammed door, but we can see a clear *meaning* — the girl is upset or sad, and the boy is angry or disturbed. Whatever caused the girl to cry or the boy to walk out the way he did may not be known for a time. To know whether softly crying "meant" that the girl was upset or sad, or that the boy was angry or disturbed, or what not, would be important first clues to look for, and the answer can sometimes be read directly from the "language of behavior" and the events that led up to the behavior.

Although an entire understanding of causation is not known, it is possible to take a first step on the basis of our interpretation of the meaning of the conduct. In the incident just described, the teacher simply reflected to each of the students involved what she saw the behavior meaning. Rather than saying to the girl, "You shouldn't feel this way" or "You must learn to control yourself," the teacher simply said, "Sally, you looked very unhappy in class today." Sally admitted that she did and was able to relate some of the sad feelings she was experiencing as the class was talking about family togetherness. The tears, as the teacher soon discovered, were very real, reflecting as they did Sally's hurt about her parents' ensuing divorce.

The teacher handled Bob, the boy who slammed out of the room, in much the same way. Rather than make a big deal about Bob's dramatic exit by saying things like, "You know better than to leave your seat," or "I really thought you were pretty childish," the teacher simply reflected what Bob's behavior seemed to mean,"Bob, you appeared very angry or upset in class." As it turned out, Bob was angry and he was specifically angry at the way he thought the teacher was sticking up for the parents' side of things without giving due consideration to the children. Significant to this incident is the fact that Bob had just that morning gotten into a hassle with his mother about how long he could stay out weekend nights. It hadn't been resolved by the time he left for school and much of the anger he felt toward the teacher really belonged to his mother. It was simply redirected at the teacher). (This goes back to the concept of "transference" discussed in Chapter 7.)

By responding to the behavior and what it may have meant, the teacher avoided making a messy situation messier, while at the same time allowing an angry student to vent his feelings.

Test hunches by action. As soon as we feel reasonably confident in our hunches, we should act on them. What we have to keep in mind is that such action is regarded as a test of the accuracy of our hunches, rather than as a course of behavior to which we are irrevocably committed.

Indeed, when a hypothesis is actually tested, it is sometimes found that it is wrong or incomplete. For instance, Richard, a boy with a very fine high school record, began not only misbehaving and acting up in his chemistry class, but was also late handing in his assignments and slow in finishing his lab work. The teacher first suspected that Richard's behavior was related to not understanding some basic concepts very well. Since the teacher's first hunch about lack of knowledge didn't fit, he reasoned that something of a more emotional sort may have been awry. With this hunch in mind, he asked Richard to stay after class for awhile one day. The teacher approached the problem directly and simply asked Richard why his chemistry work seemed so inconsistent with his high achievement in all other classes. As they talked, it became apparent there was, indeed, an emotional base to the problem—one that was directly linked to his M.D. father wanting Richard to be a doctor, too. Richard was resisting this idea (he wanted to be a lawyer), and one expression of this resistance was poor work in chemistry, which he knew was an important course to do well in to be accepted into a pre-med program. Richard ended up talking his problem through with one of the high school counselors and in the process discovered that there were more constructive ways for resisting his father than flunking chemistry.

Try new approaches when old ones fail. Richard's chemistry teacher is a good example of the basic principle here. In the process of action testing his hunch, the teacher found that he had to give up his initial hypothesis about Richard not understanding the material and develop a new one related to the possibility of an emotional problem. An essential characteristic of diagnostic thinking is that it is flexible. Our hunches are revised, not only in terms of what happens as a result of action—testing them—but also by new developments in the individual or the group.

For instance, in a tenth-grade class, we might have a boy who seemed to enjoy disrupting the class by constantly getting in arguments with one teacher or other class members over the most trivial issues. A friendship sociogram may show that the boy was an isolate. We might also know that his father was an overbearing businessman in town who had a reputation for bulldozing his employees and making a lot of enemies. One diagnosis, based on these facts, could be that the boy identified with his father and was also being excluded and rejected by his classmates and that his trouble-some argumentativeness was both a cause and effect of the total situation. We would, therefore, do what we could to help him to be more accepted by his peers. Let's assume that even though we were reasonably successful, he continued to antagonize his teacher but not his classmates. Our diagnosis, then, would change to fit these new circumstances. Quite possibly, the boy was making a better peer-level adjustment, but he was now taking the lead in the adolescent's ongoing struggle against adult authority figures, as represented by the teacher.

One final note of advice: Remember that an individual or a group, if given the opportunity, will often work out problems without interference.[22] For many persons, trouble, like pain, is a signal that something is wrong and for them to bring their own resources in to play. The wise teacher doesn't rush in when trouble occurs, but he or she takes time to first size up the situation and then intervene only if necessary. Ms. Rinehart, for example, wisely recognized that she could count on the class—or at least had enough faith to be able to *take the risk* of counting on the class—to settle the immediate problem of getting Sam to return the arithmetic assignment.

So far we've looked at what we might call a "cognitive framework" for thinking about how to handle classroom problems. Let's turn now to some specific strategies for handling problems when they occur.

STRATEGIES FOR HANDLING WOULD-BE AND ACTUAL DISCIPLINE PROBLEMS

No matter how skilled a teacher is in relating to students and conducting a class and no matter how "normal" a class may be, there will always be those moments when either an individual student or the whole class needs to be taken in tow. Before examining some practical intervention strategies, the question of *when* a teacher should intervene needs to be considered. This is an important question because school psychologists have observed that many teachers fail to set limits or intervene until they are so frustrated, angry, and choked with counter-aggressive feelings that they can't discipline in any constructive way. Long and Newman[23] have discussed seven criteria, which, in somewhat modified form, we'll examine here as guidelines to help determine when some form of disciplinary intervention is necessary.

When Are Disciplinary Measures Necessary?

1. *When there are reality dangers:* If Steve gets bonked on the head by another student or Joe tries to set fire to the rubbish basket, then these are obvious reality threats that must be curbed at once.

2. *When someone needs psychological protection:* Just as we want to protect students from physical hurt, so, too, do we want to protect them from psychological injury. A student being scapegoated or called racial names or whatever is as much in need of protection as the one who gets hit in the mouth by the class bully.

3. *When there is too much excitement:* Sometimes a teacher has to intervene in order to avoid the development of too much excitement, anxiety, and guilt in students, particularly younger ones. For example, if a game is getting out of hand and goes on for another five minutes, the children may begin to lose control, run wild, and maybe even hurt someone. It is the teacher's responsibility to stop this before it happens.

4. *When an ongoing program is threatened:* Once a class is involved in a particular task and the students have an investment in its outcome, it is not fair to have it ruined by one or two students, who for any number of reasons, want to act up. In this instance, the teacher intervenes and asks the student or students involved to change seats or sit next to him or whatever seems appropriate to insure program continuity.

5. *When there is the possibility of negative contagion:* This is related to point 4 above and refers to the disruptive behavior of one student spreading to the rest of the class. For example, when a teacher is aware that tension is mounting in the classroom and a child with high social power begins to lightly kick the legs of his desk, the teacher might ask him to stop in order to prevent this behavior from spreading to other students and disrupting the entire class.

6. *When there is the possibility of conflict with the outside world:* The outside world can mean the classroom next door or the public. It is certainly justifiable, indeed necessary, to expect that students have more control over themselves while at an assembly or on a tour of an art museum than when they are in their own classrooms.

7. *When a teacher's mental health needs protection:* This point isn't made too often, but teachers, after all, are only human. Although it is true

Unless there's the risk of someone getting really hurt, it's sometimes wise to let students work out their own problems. (Darry Dusbiber)

that he had better have a fairly high frustration level to begin with if he wants to be a successful teacher, it is also true that every person has his limits. And sometimes a teacher has to say, "Stop that" because his own upper limit has been reached.

The seven points listed above are guidelines, not mandates for action. There are, however, at least three counter indications *against* interfering. One is that it may seem to the teacher that the fuss created by the intervention is not worth it. The group confusion that usually follows might disguise the real purpose of the intervention, in which case it would be better to wait for another time. A second counter indication may be that the teacher feels that it would be wiser to wait until the misbehavior deviates to the point where it is obvious not only to the student, but to the entire group. This is one way of neutralizing the usual defenses, such as projection, i.e., "You're always picking on me," or denial, i.e., "I didn't do it." A third counter indication may be that the teacher is in too good a mood to work up enough concern to impress the student and/or the group with the seriousness of the student's behavior.

Coping Techniques Teachers Can Use

Now then, let us turn to a discussion of eleven rather specific techniques a teacher can use either to prevent or to handle disciplinary matters, depending on what the problem may be. The first ten have been discussed and elaborated in greater detail by Redl and Wineman[24] and Redl and Wattenberg[25] and, in somewhat modified form here, include: (1) deliberate ignoring, (2) signal intervention, (3) proximity control, (4) interest boosting, (5) decontamination through humor, (6) hurdle assistance, (7) program restructuring, (8) support through routine, (9) nonpunitive exile, (10) physical restraint, and (11) behavior-modification approaches, which are among the newer techniques being tried by some schools.

Deliberately ignore the misbehavior—to a point. It frequently happens that a student's misbehavior is energized by a limited power source, which is soon exhausted if not replenished. This is especially apt to be true if the misbehavior is designed to get the teacher's goat and get the student some attention. According to one teacher:

> One technique that I've found often works is to simply ignore disruptive behavior. I've learned, for instance that when Charles starts dropping his books or tapping his pencil that I'd better get over there and help him. If I confront him with his behavior, he argues and this causes more problems. If I ignore the behavior and pay attention to what may be frustrating him, I seem to have far more success.

Of course a teacher can only ignore overt misbehavior to the extent that it doesn't spread to others, but there are times when there can be a very rewarding payoff if the teacher responds to the assumed motivation behind a student's misbehavior rather than to its manifestations.

Intervene with nonverbal signals. The idea here is for the teacher to develop a repertoire of signals that communicate to the offending student(s) a message of disapproval and control. These can include any number of nonverbal cues ranging all the way from eye contact, to shaking one's finger at those involved, to a cough or a throat-clearing sound, to facial frowns, and on and on. Cues of this sort are usually most effective in misbehavior in the bud stage. As one high school student expressed it, "When Mr. Stanaway frowns at me, I *know* he means it. So I don't usually mess around after that."

Reduce the distance between the offender and you. As you may have learned from your own experience in school, it is difficult to continue acting up if you suddenly find the teacher standing right next to you. The idea here is for the teacher to reduce the physical distance between himself and the student who is beginning to misbehave until that student can control himself. An extension of this consists of a friendly, steadying touch, perhaps lightly on the shoulder or arm. This is not a restraining grab, but rather a reassuring hand, which says nonverbally, "Take it easy" or "Slow down" or "I'm here to help." For example, if a boy has been accidently poked by another student and is struggling with the possibility of poking him back, a friendly hand on the shoulder may help him win the battle.

The advantages of these three techniques, deliberate ignoring, signal intervention, and proximity control, are that they minimize the possibility of embarrassing or even identifying the student in the group. A teacher can use all these techniques while maintaining an ongoing classroom program.

Make an effort to rekindle lost interest. Frequently students will commence misbehaving because their classwork has simply become too boring. Rather than admonish the student for misconduct, it may be more helpful to communicate a genuine interest in the youngster's classroom assignment, as, for instance, asking John whether he is having trouble with problem number twelve or wondering with Sally whether she fully understands the directions. Sometimes all it takes is a concerned teacher to rekindle a student's withering flame of interest. A friendly "How are things going?" or "Is there anything I can do to help" can do wonders in helping some students to refocus their energies.

Use humor to defuse tension. We are all aware of how a humorous comment can penetrate a tense and anxiety producing situation. A skillful teacher usually has a healthy sense of humor, the sort that enables him to laugh not only at something truly funny, but also to laugh at himself. The appropriate use of humor can ease otherwise tense situations. Consider the example below, which shows how a wise teacher used this to her advantage.

> I walked into my room after lunch to find two ugly looking pictures on the blackboard, each with "teacher" written under them. The entire class was frozen to their seats wondering what I would do. Not a word was being said. I picked up a piece of chalk, walked over to one of the pictures and said that although it looked most like me, but the eyes were not quite right. So I erased the eyes and drew in two crossed eyes. Then I went to the next picture and commented that the nose was a bit small and so I drew in a hugh extension which looked more like a baseball bat than a breathing apparatus. By this time the class was almost choking in hysterics. For that matter, so was I.

This is a good example of the phenomenon called *group testing*. The pictures were put on the board to test the vulnerability of the teacher. Some teachers may have gotten defensive and reacted with anger. Other teachers may have punished the whole group by giving them more work. This teacher, however, demonstrated that she was secure, that she could not easily be driven to anger or become counter-aggressive, and that she could be counted on during stress.

Give functional assistance to perplexed students. Classroom misbehavior is not always the result of some deep inner problem. Sometimes a student acts up because he just cannot do the work, which is different than simply losing interest. Instead of asking for help and thereby running the risk of being accused of not paying attention or, worse, exposing his lack of savvy for all the class to see, he may start whispering, drawing on his desk, or in other ways diverting attention away from the assignment. The solution is to provide the student with the help he needs before the situation gets to this stage as was done by a ninth-grade teacher in the following example.

> Mark always had a lot of difficulty in math and he usually tried to stir up trouble whenever we began a new unit. I used to holler at him for this, but it never helped much. What I've learned is more effective is to make a point of briefly going over new material with Mark, before I presented the material to the class as a whole. It's remarkable to see how much this has helped. Most of all it seems to have helped Mark feel less frustrated because now, when we begin a new unit, he can understand it more readily.

Do things differently now and then. One problem that occurs now and then is a growing restlessness because the students have been sitting still for too long a period or doing the same thing for too long a time. We all tend to get restless when that happens. The other side of the coin is that the students get a bit wild, or overstimulated, or overexcited. Rather than concentrate attention on the restlessness, it may be better to change the nature of the activity or give the class a new focus of attention. This is a technique for dissolving an impending disturbance by redirecting activities in an entirely new direction. For example, if a review lesson becomes boring, a teacher could restructure it along the lines of a simulated quiz program. A listless, inattentive group of primary children may be brought to attention by the idea, "Let's pretend we're soldiers gathered together to get out instructions for the day." Another teacher, sensing that the students were being stifled by a muggy, hot day, gives the following illustration of how restructuring a class can help.

> I felt it would be useless to begin our English lesson as planned. So I asked all the children to lay their heads on their desks, and for one minute try to think of the coolest thing they could imagine in that time. Each student then shared with the class what he had been thinking. The whole procedure lasted only twelve minutes or so, and I felt it was time well spent. Given how hot it was, the English lesson went smoothly—certainly far better than if I had paid no attention to how the heat was affecting them.

Give support through routine—some students need it more than others. Although it varies from person to person, we all need a certain amount of order in our daily lives. Some students need much more than others before they can feel comfortable and secure. Some classrooms are so open-ended that they never know what is going to happen next, which is a source of much concern for the more anxious students. This is not to suggest that everything done in a classroom has to be reduced to a predictable schedule, but it is to suggest that it is helpful to most students to know about the overall organizational plan of the class. One boy summarized his anxious feelings by saying, "It's like one big surprise. Each hour you go to another teacher and each hour you don't know what's going to happen until it's too late." A daily schedule or program can greatly help these students and will go far in reducing their feelings of anxiety. They can then predict what is expected of them and prepare themselves for the next activity.

Use nonpunitive exile. It sometimes happens that a youngster may have to leave the room, not to be punished, but, rather, to regain control of himself. When a student's behavior reaches a point where the teacher questions whether the student is able to respond to verbal controls, it is usually the best course of action to ask him to leave the room for a few minutes — perhaps to wash his hands, get a drink, or deliver a message. This was done in the following situation:

> One afternoon during a study period I became aware of Maggie in the back of the room practically choking with the giggles over something. I tried signal intervention, but it only made her choke even more. Pretty soon all the kids around her were being contaged by the laughter and everybody, it seemed, was caught up in it. So, I quickly wrote to the secretary that Maggie had the giggles and asked that she keep her there waiting for a reply until she seemed under control. I then asked Maggie if she would mind delivering a message to the office and wait for an answer. Not only did she hastily agree, but looked rather relieved to leave the room. When she returned, she appeared to have herself pretty well controlled, and things went normally.

Physical restraint is sometimes necessary. Now and then an elementary age child so loses his head that he loses complete control and threatens to injure himself or others. In such emergencies there is no alternative but to physically restrain him. The intent is not to punish but to protect. It is important, therefore, that the youngster be held firmly but not roughly. Shaking, hitting, or spanking him at this time only makes it harder for a youngster to really believe that the teacher wants to help. Hurting a child, either physically or verbally, fans the flame of his anger and leads to even more intense aggression.

The preferred physical hold is for the adult to cross the child's arms around his sides while the adult stands behind him holding on to the child's wrists. Physically restraining a youngster is by no means an everyday happening, but when there is a need for it a teacher must move surely and with confidence. It is important to keep in mind that it can be a source of enormous comfort to a child to know that a teacher is both willing and able to help him control his angry impulses when he is unable to do it himself.

Use behavior-modification approaches — emphasize the positive. Behavior-modification techniques are an approach to classroom discipline that has been receiving a great deal of attention in recent years.[26-28] Essentially it is an approach that uses the basic principles of reinforcement or behavioristic theory. (You will recall that this point of view was developed more completely in Chapter 1.)

Specifically, behavior modification is strategy designed to provide systematic positive reinforcement for good behavior so that misbehavior is gradually eliminated by focusing the rewards on the good or desired behavior. The reinforcement can take almost any form, e.g., praise, tokens that can be redeemed for special privileges or prizes, or even money. Some schools, for instance, have an elaborate token system whereby the students accumulate "tokens for good behavior" throughout the day for those times that they behaved themselves and followed the rules. "Behaving oneself" can range all the way from being in your seat on time, being quiet during lunch period, lining up to wait for the bus, having your homework in on time, and so forth. In one system I am aware of, these tokens are then turned in at the end of the week and, depending on how many reward tokens a child has accumulated, converted into a pass to a school-shown movie, or candy, or a special library pass.

This may sound like a pretty mechanical system, but, like it or not, there is evidence to suggest that it works. One study, for example, found that the introduction of behavior-modification techniques resulted in increased study rates along with a concomitant reduction in classroom misbehavior. A temporary reversal during which the rewards were discontinued resulted in a return to the original symptoms. However, a return to the reward schedule once again increased study rates and decreased disruptive behavior.[29] Similar results have been reported in other studies.[30, 31]

As you may suspect, this system is not held in great favor by all teachers or psychologists. The major argument against it is that the emphasis is too little on behavior and the student's own inner controls and too much on the reward, which, it is feared, increases dependance on external controls rather than to encourage a student to greater inner or self-control.

TO THINK ABOUT

Behavior modification is a big thing these days. Sometimes an entire school will orient its disciplinary philosophy around a behavior modification frame of reference, which is, to get good behavior you

> reward good behavior at every opportunity. Some say it's too mechanical a way to control students' behavior—it's dehumanizing. Others say it works so use it. How do you feel about behavior modification as a means of controlling behavior? Would you use it? Why or why not?

Humanness need not be lost using behavior modification. Although an entire school may be organized around a behavior-modification system, this does not mean that a teacher has to turn into a dehumanized automaton who mechanically goes through a process of dispensing token buttons designed to change students' behavior in a more desirable way. Whether or not a teacher feels "mechanical" very likely depends less on the system or techniques he uses and more on his own inner feelings. A task-oriented, subject-centered teacher will probably remain that way no matter what his classroom management approaches happen to be. And the same is likely true for a more student-oriented, feeling-centered teacher.

Let's face it. Positive reinforcement, whether we call it *positive reward validation*, or *praise*, works. Research has shown that it produces positive results with practically any animal species you try it on, including rats, monkeys, dogs, porpoises—you name it (even pigeons), And it works with humans, too. As long as we don't get so wrapped up in reinforcement schedules that we lose sight of the person, and as long as we recognize that we must pay attention to his feelings in order to give his responses form and substance, the use of behavior-modification techniques can be still another tool in our repertoire for managing a classroom and helping students get the most out of their school experience as possible.

The eleven coping techniques we've just examined contain no instant magic. Each has its place and each can be effective depending on how well the teacher can communicate to the student that he cares and wants to help. Good communication is a key. How a teacher talks to students and the sorts of things he says can make a big difference in how that student behaves and feels about himself. Let's turn now to how that works.

Put-Down Messages That Cause Trouble

Each of us knows from personal experience what it feels like to be "put down" and psychologically reduced by a message that communicates blame, judgment, criticism, ridicule, or shame. Thomas Gordon,[32] a clinical psychologist, has suggested that "put-down" messages may fall into any one of four categories:

1. *Judging, Criticism, Blaming*
   "You're being very naughty."
   "You're the most inconsiderate student I've ever had."

"You ought to know better."

"You're being very thoughtless."

2. *Name-Calling, Ridiculing, Shaming*

"That's a dumb thing to do."

"You're a smart aleck, that's what you are."

"At the rate you've been going, you couldn't pass anything."

"Shame on you."

3. *Interpreting, Diagnosing, Psychoanalyzing*

"You're doing that to get attention."

"Your problem is that you're too big for your britches."

"I think what you need is a double dose of homework."

"You've probably been talking back to adults since infancy."

4. *Teaching, Instruction*

"Why don't you be good for a change?"

"It's not nice to interrupt while I'm talking."

"Good girls don't behave the way you do."

"Stop whining like a baby."

All these messages are put-downs—some subtle and others not so subtle. Each has the potential for impuning a student's character, depreciating him as a person, underscoring his inadequacies, and casting judgment on his personality. They are hardly designed to help a student feel nondefensive and open to change. What effects are these messages likely to produce in a child or adolescent?

1. *He can feel that the teacher is being unfair and unjust:* "He didn't give me a chance," or "I didn't do anything so wrong," or "I didn't mean to be so bad."

2. *He can feel guilty or remorseful:* "I'm always doing things wrong," or "Everyone blames me for everything."

3. *He can feel unliked, unwanted, and rejected:* "No one seems to like me." "Hell, why try—she won't appreciate it if I do good work anyway."

4. *He can feel very resistive, hostile, and defensive:* To change behavior that is bothersome to a teacher would be an admission of the validity of the teacher's blame or evaluation. A typical reaction might be: "Why pick on me—others are doing it, too," or "So what if I'm not doing my homework—I'm not bothering anyone."

All in all, put-down messages can have devastating effects on a youngster's developing self-image. The student who is bombarded with messages that depreciate him is encouraged to regard himself as bad, worthless, dumb, inadequate, unacceptable, and so on. Inasmuch as a negative self-image formed in childhood has a tendency to persist in the direction it started, put-down messages can sow the seeds for handicapping a person throughout his life. Troublesome students, particularly the chronically troublesome ones, are frequently among those who are unhappy and frustrated. Their misconduct is sometimes a gut reaction growing from being put down by too many adults too often. When we practice the fine art of being sensitive teachers and listen not only to *what* we say, but also are alert to the *impact* it has on students, we at least minimize the angry defensive feelings that stimulate misbehavior in the first place. How a teacher behaves and the sort of classroom procedures he or she uses *do* make a difference in either increasing or decreasing positive classroom behavior. Let's turn now to some examples of what we mean by that.

Teacher Behavior and Classroom Procedures That Make a Difference

Practices and procedures that tend to *increase negative* classroom behavior

1. *Negative statements by the teacher* — Here are a few examples of ridicule, sarcasm, criticism, negative, and tension producing statements made by a teacher. Such statements to students invariably lead to hostility, emotional disturbance, selfishness, fear and criticism of others:

   "I wish you would start acting like fourth graders instead of kindergarteners."

   "Someone is whispering again, and I guess you all know who it is."

   "Most sixth-grade classes could understand this, but I'm not sure about you."

   "Sit up straight. Don't you have a backbone."

   "Why don't you listen when I give directions? None of you seems to know how to listen."

2. *Excessively competitive situations* — Fair competition in classrooms is highly desirable. It can stimulate good work, motivate students to do their best

Practices and procedures that tend to *increase positive* classroom behavior

1. *Positive statements by the teacher* — Friendly, constructive statements by the teacher tend to reduce tension and hostility in the classroom. Here are a few examples:

   "We will all want to listen carefully in order not to miss anything Sue is going to tell us."

   "All of us did our work so well yesterday during our work period. Do you suppose we can do as well today?"

   "It is really fun for all of us when you bring such interesting things for sharing."

   "It's nice to have Dan and Greg back with us again. The boys and girls were hoping you would come back today."

2. *Successful cooperative enterprises* — The successful achievement of cooperative activities, involving all members of the class, tends to reduce hostility

Practices and procedures that tend to *increase negative* classroom behavior

Practices and procedures that tend to *increase positive* classroom behavior

and help them learn those graces associated with winning and losing. It becomes undesirable when it is of the "dog-eat-dog" variety where each child is pitted against every other child whether the competitive situation is fair or unfair.

within the group because it demands the combined efforts of everyone in the successful attainment of a common goal. Students depend upon one another in such situations and, therefore, feel a need for one another.

3. *Disregard for individual differences*—Classrooms where some students are made to feel "this place is not for me" contribute much toward breeding hostility in students. Such rooms are characterized by one level of acceptable performance applied to all, uniform assignments, one system of reward, great emphasis upon verbal, intellectual performance.

3. *Recognition of and adaptations made in accordance with individual differences*—In such classrooms, each student is challenged at a level commeasurate with his ability. Each feels that he "counts for something" in the classroom and that he belongs to it.

4. *Rigid schedule and pressure*—A rigid time schedule and constant pressure to "hurry," "finish your work," "you will be late," or stopping lessons exactly on time whether completed or not creates insecurity in students that leads to hostility. A class that is always "one jump behind the teacher" is likely to be one where pupils blame others for their failure to finish, invent excuses for themselves, and seek scapegoats.

4. *Relaxed comfortable pace*—Good teachers maintain a flexible schedule and will not place undue pressures on pupils. They will have a plan and a schedule, yet they know that life on earth and not the laws of the universe will change not at all if they deviate from their plan and schedule now and then in the interest of the need of the students they teach. Good teachers recognize that feelings of insecurity are related to hostility and will do everything they can do to develop feelings of security in the classroom on the part of the students they teach.

5. *Highly directive teaching practices*—Teachers who must make every decision themselves, give

5. *Student involvement in planning and managing the class*—Giving pupils some opportunity to plan

Practices and procedures that tend to *increase negative* classroom behavior

Practices and procedures that tend to *increase positive* classroom behavior

all the assignments, allow for very little participation on the part of students in the life of the classroom are encouraging feelings of hostility in their rooms. Such practices usually mean that teachers refer to the pupils as "my children" or in addressing the pupils, "I want you to . . . ," or more subtly, "Ms. So-and-So wasn't very proud of her class this morning."

and manage the affairs of the classroom does much to develop feelings of "we-ness," of identification with the group. Children under such circumstances are less inclined to want to think of ways to disrupt Ms. So-and-So's orderly room but will work hard to make *our* room a good place to work.

6. *Lack of closeness between teacher and pupils* — Some teachers feel they must "keep students in their place," meaning they must remain socially distant from them. This leads to a cold, objective relationship between the students and teacher, causing the students to feel that the teacher lacks affection and warmth. This "holier than thou" attitude on the part of the teacher is likely to endanger feelings of hostility in some students.

6. *Warm and friendly relationships between teacher and students* — One of the basic needs of students is that of love and affection. They need it in their homes, in their playgroups, and in school. The feeling that children do not respect the teacher if he is friendly with them is in error. They are likely to respect him more if they feel he is a "human being" capable of cordial and warm relationships with others. This is a mature relationship, however, not one of oversentimentalism and "gushiness." This does not mean that the teacher introduces himself to his class by saying, "My name is Mr. So-and-So, but my friends call me Skippy," as one beginning teacher did in introducing himself to a class of sixth graders.

7. *Lack of satisfying emotional experiences* — Some classrooms sorely lack experiences of an affective nature for students.

7. *Many opportunities for pleasurable emotional experiences* — Teachers can reduce tensions that build up in students

Everything is deadly serious business—work, work, work. Even the music, art, storytime, or dramatic activities are made to seem like work. Little time is spent on teaching students to enjoy one another, feel the inner joy that comes from a good poem or music selection, or express their feelings in some art medium.

during the course of classroom life by providing opportunities for release of such tensions through various emotional experiences. Students have the opportunity to express their feelings verbally, in writing or through art forms. They talk together, enjoy one another's company. They prepare skits, do creative dramatics, role-play situations to help get the feeling of the other fellow. All these tend to reduce feelings of hostility and discontentment in students.

POINTS TO REMEMBER ABOUT CONSTRUCTIVE CLASSROOM MANAGEMENT

1. An once of prevention is worth tons of punishment. Be sure you are using methods that will minimize the occasions for disorder. If one strategy doesn't work, try another.
2. Be yourself—your best self. This doesn't mean that we go around self-actualizing at the expense of our students, but it does mean that we keep in mind that students—no matter what grade—respond as much to who we are as what we say.
3. This seems a small matter, but keep an eye on the physical conditions—light, ventilation, temperature, and seating—any one can influence individual and group behavior for better or for worse.
4. Be firm, fair, and friendly.
5. Avoid punishing a whole class for the misbehavior of one or two. Very seldom, if ever, is every pupil involved.
6. Avoid threatening or ridiculing.
7. Be consistent.
8. Be prompt; that is, make an effort to discipline as soon after the misdeed as possible.
9. Avoid all unusual, long and cruel punishments; rather, keep the penalty to the minimum that you judge to be effective.
10. Let the punishment fit the crime. Deprivation of a possession or privilege that has been abused and rectification or reparation are the two kinds of action that most frequently fulfill this condition.

11. Be sure the student understands his case. Give an opportunity to state his case.
12. Let bygones be bygones.
13. Always search for the causes of misbehavior. If misbehavior is general, the cause may be in bad conditions or a poor curriculum. It may be in our attitude or teaching methods. The most frequent problem, however, is that of the chronic offender who is driven by circumstances beyond his control. Reform here depends not on punishment of the behavior but a cure for the cause.
14. Remember that the goal of all discipline is self-discipline.

TO DO

Self-discipline is a noble goal, but it means different things to different people. What does "self-discipline" mean for you? How would you define it for someone who wanted to know more specifically what you were talking about?

_____

_____

To achieve the goal of positive classroom management, a teacher has to be both firm and fair. (Allyn and Bacon)

EPILOGUE

Teaching a group of first graders how to read or a class of twelfth graders about the relationships between energy, mass, and speed are both demanding activities. When combined with the knowledge that different students learn at different rates and that some students not only don't want to learn, but interfere with the learning of others, then teaching and managing a classroom can be even more demanding. After several decades of investigating problems and strategies associated with classroom management, Jacob Kounin has observed that:

> . . . the business of running a classroom is a complicated technology having to do with developing a nonsatiating learning program; programming for progress, challenge, and variety in learning activities; initiating and maintaining movement in classroom tasks with smoothness and momentum; coping with more than one event simultaneously; observing and emitting feedback for many different events; directing actions at appropriate targets; maintaining a focus upon the group; and doubtless other techniques not measured in these researches.[33]

Although management skills are necessary tools in a good teacher's repertoire, their mastery should not be regarded as an end in itself. Techniques and strategies are merely facilitators. Their mastery not only enables one to do many different things, but it makes choices possible. Knowing something about group management techniques allows a teacher to accomplish his teaching goals—the absence of these skills acts as a barrier.

Classroom discipline is a complex task. What contributes to its complexity is the fact that there is no universally agreed upon criteria as to what constitutes a discipline problem in the first place. For the most part, it depends on the teacher who judges the problem and that particular teacher's tolerance for unplanned, unanticipated behavior. Some teachers actually look forward with a sense of excitment to the unexpected because it counts among those aspects of teaching that help give it flavor and zest. Other teachers have little tolerance for even the smallest infraction and, as a consequence, find themselves in a state of emotional topsy-turvy most of the time. It is probably safe to say that if you value a quiet and more or less predictable, orderly life-style, then you may want to think twice about whether teaching is really for you.

One chapter cannot hope to cover all the complexities of classroom management. Entire volumes have been devoted to this topic. What we have looked at here are some of the major factors influencing classroom discipline, along with some hints for diagnostic thinking and basic strategies for handling would-be and actual discipline situations.

Perhaps it goes without saying that all the strategies and techniques in the world will not help the teacher who doesn't particularly like teaching kids to begin with.

Write your own chapter summary (major points, ideas, and concepts that had meaning for you).

_____

_____

_____

_____

_____

_____

_____

_____

_____

REFERENCES

1. Ladd, E. T. "Perplexities of the Problem of Keeping Order." *Harvard Educational Review* 28(1958):19–28.

2. Crawford, B. M., and E. R. Harrington. "Development of a School Policy on Discipline." *California Journal of Educational Research* 12(1961):27–31.

3. Morse, W. C., and G. M. Wingo. *Psychology and Teaching*. Glenview, Ill.: Scott, Foresman, 1969.

4. Zietlin, H. "High School Discipline: Four Hundred Forty-Two Teachers Report on Discipline Problems in Seven Phoenix Schools." *California Journal of Educational Research* 13(1962):116–125.

5. Cutts, N. E., and N. Mosely. *Teaching the Disorderly Pupil*. New York: Longmans, Green, 1957, pp. 14–15.

6. Cutts, N. E., and N. Moseley. Op. cit., 1957, pp. 1–3.

7. Kelley, E. C. *In Defense of Youth*. Englewood Cliffs, N. J.: Prentice-Hall, 1962, p. 5.

8. National Education Association, Research Division. "Trouble-Makers in School." *NEA Journal* 51(November 1961):36.

9. Barker, R. G., and P. V. Gump. *Big School, Small School: High School Size and Student Behavior.* Stanford, Calif.: Stanford University Press, 1964.

10. Thomas, E. J., and C. F. Fink. "Effects of Group Size." *Psychology Bulletin* 60(1963):371–384.

11. Kaplan, L. *Education and Mental Health.* New York: Harper and Row, 1971, pp. 373–375.

12. Barclay, J. R. "Variability in Sociometric Scores and Teachers Ratings as Related to Teacher Age and Sex." *Journal of School Psychology* 5(Autumn 1966):52–59.

13. Wallen, N. E., et al. "Relationships Between Teacher Needs and Teacher Behavior in the Classroom." *Journal of Educational Psychology* 54(1963):23–32.

14. Lichter, S. O. *The Drop-Outs.* Chicago: Free Press, 1962.

15. Kestenberg, J. S. "Phases of Adolescence, Part II. Prepuberty Diffusion and Reintegration." *Journal of Child Psychiatry* 6(October 1967):577–614.

16. Redl, F. "Our Troubles with Defiant Youth." *Children* 2(January-February 1955):5–9.

17. Redl, F. "Management of Discipline Problems in Normal Students." *The Reiss-Davis Clinic Bulletin* 2(Spring 1965):38–46.

18. Bushell, D. *Classroom Behavior.* Englewood Cliffs, N.J.: Prentice-Hall, 1973.

19. Phillips, E. L., D. N. Wiener, and N. G. Haring. *Discipline Achievement in Mental Health,* 2nd ed. Englewood Cliffs, N.J.: Prentice-Hall, 1973.

20. Kaplan, L. *Education and Mental Health.* Op. cit., 1971, p. 385.

21. Redl, F., and W. W. Wattenberg. *Mental Hygiene in Teaching,* 2nd ed. New York: Harcourt, Brace, 1959, pp. 326–343.

22. Johnson, L. V., and M. A. Bany. *Classroom Management: Theory and Skill Training.* New York: Macmillan, 1970, pp. 362–400.

23. Long, N. J., and R. G. Newman. "Managing Surface Behavior of Children in School." *Bulletin of the School of Education* 37(July 1961):47–61. Bloomington, Ind.: Indiana University.

24. Redl, F., and D. Wineman. *The Aggressive Child.* Glencoe, Ill.: Free Press, 1957, pp. 395–487.

25. Redl, F., and W. W. Wattenberg. *Mental Hygiene in Teaching,* 2nd ed. Op. cit., 1959, pp. 344–381.

26. O'Leary, K. D., and S. G. O'Leary. *Classroom Management: Behavior Modification Techniques.* Elmsford, N. Y.: Pergamon Press, 1973.

27. Klein, R. D., W. G. Hapkiewicz, and A. H. Roden (eds). *Behavior Modification in Educational Settings.* Springfield, Ill.: Thomas, 1973.

28. Poteet, J. A. *Behavior Modification: A Practical Guide for Teachers.* Minneapolis, Minn.: Burgess, 1973.

29. Hall, R. V. "Instructing Beginning Teachers in Reinforcing Procedures Which Improve Classroom Control." *Journal of Applied Behavior Analysis* 1(1968):15–22.

30. Karraker, R. J. "Token Reinforcement Systems in Regular Public School Classrooms." In *Operant Conditioning in the Classroom: Readings,* edited by C. E. Pitts. New York: Crowell, 1971, pp. 301–314.

31. Thomas, D. R. "Production and Elimination of Disruptive Classroom Behavior by Systematically Varying Teacher's Behavior." *Journal of Applied Behavior Analysis* 1(1968):35–45.

32. Gordon, T. *Parent Effectiveness Training.* New York: Wyden, 1970, pp. 103–120.

33. Kounin, J. *Discipline and Group Management.* New York: Holt, Rinehart and Winston, 1970, p. 36.

REFERENCES OF RELATED INTEREST

Berkowitz, P. H., and E. P. Rothman. *The Disturbed Child: Recognition and Psychoeducational Therapy in the Classroom.* New York: New York University Press, 1960.

Blackham, G. J. *The Deviant Child in the Classroom.* Belmont, Calif.: Wadsworth, 1967.

Brown, D. *Changing Student Behavior: A New Approach to Discipline.* Dubuque, Iowa: Brown, 1971.

Clarizio, H. F. *Toward Positive Classroom Discipline.* New York: Wiley, 1971.

———, and G. F. McCoy. *Behavior Disorders in School-Aged Children.* Scranton, Ill.: Chandler, 1970.

Crisis in Child Mental Health: Challenge for the 1970's. Report of the Joint Commission on Mental Health for Children. New York: Harper & Row, 1968.

Dimick, K. M., and V. E. Huff. *Child Counseling.* Dubuque, Iowa: Brown, 1970.

Dreikurs, R. *Psychology in the Classroom: A Manual for Teachers,* 2nd ed. New York: Harper & Row, 1968.

Ginott, H. *Teacher and Child.* New York: Macmillan, 1972.

Givner, A., and P. S. Graubard. *A Handbook of Behavior Modification for the Classroom.* New York: Holt, Rinehart & Winston, 1974.

Johnson, L. V., and M. A. Bany. *Classroom Management: Theory and Skill Building.* New York: Macmillan, 1970.

Long, N. J., W. C. Morse, and R. G. Newman (eds.). *Conflict in the Classroom: The Education of Children with Problems,* 2nd ed. Belmont, Calif.: Wadsworth, 1971.

Madsen, C. H., Jr., and C. K. Madsen. *Teaching/Discipline,* 2nd ed. Boston, Mass.: Allyn and Bacon, 1974.

Quay, H. C. *Children's Behavior Disorders.* Princeton, N. J.: Van Nostrand, 1968.

Redl, F. *When We Deal with Children.* New York: Free Press, 1966.

Wiener, D. N. *Classroom Management and Discipline.* Itasca, Ill.: Peacock, 1972.

Woody, R. H. *Behavioral Problem Children in the Schools.* New York: Appleton-Century-Crofts, 1969.

A POSTSCRIPT

This is the last page of text I am writing in this book. Scattered across my desk are the fifteen chapters that lead to this final postscript. I have a generally good feeling about this volume being completed because this sort of task takes a very long time to finish, and it is a relief to have it over and look ahead to doing other things. I also have a feeling of awe. This is hard to describe, but it has to do with a sense of how incredibly big, and important, and vital teaching is, and how much there is to know and learn about to be a well-rounded "total" teacher whose behavior reflects the sort of healthy self-actualizing, fully functioning characteristics we talked about in Chapter 1. What is a "total" teacher, you ask? I suppose there are many ways to describe that sort of person, but for me a total teacher is someone who is knowledgeable, yet humble; fair, yet firm; strong, yet sympathetic; challenging, yet not overbearing; supportive, yet not totally permissive; sensitive, yet not weak.

All in all, this has been an exciting adventure in learning for me. I suppose that's one reason I have such a sense of awe about how much there is to know, and how much I have yet to learn.

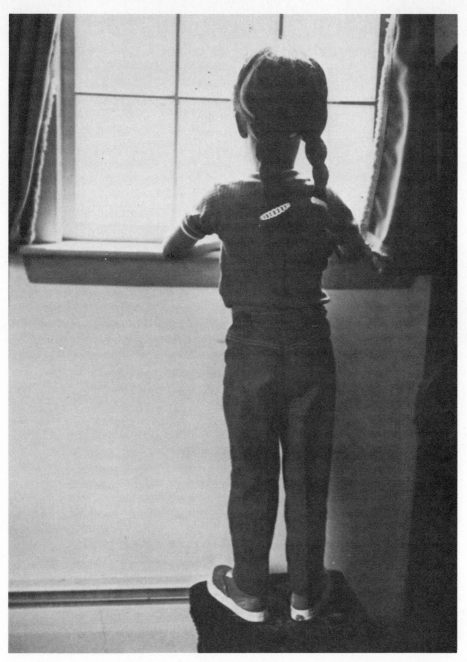

I wonder what school will be like.   I wonder if my school will be nice to me.
I wonder if I'll like my teacher.   I wonder if my teacher will like me.   I
wonder what I'll be when I grow up.   I wonder who I'll be when I grow up.
I wonder . . .

Author Index

A

Aberle, D. F., 147, 169
Aborn, M., 387, 421
Adam, J. F., 229
Adams, C. R., 338, 368
Adelson, J., 197, 205, 225, 227
Adler, A., 12, 39, 348, 369
Agranoff, B. W., 470, 481
Alexander, E. D., 546, 574
Alexander, P., 349, 369
Allebrand, G. N., 559, 576
Allender, J. S., 483
Alloway, D. N., 424
Allport, G. W., 25, 32, 38, 39, 293,
    488, 526
Alschler, R. H., 668, 683
Altman, E., 338, 368
Altman, I., 659, 682
Ames, L. B., 482, 629
Ammon, P. D., 286
Anderson, G., 639, 662, 680, 682
Anderson, H. E., 499, 527
Anderson, H. H., 298, 318, 326, 328,
    640, 680
Anderson, L., 665, 683
Anderson, R. C., 328
Anderson, R. H., 121, 549, 575
Andrews, T. G., 382, 421
Angell, G. W., 619, 629

Anttonen, R. G., 578
Appel, K. E., 371
Appelbaum, M. I., 282
Appley, M. H., 530
Aries, P., 177, 178, 223
Armstrong, C. M., 547, 574
Aronson, E., 504, 528, 647, 681
Arthur, G., 547, 574
Asher, J. W., 294, 326
Atkins, M. J., 590, 627
Atkinson, J. W., 502, 527, 529
Auglin, J. M., 445, 479
Ausubel, D. P., 208–209, 227, 296,
    326, 386, 399, 421, 422, 442, 450,
    479, 480

B

Bachman, J., 541, 573
Back, K., 663, 682
Baer, D., 146, 169
Baker, C. T., 282
Balaban, M., 482
Baldwin, A. L., 141, 169
Ball, B. S., 415, 423
Bandt, P. L., 424, 482
Bandura, A., 111, 121
Banks, J. A., 424, 578
Bany, M. A., 660, 682, 708, 725, 727
Barclay, J. R., 669, 683, 696, 725

Bard, B., 343, 368
Bardwick, J. M., 229
Barker, E. N., 168
Barker, R., 684, 695, 725
Barr, A. S., 310, 327
Barron, F., 85, 89, 285
Barzun, J., 630
Bath, J. A., 206, 227
Baughman, E. E., 424
Baumrind, D., 150–153, 154, 170, 171
Baxter, B., 342, 368
Bayley, N., 98, 119, 129, 168, 188–190,
    205, 225, 227, 263, 283
Beard, R. M., 106, 120, 168, 169, 219,
    228, 413
Becker, B. L., 452, 480
Becker, W. C., 154, 171, 451, 480
Bednar, R. L., 362, 369
Bee, H. L., 148, 170
Behrens, H. D., 148, 170
Bennett, E. L., 282, 476, 482
Bennis, W. G., 370
Benowitz, M. L., 454, 480
Bergeson, J. B., 424
Berko, J., 103, 120
Berkowits, G. K., 170
Berkowitz, P. H., 727
Bernard, H. W., 171
Berne, E., 370
Bernstein, E., 517–519, 529
Berscheid, E., 187, 224, 225, 646, 680
Bibens, R. F., 329
Biddle, B. J., 291, 325
Bigelow, R. C., 684
Bigge, M. L., 482, 529
Bills, R. E., 437, 479
Binet, A., 238, 281
Bing, E., 145, 169
Binter, A. R., 171
Bion, W. R., 684
Biran, L. A., 403, 422
Birney, R. C., 578
Bischof, L. L., 89
Blackham, G. J., 727
Block, J. H., 602, 628
Bloom, B. S., 49, 87, 135, 168,
    259–260, 262, 283, 551, 575, 591,
    602, 603, 628
Bloom, R., 304, 327
Blue, J. T., Jr., 670, 683
Bodwin, F. B., 559, 576
Bonney, M. E., 648, 669, 681, 683

Borislow, B., 559, 576
Borton, T., 424
Bovard, E., 662, 682
Bousfield, W. A., 299, 326
Bower, E. M., 328, 551, 575
Bower, G. H., 482, 530
Bowerman, G. E., 200, 226
Bowman, P. H., 305, 327
Boy, A. V., 370
Boynton, P. L., 298, 326, 342, 368
Brambs, J., 578
Branden, N., 346, 369
Bremer, J., 424, 530
Brenton, M., 367, 370
Brewer, J. E., 318, 640
Brick, M., 668, 683
Briggs, L. J., 425
Briggs, T. H., 382, 421
Brodsky, C. M., 646, 680
Bronfenbrenner, U., 148, 160, 170,
    171, 201, 202, 204, 226, 227, 665,
    683
Brookover, W. B., 560, 561, 576
Brookshire, K. H., 458, 480
Brophy, J. E., 328, 425, 578
Broudy, H. S., 328, 591, 628
Brown, D. G., 110, 121, 727
Brown, F. G., 629
Brown, J. S., 530
Brownell, W. A., 385, 421
Brubaker, D. L., 426
Bruner, J. S., 88, 221, 228, 328, 387,
    414, 421, 423, 424, 436, 443–446,
    478, 479
Brunkan, R. J., 565, 577
Brunswick, J. M., 278–279, 285
Bugental, J., 28–29, 38, 370
Burdick, H., 578
Buros, O. K., 243, 282
Burt, C., 259, 283
Burton, W. H., 439, 479
Bushell, D., 702, 725
Busse, T. V., 454, 480

C

Cabianca, W. A., 578
Calandra, A., 611, 629
Cameron, N., 356, 369
Campbell, J. D., 155, 171
Campbell, P. B., 558, 575, 578
Capehart, B. E., 402, 422

Carlsmith, J. M., 504, 528
Carroll, J. B., 602, 628
Cartwright, D., 351, 369
Cartwright, P., 653, 681
Case, D., 220, 228
Castaneda, A., 563, 576
Cattell, R. B., 263–264, 284
Cazden, C. B., 103, 120, 258, 283
Chansky, N. M., 629
Charles, D. C., 171
Chase, J. A., 549, 575
Chesebro, P. A., 482, 530
Chesler, M., 684
Chiang, H., 89, 370
Child, I. L., 31, 39
Chorost, S. B., 199, 225
Church, J., 185, 224
Clark, D. H., 424
Clark, P. M., 530
Clarizio, H. F., 89, 171, 285, 328, 370, 727
Clarke, H. H., 265, 284
Clifford, W., 556, 575
Cody, J. J., 568, 577
Cofer, C. N., 530
Coffield, W. H., 547, 574
Cogan, M. L., 300, 326
Cole, L., 229
Coleman, J., 208, 227, 349, 369
Coleman, W., 264, 284
Collinson, J. W., 220, 228
Combs, A. W., 27–28, 38–39, 285, 291–292, 306–308, 325, 327, 362, 370, 391, 422, 490, 509–510, 526, 528, 565, 577
Commoss, H. H., 648, 681
Conger, J. J., 121, 168–169, 172, 229
Conner, C., 294, 325
Conrad, H. S., 283
Cook, L. A., 649, 681
Cook, W. W., 409, 423, 547, 574
Coop, R. H., 329
Cooper, J. B., 199, 226
Coopersmith, S., 7, 37, 61, 88, 113, 121, 143–144, 153, 155, 169, 170, 171, 253, 282, 505, 527, 563, 569, 576, 578
Cordasco, F., 424
Corey, S., 391, 422
Corning, W. C., 482
Costa, P. T., 40
Cottrell, L. S., 89

Cowan, J. C., 294, 325
Cox, F. N., 503, 576
Craig, R. C., 89, 285, 328, 482
Craise, J. L., 214, 228
Cramer, P., 286
Crandall, V., 169
Crary, R. W., 424
Crawford, B. M., 690, 724
Criswell, E., 395–396
Crockenberg, S. B., 285
Croubach, L. J., 382, 421
Crowder, N. A., 407
Cuban, L., 425
Culkin, J. M., 517, 529
Cumpert, C., 569, 578
Cusick, P. A., 229
Cutts, N. E., 690, 724

D

D'Amico, L. A., 513, 529
D'Andrade, R., 143, 169
Davidson, H. H., 308, 327, 499, 527
Davis, F. B., 630
Davis, G. A., 285
Davis, M., 337, 368
Davis, R. A., 482
DeCecco, J. P., 590, 627
DeCharms, R., 226
Deci, E. L., 492–493, 527
deGroat, A. F., 497, 527
Demerest, R., 547, 574
Denny, T., 265, 284
Deutsch, J. A., 482
Deutsch, M. P., 102, 120, 513, 529
Dewey, J., 442, 479
Dillon, H. A., 548, 574
Dillon, J. C., 425
Dimick, K. M., 727
Dion, K. E., 187, 224, 225, 646, 647, 680, 681
Dizney, H., 630
Dolland, J., 22, 39
Domas, S. J., 291, 325
Douglas, V., 648, 681
Douvan, E., 197, 205, 225, 227
Downie, N. M., 630
Dreger, R. M., 137, 169
Dreikurs, R., 425, 727
Dubbé, M. C., 199, 225
Dudek, S., 301, 326
Duffy, W., 329

733

Duncan, J. K., 329
Durr, W. K., 565, 577
Dyson, E., 559, 576

E

Ebel, R. L., 531, 591, 599, 603, 612,
   616, 623, 624–625, 628, 629
Eckerson, D., 135
Eckerson, L. D., 168
Edge, D., 121, 171
Edson, L., 255
Edwards, J. A., 208, 227
Egan, G., 370, 684
Eichorn, D. H., 182, 224
Eisenstadt, J. W., 684
Eisner, E. W., 591, 628
Elashoff, J. D., 568, 577
Elder, G. H., 198, 199, 201, 225, 226
Elkind, D., 172, 365, 370
Ellena, W. J., 291, 325
Ellis, H. C., 482
Emmer, E. T., 425
Englemann, S., 425
Epstein, G. F., 504, 527
Epstein, N. B., 230
Erb, E. D., 370
Erikson, E., 39, 45–52, 55, 61, 85, 87,
   88, 141–142, 148, 161, 169, 215,
   217, 228, 545, 574
Ervin, S. M., 135, 168
Essman, W. B., 469
Estes, W. K., 22, 39
Evans, E. D., 172
Eysenck, H. J., 285, 438, 479

F

Fantini, M., 393, 422
Farls, R. J., 565, 577
Farquhar, W. W., 565, 577
Farson, R. E., 25–26, 38
Fast, J., 370
Fauls, L., 110, 121
Faust, S., 225
Feather, N. T., 529, 555
Feinberg, M. R., 210, 227
Feldhusen, J., 265, 284, 630, 648, 681
Felker, D. W., 578
Festinger, L., 656, 682
Fink, C. F., 695, 725
Fink, M. B., 558, 575

Finkelstein, M. E., 170
Fitts, W. H., 578
Fitzgerald, H. T., 459, 481
Fitzgerald, M. P., 199, 225
Flacks, R., 213, 214, 228
Flanagen, J. C., 530
Flanders, N. A., 312, 319–322, 327,
   328, 650, 681
Flavell, J. H., 137, 141, 168, 169
Fleming, E. S., 578
Foote, N. N., 89
Forlano, G., 495, 527
Foster, S. F., 362, 370
French, J. R. P., 226
Freud, S., 7–9, 37, 39, 45
Frey, S. H., 171, 229
Friedlander, B. Z., 448, 479
Fromm, E., 12, 32, 39, 82, 89, 348, 369
Frost, J. L., 122, 172, 425
Fuller, J. L., 530

G

Gage, N. L., 329
Gagne, R. M., 385, 408, 421, 423, 425
Galanter, E., 386, 421
Gallagher, J. J., 320, 328
Galloway, C. M., 425, 499, 527
Galton, F., 119, 258
Garcia, J., 261, 283
Garry, R., 482
Gartner, A., 285
Gephart, W. I., 568
Gargen, K. J., 89, 504, 528, 578
Gesell, A., 57, 88, 414, 423
Getz, H. G., 172
Getzels, J. W., 276, 285
Gibb, J. R., 673
Ginott, H., 121, 229, 727
Ginsburg, H., 141, 168, 169, 425
Givner, A., 727
Glaser, R., 403, 422
Glasser, W., 56, 62, 88, 379, 420
Gleason, J. B., 104, 120
Glock, M. D., 329
Glock, M. L., 482
Gnagey, W. J., 425, 482, 530
Goddard, I. L., 132, 168
Godfrey, E., 548, 574
Goethals, G. W., 229
Golburgh, S., 229
Gold, M., 648, 681

Goldberg, M., 416, 424
Goldfarb, W., 102, 120
Goldsmith, A., 424
Good, T. L., 328, 425, 578
Goodenough, F. L., 668, 683
Goodlad, J. I., 425, 549, 575
Gordon, T., 716, 726
Gorow, F. F., 601, 608, 628, 630
Gottesman, I., 260, 283
Gould, G., 294, 325
Gowan, J. C., 565, 577
Grace, G. L., 458, 480
Graham, R., 658, 682
Grambs, J. D., 424
Grauband, P. S., 727
Grebstein, L. C., 89
Green, R. F., 263, 283
Green, R. L., 454, 480
Greenberg, H. M., 425
Greenberg, S. B., 329
Greene, B. I., 578
Greer, C., 285
Greulich, W. W., 182, 224
Grinder, R. E., 229
Grondlund, H. E., 605, 628
Gronlund, N. E., 210, 227, 630, 664,
    665, 669, 683
Gross, R., 229
Gruen, E. W., 501, 527
Guilford, J. P., 241, 282, 388, 421
Gump, P. V., 300, 326, 684, 695, 725
Gumpert, P., 569, 578
Gurwitz, M. S., 263, 283
Guthrie, E. R., 18, 22, 38, 39

H

Haber, R. N., 530
Hadden, E. E., 425
Hales, L. W., 630
Hall, J., 530, 548, 574
Hall, R. V., 715, 725
Hall, W. F., 547, 574
Halleck, S. L., 214, 228
Hallman, R. J., 329
Hamachek, D. E., 39, 84, 89, 120, 286,
    325, 370, 384, 421, 449, 480, 578,
    684
Hapkiewicz, W. G., 715, 725
Harding, K. L., 541, 573
Haring, N. G., 702, 725
Harmon, J., 400, 422
Harris, D. B., 668, 683

Harris, R. A., 89
Harris, T. A., 371, 578
Harrison, A., Jr., 415, 424
Hartup, W. W., 208, 227
Harvey, O. J., 317, 328
Hart, F. W., 298, 326
Hass, K., 89, 370
Havighurst, R. J., 53–54, 85, 87, 195,
    225, 411, 414, 423
Havumaki, S., 650, 681
Hawk, T. L., 578
Hawkes, G. R., 172, 425
Heald, J. E., 148
Heathers, G., 113, 121
Heckhausen, H., 530
Hefferman, H., 122
Heilbrum, A. B., 204, 227
Heise, G. A., 670, 683
Helper, M. M., 204, 227
Henderson, G., 329
Hermann, G., 447, 479
Hernstein, R. J., 283
Herron, R. E., 121, 163, 171
Hertling, J. E., 172
Hess, R. D., 147, 169, 170, 201, 226
Hilgard, E. R., 386, 414, 421, 423, 433,
    478, 482
Hill, J. P., 229
Hill, W. F., 482
Hoepfner, R., 239, 281
Hoffman, B., 630
Hoffman, L. R., 204, 227
Hoffman, M. L., 199, 209, 226, 227
Hogarty, P. S., 282
Holland, J. G., 403, 423
Hollister, W. G., 328
Holmlund, W. S., 210, 227
Holt, J., 80, 89, 425, 460, 463, 481,
    509, 528, 621, 629
Honzik, M. P., 251–252, 282
Honziler, M. P., 282
Hooker, D., 370
Horn, J. L., 264, 284
Horn, T. D., 425
Horney, K., 12, 39
Hornstein, H., 642, 680
Horowitz, F. D., 649, 681
Houston, A. C., 111
Hough, J. B., 329
Howe, L. W., 34, 39, 371, 426
Howe, M. J. A., 452, 480
Hoyt, D. P., 286
Huff, V. E., 727

Hunnicutt, C. W., 495, 527
Hunter, E., 371
Hurlock, E. B., 172, 458, 480, 494, 527
Hyden, H., 472, 481

I

Ilg, F. L., 48, 88
Inhelder, B., 218, 228

J

Jackson, P. W., 291, 296–297, 325,
  326, 684
Jacobson, L., 266, 284, 509, 528
Jacobziner, H., 168
James, M., 371
James, W., 29–30, 38, 58–59, 88, 382,
  420, 537, 573
Jarrett, C. D., 630
Jarvik, M. E., 469, 481
Jenkins, G. G., 578
Jenkins, J. R., 371
Jennings, H. H., 664, 683
Jensen, A. R., 185, 224, 254–258, 282
Jensen, M. B., 401, 422
Jersild, A. T., 30, 39, 89, 121, 334, 361,
  368, 369, 537, 573
Johnson, D. W., 90, 371, 578, 639, 675,
  680, 684
Johnson, J. J., 482, 530
Johnson, L. V., 660, 682, 708, 725, 727
Johnson, R. C., 207, 227
Jones, E., 40
Jones, H. E., 263, 283
Jones, M. C., 188–190, 191, 192, 225
Jongeward, D., 371
Jordon, T. E., 645, 680
Jose, J., 568, 577
Josselyn, L. M., 229
Jourard, S. M., 180, 187, 224, 349, 369,
  371
Joyce, W. W., 425
Julian, J. W., 511, 529
Jung, C. G., 12, 40

K

Kagan, J., 102, 108, 120, 121, 154, 168,
  170, 172, 229, 257, 283, 286,
  465–466, 481
Kahn, R., 684
Kaplan, E., 104, 120

Kaplan, L., 684, 703, 725
Karmel, L. J., 630
Karraker, R. J., 715, 726
Katkovsky, W., 169
Katz, D., 684
Keislar, E., 442, 479, 483
Keliher, A. V., 671, 683
Kelley, E. C., 694, 724
Kemp, C. G., 684
Keniston, K., 215, 216, 228
Kerr, A., 648, 681
Kessler, J. W., 153, 170
Kestenberg, J. S., 699, 725
Ketcham, W. A., 264, 284
Khleif, B. B., 371
Kimble, D. P., 482
Kinch, J. W., 200, 226
King, M. L., 71
Kingsley, H. L., 482
Kingston, A. J., 630
Kirschenbaum, H., 34, 39, 371, 426,
  629, 633
Klatsin, E. H., 201, 226
Klausmeier, H. J., 383, 421
Klein, R. D., 715, 725
Klein, S. S., 365, 370
Kleinjaus, E. K., 425
Klemm, W. R., 483
Kluckhohn, C., 40
Knapp, M. L., 675, 684
Kohl, H. R., 522
Kohlberg, L., 111, 121, 550, 551, 575
Kohn, L. G., 170
Kolstoe, P., 239, 281
Kounin, J. S., 300, 326, 723, 726
Kowitz, G. T., 547, 574
Krathwohl, D. R., 591, 628
Krech, D., 239, 282, 468, 471, 474, 476
Krippner, S., 286
Kryspin, W. J., 630
Kubie, L. S., 13, 37
Kubiniec, C. M., 578
Kuethe, J. L., 425
Kumar, V. K., 483
Kvaraceus, W. C., 579

L

LaBenne, W. D., 578
LaCrosse, J., 550, 575
Ladd, E. T., 690, 724
Lambert, B. G., 229
Lambert, N. M., 667, 683

Landis, P. H., 224
Lang, G., 308, 327, 499, 527
Lantz, B., 501, 527
Larson, C. E., 675, 684
Lauterbach, C. G., 216, 228
Lavatelli, C. S., 121, 172
Laycock, S. R., 344, 369
Lecky, P., 504, 528, 553, 575
Lefebvre, A., 578
Lehmann, I. J., 599, 604, 608, 628, 629, 630
Leith, G. O., 403, 422
Lembo, J. M., 425
Lenneberg, E. H., 101, 120
Lesser, G. S., 286
Levin, H., 203
Levine, R., 436, 478
Levitt, E. E., 208, 227
Lewis, E. C., 206, 227
Lewis, G. M., 329
Lewis, H. R., 366
Libarle, M., 229
Liddle, G., 265, 284
Lien, A. S., 630
Lindeman, R. H., 630
Lindgren, H. C., 172
Lindholm, B. W., 253, 282
Lindvall, C. M., 630
Lippin, R., 204, 227
Lippitt, R., 313, 315, 328, 648, 681, 684
Lipsitt, L. P., 563, 576
Livingston, A. H., 548, 574
Long, N. J., 709, 725, 727
Looft, W. R., 171
Lord, F. M., 601, 628
Lott, A. J., 668, 683
Lott, B. E., 668, 683
Loupe, M. J., 329
Lowe, G. G., 229
Lowin, A., 504, 528
Luginbuhl, J. E. R., 570, 578
Lyon, H. C., 40, 90, 425

M

Maccoby, E., 203
MacFarlane, J. W., 251, 282
MacKinnon, D. W., 267, 271, 273, 284, 285
Maddi, S. R., 40
Maddox, H., 483
Madsen, C. H., 727

Madsen, C. K., 727
Mager, R. F., 590, 627
Mahler, D., 622, 629
Maier, H. W., 46, 87, 172
Major, J., 371
Maller, J. B., 511, 528
Maltz, M., 504, 528
Mandel, F. L., 135, 168
Mann, R. D., 659, 681
Marcus, I. M., 133, 168
Marecek, J., 505, 506, 528
Maresch, M. M., 183, 184, 224
Margaret, A., 357, 369
Marshall, J. C., 630
Marshall, M., 630
Martin, W. B., 120
Martin, W. R., 107–108
Marx, M. H., 530
Masia, B. B., 591, 628
Maslow, A. H., 12, 25, 32–33, 37, 38, 39, 40, 65–73, 75, 86, 88, 89, 267–268, 275, 284, 285, 286, 370, 371, 456, 480, 490, 491, 526
Mason, F. V., 340, 368
Mason, G. E., 415, 424
Massimo, J. L., 555, 575
Mastin, V. E., 303, 327
Mattee, D. R., 505, 506, 528
May, R., 90, 371
Mayhard, G., 170
McCall, R. B., 252, 282
McCandless, B. R., 172, 563, 576
McCarthy, D. 136, 168
McClelland, D. C., 147, 169, 201, 226
McClosky, M. G., 425
McConnell, J. V., 473–474, 481
McCoy, G. F., 171
McCroskey, J. C., 675, 684
McCuen, J. T., 557, 575
McDill, E. L., 203, 227
McDonald, F. J., 590, 627
McGaugh, J., 471, 481
McGehee, B. R., 437, 479
McGrath, J. E., 658, 682
McGuigan, F. J., 401, 422
McKeachie, W., 329
McKinney, B. T., 547
McKinnon, D. W., 286
McLaughlin, K. F., 630
Mead, M., 11, 37
Meara, N. M., 482
Mebly, E. O., 547, 574, 622, 623, 629
Medinnus, G. R., 154, 170, 207, 227

Mehrens, W. A., 285, 328, 599, 604, 608, 628, 629, 630
Meissner, W. W., 199, 225
Menninger, W. C., 359, 369
Merbaum, M., 90
Mercer, J. R., 266
Merrill, M. A., 243, 282
Miles, C. C., 262, 283
Miles, W. R., 262, 283
Miller, D. R., 201, 226
Miller, G. A., 386, 421
Miller, N., 22, 39
Miller, W. R., 168
Millet, G. B., 425
Mintz, A., 511, 528
Mischel, W., 203, 227
Mitchell, J. V., Jr., 563, 576
Moreno, J. H., 664, 683
Morris, V. C., 38
Morrison, I. E., 547, 574
Morse, W. C., 56, 87, 304, 327, 578, 690, 724, 727
Mosely, N., 690, 724
Moser, H. E., 387, 421
Moss, A., 170
Moss, H. A., 102, 108, 120, 154
Moss, J. R., 271, 284
Mosston, M., 425
Moulton, R. W., 502
Moustakes, C., 90, 329, 426
Mowrer, O. H., 22, 40, 111, 121, 454, 480
Muldoon, J. F., 651, 661, 680, 682
Munsinger, H., 172
Murphy, G., 371
Murphy, P. D., 329
Murray, E. J., 530
Murray, H. A., 32, 40
Mussen, P., 111, 121, 169, 172, 191–192, 225, 226
Muuss, R. E., 185, 224, 230

N

Naegele, K. D., 169
Napier, R. W., 623, 629
Nash, I., 172
Nash, R. J., 559, 576
Neil, L. M., 317, 328
Neill, A. S., 516–517, 529
Nelson, L. N., 329
Nelson, V. L., 282
Newman, R. G., 709, 725, 727

Nichols, M., 342, 368
Nisbet, J. D., 263, 284
Nixon, C. L., 121
Nixon, R. H., 121
Noar, G., 426
Noll, V. H., 531
Northway, M. L., 211, 227
Nuss, E. M., 730

O

Ojemann, R. H., 295, 326, 591, 627
O'Kelly, L. I., 530
O'Leary, K. D., 451, 480, 715, 725
O'Leary, S. G., 715, 725
Olson, R. G., 40
Olson, W. C., 224, 414, 423, 546
Opie, I., 171
Opie, P., 161, 171
Opper, S., 141, 169
Osler, S. F., 419, 424
Osterman, P., 729
O'Sullivan, M., 281
Otto, H. J., 547, 574
Owens, W. A., 264, 284

P

Page, E. P., 312, 327, 406, 423
Palardy, M. J., 569, 578
Palmer, F. H., 283
Palmero, D. S., 563, 576
Park, J., 511, 528
Parker, A., 111, 121
Parker, R. K., 121
Parnes, S. J., 286
Patterson, A., 560, 561, 576
Pavlov, I., 15, 37
Payne, D. A., 591, 628, 630
Pearl, A., 418, 424
Peck, L., 340, 368
Peel, E. A., 230
Pepitone, A. L., 505, 528
Perez, J. F., 230
Perry, C., 90
Perry, I. F., 547, 574
Peters, D. M., 579
Peterson, R. E., 214, 228
Peterson, S., 371
Phillips, B. N., 266, 284, 513, 529
Phillips, E. L., 702, 725
Phillips, R. C., 630
Piaget, J., 101–102, 106, 120, 134, 141,

166, 168, 218, 219, 220–221, 228, 412–414, 423
Pine, G. J., 370
Pine, P., 286
Pinneau, S. R., 168
Piper, R. M., 329
Plowman, L., 619, 629
Pope, B., 649
Poppy, K. C., 37
Postman, N., 426, 437, 478
Poteet, J. A., 715, 725
Powell, E. H., 550, 575
Preston, A., 169
Pribram, A., 386, 421
Pugh, C., 424
Purkey, W. W., 579
Putney, G. J., 90
Putney, J., 90
Putney, S., 90

Q

Quay, H. C., 727

R

Rafferty, M., 517, 529
Ragosta, T., 146, 169
Ralston, N. C., 230
Randall, H. B., 336
Raths, J., 329
Raven, B. H., 226
Read, K. H., 121
Redl, F., 172, 699, 701, 703, 725, 727
Reed, H. B., 300, 326
Reiss, A. L., 208, 227
Rethlingshafer, D., 530
Reynolds, F. H., 403, 423
Rhine, J. J., 501, 527
Richardson, K., 286
Ricks, D., 550, 555, 575
Riessman, F., 285, 461, 481
Rindlisbacher, A., 226
Ringness, T. A., 336, 368
Ringwald, B. E., 367, 370
Roark, A. E., 684
Robertson, D., 630
Robins, L. N., 549, 575
Rocchio, P. D., 310, 327
Roden, A. H., 715, 725
Roethlisberger, F. J., 675, 684
Roff, M., 159, 171

Rogers, C. R., 20, 32, 38, 40, 74–79, 86, 88, 89, 90, 273, 285, 329, 362, 369, 371, 397–398, 422, 426, 490, 526, 666, 675, 683, 684
Rogers D., 172, 215, 228
Rohwer, W. D., Jr., 426
Rosen, B. C., 147, 169
Rosen, C. R., 143
Rosen, R., 204, 227
Rosenberg, M., 200, 226, 230, 462, 481
Rosenthal, M. J., 153, 170
Rosenthal, R., 226, 284, 437, 509, 528, 567, 568, 577
Rosenzweig, M. R., 239, 282, 474, 475, 482
Rossman, M., 228
Roth, R. M., 556
Rothman, E. P., 727
Rower, W. D., Jr., 286
Royce, J. E., 40
Rubenstein, R., 457, 480
Ruch, F. L., 357, 369
Rudin, S. A., 73, 88
Ryans, D. G., 294, 300–303, 306–308, 325, 326, 341, 368

S

Sahakian, W. S., 90
Salk, L., 121, 172
Saltztein, H. D., 209, 227
Samler, J., 371
Sampson, E. E., 213, 228
Sanders, N. J., 630
Sandid, A. A., 547, 574
Sanford, E. C., 399, 422
Sarason, S. B., 563, 576
Schaefer, E. A., 260, 283
Schaefer, E. S., 205, 227
Schaie, K. W., 263, 283
Scheifeld, A., 168
Schmidt, H. O., 497, 527
Schmidt, L. D., 482
Schmuck, P. A., 90, 663, 682, 684
Schmuck, R. A., 90, 426, 642, 645, 651, 660, 663, 680, 681, 682, 684
Schmuck, R. M., 684
Schneider, F. W., 426
Schneiders, A. A., 371
Schreiber, D., 541, 573
Schutz, W. G., 371

Schwebel, A. I., 136, 168
Scott, E. M., 230
Seachrest, L. B., 498, 527
Seagoe, M. V., 401, 422, 483
Sears, P. S., 111, 121, 300, 326, 501, 527
Sears, R. R., 153, 170, 203, 226
Seashore, R. H., 135, 168
Secord, P. F., 187, 224
Seidman, J. M., 122, 172
Seitz, T. L., 271, 285
Semmelmeyer, M., 389, 422
Severin, F. T., 40, 371
Shane, H. G., 121
Shaw, M. C., 557, 575
Shaw, M. E., 511, 528
Sheni, R., 565, 577
Sherif, C. W., 653, 681
Sherif, M., 653, 681
Shipman, V. C., 147, 169
Shirley, M. M., 107, 120
Shore, M. F., 555, 575
Shulman, L. S., 329, 442, 464–465, 479, 481, 483
Shumsky, A., 329
Siegel, A. E., 170
Siegel, L., 530
Sigall, H., 647, 681
Silberman, M. L., 426, 483
Silverberg, W. V., 58, 88
Simon, S. B., 34, 39, 371, 426, 623, 629
Simon, T., 238, 281
Simun, P., 294, 326
Skeels, H. M., 260–261, 283
Skinner, B. F., 16, 17, 20, 26, 37, 40, 426, 449, 450, 451, 452, 454, 456, 457, 480, 530
Sleight, W., 382, 420
Slovic, P., 133, 168
Smallenburg, H., 622, 629
Smart, J. M., 172
Smart, M. C., 172
Smart, M. S., 120, 122
Smart, R. C., 120, 122
Smith, M. B., 31, 39
Smith, R. P., 156, 171
Smith, W. D., 110, 121
Snow, R. W., 568, 577
Snygg, D., 27–28, 38, 490, 526
Soffen, F., 579
Soloman, J. C., 364, 370

Sontag, L. W., 253, 282
Spaulding, F. T., 383, 421
Spearman, C. E., 238, 281
Spears, D., 286
Spears, M. J., 419, 424
Spence, K., 22, 40
Sperry, L., 483, 530
Spiegelman, R., 550, 575
Spitzer, H. F., 408, 423, 618, 629
Spock, B., 71
Sprinthall, N. A., 329
Spuhler, J. N., 286
Stacknik, T. J., 454, 480
Staffieri, J., 130, 168, 646, 680
Stagner, R., 73, 88
Staines, J. W., 509, 528, 565, 577
Stanford, G., 684
Stanley, J., 426
Steele, M., 630
Steigman, M. J., 501, 527
Stendler, C. B., 512, 529
Stendler, F., 121, 172
Stennett, R. G., 252, 282
Stern, G. C., 313, 327
Stevenson, H. W., 501, 527
Stewart, J. S., 34, 39
Stirdivant, L. E., 336, 368
Stolz, H. R., 191, 225
Stolz, L. M., 191, 225
Stone, G. R., 618, 629
Stone, J. C., 426
Stone, L. J., 185, 224
Strang, R., 120
Strauss, E., 254, 282
Strecker, E. A., 371
Streitfeld, H. S., 366
Stricker, G., 90
Strom, R. D., 90, 329
Strother, C. R., 283
Stroud, J. B., 619, 627
Suchman, J. R., 447, 479
Suelbecker, G., 22
Sullivan, H. S., 12, 40
Sutich, A. J., 40
Sutton-Smith, B., 121, 162–163, 171, 172
Swanson, G. D., 201, 226
Swensen, C. H., 668, 683
Symonds, P., 22–23, 38, 82, 89, 148, 170, 301, 326, 401, 410, 422, 439, 479, 549, 574
Synder, W. V., 344, 369

T

Taba, H., 447, 479
Tanner, J. M., 97, 99, 119, 120, 129, 167, 168, 183, 185, 224
Taylor, R. G., 565, 577
Taylor, T. D., 579
Teevan, R. C., 578
Templin, M., 101, 120
Terman, L. M., 203, 226, 243, 282
Terwilliger, J. S., 631
Thomas, D. R., 715, 726
Thomas, E. J., 695, 725
Thomas, S., 560, 561, 576
Thompson, G. G., 497, 527
Thompson, W., 579
Thordnike, E. L., 22, 38, 40, 239, 281, 382, 390, 420, 421, 422
Thornburg, H. D., 230
Thorndike, R. L., 568, 577, 631
Thurston, J. R., 648, 681
Thurstone, L. L., 239, 282
Tiedeman, S. C., 313, 327
Todd, V. E., 122
Torrance, E. P., 276, 285, 286, 400, 422, 464, 481, 513, 529, 645, 680
Trabasso, T., 530
Travers, R. M., 402, 403, 405, 422, 423, 452, 480, 483, 531, 677, 684
Trent, J. W., 214, 228
Turner, R. L., 365, 370
Tyler, L. E., 203, 226, 631
Tyler, R. W., 590, 627

U

Underwood, B. J., 403, 422

V

Van de Reit, H., 458, 480
Vaughn, J., 511, 528
Vaughn, W. F., 354, 369
Verplanck, W. S., 38
Vieh, M. A., 40
Vogel, W., 216, 228
Von Moschzisker, M., 530
Voyat, G., 257, 283

W

Waetjen, W. B., 531
Walberg, H. J., 639, 661, 662, 680, 682

Walker, R. N., 131, 168
Wallach, M. A., 271, 285, 286
Wallen, N. E., 696, 725
Wallin, J. E. W., 343–344, 369
Walsh, A. M., 558, 575
Walster, E., 187, 224
Wattenberg, W. W., 182
Wang, J. D., 162, 171
Ward, M. H., 452, 480
Wash, J. A., 499, 630
Washburne, C., 317, 328, 602, 628
Watson, G., 24, 38, 439, 479
Watson, J. B., 15–16, 37, 38
Watson, P., 257, 283, 286
Watson, R. L., 172
Wattenberg, W. W., 556, 575, 703, 725
Weatherly, D., 190, 191, 225
Webb, L. W., 383, 421
Wechsler, D., 282
Weigand, J. E., 329, 426
Weinberg, C., 40
Weiner, B., 531
Weiner, M. L., 371
Weinstein, G., 393, 422
Weingartner, G., 426
Welch, W. W., 662, 682
Weldon, F. A., 579
Weschler, D., 244, 282
Werner, H., 104, 120
Wesley, F., 230
Westbrook, W. H., 471, 481
Wetson, J. B., 37
Wettenberg, W. W., 224
Wheeler, R. H., 407, 423
White, K., 329
White, R. K., 313, 315, 328, 640, 680, 684
White, R. W., 55–57, 66, 86, 88, 157, 171, 447, 479, 490, 526
White, W. F., 329, 499, 527, 677, 684
Whitehall, J., 371
Wiener, D. N., 702, 725, 727
Wigdor, A., 211, 227
Wilkinson, F. R., 295, 326
Wilson, A. B., 650, 681
Winchester, J. H., 37
Wing, C. W., Jr., 286
Wingo, G. M., 690, 724
Winter, G. D., 230
Winterbottom, M. R., 169
Wittrock, M. C., 296, 326
Witty, P., 299, 326, 415, 424

Wolfbein, S. L., 541, 543, 573, 574
Wolman, R. N., 135, 168
Wood, D. A., 631
Woody, R. H., 727
Worthington, J., 342, 368
Wrenn, R. L., 371
Wright, H. F., 639, 680
Wright, N., Jr., 426
Wrinkle, W. L., 631
Wylie, R. C., 579

Y

Yamamoto, K., 122, 172, 329, 579
Yanoff, J. M., 483

Young, I., 122
Yuker, H. E., 387, 421

Z

Zander, A., 351, 369, 653, 681
Ziller, R. C., 579
Zimmerman, I. L., 559, 576
Zohorik, J. A., 426

Subject Index

A

Academic achievement:
  and early stabilization of school,
    550–552
  effects of anxiety on, 563–564
  and minority groups, 266
  the need for, 115
  parental antecedents to high,
    142–148
  prediction of, 551
  and relationship to intelligence,
    264–265
  and relationship to self-concept,
    556–562
  strategies for enhancing, 564–571
Acceptance by others, importance of,
  83–84
Accident-prone children, 133
Adirondack Mountain Humanistic
  Education Center, 366
Adjustment, the use of defense mechanisms and, 352–359
Adolescence:
  accident-proneness during, 186
  autonomy a major goal of, 205
  and development of independence,
    198–200
  developmental tasks associated
    with, 194–195
  and effects of early vs. late maturity
    on boys, 188–191
  and effects on early vs. late maturity
    on girls, 191–194
  and expressions of alienation,
    213–216
  growth spurts in, 182–184
  and health-related factors, 185–186
  hormonal output during, 184
  impact of peer relationships during,
    206–212
  influence of parents during,
    196–206
  meaning of, 177–180
  physical development during,
    181–184
  and physical growth considerations,
    186–194
  and return to parental values,
    205–206
  virtues of idealistic thinking during,
    221
Affection, effects of loss of, 204
Anxiety:
  definition of, 562
  and effects on school performance,
    563–564
  positive aspects of, 564–565
  and relationship to self-concept, 562
  and relationship to self-esteem, 563

Authoritarian classrooms, consequences of, 641
Authoritarian vs. authoritative teaching, 522–524
Autonomy, adolescents' need for, 205
Autonomy vs. shame and doubt, development of, 47–48

B

Behavior:
five factors influencing students', 694–703
learning and changes in, 434–435
looking for language of, 706–707
Behavior modification, use of, 715–716
Behavioral consistency over time, 107–109
Behavioral objectives:
examples of, 590–591
pros and cons of, 590–591 (See also Objectives)
Behavioristic psychology:
criticisms of, 20–21
explanations of, 14–15
and implications for teaching and learning, 22–24
and prediction and control of behavior, 15–20
the question of freedom and, 20–21
strategies for controlling behavior suggested by, 17–20
Belonging, the need for, 117–118
Biochemical factors and learning, 467–477
Body build as related to personality, 130–132
Brain size, research related to increasing, 474–477

C

Central tendency:
three common measures of, 595
when to use the various measures of, 595–597
Child rearing:
the authoritarian style of, 150–155
authoritarian vs. democratic practices, 199–200
consequences of permissive, 144–145

and differences in discipline for boys and girls, 203–204
and effects during adolescence, 196–206
and influences of different parenting styles, 152–155
influence of sex of parent and child on, 202–203
and influence on cognitive functioning and intellectual performance, 142–148
permissive style of, 151–155
and relationships to social class, 146–148
religious and social-class variables related to, 200–201
seven different styles of, 198
and warm-restrictive vs. warm-controlling parents, 154
and ways to encourage high self-esteem, 153
Choice, safety in one's own, 569–570
Classroom discipline:
diagnostic thinking as an approach for handling, 703–708 (See also Diagnostic thinking)
different perceptions of, 691–692
five factors that influence, 694–703
how elementary teachers view, 693
how secondary teachers view, 693
points to remember about constructive, 721–722
Classroom group cohesiveness:
antecedents to high, 660
explanation of, 659–660
varieties of, 663
ways to encourage high, 661–662
Classroom group norms:
and behavioral norms, 657–659
and cognitive norms, 654–656
and evaluative norms, 656–657
and perceptual norms, 653–654
varieties of, 652–653
Classroom group processes, communication skills for enhancing, 670–678
Classroom liking patterns, factors influencing, 644–651
Classroom social-emotional climate:
influence of authoritarian teaching on, 640–641
influence of democratic teaching on, 640–641

Classroom social-emotional climate (*cont.*)
  influence of teacher's personal style
    on, 639–640
  and influence on learning, 639
  ways to increase a positive, 642–644
    (*See also* Group processes)
Cognitive development:
  and ability to conceptualize, 136–139
  during the elementary and middle
    school years, 134–148
  and growth of concrete thinking,
    139–141
  and growth and decline of in-
    telligence, 262–264
  and implications for teachers of ele-
    mentary and middle school
    youth, 148
  and intellectual processes during
    adolescence, 218–221
  parents' influence on, 142–148
  and Piaget's three levels of intellec-
    tual activity, 101–102
  preschool years and development
    stages in, 101–104
  and social-class background,
    146–148
Competence:
  effect of early school failure experi-
    ences on feelings of, 62–63
  and importance of its growing
    during elementary years, 61–63
  and psychological health, 63–64
  relationship between self-esteem
    and, 58–60, 64
  and relationship to behavior, 57–61
  and self-esteem, 58–60, 64
Competition and cooperation:
  and effects of each as motivators,
    510–513
  and effects on learning, 510–513
  examples of constructive and
    destructive classroom, 514–516
  implications from research for the
    use of, 513–514
Communication:
  examples of positive and negative,
    716–721
  ways to improve classroom,
    671–678
Concept:
  definition of a, 136
  the role of language rules in the use
    of a, 138–139

three attributes of a, 136–137
Conceptualize, ability to, 136–139
Conditioning:
  classical, 18
  meaning of, 17–18
  operant or instrumental, 19
Confidence, development of, 49–50
Conservation, principle of, 139
Cooperation (*See* Competition and
    cooperation)
Countertransference, explanation of,
    362–364
Creative persons, characteristics of,
    271–275
Creativity:
  approaches to measurement of,
    269–271
  defined, 267–268
  and relationship to intelligence, 271
  varieties of, 267
  ways to encourage, 275–279
Criterion-referenced testing:
  arguments for and against, 603–604
  definition of, 601–602
  differences between norm-referenced
    testing and, 604–605
  mastery learning and the use of, 602
  when to use, 605–606
Criticism, and consequences of how
    given, 497–498
Curriculum, psychological content of
  a, 393–396

D

Decision making, consequences of
  shared, 641–642
Defense mechanisms, descriptions of,
  352–359
Defiance, developmental and reactive,
  699–700
Delinquency, early school experiences
  and, 550
Dependent and independent behavior
  among young children, dynamics
  of, 112–113
Developmental tasks:
  adolescents and their, 194–195
  explanation of, 53–55, 411–412
  in table form, 54
Diagnostic thinking:
  definition of, 703

Diagnostic thinking (*cont.*)
example of, 703–705
five steps involved in, 705–708
Disciplinary measures, when to take, 709–710
Discipline:
an example of harsh, 338–340 (*See also* Classroom discipline)
varieties of parental, 203–204
Discipline problems, techniques for handling, 710–716
Discovery learning:
criticisms of, 448–450
evidence supporting, 447–448
examples of, 444–445
and learning by doing, 442
ways to encourage, 446–448
Discussion, value of open, 658–659

E

Ego, definition of, 7–8
Electra complex, meaning of, 10
Elementary school:
importance of success during, 543–545
possible consequences of failing in, 547–548
Emotional-social development, influences on a child's, 149–164
Empathy, practice of, 348
Equilibration, principle of, 141
Erik Erikson's psychosocial growth stages, 45–53
Esalen Institute, 366
Examination climate, ways to create a positive, 617–618
Existential psychology, explanation of, 26–28
Expectations, psychology of teacher, 567–571
Extrinsic motivation, 491–494 (*See also* Motivation)

F

Failure experiences:
breed failure feelings, 560
consequences of, 80–81, 499–504
dropout problems related to, 541
and effect on feelings of competence, 62–63

and effects on self-esteem, 539–540
why elementary children are so vulnerable to, 544–545
and impact on self-concept development, 540–552 (*See also* Self-concept and Success experiences)
long-term consequences of early school, 549–550
and maladjustment in adulthood, 550, 575
and relation to delinquency, 550
and relationship to elementary school nonpromotion practices, 547–548
Fear of failure, consequences of, 503–504
Feelings in school, importance of having and expressing, 82–83
Friends, the importance of having honest, 351
Fully functioning person:
basic propositions related to being a, 76–77
characteristics of a, 75–76
locus of evaluation in a, 78–79
and psychological health, 77–79
role of the self in the, 76–77
and self-actualization, 74–75

G

Games, psychological significance of, 163–164 (*See also* Play)
Generativity vs. self-absorption, development of, 52
Grades, the need for confidentiality of, 515
Grading systems, alternative, 623–626
Group norms (*See* Classroom group norms)
Group processes, and interpersonal attractions, 644–651
Growth:
and the fully functioning person model (*See* Fully functioning person)
and physical development (*See* Physical development)
as related to a sense of competence, 55–57
Growth games, book of, 366

Growth stages, as expressed in psychoanalytic psychology, 8–10
Grumble theory, explanation of the, 67

H

Havighurst's developmental tasks model, explanation of, 53–55
Health considerations and middle childhood, 132–133
Healthy development, ways to encourage, 80–84
Heredity and environment, relative impact on intelligence of, 261–262, (See also Intelligence)
Human Development Institute, 366
Humanistic-perceptual psychology:
    contributions of phenomenology and existential psychology to, 26–28
    criticisms of, 30–31
    explanation of, 24–26
    implications for teaching and learning from, 32–35
    nature of man as seen in, 28–29
    place of common sense and experience in, 22
    and question of personal freedom, 26–27
    role of self in, 29–30

I

Id, definition of, 7
Identification:
    explanation of, 109–110
    and relationship to sex-typing, 109–110
    role of adult models in, 111–112
Identity vs. identity confusion, development of, 50–51
Independence, development of, 198–200
Industrious behavior, consequences of, 141–142
Industry vs. inferiority, development of, 49–50
Inferiority feelings, development of, 49–50
Initiative vs. guilt, development of, 48–49
Integrity vs. despair, development of, 52

Intellectual development:
    and abstract thinking in adolescence, 218–220
    and implications for teachers, 148
    parental influence on, 142–148
    Piaget's model of, 412–413
    stages of, 413
Intellectual growth during elementary and middle school years, 134–148
Intellectual growth, Piaget's four stages of, 139–141
Intelligence:
    as combination of different abilities, 242
    crystallized and fluid, 263–264
    definition of, 235–236, 242
    and deviation IQ, 249–250
    four different views of, 238–242
    growth and decline of, 262–264
    influence of environment on, 259–261
    influence of heredity on, 258–259
    and influence of socioeconomic status, 252–253
    and Jensen controversy, 254–258
    and learning, 238
    and mental age, 248–249
    and minority groups, 266
    personality characteristics related to changes in, 253–254
    and range, classification, and interpretation of mental abilities, 244–245
    and relationship to creativity, 271
    and school performance, 264–265
    and stability over time, 251–252
    ways to raise, 260–261
Intelligence quotients (IQs), distribution of, 245–246
Intelligence tests:
    limitations of, 265–266
    reliability of, 250–251
    three types of, 243–244
Interpersonal attractiveness:
    intellectual factors related to, 645–646
    mental health considerations related to, 647–648
    physical characteristics related to, 646–647
    social behavior related to, 648–650
    and social differences, 649

Interpersonal attractiveness (*cont.*)
  teacher preferences as influenced
      by, 650–651
Intimacy vs. isolation, development
      of, 51–52
Intrinsic motivation, 491–494 (*See
  also* Motivation)

L

Language development:
  and changes during elementary
      school years, 135–136
  and changes during preschool years,
      104–105
  and effect of environment, 102–104
  and importance of knowing lan-
      guage rules, 103–104
  and Piaget's three levels of intellec-
      tual activity, 101–102
  preschool years and developmental
      stages in, 101–104
  and vocabulary growth in preschool
      years, 101
Law of effect, 17
Learning:
  and balance between classroom
      freedom and control, 520–522
  biochemistry of, 467–477 (*See also*
      Memory)
  and conceptual vs. thematic think-
      ing, 466–467
  definitions of, 433–435
  and developmental task model,
      411–412
  differences in rate of, 546
  different points of view about,
      441–466
  discovery methods of, 442–450 (*See
      also* Discovery learning)
  and distribution of work and study,
      403–404
  effects of cooperative vs. competi-
      tive efforts on, 509–516
  effects of environment on, 474–477
  effects of failure on, 499–504
  effects of success on, 499–504
  four characteristic patterns of,
      462–465
  and importance of knowledge of re-
      sults and progress, 406–407
  and importance of objectives,
      588–589 (*See also* Objectives)

  and importance of review, 407–408
  and impulsive vs. reflective think-
      ing, 465–466
  influence of intelligence on, 438
  influence of social-emotional cli-
      mate on, 638–639 (*See also*
      Classroom social-emotional cli-
      mate)
  influence of values, needs, beliefs,
      and self-concept on, 436–438
  and issue of freedom vs. control
      456–457
  and mastery model, 603–604
  opportunities for sequential and or-
      derly, 387–388
  organism variables and, 436–437
  overlearning as a way to encourage,
      405–406
  part vs. whole, 401–402
  and pros and cons of student
      freedom, 516–524
  readiness for, 408–409
  and reinforcement approaches to,
      450–458 (*See also* Reinforce-
      ment)
  response variables and, 439
  stimulus variables influencing,
      435–536
  strategies for enhancing, 397–398
  and strategies for making it more
      lasting, 398–408
  teachable moments enhance, 411
  three styles of, 461
  transfer of, 379–385 (*See also*
      Transfer of learning)
  twenty-five important principles of,
      439–441
Level of aspiration, effects of success
      and failure on, 501, 527
Love, the need for, 115

M

Maslow's self-actualization model,
      explanation of, 65–73
Mastery learning:
  arguments for and against, 603–604
      (*See also* Learning)
  and criterion-referenced testing,
      602–604
Maturation, relationships between
      personality development and, 193
Measurement and evaluation:

Measurement and evaluation (*cont.*)
  and dangers in generalizing too
      broadly from personal experi-
      ences, 586
  meaning and functions of, 587–588
  norm-referenced testing in, 604–606
  objectives and goals in relation to,
      588–591 (*See also* Objectives)
  personal values and approaches to,
      585–586
  and problems related to grading and
      reporting, 619–626
  and standard error of a test, 600
  suggestions for creating a positive
      examination climate for,
      617–618
  test reliability related to, 593–595
  test validity related to, 592–593
  three common indices of central
      tendency related to, 595–597
  and use of criterion-referenced
      testing, 601–605
  use of essay and objective tests for,
      606–617
  use of range, percentile rank, and
      standard deviation in, 598–600
Memory:
  biochemical factors related to,
      468–473
  long-term and short-term, 468–473
  physical basis for, 472–474
  ways to enhance, long-term,
      471–473
Mental abilities (*See* Intelligence)
Mental age:
  definition of, 248
  and relationship to IQ, 248–249
Middle childhood, dynamics of,
      164–165
Minority groups and achievement, 266
Motivation:
  consequences of success and failure
      on, 499–503
  dangers in overstressing extrinsic,
      492–493
  differences between extrinsic and
      intrinsic, 491
  effects of competition and coopera-
      tion on, 509–516 (*See also*
      Competition and cooperation)
  effects of praise and criticism on,
      494–499
  influence of self-esteem on, 506–507
  and pros and cons of classroom
      freedom, 516–524 (*See also*
      Summerhill school)
  and relationship to motives,
      489–490
  value of using both extrinsic and in-
      trinsic, 493
Motives, three functions of, 489

N

National Training Laboratory Institute,
      366
Nature of man, beliefs about the, 5–37
Needs of growing children, four basic,
      114–118
Needs, the basic human, 67–68 (*See
      also* Self-actualization)
Nonpromotion:
  constructive steps to handling,
      548–549
  possible consequences of, 547–548
Norm-referenced testing:
  definition of, 604–605
  differences between criterion-
      referenced testing and, 604–605
  when to use, 605–606
Normal distribution, meaning of a,
      596

O

Objectives:
  pros and cons of behavioral,
      590–591
  three types of learning, 589
Oedipus complex, explanation of the,
      10
Overlearning, explanation of, 405–406
      (*See also* Learning)

P

Parenting styles (*See* Child rearing)
Peer culture, dynamics of the, 207
Peer group involvement:
  and differences between American
      and Russian youths, 160
  and influence during elementary
      and middle school years,
      155–158
  and three functions of, 158–161

Peer group relations:
  and academic success in adolescence, 210–211
  during adolescence, 206–212
  importance of, 212
  and seven functions during adolescence, 208–209
  and social adjustment in adolescence, 209–210
Percentile rank, calculation of a, 598–599
Percentile ranking, meaning of, 246–247
Perceptions:
  behavior related to, 552–554
  consequences of changes in, 553–554
Perfectionistic behavior, dynamics of, 78
Personal inventory questions, 359
Personality:
  and identity development, 50–51
  and relationships to changes in IQ, 253–254
  and teaching, 334–335
Personality development:
  influences of body-build on, 130–132
  and preschool years, 106–107
  relationships between maturation and, 193
Phenomenology, explanation of, 26–28
Physical characteristics, interpersonal attraction as influenced by, 646–647
Physical development:
  and adolescent growth spurts, 182–184
  and adolescent health, 185–186
  the beginnings of self-awareness as related to, 99–100
  and effects of early vs. late maturity on boys, 188–191
  and effects of early vs. late maturity on girls, 191–194
  and growth during elementary and middle school years, 126–130
  and growth in early childhood, 96–99
  hereditary factors related to, 97–98
  and hormone secretion in adolescence, 184
  and relationship to self-concept, 186
  and variations and consequences during adolescence, 181–184
  ways to predict, 97–98
Physical education, psychological content in, 396
Play, function and meaning of children's, 161–164
Power, use of functional vs. interpersonal adult, 154–155
Praise:
  and consequences of how it is given, 497–498
  effects of indiscriminately given, 496–497
  examples of the positive use of, 508–509
  how introverts and extroverts respond to, 495–496
Programmed instruction, 452–453
Psychoanalytic psychology:
  criticisms of, 11–12
  explanation of, 7–11
  and Freud, 7
  id, ego, and superego as related to, 7–8
  and implications for teaching and learning, 13–14
  importance of first five years of life in, 8–10
  and unconscious motivation, 11
  sex and its relationship to, 12
Psychosocial growth stages, 45–53

R

Readiness, opposing views about, 414–415
Reading, influence of self-concept on, 556–557
Reading readiness, differences in, 408–409
Reinforcement:
  and behavior modification practices, 715–716
  criticisms of teaching methods using, 456–459
  different effects of, 457–459
  effect of intermittent, 454–456
  and effects of punishment, 452
  good feelings through the use of, 677–678

Reinforcement (*cont.*)
  and issue of teacher control,
    456–457
  meaning of, 17
  and operant behavior, 451
  and relationship to programmed in-
    struction, 452–453
  as a way to enhance learning,
    450–451
Relevance, teaching for, 379
Reliability, and intelligence tests,
  250–251
Religious variables, child rearing and,
  200–201
Report cards:
  Consequences of poor, 620
  varieties of, 619–620
Response styles, examples of five
  frequently used, 674–675
Risk-taking behavior:
  effects of success and failure on,
    502–503
  value of, 81, 350–351
Rogers' fully functioning person
  growth model, 74–79
Rules to grow by, youths' need for,
  113–114

S

Self:
  different ways of expressing the,
    537–539
  effects of comparisons with others
    on the, 538
  two meanings of the, 536–537
Self-actualization:
  and characteristics of self-actualized
    people, 72–73
  difference between pseudo- and
    authentic, 73–74
  and examples of self-actualized
    persons, 71–72
  explanation of, 65–67
  goals of, 67
  and psychological health, 73–74
  and relationship to basic needs,
    67–71
Self-concept:
  and behavioral consistency over
    time, 107–109

  and chicken or egg question,
    555–556
  and development during preschool
    years, 106–107
  and development of dependent or
    independent behavior in young
    children, 112–113
  effect of anxiety on, 562
  effects of elementary school letter
    grades on, 546
  and humanistic-perceptual psychol-
    ogy, 29–30
  and identification or sex-typing,
    109–110
  impact of expressed perceptions on,
    131–132
  influence of adolescents' peer rela-
    tionships on, 206–212
  influence of physical characteristics
    on, 646–647
  influence of significant others on,
    560
  influence of success experiences on,
    559–560
  and influence on reading, 556–557
  and parental impact during adoles-
    cence, 196–206
  and relationship to academic
    achievement, 556–562
  and relationship to physical growth,
    186–194
  and role of adult models in develop-
    ment of, 111–112
  and self-consistency, 552–553
  strategies for enhancing, 564–571
  and underachievement, 557–559
Self-consistency:
  and school performance, 552–554
  and self-esteem, 504
Self-disclosure:
  consequences of, 349–350
  example of, 350
Self-esteem:
  effects of certain and uncertain,
    504–506
  effects of low, 505
  influence of group rejection on,
    645–646
  influence of high group cohesive-
    ness on, 663
  influence of success and failure on,
    539–540

Self-esteem (*cont.*)
  as related to competence, 57–61, 64
  and relationship to anxiety, 563
  and relationship to level of aspiration, 539
  and relationship to motivation, 506–507
  and relationship to school dropout problem, 541
  success and failure as related to certainty of, 504–506
  and ways it is influenced, 538
  ways to deal with students differing levels of, 507–509
  ways to encourage high, 153
Self-perception, influence of appearance on, 187
Self-understanding:
  importance of, 346–347
  institutes that offer programs for, 366
  therapy and growth in, 360–362
  and the use of defense mechanisms, 352–359
  ways to acquire, 347–362
Sex-typing, explanation of, 109–110
  (*See also* Identification)
Significant others, importance and influence of, 13, 560
Social adjustment, peer acceptance and, 209–210
Social behavior, social-class influences on, 649–650
Social class:
  and child-rearing practices, 146–148, 200, 201
  and influence on IQ stability, 252–253
  and influence on language development, 102–104
Sociometric approaches, necessity for, 669–670
Sociometric testing:
  examples of, 664–668
Sociometry, explanation of, 664, 683
Standard deviation, meaning of, 599
Standard error, meaning of, 600–601
Stimulus-response psychology, 15
  (*See also* Behavioristic psychology)
Students' expectations, 377–378
Success and failure, motivational consequences of, 499–503

Success, the power of, 84
Success experiences:
  consequences of, 499–506
  and effects on self-esteem, 539–540
  nothing succeeds like, 386–387, 559–560
  and their importance during the elementary school years, 543–545
Summerhill school:
  an example of total freedom, 516–517
  former students' perceptions of, 518–519
  pros and cons about, 517–518
  what we can learn from, 519
Superego, explanation of, 7–8

T

Teachable moments, importance of, 411
Teacher adjustment:
  affect of workload on, 337
  and influence on students, 336–337, 342–345
  and nervous tension, 336
  and shy behavior, 340–342
  and symptoms of possible maladjustment, 338–342
Teacher expectations:
  controversy about consequences of, 568–569
  four-factor theory of, 568
  and influence on performance, 567–568
  note of caution about, 571
  psychology of, 569–570
Teachers:
  characteristics of effective, 323
  cognitive and intellectual dimensions of good, 293–297
  differences in instructional procedures and interaction styles among, 309–315
  discipline problems caused by, 695–698
  effect of group-centered, 662–663
  influence of high-autonomy, 662
  influence of students' physical characteristics on, 646–647
  and importance of self-understanding, 346–347

Teachers (*cont.*)
and perceptions of self and others, 305–309
personal characteristics of good, 293–296
personality dimensions of good, 297–304
stimulus potential of, 23–24
students' reasons for liking and disliking, 298–299
and ways to acquire self-understanding, 347–362
Teaching:
authoritarian versus authoritative, 522–524
and balance between freedom and control, 520–522
character of material influences, 403
consequences of autocratic, laissez-faire, and democratic, 312–314
and developing appropriate mental set, 399–400
and development of trust, 654
effects of indirect and direct, 319–322
and helping students to discover personal meaning, 390–393
and importance of considering students' self-esteem, 507–509
and improving classroom communication, 671–678
and importance of trust, 676–677
influences of different student-teacher personality types on, 316–318
and the issue of freedom versus control, 456–467
and misuse of love in, 418–419
and pros and cons of student freedom, 516–524 (*See also* Summerhill school)
and psychology of teacher expectations, 567–571
and recognizing learning patterns, 462–465
and recognizing learning styles, 461–462
and relevance, 379
strategies for enhancing students' self-concepts while, 565–571
students' backgrounds should influence, 389–390

students from differing ethnic backgrounds and, 415–419
and teacher behavior to make it successful, 718–721
and transfer of learning, 379–385
and transference, counter-transference phenomena, 362–365
and use of cooperation of competition as motivators, 509–516
and use of diagnostic thinking, 703–708
and use of discovery methods, 442–450
and use of divergent and convergent questions in, 388–389
and use of praise and criticism, 494–499
and use of reinforcement methods, 451–459
and using psychological content of a curriculum, 393–396
and value of staying open to unplanned experiences, 395–396
and ways to encourage high classroom cohesiveness, 661–662
and ways to handle discipline problems, 710–716
Teaching machines, 407
Test reliability, meaning of, 593–595
Test validity:
meaning of, 592
varieties of, 592–593
Testing, examples of sociometric, 664–668 (*See also* Measurement and evaluation)
Tests:
factors to consider when preparing objective, 611–612
factors to consider when using essay, 607–609
four commonly used objective, 612–616
suggestions for scoring essay, 609–610
Therapy, value of, 360–362
Thinking:
development of concrete, 139–141
different styles of, 465–467
Transfer of learning:
misconceptions about, 381

Transfer of learning (*cont.*)
  positive and negative aspects of, 381
  teaching for, 379–381
  ways to maximize, 384–391
Transference, explanation of, 362–363
Transformation, principle of, 140–141
Trust vs. mistrust, development of,
  46–47

U

Underachievement, and relationship
  to self-concept, 557–559 (*See
  also* Self-concept)

V

Values:
  in defense of middle class, 148
  and influence on behavior, 33–34

and learning, 437
Vocabulary, growth of (*See* Language
  development)

W

White's concept of competence
  growth model, 55–57
Women's liberation, influences from,
  193

Y

Youth alienation:
  and antecedents to, 213–214
  and culturally alienated, 216
  and implications for teachers, 216
  and reasons behind the protest, 215
  and student activist, 214–215

RELATED TITLES

CONTEMPORARY ISSUES IN EDUCATIONAL PSYCHOLOGY,
Second Edition by Clarizio, Craig, and Mehrens

HELPING RELATIONSHIPS: Basic Concepts for the Helping
Professions by Combs, Avila, and Purkey

HUMAN DYNAMICS IN PSYCHOLOGY AND EDUCATION:
on by Hamachek

Allyn and Bacon, Inc.
470 Atlantic Avenue
Boston, Massachusetts 02210

224